WATERLOO REGION DISTRICT SCHOOL BOARD

B.C.I.   Book #: 11-085

Year	Form	Name
2011		Jessica Long
2011	12C	Ashley Becker
2012	12CC	Rachel McShanrock
2013	12EE	Loujaine AlMoallim

ManagementFundamentals

CANADIAN EDITION

John R. Schermerhorn, Jr.
Barry Wright

WILEY
1807 – 2007

John Wiley & Sons Canada, Ltd.

Copyright © 2007 John Wiley & Sons Canada, Ltd.

All rights reserved. No part of this work covered by the copyrights herein may be reproduced, transmitted, or used in any form or by any means—graphic, electronic, or mechanical—without the prior written permission of the publisher.

Any request for photocopying, recording, taping, or inclusion in information storage and retrieval systems of any part of this book shall be directed to The Canadian Copyright Licensing Agency (Access Copyright). For an Access Copyright License, visit www.accesscopyright.ca or call toll-free, 1-800-893-5777.

Care has been taken to trace ownership of copyright material contained in this text. The publishers will gladly receive any information that will enable them to rectify any erroneous reference or credit line in subsequent editions.

Library and Archives Canada Cataloguing in Publication

Schermerhorn, John R.
　　Management fundamentals / John R. Schermerhorn, Barry Wright.

ISBN 978-0-470-83844-0 (bound)

　　1. Management--Textbooks.　I. Wright, Barry, 1954-　II. Title.
HD31.S34 2007　　　　　658　　　　C2007-900375-3

Production Credits

Acquisitions Editor: Darren Lalonde
Editorial Manager: Karen Staudinger
Publishing Services Director: Karen Bryan
Marketing Manager: Aida Krneta
Developmental Editor: Daleara Hirjikaka
Editorial Assistant: Sheri Coombs
Design: Interrobang Graphic Design Inc.
Cover Photo: Tim Davis, Photographer's Choice, Getty Images
Anniversary Logo Design: Richard J. Pacifico
Printing & Binding: Quebecor World, Dubuque

Printed and bound in the United States of America
1 2 3 4 5 QW 11 10 09 08 07

John Wiley and Sons Canada Ltd.
6045 Freemont Blvd.
Mississauga, Ontario L5R 4J3
Visit our website at www.wiley.ca

About the Authors

Barry Wright is an Associate Professor in the Faculty of Business at Brock University in St. Catharines, Ontario. Dr. Wright has over 20 years of experience in the classroom. Prior to joining the faculty at Brock he worked as a professor at St. Francis Xavier University, taught at the International Study Centre in Herstmonceux, UK and at Queen's University in Kingston, Ontario. He has also worked as an administrator with the City of Red Deer. During his career as an educator, Barry has been nominated several times for teaching awards and was the recipient of the "PHESA Award" for excellence in academic teaching given by Queen's University.

At home in the classroom, Barry is also comfortable in the boardroom. He has provided a variety of training and research consultations to a number of Canadian private and public organizations. These services have included the development and implementation of programs in leadership, employee motivation, strategic planning, diversity management, stress management, and managing organizational change. Barry also provides one-on-one "coaching" sessions for senior executives who have expressed a desire for outside counsel.

He received his MA (Sport Psychology) and Ph.D. (Management) degrees from Queen's University. His academic research focuses on understanding and solving leadership challenges, change and its influence on organizational members, and creating effective work environments.

Barry enjoys being married and being a father, coaching sports, a trip to the art gallery, travelling, and a good laugh.

John R. Schermerhorn, Jr. is the Charles G. O'Bleness Professor of Management in the College of Business at Ohio University, where he teaches graduate and undergraduate courses in management. Dr. Schermerhorn earned a Ph.D. in Organizational Behaviour from Northwestern University, an MBA (with distinction) in Management and International Business from New York University, and a BS in Business Administration from the State University of New York at Buffalo. He has taught at Tulane University, the University of Vermont, and Southern Illinois University at Carbondale, where he also served as Head of the Department of Management and Associate Dean of the College of Business Administration.

At Ohio University Dr. Schermerhorn has been named a University Professor, the university's highest campus-wide honour for excellence in undergraduate teaching. He is committed to instructional excellence and curriculum innovation, and is working extensively with technology utilization in the classroom. He serves as a guest speaker at colleges and universities, lecturing on developments in higher education for business and management, as well as on instructional approaches and innovations. He is co-author of *Organizational Behaviour* (Wiley, 2005).

Preface

To successfully raise their young, adult Emperor penguins, pictured on the cover of this text, must work as a team through some of the harshest climate conditions on our planet.

Once born, the baby Emperor penguins must quickly adapt to their new environments, establishing their distinctive calls with their parents.

We believe this serves as a good metaphor for the study of Management. To be successful, today's management students will need to master working in teams, they will need to develop their own voice to become effective managers and leaders, and they will often be working in very competitive environments.

Management Fundamentals Philosophy

Today's students are tomorrow's leaders and managers. Just as the workplace in this new century will be vastly different from today's, so too must our teaching and learning environments be different from days gone by. New values and management approaches are appearing; the nature of work and organizations is changing; the age of information is not only with us, it is transforming our lives.

Management Fundamentals is part of the same transformation. It is based on four constructive balances that we believe remain essential to the agenda of higher education for business and management.

- *The balance of research insights with formative education.* As educators we must be willing to make choices when bringing the theories and concepts of our discipline to the attention of the introductory student. We cannot do everything in one course. The goal should be to make good content choices and to set the best possible foundations for lifelong learning.

- *The balance of management theory with management practice.* As educators we must understand the compelling needs of students to understand and appreciate the applications of the material they are reading and thinking about. We must continually bring to their attention good, interesting, and recognizable examples.

- *The balance of present understandings with future possibilities.* As educators we must continually search for the directions in which the real world of management is heading. We must select and present materials that can both point students in the right directions and help them develop the confidence and self-respect needed to best deal with them.

- *The balance of what "can" be done with what is, purely and simply, the "right" thing to do.* As educators we are role models; we set the examples. We must be willing to take stands on issues like managerial ethics and corporate social responsibility. We must be careful not to let the concept of "contingency" betray the need for positive "action" and "accountability" in managerial practice.

Today, more than ever before, our students have pressing needs for direction as well as suggestion. They have needs for application as well as information. They have needs for integration as well as presentation. Our instructional approaches and materials must deliver on all of these dimensions and more. Our goal is to put into your hands and into those of your students a learning resource that can help meet these needs. *Management Fundamentals* and its website are our contributions to the future careers of your students and ours.

MANAGEMENT FUNDAMENTALS HIGHLIGHTS

Management Fundamentals introduces the essentials of management as they apply within the contemporary work environment. The subject matter is carefully chosen to meet AACSB accreditation guidelines while allowing extensive flexibility to fit various course designs and class sizes.

Organization

- The book is organized into five parts with themes relevant to today's organizations: (1) Introducing Management, (2) Context, (3) Mission, (4) Organization, (5) Leadership.

- *Part 1: Management Today*—focuses on understanding managers, what they do, the exciting new workplace, lessons of the past and present, and ethics and social responsibility.

- *Part 2: Context*—explores the contemporary environment in terms of competition, diversity, organization cultures, globalization, crosscultural management, entrepreneurship, and small business.

- *Part 3: Mission*—addresses how managers use information, information technology, and decision making for planning and controlling, and in the process of strategic management.

- *Part 4: Organization*—reviews traditional and new developments in organization structures, organizational design contingencies and alternatives, as well as systems and work processes.

- *Part 5: Leadership*—presents the major models and current perspectives on leadership, individual behaviour and performance, teams and teamwork, communication and interpersonal skills, and change leadership.

Content

In addition to core themes of ethics, diversity, competitive advantage, quality, globalization, and empowerment, *Management Fundamentals* also covers the following topics:

- Intellectual capital • multicultural organizations • ethnocentrism • cultural relativism • strategic leadership • competitive advantage • self-management • crisis management • change leadership • customer relationship management • e-business • entrepreneurship • organizational learning • emotional intelligence • horizontal organizations • cross-functional teams • virtual teams • career readiness • virtual organizations • reengineering • work-life balance • strategic human resource planning • boundaryless organizations • performance-based rewards • personality • job stress • alternative work arrangements • cross-cultural communication • conflict management • negotiation • teamwork • innovation processes

Chapter Features

A most important feature of *Management Fundamentals* is the use of an integrated learning model to help guide students as they read and study for exams. Look for the following features in each chapter:

Planning Ahead—

- Key learning objectives and study questions
- Opening vignette

In Text—

- Learning Preview linking opening vignette to a visual chapter guide
- Learning Checks for each major section and learning objective
- Personal Management feature with recommended self-assessments
- Thematic boxes with current examples on timely themes
- Manager's Notepads with practical guidelines and suggestions
- Take-It-To-The-Case feature introducing chapter case
- Margin running glossary with definitions of key terms

End-of-Chapter Study Guide—

- Where We've Been linking back to opening vignette
- The Next Step guide to cases, projects, exercises, and assessments.
- Chapter Summary in bullet-list format
- Key Terms Review for major terms and concepts
- Chapter Self-Test with multiple-choice, short-answer, and essay questions

Management Learning Workbook

The *Management Learning Workbook* provides students and instructors with a rich variety of suggested learning activities.

- Chapter Cases—18 timely cases on well-recognized organizations
- Active Learning Projects—10 suggestions for student projects (individual or group), including management in popular culture and service learning
- Exercises in Teamwork—30 exercises for in-class and out-of-class use
- Self-Assessments—30 personality and self-reflection instruments
- Student Portfolio Builder—a special guide to building a student portfolio complete with professional résumé and competency documentations

Student Website: wiley.com/canada/highschool/schermerhorn

A robust Student Website supports *Management Fundamentals* for classroom application. This site includes the following special student learning resources:

- PowerPoint downloads for text and supplementary figures
- Student Polls introduce a key fact or survey result for every chapter
- Interactive on-line versions of self-assessments
- An online study guide for students, including PowerPoint chapter reviews and chapter self-tests

Instructor's Support

Management Fundamentals comes with a comprehensive resource package that assists the instructor in creating a motivating and enthusiastic learning environment.

- *Complete Instructor's Resource Guide* adapted by Lorie Guest and Lynda Anstett offers helpful teaching ideas, advice on course development, sample assignments, and chapter-by-chapter text highlights, learning objectives, lecture outlines, class exercises, lecture notes, answers to end-of-chapter material, and tips on using cases.

- *The Authors' Classroom*—a unique Web resource offering the author's personal classroom materials from special PowerPoint slides to quick-hitting learning activities.

- *Comprehensive Test Bank*—completely updated and linked to the chapter "Learning Checks," questions are categorized by pedagogical element, margin terms, or general text knowledge), page number, and type of questions. The entire test bank is available in a computerized version, MICROSOFT Diploma for windows, created by Brownstone Research Group.

- *Video Package*—offering video selections from business news clips.

- *Web CT and Blackboard*—full support.

- *Web Cases* by Lorie Guest and Lynda Anstett—eleven additional cases written to match the five strands of the BOH4M course as outlined by the Ministry of Education.

Acknowledgements

Writing a book is always a big task and there are many people who have contributed greatly to this project. Special thanks go to Darren Lalonde, Acquisitions Editor, for his support and vision for the project, and to Daleara Hirjikaka, Developmental Editor, for her strong, steady, and unwearied guidance on the day-to-day aspects of the project. I would also like to thank Alison Arnot for her work on the feature boxes that are an integral part of each chapter and Julie Van Tol and Laurel Hyatt for their editorial contributions. I would like to offer my particular thanks to my team of exceptional researchers who individually and collectively did an outstanding job—Wendy Dueck, Jessica Srivastava, and Michelle Leece.

I am grateful to the following colleagues who offered their insightful and very useful comments for the initial proposal for the text and those who reviewed drafts of the chapters.

Colin Boyd	University of Saskatchewan
Lewie Callahan	University of Lethbridge
Tyler Chamberlin	University of Ottawa
Choon Hian Chan	Kwantlen University College
Kay Devine	Athabasca University
Victoria Digby	Fanshawe College
Richard Field	University of Alberta
Douglas Fletcher	Kwantlen University College
Paul Gallina	Bishop's University
Jane Haddad	Seneca College
Don Haidey	Mount Royal College
Don Hill	Kwantlen University College
Cyndi Hornby	Fanshawe College
Barbara Lipton	Seneca College
Brad Long	St. Francis Xavier University
Sean MacDonald	University of Manitoba
Bonnie Milne	British Columbia Institute of Technology
Kerry Rempel	Okanagan College
Ron Shay	Kwantlen University College
Patricia Stoll	Seneca College
Susan Thompson	Trent University
Joe Trubic	Ryerson University
Debra Warren	Centennial College
Bruce Weir	Kwantlen University College
Wallace John Whistance-Smith	Ryerson University
Don Valeri	Douglas College
Heather White	Georgian College
David Wright	Kwantlen University College

I would like to particularly single out the efforts of Lorie Guest, Director of Business Studies, Waterloo Region District School Board and Lynda Anstett, Business

ACKNOWLEDGEMENTS

Teacher, Halton District School Board for their outstanding work on the Instructor's material and web cases.

I would especially like to thank my family—my lovely wife Mary and darling daughters Monica and Kit who graciously allowed me the time to take on this project. It is to my family that I dedicate this book.

Barry Wright
St. Catharines, Ontario
February 19, 2007

How to Use This Book

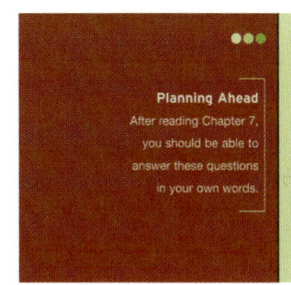

CHAPTER 7 STUDY QUESTIONS

Planning Ahead
After reading Chapter 7, you should be able to answer these questions in your own words.

1. How is information technology changing the workplace?
2. What is the role of information in the management process?
3. How do managers use information to make decisions?
4. What are the steps in the decision-making process?
5. What are the current issues in managerial decision making?

Each chapter opens with **Planning Ahead**—a set of study questions that provides learning objectives for the chapter and a framework for the end-of-chapter review.

CHAPTERS-INDIGO
A PASSION FOR BOOKS LEADS TO SUCCESS

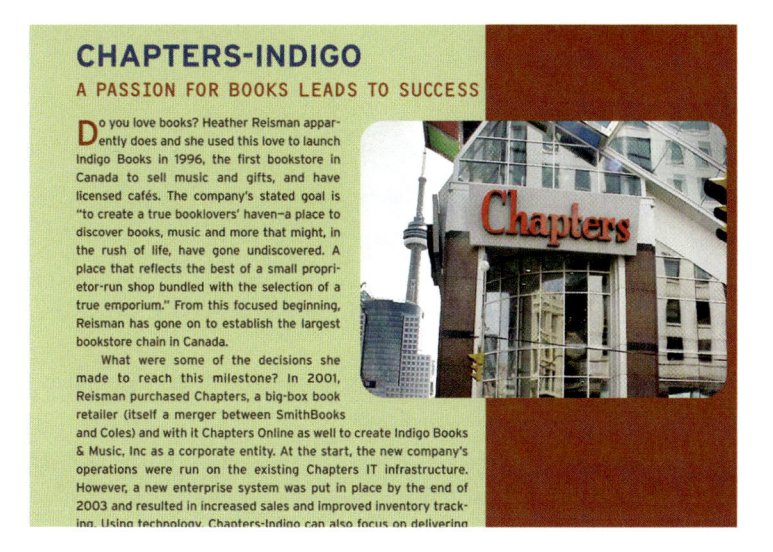

Do you love books? Heather Reisman apparently does and she used this love to launch Indigo Books in 1996, the first bookstore in Canada to sell music and gifts, and have licensed cafés. The company's stated goal is "to create a true booklovers' haven—a place to discover books, music and more that might, in the rush of life, have gone undiscovered. A place that reflects the best of a small proprietor-run shop bundled with the selection of a true emporium." From this focused beginning, Reisman has gone on to establish the largest bookstore chain in Canada.

What were some of the decisions she made to reach this milestone? In 2001, Reisman purchased Chapters, a big-box book retailer (itself a merger between SmithBooks and Coles) and with it Chapters Online as well to create Indigo Books & Music, Inc as a corporate entity. At the start, the new company's operations were run on the existing Chapters IT infrastructure. However, a new enterprise system was put in place by the end of 2003 and resulted in increased sales and improved inventory tracking. Using technology, Chapters-Indigo can also focus on delivering

The **Opening Vignette** is a timely, real-world example that highlights chapter themes. The example is visited again in the end-of chapter **Where We've Been**.

PERSONAL MANAGEMENT

Managers must have the **SELF-CONFIDENCE** to not only make decisions but also to implement them. Too many of us find all sorts of excuses for doing everything but that—we have difficulty deciding and we have difficulty acting. Opportunities to improve and develop your self-confidence abound, especially through involvement in the many student organizations on your campus. Carole Clay Winters was the first member of her family to go to college. On the encouragement of an economics professor, she joined Students in Free Enterprise (SIFE) and ended up on a team teaching business concepts to elementary school children in the local community.[27] Her team was chosen to participate in a national competition. They didn't win, but Carole did. "I felt my life had changed," she said. "I realized that if I could answer all the questions being posed by some of the country's most powerful executives, I had what I needed to become an executive myself." Carole went on to become a manager at KPMG. What about you? Do you have the self-confidence to make decisions relating to your career goals and future success? Are you taking full advantage of opportunities, on campus and off, to experience the responsibilities of leadership and gain confidence in your decision-making capabilities?

Get to know yourself better
Complete Self-Assessments #11—**Your Intuitive Ability**, and #12—**Assertiveness**, from the Workbook and Personal Management Activity #7 on the companion website.

Chapter 7 — LEARNING PREVIEW

Heather Reisman made many decisions as she shaped Chapters-Indigo into the company it is today. At each step of the way, she combined talent and business insight with risk and environmental awareness. She has gathered information effectively to turn her plans into realities. In Chapter 7 you will learn about information and decision making, with special attention to developments in information technology.

INFORMATION AND DECISION MAKING

Study Question 1	Study Question 2	Study Question 3	Study Question 4	Study Question 5
Information Technology and the Changing Workplace	Information and the Management Process	Information and Managerial Decisions	The Decision-Making Process	Issues in Managerial Decision Making
• How IT is changing business • How IT is changing organizations • How IT is changing the office	• What is useful information? • Information needs of organizations • Information systems • Managers as information processors	• Types of managerial decisions • Decision environments • Problem-solving styles	• Identify problem • Examine alternatives • Make a decision • Implement decision • Evaluate results	• Decision-making errors and traps • Individual vs. group decisions • Ethical decisions • Knowledge management and organizational learning
Learning check ①	Learning check ②	Learning check ③	Learning check ④	Learning check ⑤

The **Learning Preview** links the Opening Vignette with the major topics of the chapter and includes a graphic outline of major topics.

The **Personal Management** feature integrates each chapter with personal development issues, including how to "get to know yourself better" by using key learning resources in the end-of-chapter **Management Learning Workbook**.

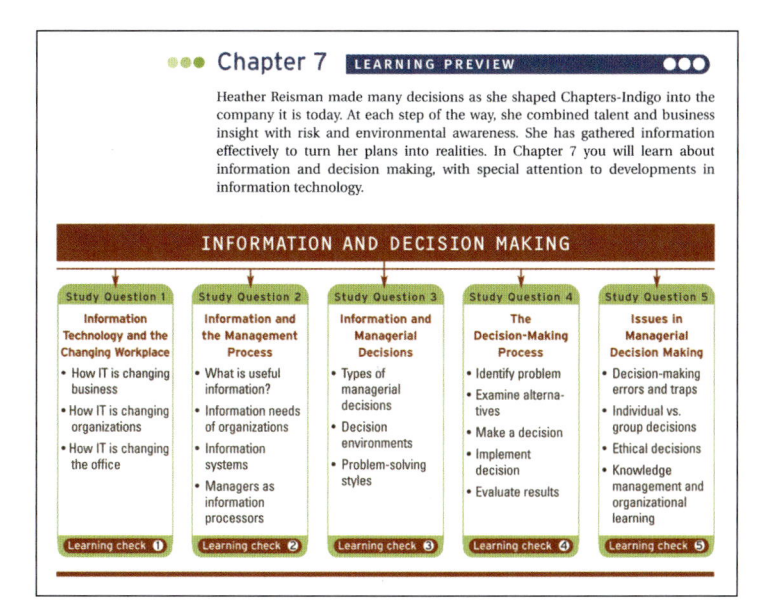

The **Canadian Company in the News** and the **Canadian Managers** features bring real-life examples of management skills and innovation into the classroom.

The **Around the World** feature introduces students to global management trends and practices.

A Critical Thinking Case for each chapter is introduced with **Take-It-To-The-Case**, which applies the case to the material being discussed.

■ **Decision support systems** help users organize and analyze data for problem solving.

■ **Groupware** is software that facilitates group collaboration and problem solving.

Key terms are called out and defined in the margins, forming a **Margin Running Glossary**.

Manager's Notepads in each chapter offer lists of helpful "do's" and "don'ts" of managerial behaviour.

HOW TO USE THIS BOOK xiii

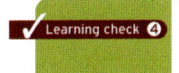

✓ Learning check ④
BE SURE YOU CAN
• list the steps in the decision-making process • apply these steps to a sample decision-making situation • explain stakeholder analysis and cost-benefit analysis • discuss the differences between the classical and behavioural decision models • define the terms optimizing and satisfying

At the end of each section, **Learning Checks** prompt you to stop and review the key points you have just studied. If you cannot answer these questions, you should go back and read the section again.

WHERE WE'VE BEEN

Back to Chapters-Indigo

The opening example of how Heather Reisman turned her love of books into a national best-selling organization shows the importance of understanding the environment and being knowledgeable when taking risks and making decisions. In Chapter 7 you learned about the information needs of organizations and how new developments in information technology are changing organizations and the way people work. You have also learned how managers use information in the decision-making process, with special attention to decision errors and traps, ethical decision making, and decision making by individuals and groups.

Each chapter ends with **Where We've Been**, which looks back at the chapter opening vignette as a helpful reminder for summary and review purposes

THE NEXT STEP
INTEGRATED LEARNING ACTIVITIES

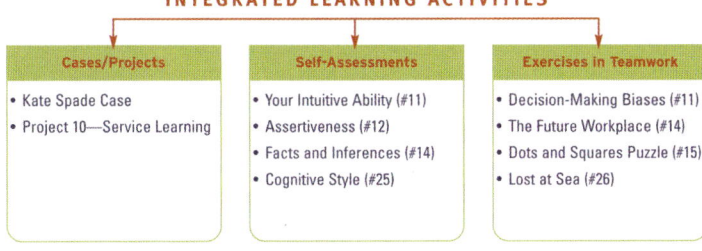

Cases/Projects
- Kate Spade Case
- Project 10—Service Learning

Self-Assessments
- Your Intuitive Ability (#11)
- Assertiveness (#12)
- Facts and Inferences (#14)
- Cognitive Style (#25)

Exercises in Teamwork
- Decision-Making Biases (#11)
- The Future Workplace (#14)
- Dots and Squares Puzzle (#15)
- Lost at Sea (#26)

The Next Step directs you to cases, projects, self-assessments, and experiential exercises included in the **Management Learning Workbook** at the back of the text.

STUDY QUESTION SUMMARY

1. How is information technology changing the workplace?
- A major and rapidly growing force in the economy are e-businesses, which use the Internet to engage in business-to-consumer and business-to-business electronic commerce.
- Within organizations and between organizations IT is breaking barriers to speed workflows and cut costs.
- Today's "electronic" offices with e-mail, instant messaging, and networked computer systems are changing the way work is accomplished in and by organizations.
- Organizations need and use internal, public, and intelligence information.
- Management information systems (MIS) collect, organize, store, and distribute data to meet the information needs of managers.
- Intranets, extranets, and Web portals allow people to share databases and communicate electronically within an organization and between the organization and its environment.

3. How do managers use information to make decisions?
- A problem is a discrepancy between an actual and a desired state of affairs.

The Summary is a bullet list summary of key points for each chapter opening Study Question.

KEY TERMS REVIEW

Behavioural decision model (p. 184)
Certain environment (p. 179)
Classical decision model (p. 184)
Corporate portals (p. 174)
Cost-benefit analysis (p. 183)
Crisis (p. 178)
Crisis management (p. 179)
Data (p. 174)
Decision (p. 178)
Decision-making process (p. 182)
Decision support system (p. 176)
Electronic commerce (p. 171)
Electronic data interchange (p. 176)
Enterprise portals (p. 174)

Escalating commitment (p. 187)
Expert system (p. 176)
Extranet (p. 176)
Framing error (p. 187)
Groupware (p. 176)
Heuristics (p. 186)
Information (p. 173)
Information system (p. 175)
Information technology (p. 170)
Instant messaging (p. 173)
Intellectual capital (p. 171)
Intranet (p. 176)
Intuitive thinking (p. 181)
Knowledge management (p. 190)
Knowledge worker (p. 171)

Learning organization (p. 190)
Management information system (p. 175)
Nonprogrammed decision (p. 178)
Optimizing decision (p. 184)
Peer-to-peer file sharing (p. 173)
Problem solving (p. 178)
Programmed decision (p. 178)
Risk environment (p. 180)
Satisficing decision (p. 184)
Strategic opportunism (p. 181)
Structured problem (p. 178)
Systematic thinking (p. 181)
Uncertain environment (p. 181)
Unstructured problem (p. 178)

SELF-TEST 7

MULTIPLE-CHOICE QUESTIONS:

1. _____ is the collective brainpower or shared knowledge of an organization and its workforce.
   (a) Artificial intelligence (b) Groupware (c) Intellectual capital (d) Intelligence information
2. _____ are special computer programs that use "if . . . then" rules to help users analyze and solve problems.
   (a) Expert systems (b) Heuristics (c) Intranets (d) Web portals
3. A manager who is reactive and works hard to address problems after they occur is known as a _____.
   (a) problem seeker (b) problem avoider (c) problem solver (d) problem manager

An end-of-chapter **Self-Test** helps assess your understanding of key chapter topics, including multiple-choice, short response and essay questions.

The **Key Terms List** is a reminder about key concepts, along with page references where they are defined.

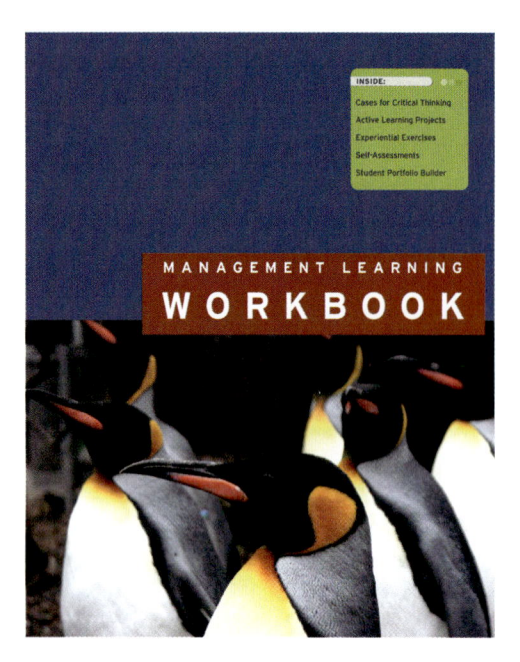

HOW TO USE THIS BOOK

The **Management Learning Workbook** is an end-of-text learning resource complete with a wide variety of cases, active learning projects, experiential exercises, self-assessments, and student portfolio builder to enrich and extend student learning.

The **Cases for Critical Thinking** section in the *Management Learning Workbook* contains 18 cases, with each based on actual organizations and specifically developed for a text chapter.

Ten **Active Learning Projects** in the *Management Learning Workbook* engage students in research and presentation projects on timely management topics, as well as in an exploration of management themes in popular culture.

A portfolio of 30 **Exercises in Teamwork** in the *Management Learning Workbook* help students experience through teamwork various issues and practical aspects of each chapter.

A set of 30 **Self-Assessment** inventories in the *Management Learning Workbook* involves students in exploring their personal managerial tendencies and perspectives.

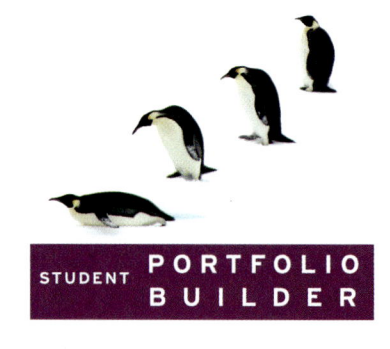

The **Student Portfolio** section of the *Management Learning Workbook* provides students with a template for building a student portfolio to summarize academic outcomes and display career credentials to potential employers.

Brief Contents

BEFORE YOU BEGIN

Memorandum to the Reader xvii

PART ONE ■ MANAGEMENT TODAY

CHAPTER 1 The Dynamic New Workplace 2
CHAPTER 2 Management–Past to Present 32
CHAPTER 3 Ethical Behaviour and Social Responsibility 58

PART TWO ■ CONTEXT

CHAPTER 4 Environment, Organizational Culture, and Diversity 88
CHAPTER 5 Global Dimensions of Management 114
CHAPTER 6 Entrepreneurship and Small Business 144

PART THREE ■ MISSION

CHAPTER 7 Information and Decision Making 168
CHAPTER 8 Planning and Controlling 194
CHAPTER 9 Strategic Management 224

PART FOUR ■ ORGANIZATION

CHAPTER 10 Organizing 252
CHAPTER 11 Organizational Design and Work Processes 278
CHAPTER 12 Human Resource Management 302

PART FIVE ■ LEADERSHIP

CHAPTER 13 Leading 330
CHAPTER 14 Motivation–Theory and Practice 356
CHAPTER 15 Individual Behaviour and Performance 382
CHAPTER 16 Teams and Teamwork 408
CHAPTER 17 Communication and Interpersonal Skills 440
CHAPTER 18 Change Leadership 470

MANAGEMENT LEARNING WORKBOOK ■

Cases for Critical Thinking W-4
Active Learning Projects W-51
Exercises in Teamwork W-57
Self-Assessments W-77
Student Portfolio Builder W-113

Contents

BEFORE YOU BEGIN

Memorandum to the Reader xvii

PART ONE ■ MANAGEMENT TODAY

CHAPTER 1

THE DYNAMIC NEW WORKPLACE 2
Planning Ahead 2
Study Questions 2
Workopolis.com—Putting Technology–and People–to Work 3
Learning Preview 4

WORKING IN THE NEW ECONOMY 5
   Intellectual Capital 5
   Globalization 6
   Technology 7
   Diversity 8
   Ethics 9
   Careers 10

ORGANIZATIONS IN THE NEW WORKPLACE 10
   What Is an Organization? 11
   Organizations as Systems 12
   Organizational Performance 12
   Changing Nature of Organizations 13

MANAGERS IN THE NEW WORKPLACE 14
   What Is a Manager? 15
   Levels and Types of Managers 15
   Managerial Performance 17
   Changing Nature of Managerial Work 18

THE MANAGEMENT PROCESS 19
   Functions of Management 19
   Managerial Activities and Roles 21
   Managerial Agendas and Networking 22

LEARNING HOW TO MANAGE 23
   Essential Managerial Skills 23
   Skill and Outcome Assessment 25
   Management Learning Framework 25

Chapter 1 Study Guide 27
   Where We've Been: Back to Workopolis.com 27
   The Next Step: Apple Computer Case, Projects, Exercises, Assessments 27
   Study Question Summary 27
   Key Terms Review 29
   Self-Test 1 29

CHAPTER 2

MANAGEMENT–PAST TO PRESENT 32
Planning Ahead 32
Study Questions 32
Google, Inc—Web-Crawler Extraordinaire! 33
Learning Preview 34

CLASSICAL MANAGEMENT APPROACHES 35
   Scientific Management 35
   Administrative Principles 37
   Bureaucratic Organization 40

BEHAVIOURAL MANAGEMENT APPROACHES 41
   The Hawthorne Studies and Human Relations 41
   Maslow's Theory of Human Needs 43
   McGregor's Theory X and Theory Y 44
   Argyris's Theory of Adult Personality 45

QUANTITATIVE MANAGEMENT APPROACHES 46
   Management Science 46
   Applied Quantitative Analysis Today 47

MODERN MANAGEMENT APPROACHES 47
   Organizations as Systems 47
   Contingency Thinking 48

CONTINUING MANAGEMENT THEMES 49
   Quality and Performance Excellence 49
   Global Awareness 51
   Learning Organizations 52
   21st-Century Leadership 52

Chapter 2 Study Guide 54
   Where We've Been: Back to Google, Inc. 54
   The Next Step: Coca-Cola Case, Projects, Exercises, Assessments 55
   Study Question Summary 55
   Key Terms Review 56
   Self-Test 2 56

CHAPTER 3

ETHICAL BEHAVIOUR AND SOCIAL RESPONSIBILITY 58
Planning Ahead 58
Study Questions 58

ALDO Shoes—*Creating a better world* 59
Learning Preview 60

WHAT IS ETHICAL BEHAVIOUR? 61
Laws, Values, and Ethical Behaviour 61
Alternative Views of Ethics 62
Cultural Issues in Ethical Behaviour 64

ETHICS IN THE WORKPLACE 65
Ethical Dilemmas at Work 65
Rationalizations for Unethical Behaviour 66
Factors Influencing Ethical Behaviour 67

MAINTAINING HIGH ETHICAL STANDARDS 70
Ethics Training 71
Whistle-blower Protection 71
Ethical Role Models 72
Codes of Ethical Conduct 72

CORPORATE SOCIAL RESPONSIBILITY 73
Stakeholder Issues and Analysis 73
Perspectives on Corporate Social Responsibility 75
Evaluating Corporate Social Performance 77
Social Entrepreneurship 79

ORGANIZATIONS AND SOCIETY 81
How Governments Influence Organizations 81
How Organizations Influence Governments 82
Role of Corporate Governance 83

Chapter 3 Study Guide 84
Where We've Been: Back to ALDO Shoes 84
The Next Step: Tom's of Maine Case, Projects, Exercises, Assessments 84
Study Question Summary 84
Key Terms Review 85
Self-Test 3 86

PART TWO ■ CONTEXT

CHAPTER 4

ENVIRONMENT, ORGANIZATIONAL CULTURE, AND DIVERSITY 88
Planning Ahead 88
Study Questions 88
BMO Financial Group—*An Employer of Choice* 89
Learning Preview 90

EXTERNAL ENVIRONMENT AND COMPETITIVE ADVANTAGE 90
What Is Competitive Advantage? 91
The General Environment 91
Stakeholders and the Specific Environment 93
Environmental Uncertainty 94

CUSTOMER-DRIVEN ORGANIZATIONS 95
Who Are the Customers? 95
What Customers Want 96
Customer Relationship Management 96

QUALITY-DRIVEN ORGANIZATIONS 97
Total Quality Management 97
Quality and Continuous Improvement 98
Quality, Technology, and Design 99

ORGANIZATIONAL CULTURE 100
What Strong Cultures Do 100
Levels of Organizational Culture 101
Value-Based Management 102
Symbolic Leadership 103

MULTICULTURAL ORGANIZATIONS AND DIVERSITY 104
What Is a Multicultural Organization? 104
Organizational Subcultures 105
Challenges Faced by Minorities and Women 106
Managing Diversity 108

Chapter 4 Study Guide 110
Where We've Been: Back to BMO Financial Group 110
The Next Step: UPS Case, Projects, Exercises, Assessments 110
Study Question Summary 110
Key Terms Review 111
Self-Test 4 112

CHAPTER 5

GLOBAL DIMENSIONS OF MANAGEMENT 114
Planning Ahead 114
Study Questions 114
Gildan—*Taking on the Giants* 115
Learning Preview 116

INTERNATIONAL MANAGEMENT AND GLOBALIZATION 117
Europe 118
The Americas 119
Asia and the Pacific Rim 119
Africa 120

INTERNATIONAL BUSINESS CHALLENGES 122
Why Companies Go International 122
Forms of International Business 122
Complications in the Global Business

Environment 124

MULTINATIONAL CORPORATIONS 125
Types of Multinational Corporations 126
Pros and Cons of Multinational Corporations 126
Ethical issues for Multinational Corporations 127

CULTURE AND GLOBAL DIVERSITY 128
Popular Dimensions of Culture 129
Values and National Cultures 131
Understanding Cultural Diversity 133

MANAGEMENT ACROSS CULTURES 134
Planning and Controlling 135
Organizing and Leading 135
Are Management Theories Universal? 136
Global Organizational Learning 137

Chapter 5 Study Guide 137
Where We've Been: Back to BMO Financial Group 139
The Next Step: Harley Davidson Case, Projects, Exercises, Assessments 139
Study Questions Summary 139
Key Terms Review 140
Self-Test 5 141

CHAPTER 6

ENTREPRENEURSHIP AND SMALL BUSINESS 144
Planning Ahead 144
Study Questions 144
ACE—*Support for the Budding Student Entrepreneur* 145
Learning Preview 146

THE NATURE OF ENTREPRENEURSHIP 147
Who Are the Entrepreneurs? 147
Characteristics of Entrepreneurs 149
Diversity and Entrepreneurship 151

ENTREPRENEURSHIP AND SMALL BUSINESS 152
Entrepreneurship and the Internet 153
International Business Entrepreneurship 153
Family Businesses 154
Why Many Small Businesses Fail 155

NEW VENTURE CREATION 156
Life Cycles of Entrepreneurial Firms 157
Writing the Business Plan 158
Choosing the Form of Ownership 159
Financing the New Venture 160

ENTREPRENEURSHIP AND BUSINESS DEVELOPMENT 161
Entrepreneurship in Large Enterprises 162
Business Incubation 162
Small Business Development Centres 163

Chapter 6 Study Guide 164
Where We've Been: Back to ACE 164
The Next Step: Domino's Pizza Case, Projects, Exercises, Assessments 164
Study Questions Summary 164
Key Terms Review 165
Self-Test 6 165

PART THREE ■ MISSION

CHAPTER 7

INFORMATION AND DECISION MAKING 168
Planning Ahead 168
Study Questions 168
Chapters-Indigo—*A Passion for Books Leads to Success* 169
Learning Preview 170

INFORMATION TECHNOLOGY AND THE CHANGING WORKPLACE 171
How IT Is Changing Business 171
How IT Is Changing Organizations 172
How IT Is Changing the Office 172

INFORMATION AND THE MANAGEMENT PROCESS 173
What Is Useful Information? 174
Information Needs in Organizations 174
Information Systems 175
Managers as Information Processors 177

INFORMATION AND MANAGERIAL DECISIONS 178
Types of Managerial Decisions 178
Decision Environments 179
Problem-Solving Styles 181

THE DECISION-MAKING PROCESS 182
Identify and Define the Problem 182
Generate and Evaluate Alternative Courses of Action 183
Decide on a Preferred Course of Action 184
Implement the Decision 185
Evaluate Results 186

ISSUES IN MANAGERIAL DECISION MAKING 186
Decision-Making Errors and Traps 186
Individual vs. Group Decision Making 188

Ethical Decision Making 189
Knowledge Management and Organizational Learning 189
Chapter 7 Study Guide 191
Where We've Been: Back to Chapters-Indigo 191
The Next Step: Kate Spade Case, Projects, Exercises, Assessments 191
Study Questions Summary 191
Key Terms Review 192
Self-Test 7 192

CHAPTER 8

PLANNING AND CONTROLLING 194
Planning Ahead 194
Study Questions 194
Cognos Inc.—*Crunching the Numbers to Succeed* 195
Learning Preview 196

HOW AND WHY MANAGERS PLAN 197
Importance of Planning 197
The Planning Process 197
Benefits of Planning 199
Planning Theories 201

TYPES OF PLANS USED BY MANAGERS 202
Short-Range and Long-Range Plans 202
Strategic and Operational Plans 203
Policies and Procedures 203
Budgets and Projects 204

PLANNING TOOLS AND TECHNIQUES 205
Forecasting 205
Contingency Planning 206
Scenario Planning 206
Benchmarking 206
Use of Staff Planners 206
Participation and Involvement 207

THE CONTROL PROCESS 208
Importance of Controlling 208
Steps in the Control Process 209
Types of Controls 211
Internal and External Control 212

ORGANIZATIONAL CONTROLS 213
MBO: Integrated Planning and Controlling 213
Employee Discipline Systems 214
Information and Financial Controls 215
Break-Even Analysis 216

Operations Management and Control 217
Chapter 8 Study Guide 220
Where We've Been: Back to Cognos Inc. 220
The Next Step: Wal-Mart Case, Projects, Exercises, Assessments 220
Study Questions Summary 220
Key Terms Review 221
Self-Test 8 222

CHAPTER 9

STRATEGIC MANAGEMENT 224
Planning Ahead 224
Study Questions 224
Taxi Invites You to be Part of the Future 225
Learning Preview 226

STRATEGIC COMPETITIVENESS 227
What Is Strategy? 227
Strategic Management 228
Strategic Management Goals 228

THE STRATEGIC MANAGEMENT PROCESS 229
Analysis of Mission, Values, and Objectives 230
Analysis of Organizational Resources and Capabilities 232
Analysis of Industry and Environment 233

STRATEGIES USED BY ORGANIZATIONS 235
Levels of Strategy 236
Growth and Diversification Strategies 236
Restructuring and Divestiture Strategies 237
Global Strategies 238
Co-operative Strategies 239
E-Business Strategies 239

STRATEGY FORMULATION 240
Porter's Generic Strategies 241
Portfolio Planning 243
Adaptive Strategies 244
Incrementalism and Emergent Strategy 244

STRATEGY IMPLEMENTATION 245
Management Practices and Systems 246
Corporate Governance 246
Strategic Leadership 247
Chapter 9 Study Guide 249
Where We've Been: Back to Taxi 249
The Next Step: Skype Case, Projects, Exercises, Assessments 249
Study Questions Summary 249
Key Terms Review 250
Self-Test 9 250

PART FOUR ■ ORGANIZATION

CHAPTER 10

ORGANIZING 252
Planning Ahead 252
Study Questions 252
Edward Jones—*Structures Supporting Strategies* 253
Learning Preview 254

ORGANIZING AS A MANAGEMENT FUNCTION 255
What Is Organization Structure? 255
Formal Structures 256
Informal Structures 256

TRADITIONAL ORGANIZATION STRUCTURES 257
Functional Structures 257
Divisional Structures 259
Matrix Structures 259

DIRECTIONS IN ORGANIZATION STRUCTURES 263
Team Structures 263
Network Structures 265
Boundaryless Organizations 267

ORGANIZING TRENDS AND PRACTICES 269
Shorter Chains of Command 269
Less Unity of Command 270
Wider Spans of Control 270
More Delegation and Empowerment 271
Decentralization with Centralization 273
Reduced Use of Staff 273

Chapter 10 Study Guide 275
Where We've Been: Back to Edward Jones 275
The Next Step: Nike Case, Projects, Exercises, Assessments 275
Study Questions Summary 275
Key Terms Review 276
Self-Test 10 276

CHAPTER 11

ORGANIZATIONAL DESIGN AND WORK PROCESSES 278
Planning Ahead 278
Study Questions 278
KPMG International—*Design for Integration, Empowerment, and Flexibility* 279
Learning Preview 280

ORGANIZATIONAL DESIGN ESSENTIALS 281
What Is Organizational Design? 281
Organizational Effectiveness 282
Organizational Design Choices 283

CONTINGENCIES IN ORGANIZATIONAL DESIGN 286
Environment 286
Strategy 287
Technology 288
Size and Life Cycle 289
Human Resources 291

SUBSYSTEMS DESIGN AND INTEGRATION 292
Subsystem Differentiation 293
Subsystem Integration 293

WORK PROCESS DESIGN 294
What Is a Work Process? 295
How to Re-engineer Core Processes 295
Process-Driven Organizations 296

Chapter 11 Study Guide 298
Where We've Been: Back to KPMG International 298
The Next Step: BET Case, Projects, Exercises, Assessments 298
Study Questions Summary 298
Key Terms Review 299
Self-Test 11 299

CHAPTER 12

HUMAN RESOURCE MANAGEMENT 302
Planning Ahead 302
Study Questions 302
DOFASCO—*"Take Care of People; They'll Take Care of Business"* 303
Learning Preview 304

WHY PEOPLE MAKE THE DIFFERENCE 305
Valuing Human Capital 305
The Diversity Advantage 305

HUMAN RESOURCE MANAGEMENT 307
Human Resource Management Process 307
Strategic Human Resource Management 307
Laws Against Employment Discrimination 308
Current Legal Issues in Human Resource Management 310

ATTRACTING A QUALITY WORKFORCE 311
Human Resource Planning 312
The Recruiting Process 313
How to Make Selection Decisions 314

DEVELOPING A QUALITY WORKFORCE 317
Employee Orientation 317
Training and Development 318
Performance Management Systems 319

MAINTAINING A QUALITY WORKFORCE 321
    Career Development 322
    Work-Life Balance 323
    Compensation and Benefits 323
    Retention and Turnover 324
    Labour – Management Relations 325
Chapter 12 Study Guide 327
    Where We've Been: Back to Dofasco 327
    The Next Step: SAS Institute Case, Projects, Exercises, Assessments 327
    Study Question Summary 327
    Key Terms Review 328
    Self-Test 12 328

PART FIVE ■ LEADERSHIP

CHAPTER 13

LEADING 330
Planning Ahead 330
Study Questions 330
J.-Robert Ouimet—*Leading with Vision, Cordon Bleu and Spirituality* 331
Learning Preview 332

THE NATURE OF LEADERSHIP 323
    Leadership and Vision 333
    Power and Influence 334
    Ethics and the Limits to Power 337
    Leadership and Empowerment 337

LEADERSHIP TRAITS AND BEHAVIOURS 338
    Search for Leadership Traits 338
    Focus on Leadership Behaviours 339
    Classic Leadership Styles 340

CONTINGENCY APPROACHES TO LEADERSHIP 341
    Fiedler's Contingency Model 341
    Hersey-Blanchard Situational Leadership Model 343
    House's Path-Goal Leadership Theory 344
    Vroom-Jago Leader-Participation Model 345

TRANSFORMATIONAL LEADERSHIP 347
    Transformational vs. Transactional Leadership 347
    Qualities of a Transformational Leader 348

CURRENT ISSUES IN LEADERSHIP DEVELOPMENT 348
    Emotional Intelligence 349
    Gender and Leadership 349
    Drucker's "Old-Fashioned" Leadership 350

    Moral Leadership 351
Chapter 13 Study Guide 353
    Where We've Been: Back to J.-Robert Ouimet 353
    The Next Step: Southwest Airlines Case, Projects, Exercises, Assessments 353
    Study Question Summary 353
    Key Terms Review 354
    Self-Test 13 354

CHAPTER 14

MOTIVATION–THEORY AND PRACTICE 356
Planning Ahead 356
Study Questions 356
Genentech—*Passion for Science and People* 356
Learning Preview 358

WHAT IS MOTIVATION? 359
    Motivation and Rewards 359
    Rewards and Performance 360

CONTENT THEORIES OF MOTIVATION 361
    Hierarchy of Needs Theory 361
    ERG Theory 362
    Two-Factor Theory 363
    Acquired Needs Theory 364
    Questions and Answers on Content Theories 365

PROCESS THEORIES OF MOTIVATION 366
    Equity Theory 366
    Expectancy Theory 367
    Goal-Setting Theory 369

REINFORCEMENT THEORY OF MOTIVATION 370
    Reinforcement Strategies 371
    Positive Reinforcement 372
    Punishment 373
    Ethical Issues in Reinforcement 373

MOTIVATION IN THE NEW WORKFORCE 374
    Integrated Model of Motivation 374
    Pay for Performance 375
    Incentive Compensation Systems 376
Chapter 14 Study Guide 379
    Where We've Been: Back to Genentech 379
    The Next Step: Nucor Case, Projects, Exercises, Assessments 379
    Study Questions Summary 379
    Key Terms Review 380
    Self-Test 14 380

CHAPTER 15

INDIVIDUAL BEHAVIOUR AND PERFORMANCE 382
Planning Ahead 382
Study Questions 382
Monitor Company—*Unlocking Everyone's Performance Potential* 383
Learning Preview 384

UNDERSTANDING PEOPLE AT WORK 385
Organizational Behaviour 385
Psychological Contracts 386
Work and the Quality of Life 387
Personality Traits 387

WORK ATTITUDES AND PERFORMANCE 390
What Is an Attitude? 390
Job Satisfaction 391
Individual Performance 392

JOB DESIGN ALTERNATIVES 393
Scientific Management 394
Job Rotation and Job Enlargement 394
Job Enrichment 395

DIRECTIONS IN JOB ENRICHMENT 396
Core Characteristics Model 396
Technology and Job Enrichment 398
Questions and Answers on Job Enrichment 398

ALTERNATIVE WORK ARRANGEMENTS 399
The Compressed Workweek 399
Flexible Working Hours 400
Job Sharing 401
Telecommuting 401
Part-Time Work 403
Chapter 15 Study Guide 398
Where We've Been: Back to Monitor Company 404
The Next Step: Steinway Piano Case, Projects, Exercises, Assessments 404
Study Question Summary 404
Key Terms Review 405
Self-Test 15 405

CHAPTER 16

TEAMS AND TEAMWORK 408
Planning Ahead 408
Study Questions 408
C.O.R.E Digital Pictures—*Teamwork in a Pod* 409
Learning Preview 410

TEAMS IN ORGANIZATIONS 411
Teamwork Pros and Cons 411
Why Meetings Fail 412
Synergy and the Usefulness of Groups 413
Formal and Informal Groups 414

TRENDS IN THE USE OF TEAMS 414
Committees, Project Teams, and Task Forces 415
Cross-Functional Teams 415
Employee Involvement Teams 416
Virtual Teams 416
Self-Managing Work Teams 417

HOW TEAMS WORK 418
What Is an Effective Team? 419
Stages of Team Development 420
Norms and Cohesiveness 423
Task and Maintenance Needs 425
Communication Networks 426

DECISION MAKING IN TEAMS 427
How Teams Make Decisions 427
Assets and Liabilities of Group Decisions 428
Groupthink 429
Creativity in Team Decision Making 430

LEADING HIGH-PERFORMANCE TEAMS 431
The Team-Building Process 431
Success Factors in Teams 433
Team Leadership Challenges 434
Chapter 16 Study Guide 436
Where We've Been: Back to C.O.R.E 436
The Next Step: Callaway Golf Case, Projects, Exercises, Assessments 436
Study Question Summary 436
Key Terms Review 437
Self-Test 16 437

CHAPTER 17

COMMUNICATION AND INTERPERSONAL SKILLS 440
Planning Ahead 440
Study Questions 440
Center for Creative Leadership—*Lead the Way with Communication* 441
Learning Preview 442

THE COMMUNICATION PROCESS 443
What Is Effective Communication? 444
Persuasion and Credibility in Communication 444
Communication Barriers 445

IMPROVING COMMUNICATION 443
    Active Listening 449
    Constructive Feedback 450
    Use of Communication Channels 450
    Interactive Management 450
    Proxemics and Space Design 452
    Technology Utilization 452
    Valuing Culture and Diversity 453

THE PERCEPTION PROCESS 454
    Perception and Attribution 455
    Perceptual Tendencies and Distortions 455

CONFLICT 457
    Functional and Dysfunctional Conflict 457
    Consequences of Conflict 458
    Causes of Conflict 458
    How to Deal with Conflict 459
    Conflict Management Styles 459

NEGOTIATION 461
    Negotiation Goals and Approaches 462
    Gaining Integrative Agreements 462
    Avoiding Negotiation Pitfalls 463
    Dispute Resolution 464
    Ethical Issues in Negotiation 465

Chapter 17 Study Guide 466
    Where We've Been: Back to Center for Creative Leadership 466
    The Next Step: United Nations Case, Projects, Exercises, Assessments 466
    Study Question Summary 466
    Key Terms Review 467
    Self-Test 17 468

CHAPTER 18

CHANGE LEADERSHIP 470
Planning Ahead 470
Study Questions 470
Meridian Credit Union—*The Call that Changed the Face of the Neighbourhood Credit Union* 471
Learning Preview 472

STRATEGIC LEADERSHIP AND INNOVATION 473
    What Is Strategic Leadership? 473
    Creativity and Innovation 473
    Characteristics of Innovative Organizations 477

ORGANIZATIONAL CHANGE 478
    Change Leaders 478
    Models of Change Leadership 479
    Transformational and Incremental Change 481
    Forces and Targets for Change 482

LEADING PLANNED CHANGE 483
    Phases of Planned Change 483
    Change Strategies 484
    Resistance to Change 487
    Challenges of Technological Change 488

ORGANIZATION DEVELOPMENT 489
    Organization Development Goals 489
    How Organization Development Works 489
    Organization Development Interventions 491

STRESS AND STRESS MANAGEMENT 492
    Sources of Stress 493
    Consequences of Stress 494
    Stress Management Strategies 495

Chapter 18 Study Guide 497
    Where We've Been: Back to Meridian Credit Union 497
    The Next Step: Disney Case, Projects, Exercises, Assessments 497
    Study Question Summary 497
    Key Terms Review 498
    Self-Test 17 499

MANAGEMENT LEARNING WORKBOOK

Cases for Critical Thinking W-4

Active Learning Projects W-51

Exercises in Teamwork W-57

Self-Assessments W-77

Student Portfolio Builder W-113

Self-test Answers AN-1

Glossary G-1

Notes EN-1

Name Index NI-1

Subject Index SI-1

managers located at the bottom. These managers aren't just order givers; they are there to mobilize and deliver the support others require to best serve customer needs. Each member of the upside-down pyramid is a value-added worker—someone who creates eventual value for the organization's customers or clients. The whole organization is devoted to serving the customer, and this is made possible with the support of managers. As noted earlier, we are in a time when the best managers are known more for "helping" and "supporting" than for "directing" and "order giving." Even in an age of high technology and "smart" machines, the human resource is indispensable. Worker involvement and empowerment are critical building blocks of organizational success. Full human resource utilization increasingly means changing the way work gets done by pushing decision-making authority to the point where the best information and expertise exist—with the operating workers.

> **BE SURE YOU CAN**
> • describe the various types and levels of managers • define the terms accountability and quality of work life and explain their importance to managerial performance • explain the role of managers in the upside-down pyramid view of organizations • list the several ways in which managerial work is changing
>
> ✓ Learning check ❸

THE MANAGEMENT PROCESS

The ultimate "bottom line" in every manager's job is to succeed in helping an organization achieve high performance by best utilizing its human and material resources. If productivity in the form of high levels of performance effectiveness and efficiency is a measure of organizational success, managers are largely responsible for its achievement. It is their job to mobilize technology and talent by creating environments within which people work hard and perform to the best of their abilities.

FUNCTIONS OF MANAGEMENT

Managers must have the capabilities to recognize performance problems and opportunities, make good decisions, and take appropriate actions. They do this through the

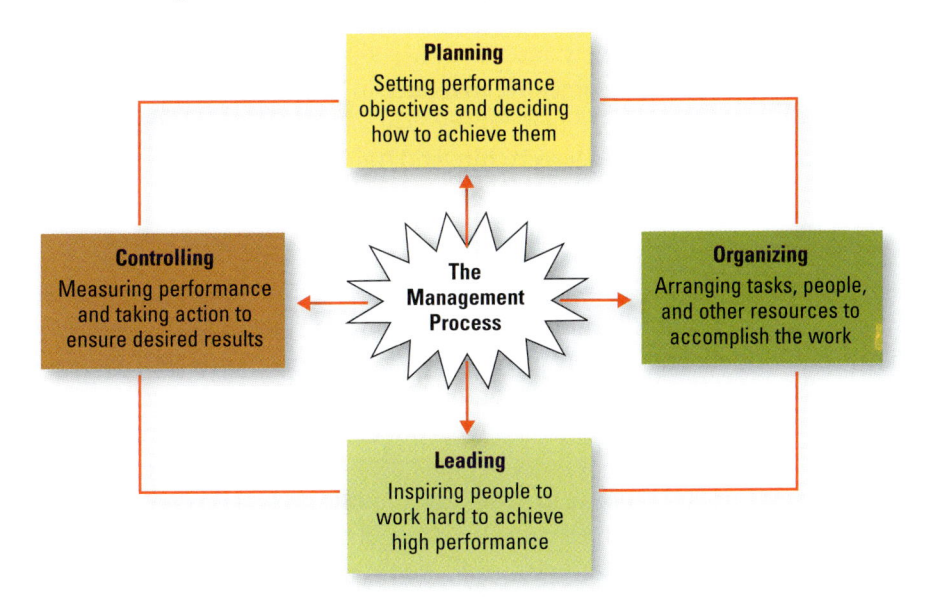

Figure 1.4 Four functions of management.

Planning — Setting performance objectives and deciding how to achieve them

Organizing — Arranging tasks, people, and other resources to accomplish the work

Leading — Inspiring people to work hard to achieve high performance

Controlling — Measuring performance and taking action to ensure desired results

The Management Process

AROUND THE WORLD

Professionalism travels the world

Ernst & Young is one of the world's top professional services firms. With operations in 130 countries, it serves the needs of business customers in all areas of public accounting as well as online security, enterprise risk management, and other business areas. Wherever in the world Ernst & Young operates, its performance commitment is expressed in the slogan "Quality in Everything We Do." Recently, Ernst & Young Poland was named by the local edition of *Newsweek* as the country's most desired employer. The firm's goal of valuing people is expressed in its emphasis on teamwork, continuous learning, work-life balance, and leadership for all employees.

Source: information found at the corporate website <www.ey.com>

■ **Management** is the process of planning, organizing, leading, and controlling the use of resources to accomplish performance goals.

process of **management**—planning, organizing, leading, and controlling the use of resources to accomplish performance goals. These four management functions and their interrelationships are shown in *Figure 1.4*. All managers, regardless of title, level, type, and organizational setting, are responsible for the four functions.[50] However, they are not accomplished in linear step-by-step fashion. The reality is that all functions are continually engaged as a manager moves from task to task and opportunity to opportunity in his or her work.

Planning

■ **Planning** is the process of setting objectives and determining what should be done to accomplish them.

In management, **planning** is the process of setting performance objectives and determining what actions should be taken to accomplish them. Through planning, a manager identifies desired results and ways to achieve them. Take, for example, an Ernst & Young initiative that was developed to better meet the needs of the firm's female professionals.[51] Top management grew concerned about the firm's retention rates for women and by a critical report from the research group Catalyst. Chairman Philip A. Laskawy, who personally headed Ernst & Young's Diversity Task Force, responded by setting a planning objective to reduce turnover rates for women. Rates at the time were running some 22 percent per year and costing the firm about 150 percent of each person's annual salary to hire and train new staff.

Organizing

■ **Organizing** is the process of assigning tasks, allocating resources, and coordinating work activities.

Even the best plans will fail without strong implementation. Success begins with **organizing**, the process of assigning tasks, allocating resources, and coordinating the activities of individuals and groups to implement plans. Through organizing, managers turn plans into actions by defining jobs, assigning personnel, and supporting them with technology and other resources. At Ernst & Young, Laskawy organized to meet his planning objective by first creating a new Office of Retention and then hiring Deborah K. Holmes to head it. As retention problems were identified in various parts of the firm, Holmes convened special task forces to tackle them and recommend location-specific solutions. A Woman's Access Program was started to give women access to senior executives for mentoring and career development.

Leading

In management, **leading** is the process of arousing people's enthusiasm to work hard and inspiring their efforts to fulfill plans and accomplish objectives. Through leading, managers build commitments to a common vision, encourage activities that support goals, and influence others to do their best work on the organization's behalf. At Ernst & Young, Deborah Holmes identified a core problem—work at the firm was extremely intense and women were often stressed because their spouses also worked. She became a champion for improved work-life balance and pursued it relentlessly. Although admitting that "there's no silver bullet" in the form of a universal solution, new initiatives from her office supported and encouraged better balance. She started "call-free holidays" where professionals did not check voice mail or e-mail on weekends and holidays. She also started a "travel sanity" program that limited staffers' travel to four days a week so that they could get home for weekends.

■ **Leading** is the process of arousing enthusiasm and inspiring efforts to achieve goals.

Controlling

The management function of **controlling** is the process of measuring work performance, comparing results to objectives, and taking corrective action as needed. Through controlling, managers maintain active contact with people in the course of their work, gather and interpret reports on performance, and use this information to plan constructive action and change. At Ernst & Young, Laskawy and Holmes both knew what the retention rates were when they started the new program, and they were subsequently able to track improvements. Through measurement they were able to compare results with objectives, and track changes in work-life balance and retention rates. They continually adjusted the program to improve it. In today's dynamic times, such control and adjustment are indispensable. Things don't always go as anticipated, and plans must be modified and redefined for future success.

■ **Controlling** is the process of measuring performance and taking action to ensure desired results.

●●● MANAGERIAL ACTIVITIES AND ROLES

Although the management process may seem straightforward, things are more complicated than they appear at first glance. In his classic book *The Nature of Managerial Work*, Henry Mintzberg describes the daily work of corporate chief executives as: "There was no break in the pace of activity during office hours. The mail…telephone calls…and meetings…accounted for almost every minute from the moment these executives entered their offices in the morning until they departed in the evenings."[52] Today, we would have to add ever-present e-mail to Mintzberg's list of executive preoccupations.[53]

In trying to systematically describe the nature of managerial work and the demands placed on those who do it, Mintzberg identified the set of 10 roles depicted in *Figure 1.5*. The roles involve managing information, people, and action. The roles are interconnected, and all managers must be prepared to perform all of them.[54] In Mintzberg's framework, a manager's *informational roles* involve the giving, receiving, and analyzing of information. The *interpersonal roles* involve interactions with people inside and outside the work unit. The *decisional roles* involve using information to make decisions to solve problems or address opportunities.

Mintzberg is careful to note that the manager's day is unforgiving in the intensity and pace of these role requirements. The managers he observed had little free time because unexpected problems and continuing requests for meetings consumed

Figure 1.5 Mintzberg's 10 managerial roles.

Interpersonal roles

How a manager interacts with other people
- Figurehead
- Leader
- Liaison

Informational roles

How a manager exchanges and processes information
- Monitor
- Disseminator
- Spokesperson

Decisional roles

How a manager uses information in decision making
- Entrepreneur
- Disturbance handler
- Resource allocator
- Negotiator

PERSONAL MANAGEMENT

SELF-AWARENESS is one of those concepts that is easy to talk about but very hard to master. What do you really know about yourself? How often do you take a critical look at your attitudes, behaviours, skills, and accomplishments? Do you ever realistically assess your personal strengths and weaknesses—both as you see them and as others do? A high degree of self-awareness is essential for personal adaptability, to be able to grow and develop in changing times. This figure, called the Johari Window, offers a way of comparing what we know about ourselves with what others know about us.[58] Our "open" areas are often small, while the "blind spot," "the unknown," and the "hidden" areas can be quite large. Think about the personal implications of the Johari Window. Are you willing to probe the unknown, uncover your blind spots, and discover talents and weaknesses that may be hidden? As your self-awareness expands, you will find many insights for personal growth and development.

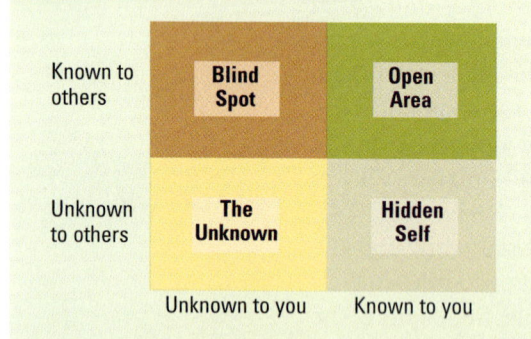

	Unknown to you	Known to you
Known to others	Blind Spot	Open Area
Unknown to others	The Unknown	Hidden Self

Get to know yourself better

Complete Self-Assessments #1—**21st Century Manager**, and #2—**Emotional Intelligence**, from the Workbook and Personal Management Activity #1 on the companion website.

---

almost all the time that became available. Their workdays were hectic, and the pressure for continuously improving performance was all-encompassing. Says Mintzberg: "The manager can never be free to forget the job, and never has the pleasure of knowing, even temporarily, that there is nothing else to do.… Managers always carry the nagging suspicion that they might be able to contribute just a little bit more. Hence they assume an unrelenting pace in their work."[55]

Managerial work is busy, demanding, and stressful not just for chief executives but for managers at all levels of responsibility in any work setting. A summary of research on the nature of managerial work offers this important reminder.[56]

- Managers work long hours.
- Managers work at an intense pace.
- Managers work at fragmented and varied tasks.
- Managers work with many communication media.
- Managers accomplish their work largely through interpersonal relationships.

MANAGERIAL AGENDAS AND NETWORKING

On her way to a meeting, a general manager (GM) bumped into a staff member who did not report to her. Using this opportunity, in a two-minute conversation she (a) asked two questions and received the information she needed; (b) reinforced their good relationship by sincerely complimenting the staff member on something he had recently done; and (c) got the staff member to agree to do something that the GM needed done.

This description of a brief incident provides a glimpse of an effective general manager in action.[57] It portrays two activities that management consultant and scholar John Kotter considers critical to a general manager's success—agenda setting and networking. Through agenda setting, good managers develop action priorities that include goals and plans spanning long and short time frames. These agendas are usually incomplete and loosely connected in the beginning, but become more specific as the manager utilizes information continually gleaned from many different sources. The agendas are always kept in mind and are "played out" whenever an opportunity arises, as in the preceding quotation. Good managers implement their agendas by working with a variety of people inside and outside the organization. In Kotter's example, the GM was getting things done through a staff member who did not report directly to her. This is made possible by networking, the process of building and maintaining positive relationships with people whose help may be needed to implement one's work agendas. In this example, the GM's networks would include relationships with peers, a boss, and higher-level executives, subordinates, and members of their work teams, as well as with external customers, suppliers, and community representatives. Such networks are indispensable to managerial success in today's complex work environments, and excellent managers devote much time and effort to their development.

> **BE SURE YOU CAN**
> • define and give examples of each of the four major functions in the management process—planning, organizing, leading, and controlling • explain Mintzberg's view of what managers do, including the key managerial roles • explain how managers use agendas and networks to fulfill their work responsibilities
>
> ✓ Learning check ④

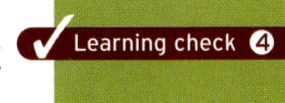

LEARNING HOW TO MANAGE

Today's turbulent times present an ever-shifting array of problems, opportunities, and performance expectations to organizations and their members. Change is a way of life, and it demands new organizational and individual responses. The quest for high performance is relentless, with workers everywhere expected to find ways to achieve high productivity under new and dynamic conditions. They are expected to become involved, participate fully, demonstrate creativity, and find self-fulfillment in their work. They are expected to be team players who understand the needs and goals of the total organization, and who use new technologies to their full advantage. All of this, of course, means that your career success depends on a real commitment to learning—not just formal learning in the classroom, but also **lifelong learning**. This is the process of continuously learning from our daily experiences and opportunities. Especially in a dynamic and ever-changing environment, a commitment to lifelong learning helps us build portfolios of skills that are always up to date, job relevant, and valuable in the emerging economy.

■ **Lifelong learning** is continuous learning from daily experiences.

●●●● ESSENTIAL MANAGERIAL SKILLS

A **skill** is the ability to translate knowledge into action that results in desired performance. Obviously, many skills are required to master the challenging nature of managerial work. The most important ones are those that allow managers to help others become more productive in their work. Harvard scholar Robert L. Katz has classified the essential skills of managers into three categories: technical, human,

■ A **skill** is the ability to translate knowledge into action that results in desired performance.

Figure 1.6 Katz's essential managerial skills.

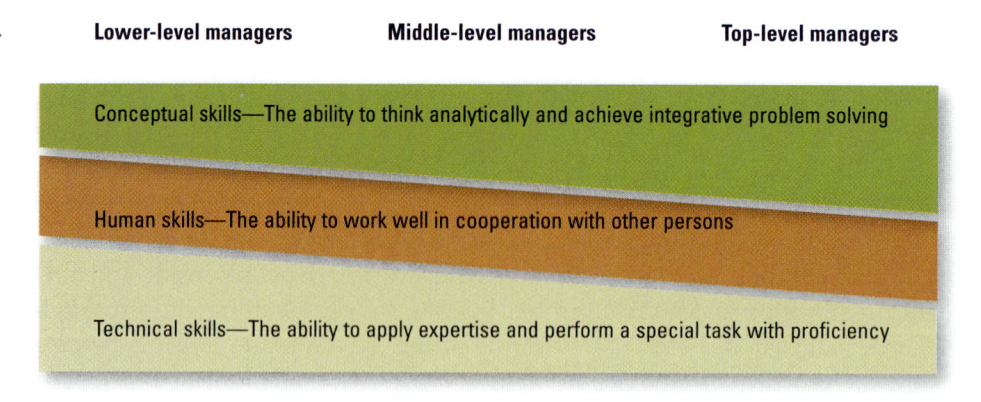

| Lower-level managers | Middle-level managers | Top-level managers |

Conceptual skills—The ability to think analytically and achieve integrative problem solving

Human skills—The ability to work well in cooperation with other persons

Technical skills—The ability to apply expertise and perform a special task with proficiency

and conceptual.[59] Although all three skills are necessary for managers, he suggests that their relative importance tends to vary by level of managerial responsibility, as shown in *Figure 1.6*.

A **technical skill** is the ability to use a special proficiency or expertise to perform particular tasks. Accountants, engineers, market researchers, financial planners, and systems analysts, for example, possess technical skills. These skills are initially acquired through formal education and are further developed by training and job experience. Technical skill in the new economy is also increasingly tied to computer literacy and utilization of the latest information technology. Figure 1.6 shows that technical skills are very important at career entry levels. The critical question to be asked and positively answered by you in this respect and in preparation for any job interview comes down to this simple test: "What can you really do for an employer?"

The ability to work well in co-operation with other persons is a **human skill**. It emerges in the workplace as a spirit of trust, enthusiasm, and genuine involvement in interpersonal relationships. A manager with good human skills will have a high degree of self-awareness and a capacity to understand or empathize with the feelings of others. An important component of the essential human skills is **emotional intelligence**.[60] Discussed in Chapter 13 for its leadership implications, "EI" is defined by scholar and consultant Daniel Goleman as the "ability to manage ourselves and our relationships effectively."[61] Given the highly interpersonal nature of managerial work, human skills and emotional intelligence are critical for all managers. Figure 1.6 shows that they are consistently important across all the managerial levels. Again, a straightforward question puts your interpersonal skills and emotional intelligence to the test: "How well do you work with others?"

All good managers ultimately have the ability to view situations broadly and to solve problems to the benefit of everyone concerned. This ability to think critically and analytically is a **conceptual skill**. It involves the capacity to break problems into smaller parts, to see the relations between the parts, and to recognize the implications of any one problem for others. As we assume ever-higher responsibilities in organizations, we are called upon to deal with more ambiguous problems that have many complications and longer-term consequences. Figure 1.6 shows that conceptual skills gain in relative importance for top managers. At this point, you should ask: "Am I developing critical thinking and problem-solving capabilities for long-term career success?"

■ **Technical skill** is the ability to use expertise to perform a task with proficiency.

■ A **human skill** is the ability to work well in co-operation with other people.

■ **Emotional intelligence** is the ability to manage ourselves and our relationships effectively.

■ **Conceptual skill** is the ability to think analytically and solve complex problems.

●●● SKILL AND OUTCOME ASSESSMENT

Business and management educators are increasingly interested in helping people acquire the essential skills and develop specific competencies that can help them achieve managerial success. A **managerial competency** is a skill-based capability that contributes to high performance in a management job.[62] A number of these competencies have been implied in the previous discussion of the management process, including those related to planning, organizing, leading, and controlling. Competencies are also implicit in the information, interpersonal, and decision-making demands of managerial roles, as well as in agenda setting and networking as managerial activities.

■ **Managerial competency** is a skill-based capability for high performance in a management job.

Listed here are some of the skills and personal characteristics business schools emphasize as foundations for continued professional development and career success. You can use this as a preliminary checklist for assessing your career readiness.

- *Communication*—ability to share ideas and findings clearly in written and oral expression—includes writing, oral presentation, giving/receiving feedback, technology utilization
- *Teamwork*—ability to work effectively as a team member and team leader—includes team contribution, team leadership, conflict management, negotiation, consensus building
- *Self-management*—ability to evaluate oneself, modify behaviour, and meet performance obligations—includes ethical reasoning and behaviour, personal flexibility, tolerance for ambiguity, performance responsibility
- *Leadership*—ability to influence and support others to perform complex and ambiguous tasks—includes diversity awareness, global understanding, project management, strategic action
- *Critical thinking*—ability to gather and analyze information for creative problem solving—includes problem solving, judgement and decision making, information gathering and interpretation, creativity/innovation
- *Professionalism*—ability to sustain a positive impression, instill confidence, and maintain career advancement—includes personal presence, personal initiative, and career management

●●● *MANAGEMENT* LEARNING FRAMEWORK

Management introduces management as an academic discipline whose understanding is important for anyone seeking career success in the new workplace. The focus is on helping you to become familiar with key concepts, theories, and terms, and to understand their practical implications. The five major parts of the book are presented in a systematic building-block fashion: (1) Introducing Management, (2) Context, (3) Mission, (4) Organization, (5) Leading. The subject matter in each has been carefully chosen, described, and illustrated in ways that encourage you to actively think about your developing managerial skills and competencies. As you read *Management* remember to take full advantage of the built-in learning framework. The chapters are written with an integrated pedagogy that makes it easier for you to do well on assignments and examinations. From the chapter-opening study questions, to the learning preview, to the embedded learning checks, through the many examples, to the end-of-chapter study guide with its summary, key terms review, and self-test, you have the opportunity to learn as you read. If you allow the book's pedagogy to work for you, the learning opportunities summarized in *Figure 1.7* should pay off in solid understanding and enhanced course performance.

Figure 1.7 *Management—Understanding Management from Theory to Practice.*

Part 1 Management Today
- The Dynamic New Workplace
- Management—Past to Present
- Ethical Behaviour and Social Responsibility

Part 2 Context
- Environment and Diversity
- Global Dimensions
- Entrepreneurship and Small Business

Part 3 Mission
- Information and Decision Making
- Planning and Controlling
- Strategic Management

Managerial Skills and Competencies

Management Learning Workbook

Part 4 Organization
- Organizing
- Organizational Design and Processes
- Human Resource Management

Part 6 Leadership
- Leading
- Motivation—Theory and Practice
- Individual, Behaviour and Performance
- Teams and Teamwork
- Communication and Interpersonal Skills
- Change Leadership

A special and unique learning resource is found in the end-of-text *Management Learning Workbook*. This feature offers the critical "next step" in learning, providing you with a rich variety of resources and activities. Explore the cases, pursue the active-learning projects, engage in the experiential exercises, take the self-assessments, and build a student portfolio. Many opportunities for learning are present in the workbook, but only you can take advantage of them. Only you can step forward and take personal responsibility for advancing your managerial skills and career readiness in today's challenging world. *Management*, from cover to cover, is a great learning resource. Now is the time to read, study, and benefit from it. Get connected with your future!

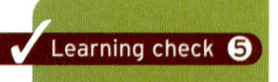

✓ **Learning check 5**

BE SURE YOU CAN
• define three essential managerial skills—technical, human, and conceptual skills • explain Katz's view of how these skills vary in importance across management levels • define emotional intelligence as an important human skill • list and give examples of several personal characteristics important for managerial success

Chapter 1 STUDY GUIDE

WHERE WE'VE BEEN

Back to workopolis.com

The opening example of workopolis.com focused on you, your career, and the great opportunities for career success that exist in today's dynamic environment. You don't need to create your own company to achieve career success, although you could. What you must do is discover the willingness to learn within yourself, and commit it to academic success and career development. In Chapter 1 you learned about the new work environment—from the challenges of technology utilization, to the forces of globalization, to diversity and ethical behaviour, and more. You also gained insight into the nature of organizations, the managerial roles, and the critical importance of developing essential managerial and leadership skills.

THE NEXT STEP
INTEGRATED LEARNING ACTIVITIES

Cases/Projects
- Apple Computer Case
- Project 1—Diversity Lessons

Self-Assessments
- A 21st Century Manager (#1)
- Emotional Intelligence (#2)
- Diversity Awareness (#7)
- Are You Cosmopolitan? (#18)

Exercises in Teamwork
- My Best Manager (#1)
- What Managers Do (#2)
- Defining Quality (#3)
- The Future Workplace (#14)

STUDY QUESTION SUMMARY

1. What are the challenges of working in the new economy?

- Today's turbulent environment challenges everyone to understand and embrace continuous change and developments in a new information-driven and global economy.
- Work in the new economy is increasingly knowledge based, and people, with their capacity to bring valuable intellectual capital to the workplace, are the ultimate foundation of organizational performance.
- The forces of globalization are bringing increased interdependencies among nations and economies, as customer markets and resource flows create intense business competition.
- Ever-present developments in information technology and the continued expansion of the Internet are reshaping organizations, changing the nature of work, and increasing the value of knowledge workers.
- Organizations must value the talents and capabilities of a workforce whose members are increasingly diverse with respect to gender, age, race and ethnicity, able-bodiedness, and lifestyles.
- Society has high expectations for organizations and their members to perform with commitment to high ethical standards and

in socially responsible ways, including protection of the natural environment and human rights.
- Careers in the new economy require great personal initiative to build and maintain skill "portfolios" that are always up to date and valuable to employers challenged by the intense competition and the information age.

2. **What are organizations like in the new workplace?**
- Organizations are collections of people working together to achieve a common purpose.
- As open systems, organizations interact with their environments in the process of transforming resource inputs into product outputs.
- Productivity is a measure of the quantity and quality of work performance, with resource costs taken into account.
- High-performing organizations are both effective, in terms of goal accomplishment, and efficient, in terms of resource utilization.
- Organizations today emphasize total quality management in a context of technology utilization, empowerment and teamwork, and concern for work-life balance, among other trends.

3. **Who are managers and what do they do?**
- Managers directly support and facilitate the work efforts of other people in organizations.
- Top managers scan the environment, create vision, and emphasize long-term performance goals; middle managers coordinate activities in large departments or divisions; team leaders and supervisors support performance at the team or work-unit level.
- Functional managers work in specific areas such as finance or marketing; general managers are responsible for larger multi-functional units; administrators are managers in public or non-profit organizations.
- Managers are held accountable for performance results that the manager depends on other persons to accomplish.

- The upside-down pyramid view of organizations shows operating workers at the top serving customer needs while being supported from below by various levels of management.
- The changing nature of managerial work emphasizes being good at "coaching" and "supporting" others, rather than simply "directing" and "order-giving."

4. **What is the management process?**
- The management process consists of the four functions of planning, organizing, leading, and controlling.
- Planning sets the direction; organizing assembles the human and material resources; leading provides the enthusiasm and direction; controlling ensures results.
- Managers implement the four functions in daily work that is intense and stressful, involving long hours and continuous performance pressures.
- Managerial success in this demanding context requires the ability to perform well in interpersonal, informational, and decision-making roles.
- Managerial success also requires the ability to utilize interpersonal networks to accomplish well-selected task agendas.

5. **How do you learn the essential managerial skills and competencies?**
- Careers in the new economy demand continual attention to lifelong learning from all aspects of daily experience and job opportunities.
- Skills considered essential for managers are broadly described as technical—ability to use expertise; human—ability to work well with other people; and conceptual—ability to analyze and solve complex problems.
- Skills and outcomes considered as foundations for managerial success include communication, teamwork, self-management, leadership, critical thinking, and professionalism.
- *Management* focuses attention on building your career potential through understanding the practical implications of important concepts and theories.

KEY TERMS REVIEW

Accountability (p. 17)
Administrator (p. 17)
Conceptual skill (p. 24)
Controlling (p. 21)
Corporate governance (p. 9)
Discrimination (p. 8)
Emotional intelligence (p. 24)
Ethics (p. 9)
Functional managers (p. 17)
General managers (p. 17)
Glass ceiling effect (p. 9)
Globalization (p. 7)
Human skill (p. 24)
Intellectual capital (p. 6)

Knowledge worker (p. 6)
Leading (p. 21)
Lifelong learning (p. 23)
Line managers (p. 7)
Management (p. 20)
Manager (p. 15)
Managerial competency (p. 25)
Middle managers (p. 16)
Open system (p. 12)
Organization (p. 11)
Organizing (p. 20)
Performance effectiveness (p. 12)
Performance efficiency (p. 13)
Planning (p. 20)

Prejudice (p. 8)
Productivity (p. 12)
Project managers (p. 16)
Quality of work life (p. 18)
Skill (p. 23)
Staff managers (p. 17)
Supervisors (p. 16)
Team leaders (p. 16)
Technical skill (p. 24)
Top managers (p. 16)
Total quality management (TQM) (p. 14)
Workforce diversity (p. 8)

SELF-TEST 1

MULTIPLE-CHOICE QUESTIONS:

1. The process of management involves the functions of planning, _____, leading, and controlling.
   (a) accounting (b) creating (c) innovating (d) organizing

2. An effective manager achieves both high-performance results and high levels of _____ among people doing the required work. (a) turnover (b) effectiveness (c) satisfaction (d) stress

3. Performance efficiency is a measure of the _____ associated with task accomplishment.
   (a) resource costs (b) goal specificity (c) product quality (d) product quantity

4. The requirement that a manager answer to a higher-level boss for results achieved by a work team is called _____.
   (a) dependency (b) accountability (c) authority (d) empowerment

5. Productivity is a measure of the quantity and _____ of work produced, with resource utilization taken into account. (a) quality (b) cost (c) timeliness (d) value

6. _____ managers pay special attention to the external environment, looking for problems and opportunities and finding ways to deal with them.
   (a) Top (b) Middle (c) Lower (d) First-line

7. The accounting manager for a local newspaper would be considered a _____ manager, whereas the editorial manager would be considered a _____ manager.
   (a) general, functional (b) middle, top (c) staff, line (d) senior, junior

8. When a team leader clarifies desired work targets and deadlines for a work team, he or she is fulfilling the management function of _____.
   (a) planning (b) delegating (c) controlling (d) supervising

9. The process of building and maintaining good working relationships with others who may help implement a manager's work agendas is called _____.
   (a) governance (b) networking (c) authority (d) entrepreneurship

10. In Katz's framework, top managers tend to rely more on their _____ skills than do first-line managers.
    (a) human (b) conceptual (c) decision-making (d) technical

11. The research of Mintzberg and others concludes that managers _____.
    (a) work at a leisurely pace (b) have blocks of private time for planning (c) always live with the pressures of performance responsibility (d) have the advantages of short work weeks

12. When someone with a negative attitude toward minorities makes a decision to deny advancement opportunities to an Indo-Canadian worker, this is an example of _____. (a) discrimination (b) emotional intelligence (c) control (d) prejudice

13. Among the trends in the new workplace, one can expect to find _____.
    (a) more order giving (b) more valuing people as human assets (c) less teamwork (d) reduced concern for work-life balance

14. The manager's role in the "upside-down pyramid" view of organizations is best described as providing _____ so that operating workers can directly serve _____.
    (a) direction, top management (b) leadership, organizational goals (c) support, customers (d) agendas, networking

15. The management function of _____ is being perfomed when a retail manager measures daily sales in the dress department and compares them with daily sales targets.
    (a) planning (b) agenda setting (c) controlling (d) delegating

SHORT-RESPONSE QUESTIONS:

16. List and explain the importance of three pressures of ethics and social responsibility that managers must be prepared to face.

17. Explain how "accountability" operates in the relationship between (a) a manager and her subordinates, and (b) the same manager and her boss.

18. Explain how the "glass ceiling effect" may disadvantage newly hired female university graduates in a large corporation.

19. What is "globalization" and what are its implications for working in the new economy?

APPLICATION QUESTION:

20. You have just been hired as the new supervisor of an audit team for a national accounting firm. With four years of experience, you feel technically well prepared for the assignment. However, this is your first formal appointment as a "manager." Things are complicated at the moment. The team has 12 members of diverse demographic and cultural backgrounds, as well as work experience. There is an intense workload and a lot of performance pressure. How will this situation challenge you to develop and use essential managerial skills and related competencies to successfully manage the team to high levels of auditing performance?

2 Management— Past to Present

Planning Ahead

After reading Chapter 2, you should be able to answer these questions in your own words.

CHAPTER 2 STUDY QUESTIONS

1. What can be learned from classical management thinking?
2. What ideas were introduced by the human resource approaches?
3. What is the role of quantitative analysis in management?
4. What is unique about the systems view and contingency thinking?
5. What are continuing management themes of the 21st century?

GOOGLE, INC.
WEB-CRAWLER EXTRAORDINAIRE!

Since its origins in a Stanford University dorm room in 1998, Google has built a reputation that usually takes most companies decades to achieve. The company recently placed third among 60 of the most prominent companies in the world, ranking behind No. 1 Johnson & Johnson and No. 2 Coca-Cola Co., business icons that are both more than a century old. Started by two young university students, Larry Page and Sergey Brin, the company has grown to 4,138 employees. In August 2004, Google became a publicly traded company; one year later its share prices had tripled and it had a market capitalization of US $125 billion. Today, Google is the world's largest search engine with 40 percent of the search market, offering its service in over 100 languages; 400 million people use Google for online searches each month. Survey respondents have called Google "indispensable" and "priceless." It's also the engine that drives both AOL and Yahoo searches. How did the com-pany attain such success? What is the Google difference? The answer is performance excellence based on speed, accuracy, and ease of use. These have been the guiding performance criteria from the beginning, the basis for generating user appeal and competitive advantage in the marketplace. Page and Brin wanted to create the "perfect search engine" that "understands exactly what you mean and gives you back exactly what you want," says Page. With such goals, talent and motivation drive the system. The company uses unique strategies to recruit the best and the brightest, once posting a billboard on a stretch of highway running through Silicon Valley that read: "Solve the complex math problem on the ad, plug the correct answer into an Internet site and you could wind up working for the world's most popular search engine." The company website describes its approach to talent this way: "Google's hiring policy is aggressively non-discriminatory, and favours ability over experience." The result is a staff that reflects the global audience the search engine serves. In all, 34 languages are spoken by Google staffers—from Turkish to Telugu. In the continuing search for motivation, the firm sticks to its historical roots—an informal culture with a small company feel. At Google, bright, creative people with diverse backgrounds and skills come together to build an ever-better search engine.[1]

GET CONNECTED!

Google is unquestionably a successful company; as you read this chapter determine what historical management practices Page and Brin appear to have drawn from as they built Google.

Chapter 2 LEARNING PREVIEW

Just as a Google search churns through billions of websites, Google's founders and staffers continuously strive to learn from past experience and apply their expertise to continuously improving the company. The same holds as scholars work within the field of management itself. In Chapter 2 you will become acquainted with the historical roots of management and learn how they created the knowledge base that today helps you and others become better managers.

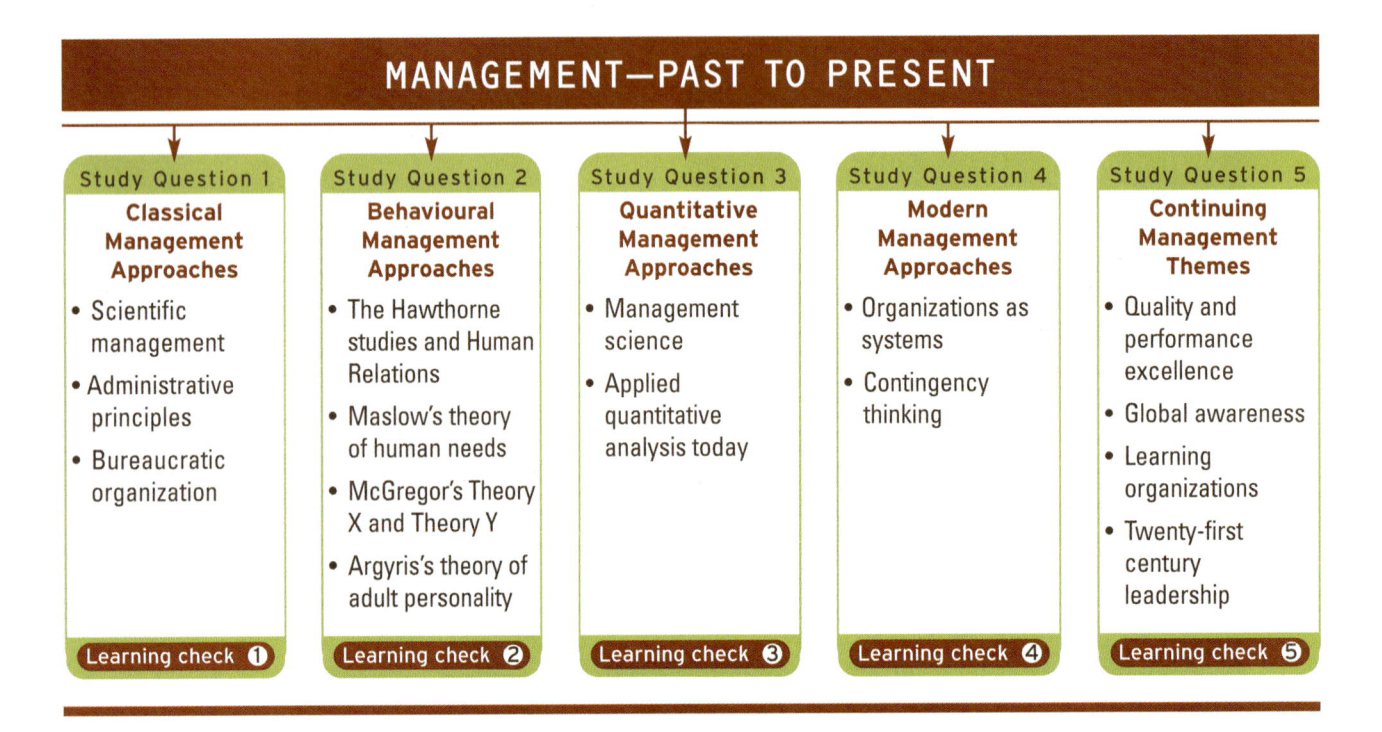

MANAGEMENT—PAST TO PRESENT

Study Question 1: Classical Management Approaches
- Scientific management
- Administrative principles
- Bureaucratic organization

Learning check 1

Study Question 2: Behavioural Management Approaches
- The Hawthorne studies and Human Relations
- Maslow's theory of human needs
- McGregor's Theory X and Theory Y
- Argyris's theory of adult personality

Learning check 2

Study Question 3: Quantitative Management Approaches
- Management science
- Applied quantitative analysis today

Learning check 3

Study Question 4: Modern Management Approaches
- Organizations as systems
- Contingency thinking

Learning check 4

Study Question 5: Continuing Management Themes
- Quality and performance excellence
- Global awareness
- Learning organizations
- Twenty-first century leadership

Learning check 5

The problems and opportunities facing organizations today are complex, ever-present, and always changing. From the anxieties of terrorism to the uncertainties of international politics to the challenges of globalization, all of society's institutions feel the pressures of a new and very challenging environment. The world of work and business as we have known it is being transformed as traditional ways of doing things are replaced by new practices and viewpoints. But even in the rush toward an exciting future, one shouldn't sell history short. Knowledge gained through past experience can and should be used as a foundation for future success.

When Harvard University Press released *Mary Parker Follett—Prophet of Management: A Celebration of Writings from the 1920s*, it clearly reminded us of the wisdom of history.[2] Although Follett wrote in a different day and age, her ideas are rich with foresight. She advocated co-operation and better horizontal relationships in organizations, taught respect for the experience and knowledge of workers, warned against the dangers of too much hierarchy, and called for visionary leadership. Today we pursue similar themes while using terms like "empowerment," "involvement," "flexibility," and "self-management." Rather than naively believe that we are reinventing management practice, it is better to recognize the historical roots of many modern ideas and admit that we are still trying to perfect them.[3]

In *The Evolution of Management Thought,* Daniel Wren traces management as far back as 5000 BC, when ancient Sumerians used written records to assist in governmental and commercial activities.[4] Management was important to the construction of the Egyptian pyramids, the rise of the Roman Empire, and the commercial success of 14th-century Venice. By the time of the Industrial Revolution in the 1700s, great social changes helped prompt a great leap forward in the manufacture of basic staples and consumer goods. Industrial development was accelerated by Adam Smith's ideas of efficient production through specialized tasks and the division of labour. By the turn of the 20th century, Henry Ford and others were making mass production a mainstay of the emerging economy. Since then, the science and practices of management have been on a rapid and continuing path of development.

To frame our "Past to Present" discussion, the history of management theory has been grouped into five eras or phases of development. The first era, the classical management approaches, begins with the work of Frederick W. Taylor and examines developments in management thinking at the beginning of the 20th century. In a search for efficiency, the classical approaches move through a number of management models, all of them based on the rationale that people will work in a manner most economically beneficial to themselves. In the 1930s the focus shifts to theories of behavioural management, which look for a more progressive workplace where employee morale and relationships are found to be important. It is in this era that the dominant thinking of "man as machine" is challenged and the human side of business examined. As a result of the demands of the Second World War, the 1940s bring in a quantitative approach to management that focuses on producing goods quickly and achieving the greatest output possible. Beginning with the 1960s, the modern era of management theory concerns itself with an examination of organizations within their environment and the things that could be learned from the interactions between the two. Strategy and structure discussions are in vogue as management fully explores contingency theories. In the 1980s, up until the present, management theory focuses on the issues of quality, excellence, globalization, learning, technology, and cross-cultural aspects of management. You will discover that much of current management thought is built on the theories and lessons of the past.

CLASSICAL MANAGEMENT APPROACHES

Our study of management begins with the classical approaches: (1) scientific management, (2) administrative principles, and (3) bureaucratic organization.[5] *Figure 2.1* associates each with a prominent person or people in the history of management thought. These names are important to know since they are still widely used in management conversations today. Also, the figure shows that the classical approaches share a common assumption: people at work act in a rational manner that is primarily driven by economic concerns. Workers are expected to rationally consider opportunities made available to them and do whatever is necessary to achieve the greatest personal and monetary gain.[6]

●●●● SCIENTIFIC MANAGEMENT

In 1911 Frederick W. Taylor published *The Principles of Scientific Management,* in which he makes the following statement: "The principal object of management should be to secure maximum prosperity for the employer, coupled with the

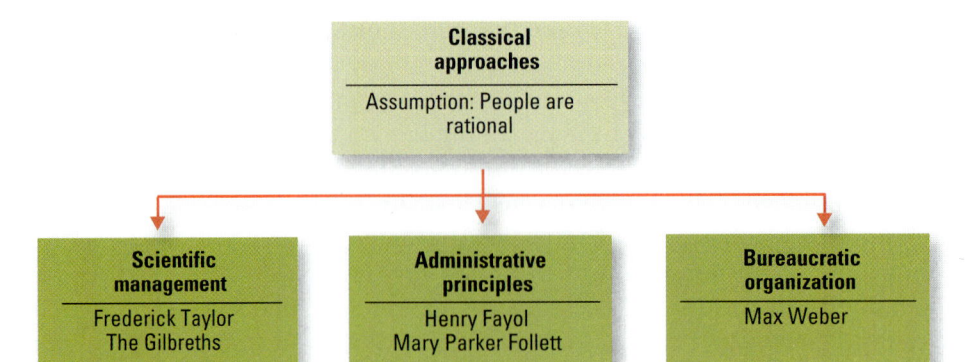

Figure 2.1 Major branches in the classical approach to management.

```
                    Classical
                    approaches
            Assumption: People are
                     rational
            ┌───────────┼───────────┐
            ▼           ▼           ▼
      Scientific   Administrative  Bureaucratic
      management     principles    organization
      Frederick Taylor  Henry Fayol    Max Weber
      The Gilbreths  Mary Parker Follett
```

maximum prosperity for the employee."[7] Taylor, often called the "father of scientific management," noticed that many workers did their jobs their own way and without clear and uniform specifications. He believed that this caused them to lose efficiency and perform below their true capacities. He also believed that this problem could be corrected if workers were taught and then helped by supervisors to always perform their jobs in the right way.

Taylor's goal was to improve the productivity of people at work. He used the concept of "time study" to analyze the motions and tasks required in any job and to develop the most efficient ways to perform them.[8] He then linked these job requirements with both training for the worker and support from supervisors in the form of proper direction, work assistance, and monetary incentives. The implications of his efforts are found in many management settings today, as summarized in *Manager's Notepad 2.1*. Taylor's approach is known as **scientific management** and includes these four guiding action principles.

■ **Scientific management** emphasizes careful selection and training of workers and supervisory support with an emphasis on improving efficiency.

1. Develop for every job a "science" that includes rules of motion, standardized work implements, and proper working conditions.

2. Carefully select workers with the right abilities for the job.

3. Carefully train workers to do the job and give them the proper incentives to co-operate with the job "science."

MANAGER'S
Notepad 2.1

Practical lessons from scientific management

- Produce safe products and services.
- Make results-based compensation a performance incentive.
- Carefully design jobs with efficient work methods.
- Carefully select workers with the abilities to do these jobs.
- Train workers to perform jobs to the best of their abilities.
- Train supervisors to support workers so that they can perform jobs to the best of their abilities.

4. Support workers by carefully planning their work and by smoothing the way as they go about their jobs.

Expanding on his first guiding principle, Taylor highlighted the importance of studying the motions involved in a task in order to understand the most efficient way of working. This approach, called **motion study**, is the science of reducing a job or task to its basic physical motions. Two contemporaries of Taylor, Frank and Lillian Gilbreth, pioneered motion studies as a management tool. In one famous study, they reduced the number of motions used by bricklayers and tripled their productivity.[9] The Gilbreths' work established the foundation for later advances in the areas of job simplification, work standards, and incentive wage plans—all techniques still used in the modern workplace.

An example of the continuing influence of Taylor and the Gilbreths can be seen at United Parcel Service (UPS), where workers are guided by carefully calibrated productivity standards. At regional centres, sorters are timed according to strict task requirements and are expected to load vans at a set number of packages per hour. Delivery stops on regular van routes are studied and carefully timed, and supervisors generally know, within a few minutes, how long a driver's pickups and deliveries will take. Industrial engineers devise precise routines for drivers, who are trained to knock on customers' doors rather than spend even a few seconds looking for the doorbell. Handheld computers further enhance delivery efficiencies. At UPS, savings of seconds on individual stops add up to significant increases in productivity.

■ **Motion study** is the science of reducing a task to its basic physical motions.

ADMINISTRATIVE PRINCIPLES

A second branch in the classical approaches to management includes attempts to document and understand the experiences of successful managers. Two prominent writers in this school of thought are Henri Fayol and Mary Parker Follett.

Henri Fayol

In 1916, after a career in French industry, Henri Fayol published *Administration Industrielle et Générale*.[10] The book outlines his views on the proper management of organizations and the people within them. Henri Fayol identified 14 principles of management that he felt should be taught to all aspiring managers like yourselves. Fayol derived these principles from his own experiences as an engineer leading large-scale enterprises of thousands of employees. His 14 principles are as follows:

1. *Division of Labour*—Specialization of work will result in continuous improvements in skills and methods.
2. *Authority*—Managers and workers need to understand that managers have the right to give orders.
3. *Discipline*—Behaviour needs to be grounded in obedience and derived from respect. There will be no slacking or bending of rules.
4. *Unity of command*—Each employee should have one, and only one, manager.
5. *Unity of direction*—The leader generates a single plan, and all play their part in executing that plan.

6. *Subordination of Individual Interests*—While at work, only work issues should be undertaken or considered.

7. *Remuneration*—All should receive fair payment for their work; employees are valuable and not simply an expense.

8. *Centralization*—While recognizing the difficulties in large organizations, decisions are primarily made from the top.

9. *Scalar Chain* (line of authority)—Organizations must have clear, formal chains of command running from the top to the bottom of the organization.

10. *Order*—There is a place for everything, and all things should be in their place.

11. *Equity*—Managers should be kind and fair.

12. *Personnel Tenure*—Unnecessary turnover is to be avoided, and there should be lifetime employment for good workers.

13. *Initiative*—Undertake work with zeal and energy.

14. *Esprit de corps*—Work to build harmony and cohesion among personnel.

The following five "rules" or "duties" of management identified by Fayol in his book closely resemble the four functions of management—planning, organizing, leading, and controlling—that we talk about today:

1. *Foresight*—to complete a plan of action for the future.

2. *Organization*—to provide and mobilize resources to implement the plan.

3. *Command*—to lead, select, and evaluate workers to get the best work toward the plan.

4. *Coordination*—to fit diverse efforts together, and ensure information is shared and problems solved.

5. *Control*—to make sure things happen according to plan, and to take necessary corrective action.

What lessons can we derive from Fayol today? Most importantly, Fayol believed that management could be taught. He was very concerned about improving the quality of management and set forth a number of "principles" to guide managerial action. Fayol showed us that management can be seen as a variety of activities or actions that can be worked on in order to improve one's managerial skill set. A number of them are still part of the management vocabulary. They include Fayol's *scalar chain principle*—there should be a clear and unbroken line of communication from the top to the bottom in the organization; the *unity of command principle*—each person should receive orders from only one boss; and the *unity of direction principle*—one person should be in charge of all activities that have the same performance objective.

AROUND THE WORLD

When Mercedes Benz set up manufacturing in North America, the best of its German management practices came, too. The German automaker expects and teaches its American workers to follow precise standards known at SMPs (standard methods and procedures). The SMPs specify everything right down to the way a lug nut should be tightened and where a tool should be placed when not in use. Mercedes believes this is the key to maintaining high-quality and high-performance standards, no matter where in the world its automobiles are manufactured.

Sources: Information from Justin Martin, "Mercedes: Made in Alabama," *Fortune* (July 7, 1997), pp. 150–158; and "A Plant Grows in Alabama," *Mercedes Momentum* (Spring 1998), pp. 56–61.

Quality practices readily travel the world

Mary Parker Follett

Another contributor to the administrative principles school was Mary Parker Follett, who was eulogized at her death in 1933 as "one of the most important women America has yet produced in the fields of civics and sociology."[11] In her writings about businesses and other organizations, Follett displayed an understanding of groups and a deep commitment to human cooperation—ideas that are highly relevant today. For her, groups were mechanisms through which diverse individuals could combine their talents for a greater good. She viewed organizations as "communities" in which managers and workers should labour in harmony, without one party dominating the other and with the freedom to talk over and truly reconcile conflicts and differences. She believed it was the manager's job to help people in organizations co-operate with one another and achieve an integration of interests.

A review of *Dynamic Administration: The Collected Papers of Mary Parker Follett* helps to illustrate the modern applications of her management insights.[12] Follett believed that making every employee an owner in the business would create feelings of collective responsibility. Today, we address the same issues under such labels as "employee ownership," "profit sharing," and "gain-sharing plans." Follet believed that business problems involve a wide variety of factors that must be considered in relationship to one another. Today, we talk about "systems" when describing the same phenomenon. Follett believed that businesses were services and that private profits should always be considered vis-à-vis the public good. Today, we pursue the same issues under the labels of "managerial ethics" and "corporate social responsibility."

● ● ● BUREAUCRATIC ORGANIZATION

Max Weber was a late-19th-century German intellectual whose insights have had a major impact on the field of management and the sociology of organizations. His ideas developed somewhat in reaction to what he considered to be performance deficiencies in the organizations of his day. Among other things, Weber was concerned that people were in positions of authority not because of their job-related capabilities, but because of their social standing or "privileged" status in German society. For this and other reasons, he believed that organizations largely failed to reach their performance potential.

At the heart of Weber's thinking was a specific form of organization he believed could correct the problems just described—a **bureaucracy**.[13] This is an ideal, intentionally rational, and very efficient form of organization founded on principles of logic, order, and legitimate authority. The defining characteristics of Weber's bureaucratic organization are as follows:

- *Clear division of labour:* Jobs are well defined, and workers become highly skilled at performing them.

- *Clear hierarchy of authority:* Authority and responsibility are well defined for each position, and each position reports to a higher-level one.

- *Formal rules and procedures:* Written guidelines direct behaviour and decisions in jobs, and written files are kept for historical record.

- *Impersonality:* Rules and procedures are impartially and uniformly applied with no one receiving preferential treatment.

- *Careers based on merit:* Workers are selected and promoted on ability and performance, and managers are career employees of the organization.

Weber believed that organizations would perform well as bureaucracies. They would have the advantages of efficiency in utilizing resources and of fairness or equity in the treatment of employees and clients. In his words:

> *The purely bureaucratic type of administrative organization…is, from a purely technical point of view, capable of attaining the highest degree of efficiency. …It is superior to any other form in precision, in stability, in the stringency of its discipline, and in its reliability. It thus makes possible a particularly high degree of calculability of results for the heads of the organization and for those acting in relation to it. It is finally superior both in intensive efficiency and in the scope of its operations and is formally capable of application to all kinds of administrative tasks.*[14]

This is the ideal side of bureaucracy. However, the terms "bureaucracy" and "bureaucrat" are now often used with negative connotations. The possible disadvantages of bureaucracy include excessive paperwork or "red tape," slowness in handling problems, rigidity in the face of shifting customer or client needs, resistance to change, and employee apathy. These disadvantages are most likely to cause problems for organizations that must be flexible and quick in adapting to changing circumstances—a common situation today. Thus researchers now try to determine when and under what conditions bureaucratic features work best. They

■ A **bureaucracy** is a rational and efficient form of organization founded on logic, order, and legitimate authority.

also want to identify alternatives to the bureaucratic form. Current trends in management include many innovations that seek the same goals as Weber but with different approaches to how organizations can be structured.

> **BE SURE YOU CAN**
> • list the principles of Taylor's scientific management • list key points raised by Fayol such as "unity of command" • understand Follett's view of an "integration of interests" • list the key characteristics of bureaucracy and explain why Weber considered it an ideal form of organization • identify possible disadvantages of bureaucracy in today's environment

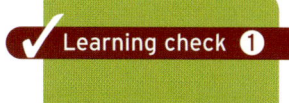

BEHAVIOURAL MANAGEMENT APPROACHES

During the 1920s, an emphasis on the human side of the workplace began to influence management thinking. Major branches in the behavioural, or human resource, approaches to management are shown in *Figure 2.2*. They include the famous Hawthorne studies and Maslow's theory of human needs, as well as theories generated from these foundations by Douglas McGregor, Chris Argyris, and others. The behavioural approaches maintain that people are social and self-actualizing. People at work are assumed to seek satisfying social relationships, respond to group pressures, and search for personal fulfillment.

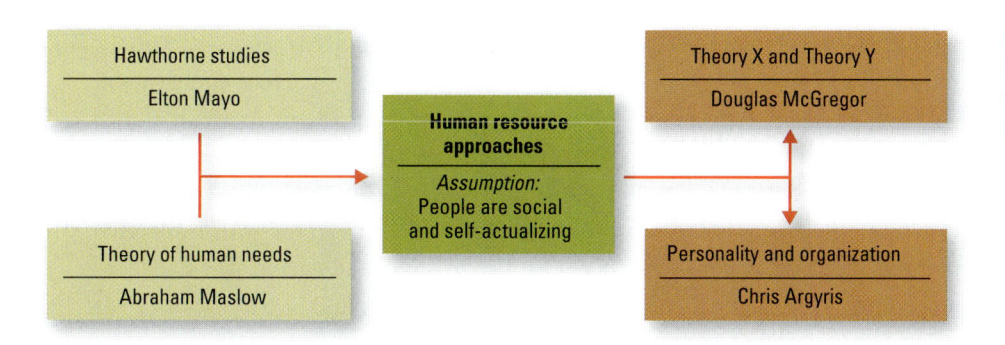

Figure 2.2 Foundations in the behavioural or human resource approaches to management.

●●● THE HAWTHORNE STUDIES AND HUMAN RELATIONS

In 1924, the Western Electric Company (predecessor to today's Lucent Technologies) commissioned a research program to study individual productivity at the Hawthorne Works of the firm's Chicago plant.[15] The initial "Hawthorne studies" had a scientific management perspective and sought to determine how economic incentives and the physical conditions of the workplace affected the output of workers. An initial focus was on the level of illumination in the manufacturing facilities; it seemed reasonable to expect that better lighting would improve performance. After failing to find this relationship, however, the researchers concluded that unforeseen "psychological factors" somehow interfered with their illumination experiments. This finding and later Hawthorne studies directed attention toward human interactions in the workplace and ultimately had a major influence on the field of management.

Relay Assembly Test-Room Studies

In 1927, a team led by Harvard's Elton Mayo began more research to examine the effect of worker fatigue on output. Care was taken to design a scientific test that would be free of the psychological effects thought to have confounded the earlier illumination studies. Six workers who assembled relays were isolated for intensive study in a special test room. They were given various rest pauses and workdays and workweeks of various lengths, and production was regularly measured. Once again, researchers failed to find any direct relationship between changes in physical working conditions and output. Productivity increased regardless of the changes made.

Mayo and his colleagues concluded that the new "social setting" created for workers in the test room accounted for the increased productivity. Two factors were singled out as having special importance. One was the group atmosphere; the workers shared pleasant social relations with one another and wanted to do a good job. The other was more participative supervision. Test-room workers were made to feel important, were given a lot of information, and were frequently asked for their opinions. This was not the case in their regular jobs elsewhere in the plant.

CANADIAN COMPANY IN THE NEWS — Four Seasons Hotels and Resorts

PEOPLE HOLD THE KEYS TO LONG-TERM PERFORMANCE SUCCESS

Toronto-based Four Seasons Hotels and Resorts seeks employees who are friendly, committed to teamwork, and, of course, highly talented. The firm declares that quality of service is "so critically important to our guests, and the degree to which we can provide and evolve it, worldwide, is also the degree to which we can differentiate ourselves and stay ahead of the rest." Four Seasons is a leader in the luxury segment of the hospitality industry. Its strengths and reputation are cultivated with leadership commitment to a fundamental principle: The key to sustained performance success is people. Among the guiding values of the firm is: "we believe that each of us needs a sense of dignity, pride, and satisfaction in what we do."

Source: Information from corporate website, <www.fourseasons.com>

Employee Attitudes, Interpersonal Relations, and Group Processes

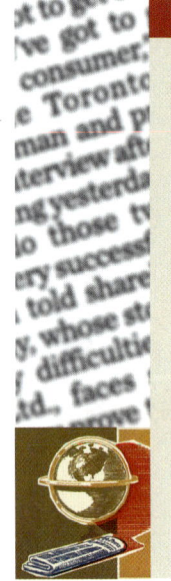

Mayo's research continued until the worsening economic conditions of the Depression forced its termination in 1932. By then, interest in the human factor had broadened to include employee attitudes, interpersonal relations, and group relations. In one study, over 21,000 employees were interviewed to learn what they liked and disliked about their work environment. "Complex" and "baffling" results led the researchers to conclude that the same things (e.g., work conditions or wages) could be sources of satisfaction for some workers and of dissatisfaction for others. The final Hawthorne study was conducted in a bank wiring room and centred on the role of the work group. A surprise finding here was that people would restrict their output in order to avoid the displeasure of the group, even if it meant sacrificing pay that could otherwise be earned by increasing output. Thus, it was recognized that groups can have strong negative, as well as positive, influences on individual productivity.

Lessons of the Hawthorne Studies

As scholars now look back, the Hawthorne studies are criticized for poor research design, weak empirical support for the conclusions drawn, and the tendency of researchers to overgeneralize their findings.[16] Yet their significance as turning points in the evolution of management thought remains intact. The Hawthorne studies helped shift the attention of managers and management researchers away from the technical and structural concerns of the classical approach and toward social and human concerns as keys to productivity. They showed that people's feelings, attitudes, and relationships with co-workers affected their work. They recognized the importance of group influences on individuals. They also identified the **Hawthorne effect**—the tendency of people who are singled out for special attention to perform as anticipated merely because of expectations created by the situation.

The Hawthorne studies contributed to the emergence of the **human relations movement**, which influenced management thinking during the 1950s and 1960s. This movement was largely based on the viewpoint that managers who used good human relations in the workplace would achieve productivity. Importantly, this movement combined with related developments in the social sciences to set the stage for what has now evolved as the field of **organizational behaviour**, the study of individuals and groups in organizations.

> ■ The **Hawthorne effect** is the tendency of persons singled out for special attention to perform as expected.
>
> ■ The **human relations movement** suggests that managers using good human relations will achieve productivity.
>
> ■ **Organizational behaviour** is the study of individuals and groups in organizations.

●●● MASLOW'S THEORY OF HUMAN NEEDS

Among the insights of the human relations movement, the work of psychologist Abraham Maslow in the area of human "needs" is a key foundation.[17] A **need** is a physiological or psychological deficiency a person feels the compulsion to satisfy. This is a significant concept for managers because needs create tensions that can influence a person's work attitudes and behaviours.

> ■ A **need** is a physiological or psychological deficiency that a person wants to satisfy.

Maslow identified the five levels of human needs, shown in *Figure 2.3*. From lowest to highest in order, they are physiological, safety, social, esteem, and self-actualization needs. Maslow's theory is based on two underlying principles. The first is the *deficit principle*—a satisfied need is not a motivator of behaviour. People act to satisfy "deprived" needs, those for which a satisfaction "deficit" exists. The second is the *progression principle*—the five needs exist in a hierarchy of "prepotency." A need at any level is only activated when the next-lower-level need is satisfied.

According to Maslow, people try to satisfy the five needs in sequence. They progress step by step from the lowest level in the hierarchy up to the highest. Along the way, a deprived need dominates individual attention and determines behaviour until it is satisfied. Then, the next-higher-level need is activated. At the level of self-actualization, the deficit and progression principles cease to operate. The more this need is satisfied, the stronger it grows.

Consistent with human relations thinking, Maslow's theory implies that managers who help people satisfy their important needs at work will achieve productivity. Although scholars now recognize that things are more complicated than this, as

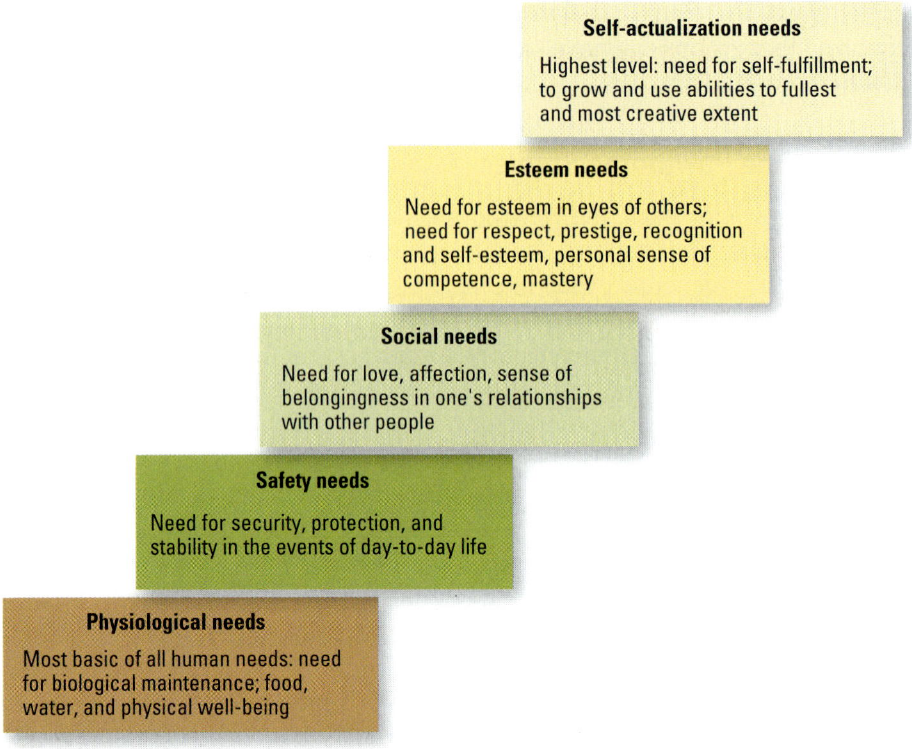

Figure 2.3 Maslow's hierarchy of human needs.

Self-actualization needs
Highest level: need for self-fulfillment; to grow and use abilities to fullest and most creative extent

Esteem needs
Need for esteem in eyes of others; need for respect, prestige, recognition and self-esteem, personal sense of competence, mastery

Social needs
Need for love, affection, sense of belongingness in one's relationships with other people

Safety needs
Need for security, protection, and stability in the events of day-to-day life

Physiological needs
Most basic of all human needs: need for biological maintenance; food, water, and physical well-being

discussed in Chapter 14 on motivation, Maslow's ideas are still relevant. Consider, for example, the case of volunteer workers who do not receive any monetary compensation. Managers in non-profit organizations have to create jobs and work environments that satisfy the many different needs of volunteers. If their work isn't fulfilling, the volunteers will lose interest and probably redirect their efforts elsewhere.

McGREGOR'S THEORY X AND THEORY Y

Douglas McGregor was heavily influenced by both the Hawthorne studies and Maslow. His classic book *The Human Side of Enterprise* advances the thesis that managers should give more attention to the social and self-actualizing needs of people at work.[18] McGregor called upon managers to shift their view of human nature away from a set of assumptions he called "Theory X" and toward ones he called "Theory Y."

According to McGregor, managers holding **Theory X** assumptions approach their jobs believing that those who work for them generally dislike work, lack ambition, are irresponsible, are resistant to change, and prefer to be led rather than to lead. McGregor considers such thinking inappropriate. He argues instead for the value of **Theory Y** assumptions in which the manager believes people are willing to work, are capable of self-control, are willing to accept responsibility, are imaginative and creative, and are capable of self-direction.

An important aspect of McGregor's ideas is his belief that managers who hold either set of assumptions can create **self-fulfilling prophecies**—that is, through their behaviour they create situations where others act in ways that confirm the original expectations. *Managers with Theory X assumptions*, for example, act in a very

■ **Theory X** assumes people dislike work, lack ambition, are irresponsible, and prefer to be led.

■ **Theory Y** assumes people are willing to work, accept responsibility, are self-directed and creative.

■ A **self-fulfilling prophecy** occurs when a person acts in ways that confirm another's expectations.

directive "command-and-control" fashion that gives people little personal say over their work. These supervisory behaviours create passive, dependent, and reluctant subordinates who tend to do only what they are told to or required to do. This reinforces the original Theory X viewpoint.

In contrast, *managers with Theory Y perspectives* behave in "participative" ways that allow subordinates more job involvement, freedom, and responsibility. This creates opportunities to satisfy esteem and self-actualization needs, and workers tend to perform as expected with initiative and high performance. The self-fulfilling prophecy thus becomes a positive one. Theory Y thinking is consistent with developments in the new workplace and its emphasis on valuing workforce diversity. It is also central to the popular notions of employee participation, involvement, empowerment, and self-management.[19] In summary, Theory X and Y are assumptions about human nature that guide our thoughts, but this approach to managing people has its limitations. Rather than thinking that all workers belong to either the X or Y camp, managers need to understand that both approaches to dealing with people work (and do not work) under certain conditions. We will discuss this later in the chapter under the topic "contingency thinking."

●●● ARGYRIS'S THEORY OF ADULT PERSONALITY

Ideas set forth by the well-regarded scholar, and consultant, Chris Argyris also reflect the belief in human nature advanced by Maslow and McGregor. In his book *Personality and Organization*, Argyris contrasts the management practices found in traditional and hierarchical organizations with the needs and capabilities of mature adults.[20] He concludes that some practices, especially those influenced by the classical management approaches, are inconsistent with the mature adult personality.

Canadian Managers
Measuring Innovation

Zenon Environmental, known for its innovative membrane for water filtration, has thrived largely due to the quantitative management approach of former COO Rafael Simon. While at Zenon, Simon created a single metric to measure all costs at Zenon: the cost per gallon of water treated. This encompasses everything that goes into the final product, and links the company's efforts with customers' interests. In the three years after Simon introduced the metric in 2001, the cost per gallon of water treated fell more than 25%. Simon's approach has become part of the corporate culture. It has changed the way the company works—how it bids on contracts and how departments collaborate. Still, simple cost-cutting isn't enough. In an interview Simon once said that as COO he faced the challenge " to make sure that, as we improve our profitability, as we tighten up our operations, and as we install the necessary policies and procedures, we never lose that entrepreneurial spark."

Source: Andrew Wahl, "The Best Managers in Canada: Top in Operations," *Canadian Business*, April 26–May 9, 2004, Vol. 77, Iss. 9.

At Bell Canada Enterprises (BCE) their code of ethical conduct offers that "what we do is who we are." As President and CEO, Michael Sabia, states, "To maintain these high standards and our reputation, we cannot just read the code and sign compliance forms. We must live it and apply the code to every action and decision we take."[35]

■ A **code of ethics** is a formal statement of an organization's values and beliefs.

In the increasingly complex world of international business, codes of conduct for manufacturers and contractors are becoming more prevalent. At Gap Inc., global manufacturing is governed by a formal Code of Vendor Conduct.[37] The document specifically deals with *discrimination*—"Factories shall employ workers on the basis of their ability to do the job, not on the basis of their personal characteristics or beliefs"; *forced labour*—"Factories shall not use any prison, indentured or forced labour"; *working conditions*—"Factories must treat all workers with respect and dignity and provide them with a safe and healthy environment"; and *freedom of association*—"Factories must not interfere with workers who wish to lawfully and peacefully associate, organize, or bargain collectively."

Although codes of ethical conduct are now common, it must be remembered that they have limits. While helpful, codes alone cannot guarantee ethical conduct. Ultimately, the value of any ethics code still rests on the human resource foundations of the organization. There is no replacement for effective hiring practices that staff organizations with honest and moral people. And there is no replacement for leadership by committed managers who set positive examples and always act as ethical role models.

> **BE SURE YOU CAN**
> • define the term whistle-blower • list three organizational barriers to whistle-blowing • compare and contrast ethics training, codes of ethical conduct, and ethical role models as methods for encouraging ethical behaviour in organizations

✓ Learning check ❸

CORPORATE SOCIAL RESPONSIBILITY

It is now time to shift our interest in ethical behaviour from the level of the individual to that of the organization. To begin, it is important to remember that all organizations exist in an "open system" or in a complex relationship with elements in their external environment. In this context, **corporate social responsibility** is defined as an obligation of the organization to act in ways that serve both its own interests and the interests of society at large.[38]

■ **Corporate social responsibility** is the obligation of an organization to serve its own interests and those of society.

●●● STAKEHOLDER ISSUES AND ANALYSIS

A popular and useful way to examine the concept of corporate social responsibility is through a stakeholder analysis. *Figure 3.4* describes the environment of a typical business as a network of **organizational stakeholders**—those persons, groups, and other organizations directly affected by the behaviour of the organization and holding a stake in its performance.[39] In this perspective, the organization has a social responsibility to serve the interests of its many stakeholders, including:

■ **Organizational stakeholders** are directly affected by the behaviour of the organization and hold a stake in its performance.

- *Employees*—employees and contractors who work for the organization.
- *Customers*—consumers and clients who purchase the organization's goods and/or use its services.
- *Suppliers*—providers of the organization's human, information, material, and financial resources.
- *Owners*—stockholders, investors, and creditors with claims on assets and profits of the organization.
- *Competitors*—other organizations producing the same or similar goods and services.
- *Regulators*—the local, provincial, and federal government agencies that enforce laws and regulations.
- *Interest groups*—community groups, activists, and others representing interests of citizens and society.

The unethical practices at Bre-X, WorldCom, Enron, and Andersen, as discussed previously, had an adverse impact on these firms' stakeholders. Everyone from investors to employees to customers suffered, with even competitors feeling the spillover effects as new government regulations were put into place. But even when it seems that "bad" things dominate the news, remember that there are also a lot of good things happening in organization–stakeholder relationships.

Figure 3.4 Multiple stakeholders in the environment of organization.

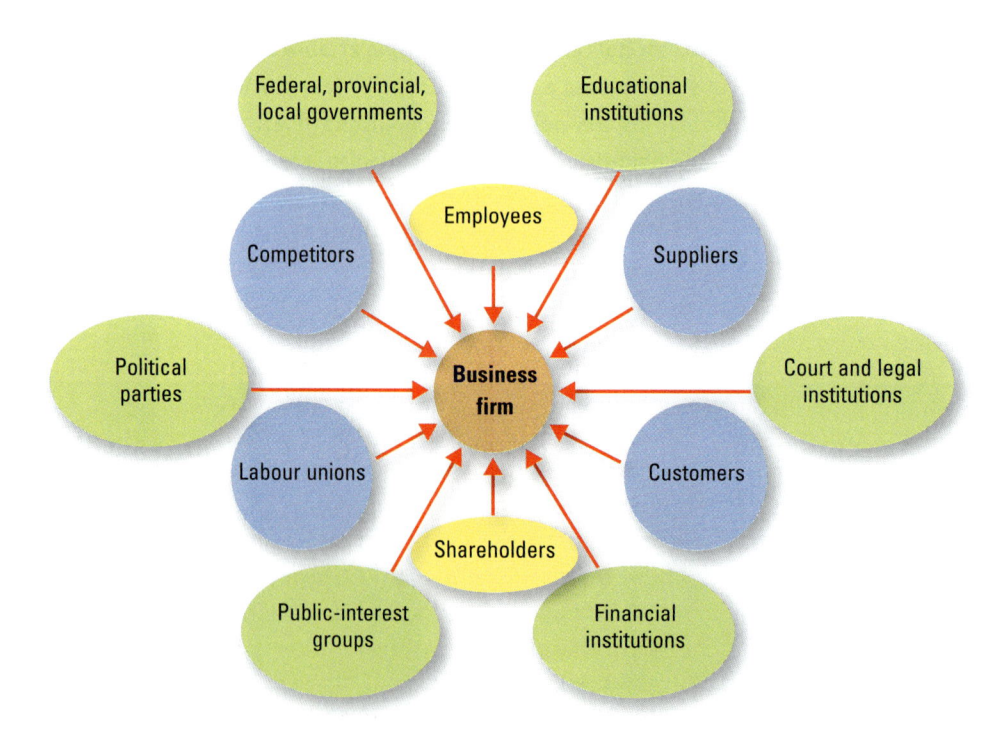

Several Canadian organizations have worked extensively with stakeholders to achieve positive results within their communities. Dupont Canada initiated a multi-stakeholder round table entitled the Social Innovation Enterprise Program in order to ensure that the company is contributing to the communities in which it operates. Home Depot encourages a culture of volunteerism among their employees. The company's community investments target four priority areas: environment; affordable housing; at-risk youth; and emergency preparedness. The Moose Deer Point First Nations Sustainable Community Project, initiated by Husky Injection Molding, has proven to be a truly innovative partnership successfully linking private industry, the government, and First Nations communities.[40]

Consumers, activist groups, non-profit organizations, and governments are increasingly vocal and influential in directing organizations toward socially responsible practices. In today's information age, business activities are increasingly transparent. Irresponsible practices are difficult to hide for long, wherever in the world they take place. Not only do news organizations find and disseminate the information, activist organizations also lobby, campaign, and actively pressure organizations to respect and protect everything from human rights to the natural environment. Increasingly important too are investor groups such as the Ethical Funds Company.

Ultimately, leaders exert a critical influence on the behaviour of organizations and their members. The leadership beliefs that guide socially responsible practices have been described as:[41]

- *People*—people do their best in healthy work environments with a balance of work and family life.

- *Communities*—organizations perform best when located in healthy communities.

- *Natural environment*—organizations gain by treating the natural environment with respect.

- *Term*—organizations must be managed and led for long-term success.

- *Reputation*—one's reputation must be protected to ensure customer and stakeholder support.

●●● PERSPECTIVES ON CORPORATE SOCIAL RESPONSIBILITY

Two contrasting views of corporate social responsibility have stimulated debate in academic and public-policy circles.[42] The *classical view* holds that management's only responsibility in running a business is to maximize profits. In other words, "the business of business is business," and the principal concern of management should always be to maximize shareholder value. This view is supported by Milton Friedman, a respected economist and Nobel Laureate. He says, "Few trends could so thoroughly undermine the very foundations of our free society as the acceptance by corporate officials of social responsibility other than to make as much money for their stockholders as possible."[43] The *arguments against corporate social responsibility* include fears that its pursuit will reduce business profits, raise business costs, dilute business purpose, give business too much social power, and do so without business accountability to the public.

By contrast, the *socio-economic view* holds that management of any organization must be concerned with broader social welfare and not just with corporate profits. This broad-based stakeholder perspective is supported by Paul Samuelson, another distinguished economist and Nobel Laureate. He states, "A large corporation these days not only may engage in social responsibility, it had damn well better try to do so."[44] Among the *arguments in favour of corporate social responsibility* are that it will add long-run profits for businesses, improve the public image of businesses, and help them avoid government regulation. Furthermore, businesses have the resources and ethical obligation to act responsibly.

Today, there is little doubt that the public at large wants businesses and other organizations to act with genuine social responsibility. Stakeholder expectations are increasingly well voiced and include demands that organizations integrate social responsibility into their core values and daily activities. And research indicates that social responsibility can be associated with strong financial performance and, at worst, has no adverse financial impact.[45] The argument that acting with a commitment to social responsibility will negatively affect the "bottom line" is hard to defend. Indeed, evidence points toward a *virtuous circle* in which corporate social responsibility leads to improved financial performance for the firm and this in turn leads to more socially responsible actions in the future.[46]

There seems little reason to believe that businesses cannot serve the public good while advancing the financial interests of their shareholders. Even as the research continues on this important concept, these historical comments by management theorist Keith Davis still confirm the importance of corporate social responsibility.[47]

Society wants business as well as all other major institutions to assume significant social responsibility. Social responsibility has become the hallmark

---

CANADIAN COMPANY IN THE NEWS — **Mountain Equipment Co-op**

CANADIAN STORE IS NUMBER ONE AT DOING GOOD

Vancouver-based Mountain Equipment Co-op (MEC) ranks at the top of big retail chains when it comes to corporate social responsibility (CSR), according *Report on Business* magazine. *ROB* ranked companies that operate in Canada on the basis of their CSR performance, focusing on five specific industries, rather than on a broad range of sectors. MEC scored well above its peer group in the big retail category. The main reasons for this are the co-operative membership structure, which encourages employee and customer involvement, and the fact that it's the only Canadian retailer participating in the Fair Labour Association, a non-profit coalition working to improve labour standards and working conditions worldwide. Also, MEC is committed to generating zero waste in its operations. In 2004, it diverted about 76 percent of waste from its stores that would otherwise have gone to landfill.

Source: "Corporate Social Responsibility Ranking," *Report on Business*, February 23, 2006.

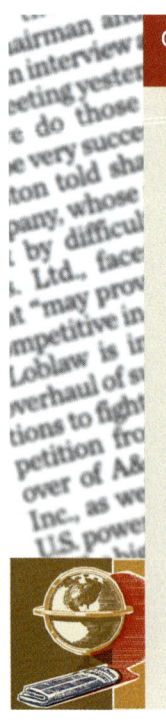

of a mature, global organization.... The business which vacillates or chooses not to enter the arena of social responsibility may find that it gradually will sink into customer and public disfavour.

EVALUATING CORPORATE SOCIAL PERFORMANCE

A **social responsibility audit** can be used at regular intervals to report on, and systematically assess, an organization's accomplishments in various areas of corporate social responsibility. You might think of social responsibility audits as attempts to assess the social performance of organizations, much as accounting audits assess their financial performance. Typical audit areas include concerns for ecology and environmental quality, truth in lending, product safety, consumer protection, and aid to education. They also include service to communities, employment practices, diversity practices, progressive labour relations and employee assistance, and general corporate philanthropy, among other possibilities.

■ A **social responsibility audit** assesses an organization's accomplishments in areas of social responsibility.

Criteria for Evaluating Social Performance

The social performance of business firms and other organizations can be described as driven by *compliance*—acting to avoid adverse consequences, or by *conviction*—acting to create positive impact.[48] Obviously, those of us who highly value corporate social responsibility believe that organizations should act with both. *Figure 3.5* links compliance and conviction with four criteria of social responsibility identified by management scholar Archie Carroll—economic, legal, ethical, and discretionary.[49] An audit of corporate social performance might include questions posed for each criterion: (1) Is the organization's *economic responsibility* met—is it profitable? (2) Is the organization's *legal responsibility* met—does it obey the law? (3) Is the organization's *ethical responsibility* met—is it doing the "right" things? (4) Is the organization's *discretionary responsibility* met—does it contribute to the broader community?

As the audit moves step-by-step through these criteria, the assessment inquires into ever-greater demonstrations of social performance. An organization is meeting its economic responsibility when it earns a profit through the provision of goods and services desired by customers. Legal responsibility is fulfilled when an organization operates within the law and according to the requirements of various external regulations. An organization meets its ethical responsibility when its actions voluntarily conform not only to legal expectations but also to the broader values and moral expectations of society. The highest level of social performance comes through the

Zone of Compliance: Economic Responsibility: *Be Profitable*; Legal Responsibility: *Obey the Law*

Zone of Conviction: Ethical Responsibility: *Do What Is Right*; Discretionary Responsibility: *Contribute to Community*

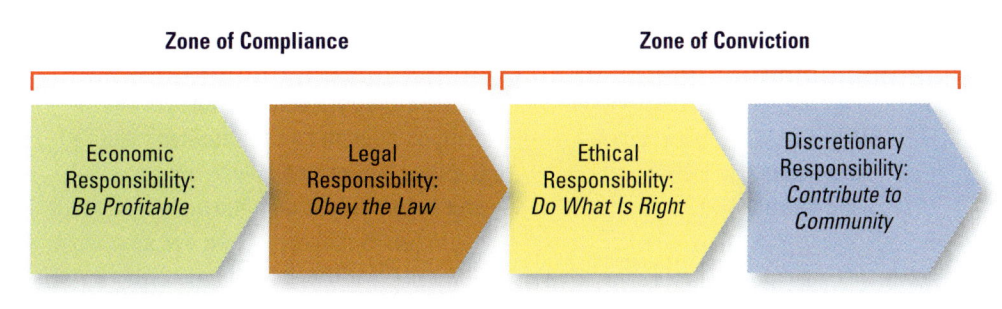

Figure 3.5 Criteria for evaluating corporate social performance.

satisfaction of an organization's discretionary responsibility. Here, the organization voluntarily moves beyond basic economic, legal, and ethical expectations to provide leadership in advancing the well-being of individuals, communities, and society as a whole.

Social Responsibility Strategies

The social performance of organizations can also be analyzed in respect to the apparent "strategy" being followed. *Figure 3.6* describes a continuum of four corporate social responsibility strategies, with the commitment increasing as the strategy shifts from "obstructionist" at the lowest end to "proactive" at the highest.[50]

An **obstructionist strategy** ("Fight the social demands") reflects mainly economic priorities; social demands lying outside the organization's perceived self-interests are resisted. If the organization is criticized for wrongdoing, it can be expected to deny the claims. A **defensive strategy** ("Do the minimum legally required") seeks to protect the organization by doing the minimum legally necessary to satisfy expectations. Corporate behaviour at this level conforms only to legal requirements, competitive market pressure, and perhaps activist voices. If criticized, intentional wrongdoing is likely to be denied.

Organizations pursuing an **accommodative strategy** ("Do the minimum ethically required") accept their social responsibilities. They try to satisfy economic, legal, and ethical criteria. Corporate behaviour at this level is congruent with society's prevailing norms, values, and expectations. But, it may be so only because of outside pressures. An oil firm, for example, may be willing to "accommodate" with cleanup activities when spills occur but remain quite slow in taking actions to prevent them in the first place. The **proactive strategy** ("Take leadership in social initiatives") is designed to meet all the criteria of social performance, including discretionary performance. Corporate behaviour at this level takes preventive action to avoid adverse social impacts from company activities, and it takes the lead in identifying and responding to emerging social issues.

■ An **obstructionist strategy** avoids social responsibility and reflects mainly economic priorities.

■ A **defensive strategy** seeks protection by doing the minimum legally required.

■ An **accommodative strategy** accepts social responsibility and tries to satisfy economic, legal, and ethical criteria.

■ A **proactive strategy** meets all the criteria of social responsibility, including discretionary performance.

Figure 3.6 Four strategies of corporate social responsibility—from obstructionist to proactive behaviour.

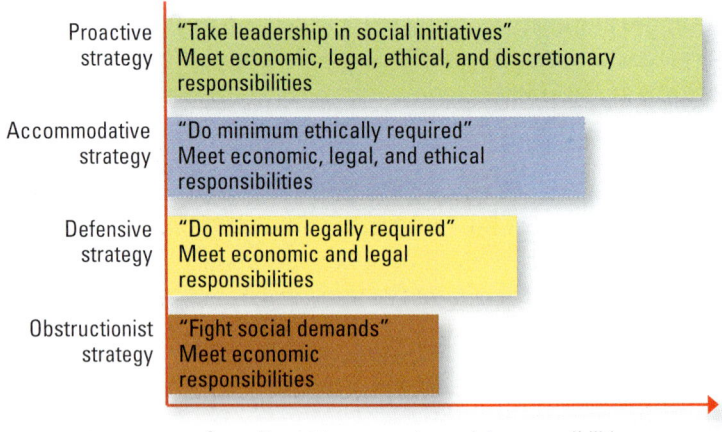

Proactive strategy: "Take leadership in social initiatives" Meet economic, legal, ethical, and discretionary responsibilities

Accommodative strategy: "Do minimum ethically required" Meet economic, legal, and ethical responsibilities

Defensive strategy: "Do minimum legally required" Meet economic and legal responsibilities

Obstructionist strategy: "Fight social demands" Meet economic responsibilities

Commitment to corporate social responsibilities

●●● SOCIAL ENTREPRENEURSHIP

Social entrepreneurs recognize that certain groups in their communities are experiencing difficulties and they seek new ways to solve the problems. Loosely defined, social entrepreneurial behaviour involves undertaking tasks for the benefit of society rather than for personal profit. For example, as a nurse, Veronica Khosa was frustrated with the health care system in her native country of South Africa. She saw sick people not being helped and thus becoming sicker, aged people physically unable to make the trip to a doctor, and hospitals with empty beds but apparently with no room for people with HIV-related illnesses. In response to these things, Khosa began a "home care" program in her country, calling it Tateni Home Care Nursing Services.[51] Her not-for-profit team took to the streets to provide care to the sick in the comfort and security of their own homes. Years later, the South African government recognized the wisdom of this plan and adopted her model of health care. Social entrepreneurs like Veronica Khosa redefine their field and go on to solve systemic social problems on a larger scale.

Social entrepreneurs search out things that are not working for those who need them. They seek to solve the problem first by changing the system, then by spreading the solution, and lastly by working to persuade entire societies to take up the challenge to change. For example, Ashoka, which serves to develop the concept of social entrepreneurship and support these individuals, sees social entrepreneurs as people who "are not content just to give a fish to a starving person nor are they satisfied with teaching them how to fish. Social entrepreneurs will not rest until they have revolutionized the fishing industry."[52]

Social Entrepreneurship and Business

Central to any discussion of social entrepreneurship is the question of who should take responsibility for the needs of our collective society? As such, you might ask how social entrepreneurship fits within the business world. Traditionally, governments have been regarded as having responsibility for social initiatives. As discussed earlier in the chapter, modern perspectives now recognize that our communities are everyone's responsibility. The growing number of businesses helping out in communities indicates that many social entrepreneurs are experienced and successful business executives who clearly wish to "give something back" to the communities in which their businesses operate.

For example, business social entrepreneurs ensure that profits generated from a specific project are used for the benefit of a specific group. An example of this is the CIBC's partnership with the Canadian Breast Cancer Foundation in order to organize and promote the "Run for the Cure" event. Overall, there is a movement to formalize the links between corporate donations and social causes. A key focus of Imagine Canada, a non-profit organization, is to champion corporate citizenship and help businesses partner in the community. The Imagine challenge asks Canadian companies to donate a minimum of 1 percent of their domestic, pre-tax profits to a Canadian charitable or non-profit organization.

Taking the social entrepreneurship idea a step further, others have argued that a realistic and desirable way for businesses to be socially responsible is through "strategic philanthropy," whereby a business makes donations in areas that support the company's interests and to organizations that they might have a connection with. For example, a construction company might be active in social initiatives that promote the building of low-cost housing in a community. This is the case with Home Depot. Through employee engagement programs, Home Depot has given paid time off to employees to allow them to help build affordable housing in their communities.

Many Canadian organizations, both for profit and not-for-profit, encourage employees to take up the change the community for the better challenge. Microsoft donates $17 per hour to a registered charity for each hour their employee volunteers there, and also loans out their executives to volunteer for the United Way. PricewaterhouseCoopers Canada also provides funding to organizations where their employees volunteer; last year over 1,000 employees were active in making a difference in their communities. The term "caring capitalism" has been coined to describe this type of activity in which the achievement of relevant social goals relies on competitiveness in the marketplace.

On Becoming a Social Entrepreneur

In one of the first studies aimed at understanding social entrepreneurs, Charles Leadbeater, a visiting fellow at Oxford University, identified several social entrepreneurs and looked for common traits among them. These individuals endeavoured to address local issues, some of which, over time, spread from their neighborhood beginnings to have a national or even international focus. Leadbeater established that while social entrepreneurs possessed many of the qualities of successful business entrepreneurs, they also had a strong commitment to help others.[53] These attributes and abilities allowed a social entrepreneur to follow a distinctive course of action, which was often characterized by the following steps:

1. identify a "needs gap" and fully understand the related opportunity,
2. inject imagination and vision into their approach,

Canadian Managers
Volunteer Now!

Marc Kielburger is a Canadian social entrepreneur. He started Volunteer Now! in order to make social advocacy "cool" in Toronto high schools. His organization was founded on the principle that young people have within them the power to change the world. Volunteer Now! seeks to motivate young people to become active in both their local and global communities. It is primarily a student-run program that serves to educate teachers about how to introduce the concept into classrooms, organizes student leadership programs, and educates student "volunteer ambassadors" who go out to inspire fellow students to work with their communities as agents of positive change.

Source: Information taken from <www.volunteernow.ca> (January 2007).

3. recruit and motivate others to the cause and build essential networks,
4. secure the needed resources,
5. overcome obstacles and challenges and handle the associated risks, and
6. introduce proper control systems for the venture.

Social entrepreneurship is a growing opportunity. How might you make a difference in your community?

> **BE SURE YOU CAN**
> • define the term corporate social responsibility • summarize the arguments for and against social responsibility by businesses • defend a personal preference between these arguments • identify four criteria for measuring corporate social performance • identify these criteria with four possible social responsibility strategies • understand the goals of social entrepreneurs
>
> ✓ Learning check ❹

ORGANIZATIONS AND SOCIETY

The fact remains that not all managers and not all organizations accept the challenge of acting with conviction and proactive commitment to social responsibility. Government, as the voice and instrument of the people, is often called upon to step in and act on the public's behalf.

●●●● HOW GOVERNMENTS INFLUENCE ORGANIZATIONS

Governments influence organizations by passing laws and establishing regulating agencies to control and direct their behaviour. It may not be too far-fetched to say that behind every piece of legislation—federal, provincial, or muncipal—is a government agency charged with the responsibility of monitoring and ensuring compliance with its mandates. These include groups like the Transportation Safety Board of Canada, provincial ministries of the environment and of health, and the Canadian Food Inspection Agency.

Business executives often complain that many laws and regulations are overly burdensome. Public outcries to "dismantle the bureaucracy" and/or "deregulate business" express concerns that some agencies and legislation are not functional. But the reality is that the legal environment is both complex and constantly changing. Managers must stay informed about new and pending laws as well as existing ones. As a reminder, consider four areas in which the Canadian government takes an active role in regulating business affairs.

The first area is *occupational health and safety*. The *Occupational Health and Safety Act* of 1973 firmly established that the federal government is concerned about worker health and safety on the job. Even though some complain that the regulations are still not strong enough, the act continues to influence the concerns of employers and government policy-makers for worker safety. Second is the area of *fair labour* practices. Legislation and regulations that prohibit discrimination in labour practices are discussed in Chapter 12, which deals with human resource management. For example, in Canada, the *Employment Equity Act*, originally passed in 1985 and adapted in 1995, is designed to reduce employment barriers for visible minorities, women, Aboriginals, and persons with disabilities. Unfortunately, the act applies only to federal government employees or employees of companies that have contracts

82   CHAPTER 3   Ethical Behaviour and Social Responsibility

AROUND THE WORLD

Non-profit supports social accountability worldwide

Among the important social contributions of non-profit organizations, Social Accountability International stands tall for its dedication to workers and their communities around the world. Its mission is described as, "Setting standards for a just world." In practice, this involves the organization's commitment to improving workplaces and combatting sweatshops through the expansion and further development of the international workplace standards known as SA8000 and S8000. The nine dimensions of accountability it measures are child labour, forced labour, health and safety, freedom of association and the right to collective bargaining, discrimination, discipline, working hours, remuneration, and management systems. Certification is voluntary but is highly regarded by unions and non-governmental organizations (NGOs). At present there are certified firms in more than 30 countries and industries.

Source: Information from <www.cepaa.org/AboutSAI/>.

with the federal government. Third is *consumer protection*. The *Hazardous Product Act* gives government the authority to examine and force a business to withdraw from sale any product that it feels is hazardous to the consumer. Children's toys and flammable fabrics are within the great range of products affected by such regulation. The fourth area concerns *environmental protection*. Several anti-pollution acts, including the Canadian *Environmental Protection Act* of 1999, are designed to eliminate careless pollution of the air, water, and land.

●●● HOW ORGANIZATIONS INFLUENCE GOVERNMENTS

Just as governments influence organizations, the leaders of organizations may take action to influence governments. There are a number of ways in which businesses

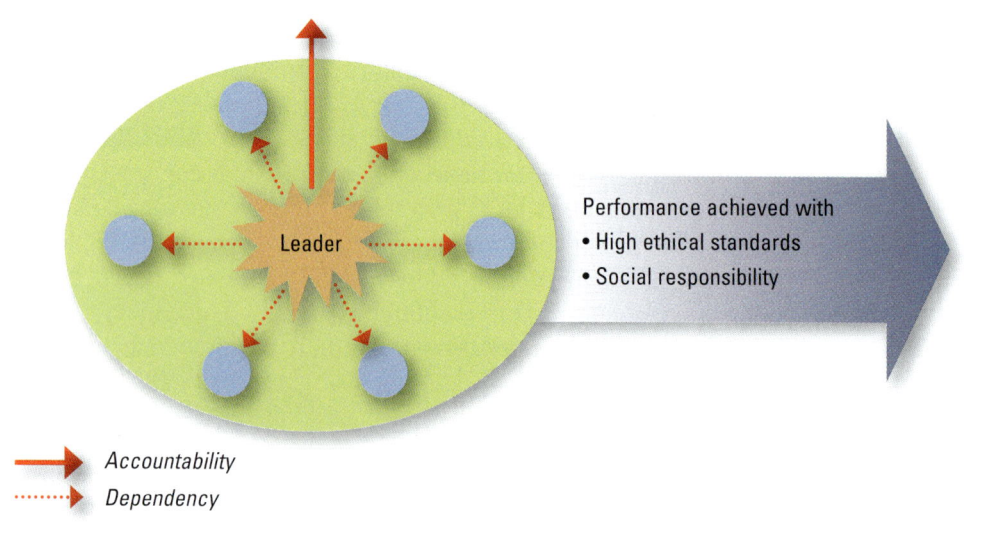

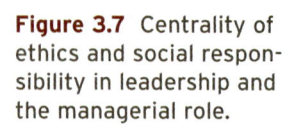

Figure 3.7 Centrality of ethics and social responsibility in leadership and the managerial role.

Performance achieved with
- High ethical standards
- Social responsibility

→ Accountability
⇢ Dependency

in particular attempt to influence government to adopt and pursue policies favourable to them.

Through *personal contacts and networks*, executives get to know important people in government and try to gain their support for special interests. Through *public relations campaigns*, executives try to communicate positive images of their organizations to the public at large. Through **lobbying**, often with the assistance of professional lobbyists, executives can have their desires communicated directly to government officials. Executives also seek influence through financial contributions to **political action committees** (PACs) that collect money and donate it to support favoured political candidates. Unfortunately, illegal acts also occur. Executives sometimes resort to bribes or illegal financial campaign contributions in the attempt to gain influence over public officials.

■ **Lobbying** expresses opinions and preferences to government officials.

■ **Political action committees** collect money for donation to political campaigns.

●●● ROLE OF CORPORATE GOVERNANCE

In Chapter 1, **corporate governance** was defined as oversight of the top management of an organization by a board of directors. Governance most typically involves hiring, firing, and compensating the CEO, assessing strategy, and verifying financial records. One board member describes the responsibilities of corporate governance as, "It's really about setting and maintaining high standards."[54] But even though the purpose is clear, there is a lot of concern that corporate governance can be inadequate and in some cases ineffectual. For example, the news contains critical reports that CEO pay is too high; we also read about continuing accounting scandals that reveal misuse of corporate assets and wrongful financial reporting.[55] All this raises stakeholder concerns to ensure high standards of ethical conduct by executives and socially responsible behaviour by organizations.

■ **Corporate governance** is the oversight of top management by a board of directors.

There is no doubt that the pressure is on to restore corporate governance to its rightful place as a key guarantor that businesses and other organizations are run properly. And importantly, the responsibilities of "governance" in respect to day-to-day managerial control are being well communicated throughout organizations. Trends in social values are reflected in ever-increasing demands, from governments and other stakeholders, that managerial decisions reflect ethical as well as high-performance standards. All managers must accept personal responsibility for doing the "right" things. Decisions must be made and problems solved with ethical considerations standing side by side with performance objectives.

Management focuses your attention throughout on the responsibilities depicted in *Figure 3.7*. It presents the manager's or team leader's challenge this way: to fulfill an accountability for achieving performance objectives, while always doing so in an ethical and socially responsible manner. The full weight of this responsibility applies to every organizational setting from small to large and from private to non-profit. It applies also at every managerial level, from bottom to top. There is no escaping the ultimate reality—being a manager is a very socially responsible job!

BE SURE YOU CAN
• explain and give examples of how governments use legislation to influence business behaviour • identify methods used by businesses to influence governments to adopt favourable policies toward them
• define corporate governance and discuss its importance in organization–society relationships

✓ Learning check ❺

Chapter 3 STUDY GUIDE

WHERE WE'VE BEEN

Back to Aldo Shoes

The opening example of Aldo Shoes provided a clear benchmark for how business performance, ethical behaviour, and social responsibility can go hand in hand. Aldo Shoes, along with other positive examples in the chapter, helps offset the bad side of business and managerial behaviour sensationalized in the cases of Bre-X, Enron, Andersen, WorldCom, and others. In Chapter 3 you learned more about the issues and complexities of personal ethics and corporate social responsibility. As you read further in *Management*, always keep these themes in mind as a learning context. Never forget that there is no substitute for ethical and socially responsible behaviour.

THE NEXT STEP
INTEGRATED LEARNING ACTIVITIES

Cases/Projects
- Tom's of Maine Case
- Project 2—Corporate Social Responsibility
- Project 6—CEO Pay

Self-Assessments
- Terminal Values (#5)
- Instrumental Values (#6)
- Diversity Awareness (#7)
- Internal/External Control (#26)

Exercises in Teamwork
- Confronting Ethical Dilemmas (#6)
- What Do You Value in Work? (#7)
- Case of the Contingency Workforce (#22)

STUDY QUESTION SUMMARY

1. What is ethical behaviour?
- Ethical behaviour is that which is accepted as "good" or "right" as opposed to "bad" or "wrong."
- Simply because an action is not illegal does not necessarily make it ethical in a given situation.
- Because values vary, the question of "What is ethical behaviour?" may be answered differently by different people.
- Four ways of thinking about ethical behaviour are the utilitarian, individualism, moral-rights, and justice views.
- Cultural relativism argues that no culture is ethically superior to any other.

2. How do ethical dilemmas complicate the workplace?
- When managers act ethically they have a positive impact on other people in the workplace and on the social good performed by organizations.
- An ethical dilemma occurs when someone must decide whether to pursue a course of action that, although offering the potential for personal or organizational benefit or both, may be considered potentially unethical.
- Managers report that their ethical dilemmas often involve conflicts with superiors, customers, and subordinates over such matters as dishonesty in advertising and communications as well as pressure from their bosses to do unethical things.

- Common rationalizations for unethical behaviour include believing the behaviour is not illegal, is in everyone's best interests, will never be noticed, or will be supported by the organization.

3. How can high ethical standards be maintained?
- Ethics training in the form of courses and training programs helps people better deal with ethical dilemmas in the workplace.
- Whistle-blowers expose the unethical acts of others in organizations, even while facing career risks for doing so.
- Top management sets an ethical tone for the organization as a whole, and all managers are responsible for acting as positive models of appropriate ethical behaviour.
- Written codes of ethical conduct formally state what an organization expects of its employees regarding ethical conduct at work.

4. What is corporate social responsibility?
- Corporate social responsibility is an obligation of the organization to act in ways that serve both its own interests and the interests of its many external publics, often called stakeholders.
- Criteria for evaluating corporate social performance include economic, legal, ethical, and discretionary responsibilities.
- Corporate strategies in response to social demands include obstruction, defence, accommodation, and proaction, with more progressive organizations taking proactive stances.

5. How do organizations and governments work together in society?
- Government agencies are charged with monitoring and ensuring compliance with the mandates of law.
- Managers must be well informed about existing and pending legislation in a variety of social responsibility areas, including environmental protection and other quality-of-life concerns.
- Organizations exert their influence on government in many ways, including interpersonal contacts of executives, use of lobbyists, and financial contributions to PACs.
- All managerial decisions and actions in every workplace should fulfill performance accountability with commitments to high ethical standards and socially responsible means.

KEY TERMS REVIEW

Accommodative strategy (p. 78)
Code of ethics (p. 73)
Corporate governance (p. 83)
Corporate social responsibility (p. 73)
Cultural relativism (p. 64)
Defensive strategy (p. 78)
Distributive justice (p. 63)
Ethical behaviour (p. 61)
Ethical dilemma (p. 65)
Ethical imperialism (p. 64)

Ethics (p. 61)
Ethics training (p. 71)
Individualism view (p. 63)
Instrumental values (p. 62)
Interactional justice (p. 63)
Justice view (p. 63)
Lobbying (p. 83)
Moral-rights view (p. 63)
Obstructionist strategy (p. 78)
Organizational stakeholders (p. 73)

Political action committees (p. 83)
Proactive strategy (p. 78)
Procedural justice (p. 63)
Social responsibility audit (p. 77)
Terminal values (p. 62)
Universalism (p. 64)
Utilitarian view (p. 62)
Values (p. 62)
Whistle-blowers (p. 71)

SELF-TEST 3

MULTIPLE-CHOICE QUESTIONS:

1. Values are personal beliefs that help determine whether a behaviour will be considered ethical or unethical. An example of a terminal value is _____ .
   (a) ambition (b) self-respect (c) courage (d) imagination

2. Under the _____ view of ethical behaviour, a business owner would be considered ethical if she reduced a plant's workforce by 10 percent in order to cut costs and be able to save jobs for the other 90 percent.
   (a) utilitarian (b) individualism (c) justice (d) moral-rights

3. A manager's failure to enforce a late-to-work policy the same way for all employees is an ethical violation of _____ justice.
   (a) ethical (b) moral (c) distributive (d) procedural

4. The *Sarbanes-Oxley Act* of 2002 makes it easier for corporate executives to _____.
   (a) protect themselves from shareholder lawsuits (b) sue employees who commit illegal acts (c) be tried and sentenced to jail for financial misconduct (d) shift blame for wrongdoing to boards of directors

5. Two "spotlight" questions for conducting the ethics double-check of a decision are: (a) "How would I feel if my family found out about this?" and (b) "How would I feel if _____?"
   (a) my boss found out about this (b) my subordinates found out about this (c) this was printed in the local newspaper (d) this went into my personnel file

6. Research on ethical dilemmas indicates that _____ is/are often the cause of unethical behaviour by people at work.
   (a) declining morals in society (b) lack of religious beliefs (c) the absence of whistle-blowers (d) pressures from bosses and superiors

7. Customers, investors, employees, and regulators are examples of _____ that are important in the analysis of corporate social responsibility.
   (a) special-interest groups (b) stakeholders (c) ethics advocates (d) whistle-blowers

8. A(n) _____ is someone who exposes the ethical misdeeds of others.
   (a) whistle-blower (b) ethics advocate (c) ombudsman (d) stakeholder

9. Two employees are talking about their employers. Sean says that ethics training and codes of ethical conduct are worthless; Maura says these are the best ways to ensure ethical behaviour in the organization. Who is right and why?
   (a) Sean—no one cares. (b) Maura—only the organization can influence ethical behaviour. (c) Neither Sean nor Maura—training and codes can aid but never guarantee ethical behaviour. (d) Neither Sean nor Maura—only the threat of legal punishment will make people act ethically.

10. A proponent of the classical view of corporate social responsibility would most likely agree with which of these statements?
    (a) Social responsibility improves the public image of business. (b) The primary responsibility of business is to maximize business profits. (c) By acting responsibly, businesses avoid government regulation. (d) Businesses can and should do "good" while doing business.

11. Which criterion for evaluating corporate social performance ranks highest in terms of conviction to operate in a responsible manner?
    (a) economic (b) legal (c) ethical (d) discretionary

12. An organization that takes the lead in addressing emerging social issues is being _____, showing the most progressive corporate social responsibility strategy.

    (a) accommodative (b) defensive (c) proactive (d) obstructionist

13. _____ seek to influence governments to adopt favourable policies toward business by raising money and donating it to support political candidates.
    (a) Stakeholders (b) Lobbyists (c) PACs (d) Auditors

14. In the final analysis, managers must make sure that high-performance goals in and by organizations are achieved by _____ means.
    (a) any possible (b) cultural relativism (c) ethical imperialism (d) ethical and socially responsible

15. A social entrepreneur _____ . (a) looks for opportunities to make money (b) seeks out social problems and works to find solutions (c) adheres to the status quo (d) is a small business owner

SHORT-RESPONSE QUESTIONS:

16. Explain the difference between the individualism and justice views of ethical behaviour.

17. List four common rationalizations for unethical managerial behaviour.

18. What are the major elements in the socio-economic view of corporate social responsibility?

19. What role do government agencies play in regulating the socially responsible behaviour of businesses?

APPLICATION QUESTION:

20. A small outdoor clothing company has just received an attractive offer from a business in Bangladesh to manufacture its work gloves. The offer would allow for substantial cost savings over the current supplier. The company manager, however, has read reports that some Bangladeshi businesses break their own laws and operate with child labour. How would differences in the following corporate responsibility strategies affect the manager's decision regarding whether to accept the offer: obstruction, defence, accommodation, and proaction?

4 Environment, Organizational Culture, and Diversity

CHAPTER 4 STUDY QUESTIONS

1. What is the external environment of organizations?
2. What is a customer-driven organization?
3. What is a quality-driven organization?
4. What is organizational culture?
5. How is diversity managed in a multicultural organization?

Planning Ahead

After reading Chapter 4, you should be able to answer these questions in your own words.

BMO FINANCIAL GROUP
AN EMPLOYER OF CHOICE

Would you like to work for a company that is "committed to ensuring a workplace where the voice of every colleague is listened to and encouraged"? That's what BMO Financial Group prides itself in providing. Established in 1817 as Bank of Montreal, BMO Financial Group's core values have been fundamental in the development of many diverse and innovative programs. These have helped drive the institution's stated vision to be the top performing financial services company in North America. The bank's core values create an inclusive organizational culture:

- We care about our customers, shareholders, communities and each other.

- We draw our strength from the diversity of our people and our businesses.

- We insist upon respect for everyone and encourage all to have a voice.

- We keep our promises and stand accountable for our every action.

- We share information, learn, and innovate to create consistently superior customer service.

Since 1990, there have been several groundbreaking task forces within the company to ensure a diverse and equitable working population. This, coupled with the flexible working hours and generous allowances for employee education, have resulted in continuing high job satisfaction rates reported by employees. The bank believes that "its revenue growth and the advancement of workplace equality are inextricably linked."

It's not surprising then that the institution was recently awarded the 2005 Canada's Best Corporate Citizen of the Year award by the magazine *Corporate Knights*, that it is consistently ranked as one of the best places to work in Canada and, according to *Canadian Business* magazine's annual corporate governance survey, ranked among the top 25 boards in Canada. BMO Financial Group is an "employer of choice." [1]

GET CONNECTED!

Find out more about the BMO Financial Group's core values. Examine the firm's environment, which they call their corporate community. Think about the roles leaders play in building high-performing organizations.

Chapter 4 LEARNING PREVIEW

The BMO Financial Group keeps its high-performance edge with a unique commitment to environment and diversity. Externally, the firm values all stakeholders, including its communities. Internally, it values people, respects diversity, and engages employees through participation in the affairs of the enterprise. The purpose of Chapter 4 is to introduce you to the external and internal environments of organizations. As you read, check your learning progress in these major areas.

ENVIRONMENT, ORGANIZATIONAL CULTURE, AND DIVERSITY

Study Question 1: Environment and Competitive Advantage
- What is competitive advantage?
- The general environment
- Stakeholders and the specific environment
- Environmental uncertainty

Learning check 1

Study Question 2: Customer-Driven Organizations
- Who are the customers?
- What customers want
- Customer relationship management

Learning check 2

Study Question 3: Quality-Driven Organizations
- Total quality management
- Quality and continuous improvement
- Quality, technology, and design

Learning check 3

Study Question 4: Organizational Culture
- What strong cultures do
- Levels of organizational culture
- Value-based management
- Symbolic leadership

Learning check 4

Study Question 5: Multicultural Organizations and Diversity
- What is a multicultural organization?
- Organizational subcultures
- Challenges faced by minorities and women
- Managing diversity

Learning check 5

Once a benchmark for science fiction writers, the dawning of the 21st century is now placing unrelenting new demands on organizations and their members. Managers today are learning to operate in a world that places a premium on information, technology utilization, quality, customer service, and speed. They are learning how to succeed in a world of intense competition, continued globalization of markets and business activities, and rapid technological change. And they are facing renewed demands for ethical behaviour and social responsibility.

This chapter introduces the external and internal environments of organizations, along with their performance implications. The chapter opening example, the BMO Financial Group, sets the stage. It introduces the importance of core values and it raises the following question: What must organizations do to remain successful in our dynamic, complex, and ever-changing environment?

ENVIRONMENT AND COMPETITIVE ADVANTAGE

In his book *The Future of Success*, Robert Reich writes: "The emerging economy is offering unprecedented opportunities, an ever-expanding choice of terrific deals, fabulous products, good investments, and great jobs for people with the right talents and skills. Never before in human history have so many had access to so much so easily."[2] In these terms, things couldn't be better for organizations and career seekers. But there are also major challenges to be faced. When looking at things from a business vantage point, IBM's former CEO Louis V. Gerstner, Jr., described the challenge this way: "We believe very strongly that the age-old levers of competition—labour, capital, and land—are being supplemented by knowledge, and that most successful companies in the future will be those that learn how to exploit knowledge—knowledge about customer behaviour, markets, economies, technology—faster than their competitors."[3]

Knowledge and speed are indispensable to success in this new economy. Even as managers strive to lead their organizations toward a high-performance edge, they cannot afford for a minute to rest on past laurels. The world is too uncertain and the competition too intense for that. "In order to survive," Reich points out, "all organizations must dramatically and continuously improve—cutting costs, adding value, creating new products."[4]

WHAT IS COMPETITIVE ADVANTAGE?

Astute executives understand the management implications in the prior observations. They are ever alert to environmental trends that require adjustments in the ways their organizations operate and that offer opportunities to gain **competitive advantage**.[5] This term refers to a core competency that clearly sets an organization apart from its competitors and gives it an advantage over them in the marketplace. Simply put, it comes from an ability to do things better than one's competitors. An organization may achieve competitive advantage in many ways, including through its products, pricing, customer service, cost efficiency, and quality, among other aspects of operating excellence. But regardless of how competitive advantage is achieved, the key result is the same—an ability to consistently do something of high value that one's competitors cannot replicate quickly or do as well.

■ A **competitive advantage** allows an organization to deal with market and environmental forces better than its competitors.

Some years ago, at a time when the North American industry was first coming to grips with fierce competition from Japanese products, quality pioneer J. M. Juran challenged an audience of Japanese executives with a prediction. He warned them against complacency, suggesting that North America would bounce back in business competitiveness.[6] There seems little doubt today that Juran's prediction was accurate.

There was a resurgence of business excellence in North America partly because business leaders could better understand the interdependencies of their organizations with the external environment. Competitive advantage in the demanding global economy can be achieved only by continuously scanning the environment for opportunities and taking effective action based on what is learned.[7] The ability to do this begins with the answer to a basic question: What is present in the external environment of organizations?

THE GENERAL ENVIRONMENT

The **general environment** consists of all conditions in the external environment that form a background context for managerial decision making. The following are typical external environmental issues:

■ The **general environment** is composed of cultural, economic, legal-political, and educational conditions.

- *Economic conditions*—health of the economy in terms of inflation, income levels, gross domestic product, unemployment, and job outlook.

- *Social-cultural conditions*—norms, customs, and social values on such matters as human rights, trends in education and related social institutions, as well as demographic patterns in society.

- *Legal-political conditions*—prevailing philosophy and objectives of the political party or parties running the government, as well as laws and government regulations.

- *Technological conditions*—development and availability of technology, including scientific advancements.

- *Natural environment conditions*—nature and conditions of the natural environment, including levels of public concern expressed through environmentalism.

If we take the natural environment as an example, Japanese automakers Honda and Toyota seem to be finding the potential for competitive advantage. The two firms are on the leading edge of new markets for hybrid cars that combine gas and electric power. While North America's automakers were betting that customers would stay loyal to large gas-fuelled and often gas-hungry vehicles, their Japanese competitors saw the potential for competitive advantage. Now they have experience and a reputation gained from being first to market with the more environmentally friendly vehicles.

In respect to the socio-cultural environment, population demographics are a key feature. Managers who understand demographic profiles and trends can anticipate shifts in the customer base and labour markets that affect their organizations. For example, *Manager's Notepad 4.1* highlights important diversity trends in the demographic characteristics of Canadian society.[8] These and other differences in general environment factors are especially noticeable internationally. External conditions vary significantly from one country and culture to the next, and managers must understand these differences. Like many large firms, the pharmaceutical giant

MANAGER'S Notepad 4.1

Diversity trends in the socio-cultural environment

- Visible minority groups and new Canadians from a variety of ethnic populations are an increasing percentage of the workforce.
- More women are working.
- People with disabilities are gaining more access to the workplace.
- More workers come from non-traditional families (e.g., single parents, dual wage earners).
- The average age of workers is increasing.
- The number of different faith backgrounds is increasing.

Merck derives a substantial portion of its business from overseas operations. Its executives recognize the need to be well informed about, and responsive to, differing local conditions. In Europe, for example, they have entered into co-operative agreements with local companies, conducted research with local partners, and worked with local governments on legal matters.

STAKEHOLDERS AND THE SPECIFIC ENVIRONMENT

The **specific environment** consists of the actual organizations, groups, and persons with whom an organization interacts and conducts business. These are environmental elements of direct consequence to the organization as it operates on a day-to-day basis. The specific environment is often described in terms of **stakeholders**, defined in Chapter 3 as the persons, groups, and institutions who are affected in one way or another by the organization's performance. They are key constituencies that have a stake in the organization's performance, are influenced by how it operates, and can influence it in return.

Sometimes called the *task environment*, the specific environment and the stakeholders are distinct for each organization. They can also change over time according to the company's unique customer base, operating needs, and circumstances. Important stakeholders common to the specific environment of most organizations include customers, suppliers, competitors, regulators, and investors/owners from the external environment, as well as employees from the internal environment.

Figure 4.1 shows the typical business firm as an open system, with the interests of several stakeholder groups linked by stages in the input-transformation-output process. This type of stakeholder analysis can be used to both assess the current performance of organizations vis-à-vis *strategic constituencies* and to develop ideas for improving performance in the future. The analysis helps focus management attention on **value creation**, the extent to which the organization is creating value for, and satisfying the needs of, important constituencies.

■ The **specific environment** includes the people and groups with whom an organization interacts.

■ **Stakeholders** are the persons, groups, and institutions directly affected by an organization.

■ **Value creation** is creating value for, and satisfying needs of, constituencies.

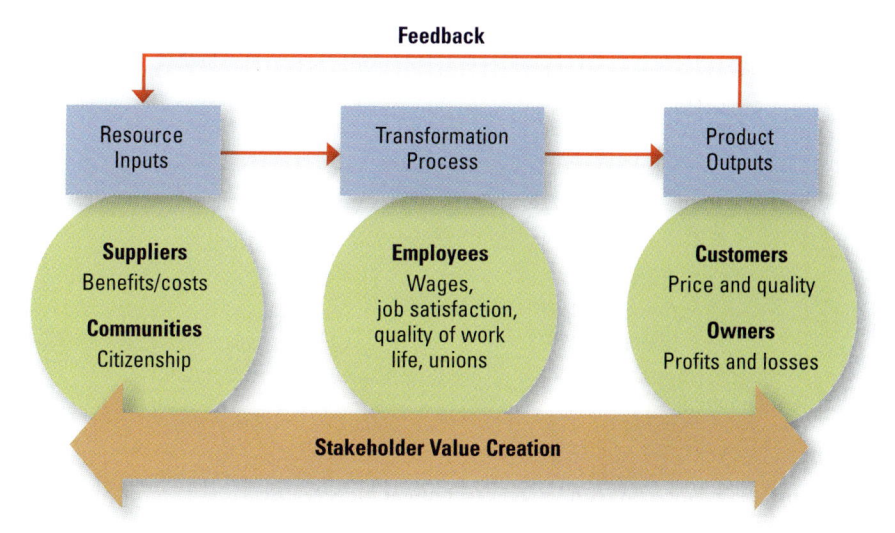

Figure 4.1 Stakeholder analysis of value creation for key constituencies of a business firm: an open-systems approach.

As suggested in *Figure 4.1*, value creation is important to stakeholders from both the specific environment, reflected on the input and output boundaries of the business firm as an open system, and from the internal environment, reflected in the transformation process itself. In respect to product outputs, for example, businesses create value for customers through product price and quality, and for owners by realized profits and losses. In respect to inputs, businesses create value for suppliers through the benefits of long-term business relationships, and for communities in such areas as the citizenship they display in using and contributing to public services. And in respect to throughputs, businesses create value for employees through the wages and satisfaction gained through their work of transforming resource inputs into product outputs. Wal-Mart is an example of an organization that manages the value creation chain quite well. By managing costs at both the input and throughput stages, they are able to offer products at a price and quality that appeal to customers.

ENVIRONMENTAL UNCERTAINTY

■ **Environmental uncertainty** is a lack of complete information about the environment.

There is a lot of uncertainty in the external environments of many organizations. **Environmental uncertainty** means that there is a lack of complete information regarding what exists and what developments may occur. This makes it difficult to analyze constituencies and their needs, predict future states of affairs, and understand their potential implications for the organization. *Figure 4.2* describes two dimensions of environmental uncertainty: (1) complexity, or the number of different factors in the environment, and (2) the rate of change in these factors.[9]

Environmental uncertainty presents a host of management challenges. Greater uncertainty requires more concentrated attention. An uncertain environment has to be continually studied and monitored to spot emerging trends. Also, the greater the environmental uncertainty, the greater the need for flexibility and adaptability in organizational designs and work practices. Because of uncertainty, organizations must be able to respond quickly as new circumstances arise and information becomes available. The airline industry is an example of an uncertain environment arising from a

Figure 4.2 Dimensions of uncertainty in organizational environments.

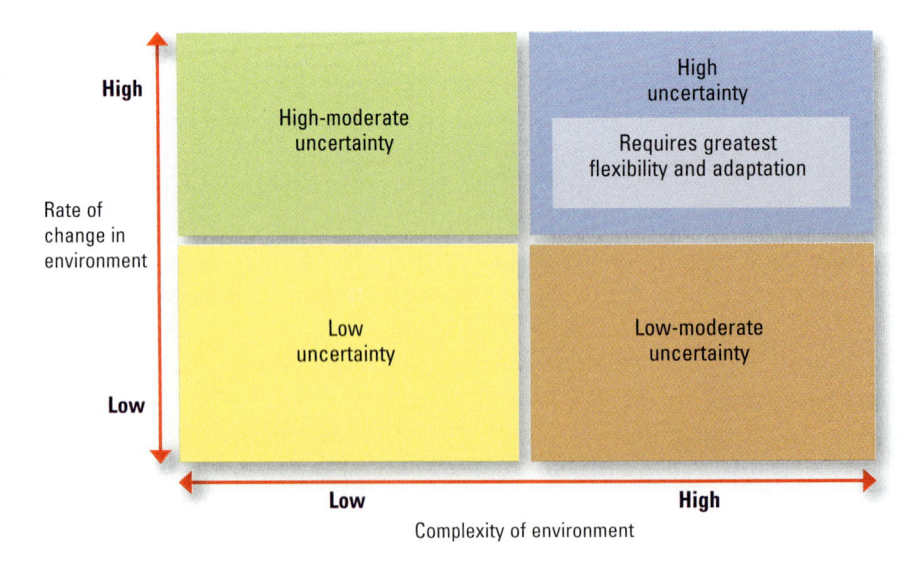

number of factors: threats of terrorism, fuel costs, deregulation, and currency fluctuations. One need only look at the management challenges faced by companies such as the now-defunct CanJet and Jetsgo to appreciate this fact. Throughout this book you will find many examples of how organizations try to stay adaptable in order to best deal with the high uncertainty that so often prevails in their environments.

> **BE SURE YOU CAN**
> • list key elements in the general and specific environments of organizations • define the terms competitive advantage, stakeholders, and environmental uncertainty • describe the stakeholders for a business in your local community
>
> ✓ Learning check ❶

CUSTOMER-DRIVEN ORGANIZATIONS

Question: What's your job?

Answer: I run the cash register and sack groceries.

Question: But isn't it your job to serve the customer?

Answer: I guess, but it's not in my job description.

This conversation illustrates what often becomes the missing link in the quest for competitive advantage: customer service. Contrast this conversation with the example of a customer who called the Vermont Teddy Bear Company to complain that her new mail-order teddy bear had a problem. The company responded promptly, she said, and arranged to have the bear picked up and replaced. She wrote the firm to say "thank you for the great service and courtesy you gave me."[10] As demonstrated, responding quickly to customer requests can turn a potentially negative situation into a very positive one.

●●● WHO ARE THE CUSTOMERS?

Figure 4.3 expands the open-systems view of organizations to now depict the complex internal operations of the organization as well as its interdependence with the external environment. In this figure the organization's *external customers* purchase the goods produced or utilize the services provided. They may be industrial customers, that is, other firms that buy a company's products for use in their own operations; or they may be retail customers or clients who purchase or use the goods and services directly. *Internal customers*, by contrast, are found within the organization. They are the individuals and groups who use or otherwise depend on one another's work in order to do their own jobs well. The notion of customer service applies equally well to external and internal customers. For example, the customer is "captain" of the supply chain for Dell Computer. Founder and chairman Michael Dell firmly believes that customers drive competitive advantage. The firm is a leader in using information technology to efficiently deliver products meeting customer preferences.

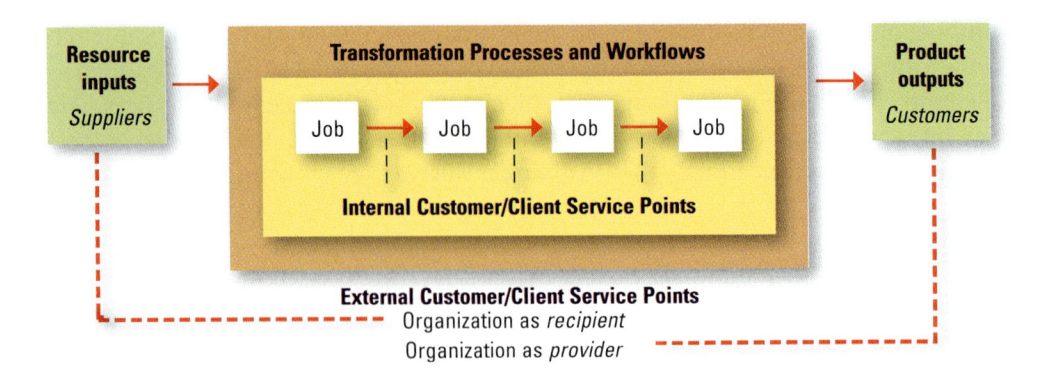

Figure 4.3 The importance of external and internal customers.

[Figure 4.3: Diagram showing Resource inputs (Suppliers) → Transformation Processes and Workflows (Job → Job → Job → Job, with Internal Customer/Client Service Points) → Product outputs (Customers). External Customer/Client Service Points shown below with Organization as *recipient* and Organization as *provider*.]

●●● WHAT CUSTOMERS WANT

Customers are always key stakeholders; they sit at the top when organizations are viewed as the upside-down pyramids described in Chapter 1. And without any doubt, customers put today's organizations to a very stiff test. They primarily want at least one of four things in the goods and services they buy: (1) high quality, (2) reasonable price, (3) on-time delivery, and (4) excellent service.

Organizations that can't meet customer expectations suffer the market consequences; they lose competitive advantage. Some time ago, for example, Intel Corporation faced a crisis in customer confidence when a defect was found in one of its computer chips. At first, top management of this highly regarded company balked at replacing the chips, suggesting that the defect wasn't really important. But customers were angry and unrelenting in their complaints. Eventually the customers won, as they should. Intel agreed to replace the chips without any questions asked. Company executives also learned two important lessons of successful business practices: (1) always protect your reputation for quality products—it is hard to get and easy to lose, and (2) always treat your customers well—they, too, are hard to get and easy to lose.

●●● CUSTOMER RELATIONSHIP MANAGEMENT

A *Harvard Business Review* survey reports that North American business leaders rank customer service and product quality as the first and second most important goals in the success of their organizations.[11] In a survey by the market research firm Michelson & Associates, poor service and product dissatisfaction were the first and second reasons respectively for customers abandoning a retail store.[12] Reaching the goals of providing great service and quality products isn't always easy. But when pursued relentlessly they can be important sources of competitive advantage. Just imagine the ramifications if every customer or client contact for an organization were positive. Not only would these customers return again and again, they would also tell others and expand the customer base.

Progressive managers use the principles of **customer relationship management** to establish and maintain high standards of customer service. Known as

■ **Customer relationship management** strategically tries to build lasting relationships with, and add value for, customers.

"CRM," this approach uses the latest information technologies to maintain intense communication with customers as well as to gather and utilize data regarding their needs and desires. At Marriott International, for example, CRM is supported by special customer management software that tracks information on customer preferences. When you check in, the likelihood is that your past requests for things like a king-size bed, no-smoking room, and Internet access are already in your record. Says Marriott's chairman: "It's a big competitive advantage."[13]

Just as organizations need to manage their customers on the output side, supplier relationships on the input side must be well managed, too. The concept of **supply chain management** (SCM) involves strategic management of all operations involving an organization's suppliers. This includes the use of information technology to improve purchasing, manufacturing, transportation, and distribution.[14] The goals of SCM are straightforward: achieve efficiency in all aspects of the supply chain while ensuring on-time availability of quality resources for customer-driven operations. As retail sales are made at Wal-Mart, for example, an information system updates inventory records and sales forecasts. Suppliers access this information electronically, allowing them to adjust their operations and rapidly ship replacement products to meet the retailer's needs.

■ **Supply chain management** strategically links all operations dealing with resource supplies.

> **BE SURE YOU CAN**
> • explain the difference between internal and external customers of a firm • list the four primary things customers want in what they buy • discuss the importance of customer relationship management in a competitive business environment

✓ Learning check ❷

QUALITY-DRIVEN ORGANIZATIONS

If managing for high performance and competitive advantage is the theme of the day, "quality" is one of its most important watchwords. Customers want quality whether they are buying a consumer product or receiving a service. The achievement of quality objectives in all aspects of operations is a global criterion of organizational performance in manufacturing and service industries alike. **ISO certification** by the International Organization for Standardization in Geneva, Switzerland has been adopted by many countries of the world as a quality benchmark. Businesses that want to compete as "world-class companies" are increasingly expected to have ISO certification at various levels. To do so, they must refine and upgrade quality in all operations and then undergo a rigorous assessment by outside auditors to determine whether they meet ISO requirements.

■ **ISO certification** indicates conformance with a rigorous set of international quality standards.

●●● TOTAL QUALITY MANAGEMENT

The term **total quality management** (TQM) was introduced in Chapter 1. It describes the process of making quality principles part of the organization's strategic objectives, applying them to all aspects of operations, committing to continuous improvement, and striving to meet customers' needs by doing things right the first time.[15]

Most TQM approaches begin with an insistence that the total quality commitment apply to everyone in an organization and to all aspects of operations, right

■ **Total quality management** is managing with an organization-wide commitment to continuous improvement, product quality, and customer needs.

from resource acquisition through to the production and distribution of finished goods and services.[16] Philip Crosby, a consultant, became quite famous for offering these "four absolutes" of management for total quality control: (1) *quality means conformance to standards*—workers must know exactly what performance standards they are expected to meet; (2) *quality comes from defect prevention, not defect correction*—leadership, training, and discipline must prevent defects in the first place; (3) *quality as a performance standard must mean defect-free work*—the only acceptable quality standard is perfect work; and (4) *quality saves money*—doing things right the first time saves the cost of correcting poor work.[17]

take it to the case!

United Parcel Service
Where technology rules a total quality road

Once named company of the year by *Forbes* magazine, UPS is the world's largest package delivery company. It's also a leader in technology utilization for competitive advantage. Log on to the UPS website and the company literally takes you around the world of package delivery. Operating efficiency and customer service are rules of the day every day at UPS. The company claims "a technology infrastructure second to none, enabling customers to link product shipments, services and information throughout the transaction value chain." Customers find IT working for them through an efficient online package tracking system and transit and delivery times. Operations are streamlined through the firm's seamless supply chain.

Source: With information from the corporate websites www.ups.com and www.ups-scs.ca

●●● QUALITY AND CONTINUOUS IMPROVEMENT

The work of W. Edwards Deming is a cornerstone of the total quality movement. The story begins in 1951 when he was invited to Japan to explain quality control techniques that had been developed in the United States. The result was a lifelong relationship epitomized in the Deming Prize, which is still annually awarded in Japan for excellence in quality. "When Deming spoke," we might say, "the Japanese listened." The principles he taught the Japanese were straightforward . . . and they worked: tally defects, analyze and trace them to the source, make corrections, and keep a record of what happens afterward.[18] Deming's "14 points of quality" emphasize constant innovation, use of statistical methods, and commitment to training in the fundamentals of quality assurance.

The search for quality is closely tied to the emphasis on **continuous improvement**—always looking for new ways to improve on current performance.[19] The

■ **Continuous improvement** involves always searching for new ways to improve work quality and performance.

notion is that one can never be satisfied; something always can and should be improved on. Continuous improvement must be a way of life. Another important aspect of total quality operations is cycle time—the elapsed time between receipt of an order and delivery of the finished product. The quality objective here is to reduce cycle time by finding ways to serve customer needs more quickly.

One way to combine employee involvement and continuous improvement is through the popular **quality circle** concept.[20] This is a small group of workers that meets regularly to discuss ways of improving the quality of their products or services. Their objective is to assume responsibility for quality and apply every member's full creative potential to ensure that it is achieved. Such worker empowerment can result in cost savings from improved quality and greater customer satisfaction. It can also improve morale and commitment, as the following remarks from quality circle members indicate: "This is the best thing the company has done in 15 years." . . . "The program proves that supervisors have no monopoly on brains." . . . "It gives me more pride in my work."[21]

■ Members of a **quality circle** meet periodically to discuss ways of improving the quality of products or services.

●●● QUALITY, TECHNOLOGY, AND DESIGN

Technology utilization is improving the quality of manufacturing today by helping firms better integrate their operations with customer preferences, and by allowing production changes to be made quickly and at low cost. For example, *lean production* uses technologies to streamline systems and allow work to be performed with fewer workers and smaller inventories. *Flexible manufacturing* allows processes to be changed quickly and efficiently to produce different products or modifications to existing ones. Through such techniques as *agile manufacturing* and *mass customization*, organizations are able to make individualized products quickly and with production efficiencies once only associated with the mass production of uniform products.[22]

Another timely and important contribution to quality management is found in *product design*. We are all aware of design differences among products, be they cars, computers, cell phones, stereos, watches, clothes, or whatever. But what may not be recognized is that design makes a difference in how things are produced and at what level of cost and quality. In today's competitive global economy, product designs are strategic weapons. A "good" design has both eye appeal to the customer and is easy to manufacture with regards to productivity. *Design for manufacturing* means that products are styled to lower production costs and smooth the way toward high-quality results in all aspects of the manufacturing processes. A manufacturing approach that shows respect for the natural environment is *design for disassembly*. The goal is to design products while taking into account how their component parts will be recycled at the end of their lives.

> **BE SURE YOU CAN**
> • define the term ISO certification • explain the role of continuous improvement in TQM • describe what a quality circle is and how its use can increase performance quality • discuss how good use of technology and product design can improve quality

✓ Learning check ❸

ORGANIZATIONAL CULTURE

"Culture" is a popular word in management these days. Important differences in national cultures will be discussed in Chapter 5 on the global dimensions of management. Here, it is time to talk about cultural differences in the internal environments of organizations. **Organizational culture** is defined by noted scholar and consultant Edgar Schein as the system of shared beliefs and values that develops within an organization and guides the behaviour of its members.[23] Sometimes called the *corporate culture*, it is a key aspect of any organization and work setting. Whenever someone, for example, speaks of "the way we do things here," they are talking about the culture.

■ **Organizational culture** is the system of shared beliefs and values that guides behaviour in organizations.

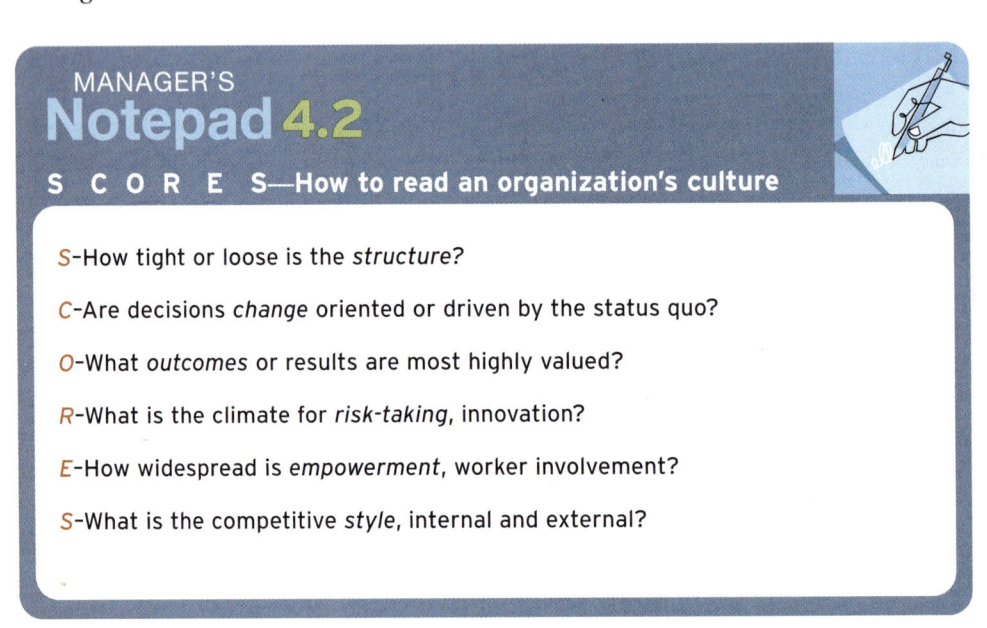

MANAGER'S Notepad 4.2

S C O R E S—How to read an organization's culture

S-How tight or loose is the *structure*?

C-Are decisions *change* oriented or driven by the status quo?

O-What *outcomes* or results are most highly valued?

R-What is the climate for *risk-taking*, innovation?

E-How widespread is *empowerment*, worker involvement?

S-What is the competitive *style*, internal and external?

●●● WHAT STRONG CULTURES DO

Although it is clear that culture is not the sole determinant of what happens in organizations, it is an important influence on what they accomplish . . . and how. The internal culture has the potential to shape attitudes, reinforce beliefs, direct behaviour, and establish performance expectations and the motivation to fulfill them. A widely discussed study of successful businesses concluded that organizational culture made a major contribution to their long-term performance records.[24] Importantly, the cultures in these organizations provided for a clear vision of what the organization was attempting to accomplish, allowing individuals to rally around the vision and work hard to support and accomplish it.[25] *Manager's Notepad 4.2* offers ideas for reading differences among organizational cultures.

Strong cultures, ones that are clear and well defined and widely shared among members, discourage dysfunctional work behaviours and encourage positive ones. They commit members to doing things for and with one another that are in the best interests of the organization. The best organizations are likely to have cultures that are performance oriented, emphasize teamwork, allow for risk taking, encourage innovation, and make the well-being of people a top management priority.[26] Only 36 percent of Canadian executives surveyed by Waterstone Human Capital Ltd., a Toronto-based executive search firm, felt that their companies could be classified as having strong, adaptive cultures, while a large portion (55 percent) felt that their organizations were weak and plagued by problems such as top-down managerial haughtiness, a fear of risk-taking, too much of an inward focus, and too much bureaucracy.[27] In the recent study by Waterstone, WestJet stood out as having the most admired Canadian corporate culture. WestJet, based in Calgary, Alberta, is noted for its "entrepreneurial spirit," "delivering what they promise," and its "winning attitude."[28] Honda is another good example. The firm's culture is tightly focused around what is known as "The Honda Way"—a set of principles emphasizing ambition, respect for ideas, open communication, work enjoyment, harmony, and hard work.

LEVELS OF ORGANIZATIONAL CULTURE

Organizational culture is usually described from the perspective of the two levels shown in *Figure 4.4*—the "observable" culture and the "core" culture.[29] The *observable culture* is visible; it is what one sees and hears when walking around an organization as a visitor, a customer, or an employee. The observable culture is apparent in the way people dress at work, how they arrange their offices, how they speak to and behave toward one another, the nature of their conversations, and how they talk about and treat their customers. It is also found in the following elements of daily organizational life—through them, new members learn the organization's culture and all members share and reinforce its special aspects over time:

- *Stories*—oral histories and tales, told and retold among members, about dramatic sagas and incidents in the life of the organization.

- *Heroes*—the people singled out for special attention and whose accomplishments are recognized with praise and admiration among members; they include founders and role models.

Observable Culture

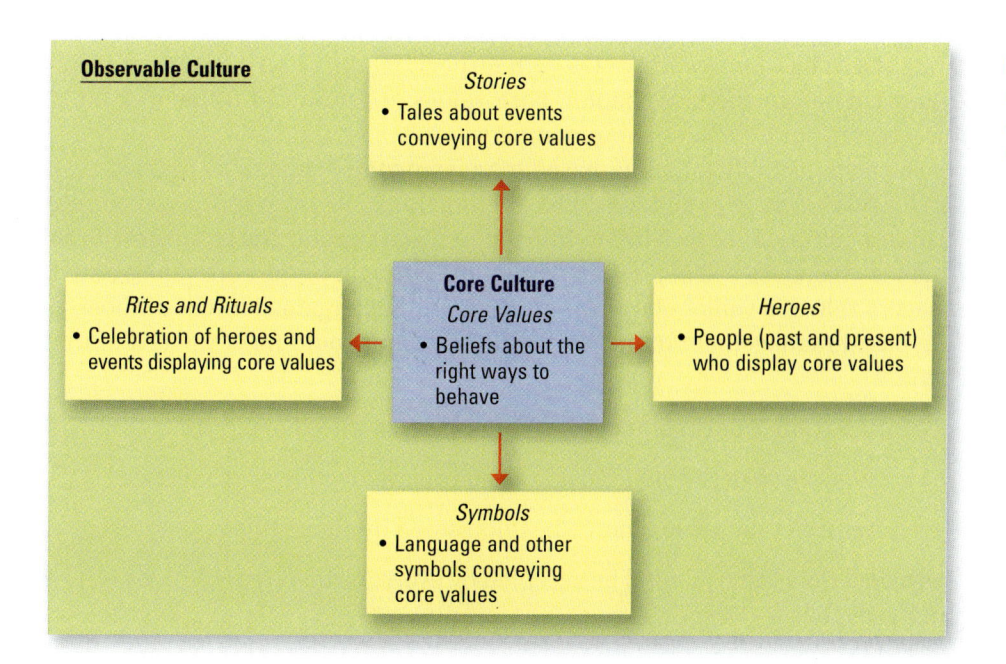

- *Stories* — Tales about events conveying core values
- *Rites and Rituals* — Celebration of heroes and events displaying core values
- **Core Culture** — Core Values — Beliefs about the right ways to behave
- *Heroes* — People (past and present) who display core values
- *Symbols* — Language and other symbols conveying core values

Figure 4.4 Levels of organizational culture—observable culture and core culture.

- *Rites and rituals*—the ceremonies and meetings, planned and spontaneous, that celebrate important occasions and performance accomplishments.

- *Symbols*—the special use of language and other non-verbal expressions to communicate important themes of organizational life.

For example, at the eBay Canada office in Toronto, an organizational ritual has all 30 employees voting on the "Hat Trick Award." The award is given quarterly to a person who has achieved "great performance." As Jordon Banks, eBay Canada's managing director, states, the award is given for "not only what is done, but more importantly, how it is done."[30]

The second and deeper level of organizational culture is the *core culture*. It consists of the **core values** or underlying assumptions and beliefs that shape and guide people's behaviours, and actually contribute to the aspects of observable culture just described. Strong-culture organizations operate with a small but enduring set of core values. Researchers point out that commitment to core values is a major contributor to long-term success.[31] Highly successful companies typically emphasize the values of performance excellence, innovation, social responsibility, integrity, worker involvement, customer service, and teamwork. Examples of core values that drive the best firms include "service above all else" at Nordstrom; "science-based innovation" at Merck; "encouraging individual initiative and creativity" at Sony; and "fanatical attention to consistency and detail" at Disney.

> ■ **Core values** are beliefs and values shared by organization members.

●●● VALUE-BASED MANAGEMENT

The core values espoused by organizations are widely publicized in corporate mission statements and on their official websites. But mere testimonies to values are not enough to create a strong core culture and derive its benefits. The values must be practised. They must be real, they must be shared, and they must be modelled and reinforced by managers from top to bottom. The term value-based management describes managers who actively help develop, communicate, and enact shared values within an organization. Importantly, one area where **value-based management** has a major impact is with respect to ethics and social responsibility. As discussed in the last chapter, core values are powerful influences on the ethical behaviour of organization members.

> ■ **Value-based management** actively develops, communicates, and enacts shared values.

The responsibility for value-based management extends to all managers and team leaders working at all levels. Like the organization, any work team or group will have a culture. How well this culture operates to support the group and its performance objectives will depend in part on the strength of the core values and the manager's role as a values champion. Just as with the organization as a whole, the value-based management of any work unit or team should meet the test of these criteria.[32]

- *Relevance*—Core values should support key performance objectives.

- *Integrity*—Core values should provide clear, consistent ethical anchors.

- *Pervasiveness*—Core values should be understood by all members.

- *Strength*—Core values should be accepted by everyone involved.

AROUND THE WORLD

Value-based initiative encourages Latin American entrepreneurs

Entrepreneurship accounts for most new job creation, business innovation, and inventions around the world. With the vision of helping Latin America's sagging economies, Linda Rottenberg and Peter Kellner formed the non-profit organization Endeavor Global to help owners of small and medium-sized businesses in Latin America to become entrepreneurs. In six years their approach has created over 6,000 new jobs and generated more than $400 million in local entrepreneurial revenues. Former World Bank president, James D. Wolfensohn calls the firm "a model that should be replicated around the world." After examining its successes in Latin America, he wants to support its expansion to Africa. Endeavor's founders Rottenberg and Kellner are committed to the belief that "new ventures create jobs, spread wealth, expand opportunity and increase social mobility."

Source: Information from Michael Allen, "Endeavor Bets on Latin American entrepreneurs," *Wall Street Journal* (April 15, 2002), p. B4.

●●● SYMBOLIC LEADERSHIP

A **symbolic leader** is someone who uses symbols to establish and maintain a desired organizational culture. Symbolic managers and leaders both act and talk the "language" of the organization. They are always careful to behave in ways that live up to the espoused core values; they are ever-present role models for others to emulate and follow. Symbolic leaders also communicate values in their spoken and written words, taking advantage of every opportunity to do so. They use language very well to describe people, events, and even the competition in ways that reinforce and communicate core values. *Language metaphors*—the use of positive examples from another context—are very powerful in this regard. For example, newly hired workers at Disney World and Disneyland are counselled to always think of themselves as more than employees; they are key "members of the cast," and they work "on stage." After all, they are told, Disney isn't just any business, it is an "entertainment" business.

■ A **symbolic leader** uses symbols to establish and maintain a desired organizational culture.

Good symbolic leaders highlight and even dramatize core values and the observable culture. They tell key stories over and over again, and they encourage others to tell them. They often refer to the "founding story" about the entrepreneur whose personal values set a key tone for the enterprise. They remind everyone about organizational heroes, past and present, whose performances exemplify core values. They often use rites and rituals to glorify the performance of the organization and its members. At Mary Kay Cosmetics, gala events at which top sales performers share their tales of success are legendary. So, too, are the lavish incentive awards presented at these ceremonies, especially the pink luxury cars given to the most successful salespeople.[33]

> **Learning check 4**
>
> **BE SURE YOU CAN**
> - define the term organizational culture and explain the importance of strong cultures to organizations
> - distinguish between the observable and core cultures • explain the concept of value-added management
> - discuss how symbolic leaders build high-performance organizational cultures

MULTICULTURAL ORGANIZATIONS AND DIVERSITY

At the very time that we talk about the culture of an organization as a whole, we must also recognize diversity in its membership. Organizations are made up of many individuals, each of them unique. An important key to competitive advantage is respecting this diversity and allowing everyone's talents to be fully utilized.

■ The term **diversity** describes race, gender, age, and other individual differences.

As first introduced in Chapter 1, **diversity** is a term used to describe differences among people at work. Primary dimensions of diversity include age, race, ethnicity, gender, physical ability, and sexual orientation. But workplace diversity also includes differences in religious beliefs, education, experience, and family status, among others.[34] In his book *Beyond Race and Gender*, consultant R. Roosevelt Thomas, Jr., makes the point that "diversity includes everyone." He says, "In this expanded context, white males are as diverse as their colleagues."[35] Thomas also links diversity with organizational culture, believing that the way people are treated at work—with respect and inclusion, or with disrespect and exclusion—is a direct reflection of the organization's culture.

Thomas's diversity message to those who lead and manage organizations is pointed. Diversity is a potential source of competitive advantage, offering organizations a mixture of talents and perspectives that is ready and able to deal with complexities and uncertainty in the ever-changing 21st-century environment. If you do the right things in organizational leadership, in other words, you'll gain competitive advantage through diversity. If you don't, you'll lose it. This message is backed by recent research on the relationship of diversity and performance. In a study of the business case for diversity, Thomas Kochan found that the presence of diversity alone does not guarantee a positive performance impact.[36] Only when diversity is leveraged through training and supportive human resource practices are the advantages gained. The study offers this guidance:

> *To be successful in working with and gaining value from diversity requires a sustained, systemic approach and long-term commitment. Success is facilitated by a perspective that considers diversity to be an opportunity for everyone in an organization to learn from each other how better to accomplish their work and an occasion that requires a supportive and cooperative organizational culture as well as group leadership and process skills that can facilitate effective group functioning.*

●●● WHAT IS A MULTICULTURAL ORGANIZATION?

■ **Multiculturalism** involves pluralism and respect for diversity.

A key issue in the culture of any organization is *inclusivity*—the degree to which the organization is open to anyone who can perform a job, regardless of their race, sexual preference, gender, or other diversity attribute.[37] The term **multiculturalism** refers to inclusivity, pluralism, and respect for diversity in the workplace. There is no reason why organizational cultures cannot communicate core values that respect and empower the full demographic and cultural diversity that is now characteristic of our workforces. The "best" organizational cultures in this sense are inclusive. They value the talents, ideas, and creative potential of all members. The model in this regard is the truly **multicultural organization** with these characteristics:[38]

- *Pluralism*—Members of both minority cultures and majority cultures are influential in setting key values and policies.

- *Structural integration*—Minority-culture members are well represented in jobs at all levels and in all functional responsibilities.

- *Informal network integration*—Various forms of mentoring and support groups assist in the career development of minority-culture members.

- *Absence of prejudice and discrimination*—A variety of training and task force activities address the need to eliminate culture-group biases.

- *Minimum inter-group conflict*—Diversity does not lead to destructive conflicts between members of majority and minority cultures.

■ A **multicultural organization** is based on pluralism and operates with inclusivity and respect for diversity.

ORGANIZATIONAL SUBCULTURES

Like society as a whole, organizations contain a mixture of **subcultures**, that is, cultures common to groups of people with similar values and beliefs based on shared work responsibilities and personal characteristics. Whereas the pluralism that characterizes multicultural organizations conveys respect for different subcultures, working relations in organizations are too often hurt by the opposite tendency. Just as with life in general, **ethnocentrism**—the belief that one's membership group or subculture is superior to all others—can creep into the workplace and adversely affect the way people relate to one another.

The many possible subcultures in organizations include *occupational subcultures*.[39] Salaried professionals such as lawyers, scientists, engineers, and accountants have been described as having special needs for work autonomy and empowerment that may conflict with traditional management methods of top-down direction and control. Unless these needs are recognized and properly dealt with, salaried professionals may prove difficult to integrate into the culture of the larger organization.

There are also *functional subcultures* in organizations, and people from different functions often have difficulty understanding and working well with one another. For example, employees of a business may consider themselves "systems people" or "marketing people" or "manufacturing people" or "finance people." When such identities are overemphasized, members of the functional groups may spend most of their time with each other, develop a "jargon" or technical language that is shared among themselves, and view their role in the organization as more important than the contributions of the other functions.

Differences in *ethnic or national cultures* will be discussed in Chapter 5 on the global dimensions of management.[40] Although it is relatively easy to recognize that people from various countries and regions of the world have different cultures, it is far harder to turn this awareness into the ability to work well with persons whose backgrounds differ from our own. The best understanding is most likely gained through direct contact and being open-minded. The same advice holds in respect to *racial*

■ Organizational **subcultures** exist among people with similar values and beliefs based on shared work responsibilities and personal characteristics.

■ **Ethnocentrism** is the belief that one's membership group or subculture is superior to all others.

subcultures. Although one may speak in everyday conversations about "African-American" or "Aboriginal" or "Asian" cultures, one has to wonder what we really know about them.[41] Importantly, a key question remains largely unanswered: Where can we find frameworks for understanding them? If improved cross-cultural understandings can help people work better across national boundaries, how can we create the same to help people from different racial subcultures work together better?

We live at a time when the influence of *generational subcultures* at work is of growing importance. But the issues are more subtle than young–old issues alone. It is possible to identify "generational gaps" among "baby boomers" now in their 50s, "Generation Xers" now in their 30s and early 40s, "Nexters" now in their 20s, and the "Millennial Generation" in high school at the turn of the century. Members of these generations grew up in quite different worlds and were influenced by different values and opportunities. Their work preferences and attitudes tend to reflect these differences. Someone who is 60 years old today, a common age for senior managers, was a teenager in the 1960s. Such a person may have difficulty understanding, supervising, and working with younger managers who were teens during the 1970s, 1980s, and even the 1990s.[42]

Issues of relationships and discrimination based on *gender subcultures* also continue to complicate the workplace. Some research shows that when men work together, a group culture forms around a competitive atmosphere. Sports metaphors are common, and games and stories often deal with winning and losing.[43] When women work together, a rather different culture may form, with more emphasis on personal relationships and collaboration.[44]

●●● CHALLENGES FACED BY MINORITIES AND WOMEN

The very term "diversity" basically means the presence of differences. But what does it mean when those differences are distributed unequally in the organizational power structure? What difference does it make when one subculture is in "majority" status while others become "minorities" in respect to representation within the organization? Even though organizations are changing today, most senior executives in large organizations are older, white, and male. There is still likely to be more workforce diversity at lower and middle levels of most organizations than at the top.

Take a look at the situation shown by *Figure 4.5*. It depicts the operation of the **glass ceiling**, defined in Chapter 1 as an invisible barrier that limits the advancement of women and minorities in some organizations. What are the implications for visible minorities and women, seeking to advance and prosper in organizations traditionally dominated by a majority culture, such as white males?

■ The **glass ceiling** is a hidden barrier to the advancement of women and minorities.

The daily work challenges faced by minorities and women can range from misunderstandings and lack of sensitivity on the one hand, to glass ceiling limitations, to even outright harassment and discrimination. *Sexual harassment* in the form of unwanted sexual advances, requests for sexual favours, and sexually laced communications is a problem female employees in particular may face. Minority workers can also be targets of cultural jokes; one survey reports some 45 percent of respondents had been the targets of such abuse. *Pay discrimination* is also an issue. A senior executive in the computer industry reported her surprise at finding out that the top performer in her work group, an African-American male, was paid 25 percent less than anyone else. This wasn't because his pay had been cut to that

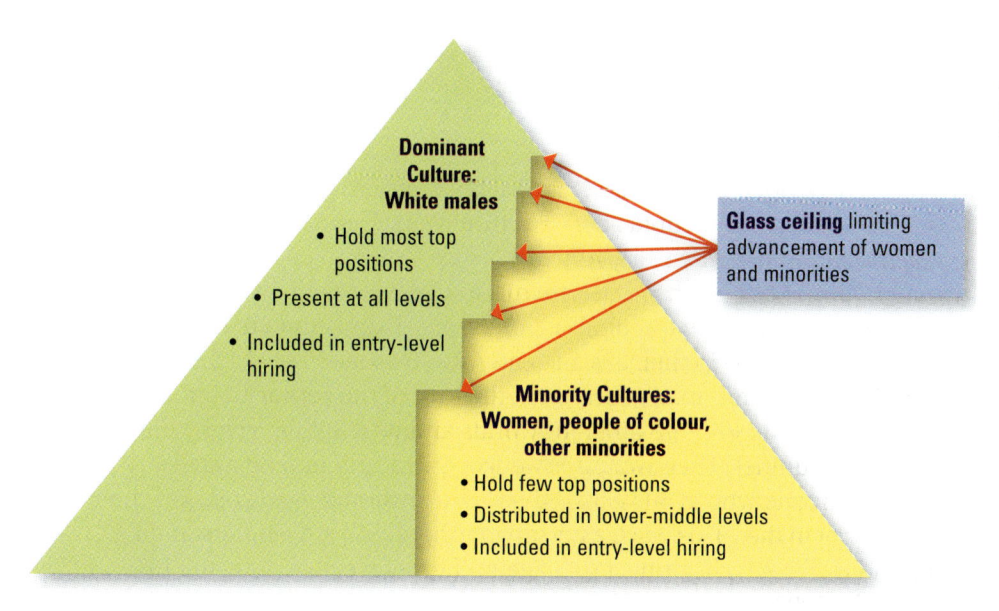

Figure 4.5 Glass ceilings as barriers to women and minority cultures in traditional organizations.

Dominant Culture: White males
- Hold most top positions
- Present at all levels
- Included in entry-level hiring

Glass ceiling limiting advancement of women and minorities

Minority Cultures: Women, people of colour, other minorities
- Hold few top positions
- Distributed in lower-middle levels
- Included in entry-level hiring

Canadian Managers
Balanced Leadership

Annette Verschuren is a leader in the traditionally male-dominated world of home renovation. As head of Home Depot Canada, Verschuren is responsible for the retailer's operations in all 10 provinces. Verschuren ventured into big-box retailing by bringing the arts and crafts store Michaels to Canada. She left Michaels in 1996, taking over Home Depot's Canadian operations when it had 19 stores with 4,500 associates. A decade later, it has approximately 151 stores and 23,000 associates. How does she manage such a large company? "I delegate and juggle well," Verschuren says. "I think a lot of my success comes from putting a team together… I believe better teams usually have a more diverse group of people… I like to be among balanced groups."

Source: "Flexibility is key, says Home Depot chief," *Business Edge*, May 12, 2005; Sarah Thomson, "Annette Verschuren: president of Home Depot," *Women's Post*, November 2005.

---

level, she said, but because his pay increases over time had always trailed those given to his white co-workers. The differences added up significantly over time, but no one noticed or stepped forward to make the appropriate adjustment.[45] Minority members may also face *job discrimination*. Microsoft, for example, has been criticized for treating the firm's 5,000 or more temporary workers unfairly in terms of access to benefits and work assignments. Some temporary employees (who wore orange identification badges at work) claimed that they were treated as second-class citizens by the permanent employees (who wore blue badges).[46]

Sometimes the adaptation of minorities to organizations dominated by a majority culture takes the form of tendencies toward **biculturalism**. This is the

■ **Biculturalism** is when minority members adopt characteristics of majority cultures in order to succeed.

CANADIAN COMPANY IN THE NEWS — Xerox Canada

RECOGNIZING DIVERSITY

The Canadian Council for Aboriginal Business's Progressive Aboriginal Relations (PAR) program assesses the performance of corporations and their relations and involvement with Native Canadian communities. PAR provides a framework for setting organizational objectives, developing action plans, measuring performance, and achieving results. PAR participants measure their performance through a self-assessment and external verification process, and use the results to determine the success of their efforts.

Toronto-based Xerox Canada achieved gold-level recognition in 2006, after receiving silver-level recognition in 2003. In addition to financial and in-kind donations, employee recruitment, and cultural awareness training, Xerox Canada's support includes an annual Aboriginal Scholarship Program, a "CEO for a Day" program, and the creation of the Aboriginal Community Records Information Management program at the Southern Alberta Institute of Technology.

Sources: "Xerox recognized for work with Native community," *The Globe and Mail*, February 21, 2006. CCAB web site: <http://www.ccab.com/par.htm>

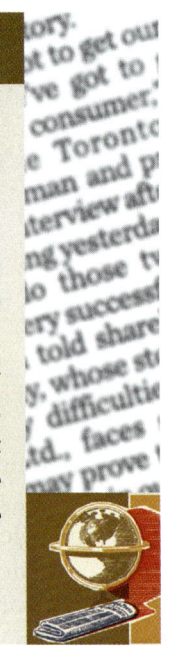

display, by members of minority cultures, of majority-culture characteristics that seem necessary to succeed in the work environment. For example, one might find gays and lesbians hiding their sexual orientation from co-workers out of fear of prejudice or discrimination. Similarly, one might find an employee of colour carefully training herself to not use, at work, certain words or phrases that might be considered by white co-workers as subculture slang.

The special economic and work challenges faced by minorities are not always highly visible. Over a recent period of economic expansion, most Canadians and Americans benefitted from a growth in jobs and employment opportunities. But how many of us know that disabled workers largely failed to share in the gains? At the same time that demand for workers in general rose, the employment rate of the disabled fell over 10 percent for men and 5 percent for women.[47]

●●● MANAGING DIVERSITY

There's no doubt today what minority workers want.[48] They want the same thing everyone wants. They want respect for their talents and a work setting that allows them to achieve their full potential. It takes the best in diversity leadership at all levels of organizational management to meet these expectations. R. Roosevelt Thomas defines **managing diversity** as building an organizational culture that allows all members, minorities and women included, to reach their full potential.

Figure 4.6 describes a continuum of leadership approaches to diversity. The first is *advancing action*, in which leadership commits the organization to hiring and advancing minorities and women. The second is *valuing diversity*, in which leadership commits the organization to education and training programs designed to help people better understand and respect individual differences. The third, and most comprehensive, is *managing diversity*, in which leadership commits to changing the organizational culture to empower and include all people.

Thomas believes that managing diversity holds the most value in respect to competitive advantage.[49] A diverse workforce offers a rich pool of talents, ideas, and viewpoints for solving the complex problems of often-uncertain environments. And a

■ **Managing diversity** is building an inclusive work environment that allows everyone to reach their full potential.

Figure 4.6 Leadership approaches to diversity—from advancing action to managing diversity.

- **Advancing Action**: Create upward mobility for minorities and women
- **Valuing Differences**: Build quality relationships with respect for diversity
- **Managing Diversity**: Achieve full utilization of diverse human resources

Source: Adapted by permission of the publisher, from *Beyond Race and Gender* by R. Roosevelt Thomas © 1991 R. Roosevelt Thomas Jr., AMACOM books, division of American Management Association, New York, NY. All rights reserved. www.amacombooks.org

diverse workforce is best aligned with the needs and expectations of a diverse customer and stakeholder base. Organizations that Thomas calls "diversity mature" are well positioned to derive these and other sources of competitive advantage. In these organizations there is a diversity mission as well as an organizational mission; diversity is viewed as a strategic imperative, and the members understand diversity concepts.[50] Ultimately, however, he considers the basic building block of a diversity-mature organization to be the *diversity-mature individual*.[51]

Perhaps the most important word in human resource management today is "inclusiveness." By valuing diversity and building multicultural organizations that include everyone, organizations of all types can be strengthened and brought into better alignment with the challenges and opportunities of today's environment. Research reported in the *Gallup Management Journal*, for example, shows that establishing a racially and ethnically inclusive workplace is good for morale.[52] In a study of 2,014 workers, those who felt included were more likely to stay with their employers and recommend them to others. Survey questions asked such things as: "Do you always trust your company to be fair to all employees?" "At work, are all employees always treated with respect?" "Does your supervisor always make the best use of employees' skills?" Clearly, inclusivity counts; it counts in terms of respect for people, and it counts in building organizational capacities for high performance and sustainable competitive advantage. As Michael R. Losey, president of the Society for Human Resource Management (SHRM), says: "Companies must realize that the talent pool includes people of all types, including older workers; persons with disabilities; persons of various religious, cultural, and national backgrounds; persons who are not heterosexual; minorities; and women."[53]

PERSONAL MANAGEMENT

DIVERSITY MATURITY is essential if you are to work well in today's organizations. It is a cornerstone for personal inclusivity. Consultant Roosevelt Thomas uses the following questions when testing diversity maturity among people in the workplace. Answer the questions. Be honest; admit where you still have work left to do. Use your answers to help set future goals to ensure that your actions, not just your words, consistently display positive diversity values.

- Do you accept responsibility for improving your performance?
- Do you understand diversity concepts?
- Do you make decisions about others based on their abilities?
- Do you understand that diversity issues are complex?
- Are you able to cope with tensions in addressing diversity?
- Are you willing to challenge the way things are?
- Are you willing to learn continuously?

Get to know yourself better

Complete Self-Assessments #7—**Diversity Awareness**, and Exercise #7—**What Do You Value in Work?**, from the Workbook and Personal Management Activity #4 on the companion website.

> **BE SURE YOU CAN**
> - explain multiculturalism and list key characteristics of multicultural organizations • identify typical organizational subcultures • discuss the common employment problems faced by minorities and women
> - explain Thomas's concept of managing diversity • realistically assess your diversity maturity

✓ Learning check 5

Chapter 4 STUDY GUIDE

WHERE WE'VE BEEN

Back to BMO Financial Group

The opening example describes BMO Financial Group as a vanguard company noted for its values and performance success. In Chapter 4 you learned more about the complex nature of the external environments faced by organizations like BMO Financial Group. You also learned how organizations can benefit from strong and positive cultures and from internal environments committed to managing diversity and inclusivity for all employees. All of this, of course, doesn't just happen. Great managers make it happen. And that is what *Management* is all about.

THE NEXT STEP
INTEGRATED LEARNING ACTIVITIES

Cases/Projects
- UPS Case
- Project 1—Diversity Lessons
- Project 7—Gender and Leadership

Self-Assessments
- Diversity Awareness (#7)
- Organizational Design Preferences (#17)
- Are You Cosmopolitan? (#18)

Exercises in Teamwork
- Defining Quality (#3)
- Which Organization Culture Fits You? (#8)
- Case of the Contingency Workforce (#22)

STUDY QUESTION SUMMARY

1. What is the external environment of organizations?
- Competitive advantage and distinctive competency can only be achieved by organizations that deal successfully with dynamic and complex environments.
- The external environment of organizations consists of both general and specific parts.
- The general environment includes background economic, socio-cultural, legal-political, technological, and natural environment conditions.
- The specific or task environment consists of suppliers, customers, competitors, regulators, and pressure groups that an organization interacts with.
- Environmental uncertainty challenges organizations and managers to be flexible and responsive to new and changing conditions.

2. What is a customer-driven organization?
- A customer-driven organization recognizes customer service and product quality as foundations of competitive advantage.

- Total quality operations address needs of both internal customers and external customers.
- Customer relationship management builds and maintains strategic relationships with customers.
- Supply chain management builds and maintains strategic relationships with suppliers.

3. What is a quality-driven organization?
- To compete in the global economy, organizations are increasingly expected to meet ISO 9000 quality standards.
- Total quality management makes quality a strategic objective of the organization and supports it by continuous improvement efforts.
- Total quality operations try to meet customers' needs—on time, the first time, and all the time.
- Quality circles are groups of employees working together to solve quality problems.

4. What is organizational culture?
- The organizational culture is an internal environment that establishes a personality for the organization and has a strong influence on the behaviour of its members.
- The observable culture is found in the rites, rituals, stories, heroes, and symbols of the organization.
- The core culture consists of the core values and fundamental beliefs on which the organization is based.
- In organizations with strong cultures, members behave with shared understandings that support the organizational objectives.
- Symbolic managers build shared values, and use stories, ceremonies, heroes, and language to reinforce these values.

5. How is diversity managed in a multicultural organization?
- The organizational culture should create a positive ethical climate, or shared set of understandings about what is considered ethical.
- Multicultural organizations operate through a culture that values pluralism and respects diversity.
- Organizations have many subcultures, including those based on occupational, functional, ethnic, racial, age, and gender differences in a diverse workforce.
- Challenges faced by organizational minorities include sexual harassment, pay discrimination, job discrimination, and the glass ceiling effect.
- Managing diversity is the process of developing a work environment that is inclusive and allows everyone to reach their full potential.

KEY TERMS REVIEW

Biculturalism (p. 107)
Competitive advantage (p. 91)
Continuous improvement (p. 98)
Core values (p. 102)
Customer relationship management (p. 96)
Diversity (p. 104)
Environmental uncertainty (p. 94)
Ethnocentrism (p. 105)

General environment (p. 91)
Glass ceiling (p. 106)
ISO certification (p. 97)
Managing diversity (p. 108)
Multicultural organization (p. 105)
Multiculturalism (p. 104)
Organizational culture (p. 100)
Quality circle (p. 99)

Specific environment (p. 93)
Stakeholders (p. 93)
Subcultures (p. 105)
Supply chain management (p. 97)
Symbolic leader (p. 103)
Total quality management (p. 97)
Value-based management (p. 102)
Value creation (p. 93)

SELF-TEST 4

MULTIPLE-CHOICE QUESTIONS:

1. The general environment of an organization would include _____.
   (a) population demographics (b) activist groups (c) competitors (d) customers

2. In terms of value creation for stakeholders, _____ have a major interest in a business firm's profits and losses.
   (a) employees (b) communities (c) owners (d) suppliers

3. Two dimensions that determine the level of environmental uncertainty are the number of factors in the external environment and the _____ of these factors.
   (a) location (b) rate of change (c) importance (d) interdependence

4. Benchmarking, continuous improvement, and reduced cycle times are examples of organizational practices that show a commitment to _____.
   (a) affirmative action (b) total quality management (c) cost containment (d) supply chain management

5. A quality standard that has become essential for world-class companies competing in global markets is _____.
   (a) the Deming Prize (b) the Baldrige Award (c) CRM (d) ISO certification

6. New computer technologies have made possible _____ that quickly and efficiently produces individualized products for customers.
   (a) flexible manufacturing (b) mass production (c) mass customization (d) design for disassembly

7. Planned and spontaneous ceremonies and celebrations of work achievements illustrate how _____ help build strong corporate cultures.
   (a) rewards (b) heroes (c) rites and rituals (d) core values

8. When managers at Disney World use language metaphors, telling workers they are "on stage" as "members of the cast," they are engaging in _____ leadership.
   (a) symbolic (b) competitive (c) multicultural (d) stakeholder

9. Pluralism and the absence of discrimination and prejudice in policies and practices are two important hallmarks of _____.
   (a) the glass ceiling effect (b) a multicultural organization (c) quality circles (d) affirmative action

10. When members of minority cultures feel that they have to behave in ways similar to the majority, this is called _____.
    (a) biculturalism (b) symbolic leadership (c) the glass ceiling effect (d) inclusivity

11. Wal-Mart's suppliers electronically access inventory data and sales forecasts in the stores and automatically ship replacement products. This is an example of IT utilization in _____.
    (a) supply chain management (b) customer relationship management (c) total quality management (d) strategic constituencies analysis

12. Whether a structure is tight or loose and whether decisions are change oriented or driven by the status quo are indicators of an organization's _____.
    (a) inclusivity (b) culture (c) competitive advantage (d) multiculturalism

13. Performance with honesty, innovation, and social responsibility are among the _____ often espoused in corporate mission statements.
    (a) core values (b) stakeholder interests (c) TQM practices (d) ISO standards

14. _____ means that an organization fully integrates members of minority cultures and majority cultures.
    (a) Equal employment opportunity (b) Managing diversity (c) Symbolic leadership (d) Pluralism

15. The beliefs that older workers are not creative and are more interested in routine jobs are examples of stereotypes that can create bad feelings among members of different _____ subcultures in organizations.
    (a) occupational (b) generational (c) gender (d) functional

SHORT-RESPONSE QUESTIONS:

16. What operating objectives are appropriate for an organization seeking competitive advantage through improved customer service?

17. What is the difference between an organization's external customers and its internal customers?

18. What is value-based management?

19. Why is it important for managers to understand subcultures in organizations?

APPLICATION QUESTION:

20. Two businesswomen, former college roommates, are discussing their jobs and careers over lunch. You overhear one saying to the other, "I work for a large corporation, while you own a small retail business. In my company there is a strong corporate culture and everyone feels its influence. In fact, we are always expected to act in ways that support the culture and serve as role models for others to do so as well. This includes a commitment to diversity and multi-culturalism. Because of the small size of your firm, things like corporate culture, diversity, and multiculturalism are not so important to worry about." Do you agree or disagree with this statement? Why?

5 Global Dimensions of Management

CHAPTER 5 STUDY QUESTIONS

1. What are the international management challenges of globalization?
2. What are the forms and opportunities of international business?
3. What are multinational corporations and what do they do?
4. What is culture and how does it relate to global diversity?
5. How do management practices and learning transfer across cultures?

Planning Ahead
After reading Chapter 5, you should be able to answer these questions in your own words.

GILDAN
TAKING ON THE GIANTS

A Montreal based clothing company deciding to take on the Chinese manufacturing might-seems foolish, right? Well that's exactly what Gildan is doing. Most experts agreed that high Canadian labour costs, together with the removal of quotas under the World Trade Organization's Agreement on textiles and clothing (in 1995), meant a surefire decline in the North American textile business. Not so for Gildan Activewear Inc. which has not only survived, but is set to expand further by venturing into the world of retail. Until now, Gildan has focused on selling only into the screen printing channel. How did they take on the giants?

Starting in 1999, the company undertook a global survey of clothing prices. "The first thing we did from Day 1 was to make sure that we benchmarked ourselves against the global market," says Glenn Chamandy, the CEO of Gildan. Gildan worked diligently to achieve their current level of pricing, which is approximately 35% lower than their Chinese competitors, in the U.S. market.

To maintain its competitive advantage and remain a global player, Gildan recognized that it also had to establish operations offshore, first in Honduras in 1997, later expanding to Mexico, Haiti, the Dominican Republic, and Nicaragua. Locating offshore was not clear sailing. Initially, they were accused of poor working conditions and infringements on workers' rights, which may have negatively impacted the company's share price at the time. However, Gildan worked hard to develop a good working relationship and positive reputation for corporate social responsibility with non-governmental organizations, and joined the Fair Labor Association.

The strategic placement of these facilities has allowed Gildan to benefit from bilateral and multilateral trade agreements. It can ship duty-free anywhere in North America, the European Union, and Australia. This together with fair labour practices and advanced technology has kept the Chinese giants at bay. As Chamandy notes, 2005 was the year in which Gildan not only began to truly achieve its goals in economic terms but also reinforced its excellent financial performance by positioning itself "as a leader in corporate social responsibility and governance." [1]

GET CONNECTED!

Browse the Web for information on the retailing industry, at home and around the world. Is Gildan Activewear Inc. still successful in taking on the giants?

Chapter 5 LEARNING PREVIEW

There is more to Gildan than its manufacturing centres. Standing behind the T-shirts and clothing line is a large operation that depends on worldwide networks of suppliers and subcontractors to produce its products. But as Gildan strives for world markets it must continue to be well managed and to maintain high ethical standards. In Chapter 5 you will learn about international management with special attention to multinational corporations and the implications of global cultural diversity.

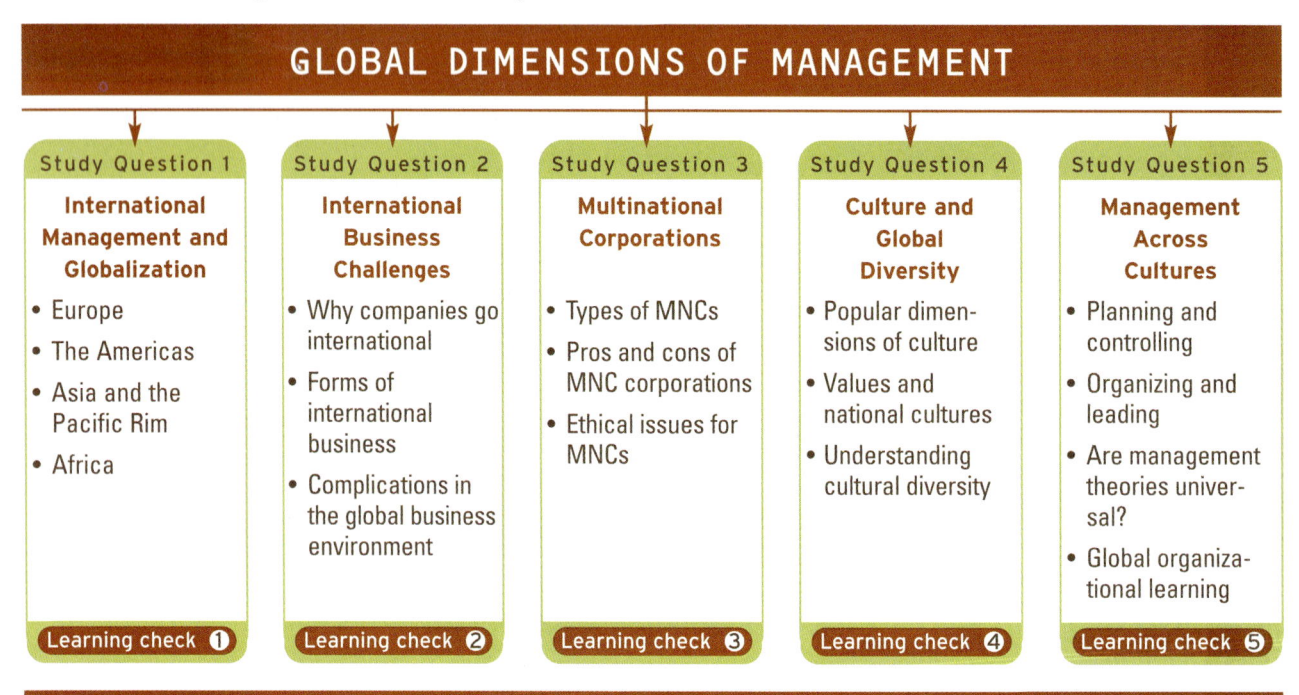

GLOBAL DIMENSIONS OF MANAGEMENT

Study Question 1
International Management and Globalization
- Europe
- The Americas
- Asia and the Pacific Rim
- Africa

Learning check 1

Study Question 2
International Business Challenges
- Why companies go international
- Forms of international business
- Complications in the global business environment

Learning check 2

Study Question 3
Multinational Corporations
- Types of MNCs
- Pros and cons of MNC corporations
- Ethical issues for MNCs

Learning check 3

Study Question 4
Culture and Global Diversity
- Popular dimensions of culture
- Values and national cultures
- Understanding cultural diversity

Learning check 4

Study Question 5
Management Across Cultures
- Planning and controlling
- Organizing and leading
- Are management theories universal?
- Global organizational learning

Learning check 5

There is no doubt about it. We live and work in a global community, one that grows smaller and more immediately accessible by the day. The Internet and television bring on-the-spot news from around the world into our homes, 24 hours a day. The world's newspapers, from *The Globe and Mail*, to *El Financiero* (Mexico), to *Le Monde* (France), to the *Japan Times* can be read at the touch of a keyboard on your PC. It is possible to board a plane in Vancouver and fly non-stop to Beijing; it is sometimes less expensive to fly from Montreal to Paris than Montreal to Toronto. Colleges and universities offer a growing variety of study-abroad programs. For example, students at St. Francis Xavier University travel to places such as Grenada, Mexico, and Cuba to further understand global issues.

This world of international opportunities isn't just for tourists and travellers; it has major implications for businesses and those who work for them. Just take a look at the automobile industry. The Chrysler PT Cruiser is built in Mexico for Daimler-Chrysler of Germany; Ford owns Volvo; Toyota has produced more than 10 million cars at its North American plants; the "big three" Japanese automakers—Honda, Nissan, Toyota—get as much as 80 to 90 percent of their profits from sales in North America. And when the last of the original Volkswagen Beetles was made in mid-2003, it wasn't a German band that heralded its departure to the museum. *Mariachi* music greeted the car as it rolled off the line at Volkswagen's Puebla, Mexico, plant.[2] The same trends and patterns are evident in other industries and countries. National boundaries are fast blurring as businesses of all sizes and types now travel the trade routes of the world.

Astute business investors know all this and more. They buy and sell only with awareness of the latest financial news from Hong Kong, London, Tokyo, New York, Sao Paulo, Johannesburg, and other financial centres of the world. There is no doubt that we live and work today in a truly global village. You, like the rest of us, must get connected with its implications for everyday living and careers.

And, what does the world think of Canada's place in the world economy? The Merrill Lynch Misery Index ranks nations based on unemployment, inflation, budgets, and trade balance; an economy with an increasing index is in poor economic shape. According to this Index, Canada ranks second in the developed world with Japan topping the index; this rating shows to the world that the Canadian economy is strong and vibrant. Merrill's chief North American economist, David Rosenberg, states that because of the volatility in Japan's economic fortunes, Canada is the most likely recipient of foreign-equity investment dollars in the next few years. It appears that the world is noticing what is happening in Canada, and likes it.[3]

INTERNATIONAL MANAGEMENT AND GLOBALIZATION

This is the age of the **global economy** in which resource supplies, product markets, and business competition are worldwide rather than purely local or national in scope.[4] It is also a time heavily influenced by the forces of **globalization**, the process of growing interdependence among these components in the global economy.[5] Harvard scholar and consulant Rosabeth Moss Kanter describes it as: "one of the most powerful and pervasive influences on nations, businesses, workplaces, communities, and lives…"[6]

The global economy offers great opportunities for worldwide sourcing, production, and sales capabilities. But as businesses spread their reach around the world, the processes of globalization also bring many adjustments to traditional patterns.[7] Large multinational businesses are increasingly adopting transnational or "global" identities, rather than being identified with a national home. The growing strength and penetration of these businesses worldwide are viewed by some as a potential threat to national economies and their local business systems, labour markets, and cultures. All this adds up to great uncertainty as executives move into new and uncharted competitive territories. America Online's co-founder Stephen M. Case once described the scene: "I sometimes feel like I'm behind the wheel of a race car. One of the biggest challenges is there are no road signs to help navigate. And in fact… no one has yet determined which side of the road we're supposed to be on."[8]

The term used to describe management in organizations with business interests in more than one country is **international management**. There is no denying its importance. Procter & Gamble, for example, pursues a global strategy with a presence in more than 70 countries; the majority of McDonald's sales are now coming from outside North America, with some of its most profitable restaurants located in places like Moscow, Budapest, and Beijing. As the leaders of these and other companies press forward with global initiatives, the international management

■ In the **global economy**, resources, markets, and competition are worldwide in scope.

■ **Globalization** is the process of growing interdependence among elements of the global economy.

■ **International management** involves managing operations in more than one country.

- A **global manager** is culturally aware and informed about international affairs.

challenges and opportunities of working across borders—national and cultural—must be mastered. A new breed of manager, the **global manager**, is increasingly sought after. This is someone informed about international developments, transnational in outlook, competent in working with people from different cultures, and always aware of regional developments in a changing world.

What about you? Are you prepared for the challenges of international management? Are you informed about the world and the forces of globalization?

EUROPE

The new Europe is a place of dramatic political and economic developments.[9] The **European Union** (EU) is expanding to 22 countries that agree to support mutual economic growth by removing barriers that previously limited cross-border trade and business development. As an economic union, the EU is putting the rest of the world on notice that European business is a global force to be reckoned with. Members are linked through favourable trade and customs laws intended to facilitate the free flow of workers, goods and services, and investments across national boundaries. Businesses in each member country have access to a market of over 375 million consumers.

- The **European Union** is a political and economic alliance of European countries.

Among the important business and economic developments in the EU are agreements to eliminate frontier controls and trade barriers, create uniform minimum technical product standards, open government procurement to businesses from all member countries, unify financial regulations, lift competitive barriers in banking and insurance, and offer a common currency—the **Euro**. The growing worldwide impact of the Euro is being watched carefully. Although there are still political and economic uncertainties, the expected regional benefits of an expanding EU include higher productivity, lower inflation, and steady growth.

- The **Euro** is the common European currency.

take it to the case!

Harley-Davidson Motor Company
Where style and strategy travel the globe

Harley-Davidson motorcycles rule the road these days. Along with the popular "Harley"-branded clothing and accessories, the company is on a roll. It wasn't always that way. During the late 1970s, the firm's sales suffered in the face of new and stiff competition from Japan. The U.S. International Trade Commission granted Harley short-term tariff protection from Japanese motorcycles in 1983; the firm regrouped, put its house in order, and hasn't looked back since. The Harley Owner's Group has over a million members worldwide. Harley has a solid market in Japan, where its bikes are a mark of prestige for their owners. Harley is secure in pursuing its mission with a clear sense of its global markets: "We fulfill dreams through the experience of motorcycling."

Photographs courtesy of Harley-Davidson Photography & Imaging. Copyright Harley-Davidson.

Sources: Information from Rich Teerlink, "Harley's Leadership U-Turn," *Harvard Business Review* (March–April 2000), pp. 3–4. See also Rich Teerlink and Lee Ozley, *More Than a Motorcycle: The Leadership Journey at Harley-Davidson* (Cambridge, MA: Harvard Business School Press 2000); and corporate website: <www.harley-davidson.com.>

●●● THE AMERICAS

Canada, the United States, and Mexico are joined in the North American Free Trade Agreement (**NAFTA**). This agreement largely frees the flow of goods and services, workers, and investments within a region that has more potential consumers than its European rival, the EU. Getting approval of NAFTA from all three governments was not easy. Whereas Canadian firms worried about domination by US manufacturers, American politicians were concerned about the potential loss of jobs to Mexico. Some calls were made for more government legislation and support to protect domestic industries from foreign competition. While Mexicans feared that free trade would bring a further intrusion of US culture and values into their country, Americans complained that Mexican businesses did not operate by the same social standards—particularly with respect to environmental protection and the use of child labour.

■ **NAFTA** is the North American Free Trade Agreement linking Canada, the United States, and Mexico in an economic alliance.

At times an issue in NAFTA controversies, *maquiladoras* are foreign manufacturing plants allowed to operate in Mexico with special privileges in return for employing Mexican labour.[10] These firms import materials, components, and equipment duty free. They employ lower-cost Mexican labour to assemble these materials into finished products, which are then exported with duty paid only on the "value added" in Mexico. Critics of *maquiladoras* accuse them of exploiting Mexican workers and giving away jobs that would otherwise go to Canadians and Americans. They also point to high "social costs" as a continuing influx of workers overburdens services in Mexican border towns and the region becomes increasingly "Americanized." Advocates argue that *maquiladoras* increase employment and prosperity, and help develop skilled local workers.

■ *Maquiladoras* are foreign manufacturing plants that operate in Mexico with special privileges.

Optimism regarding business and economic growth extends throughout the Americas. Countries of the region are cutting tariffs, updating their economic policies, and welcoming foreign investors. An agreement has been reached by trade ministers to create a Free Trade Area of the Americas (FTAA), a proposed free-trade zone that would stretch from Point Barrow, Alaska, all the way to Tierra del Fuego, Chile. In addition, the *MERCOSUR* agreement links Bolivia, Brazil, Paraguay, Uruguay, and Argentina; the Andean Pact links Venezuela, Colombia, Equador, Peru, and Bolivia; and the Carribean Community, CARICOM, is growing as an economic linkage.

●●● ASIA AND THE PACIFIC RIM

When one looks toward Asia, China looms centre stage. The country of 1.3 billion people is the world's largest consumer marketplace. It is projected that China will top world performance charts for the next several years, growing by an average of 8.5–9 percent annually. However, another Asian giant, India, is not far behind as it cruises along at a 7–7.5 percent rate. While their economic structures differ noticeably, they do share a number of similarities. Both have economies that are growing at more than three times the average rate of other industrialized countries. Each nation has more people than the combined populations of Canada, the United States, the Eurozone (the collective group of countries which use the Euro as their common currency), and Japan. Combined, China and India add approximately 25 million people—a mini-Canada—to their economic base each year.[11] China's firms are major exporters of apparel and clothing and are direct competitors to firms like Gildan, featured in the chapter opener. It is also a top exporter of computers, electrical parts and components, telecommunications equipment, and sporting goods, among other products.[12] Over $120 billion worth of exports find their way annually from China to North America alone. But in Asia, one also has to recognize the historical strength of Japanese businesses—Honda, Toyota, Sony, to name just three—the growing prominence of firms like Samsung and Hyundai of South Korea, as well as other regional powers like Taiwan and Singapore. Together, they add another $200+ billion in exports to North America.

Elsewhere in Southeast Asia, countries like Malaysia and Thailand are prominent, Vietnam is fast advancing, and the Philippines is making a strategic move. With a high literacy rate, an educated workforce, and a population that speaks English, it intends to become a world centre for business process outsourcing. Goals include expanding its growing presence in global markets for medical transcription and accounting services, as well as customer call centres.[13] The 2003 agreement among 10 Southeast Asian nations to form an economic community along the lines of the EU model is designed to further growth in this region.

"Opportunity" is the watchword of the day wherever you travel or do business in Asia. Asian countries already represent a third of the global marketplace and rank as the world's top market for cars and telecommunications equipment. It is not just "low-cost" labour that attracts businesses to Asia; the growing availability of highly skilled "brainpower" is increasingly high on its list of advantages. India is a good example. The country is in the midst of economic expansion, with a high literacy rate and relatively inexpensive skilled labour. It is emerging as a world-class base for technology development and software engineering.

●●● AFRICA

Africa (*see Figure 5.1*) is a continent in the news.[14] Although often the focus of reports on ethnic turmoil and civil strife in countries struggling along pathways to peace and development, the region beckons international investments. Whereas foreign businesses tend to avoid the risk of trouble spots, they are giving

Figure 5.1 Africa, continent of opportunity.

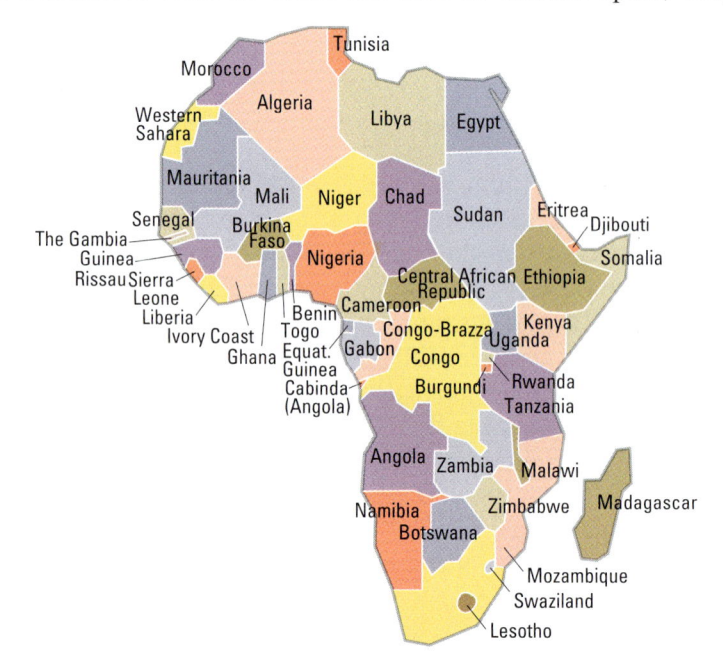

> ### AROUND THE WORLD
>
> **Mozambique is just one of Africa's opportunities**
>
> A turnaround is underway in the East African nation of Mozambique as the former Portuguese colony continues to emerge from years of civil war that began with its independence in 1975. Considered the world's poorest country in 1990, Mozambique's new economy offers citizens hope and advancement. A local entrepreneur says, "Mozambicans, sick of war, want a working society." Mozambique is rich with natural resources and is in an ideal trading location. The country is now home to billion-dollar infrastructure projects financed by development agencies. A railroad and highway corridor from the capital city of Maputo to South Africa is fast developing. Mozambique is a member of the Southern African Development Community.
>
> Source: Quotes from Mort Rosenblum, "Turnaround: Once a Basket Case, Mozambique Now a Free-Market Example," *Columbus Dispatch* (December 14, 1997), p. 4c.

increased attention to stable countries with growing economics. One is Ghana, which has established a growing presence in the market for business process outsourcing.[15] On the discouraging side, the rates of economic growth in sub-Saharan Africa are among the lowest in the world; many parts of Africa suffer from terrible problems of poverty and the ravishment of a continuing AIDS epidemic. The region's need for sustained assistance from business investments and foreign aid is well established.

A report by two Harvard professors recently analyzed the foreign investment environment of Africa and concluded that the region's contextual problems are manageable.[16] "In fact they should be viewed as opportunities," says James A. Austin, one of the co-authors. He adds: "If a company has the managerial and organizational capabilities to deal with the region's unique business challenges, then it will be able to enter a promising market."[17]

The Southern African Development Community (SADC) links 14 countries of southern Africa in trade and economic development efforts. The objectives of SADC include harmonizing and rationalizing strategies for sustainable development among member countries.[18] Post-apartheid South Africa, in particular, has benefitted from political revival. A country of almost 50 million people and great natural resources, South Africa is experiencing economic recovery and attracting outside investors. It already accounts for half the continent's purchasing power.[19] Foreign investments in the country increased sharply after minority white rule ended and Nobel Prize winner Nelson Mandela became the nation's first black president.

> **BE SURE YOU CAN**
> • define the terms global economy and globalization • discuss the implications of globalization for international management • illustrate the significance of regional economic alliances by describing how NAFTA and the EU operate • discuss the pros and cons of *maquiladora* operations
>
> ✓ Learning check ❶

INTERNATIONAL BUSINESS CHALLENGES

John Chambers, CEO of Cisco Systems Inc., says: "I will put my jobs anywhere in the world where the right infrastructure is, with the right educated workforce, with the right supportive government."[20] Cisco and other firms like it are **international businesses**. They conduct for-profit transactions of goods and services across national boundaries.

■ An **international business** conducts commercial transactions across national boundaries.

●●● WHY COMPANIES GO INTERNATIONAL

International businesses of all types and sizes are the foundations of world trade. They are the engines for moving raw materials, finished products, and specialized services from one country to another in the global economy. The reasons *why businesses go international* include these attractions of the marketplaces of the world:

- *Profits*—Global operations offer greater profit potential.
- *Customers*—Global operations offer new markets to sell products.
- *Suppliers*—Global operations offer access to needed raw materials.
- *Capital*—Global operations offer access to financial resources.
- *Labour*—Global operations offer access to lower labour costs.

CANADIAN COMPANY IN THE NEWS — Toyota Canada Inc.

MULTINATIONAL CORPORATION (MNC) COMMITS TO ONTARIO TOWNS

The towns of Simcoe and Woodstock, Ontario, are certainly benefiting from the expansion of one multinational corporation—Toyota Motor Corp. The Japanese car maker's truck subsidiary Hino Motors Ltd. opened the first Japanese commercial truck assembly factory in Canada in Woodstock in 2006, hiring 45 people, with the possibility of another 15 to 20 jobs with the addition of a second shift. While it's not a major employer, analysts describe the move as an indication of the Japanese company's further commitment to Canada. Toyota also announced plans for a $50-million auto parts plant in Simcoe, to begin operations in 2007 with the creation of 250 jobs. Run by Toyotetsu Canada Inc., the auto parts plant will supply parts to the Toyota plant in Cambridge, Ontario, with another plant set to open in Woodstock in 2008.

Sources: Omar El Akkad, "Toyota to build auto parts factory in Ontario," *The Globe and Mail*, March 15, 2006, p. B4; Gary Norris, "Toyota opening truck plant in Woodstock, Ont.," *Canadian Press*, March 7, 2006.

●●● FORMS OF INTERNATIONAL BUSINESS

The common forms of international business are shown in *Figure 5.2*. When a business is just getting started internationally, global sourcing, exporting/importing, and licensing and franchising are the usual ways to begin. These are *market entry strategies* that involve the sale of goods or services to foreign markets but do not require expensive capital investments. Joint ventures and wholly owned subsidiaries are *direct investment strategies*. They require major capital commitments but create rights of ownership and control over operations in the foreign country.

Figure 5.2 Common forms of international business—from market entry to direct investment strategies.

Market entry strategies: Global sourcing | Exporting and importing | Licensing and franchising

Direct investment strategies: Joint ventures | Foreign subsidiaries

Increasing involvement in ownership and control of foreign operations

Market Entry Strategies

A common first step into international business is **global sourcing**—the process of purchasing materials, manufacturing components, or business services from around the world. It is an international division of labour in which activities are performed in countries where they can be done well at the lowest cost. In manufacturing, global sourcing of components for cars may mean purchasing windshields and instrument panels from Mexico, and anti-lock braking systems from Germany. In services, it may mean setting up toll-free customer support call centres in the Philippines, or contracting for computer software programs in India. The goal of global sourcing is to take advantage of international wage gaps and the availability of skilled labour by contracting for goods and services in low-cost foreign locations.

A second form of international business involves **exporting**—selling locally made products in foreign markets, and/or **importing**—buying foreign-made products and selling them in domestic markets. Because the growth of export industries creates local jobs, governments often offer special advice and assistance to businesses that are trying to develop or expand their export markets. According to Statistics Canada, in 2005 Canada exported over $450 billion worth of goods, with the United States purchasing approximately 85 percent of that total. Our second trading partner, Japan, was a distant second place at 2 percent. Despite efforts to expand our trading partners, it is easy to see that the Canadian economy is extensively entwined with our neighbour to the south.[21]

Another form of international business is the **licensing agreement**, where foreign firms pay a fee for rights to make or sell another company's products in a specified region. The licence typically grants access to a unique manufacturing technology, special patent, or trademark. **Franchising** is a form of licensing in which the foreign firm buys the rights to use another's name and operating methods in its home country. As in domestic franchising agreements, firms like McDonald's, Wendy's, Subway, and others sell facility designs, equipment, product ingredients and recipes, and management systems to foreign investors, while retaining certain product and operating controls.

■ In **global sourcing**, materials or services are purchased around the world for local use.

■ In **exporting**, local products are sold abroad.

■ **Importing** is the process of acquiring products abroad and selling them in domestic markets.

■ In a **licensing agreement** one firm pays a fee for rights to make or sell another company's products.

■ In **franchising** a fee is paid for rights to use another firm's name and operating methods.

Direct Investment Strategies

To establish a direct investment presence in a foreign country, many firms enter into **joint ventures**. These are co-ownership arrangements that pool resources and share risks and control for business operations. A joint venture may be established by equity purchases and/or direct investments by a foreign partner in an existing operation; it may also involve the creation of an entirely new business by a foreign and local partner. International joint ventures are *strategic alliances* that help partners gain things through co-operation that otherwise would be difficult to achieve independ-

■ A **joint venture** operates in a foreign country through co-ownership with local partners.

■ A **foreign subsidiary** is a local operation completely owned by a foreign firm.

ently. In return for its investment in a local operation, for example, the outside or foreign partner often gains both access to new markets and the assistance of a local partner who understands them. In return for its investment, the local partner often gains new technology as well as opportunities for its employees to learn new skills. *Manager's Notepad 5.1* offers a checklist for choosing joint venture partners.[22]

A **foreign subsidiary** is a local operation completely owned and controlled by a foreign firm. Like joint ventures, foreign subsidiaries may be formed through direct investment in start-up operations called *greenfield ventures*, or through equity purchases in existing ones. When making such investments, foreign firms are clearly taking a business risk. They must be confident that they possess the expertise needed to manage and conduct business affairs successfully in the new environment. This is where prior experience gained through joint ventures can prove very beneficial. Although establishing a foreign subsidiary represents the highest level of involvement in international operations, it can make very good business sense. Toyota recently agreed to open a second Canadian plant in Woodstock, Ontario. According to the president of Toyota Motor Corp., Katsuaki Watanabe, the expectation is to build 100,000 vehicles annually.[23] An auto analyst for a Japanese brokerage firm says: "It's a smart strategy to shift production to North America. They're reducing their exposure through building more in their regional markets, as well as being able to meet consumers' needs more quickly."[24]

MANAGER'S Notepad 5.1
Checklist for successful joint ventures

Choose a partner with
- experience with your firm's major business,
- a strong local workforce,
- future expansion possibilities,
- a strong local market for its own products,
- shared interests in meeting customer needs,
- good profit potential, and
- in sound financial standing.

●●● COMPLICATIONS IN THE GLOBAL BUSINESS ENVIRONMENT

The environment of international business in any form is complex and dynamic—and highly competitive. Global business executives must master task demands of operating with worldwide suppliers, distributors, customers, and competitors. They must understand and deal successfully with general environment differences in economic, legal-political, and educational systems, among other aspects of business infrastructure. Percy Barnevik, when chairman of the global corporation Asea Brown Boveri (ABB), once said: "Too many people think you can succeed in the long run just by exporting from America to Europe. But you need to establish yourself locally and become, for example, a Chinese, Indonesian, or Indian citizen."[25]

Differences in legal environments among nations create substantial international business challenges. Organizations are expected to abide by the laws of the host country in which they are operating. In the United States, for example, executives of foreign-owned companies must worry about antitrust issues that prevent competitors from regularly talking to one another. They also must deal with a variety of special laws regarding occupational health and safety, equal employment opportunity, sexual harassment, and other matters—all constraints potentially different from those they find at home.

The more home- and host-country laws differ, the more difficult and complex it is for international businesses to adapt to local ways. Common legal problems in international business involve incorporation practices and business ownership; negotiating and implementing contracts with foreign parties; protecting patents, trademarks, and copyrights; and handling foreign exchange restrictions. Intellectual property rights have long been a source of dispute between western businesses and China. Software piracy and copyright violations of CDs and books, for example, are well known. But General Motors recently had its own problems there. The firm's China executives noticed that a new model from a fast-growing local competitor—Chery Automobile, partially owned by GM's Chinese partner—looked very similar to one of their own cars due out in the near future. GM claims in local courts that their design was copied; the competitor denies the charges.[26]

When disputes between nations relate to international trade, they can end up before the **World Trade Organization**. This is a global institution established to promote free trade and open markets around the world. In the WTO some 140+ members agree to give one another **most favoured nation status**—the most favourable treatment for imports and exports. Although members agree to ongoing negotiations and the reduction of tariffs and trade restrictions, trading relationships are often difficult. The WTO offers a mechanism for monitoring international trade and resolving disputes among countries. **Protectionism** in the form of political calls for tariffs and favourable treatments to help protect domestic businesses from foreign competition is a common and complicating theme. Government leaders, such as the prime minister of Canada, face internal political dilemmas involving the often-conflicting goals of seeking freer international trade while still protecting domestic industries. These dilemmas make it difficult to reach international agreement on trade matters, and create controversies for the WTO.

■ **World Trade Organization** member nations agree to negotiate and resolve disputes about tariffs and trade restrictions.

■ **Most favoured nation status** gives a trading partner most favourable treatment for imports and exports.

■ **Protectionism** is a call for tariffs and favourable treatments to protect domestic firms from foreign competition.

> **BE SURE YOU CAN**
> • list five reasons that companies pursue international business opportunities • describe and give examples of each of these international business strategies—global sourcing, exporting/importing, franchising/licensing, joint ventures, and foreign subsidiaries • explain the operations of the WTO • discuss how differences in legal environments can affect businesses operating internationally

✓ Learning check ❷

MULTINATIONAL CORPORATIONS

A true **multinational corporation** (MNC) is a business firm with extensive international operations in more than one foreign country. Premier MNCs found in annual listings such as *Fortune* magazine's Global 500 include such global giants as General Electric, Exxon, and Wal-Mart from the United States; Mitsubishi, Toyota, and NTT

■ A **multinational corporation** is a business with extensive international operations in more than one foreign country.

DoCoMo of Japan; DaimlerChrysler of Germany; Barrick Gold, En Cana Corp., and Enbridge International of Canada; and Royal Dutch/Shell Group of the Netherlands and Great Britain. Also important on the world scene are *multinational organizations* (MNOs)—like the International Federation of Red Cross and Red Crescent Societies, the United Nations, and the World Bank—whose non-profit missions and operations span the globe.

TYPES OF MULTINATIONAL CORPORATIONS

A typical MNC operates in many countries but has corporate headquarters in one home or host country. Microsoft, Apple Computer, and McDonald's are among the ready examples. Although deriving substantial sales and profits from international sources, these firms and others like them typically also have strong national identifications. But as the global economy grows more competitive, many multinationals are acting more like **transnational corporations**. They increasingly try to operate worldwide without being identified with one national home.[27] Executives of transnationals view the entire world as their domain for acquiring resources, locating production facilities, marketing goods and services, and promoting its brand image. They seek total integration of global operations, try to operate across borders without home-based prejudices, make major decisions from a global perspective, distribute work among worldwide points of excellence, and employ senior executives from many different countries. Nestlé is a good example in foods; Asea Brown Boveri (ABB) is another in diversified conglomerates. When one buys a Nestlé product in Brazil or has a neighbour working for ABB in Toronto, Ontario, who would know that both are actually registered Swiss companies?

■ A **transnational corporation** is an MNC that operates worldwide on a borderless basis.

PROS AND CONS OF MULTINATIONAL CORPORATIONS

In this time when consumer demand, resource supplies, product flows, and labour markets increasingly span national boundaries, the actions of MNCs are increasingly influential in the global economy. The United Nations has reported that MNCs hold one-third of the world's productive assets and control 70 percent of world trade. Furthermore, more than 90 percent of these MNCs are based in the Northern Hemisphere. While this may bring a sense of both accomplishment and future opportunity to business leaders, it can also be very threatening to small and less-developed countries and their domestic industries.

Host-Country Issues

Ideally, global corporations and the countries that "host" their foreign operations should both benefit. *Figure 5.3* shows how things can and do go both right and wrong in MNC–host-country relationships. The *potential host-country benefits* include larger tax bases, increased employment opportunities, technology transfers, the introduction of new industries, and the development of local resources. The *potential host-country costs* include complaints that MNCs extract excessive profits, dominate the local economy, interfere with the local government, do not respect local customs and laws, fail to help domestic firms develop, hire the most talented of local personnel, and do not transfer their most advanced technologies.[28]

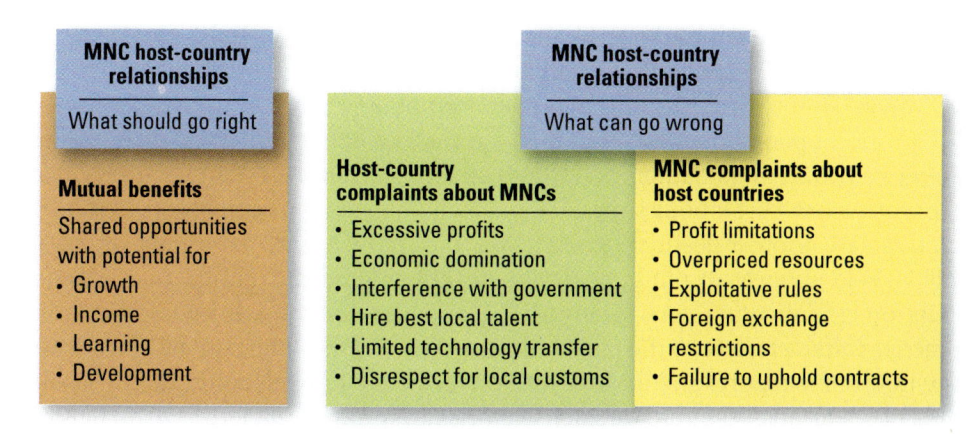

Figure 5.3 What should go right and what can go wrong in MNC–host-country relationships.

MNC host-country relationships — What should go right

Mutual benefits

Shared opportunities with potential for
- Growth
- Income
- Learning
- Development

MNC host-country relationships — What can go wrong

Host-country complaints about MNCs
- Excessive profits
- Economic domination
- Interference with government
- Hire best local talent
- Limited technology transfer
- Disrespect for local customs

MNC complaints about host countries
- Profit limitations
- Overpriced resources
- Exploitative rules
- Foreign exchange restrictions
- Failure to uphold contracts

Of course executives of MNCs sometimes feel exploited as well in their relations with host countries. Consider China once again, a setting where major cultural, political, and economic differences confront the outsider.[29] Profits have proved elusive for some foreign investors; some have found it difficult to take profits out of the country; some have struggled to get the raw materials needed for operations.[30] The protection of intellectual property was mentioned earlier as an ongoing concern of foreign manufacturers, and managing relationships with Chinese government agencies can be very complicated.

Home-Country Issues

MNCs may also encounter difficulties in the "home" country where their headquarters are located. Even as many MNCs try to operate more globally, home-country governments and citizens still tend to identify them with local and national interests. When an MNC outsources, cuts back, or closes a domestic operation to shift work to lower-cost international destinations, the loss of local jobs is controversial. Corporate decision makers are likely to be engaged by government and community leaders in critical debate about a firm's domestic social responsibilities. *Home-country criticisms of MNCs* include complaints about transferring jobs out of the country, shifting capital investments abroad, and engaging in corrupt practices in foreign settings.

●●● ETHICAL ISSUES FOR MULTINATIONAL CORPORATIONS

The ethical aspects of international business deserve special attention and were introduced in Chapter 3 on ethics and social responsibility. **Corruption**, engaging in illegal practice to further one's business interests, is a source of continuing controversy. The Canadian *Corruption of Foreign Public Officials Act* (1998) makes it illegal for firms and their managers to engage in corrupt practices overseas, including giving bribes and excessive commissions to foreign officials in return for business favours. This law specifically bans payoffs to foreign officials to obtain or keep business, provides punishments for executives who know about or are involved in such activities, and requires detailed accounting records for international business transactions. Critics, however, believe the law fails to recognize the "reality" of business as practised in many foreign nations. They complain that Canadian companies are at a

■ **Corruption** involves illegal practices to further one's business interests.

Sweatshops employ workers at very low wages, for long hours, and in poor working conditions.

competitive disadvantage because they can't offer the same "deals" as competitors from other nations—deals that locals may regard as standard business practices.

Sweatshops, business operations that employ workers at low wages for long hours and in poor working conditions, are another concern in the global business arena. Networks of outsourcing contracts are now common as manufacturers follow the world's low-cost labour supplies—countries like the Philippines, Sri Lanka, and Vietnam are popular destinations. Yet Nike, Inc., has learned that a global company will be held publicly accountable for the work standards and employment practices of its foreign subcontractors. Facing activist criticism, the company revised its labour practices after a review by the consulting firm GoodWorks International. Nike's website now offers reports and audit results on its international labour practices. Nike's international business web is extensive, including more than 750 manufacturing sites and contractors in some 50 countries.[31]

Child labour is the full-time employment of children for work otherwise done by adults.

Child labour, the full-time employment of children for work otherwise done by adults, is an international business ethics issue covered in Chapter 4. It has been made especially visible by activist concerns regarding the manufacture of handmade carpets in countries like Pakistan. Initiatives to eliminate child labour include an effort by the Rugmark Foundation to discourage purchases of carpets that do not carry its label. The "Rugmark" label is earned by a certification process to guarantee that a carpet manufacturer does not use illegal child labour.[32]

Sustainable development meets the needs of the present without hurting future generations.

ISO 14000 offers a set of certification standards for responsible environmental policies.

Yet another ethical issue relates to global concerns for environmental protection. The world's citizenry expects global corporations to respect the natural environment. Industrial pollution of cities, hazardous waste, depletion of natural resources, and related concerns are now worldwide issues. The concept of **sustainable development** is a popular guideline advanced by activist groups. It is "development that meets the needs of the present without compromising the ability of future generations to meet their own needs."[33] As global corporate citizens, MNCs are increasingly expected to uphold high standards in dealing with sustainable development and protection of the natural environment—whenever and wherever they operate. The available guidelines for responsible environmental policies include **ISO 14000** certification standards of the International Organization for Standardization.

✓ Learning check 3

BE SURE YOU CAN
• differentiate a multinational corporation from a transnational corporation • list at least three host-country complaints and three home-country complaints about MNC operations • define the terms corruption, sweatshop, and child labour • illustrate how each of these practices can create ethical problems for international businesses

CULTURE AND GLOBAL DIVERSITY

Culture is a shared set of beliefs, values, and patterns of behaviour common to a group of people.

Culture shock is the confusion and discomfort a person experiences when in an unfamiliar culture.

Culture is the shared set of beliefs, values, and patterns of behaviour common to a group of people. Anyone who has visited another country knows that cultural differences exist. **Culture shock**, the confusion and discomfort a person experiences when in an unfamiliar culture, is a reminder that many of these differences must be mastered just to travel comfortably around the world. But the business implications of cultural differences are also important to understand. An American exporter, for example, once went to see a Saudi Arabian official. He sat in the office with crossed legs and the sole of his shoe exposed—an unintentional sign of disrespect in the

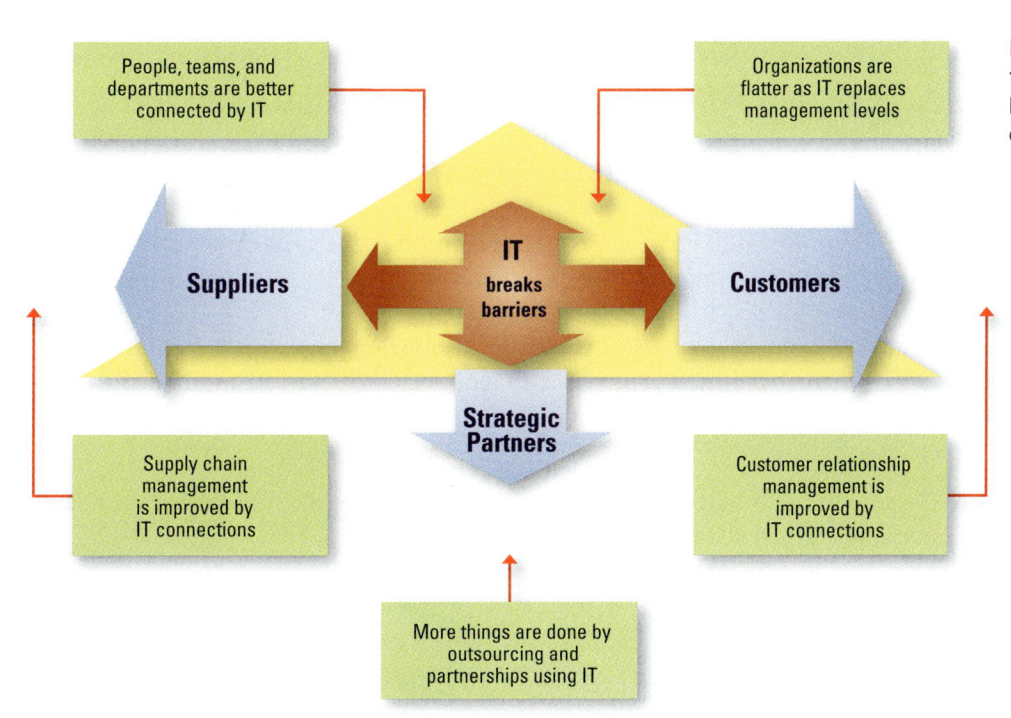

Figure 7.1 Information technology is breaking barriers and changing organizations.

- People, teams, and departments are better connected by IT
- Organizations are flatter as IT replaces management levels
- Supply chain management is improved by IT connections
- Customer relationship management is improved by IT connections
- More things are done by outsourcing and partnerships using IT

IT breaks barriers — Suppliers, Customers, Strategic Partners

And that's not all. There are more developments coming to the networked office every day, and you most probably are already familiar with them. **Instant messaging**, instantaneous communication among persons online at the same time, isn't just for friends; it is a work facilitator as well. **Peer-to-peer file sharing** (P2P), PCs connected directly to one another over the Internet, gained fame as a way for friends to swap music and video files. It is now becoming indispensable as a way for workers to share information and otherwise collaborate "peer-to-peer."

At Nortel, the company's Multimedia Communications Server uses voice over internet protocol (VoIP) to allow telecommuters to make calls from anywhere, and a "find me–follow me" feature lets colleagues and customers know where they are and what they are doing. Instant messenger and other IP features allow workers to easily set up video and teleconferences with colleagues, while white board and other application sharing programs encourage team communication and collaboration.[9]

■ **Instant messaging** is instantaneous communication between people online at the same time.

■ **Peer-to-peer file sharing** connects PCs directly to one another over the Internet.

> **BE SURE YOU CAN**
> • define the terms electronic commerce, B2B, and B2C • discuss how IT is breaking barriers within organizations and between organizations and their environments • describe the way IT is changing the office

✓ Learning check ❶

INFORMATION AND THE MANAGEMENT PROCESS

Organizations are changing as continuing developments in information technology exert their influence. Information departments, or centres, are now mainstream on organization charts. The number and variety of information career fields is rapidly expanding. Managers are increasingly expected to excel in their information processing roles. All of this, and more, is characteristic of the great opportunities of an information age.

WHAT IS USEFUL INFORMATION?

■ **Data** are raw facts and observations.

■ **Information** is data made useful for decision making.

Data are raw facts and observations. **Information** is data made useful and meaningful for decision making. In the music industry, for example, lots of data are available on the demographic profiles of customers—such as which age groups are buying which CDs and where they are buying them. Not everyone with access to this data, however, uses it well. But those who do may gain competitive advantage, perhaps by changing their advertising because younger customers do a lot of buying on the Internet while older customers shop mainly in retail stores.

The management process of planning, organizing, leading, and controlling is ultimately driven by information, not data alone. Managers need good information, and they need it all the time. Information that is truly useful meets the test of these five criteria:

1. *Timely*—the information is available when needed; it meets deadlines for decision making and action.
2. *High quality*—the information is accurate, and it is reliable; it can be used with confidence.
3. *Complete*—the information is complete and sufficient for the task at hand; it is as up-to-date as possible.
4. *Relevant*—the information is appropriate for the task at hand; it is free from extraneous or irrelevant materials.
5. *Understandable*—the information is clear and easily understood by the user; it is free from unnecessary detail.

INFORMATION NEEDS OF ORGANIZATIONS

Driven largely by IT, information serves the variety of needs described in *Figure 7.2*. At the organization's boundaries, information in the external environment is accessed. Managers use this *intelligence information* to deal effectively with competitors and key stakeholders such as government agencies, creditors, suppliers, and

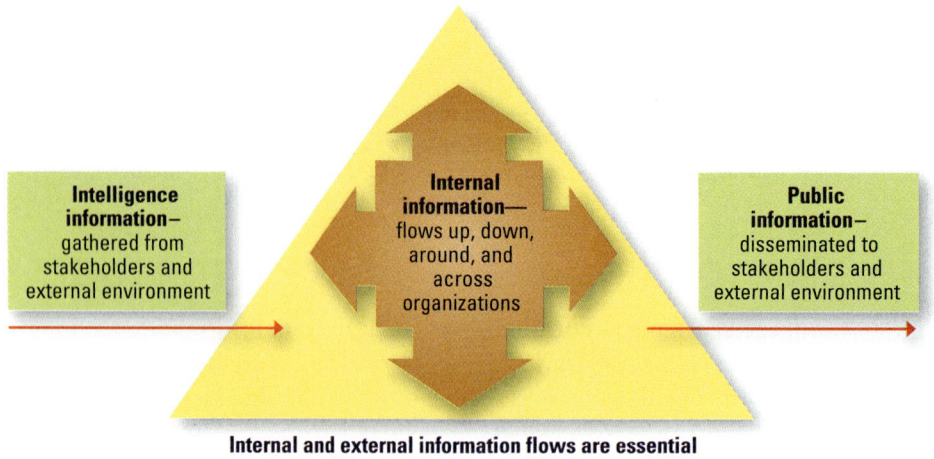

Figure 7.2 External and internal information needs of organizations.

- **Intelligence information**—gathered from stakeholders and external environment
- **Internal information**—flows up, down, around, and across organizations
- **Public information**—disseminated to stakeholders and external environment

Internal and external information flows are essential to problem solving and decision making in organizations

stockholders. Peter Drucker said that "a winning strategy will require information about events and conditions outside the institution," and that organizations must have "rigorous methods for gathering and analyzing outside information."[10] Organizations also send many types of *public information* to stakeholders and the external environment. This serves a variety of purposes ranging from image building to product advertising to financial reporting for taxes.

Within organizations, people need vast amounts of information to make decisions and solve problems in their daily work. The ability of IT to gather and move information quickly allows top levels to stay informed while freeing lower levels to make speedy decisions and take the actions they need to best perform their jobs. Silicon Valley giant and Cisco Systems' CEO John Chambers, for example, points out that he always has the information he needs in order to be in control—be it information on earnings, expenses, profitability, gross margins, and more. He also says, importantly: "Because I have my data in that format, every one of my employees can make decisions that might have had to come all the way to the president. …Quicker decision making at lower levels will translate into higher profit margins. …Companies that don't do that will be non-competitive."[11]

●●● INFORMATION SYSTEMS

In order to perform well, people in any work setting, large or small, must have available to them the right information at the right time and in the right place. **Information systems** use the latest in information technology to collect, organize, and distribute data in such a way that they become meaningful as information. **Management information systems**, or MIS, meet the specific information needs of managers as they make a variety of day-to-day decisions. Although it is important to avoid common mistakes (see *Manager's Notepad 7.1*), today's developments in MIS make possible performance levels that are truly extraordinary. C.R. England, Inc., a long-haul refrigerated trucking company, for example, uses a computerized MIS to monitor more than 500 aspects of organizational performance. The system tracks everything from billing accuracy to arrival times to driver satisfaction with company maintenance on their vehicles. Says CEO Dean England: "Our view was, if we could measure it, we could manage it."[12]

■ **Information systems** use IT to collect, organize, and distribute data for use in decision making.

■ **Management information systems** meet the information needs of managers in daily decisions.

MANAGER'S Notepad 7.1
Avoiding common information systems mistakes

- Don't assume more information is always better.
- Don't assume that computers eliminate human judgement.
- Don't assume that the newest technology is always best.
- Don't assume that nothing will ever go wrong with your computer.
- Don't assume that everyone understands how the system works.

Decision Support and Expert Systems

■ **Decision support systems** help users organize and analyze data for problem solving.

A **decision support system** (DSS) is an interactive information system that allows users to organize and analyze data for solving complex and sometimes unstructured problems. Decision support systems are now available to assist in such business decisions as mergers and acquisitions, plant expansions, new product developments, and stock portfolio management, among many others. A fast-growing application involves *group decision support systems* (GDSS) that facilitate group efforts to solve complex and unstructured problems. GDSS software, called **groupware**, allows several people to simultaneously access a file or database and work together virtually. It facilitates information exchange, group decision making, work scheduling, and other forms of group activity without the requirement of face-to-face meetings.

■ **Groupware** is software that facilitates group collaboration and problem solving.

An exciting area is *artificial intelligence* (AI), a field of science that is interested in building computer systems with the capacity to reason the way people do. **Expert systems** use AI to mimic the thinking of human experts, even to the point of dealing with ambiguities and difficult issues of judgement. In so doing, they offer consistent and "expert" decision-making advice to the user. Some use a complicated set of "if . . . then" rules developed by human experts to analyze problems. A good example is automatic approval for credit card purchases. Behind this system is an AI platform that analyzes the purchaser's credit worthiness using a set of predetermined rules, the same ones that a human expert would apply.

■ **Expert systems** allow computers to mimic the thinking of human experts for applied problem solving.

Web Portals and Networks

The growth of the World Wide Web has created many advantages in the area of information systems. Rather than relying solely on their own networks for computer interfacing, organizations are actively utilizing Web portals to facilitate information processing. It is now very common for organizations to have **intranets** and **corporate portals** that allow employees, by password access, to share databases and communicate electronically. The goal is to efficiently improve integration and communication throughout the organization, while making it easy for employees to access key services. At Hewlett-Packard, for example, a corporate portal has saved over $50 million in reduced paperwork and administrative costs. Employees use the portal to stay up to date on company news, access benefit information, participate in focus groups and special surveys, and locate one another for business communications.[13]

■ **Intranets** and **corporate portals** use the Web for communication and data sharing within an organization.

Extranets and **enterprise portals** allow communication and data sharing between the organization and special elements in its external environment. They typically link organizations with strategic partners, vendors, outsourcers, suppliers, and consultants. An important and rapidly expanding development in this area is called **electronic data interchange,** or EDI. It uses controlled access to enterprise portals and supporting software to enable firms to electronically transact business with one another, for example by sharing purchase orders, bills, receipt confirmations, and payments. The goals of EDI include improved transaction speed and cost savings. In the retailing industry where profit margins are tiny, Wal-Mart aggressively pursues these goals as a state-of-the art user of EDI. Its suppliers are required to purchase the necessary software and then electronically work with the firm to handle all order, purchasing, and delivery details.[14]

■ **Extranets** and **enterprise portals** use the Web for communication and data sharing between the organization and its environment.

■ **Electronic data interchange** uses controlled access to enterprise portals to enable firms to electronically transact business with one another.

●●● MANAGERS AS INFORMATION PROCESSORS

The manager's job as shown in *Figure 7.3* is a nerve centre of information flows, with information being continually gathered, given, and received from many sources. All of the managerial roles identified by Henry Mintzberg and discussed in Chapter 1—interpersonal, decisional, and informational—involve communication and information processing.[15] So too, do all aspects of the management process—planning, organizing, leading, and controlling. Success in management is increasingly tied to the opportunities of IT.

- *Planning advantages*—better and more timely access to useful information, involving more people in the planning process.

- *Organizing advantages*—more ongoing and informed communication among all parts, improving coordination and integration.

- *Leading advantages*—more frequent and better communication with staff and stakeholders, keeping objectives clear.

- *Controlling advantages*—more immediate measures of performance results, allowing real-time solutions to problems.

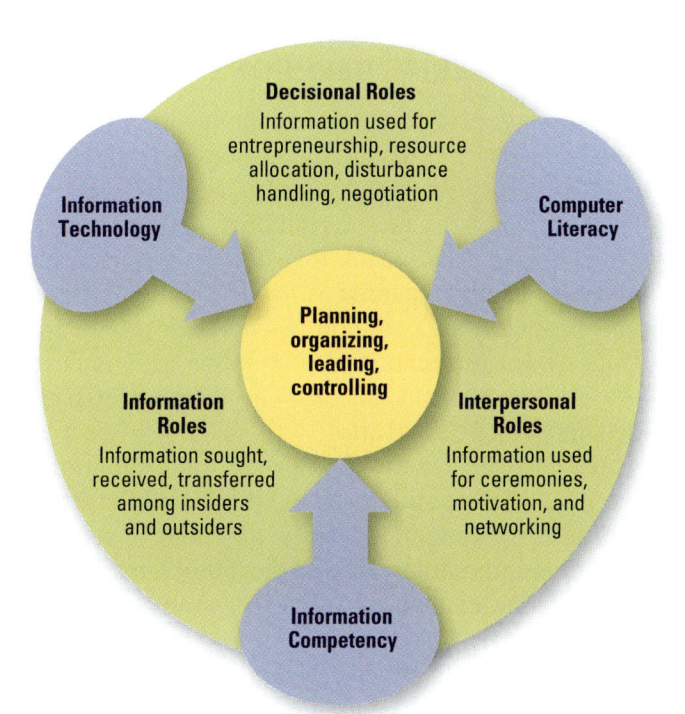

Figure 7.3 The manager as an information-processing nerve centre.

> **BE SURE YOU CAN**
>
> • differentiate data and information • list the criteria of useful information • describe the information needs of organizations • explain the role of information systems in organizations • illustrate the use of corporate portals and enterprise portals • describe how IT influences the four functions of management

✓ Learning check ❷

INFORMATION AND MANAGERIAL DECISIONS

One way to describe what managers do is that they use information to solve a continuous stream of daily problems. The most obvious problem situation is a *performance deficiency*; that is, when actual performance is less than desired. For example, a manager faces a possible problem when turnover or absenteeism suddenly increases in the work unit, when a subordinate's daily output decreases, or when a higher executive complains about something that has been said or done. Another important problem situation emerges as a *performance opportunity* when an actual situation either turns out better than anticipated or offers the potential to be so.

The challenge in dealing with any performance deficiency or performance opportunity is to proceed with effective **problem solving**—the process of identifying a discrepancy between an actual and desired state of affairs and then taking action to resolve the deficiency or taking advantage of the opportunity. Success in problem solving is dependent on the right information being available to the right people at the right times so that they can make good problem-solving decisions. A **decision**, to be precise, is a choice among alternative possible courses of action. In today's IT-enriched organizations, information systems assist managers in gathering data, turning them into useful information, and utilizing that information individually and collaboratively to make problem-solving decisions.

- **Problem solving** involves identifying and taking action to resolve problems.

- A **decision** is a choice among possible alternative courses of action.

●●● TYPES OF MANAGERIAL DECISIONS

Managers make different types of decisions in their day-to-day work. **Programmed decisions** use solutions already available from past experience to solve **structured problems**—ones that are familiar, straightforward, and clear with respect to information needs. These problems are routine; although perhaps not predictable, they can at least be anticipated. This means that decisions can be planned or programmed in advance to be implemented as needed. In human resource management, for example, problems are common whenever decisions are made on pay raises and promotions, vacation requests, committee assignments, and the like. Knowing this, forward-looking managers plan ahead on how to handle complaints and conflicts when and if they should arise.

Managers must also deal with new or unusual situations that present **unstructured problems**, full of ambiguities and information deficiencies. These problems require **nonprogrammed decisions** that craft novel solutions to meet the demands of the unique situation at hand. Most problems faced by higher-level managers are of this type, often involving choice of strategies and objectives in situations of some uncertainty.

An extreme type of nonprogrammed decision must be made in times of **crisis**—the occurrence of an unexpected problem that can lead to disaster if not resolved quickly and appropriately. Terrorism in a post–9/11 world, outbreaks of workplace violence, man-made environmental catastrophes, ethical scandals, and IT failures are examples. The ability to handle crises (see *Manager's Notepad 7.2*) may be the ultimate test of a manager's problem-solving capabilities. Unfortunately, research indicates that managers may react to crises by doing the wrong things. They isolate themselves and try to solve the problem alone or in a small "closed" group.[16] This denies them access to crucial information and assistance at the very time they are most needed. The crisis can even be accentuated when more problems are created

- A **programmed decision** applies a solution from past experience to a routine problem.

- **Structured problems** are straightforward and clear in information needs.

- **Unstructured problems** have ambiguities and information deficiencies.

- A **nonprogrammed decision** applies a specific solution crafted for a unique problem.

- A **crisis** is an unexpected problem that can lead to disaster if not resolved quickly and appropriately.

> **MANAGER'S Notepad 7.2**
>
> **Six rules for crisis management**
>
> 1. *Figure out what is going on:* Take the time to understand the situation, what's happening, and the conditions under which the crisis must be resolved.
> 2. *Remember that speed matters:* Attack the crisis as quickly as possible, trying to catch it when it is as small as possible.
> 3. *Remember that slow counts, too:* Know when to back off and wait for a better opportunity to make progress with the crisis.
> 4. *Respect the danger of the unfamiliar:* Understand that the most dangerous crisis is the all-new territory where you and others have never been before.
> 5. *Value the skeptic:* Don't look for and get too comfortable with agreement; appreciate skeptics and let them help you to see things differently.
> 6. *Be ready to "fight fire with fire":* When things are going wrong but others don't seem to care, you may have to start a crisis of your own to get their attention.

because critical decisions are made with poor or inadequate information and from a limited perspective. The organizational consequences of alienated customers, lost profits, damaged reputations, and increased costs can be very severe.

When the power went out at the offices of Ottawa-based Magma Communications Ltd., the Internet service provider went on with business as usual. The emergency diesel generators were automatically started, staff members were immediately reallocated to reassure customers, and an order was placed to replenish the two-day supply of generator fuel. When the power came back on 12 hours later, Ron Ethier, Magma's vice-president of technology, stated, "The blackout wasn't a disaster for us; it was more of a hands-on test of our emergency plan."[17]

For these and other reasons, many organizations are developing formal **crisis management** programs. They are designed to help managers and others prepare for unexpected high-impact events that threaten an organization's health and well-being. Anticipation is one aspect of crisis management; preparation is another. People can be assigned ahead of time to *crisis management teams*, and *crisis management plans* can be developed to deal with various contingencies. Just as police departments and community groups plan ahead and train to best handle civil and natural disasters, so too can managers and work teams plan ahead and train to best deal with organizational crises.[18]

■ **Crisis management** is preparation for the management of crises that threaten an organization's health and well-being.

●●● DECISION ENVIRONMENTS

Figure 7.4 shows three different decision environments—certainty, risk, and uncertainty. Although managers make decisions in each, the conditions of risk and uncertainty are common at higher management levels where problems are more complex and unstructured. Former Coca-Cola CEO Roberto Goizueta, for example, was known as a risk taker. Among his risky moves were introducing Diet Coke to the market, changing the formula of Coca-Cola to create New Coke, and then reversing direction after New Coke flopped.[19]

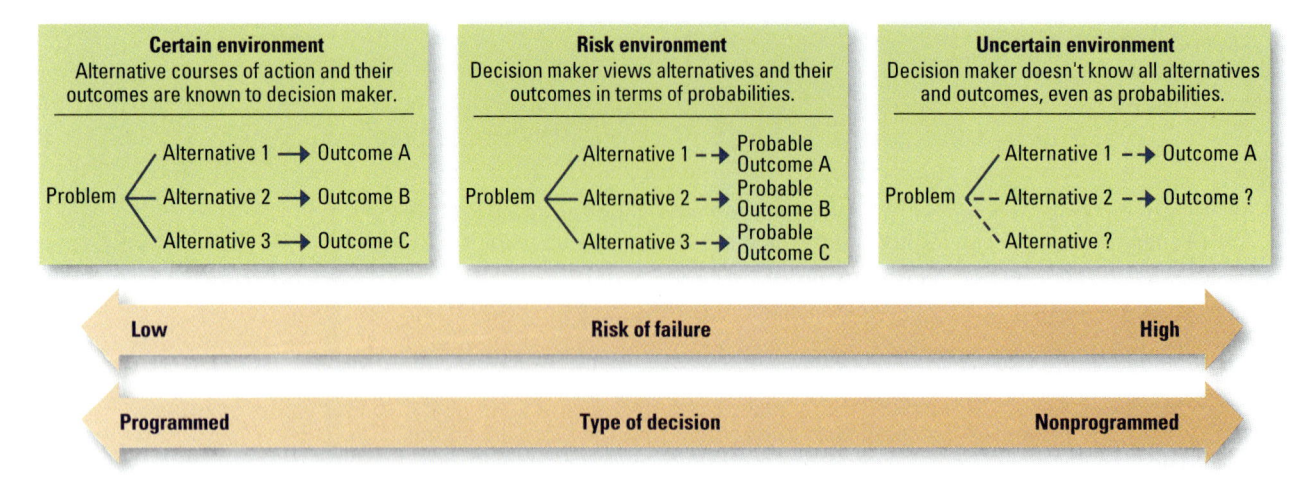

Figure 7.4 Three environments for managerial decision making and problem solving.

Certain environment
Alternative courses of action and their outcomes are known to decision maker.

Problem → Alternative 1 → Outcome A
Problem → Alternative 2 → Outcome B
Problem → Alternative 3 → Outcome C

Risk environment
Decision maker views alternatives and their outcomes in terms of probabilities.

Problem → Alternative 1 → Probable Outcome A
Problem → Alternative 2 → Probable Outcome B
Problem → Alternative 3 → Probable Outcome C

Uncertain environment
Decision maker doesn't know all alternatives and outcomes, even as probabilities.

Problem → Alternative 1 → Outcome A
Problem → Alternative 2 → Outcome ?
Problem → Alternative ?

Risk of failure: Low ←→ High

Type of decision: Programmed ←→ Nonprogrammed

■ A **certain environment** offers complete information on possible action alternatives and their consequences.

■ A **risk environment** lacks complete information but offers "probabilities" of the likely outcomes for possible action alternatives.

The decision to market any new product is made in conditions quite different from the relative predictability of a **certain environment**. This is an ideal decision situation where factual information is available about the possible alternative courses of action and their outcomes. The decision maker's task is simply to study the alternatives and choose the best solution. But very few managerial problems are like this. It is more common to face a **risk environment** where facts and information on action alternatives and their consequences are incomplete, but some estimates of "probabilities" can be made. A *probability* is the degree of likelihood (e.g., 4 chances out of 10) that an event will occur. Risk is typical for entrepreneurs and organizations that depend on ideas and continued innovation for their success. Steps can be taken to reduce risk in many situations. In the case of a new Coke product, for example, the firm can make the go-ahead decision only after receiving favourable reports from special focus groups testing it.

Canadian Managers
Establishing an IT Tradition

The history of Mississauga, Ontario-based metals distributor Russel Metals Inc. dates back to 1866 and a one-man iron-trading operation. Today, the company has to manage inventories, meet just-in-time demands, and provide customized steel processing at 58 metals service centres in Canada and four in the United States. When Maureen Kelly joined Russel Metals in 1998 as vice president of information systems, her first task was to replace the 20-year-old Enterprise Resource Planning system with one that was Y2K-compliant, which she completed by July 1, 1999. She and her 29 staff members have digitized the company's paper systems with central document management, electronic fund transfers, and e-mail, and a purchasing portal now provides branches with immediate access to inventory data. And, while making these investments, Kelly has reduced IT costs each year.

Source: Andrew Wahl and John Gray, "Top in technology 2005: Maureen Kelly, Russel Metals Inc.," *Canadian Business*, April 25–May 8, 2005.

When facts are few and information is so poor that managers are unable even to assign probabilities to the likely outcomes of alternatives, an **uncertain environment** exists. This is the most difficult decision making condition.[20] The high level of uncertainty forces managers to rely heavily on creativity in solving problems. Because uncertainty requires unique, novel, and often totally innovative alternatives, groups are frequently used for problem solving. In all cases, the responses to uncertainty depend greatly on intuition, judgement, informed guessing, and hunches—all of which leave considerable room for error.

■ An **uncertain environment** lacks so much information that it is difficult to assign probabilities to the likely outcomes of alternatives.

●●● PROBLEM-SOLVING STYLES

In practice, managers display three quite different approaches or "styles" in the way they process information and deal with problems. Some are *problem avoiders* who ignore information that would otherwise signal the presence of an opportunity or performance deficiency. They are inactive in information gathering, not wanting to make decisions and deal with problems. *Problem solvers*, by contrast, are willing to make decisions and try to solve problems, but only when forced to by the situation. They are reactive in gathering information and responding to problems after they occur. They may deal reasonably well with performance deficiencies, but they miss many performance opportunities. *Problem seekers* actively process information and constantly look for problems to solve or opportunities to explore. True problem seekers are proactive and forward thinking. They anticipate problems and opportunities and take appropriate action to gain the advantage. Success at problem seeking is one of the ways exceptional managers distinguish themselves from the merely good ones.

Managers also differ in tendencies toward "systematic" and "intuitive" thinking. In **systematic thinking** a person approaches problems in a rational, step-by-step, and analytical fashion. This type of thinking involves breaking a complex problem into smaller components and then addressing them in a logical and integrated fashion. Managers who are systematic can be expected to make a plan before taking action and then to search for information to facilitate problem solving in a step-by-step fashion.

■ **Systematic thinking** approaches problems in a rational and analytical fashion.

Someone using **intuitive thinking**, by contrast, is more flexible and spontaneous and also may be quite creative.[21] This type of thinking allows us to respond imaginatively to a problem based on a quick and broad evaluation of the situation and the possible alternative courses of action. Managers who are intuitive can be expected to deal with many aspects of a problem at once, jump quickly from one issue to another, and consider "hunches" based on experience or spontaneous ideas. This approach tends to work best in situations of high uncertainty where facts are limited and few decision precedents exist.

■ **Intuitive thinking** approaches problems in a flexible and spontaneous fashion.

Senior managers, in particular, must deal with portfolios of problems and opportunities that consist of multiple and interrelated issues. This requires *multidimensional thinking*, or the ability to view many problems at once, in relationship to one another, and across long and short time horizons.[22] The best managers "map" multiple problems into a network that can be actively managed over time as priorities, events, and demands continuously change. And importantly, they are able to make decisions and take actions in the short run that benefit longer-run objectives. They avoid being sidetracked while sorting through a shifting mix of daily problems. This requires skill at **strategic opportunism**—the ability to remain focused on long-term objectives while being flexible enough to resolve short-term problems and opportunities in a timely manner.[23]

■ **Strategic opportunism** focuses on long-term objectives while being flexible in dealing with short-term problems.

Learning check 3

BE SURE YOU CAN

• define the terms problem solving and decision • differentiate among programmed, nonprogrammed, and crisis decisions • explain the challenges of decision making in certain, risk, and uncertain environments • describe three problem-solving styles of managers • discuss the differences between systematic and intuitive thinking

THE DECISION-MAKING PROCESS

■ The **decision-making process** begins with identification of a problem and ends with evaluation of implemented solutions.

The **decision-making process** involves a set of activities that begins with identification of a problem, includes making a decision, and ends with the evaluation of results.[24] As shown in *Figure 7.5*, the steps in managerial decision making are to (1) identify and define the problem, (2) generate and evaluate alternative solutions, (3) choose a preferred course of action and conduct the "ethics double-check," (4) implement the decision, and (5) evaluate results. Importantly, Step 3 in this model includes a built-in "checkpoint" as a way to verify the ethical aspects of a decision before any action is taken. Working with the following short-but-true case will help put all five steps into perspective.

> *The Ajax Case.* On December 31, the Ajax Company decided to close down its Murphysboro plant. Market conditions were forcing layoffs, and the company could not find a buyer for the plant. Of 172 employees, some had been with the company as long as 18 years, others as little as 6 months. All were to be terminated. Under company policy, they would be given severance pay equal to one week's pay per year of service. Top management faced a difficult problem: how to minimize the negative impact of the plant closing on employees, their families, and the small town of Murphysboro.

This case reflects how competition, changing times, and the forces of globalization can take their toll on organizations, the people that work for them, and the communities in which they operate. Think about how you would feel as the CEO of Ajax Company contemplating this decision, as one of the affected employees, and as the mayor of this small town.

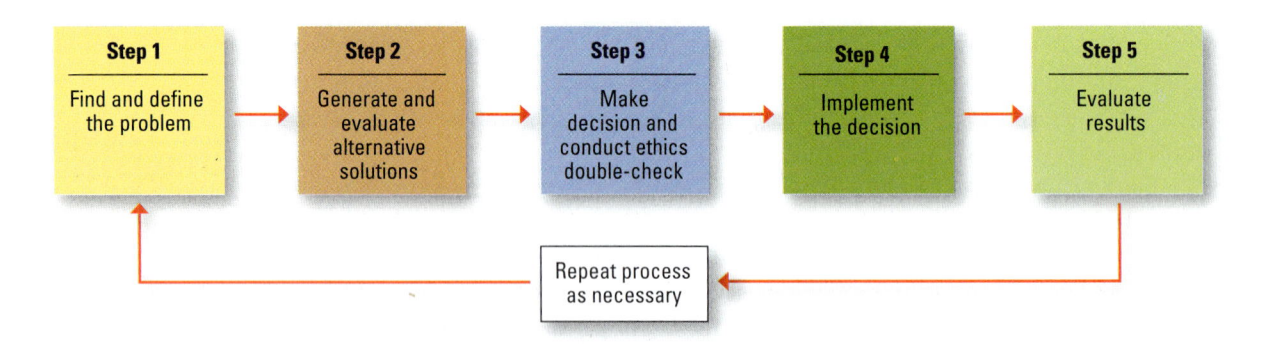

Figure 7.5 Steps in managerial decision making and problem solving.

Step 1	Step 2	Step 3	Step 4	Step 5
Find and define the problem	Generate and evaluate alternative solutions	Make decision and conduct ethics double-check	Implement the decision	Evaluate results

Repeat process as necessary

●●● IDENTIFY AND DEFINE THE PROBLEM

The first step in decision making is to find and define the problem. This is a stage of information gathering, information processing, and deliberation.[25] It is important at this step to clarify goals by identifying exactly what a decision should accomplish.

The more specific the goals, the easier it is to evaluate results after the decision is actually implemented. Importantly, the way a problem is defined can have a major impact on how it is resolved.

Three common mistakes occur in this critical first step in decision making. *Mistake number one* is defining the problem too broadly or too narrowly. To take a classic example, the problem stated as "Build a better mousetrap" might be better defined as "Get rid of the mice." That is, managers should define problems in ways that give them the best possible range of problem-solving options. *Mistake number two* is focusing on symptoms instead of causes. Symptoms are indicators that problems may exist, but they shouldn't be mistaken for the problems themselves. Managers should be able to spot problem symptoms (e.g., a drop in performance). But instead of treating symptoms (such as simply encouraging higher performance), managers should address their root causes (such as discovering the worker's need for training in the use of a complex new computer system). *Mistake number three* is choosing the wrong problem to deal with. Managers should set priorities and deal with the most important problems first. They should also give priority to problems that are truly solvable.

> *Back to the Ajax Case.* Closing the Ajax plant will put a substantial number of people from this small community of Murphysboro out of work. The unemployment created will have a negative impact on individuals, their families, and the community as a whole. The loss of the Ajax tax base will further hurt the community. The local financial implications of the plant closure will be great. The problem for Ajax management is how to minimize the adverse impact of the plant closing on the employees, their families, and the community.

●●● GENERATE AND EVALUATE ALTERNATIVE COURSES OF ACTION

Once the problem is defined, it is time to assemble the facts and information that will be helpful for problem solving. It is important here to clarify exactly what is known and what needs to be known. Extensive information gathering should identify alternative courses of action, as well as their anticipated consequences. The process of evaluating alternatives often benefits from a *stakeholder analysis*. Key stakeholders in the problem should be identified and the effects of each possible course of action on them considered. Another useful approach for the evaluation of alternatives is **cost-benefit analysis**, the comparison of what an alternative will cost in relation to the expected benefits. At a minimum, the benefits of an alternative should be greater than its costs. Typical criteria for evaluating alternatives include the following:

■ **Cost-benefit analysis** involves comparing the costs and benefits of each potential course of action.

- *Benefits:* What are the "benefits" of using the alternative to solve a performance deficiency or take advantage of an opportunity?

- *Costs:* What are the "costs" of implementing the alternative, including resource investments as well as potential negative side effects?

- *Timeliness:* How fast will the benefits occur and how soon can a positive impact be achieved?

- *Acceptability:* To what extent will the alternative be accepted and supported by those who must work with it?

- *Ethical soundness:* How well does the alternative meet acceptable ethical criteria in the eyes of the various stakeholders?

The end result of this step can only be as good as the quality of the options considered; the better the pool of alternatives, the more likely that a good solution will be achieved. A common error is abandoning the search for alternatives too quickly. This often happens under pressures of time and other circumstances. But just because an alternative is convenient doesn't make it the best. It could have damaging side effects, or it might not be as good as others that might be discovered with extra effort. One way to minimize this error is through participation and involvement, bringing more people into the process, and bringing more information and perspectives to bear on the problem.

Back to the Ajax Case. The Ajax plant is going to be closed. Among the possible alternatives that can be considered are (1) close the plant on schedule and be done with it; (2) delay the plant closing until all efforts have been made to sell it to another firm; (3) offer to sell the plant to the employees and/or local interests; (4) close the plant and offer transfers to other Ajax plant locations; or (5) close the plant, offer transfers, and help the employees find new jobs in and around Murphysboro.

●●● DECIDE ON A PREFERRED COURSE OF ACTION

This is the point of choice, where an actual decision is made to select a preferred course of action. Just how this is done, and by whom, must be successfully resolved in each problem situation. Management theory recognizes differences between the classical and behavioural models of decision making shown in *Figure 7.6*. The **classical decision model** views the manager as acting rationally in a certain world. Here, the manager faces a clearly defined problem and knows all possible action alternatives as well as their consequences. As a result, he or she makes an **optimizing decision** that gives the absolute best solution to the problem. The classical approach is a rational model that assumes perfect information is available for decision making.

■ The **classical decision model** describes decision making with complete information.

■ An **optimizing decision** chooses the alternative giving the absolute best solution to a problem.

■ The **behavioural decision model** describes decision making with limited information and bounded rationality.

■ A **satisficing decision** chooses the first satisfactory alternative that comes to one's attention.

Behavioural scientists question these assumptions. Perhaps best represented by the work of Herbert Simon, they recognize limits to our human information-processing capabilities.[26] These *cognitive limitations* make it hard for managers to become fully informed and make perfectly rational decisions. They create a *bounded rationality* such that managerial decisions are rational only within the boundaries defined by the available information. The **behavioural decision model**, accordingly, assumes that people act only in terms of what they perceive about a given situation. Because such perceptions are frequently imperfect, the decision maker has only partial knowledge about the available action alternatives and their consequences. Consequently, the first alternative that appears to give a satisfactory resolution of the problem is likely to be chosen. Simon, who won a Nobel Prize for his work, calls this the tendency toward **satisficing decisions**—choosing the first satisfactory alternative that comes to your attention. This model seems especially accurate in describing how people make decisions about ambiguous problems in risky and uncertain conditions.

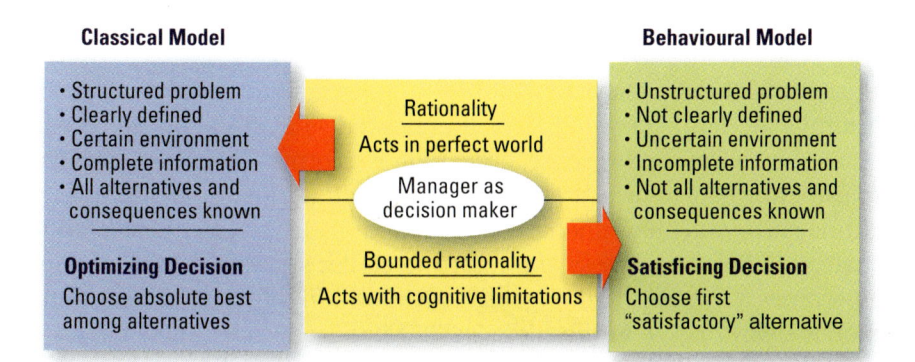

Figure 7.6 Differences in the classical and behavioural models of managerial decision making.

Classical Model
- Structured problem
- Clearly defined
- Certain environment
- Complete information
- All alternatives and consequences known

Optimizing Decision
Choose absolute best among alternatives

Rationality
Acts in perfect world

Manager as decision maker

Bounded rationality
Acts with cognitive limitations

Behavioural Model
- Unstructured problem
- Not clearly defined
- Uncertain environment
- Incomplete information
- Not all alternatives and consequences known

Satisficing Decision
Choose first "satisfactory" alternative

Back to the Ajax Case. Management at Ajax decided to follow alternative five as described in Step 2 of the decision-making process. They would close the plant, offer transfers to company plants in another state, and offer to help displaced employees find new jobs in and around Murphysboro.

IMPLEMENT THE DECISION

Once a preferred solution is chosen, actions must be taken to fully implement it. Nothing new can or will happen unless action is taken to actually solve the problem. Managers not only need the determination and creativity to arrive at a decision, they also need the ability and willingness to implement it.

The "ways" in which previous steps have been accomplished can have a powerful impact on this stage of implementation. Difficulties encountered at this point can often be traced back to the *lack-of-participation error*. This is a failure to adequately involve in the process those persons whose support is necessary to implement the decision. Managers who use participation wisely get the right people involved in problem solving right from the beginning. When they do, implementation typically follows quickly, smoothly, and to everyone's satisfaction. Participation in decision making not only makes everyone better informed, it also builds the commitments needed for implementation.

Back to the Ajax Case. Ajax ran an ad in the local and regional newspapers for several days. The ad called attention to an "Ajax skill bank" composed of "qualified, dedicated, and well-motivated employees with a variety of skills and experiences." Interested employers were urged to contact Ajax for further information.

PERSONAL MANAGEMENT

Managers must have the **SELF-CONFIDENCE** to not only make decisions but also to implement them. Too many of us find all sorts of excuses for doing everything but that—we have difficulty deciding and we have difficulty acting. Opportunities to improve and develop your self-confidence abound, especially through involvement in the many student organizations on your campus. Carole Clay Winters was the first member of her family to go to college. On the encouragement of an economics professor, she joined Students in Free Enterprise (SIFE) and ended up on a team teaching business concepts to elementary school children in the local community.[27] Her team was chosen to participate in a national competition. They didn't win, but Carole did. "I felt my life had changed," she said. "I realized that if I could answer all the questions being posed by some of the country's most powerful executives, I had what I needed to become an executive myself." Carole went on to become a manager at KPMG. What about you? Do you have the self-confidence to make decisions relating to your career goals and future success? Are you taking full advantage of opportunities, on campus and off, to experience the responsibilities of leadership and gain confidence in your decision-making capabilities?

Get to know yourself better

Complete Self-Assessments #11—**Your Intuitive Ability,** and #12—**Assertiveness**, from the Workbook and Personal Management Activity #7 on the companion website.

●●● EVALUATE RESULTS

The decision-making process is not complete until results are evaluated. If the desired results are not achieved and/or if undesired side effects occur, corrective action should be taken. In this sense, evaluation is a form of managerial control. It involves gathering data to measure performance results against goals. Both the positive and negative outcomes should be examined. If the original choice appears inadequate, it is time to reassess and return to earlier steps. In this way, problem solving becomes a dynamic and ongoing activity within the management process. Evaluation is always easier, furthermore, when clear goals, measurable targets, and timetables were established to begin with.

> *Back to the Ajax Case.* The advertisement ran for some 15 days. The plant's industrial relations manager commented, "I've been very pleased with the results." That's all we know. You can look back on the case and problem-solving process just described and judge for yourself. How well did Ajax management do in dealing with this very difficult problem? Perhaps you would have approached the situation and the five steps in decision making somewhat differently.

✓ Learning check 4

BE SURF YOU CAN

• list the steps in the decision-making process • apply these steps to a sample decision-making situation • explain stakeholder analysis and cost-benefit analysis • discuss the differences between the classical and behavioural decision models • define the terms optimizing and satisfying

ISSUES IN MANAGERIAL DECISION MAKING

In settings rich in information technology but complicated by risk and uncertainty, managers with their limited human capacities face many decision-making challenges. It helps to be aware of the common decision-making errors and traps, the advantages and disadvantages of individual and group decision making, the imperative of ethical decision making, and the growing importance of knowledge management and organizational learning.

●●● DECISION-MAKING ERRORS AND TRAPS

■ **Heuristics** are strategies for simplifying decision making.

Faced with limited information, time and even energy, people often use simplifying strategies for decision making. These strategies, known as **heuristics**, can cause decision-making errors.[28] The *availability heuristic* occurs when people use information "readily available" from memory as a basis for assessing a current event or situation. An example is deciding not to invest in a new product based on your recollection of how a similar new product performed in the recent past. The potential bias is that the readily available information may be fallible and irrelevant. The new product that recently failed may have been a good idea that was released to market at the wrong time of year.

The *representativeness heuristic* occurs when people assess the likelihood of something occurring based on its similarity to a stereotyped set of occurrences. An example is deciding to hire someone for a job vacancy simply because he or she graduated from the same school attended by your last and most successful new hire.

The potential bias is that the representative stereotype may mask the truly important factors relevant to the decision. For instance, the abilities and career expectations of the newly hired person may not fit the job requirements.

The *anchoring and adjustment heuristic* involves making decisions based on adjustments to a previously existing value or starting point. An example is setting a new salary level for an employee by simply raising the prior year's salary by a reasonable percentage. This may inappropriately bias a decision toward only incremental movement from the starting point. For instance, the individual's market value may be substantially higher than the existing salary. An incremental adjustment won't keep this person from looking for another job.

In addition to the biases of judgemental heuristics, managers can suffer from **framing error** when making decisions. Framing occurs when a problem is evaluated and resolved in the context in which it is perceived—either positive or negative. An example from the world of marketing is a product that data show has a 40-percent market share. A negative frame views the product as being deficient because it is missing 60 percent of the market. The likely discussion and problem solving in this frame would focus on the question: "What are we doing wrong?" Alternatively, the frame could be a positive one, looking at the 40-percent share as a good accomplishment. In this case the discussion is more likely to proceed with the question: "How do we do things better?" Sometimes people use framing as a tactic for presenting information in a way that gets other people to think inside the desired frame. In politics this is often referred to as "spinning" the data. In the marketing example, the data could be "spun" to the negative or positive by a presenter in an attempt to influence the decision-making process one way or the other.

■ **Framing error** is solving a problem in the context perceived.

Good managers are also aware of another decision-making trap known as **escalating commitment**. This is a decision to increase effort and perhaps apply more resources to pursue a course of action that is not working.[29] In such cases, managers let the momentum of the situation overwhelm them. They are unable to decide to "call it quits," even when experience otherwise indicates that this is the most appropriate thing to do. *Manager's Notepad 7.3* offers advice on avoiding tendencies toward escalating commitments to previously chosen courses of action.

■ **Escalating commitment** is the continuation of a course of action even though it is not working.

MANAGER'S Notepad 7.3

How to avoid the escalation trap

- Set advance limits on your involvement and commitment to a particular course of action; stick with these limits.

- Make your own decisions; don't follow the lead of others, since they are also prone to escalation.

- Carefully determine just why you are continuing a course of action; if there are insufficient reasons to continue, don't.

- Remind yourself of what a course of action is costing; consider saving these costs as a reason to discontinue.

- Watch for escalation tendencies; be on guard against their influence on both you and others involved in the course of action.

●●● INDIVIDUAL VS. GROUP DECISION MAKING

One of the important issues in decision making is the choice of whether to make the decision individually or with the participation of a group. The best managers and team leaders don't limit themselves to just one way. Instead, they switch back and forth among individual and group decision making to best fit the problems at hand. A managerial skill is the ability to choose the "right" decision method—one that provides for a timely and quality decision, and one to which people involved in the implementation will be highly committed. To do this well, however, managers must understand both the potential assets and potential liabilities of moving from individual to more group-oriented decision making.[30]

The potential *advantages of group decision making* are highly significant, and they should be actively sought whenever time and other circumstances permit. Team decisions make greater amounts of knowledge, and expertise available to solve problems. They expand the number of action alternatives that are examined; they help to avoid tunnel vision and consideration of only limited options. Team decisions increase the understanding and acceptance of outcomes by members. And importantly, team decisions increase the commitments of members to work hard to implement final plans.

The *potential disadvantages of group decision making* can be traced largely to the difficulties that can be experienced in a group process. In a team decision there may be social pressure to conform. Some individuals may feel intimidated or compelled to go along with the apparent wishes of others. There may be minority domination, where some members feel forced or "railroaded" to accept a decision advocated by one vocal individual or small coalition. Another problem that might occur is "groupthink," where cohesion among group members and a desire for unanimity overrides their motivation to realistically appraise a situation.[31] Also, there is no doubt that the time required to make team decisions can sometimes be a disadvantage. As more people are involved in the dialogue and discussion, decision making takes longer. This added time may be costly, even prohibitively so, in certain circumstances.[32]

take it to the case!

Kate Spade turns risk into opportunities

If you begin with an idea to create a better handbag, a vacation in Provincetown, Massachusetts, and a woman's first name along with her future husband's last, what do you get? Kate Spade—one of the best-known and fastest-growing brands in the fashion business. Kate wanted to start her own business and believed she knew what the fashion handbag market was missing. The risk was high; the odds were against her. But starting in 1992 with six construction-paper design mock-ups, she hasn't looked back since. Her company is now a $70-million business, with retail stores in the United States, Canada, and Japan, and products sold globally at high-quality department and specialty stores. Her brand communicates sophistication. And with a continued and laser-sharp eye on the market, Kate Spade continues to grow. Her lines now include luggage, shoes, glasses, and paper products; more are on the way. And then there's husband Andy—watch out for Andy Spade, he's on the move too.

Source: Information from Bart Boehlert, "Kate Spade and Her Hip Handbags," *Urban Desires* 1996, http://desires.com/2.1/Style/Spade/spade.html; "Kate and Andy Spade," *Fortune Small Business* (September 2003), pp. 51–57; and company website: www.katespade.com.

●●● ETHICAL DECISION MAKING

Chapter 3 was devoted to ethics and social responsibility issues in management. As a reminder, however, it is important to restate the expectation that any decision should be ethical. It should at least meet the test described in Step 3 of decision making as the "ethics double-check." This involves asking and answering two straightforward but powerful *spotlight questions:* (1) "How would I feel if my family found out about this decision?", and (2) "How would I feel if this decision were published in the local newspaper?" The Josephson Institute model for ethical decision making suggests a third question to further strengthen the ethics double-check: "Think of the person you know or know of (in real life or fiction) who has the strongest character and best ethical judgement. Then ask yourself—what would that person do in your situation?"[33]

Although it adds time to decision making, the ethics double-check is necessary to ensure that the ethical aspects of a problem are properly considered in all situations. It is also consistent with the demanding moral standards of modern society. A willingness to pause to examine the ethics of a proposed decision may well result in both a better decision and the prevention of costly litigation. Ethicist Gerald Cavanaugh and his associates suggest that managers can proceed with the most confidence when the following criteria are met.[34]

1. *Utility*—Does the decision satisfy all constituents or stakeholders?
2. *Rights*—Does the decision respect the rights and duties of everyone?
3. *Justice*—Is the decision consistent with the canons of justice?
4. *Caring*—Is the decision consistent with my responsibilities to care?

●●● KNOWLEDGE MANAGEMENT AND ORGANIZATIONAL LEARNING

Now that the process of managerial decision making is clear, let's return to its context—a technology-driven world rich with information and demanding in the pace

AROUND THE WORLD

It's hard to find an executive conversation about computer software today without hearing a reference to India. The country's talented computer scientists offer great advantages to organizations willing to invest in global sourcing. Wipro Technologies, based in the Indian high-tech capital of Bangalore, is one of India's most valuable companies. It was named by *Business Week* magazine as one of the seven top software services firms in the world. Wipro's website includes this testimonial from former GE CEO Jack Welch: "From the first day in dealing with Wipro, there's been nothing but quality, character, highest integrity, highest quality work. As a joint venture, you wouldn't find a better partner. As a supplier, you wouldn't find a higher quality partner."

Source: Information and quote from corporate website: <www.wipro.com.>

Global sourcing rules computer software services

and uncertainty of change. This is the setting in which knowledge workers with intellectual capital become the most critical assets of organizations. Management theorist Peter Drucker, however, warned us that "knowledge constantly makes itself obsolete."[35] His message must be taken to heart. People and organizations cannot rest on past laurels; future success will be earned only by those who continually learn through experience.

■ **Knowledge management** is the processes using intellectual capital for competitive advantage.

The term **knowledge management** describes the processes through which organizations develop, organize, and share knowledge to achieve competitive advantage.[36] The significance of knowledge management as a strategic and integrating force in organizations is represented by the emergence of a new executive job title—*chief knowledge officer* (CKO). The CKO is responsible for energizing learning processes and making sure that an organization's portfolio of intellectual assets are well managed and continually enhanced. These assets include such things as patents, intellectual property rights, trade secrets, and special processes and methods, as well as the accumulated knowledge and understanding of the entire workforce.

■ A **learning organization** continuously changes and improves using the lessons of experience.

Knowledge management requires the creation of an organizational culture that truly values learning. Progressive organizations strive to build the foundations of what consultant Peter Senge calls a true **learning organization**. This is an organization, first described in Chapter 2, that "by virtue of people, values, and systems is able to continuously change and improve its performance based upon the lessons of experience."[37] Browne says that organizations can learn from many sources. They can learn from their own experience. They can learn from the experiences of their contractors, suppliers, partners, and customers. And they can learn from firms in unrelated businesses.[38] All of this, of course, depends on a willingness to seek out learning opportunities from these sources and to make information sharing an expected and valued work behaviour.

✓ **Learning check 5**

BE SURE YOU CAN

• explain the availability, representativeness, anchoring, and adjustment heuristics • illustrate the concepts of framing error and escalating commitment in decision making • list questions that can be asked to double check the ethics of a decision • discuss why the best organizations today give high priority to knowledge management and organizational learning

Chapter 7 STUDY GUIDE

WHERE WE'VE BEEN

Back to Chapters-Indigo

The opening example of how Heather Reisman turned her love of books into a national best-selling organization shows the importance of understanding the environment and being knowledgeable when taking risks and making decisions. In Chapter 7 you learned about the information needs of organizations and how new developments in information technology are changing organizations and the way people work. You have also learned how managers use information in the decision-making process, with special attention to decision errors and traps, ethical decision making, and decision making by individuals and groups.

THE NEXT STEP
INTEGRATED LEARNING ACTIVITIES

Cases/Projects
- Kate Spade Case
- Project 10—Service Learning

Self-Assessments
- Your Intuitive Ability (#11)
- Assertiveness (#12)
- Facts and Inferences (#14)
- Cognitive Style (#25)

Exercises in Teamwork
- Decision-Making Biases (#11)
- The Future Workplace (#14)
- Dots and Squares Puzzle (#15)
- Lost at Sea (#26)

STUDY QUESTION SUMMARY

1. How is information technology changing the workplace?
- A major and rapidly growing force in the economy are e-businesses, which use the Internet to engage in business-to-consumer and business-to-business electronic commerce.
- Within organizations and between organizations IT is breaking barriers to speed workflows and cut costs.
- Today's "electronic" offices with e-mail, instant messaging, and networked computer systems are changing the way work is accomplished in and by organizations.

2. What is the role of information in the management process?
- Information is data made useful for decision making.
- Organizations need and use internal, public, and intelligence information.
- Management information systems (MIS) collect, organize, store, and distribute data to meet the information needs of managers.
- Intranets, extranets, and Web portals allow people to share databases and communicate electronically within an organization and between the organization and its environment.

3. How do managers use information to make decisions?
- A problem is a discrepancy between an actual and a desired state of affairs.
- The most threatening type of problem is the crisis, which occurs unexpectedly and can lead to disaster if it is not handled quickly and properly.

- Managers face structured and unstructured problems in environments of certainty, risk, and uncertainty.
- Managers vary in their willingness to deal with problems, and in their use of systematic and intuitive thinking.

4. **What are the steps in the decision-making process?**
- The steps in the decision-making process are: find and define the problem, generate and evaluate alternatives, decide on the preferred course of action, implement the decision, and evaluate the results.
- An optimizing decision, following the classical model, chooses the absolute best solution from a known set of alternatives.
- A satisfying decision, following the behavioural decision model, chooses the first satisfactory alternative that comes to attention.

5. **What are the current issues in managerial decision making?**
- Judgmental heuristics, framing errors, and escalating commitment can bias decision making.
- Group decisions offer the potential advantages of greater information and expanded commitment, but they are often slower than individual decisions.
- Decision makers should always take time to double-check the ethics of their decisions.
- Knowledge management captures, develops, and uses knowledge for competitive advantage; a learning organization is committed to continuous change and improvement based on the lessons of experience.

KEY TERMS REVIEW

Behavioural decision model (p. 184)
Certain environment (p. 179)
Classical decision model (p. 184)
Corporate portals (p. 174)
Cost-benefit analysis (p. 183)
Crisis (p. 178)
Crisis management (p. 179)
Data (p. 174)
Decision (p. 178)
Decision-making process (p. 182)
Decision support system (p. 176)
Electronic commerce (p. 171)
Electronic data interchange (p. 176)
Enterprise portals (p. 174)

Escalating commitment (p. 187)
Expert system (p. 176)
Extranet (p. 176)
Framing error (p. 187)
Groupware (p. 176)
Heuristics (p. 186)
Information (p. 173)
Information system (p. 175)
Information technology (p. 170)
Instant messaging (p. 173)
Intellectual capital (p. 171)
Intranet (p. 176)
Intuitive thinking (p. 181)
Knowledge management (p. 190)
Knowledge worker (p. 171)

Learning organization (p. 190)
Management information system (p. 175)
Nonprogrammed decision (p. 178)
Optimizing decision (p. 184)
Peer-to-peer file sharing (p. 173)
Problem solving (p. 178)
Programmed decision (p. 178)
Risk environment (p. 180)
Satisficing decision (p. 184)
Strategic opportunism (p. 181)
Structured problem (p. 178)
Systematic thinking (p. 181)
Uncertain environment (p. 181)
Unstructured problem (p. 178)

SELF-TEST 7

MULTIPLE-CHOICE QUESTIONS:

1. _____ is the collective brainpower or shared knowledge of an organization and its workforce.
   (a) Artificial intelligence (b) Groupware (c) Intellectual capital (d) Intelligence information

2. _____ are special computer programs that use "if . . . then" rules to help users analyze and solve problems.
   (a) Expert systems (b) Heuristics (c) Intranets (d) Web portals

3. A manager who is reactive and works hard to address problems after they occur is known as a _____.
   (a) problem seeker (b) problem avoider (c) problem solver (d) problem manager

4. When businesses like Chapters-Indigo and Dell use the Internet to sell products directly to customers, they are pursuing a form of e-commerce known as _____.
 (a) optimizing (b) B2B (c) B2C (d) networking

5. A problem is a discrepancy between a(n) _____ situation and a desired situation.
 (a) unexpected (b) past (c) actual (d) anticipated

6. A(n) _____ thinker approaches problems in a rational and analytic fashion.
 (a) systematic (b) intuitive (c) internal (d) external

7. The first step in the decision-making process is to _____.
 (a) identify alternatives (b) evaluate results (c) find and define the problem (d) choose a solution

8. Being asked to develop a plan to increase international sales of a product is an example of the types of _____ problems that managers must be prepared to deal with.
 (a) routine (b) unstructured (c) crisis (d) structured

9. Costs, timeliness, and _____ are among the recommended criteria for evaluating alternative courses of action.
 (a) ethical soundness (b) competitiveness (c) availability (d) simplicity

10. The _____ decision model views managers as making optimizing decisions, whereas the _____ decision model views them as making satisfying decisions.
 (a) behavioural, human relations (b) classical, behavioural (c) heuristic, humanistic (d) quantitative, behavioural

11. Top managers in organizations commonly use information to make decisions about _____.
 (a) strategy formulation (b) operational plans (c) day-to-day operations (d) short-term plans

12. Among the ways IT is changing organizations today, _____ is one of its most noteworthy characteristics.
 (a) eliminating the need for top managers (b) reducing the amount of information available for decision making (c) breaking down barriers internally and externally (d) decreasing the need for environmental awareness

13. When a problem is addressed according to the positive or negative context in which it is presented, this is an example of _____.
 (a) framing error (b) escalating commitment (c) availability and adjustment (d) strategic opportunism

14. A manager who asks whether or not the decision will satisfy all stakeholders is using the criterion of _____ to check the ethical soundness of the intended course of action.
 (a) justice (b) rights (c) cost vs. benefit (d) utility

15. Among the environments for managerial decision making, certainty is the most favourable and it can be addressed through _____ decisions.
 (a) programmed (b) risk (c) satisfying (d) intuitive

SHORT-RESPONSE QUESTIONS:

16. What is the difference between an optimizing decision and a satisficing decision?
17. How can a manager double-check the ethics of a decision?
18. How would a manager use systematic thinking and intuitive thinking in problem solving?
19. How can the members of an organization be trained in crisis management?

APPLICATION QUESTION:

20. As a participant in a new "mentoring" program between your university and a local high school, you have volunteered to give a presentation to a class on the challenges in the new "electronic office." The goal is to sensitize them to developments in IT and motivate them to take the best advantage of their high school program so as to prepare themselves for the workplace of the future. What will you say to them?

8 Planning and Controlling

CHAPTER 8 STUDY QUESTIONS

Planning Ahead
After reading Chapter 8, you should be able to answer these questions in your own words.

1. How do managers plan?
2. What types of plans do managers use?
3. What are the useful planning tools and techniques?
4. What is the control process?
5. What are the common organizational controls?

COGNOS INC.
CRUNCHING THE NUMBERS TO SUCCEED

The aim of Cognos Inc., a software company operating from Ottawa, Ontario, is to help businesses "crunch the numbers" in order to yield better organizational planning and control. Established in 1969, Cognos is now located in over 135 countries, with over 3,500 employees.

With businesses facing an ever-changing marketplace, Cognos has set out to help companies gain a flexible approach to their strategic plans by providing software to analyze business data. A world leader in business intelligence and performance planning software, the company provides businesses with a competitive advantage by integrating key areas of budgeting, performance, and sales so companies can analyze the numbers to monitor and re-engineer strategic direction. This ensures resources are directed toward areas that are financially and commercially viable. According to their website, "Cognos is the only company to support all these key management activities with a complete solution."

What is Cognos's own plan? They continue to research and develop new software. Recently, they launched Cognos 8 Business Intelligence, a product they state delivers "the complete range of BI capabilities: reporting, analyzing, scorecarding, dashboarding, business event management." The company has also created the Cognos Innovation Centre, a venue for executives and senior managers to dialogue and to create, implement, and sustain various innovative practices.

With customers in all sectors of industry, including Yamaha, Lufthansa, and Dow Chemical, the company looks set to take on the big enterprise resource planners (ERPs) and even Microsoft. As Philip Howard notes, "What Cognos has recognized is that planning is more than just a financial activity—that it is something that needs to spread across the enterprise and be coordinated across multiple departments. However, appreciating that fact and supporting it in principle in the planning software is one thing; supporting it in practice is another. This is where the Cognos blueprints come in, enabling users to adopt these practices relatively easily." It sounds as if Cognos has a plan.[1]

GET CONNECTED!
In business and in a career you need to look ahead to plan where you will fit into the future. Visit *Fortune,* or *Business Week, Canadian Business,* or *The Economist* magazines online to find current business and economic forecasts.

Chapter 8 LEARNING PREVIEW

To survive and succeed, Cognos knows it has to plan for the future by constantly reinventing itself and its products. In Chapter 8 you will learn how managers use planning to help turn insight and opportunity into real performance accomplishments. You will find also that what you learn about planning has important personal applications. And you will learn why the management function of controlling is essential if we are to ensure that things do, in fact, happen according to plans.

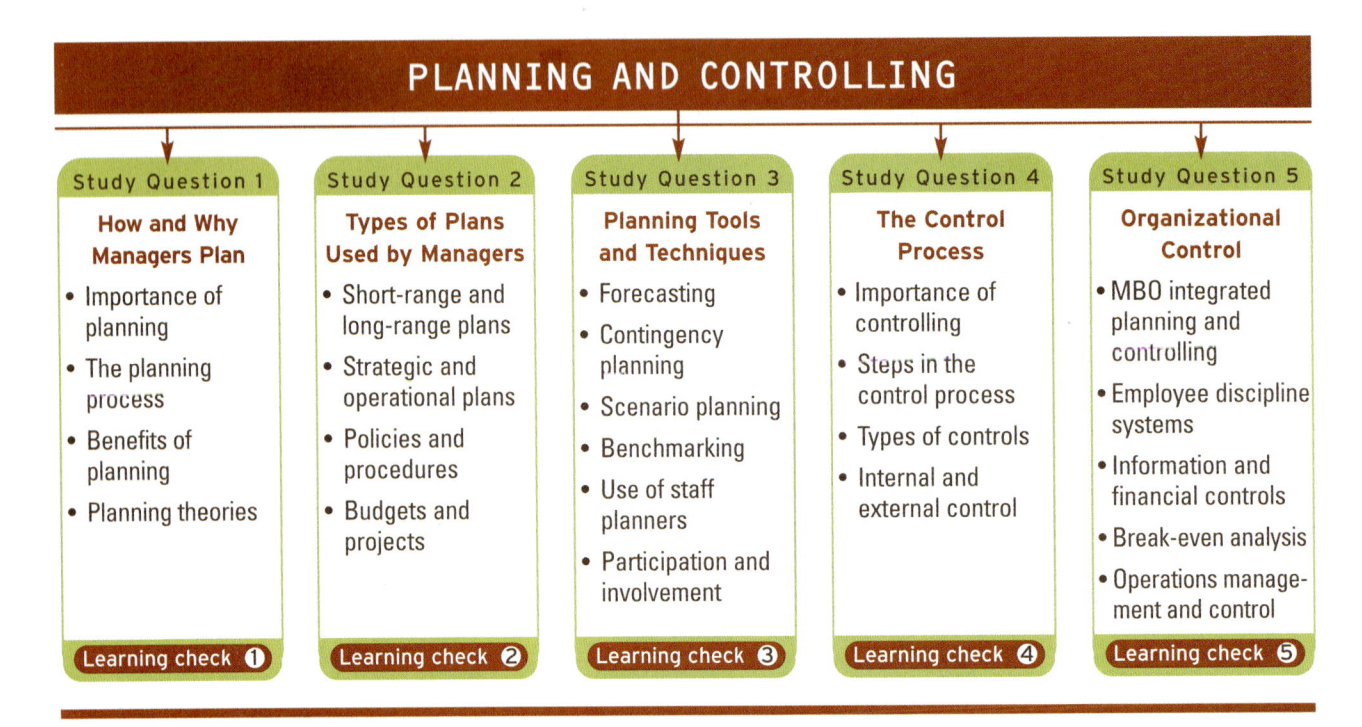

PLANNING AND CONTROLLING

Study Question 1
How and Why Managers Plan
- Importance of planning
- The planning process
- Benefits of planning
- Planning theories

Learning check ❶

Study Question 2
Types of Plans Used by Managers
- Short-range and long-range plans
- Strategic and operational plans
- Policies and procedures
- Budgets and projects

Learning check ❷

Study Question 3
Planning Tools and Techniques
- Forecasting
- Contingency planning
- Scenario planning
- Benchmarking
- Use of staff planners
- Participation and involvement

Learning check ❸

Study Question 4
The Control Process
- Importance of controlling
- Steps in the control process
- Types of controls
- Internal and external control

Learning check ❹

Study Question 5
Organizational Control
- MBO integrated planning and controlling
- Employee discipline systems
- Information and financial controls
- Break-even analysis
- Operations management and control

Learning check ❺

In his book *Leading the Revolution*,[2] management consultant Gary Hamel argues that many of today's companies won't make it in the long run. "Organizations that succeed in this new century will be as different from industrial-era organizations as those companies themselves were different from craft-based industries," he says. "Companies are going to have to re-invent themselves much more frequently than before.[3] Cognos seems to be meeting this challenge. Although there are no guarantees about the future, it keeps changing to stay on top of its markets.

Managers need the ability to look ahead, make good plans, and then help others meet the challenges of the future. With the future uncertain, however, the likelihood is that even the best of plans will have to be changed at some point. Thus, managers also need the courage to be flexible in response to new circumstances and the discipline to maintain control even as situations become hectic and the performance pressures stay unrelenting. In the ever-changing technology industry, for example, CEO T. J. Rodgers of Cypress Semiconductor Corp., which has six offices in Canada, is known for valuing both performance goals and accountability. Cypress employees work with clear and quantified work goals, which they help set. Rodgers believes the system helps find problems before they interfere with performance. He says: "Managers monitor the goals, look for problems, and expect people who fall behind to ask for help before they lose control of, or damage, a major project."[4]

HOW AND WHY MANAGERS PLAN

In Chapter 1 the management process was described as planning, organizing, leading, and controlling the use of resources to achieve performance objectives. The first of these functions, **planning**, sets the stage for the others by providing a sense of direction. It is a process of setting objectives and determining how to best accomplish them. Said a bit differently, planning involves deciding exactly what you want to accomplish and how to best go about it.

■ **Planning** is the process of setting objectives and determining how to accomplish them.

IMPORTANCE OF PLANNING

When planning is done well it creates a solid platform for the other management functions: *organizing*—allocating and arranging resources to accomplish tasks; *leading*—guiding the efforts of human resources to ensure high levels of task accomplishment; and *controlling*—monitoring task accomplishments and taking necessary corrective action.

The centrality of planning in management, as shown in *Figure 8.1*, is important to understand. In today's demanding organizational and career environments it is essential to stay one step ahead of the competition. This involves striving always to become better at what you are doing and to be action oriented. An Eaton Corporation annual report, for example, once stated: "Planning at Eaton means taking the hard decisions before events force them upon you, and anticipating the future needs of the market before the demand asserts itself."[5]

THE PLANNING PROCESS

In the planning process, **objectives** identify the specific results, or desired outcomes, that one intends to achieve. The **plan** is a statement of action steps to be taken in order to accomplish the objectives. The steps in the systematic planning process include the following:

■ **Objectives** are specific results that one wishes to achieve.

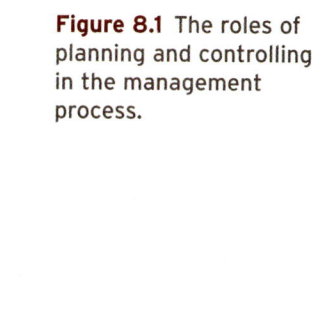

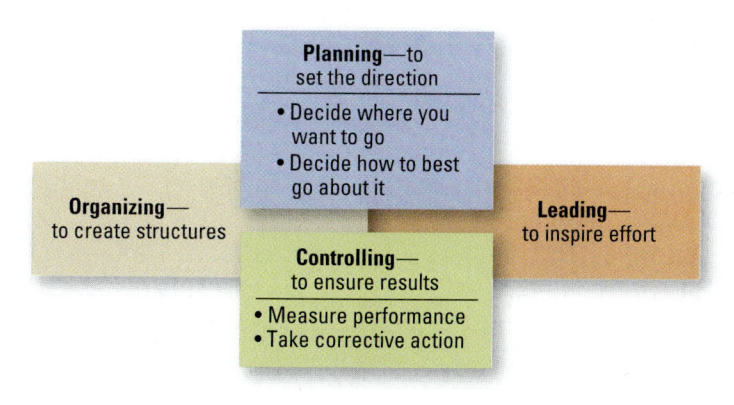

■ A **plan** is a statement of intended means for accomplishing objectives.

Figure 8.1 The roles of planning and controlling in the management process.

Planning—to set the direction
- Decide where you want to go
- Decide how to best go about it

Organizing—to create structures

Leading—to inspire effort

Controlling—to ensure results
- Measure performance
- Take corrective action

1. *Define your objectives:* Identify desired outcomes or results in very specific ways. Know where you want to go; know how far off the mark you are at various points along the way and be specific enough to know exactly when you have arrived.

2. *Determine where you stand vis-à-vis objectives:* Evaluate current accomplishments relative to the desired results. Know where you stand in reaching the objectives; know what strengths work in your favour and what weaknesses may hold you back.

3. *Develop premises regarding future conditions:* Try to anticipate future events. Generate alternative "scenarios" for what may happen; identify, for each scenario, things that may help or hinder progress toward your objectives.

4. *Analyze and choose among action alternatives:* List and carefully evaluate the possible actions that may be taken. Choose the alternative(s) most likely to accomplish your objectives; describe step-by-step what must be done to follow the chosen course of action.

5. *Implement the plan and evaluate results:* Take action and carefully measure your progress toward your objectives. Do what the plan requires; evaluate results, take corrective action, and revise plans as needed.

The planning process just described is an application of the decision-making process discussed in Chapter 7. It is a systematic way to approach two important tasks: (1) setting performance objectives and (2) deciding how to best achieve them. This is not something managers do while working alone in quiet rooms, free from distractions, and at scheduled times. Planning should be ongoing, continuously done even while dealing with an otherwise hectic and demanding work setting.[6] Importantly, the best planning is always done with the active participation and involvement of those people whose work efforts will eventually determine whether or not the objectives are accomplished.

CANADIAN COMPANY IN THE NEWS — **Air Canada**

AIRLINE'S RESTRUCTURING PUTS IT BACK IN THE AIR

Air Canada successfully recovered from bankruptcy protection in 2004 largely because of a creative and effective change management plan, which included reduced operating costs, a stronger balance sheet, corporate reorganization, and a fleet renewal and marketing strategy. "We're emerging from CCAA [bankruptcy] focused and well on our way to becoming a profitable, growing and competitive company in a rapidly changing industry," Robert Milton, then chairman, president, and CEO of ACE Aviation Holdings Inc., said at the time. "We have not only reduced our cost structure and strengthened our balance sheet; we have fundamentally reinvented who we are." Air Canada's various businesses segments—Aeroplan, Air Canada Jazz, Touram, Air Canada Technical Services, Air Canada Cargo, and Air Canada Ground-handling Services—now operate as separate legal entities under parent holding company ACE Aviation Holdings Inc. Along with the creation of ACE came new by-laws and a new board of directors. Air Canada developed their plan and were successful at implementing it.

Source: Air Canada news release, Sept. 30, 2004; Schermerhorn et al., "Renewed Airline Takes Flight," *Organizational Behaviour*, (Toronto: John Wiley & Sons Canada, 2005) p. 380

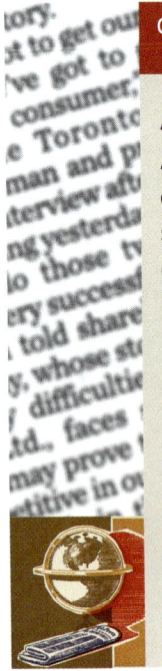

●●● BENEFITS OF PLANNING

Organizations in today's dynamic times are facing pressures from many sources. Externally, these include ethical expectations, government regulations, ever-more-complex technologies, the uncertainties of a global economy, changing technologies, and the sheer cost of investments in labour, capital, and other supporting resources. Internally, they include the quest for operating efficiencies, new structures and technologies, alternative work arrangements, greater diversity in the workplace, and related managerial challenges. As you would expect, planning in such conditions offers a number of benefits.

Decima Research Inc. is a company focused on its core strengths: telephone survey and research. It has used its planning process to evolve and meet the market's changing needs: balancing customers' need for more precision with the fact that fewer people want to answer phone surveys. Decima, listed as one of Canada's best managed companies, is showing focus and innovation by building a large panel of Canadians willing to do telephone surveys, thereby providing researchers with a steady pool of respondents.[7]

Planning Improves Focus and Flexibility

Good planning improves focus and flexibility, both of which are important for performance success. An *organization with focus* knows what it does best, knows the needs of its customers, and knows how to serve them well. An *individual with focus* knows where he or she wants to go in a career or situation, and is able to retain that objective even when difficulties arise. An *organization with flexibility* is willing and able to change and adapt to shifting circumstances, and operates with an orientation toward the future rather than the past. An *individual with flexibility* adjusts career plans to fit new and developing opportunities.

Planning Improves Action Orientation

Planning is a way for people and organizations to stay ahead of the competition and always become better at what they are doing. It helps avoid the complacency trap of simply being carried along by the flow of events or of being distracted by successes or failures of the moment. It keeps the future visible as a performance target and reminds us that the best decisions are often made before events force them upon us. Management consultant Stephen R. Covey talks about the importance of priorities. He points out that the most successful executives "zero in on what they do that 'adds value' to an organization." Instead of working on too many things, they work on the things that really count. Covey says that good planning makes us more (1) *results oriented*—creating a performance-oriented sense of direction; (2) *priority oriented*—making sure the most important things get first attention; (3) *advantage oriented*—ensuring that all resources are used to best advantage; and (4) *change oriented*—anticipating problems and opportunities so they can be best dealt with.[8]

Planning Improves Coordination

Planning improves coordination. The many different individuals, groups, and subsystems in organizations are each doing many different things at the same time.

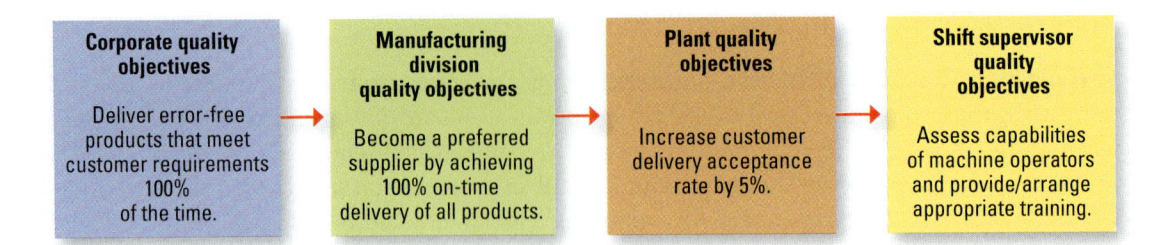

```
[Corporate quality objectives: Deliver error-free products that meet customer requirements 100% of the time.]
→ [Manufacturing division quality objectives: Become a preferred supplier by achieving 100% on-time delivery of all products.]
→ [Plant quality objectives: Increase customer delivery acceptance rate by 5%.]
→ [Shift supervisor quality objectives: Assess capabilities of machine operators and provide/arrange appropriate training.]
```

Figure 8.2 A sample means–ends chain for total quality management.

■ In a **means–ends chain**, lower-level objectives help accomplish higher-level ones.

But even as they pursue their specific tasks and objectives, their accomplishments must add up to meaningful contributions to the needs of the organization as a whole. Good planning throughout an organization creates a **means–ends chain** or *hierarchy of objectives* in which lower-level objectives lead to the accomplishment of higher-level ones. Higher-level objectives as *ends* are directly tied to lower-level objectives as the means for their accomplishment. *Figure 8.2* uses the example of quality management to show how a means–ends chain helps guide and integrate quality efforts within a large manufacturing firm.

Planning Improves Time Management

One of the side benefits that planning offers is better time management. Lewis Platt, former chairman of Hewlett-Packard, says: "Basically, the whole day is a series of choices."[9] These choices have to be made in ways that allocate your time to the most important priorities. Platt says that he was "ruthless about priorities" and that you "have to continually work to optimize your time."

Most of us have experienced the difficulties of balancing available time with the many commitments and opportunities we would like to fulfill. It is easy to lose track of time and fall prey to what consultants identify as "time wasters." Too many of us allow our time to be dominated by other people and/or by non-essential activities.[10] "To-do" lists can help, but they have to contain the right things. In daily living and in management, it is important to distinguish between things that you *must do* (top priority), *should do* (high priority), would be *nice to do* (low priority), and really *don't need to do* (no priority).

Planning Improves Control

When planning is done well it facilitates control, making it easier to measure performance results and take action to improve things as necessary. Planning helps make this possible by defining the objectives along with the specific actions through which they are to be pursued. If results are less than expected, either the objectives or the action being taken, or both, can be evaluated and then adjusted through the control process. In this way planning and controlling work closely together in the management process. Without planning, control lacks a framework for measuring how well things are going and what could be done to make them go better. Without control, planning lacks the follow-through needed to ensure that things work out as planned.

●●● PLANNING THEORIES

Two different theoretical approaches to planning are rational comprehensive planning and incrementalism. **Rational comprehensive planning** (RCP) focuses on a logical decision-making approach and advocates that problem solving should be looked at from a holistic or integrated systems viewpoint. RCP uses conceptual or mathematical models that relate ends (objectives) to means (resources and constraints) with a heavy reliance on statistical analysis. Planners using this approach gather information from the environment in order to run models that will allow them to determine what the future will be like so that the organization may be adapted accordingly.

RCP's major advantage is its simplicity. By following a logical, deliberate process, this type of planning is easily understood, the analytical techniques easy to use, and the corresponding plan of action easy to defend. RCP is, however, somewhat unrealistic. It can only be applied to relatively simple problems. In the real world, the limitations of resources, information, and time make it extremely difficult to use RCP in its purest form. Caveats and assumptions abound when using this approach, as the statistical modelling tools used cannot address the many subtle nuances of the complex world that businesses operate within. The costs of developing more comprehensive models often exceed the benefits derived from undertaking this analysis.

The perspective of *incrementalism* is to "muddle through." Recognizing the problems with RCP, planners examined alternative approaches. Eminent sociologist Amitai Etzioni provided the foundation for an incrementalist approach with his six key procedures for "disjointed incrementalism."

1. Rather than attempting a comprehensive survey and the evaluation of all alternatives, the decision maker focuses only on those policies that differ incrementally from existing policies.

2. Only a relatively small number of policy alternatives are considered.

3. For each policy alternative, only a restricted number of "important" consequences are evaluated.

4. The problem confronting the decision maker is continually redefined: incrementalism allows for countless ends–means and means–ends adjustments, which, in effect, make the problem more manageable.

5. Thus, there is no one decision or "right" solution but a "never-ending series of attacks" on the issues at hand through serial analyses and evaluation.

6. As such, incremental decision making is described as remedial, geared more to the alleviation of present, concrete social imperfections than to the promotion of future goals.[11]

Incremental planning's strength is that, rather than trying to be both rational and comprehensive, it looks at decision making as it generally occurs—quickly and with imperfect information. The model recognizes that planning is continually being undertaken and revised. Thus, changes are made in small doses rather than through a radical action, as is proposed with RCP. Incrementalism has fewer information demands and examines the consequences of smaller change, both of which allow decision makers to act more quickly in response to environmental changes. However, critics state that incremental planning is limited in scope as it generally

■ **Rational comprehensive planning** (RCP) focuses on a logical decision-making approach and advocates a holistic approach to problem solving.

addresses only a small range of alternatives. By focusing only on the very near future, incremental planning fails to take advantage of innovations and innovating thinking. Small steps are taken rather than big and bold ones that might be necessary.

In practice, planners initially examine a problem using an incremental planning approach and switch over to be more comprehensive depending upon the depth of the problem. Planners thus take advantage of the strengths of both approaches while attempting to avoid the weaknesses of each. This collectivist approach blends both types to yield successful planning. Some planners operate in an opposite direction—they use the RCP approach first to develop an "official plan" and then utilize an incremental approach in daily planning practice in order to successfully achieve their goal.[12]

✓ Learning check ❶

BE SURE YOU CAN
• define planning as a management function • list the steps in the formal planning process • illustrate the benefits of planning for a business or organization that is familiar to you • illustrate the benefits of planning for personal career development

PERSONAL MANAGEMENT

Time is one of our most precious resources, and **TIME MANAGEMENT** is an essential skill in today's high-pressure and fast-paced world of work. Some 77 percent of managers in one survey said that the new digital age has increased the number of decisions they have to make; 43 percent complained there was less time available to make them. Others say that 20 percent of their telephone time is wasted.[13] Of course, you have to be careful in defining "waste." It isn't a waste of time to occasionally relax, take a breather from work, and find humour and pleasure in social interaction. Such breaks help us gather energies to do well in our work. But it is a waste to let friends dominate your time so that you don't work on a term paper until it is too late to write a really good one, or delay a decision to apply for an internship until the deadline is passed. Perhaps you are one of those who plans to do so many things in a day that you never get to the most important ones. Perhaps you don't plan, let events take you where they may, and on many days don't accomplish much at all. Learning to manage your time better will serve you very well in the future, both at work and in your personal life.

Get to know yourself better

Complete Self-Assessments #13—**Time Management Profile,** and Exercise #9—**Beating the Time Wasters**, from the Workbook and Personal Management Activity #8 on the companion website.

TYPES OF PLANS USED BY MANAGERS

Managers face different planning challenges in the flow and pace of activities in organizations. In some cases the planning environment is stable and quite predictable; in others it is more dynamic and uncertain. A variety of plans are available to meet these different needs.

SHORT-RANGE AND LONG-RANGE PLANS

A rule of thumb is that *short-range plans* cover one year or less, *intermediate-range plans* cover one to two years, and *long-range plans* look three or more years into the future. Top management is most likely to be involved in setting long-range plans and directions for the organization as a whole, while lower management levels focus more on short-range plans that help achieve long-term objectives. But everyone should understand an organization's long-term plans. In the absence of a hierarchy of objectives tied to a long-range plan, there is always a risk that the pressures of daily events may create confusion and divert attention from important tasks. In other words, without a sense of long-term direction, people can end up working hard but without achieving significant results.

EllisDon Corp. is a good example of a company that looks to the future. Five years ago, this Ontario construction company decided to change their business model and become a client-focused company, a new idea in this industry sector. They are now benefiting from increased profits and new markets, including setting up a permanent office in Dubai.

Management researcher Elliott Jaques suggests that people vary in their capability to think out, organize, and work through events of different time horizons.[14] In fact, he believes that most people work comfortably with only three-month time spans; a smaller group works well with a one-year span; and only about one person in several million can handle a 20-year time frame. These are provocative ideas. Although a team leader's planning challenges may rest mainly in the weekly or monthly range, a chief executive is expected to have a vision extending several years into the future. Career progress to higher management levels requires the conceptual skills to work well with longer-range time frames.[15]

Complexities and uncertainties in today's environments are putting pressure on these planning horizons. In an increasingly global economy, planning opportunities and challenges are often worldwide in scope, not just local. And, of course, the information age is ever present in its planning implications. We now talk about planning in *Internet time*, where businesses are continually changing and updating plans. Even top managers now face the reality that Internet time keeps making the "long" range of planning shorter and shorter.

STRATEGIC AND OPERATIONAL PLANS

Plans differ not only in time horizons but also in scope. **Strategic plans** set broad, comprehensive, and longer-term action directions. Strategic planning by top management involves determining objectives for the entire organization and describing what and where the organization wants to be in the future. There was a time, for example, when many large businesses strategically sought to diversify into unrelated areas. A successful oil firm might have acquired an office products company or a successful cereal manufacturer might have acquired an apparel company. In the next chapter, "Strategic Management," we will examine the process through which such strategic choices are made and how they can be analyzed. For now, suffice it to say that diversification strategies haven't always proved successful. Many companies following them have since reversed course, choosing instead to strategically focus on core areas of expertise. Take for example A&W Food Services of Canada Inc., which wants to be the number-one burger choice of the baby boom generation and is doing so by creating a new/old relationship with the drive-in generation. Over the last 15 years, its strategic plan for attracting baby boomers has included expanding its free-standing street presence with retro designs and "cruising events." Initially focusing on British Columbia, the chain is now bringing these ideas to Ontario and Quebec.

■ A **strategic plan** identifies long-term directions for the organization.

Operational plans define what needs to be done in specific functions or work units to implement strategic plans. Typical operational plans in a business firm include: *production plans*—dealing with the methods and technology needed by people in their work; *financial plans*—dealing with money required to support various operations; *facilities plans*—dealing with facilities and work layouts; *marketing plans*—dealing with the requirements of selling and distributing goods or services; and *human resource plans*—dealing with the recruitment, selection, and placement of people into various jobs.

■ An **operational plan** identifies activities to implement strategic plans.

POLICIES AND PROCEDURES

Among the many plans in organizations, *standing plans* in the form of organizational policies and procedures are designed for use over and over again. A **policy** communicates broad guidelines for making decisions and taking action in specific circumstances. For

■ A **policy** is a standing plan that communicates broad guidelines for decisions and action.

example, typical human resource policies address such matters as employee hiring, termination, performance appraisals, pay increases, promotions, and discipline. Another policy area of special organizational consequence is sexual harassment. Enlightened employers take great pains to clearly spell out their policies on sexual harassment and the methods for implementing them. When Judith Nitsch started her own engineering consulting business, for example, she defined a sexual harassment policy, took a hard line in its enforcement, and appointed both a male and a female employee for others to talk with about sexual harassment concerns.[16]

■ A **procedure** or **rule** precisely describes actions that are to be taken in specific situations.

Rules or **procedures** describe exactly what actions are to be taken in specific situations. They are often found stated in employee handbooks or manuals as "SOPs"—standard operating procedures. Whereas a policy sets a broad guideline for action, procedures define precise actions to be taken. In the prior example, Judith Nitsch will want to put in place procedures that ensure everyone receives fair, equal, and nondiscriminatory treatment under the sexual harassment policy. Everyone should know how to file a sexual harassment complaint and how that complaint will be handled.

●●● BUDGETS AND PROJECTS

In contrast to standing plans, *single-use plans* are used once, serving the needs and objectives of well-defined situations in a timely manner. **Budgets** are single-use plans that commit resources to activities, projects, or programs. They are powerful tools that allocate scarce resources among multiple and often competing uses. Good managers are able to bargain for, and obtain, adequate budgets to support the needs of their work units or teams. They also achieve performance objectives while keeping within the allocated budget.

■ A **budget** is a plan that commits resources to projects or activities.

A *fixed budget* allocates a fixed amount of resources for a specific purpose. For example, a manager may have a $25,000 budget for equipment purchases in a given year. A *flexible budget* allows the allocation of resources to vary in proportion with various levels of activity. For example, a manager may have flexibility to hire extra temporary workers if production orders exceed a certain volume.

A common problem with budgets is that resource allocations get "rolled over" from one budgeting period to the next, often without a rigorous performance review. A **zero-based budget** deals with this problem by approaching each new budget period as if it were brand new. There is no guarantee that any past funding will be renewed; all proposals compete anew for available funds at the start of each new budget cycle. In a major division of the company Campbell Soup, for example, managers using zero-based budgeting once discovered that 10 percent of the marketing budget was going to sales promotions no longer relevant to current product lines.

■ A **zero-based budget** allocates resources as if each budget were brand new.

■ **Projects** are one-time activities that have clear beginning and end points.

A lot of work in organizations takes the form of **projects**, one-time activities that have clear beginning and end points. Examples are the completion of a new student activities building on a campus, the development of a new computer software program, or the implementation of a new advertising campaign for a sports team. **Project management** involves making sure that the activities required to complete a project are completed on time, within budget, and in ways that otherwise meet objectives. Managers of projects make extensive use of *project schedules* that define specific task objectives, link activities to be accomplished with due dates, and identify the amounts and time of resource requirements.

■ **Project management** makes sure that activities required to complete a project are accomplished on time and correctly.

> **BE SURE YOU CAN**
> • differentiate short-range and long-range plans • differentiate strategic and operational plans and explain their relationships to one another • define the terms policy and procedure, and give an example of each in the university setting • explain the unique operation of a zero-based budget
>
> ✓ Learning check ❷

PLANNING TOOLS AND TECHNIQUES

The benefits of planning are best realized when the foundations are strong. The useful tools and techniques of managerial planning include forecasting, contingency planning, scenarios, benchmarking, participative planning, and the use of staff planners.

●●● FORECASTING

Forecasting is the process of predicting what will happen in the future.[17] All plans involve forecasts of some sort. Periodicals such as *Business Week*, *Fortune*, *Canadian Business*, and *The Economist* regularly report forecasts of economic conditions, interest rates, unemployment, and trade deficits, among other issues. Some are based on *qualitative forecasting*, which uses expert opinions to predict the future. Others involve *quantitative forecasting*, which uses mathematical models and statistical analysis of historical data and surveys to predict future events. Although useful, all forecasts should be treated cautiously. They are planning aids, not substitutes. It is said that a music agent once told Elvis Presley: "You ought to go back to driving a truck because you ain't going nowhere." He was obviously mistaken. That's the problem with forecasts—they can be wrong. In the final analysis, forecasting always relies on human judgement. Planning involves deciding what to do about the implications of forecasts once they are made.

■ **Forecasting** attempts to predict the future.

AROUND THE WORLD

Coke and Pepsi spend hundreds of millions of dollars on advertising as they engage one another in the ongoing "Cola War." It may seem that they have nothing to worry about but each other and a few discounters. Not so. There is an ever-changing world out there, and more than 50 percent of their revenues come internationally. Now factor into the planning equation current events, and what do you get? Mecca Cola and Qibla Cola for one thing! Both new colas entered European markets riding a wave of resentment of US brands and multinationals. The founder of Qibla says: "By choosing to boycott major brands, consumers are sending an important signal: that the exploitation of Muslims cannot continue unchecked." Although Coke and Pepsi may have little to fear from these competitors, the emerging international consumer voice has to be heard inside the executive suites of all multinational companies.

Source: Information from Associated Press, "Cola Jihad Bubbling in Europe," *Columbus Dispatch* (February 11, 2003), pp. C1, C2.

There may be more to competition than meets the eye

●●● CONTINGENCY PLANNING

Planning, by definition, involves thinking ahead. But the more uncertain the planning environment, the more likely that one's original assumptions, forecasts, and intentions may prove inadequate or wrong. **Contingency planning** identifies alternative courses of action that can be implemented to meet the needs of changing circumstances. Although one can't always predict when things will go wrong, it can be anticipated that they will. It is highly unlikely that any plan will ever be perfect; changes in the environment will sooner or later occur, as will crises and emergencies. And when they do, the best managers and organizations have contingency plans ready to be implemented. Contingency plans contain "trigger points" that indicate when pre-selected alternative plans should be activated.

■ **Contingency planning** identifies alternative courses of action to take when things go wrong.

●●● SCENARIO PLANNING

A long-term version of contingency planning, called **scenario planning**, involves identifying several alternative future scenarios or states of affairs that may occur. Plans are then made to deal with each should it actually occur.[18] When the Heart and Stroke Foundation of Ontario set out to design a new model for health care funding, they wanted to challenge the organization to think in different ways about the future. A scenario planning process helped the board and other invited experts to rehearse strategic development plans and tactics in five different but realistic scenarios from the world of cardiovascular research and health care in 2020. This scenario planning helped the foundation balance tools, evidence, and insight in order to develop a new way of doing business that would take them into the future.[19]

■ **Scenario planning** identifies alternative future scenarios and makes plans to deal with each.

●●● BENCHMARKING

All too often planners become too comfortable with the ways things are going and overconfident that the past is a good indicator of the future. Successful planning must challenge the status quo; it cannot simply accept things as they are. One way to do this is through **benchmarking**, a technique that makes use of external comparisons to better evaluate one's current performance and identify possible actions for the future.[20] The purpose of benchmarking is to find out what other people and organizations are doing very well, and plan how to incorporate these ideas into one's own operations. One benchmarking technique is to search for **best practices**, those things done by competitors and non-competitors alike that help them to achieve superior performance. This powerful planning technique is a way for progressive companies to learn from other "excellent" companies. The best-run organizations also emphasize internal benchmarking that encourages all members and work units to learn and improve by sharing one another's best practices.

■ **Benchmarking** uses external comparisons to gain insights for planning.

■ **Best practices** are things that lead to superior performance.

●●● USE OF STAFF PLANNERS

As organizations grow, there is a corresponding need to increase the sophistication of the planning system itself. In some cases, staff planners are employed to help coordinate planning for the organization as a whole or for one of its major components.

These planning specialists are skilled in all steps of the planning process, as well as planning tools and techniques. They can help bring focus and energy to accomplish important, often strategic, planning tasks. But one risk is a tendency for a communication "gap" to develop between staff planners and line managers. Unless everyone works closely together, the resulting plans may be inadequate and people may lack commitment to implement the plans no matter how good they are.

●●● PARTICIPATION AND INVOLVEMENT

"Participation" is a key word in the planning process. **Participatory planning** includes, in all planning steps, the people who will be affected by the plans and/or who will be asked to help implement them. This process, as shown in *Figure 8.3*, brings many benefits to the organization. Participation can increase the creativity and information available for planning. It can also increase the understanding and acceptance of plans, as well as commitment to their success. Even though participatory planning takes more time, it can improve results by improving implementation. When 7-Eleven executives planned for new "up-scale" products and services such as selling fancy meals-to-go, they received a hard lesson. Although their ideas sounded good at the top, franchisees balked at the shop level. The executives learned the value of taking time to involve franchise owners in the process of planning new corporate strategies.[21] At Mackinnon Transport Inc. in Guelph, Ontario, participatory planning has resulted in an employee value-driven culture. All employees participate in the planning process and are regularly updated about the company's program toward its goals.

■ **Participatory planning** includes the persons who will be affected by plans and/or who will implement them.

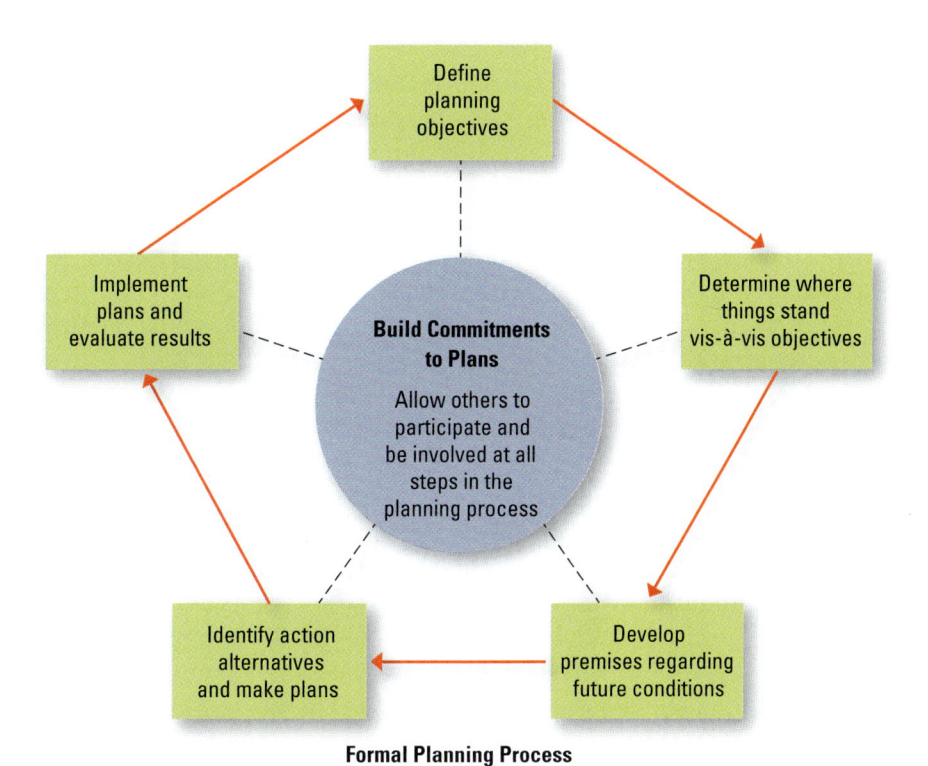

Figure 8.3 How participation and involvement help build commitments to plans.

✓ Learning check ③

BE SURE YOU CAN
• define the terms forecasting, contingency planning, scenario planning, and benchmarking • explain the value of contingency planning and scenario planning • explain the concept of participatory planning and defend its importance in organizations today

THE CONTROL PROCESS

"Keeping in touch . . . Staying informed . . . Being in control." In addition to planning, these are important responsibilities for every manager. But "control" is a word like "power." If you aren't careful when it is used, it leaves a negative connotation. However, it is important to know that control plays a positive and necessary role in the management process. To have things "under control" is good; for things to be "out of control" is generally bad.

IMPORTANCE OF CONTROLLING

■ **Controlling** is the process of measuring performance and taking action to ensure desired results.

In the management process, **controlling** is a process of measuring performance and taking action to ensure desired results. Its purpose is straightforward—to make sure that plans are achieved, that actual performance meets or surpasses objectives. The foundation of control is information. Henry Schacht, former CEO of Cummins Engine Company, once discussed control in terms of what he called "friendly facts." He stated, "Facts that reinforce what you are doing . . . are nice, because they help in terms of psychic reward. Facts that raise alarms are equally friendly, because they give you clues about how to respond, how to change, and where to spend the resources."[22]

If you refer back to *Figure 8.1*, it shows how controlling fits in with the other management functions. Planning sets the directions and allocates resources. Organizing brings people and material resources together in working combinations. Leading inspires people to best utilize these resources. Controlling sees to it that the right things happen, in the right way, and at the right time. It helps ensure that performance by individuals and groups is consistent with plans. It helps ensure that accomplishments throughout an organization are coordinated in means–ends fashion. And, it helps ensure that people comply with organizational policies and procedures.

■ An **after-action review** identifies lessons learned in a completed project, task force, or special operation.

Effective control is also important to organizational learning. It offers the great opportunity of learning from experience. Consider, for example, the program of **after-action review** pioneered by the US Army and now utilized by the Canadian military, firefighters, and in many corporate settings. This is a structured review of lessons learned and results accomplished on a completed project, task force, or special operation. Participants are asked to answer questions like: "What was the intent?" "What actually happened?" "What did we learn?"[23] The review helps make continuous improvement a part of the organizational culture. It encourages everyone involved to take responsibility for their performance efforts and accomplishments.

chosen from other organizations and positions external to the organization. In some cases insiders may have too much control; in others the outsiders may be selected because they are friends of top management or at least sympathetic to them. The concern is that the boards may be too compliant in endorsing or confirming the strategic initiatives of top management. Today, board members are increasingly expected to exercise control and take active roles in ensuring that the strategic management of an enterprise is successful. They are also being selected because of special expertise that they can bring to the governance process.

If anything, the current trend is toward greater emphasis on the responsibilities of corporate governance. Top managers probably feel more performance accountability today than ever before to boards of directors and other stakeholder interest groups. Furthermore, this accountability relates not only to financial performance but also to broader ethical and social responsibility concerns. At GE, for example, CEO Jeffrey Immelt makes it a practice to absent himself at times from directors' meetings.[48] His predecessor, Jack Welch, always wanted to be present when directors met, but Immelt believes differently. His practice helps ensure that the governance responsibilities of the board, including oversight of the CEO's decisions and actions, are independently exercised.

STRATEGIC LEADERSHIP

Effective strategy implementation depends on the full commitment of all managers to support and lead strategic initiatives within their areas of supervisory responsibility. In our dynamic and often-uncertain environment, the premium is on **strategic leadership**—the capability to inspire people to successfully engage in a process of continuous change, performance enhancement, and implementation of organizational strategies.[49] The broad issues associated with strategic leadership are so important that Part 5 of *Management* is devoted in its entirety to leadership and issues related to leadership development—including leadership models, motivation, communication, interpersonal dynamics, teamwork, and change leadership.

■ **Strategic leadership** inspires people to continuously change, refine, and improve strategies and their implementation.

Porter argues that the CEO of a business has to be the chief strategist, someone who provides strategic leadership.[50] He describes the task in the following way. A strategic leader has to be the *guardian of trade-offs*. It is the leader's job to make sure that the organization's resources are allocated in ways consistent with the strategy. This requires the discipline to sort through many competing ideas and alternatives to stay on course and not get sidetracked. A strategic leader also needs to *create a sense of urgency*, not allowing the organization and its members to grow slow and complacent. Even when doing well, the leader keeps the focus on getting better and being alert to conditions that require adjustments to the strategy. A strategic leader needs to *make sure that everyone understands the strategy*. Unless strategies are understood, the daily tasks and contributions of people lose context and purpose. Everyone might work very hard, but without alignment to strategy the impact is dispersed rather than advancing in a common direction to accomplish the goals. Importantly, a strategic leader must *be a teacher*. It is the leader's job to teach the strategy and make it a "cause," says Porter. In order for strategy to work, it must become an ever-present commitment throughout the organization.

PERSONAL MANAGEMENT

CRITICAL THINKING is essential for executive leadership success. It is an analytical skill that involves the ability to gather and interpret information for decision making in a problem context. A good way to develop this skill is through case studies and problem-solving projects in your courses. But beware! One of the risks of our information-rich environment is over-reliance on what we hear or read—especially when it comes from the Web. A lot of what circulates on the Web is anecdotal, superficial, irrelevant, and even just plain inaccurate. You must be disciplined, cautious, and discerning in interpreting the credibility and usefulness of any information that you retrieve. Once you understand this and are willing to invest the time for critical thinking, the Web offers a world of opportunities. Consider your personal career strategy: How well prepared are you to succeed in the *future* job market, not just the present one?

Get to know yourself better

Complete Self-Assessments #14—**Facts and Inferences**, and Exercise #10—**Personal Career Planning**, from the Workbook and Personal Management Activity #9 on the companion website.

This means that a strategic leader must *be a great communicator*. Everyone must understand the strategy and how it makes their organization different from others.

Finally, it is important to note that the challenges faced by organizations today are so complex that it is difficult for any one individual to fulfill all strategic leadership needs. Strategic management is increasingly viewed as a team leadership responsibility. When Michael Dell founded Dell Computer, he did it in his dormitory room at university. Now the firm operates globally with $30 billion in sales. Dell is still Chairman and CEO, but he operates with a top management team. "I don't think you could do it with one person," he says, "there's way too much to be done."[51] As discussed in Chapter 16 on teams and teamwork, it takes hard work and special circumstances to create a real team, at the top or anywhere else in the organization.[52] Top management teams must work up to their full potential in order to bring the full advantages of teamwork to strategic leadership. Dell believes his top management team has mastered the challenge. "We bounce ideas off each other," he says, "and at the end of the day if we say who did this, the only right answer is that we all did. Three heads are better than one."

Learning check 5

BE SURE YOU CAN

• explain how the management process supports strategy implementation • define the term corporate governance • explain why boards of directors sometimes fail in their governance responsibilities • define the term strategic leadership • list the responsibilities of a strategic leader in today's organizations

Chapter 9 STUDY GUIDE

WHERE WE'VE BEEN

Back to Taxi

The opening vignette, Taxi, introduced you to a firm that has successfully followed a growth strategy by differentiating themselves from others. In Chapter 9 you learned more about the concept of strategy and its relationship to the achievement of sustainable competitive advantage. You also learned how the strategic management process analyzes organization and environment, and utilizes various frameworks to select effective strategies. Finally, you learned that even the best strategies deliver high-performance results only when they are well implemented.

THE NEXT STEP
INTEGRATED LEARNING ACTIVITIES

Cases/Projects
- Skype Case
- Project 3—Globalization
- Project 10—Service Learning

Self-Assessments
- A 21st-century Manager (#1)
- Facts and Inferences (#14)
- Empowering Others (#15)
- Turbulence Tolerance Test (#16)

Exercises in Teamwork
- Personal Career Planning (#10)
- Decision-making Bases (#11)
- Strategic Scenarios (#12)
- The Future Workplace (#14)

STUDY QUESTION SUMMARY

1. What are the foundations of strategic competitiveness?
- Competitive advantage is achieved by operating in ways difficult for competitors to imitate.
- A strategy is a comprehensive plan that sets long-term direction and guides resource allocation for sustainable competitive advantage.
- Strategic intent directs organizational resources and energies toward a compelling goal.
- The strategic goals of a business should include superior profitability and the generation of above-average returns for investors.

2. What is the strategic management process?
- Strategic management is the process of formulating and implementing strategies that achieve goals in a competitive environment.
- The strategic management process begins with analysis of mission, clarification of core values, and identification of objectives.
- A SWOT analysis systematically assesses organizational resources and capabilities and industry/environmental opportunities and threats.
- Porter's five forces model analyzes industry attractiveness in terms of competititors, new entrants, substitute products, and the bargaining powers of suppliers and buyers.

3. What types of strategies are used by organizations?
- Corporate strategy sets direction for an entire organization; business strategy sets direction for a business division or product/service line; functional strategy sets direction for the operational support of business and corporate strategies.
- The grand or master strategies used by organizations include growth—pursuing expansion through concentration and diversification; they also include retrenchment—pursuing ways to scale back operations through restructuring and divestiture.
- Global strategies take advantage of international business opportunities; co-operative strategies, such as international joint ventures, use strategic alliances for performance gains.
- E-business strategies use IT and the Internet to pursue competitive advantage.

4. How are strategies formulated?
- The three options in Porter's model of competitive strategy are: differentiation—distinguishing one's products from the competition; cost leadership—minimizing costs relative to the competition; and focus—concentrating on a special market segment.
- The BCG matrix is a portfolio planning approach that classifies businesses or product lines as "stars," "cash cows," "question marks," or "dogs."
- The adaptive model focuses on the congruence of prospector, defender, analyzer, or reactor strategies with demands of the external environment.
- The incremental or emergent model recognizes that many strategies are formulated and implemented incrementally over time.

5. What are current issues in strategy implementation?
- Management practices and systems—including the functions of planning, organizing, leading, and controlling—must be mobilized to support strategy implementation.
- Pitfalls that inhibit strategy implementation include failures of substance—such as poor analysis of the environment; and failures of process—such as lack of participation in the planning process.
- Boards of directors play important roles in corporate governance, monitoring top management, and organizational strategies and performance.
- Strategic leadership inspires the process of continuous evaluation and improvement of strategies and their implementation.
- Success in strategic leadership requires the ability to manage trade-offs in resource allocations, maintain a sense of urgency in strategy implementation, and effectively communicate the strategy to key constituencies.

KEY TERMS REVIEW

Above-average returns (p. 228)
B2B business strategy (p. 239)
B2C business strategy (p. 240)
BCG matrix (p. 243)
Business strategy (p. 236)
Competitive advantage (p. 227)
Concentration (p. 237)
Core competency (p. 232)
Corporate governance (p. 246)
Corporate strategy (p. 236)
Cost leadership strategy (p. 242)
Differentiation strategy (p. 242)
Diversification (p. 237)
Divestiture (p. 238)
Downsizing (p. 237)

E-business strategy (p. 239)
Emergent strategy (p. 245)
Focused cost leadership strategy (p. 243)
Focused differentiation strategy (p. 242)
Functional strategy (p. 236)
Globalization strategy (p. 238)
Growth strategy (p. 236)
Mission (p. 231)
Multidomestic strategy (p. 238)
Operating objectives (p. 232)
Organizational culture (p. 232)
Portfolio planning (p. 243)
Restructuring (p. 237)

Retrenchment strategy (p. 237)
Stakeholders (p. 231)
Strategic alliance (p. 239)
Strategic business unit (SBU) (p. 236)
Strategic intent (p. 227)
Strategic leadership (p. 247)
Strategic management (p. 228)
Strategy (p. 227)
Strategy formulation (p. 229)
Strategy implementation (p. 230)
SWOT analysis (p. 232)
Transnational strategy (p. 238)
Vertical integration (p. 237)

SELF-TEST 9

MULTIPLE-CHOICE QUESTIONS:

1. The most appropriate first question to ask in strategic planning is _____.
   (a) "Where do we want to be in the future?" (b) "How well are we currently doing?" (c) "How can we get where we want to be?" (d) "Why aren't we doing better?"

2. The ability of a firm to consistently outperform its rivals is called _____.
   (a) vertical integration (b) competitive advantage (c) incrementalism (d) strategic intent

3. In a complex conglomerate business such as General Electric, a(n) _____-level strategy sets strategic direction for a strategic business unit or product division.
   (a) institutional (b) corporate (c) business (d) functional

4. An organization that is downsizing to reduce costs is implementing a grand strategy of _____.
    (a) growth (b) cost differentiation (c) retrenchment (d) stability

5. The _____ is a predominant value system for an organization as a whole.
    (a) strategy (b) core competency (c) mission (d) corporate culture

6. A _____ in the BCG matrix would have a high market share in a low-growth market.
    (a) dog (b) cash cow (c) question mark (d) star

7. In Porter's five forces framework, which of the following increases industry attractiveness?
    (a) many rivals (b) many substitute products (c) low bargaining power of suppliers (d) few barriers to entry

8. When PepsiCo acquired Tropicana, a maker of fruit juice, the firm's strategy was one of _____.
    (a) related diversification (b) concentration (c) vertical integration (d) co-operation

9. Cost efficiency and product quality are two examples of _____ objectives of organizations.
    (a) official (b) operating (c) informal (d) institutional

10. The customer generally gains through the lower prices and greater innovation characteristic of _____ environments.
    (a) monopoly (b) oligopoly (c) hypercompetition (d) central planning

11. In the Miles and Snow model of adaptive strategy, the _____ strategy is largely a copycat approach that seeks to do whatever seems to be working well for someone else.
    (a) prospector (b) reactor (c) defender (d) analyzer

12. The role of the board of directors as an oversight body that holds top executives accountable for the success of business strategies is called _____.
    (a) strategic leadership (b) corporate governance (c) logical incrementalism (d) strategic opportunism

13. Among the global strategies that might be pursued by international businesses, the _____ strategy is the most targeted on local needs, local management, and local products.
    (a) ethnocentric (b) transnational (c) geocentric (d) multidomestic

14. Restructuring by downsizing operations and reducing staff is a form of _____ strategy.
    (a) retrenchment (b) growth (c) concentration (d) incremental

15. According to Porter's model of generic strategies, a firm that wants to compete with its rivals by selling a very low priced product would need to succesfully implement a _____ strategy.
    (a) retrenchment (b) differentiation (c) cost leadership (d) diversification

SHORT-RESPONSE QUESTIONS:

16. What is the difference between corporate strategy and functional strategy?
17. How would a manager perform a SWOT analysis?
18. Explain the difference between B2B and B2C as e-business strategies.
19. What is strategic leadership?

APPLICATION QUESTION:

20. Kim Harris owns and operates a small retail store selling the outdoor clothing of a Canadian manufacturer to a predominately college and university student market. Lately, a large department store outside of town has started selling similar but lower-priced clothing manufactured in China, Thailand, and Bangladesh. Kim believes he is starting to lose business to this store. Assume you are part of a student team assigned to do a management class project for Kim. His question for the team is: "How can I best deal with my strategic management challenges in this situation?" How will you reply?

10 Organizing

CHAPTER 10 STUDY QUESTIONS

1. What is organizing as a management function?
2. What are the major types of organization structures?
3. What are the new developments in organization structures?
4. What organizing trends are changing the workplace?

Planning Ahead

After reading Chapter 10, you should be able to answer these questions in your own words.

EDWARD JONES
STRUCTURES SUPPORTING STRATEGIES

Edward Jones is an investment firm that does not operate like other investment firms. Its way of organizing its business sets them apart from the rest. Rather than develop large offices with many employees, Edward Jones has opened up many smaller offices, each staffed with one investment representative and one branch office administrator. Edward Jones' core strategic belief is that face-to-face interaction with clients is the best way to build their business; something best done at small, highly personal, focused centres. Offices are generally staffed by one investment representative who is a licensed broker and at least one office administrator. Some branches may have additional brokers and office staff depending on the level of business. Edward Jones believes that the one-broker-per-office model allows clients the opportunity to choose their broker and then to deal only with that broker.

With a strong core surrounded by largely independent satellite units, the Edward Jones structure is unique. Noted organizational theorist Peter Drucker described this company as "a confederation of highly autonomous entrepreneurial units bound together by a highly centralized core of values and services." And their approach is working. In the 1980s they were a small regional firm in the United States, with just over 300 offices. Today, Edward Jones has nearly 10,000 offices in three countries, including Canada. Edward Jones established its first office in Canada in 1994, and today it has more than 550 branches here.

Their satellite set-up appeals to employees of Edward Jones. *Report on Business* magazine recently named it one of the "50 Best Employers in Canada." Employees like working for the company because of the family atmosphere. Edward Jones also has a strong emphasis on work/life balance, which allows employees flexible work scheduling, training for staff, and realistic sales expectations.

Edward Jones's way of organizing also seems to be working for its clients. Edward Jones ranked "Highest in Investor Satisfaction with Full Service Brokerage Firms" by J.D. Power and Associates. The J.D. Power and Associates 2006 Canadian Full Service Investor Satisfaction Study is based on responses from 5,190 investors who used one of the 14 firms profiled in the study. It is easy to see that Edward Jones has found both an inventive and a successful way to organize.[1]

GET CONNECTED!

Examine the financial services industry. What are the differences among major firms? Make sure you can manage your personal finances.

Chapter 10 LEARNING PREVIEW

The opening example of Edward Jones shows how one firm has organized itself for high performance in the financial services industry. Part of the challenge faced by the company is to maintain success with its entrepreneurial strategy and small-firm ways even while experiencing the pressures of growth. This chapter introduces you to organizing as a management function. It reviews the traditional ways of structuring organizations as well as new directions such as those taken by Edward Jones. Current trends and organizing practices in the new workplace are also described.

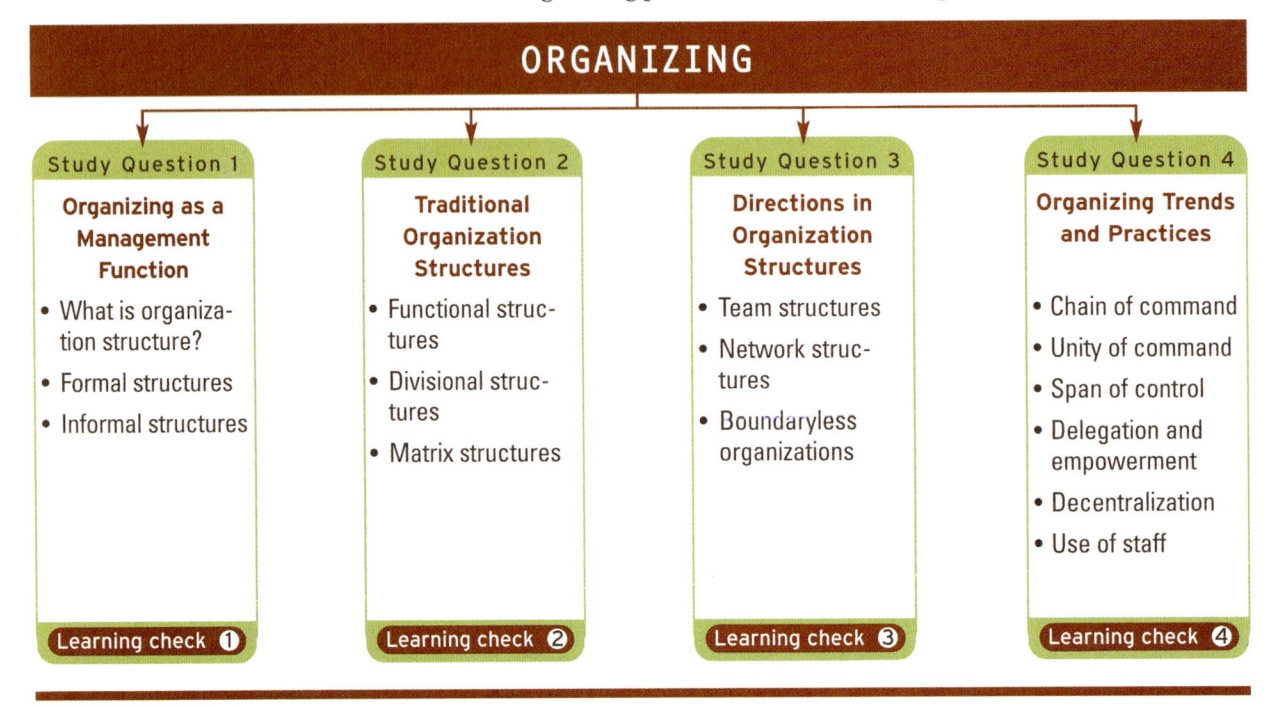

ORGANIZING

Study Question 1

Organizing as a Management Function
- What is organization structure?
- Formal structures
- Informal structures

Learning check 1

Study Question 2

Traditional Organization Structures
- Functional structures
- Divisional structures
- Matrix structures

Learning check 2

Study Question 3

Directions in Organization Structures
- Team structures
- Network structures
- Boundaryless organizations

Learning check 3

Study Question 4

Organizing Trends and Practices
- Chain of command
- Unity of command
- Span of control
- Delegation and empowerment
- Decentralization
- Use of staff

Learning check 4

Management scholar and consultant Henry Mintzberg points out that organizations are changing very quickly in today's world and people within them are struggling to find their place.[2] His point is that people need to understand how their organizations work if they are to work well within them. Mintzberg notes some common questions: "What parts connect to one another?" "How should processes and people come together?" "Whose ideas have to flow where?" These and related questions raise critical issues about organization structures and how well they meet an organization's performance needs.

The organizing approach of Edward Jones—management through a strong central core surrounded by small and autonomous units—is one entrepreneurial benchmark. By building a well-focused yet market-responsive structure, the firm has established and sustained a niche in the highly competitive financial services industry. But this is only one of the ways to structure for success. There are many options as organizations in all industries try new forms in the quest for sustained competitive advantage. Some are using designs that we will discuss as team, network, or even "boundaryless" and "virtual" organizations. Others involve downsizing, rightsizing, and delayering organizations in the search for productivity gains.

Among the best organizations, those that consistently deliver above-average returns and outperform their competitors, one does find consistent themes.[3] They emphasize empowerment, support for employees, responsiveness to client or customer needs, flexibility in dealing with a dynamic environment, and continual attention to quality improvements. They strive for positive cultures and high quality-of-work-life experiences for members and employees. And, importantly, they accept that nothing is constant, at least not for long. They are always seeking new ways of organizing the workplace to best support strategies and achieve high-performance goals.

ORGANIZING AS A MANAGEMENT FUNCTION

Organizing is the process of arranging people and other resources to work together to accomplish a goal. As one of the basic functions of management, it involves both creating a division of labour for tasks to be performed and then coordinating results to achieve a common purpose. *Figure 10.1* shows the central role that organizing plays in the management process. Once plans are created, the manager's task is to see to it that they are carried out. Given a clear mission, core values, objectives, and strategy, *organizing* begins the process of implementation by clarifying jobs and working relationships. It identifies who is to do what, who is in charge of whom, and how different people and parts of the organization relate to and work with one another. All of this, of course, can be done in different ways. The strategic leadership challenge is to choose the best organizational form to fit the strategy and other situational demands.

■ **Organizing** arranges people and resources to work toward a goal.

●●●● WHAT IS ORGANIZATION STRUCTURE?

The way in which the various parts of an organization are formally arranged is usually referred to as the **organization structure**. It is the system of tasks, workflows, reporting relationships, and communication channels that link together the work of diverse individuals and groups. Any structure should both allocate tasks through a division of labour and provide for the coordination of performance results. A structure that does both of these things well is an important asset, helping to implement an organization's strategy.[4] Unfortunately, it is easier to talk about good structures

■ **Organization structure** is a system of tasks, reporting relationships, and communication linkages.

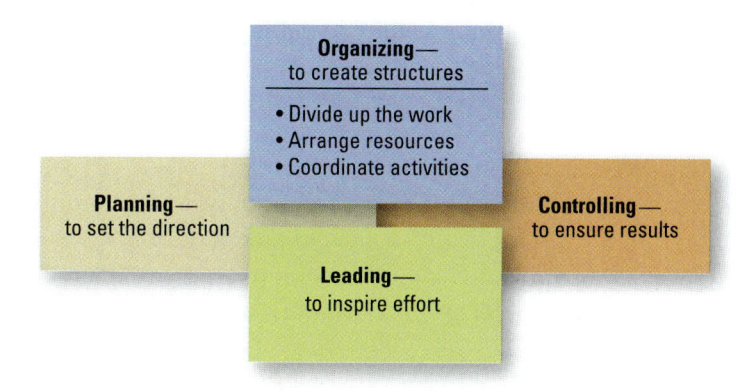

Figure 10.1 Organizing viewed in relationship with the other management functions.

than it is to actually create them. This is why you often read and hear about organizations changing their structures in an attempt to improve performance. There is no one best structure that meets the needs of all circumstances; structure must be addressed in a contingency fashion. As environments and situations change, structures must often be changed too. To make good choices, a manager must understand how structures work and know the available alternatives.

●●● FORMAL STRUCTURES

You may know the concept of structure best in the form of an **organization chart.** This is a diagram that shows reporting relationships and the formal arrangement of work positions within an organization.[5] A typical organization chart identifies various positions and job titles as well as the lines of authority and communication between them. This is the **formal structure**, or the structure of the organization in its official state. It represents the way the organization is intended to function. By reading an organization chart, you can learn the basics of an organization's formal structure, including the following:

- *Division of work:* Positions and titles show work responsibilities.
- *Supervisory relationships:* Lines show who reports to whom.
- *Communication channels:* Lines show formal communication flows.
- *Major subunits:* Positions reporting to a common manager are shown.
- *Levels of management:* Vertical layers of management are shown.

■ An **organization chart** describes the arrangement of work positions within an organization.

■ **Formal structure** is the official structure of the organization.

●●● INFORMAL STRUCTURES

Behind every formal structure typically lies an **informal structure**. This is a "shadow" organization made up of the unofficial, but often critical, working relationships between organizational members. If the informal structure could be drawn, it would show who talks to and interacts regularly with whom regardless of their formal titles and relationships. The lines of the informal structure would cut across levels and move from side to side. They would show people meeting for coffee, in exercise groups, and in friendship groups, among other possibilities. Importantly, no organization can be fully understood without gaining insight into the informal structure as well as the formal one.[6]

Informal structures can be very helpful in getting work accomplished. Indeed, they may be essential in many ways to organizational success. This is especially true during times of change, when out-of-date formal structures may fail to provide the support people need to deal with new or unusual situations. Because it takes time to change or modify formal structures, this happens quite often. In many cases, the informal structure helps fill the void. Through the emergent and spontaneous relationships of informal structures, people benefit in task performance by being in personal contact with others who can help them get things done when necessary. They gain the advantages of *informal learning* that takes place while working and interacting together throughout the workday. Informal structures are also helpful in giving people access to interpersonal networks of emotional support and friendship that satisfy important social needs.

■ **Informal structure** is the set of unofficial relationships among an organization's members.

Nortel Networks, headquartered in Brampton, Ontario, recognizes the value of internal networking in increasing learning within their organization. Among the methods Nortel uses to promote the sharing of knowledge and experience among staff are social events, locating a project's staff in close proximity to each other, setting up informal coffee groups, and organizing formal meetings to discuss common concerns and important issues. Nortel also ensures networking throughout their global operations by implementing quarterly get-togethers and by using video conferencing extensively.[7]

Of course, informal structures also have potential disadvantages. Because they exist outside the formal authority system, the activities of informal structures can sometimes work against the best interests of the organization as a whole. They can be susceptible to rumour, carry inaccurate information, breed resistance to change, and even divert work efforts from important objectives. Also, "outsiders," or people who are left out of informal groupings, may feel less a part of daily activities and suffer a loss of satisfaction. Some North American managers of Japanese firms, for example, have complained about being excluded from what they call the "shadow cabinet"—an informal group of Japanese executives who hold the real power to get things done and sometimes act to the exclusion of others.[8]

> **BE SURE YOU CAN**
> • define organizing as a management function • explain the difference between formal and informal structures • discuss the potential advantages and disadvantages of informal structures in organizations

✓ Learning check 1

TRADITIONAL ORGANIZATION STRUCTURES

A traditional principle of organizing is that performance improves when people are allowed to specialize and become expert in specific jobs or tasks. Given this division of labour, however, decisions must then be made on **departmentalization**, how to group work positions into formal teams or departments that are linked together in a coordinated way. These decisions have traditionally resulted in three major types of organizational structures—the functional, divisional, and matrix structures.[9]

■ **Departmentalization** is the process of grouping together people and jobs into work units.

●●● FUNCTIONAL STRUCTURES

In **functional structures**, people with similar skills and performing similar tasks are grouped together into formal work units. Members of functional departments share technical expertise, interests, and responsibilities. The first example in *Figure 10.2* shows a functional structure common in business firms: top management is arranged by the functions of marketing, finance, production, and human resources. In this functional structure, manufacturing problems are the responsibility of the production vice-president, marketing problems are the province of the marketing vice-president, and so on. The key point is that members of each function work within their areas of expertise. If each function does its work properly, the expectation is that the business will operate successfully.

Functional structures are not limited to businesses. The figure also shows how this form of departmentalization can be used in other types of organizations, such as banks and hospitals. Functional structures typically work well for small organizations

■ A **functional structure** groups together people with similar skills who perform similar tasks.

Figure 10.2 Functional structures in a business, bank branch, and community hospital.

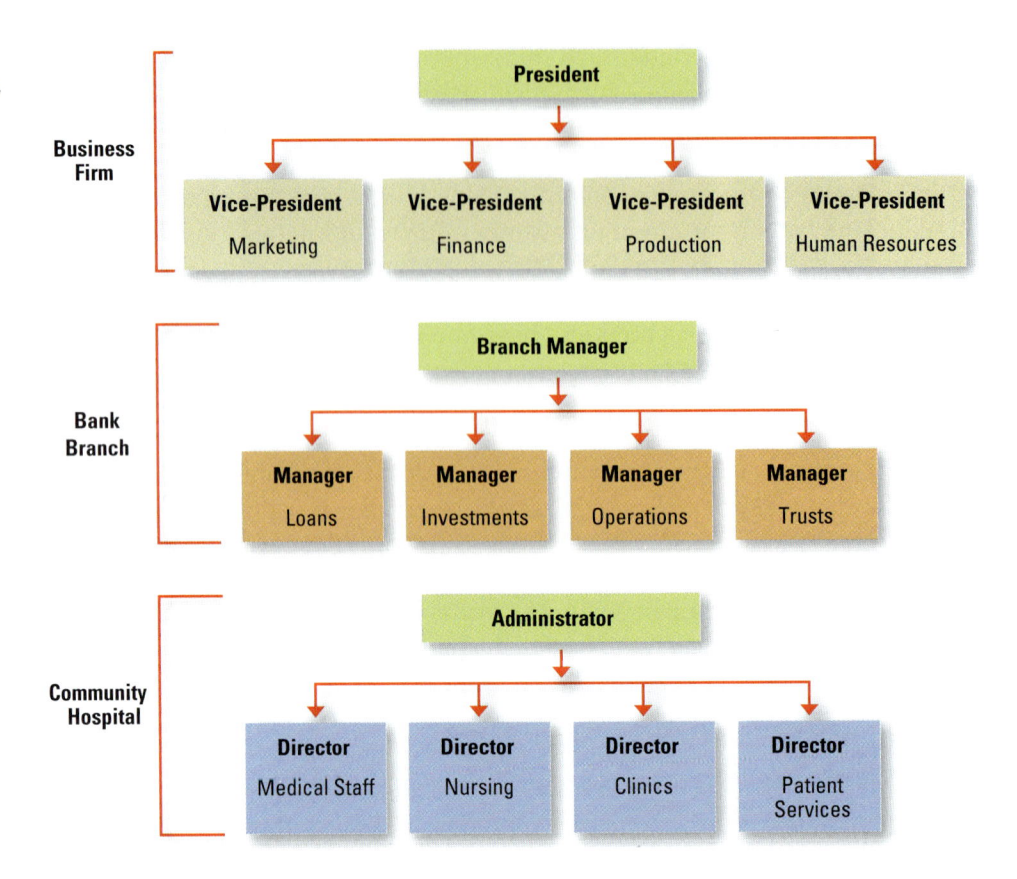

that produce only one or a few products or services. They also tend to work best in relatively stable environments where problems are predictable and the demands for change and innovation are limited. The major *advantages of a functional structure* include the following:

- Economies of scale with efficient use of resources.
- Task assignments consistent with expertise and training.
- High-quality technical problem solving.
- In-depth training and skill development within functions.
- Clear career paths within functions.

There are also potential *disadvantages of functional structures*. Common problems include difficulties in pinpointing responsibilities for things like cost containment, product or service quality, timeliness, and innovation. A significant concern is with the **functional chimneys problem**—lack of communication, coordination, and problem solving across functions. Because the functions become formalized, not only on an organization chart but also in the mindsets of people, the sense of co-operation and common purpose breaks down. The total system perspective is lost to self-centred and narrow viewpoints. When problems occur between functions, they are too often referred up to higher levels for resolution

■ The **functional chimneys problem** is a lack of communication and coordination across functions.

rather than being addressed by people at the same level. This slows decision making and problem solving, and can result in a loss of advantage in competitive situations. For example, when Ford took over as the new owner of Jaguar it had to resolve many quality problems. The quality turnaround took longer than anticipated, in part because of what Jaguar's chairman called "excessive compartmentalization." In building cars, the different departments did very little talking and working with one another. Ford's response was to push for more interdepartmental coordination and consensus decision making.[10]

●●● DIVISIONAL STRUCTURES

A second organizational alternative is the **divisional structure**. It groups together people who work on the same product or process, serve similar customers, and/or are located in the same area or geographical region. As illustrated in *Figure 10.3*, divisional structures are common in complex organizations with diverse operations that extend across many products, territories, customers, and work processes.[11]

■ A **divisional structure** groups together people working on the same product, in the same area, with similar customers, or on the same processes.

Divisional structures attempt to avoid problems common to functional structures. The potential *advantages of divisional structures* include the following:

- More flexibility in responding to environmental changes.
- Improved coordination across functional departments.
- Clear points of responsibility for product or service delivery.
- Expertise focused on specific customers, products, and regions.
- Greater ease in changing size by adding or deleting divisions.

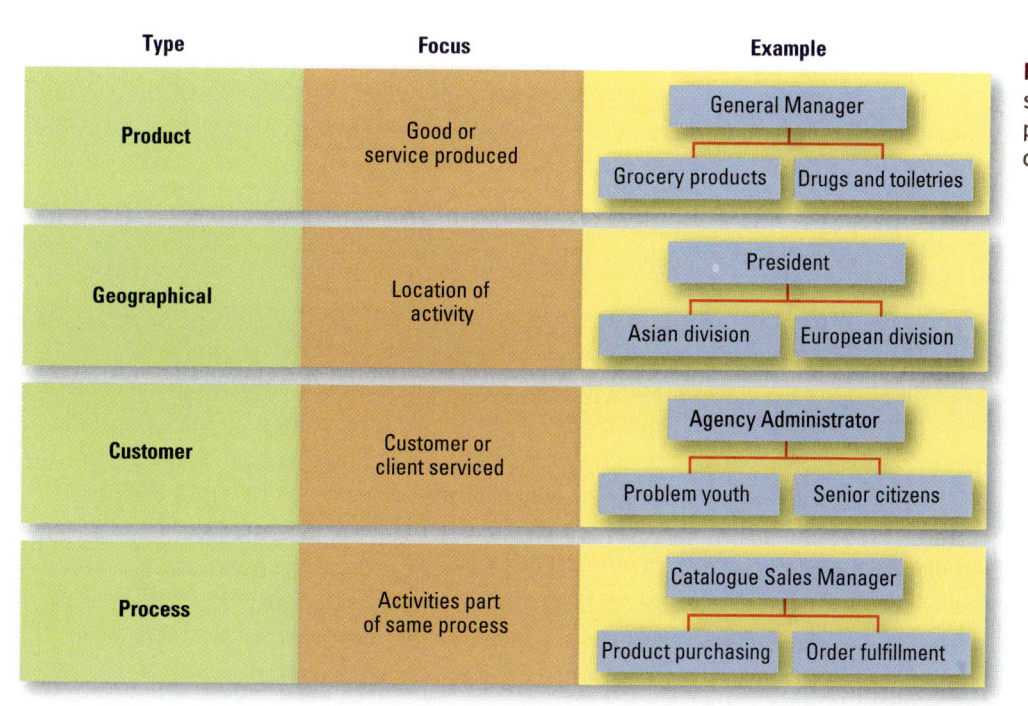

Type	Focus	Example
Product	Good or service produced	General Manager — Grocery products, Drugs and toiletries
Geographical	Location of activity	President — Asian division, European division
Customer	Customer or client serviced	Agency Administrator — Problem youth, Senior citizens
Process	Activities part of same process	Catalogue Sales Manager — Product purchasing, Order fulfillment

Figure 10.3 Divisional structures based on product, geography, customer, and process.

As with other alternatives, there are potential *disadvantages of divisional structures*. They can reduce economies of scale and increase costs through the duplication of resources and efforts across divisions. They can also create unhealthy rivalries as divisions compete for resources and top-management attention, and as they emphasize division needs to the detriment of the goals of the organization as a whole.

Product Structures

■ A **product structure** groups together people and jobs related to a single product or service.

Product structures, sometimes called *market structures*, group together jobs and activities related to a single product or service. They clearly identify costs, profits, problems, and successes in a market area with a central point of accountability. Consequently, managers are encouraged to be responsive to changing market demands and customer tastes. Common in large organizations, product structures may even extend into global operations. When taking over as H.J. Heinz's new CEO, William R. Johnson became concerned about the company's international performance. He decided a change in structure could help improve performance. The existing structure that emphasized countries and regions was changed to global product divisions. The choice was based on his belief that a product structure would bring the best brand management to all countries and increase co-operation around the world within product businesses.

Geographical Structures

■ A **geographical structure** groups together people and jobs performed in the same location.

Geographical structures, sometimes called *area structures*, group together jobs and activities being performed in the same location or geographical region. They are typically used when there is a need to differentiate products or services in various locations, such as in different regions of a country. They are also quite common in international operations, where they help to focus attention on the unique cultures and requirements of particular regions. As UPS operations expanded worldwide, for example, the company announced a change from a product to geographical organizational structure. Two geographical divisions were created—the Americas and Europe/Asia. Each area was given responsibility for its own logistics, sales, and other business functions.

CANADIAN COMPANY IN THE NEWS — Workbrain Corp.

ORGANIZING FOR SUCCESS

Workbrain Corp., a Toronto based HR software developer, knows the importance of organizing. The company produces scheduling software for "supersized" corporations (10,000 or more staff)—the software is designed to simplify the mind-numbing complexities of organizing staff schedules, forecasting labour needs, tracking absences, and ensuring that staffing plans comply with obey labour laws. A key success factor for the company was how they organized themselves. Initially, they partnered with systems integrators like IBM and Accenture that worked with prospective key clients. Their partners opened the doors for Workbrain, and with their early successes they were able to tackle new business sectors one at a time. Their approach to organizing and keeping others organized is working; *Profit Magazine* has them ranked as the number 2 company on their fastest growing Canadian companies list.

Source: Camilla Cornell, "The Dream Team: Supersize Me," *Canadian Business*, June 2006.

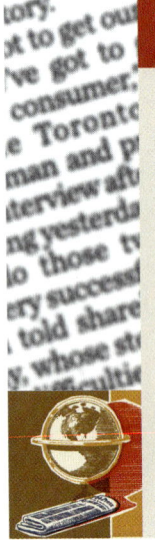

Customer Structures

Customer structures, sometimes also called *market structures* or *product structures*, group together jobs and activities that are serving the same customers or clients. The major appeal is the ability to best serve the special needs of the different customer groups. This is a common form of structure for complex businesses in the consumer products industries. 3M Corporation structures itself to focus attention around the world on its six business areas: consumer and office products, display and graphics products, electronic and communications solutions, health care products and services, industrial and transportation services, and security and safety services. Customer structures are also useful in the services sector. For example, banks use them to give separate attention to consumer and commercial loan customers. The example used in *Figure 10.3* also shows a government agency serving different client populations.

■ A **customer structure** groups together people and jobs that serve the same customers or clients.

Process Structures

A *work process* is a group of tasks related to one another that collectively creates something of value to a customer.[12] An example is order fulfillment, for example, when you telephone a catalogue retailer and request a particular item. The process of order fulfillment takes the order from point of initiation by the customer to point of fulfillment by a delivered product. A **process structure** groups together jobs and activities that are part of the same processes. In the example of Figure 10.3, this might take the form of product-purchasing teams, order-fulfillment teams, and systems-support teams for the mail-order catalogue business. The importance of understanding work processes and designing process-driven organizations has been popularized by management consultant and author Michael Hammer.[13] The essentials of Hammer's ideas on work process design are discussed in the next chapter.

■ A **process structure** groups jobs and activities that are part of the same processes.

Matrix Structures

The **matrix structure**, often called the *matrix organization*, combines the functional and divisional structures just described. In effect, it is an attempt to gain the advantages and minimize the disadvantages of each. This is accomplished in the matrix by using permanent cross-functional teams to support specific products, projects, or programs.[14] As shown in *Figure 10.4*, workers in a matrix structure belong to at least two formal groups at the same time—a functional group and a product, program, or project team. They also report to two bosses—one within the function and the other within the team.

■ A **matrix structure** combines functional and divisional approaches to emphasize project or program teams.

The matrix organization has gained a strong foothold in the workplace, with applications in such diverse settings as manufacturing (e.g., aerospace, electronics, pharmaceuticals), service industries (e.g., banking, brokerage, retailing), professional fields (e.g., accounting, advertising, law), and the non-profit sector (e.g., city, state, and federal agencies, hospitals, universities). Matrix structures are also found in multinational corporations, where they offer the flexibility to deal with regional differences as well as multiple product, program, or project needs.

The main contribution of matrix structures to organizational performance lies with the cross-functional teams whose members work closely together to share expertise and information in a timely manner to solve problems. The potential *advantages of matrix structures* include the following:

Figure 10.4 Matrix structure in a small multiproject business firm.

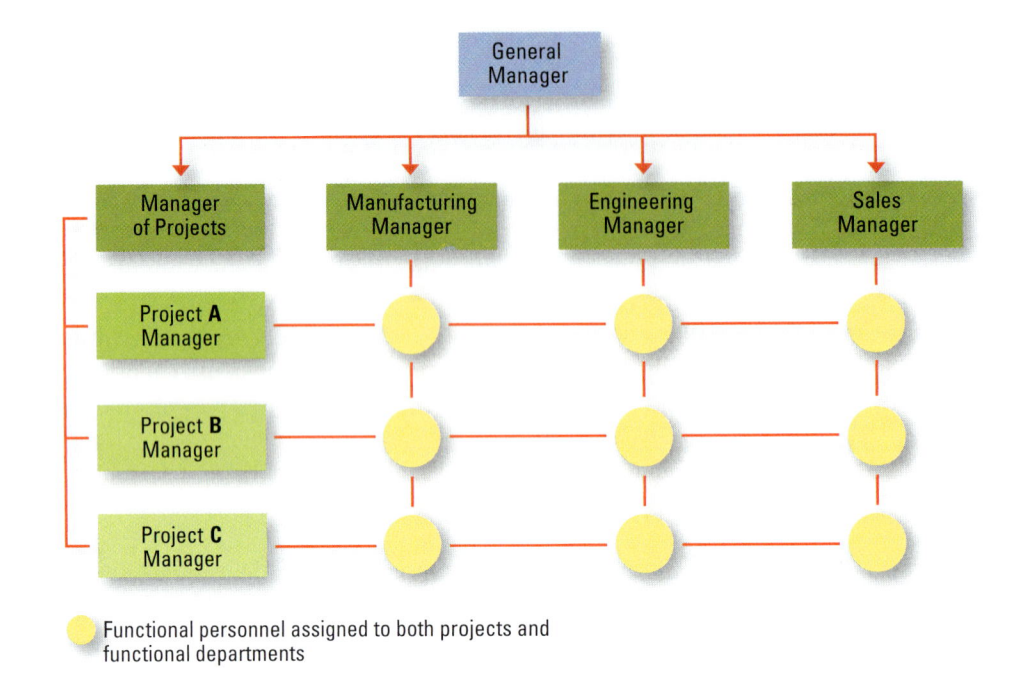

[Organizational chart showing General Manager at top, with Manager of Projects, Manufacturing Manager, Engineering Manager, and Sales Manager reporting to him. Below Manager of Projects are Project A Manager, Project B Manager, and Project C Manager. Yellow circles at intersections represent functional personnel assigned to both projects and functional departments.]

○ Functional personnel assigned to both projects and functional departments

- Better co-operation across functions.
- Improved decision making as problem solving takes place at the team level, where the best information is available.
- Increased flexibility in adding, removing, and/or changing operations to meet changing demands.
- Better customer service, since there is always a program, product, or project manager informed and available to answer questions.
- Better performance accountability through the program, product, or project managers.
- Improved strategic management, since top managers are freed from unnecessary problem solving to focus time on strategic issues.

Predictably, there are also potential *disadvantages of matrix structures*. The two-boss system is susceptible to power struggles, as functional supervisors and team leaders vie with one another to exercise authority. The two-boss system can also be frustrating for matrix members if it creates task confusion and conflicting work priorities. Team meetings in the matrix are also time consuming. Teams may develop "groupitis," or strong team loyalties that cause a loss of focus on larger organizational goals. And the requirements of adding the team leaders to a matrix structure can result in increased costs.[15]

Learning check 2

BE SURE YOU CAN
• explain the differences between functional, divisional, and matrix structures • list advantages and disadvantages of a functional structure, and draw a chart to show its use in an organization familiar to you • list advantages and disadvantages of a divisional structure • draw a chart to show use of each divisional type in an organization familiar to you • list advantages and disadvantages of a matrix structure, and draw a chart to show its use in an organization familiar to you

DIRECTIONS IN ORGANIZATION STRUCTURES

The realities of a global economy and the demands of strategies driven by hyper competition are putting increasing pressures on organization structures. The performance demands are for more speed to market, greater customer orientation, constant productivity improvements, better technology utilization, and more. The environment is unrelenting in such demands. As a result, managers are continually searching for new ways to better structure their organizations.

Structural innovation is always important in the search for productivity improvement and competitive advantage. The right structure is a performance asset; the wrong one is a liability. Today, the vertical and control-oriented structures of the past are proving less and less sufficient to master the tasks at hand. The matrix structure was a first step toward improving flexibility and problem solving through better cross-functional integration. It is now part of a broader movement toward more horizontal structures that decrease hierarchy, increase empowerment, and better mobilize technology and the talents of people to drive organizational performance. *Manager's Notepad 10.1* offers guidelines for tapping the opportunities of horizontal structures.[16]

MANAGER'S Notepad 10.1
Guidelines for mobilizing horizontal structures

- Focus the organization around processes, not functions.
- Put people in charge of core processes.
- Decrease hierarchy and increase the use of teams.
- Empower people to make decisions critical to performance.
- Utilize information technology.
- Emphasize multi-skilling and multiple competencies.
- Teach people how to work in partnership with others.
- Build a culture of openness, collaboration, and performance commitment.

●●●● TEAM STRUCTURES

As the traditional vertical structures give way to more horizontal ones, teams are serving as the basic building blocks.[17] Organizations with **team structures** extensively use both permanent and temporary teams to solve problems, complete special projects, and accomplish day-to-day tasks.[18] As illustrated in *Figure 10.5*, these are often **cross-functional teams** composed of members from different areas of work responsibility.[19] The intention is to break down the functional chimneys, or barriers, inside the organization and create more effective lateral relations for problem solving and work performance. They are also often **project teams** that are convened for a particular task or "project" and are disbanded once the task is completed. The intention here is to quickly convene people with the needed talents and focus their efforts intensely to solve a problem or take advantage of a special opportunity.

■ A **team structure** uses permanent and temporary cross-functional teams to improve lateral relations.

■ A **cross-functional team** brings together members from different functional departments.

■ **Project teams** are convened for a particular task or project and disbanded once it is completed.

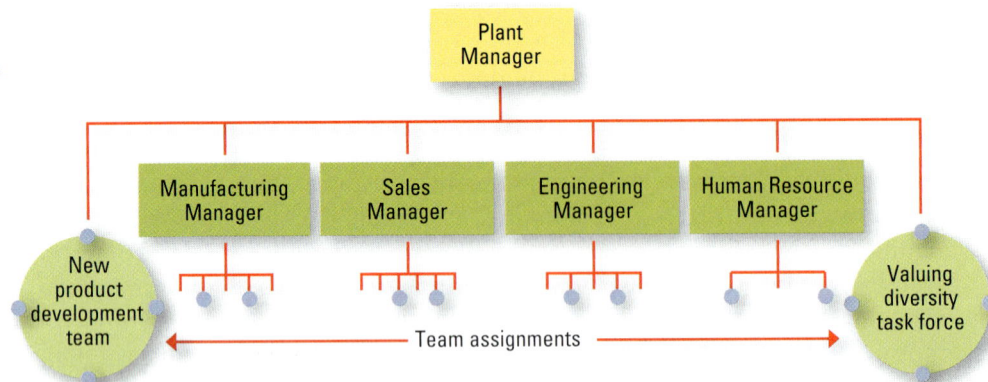

Figure 10.5 How a team structure uses cross-functional teams for improved lateral relations.

There are many potential *advantages of team structures*. They help eliminate difficulties with communication and decision making due to the functional chimneys problem described earlier. Team assignments help to break down barriers between operating departments as people from different parts of an organization get to know one another. They can also boost morale; people working in teams often experience a greater sense of involvement and identification, increasing their enthusiasm for the job. Because teams focus shared knowledge and expertise on specific problems, they can also improve the speed and quality of decisions in many situations. After a research team at Polaroid Corporation developed a new medical imaging system in three years when most had predicted it would take six, a senior executive said, "Our researchers are not any smarter, but by working together they get the value of each other's intelligence almost instantaneously."[20]

The complexities of teams and teamwork contribute to the potential *disadvantages of team structures*. These include conflicting loyalties for persons with both team and functional assignments. They also include issues of time management and

AROUND THE WORLD

Team organization becomes part of borderless world

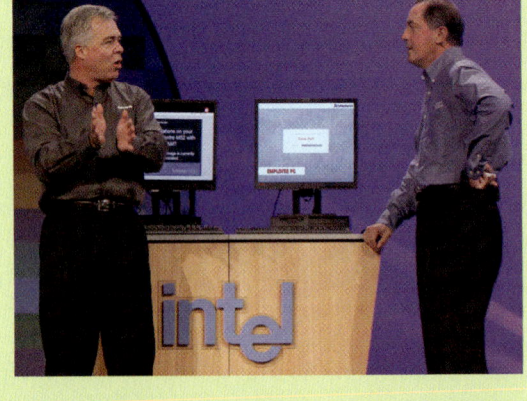

Intel is a well-known global competitor in the dynamic computer chip industry. But a visit to the firm's website is an eye opener. A quick look finds a listing of over 70 locations worldwide, from Belarus to the Philippines to Tajikistan. A fast-moving company in an industry that never sleeps, the firm taps the talents of the globe to keep its chips ahead of the pack. Intel relies heavily on a team organization; hierarchy takes a back seat to teamwork. Says one team member, "We report to each other." This commitment knows no boundaries. The County Kildare plant in Ireland was named recently by *Fortune* magazine as one of 10 "Great Companies to Work For" in Europe. Judges highlighted the importance of egalitarianism at the Irish facility, stating: "Intel has brought to Ireland the Silicon Valley culture of no reserved parking spaces, no executive dining rooms, and small cubicles for all employees. Everyone is on a first-name basis."

Source: Information and quotes from corporate website and <www.intel.com/ireland>

group process. By their very nature, teams spend a lot of time in meetings. Not all of this time is productive. How well team members spend their time together often depends on the quality of interpersonal relations, group dynamics, and team management. All of these concerns are manageable, as will be described in Chapter 16 on teams and teamwork.

●●● NETWORK STRUCTURES

Organizations using a **network structure** operate with a central core that is linked through "networks" of relationships with outside contractors and suppliers of essential services.[21] The old model was for organizations to own everything. The new model is to own only the most essential or "core" components of the business, and to engage in strategic alliances and "outsourcing" to provide the rest. The *strategic alliance*, discussed in the last chapter, is a co-operative strategy through which partners do things of mutual value for one another. For example, Bombardier's recreational products division began developing strategic supplier alliances in 1994, initially with just four subcontractors. Since then, Bombardier has increased the number of supplier partnerships and has developed a true network of firms around itself. The synergy generated by these relationships has promoted shared innovation, and, under the leadership of subcontractors, a number of products have been developed or improved to the benefit of all the partners.[22] **Outsourcing** is the contracting of business functions to outside suppliers. For example, a bank may contract with local firms to provide mailroom, cafeteria, and legal services; an airline might contract out customer service jobs at various airports.

Figure 10.6 illustrates a network structure as it might work for a mail-order company selling lawn and deck furniture through a catalogue. The firm itself is very small, consisting of a relatively few full-time core employees working from a central

■ A **network structure** uses IT to link with networks of outside suppliers and service contractors.

■ **Outsourcing** is when a business function is contracted to an outside supplier.

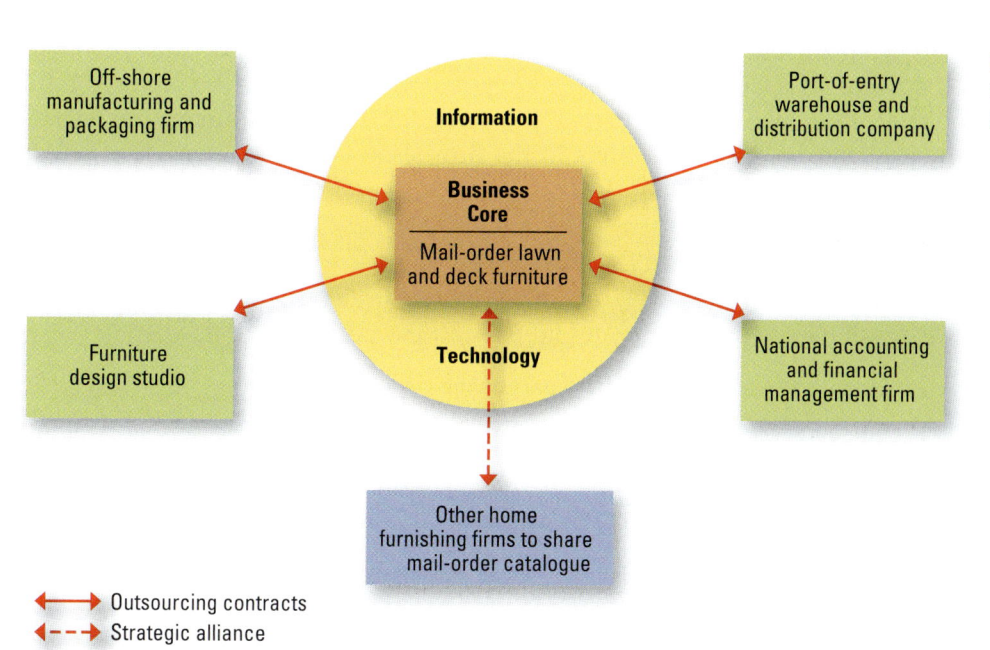

Figure 10.6 A network structure for a Web-based retail business.

headquarters. Beyond that, it is structured as a network of outsourcing and partner relationships, maintained operationally using the latest in information technology. Merchandise is designed on contract with a furniture design firm—which responds quickly as designs are shared and customized via computer networking; it is manufactured and packaged by subcontractors located around the world—wherever materials, quality, and cost are found at best advantage; stock is maintained and shipped from a contract warehouse—ensuring quality storage and on-time expert shipping; all of the accounting and financial details are managed on contract with an outside firm—providing better technical expertise than the firm could afford to employ on a full-time basis; and the quarterly catalogue is designed, printed, and mailed co-operatively as a strategic alliance with two other firms that sell different home furnishings with a related price appeal. All of this, of course, is supported by a company website also maintained by an outside contractor.

The creative use of information technology adds to the potential *advantages of network structures*. With the technological edge, the mail-order company in the prior example can operate with fewer full-time employees and less-complex internal systems. Network structures are thus very lean and streamlined. They help organizations stay cost competitive through reduced overhead and increased operating efficiency. Network concepts allow organizations to employ outsourcing strategies and contract out specialized business functions rather than maintain full-time staff to do them. Information technology now makes it easy to manage these contracts and business alliances, even across great distances. Within the operating core of a network structure, furthermore, a variety of interesting jobs are created for those who must coordinate the entire system of relationships.

The potential *disadvantages of network structures* largely lie with the demands of new management responsibilities. The more complex the business or mission of the organization, the more complicated the network of contracts and alliances that must be maintained. It may be difficult to control and coordinate among them. If one part of the network breaks down or fails to deliver, the entire system suffers the consequences. Also, there is the potential for loss of control over activities contracted out and for a lack of loyalty to develop among contractors who are used infrequently rather than on a long-term basis. Some worry that outsourcing can become so aggressive as to be dangerous to the firm, especially when ever-more-critical

---

MANAGER'S
Notepad 10.2

Seven deadly sins of outsourcing

1. Outsourcing activities that are part of the core.
2. Outsourcing to untrustworthy vendors.
3. Not having good contracts with the vendor.
4. Overlooking impact on existing employees.
5. Not maintaining adequate supervision; losing control to vendors.
6. Overlooking hidden costs of managing contracts.
7. Failing to anticipate need to change vendors, cease outsourcing.

activities such as finance, logistics, and human resource management are outsourced. *Manager's Notepad 10.2* lists the "seven deadly sins" of outsourcing that were developed by research on the practice.[23] Overall, the conclusion is that outsourcing works well, but, like anything else, it must be strategically directed and then controlled for results.

●●● BOUNDARYLESS ORGANIZATIONS

It is popular today to speak about creating a **boundaryless organization** that eliminates internal boundaries among subsystems and external boundaries with the external environment.[24] The boundaryless organization can be viewed as a combination of the team and network structures just described, with the addition of "temporariness." Within the organization, teamwork and communication—spontaneous, as needed, and intense—replace formal lines of authority. There is an absence of boundaries that traditionally and structurally separate organizational members from one another. In the external context, organizational needs are met by a shifting mix of outsourcing contracts and operating alliances that form and disband with changing circumstances. A "photograph" that documents an organization's configuration of external relationships today will look different from one taken tomorrow, as the form naturally adjusts to new pressures and circumstances. *Figure 10.7* shows how the absence of internal and external barriers helps people work in ways that bring speed and flexibility to the boundaryless firm.

Key requirements of boundaryless organizations are the absence of hierarchy, empowerment of team members, technology utilization, and acceptance of impermanence. Work is accomplished by empowered people who come together voluntarily and temporarily to apply their expertise to a task, gather additional expertise from whatever sources may be required to perform it successfully, and stay together only as long as the task is a work in process. The focus is on talent for the task. The assumption is that empowered people working together without bureaucratic restrictions can accomplish great things. Such a work setting is supposed to encourage creativity, quality, timeliness, and flexibility, while reducing inefficiencies and increasing speed. At General Electric, for example, the drive toward boundaryless operations is

■ A **boundaryless organization** eliminates internal boundaries among subsystems and external boundaries with the external environment.

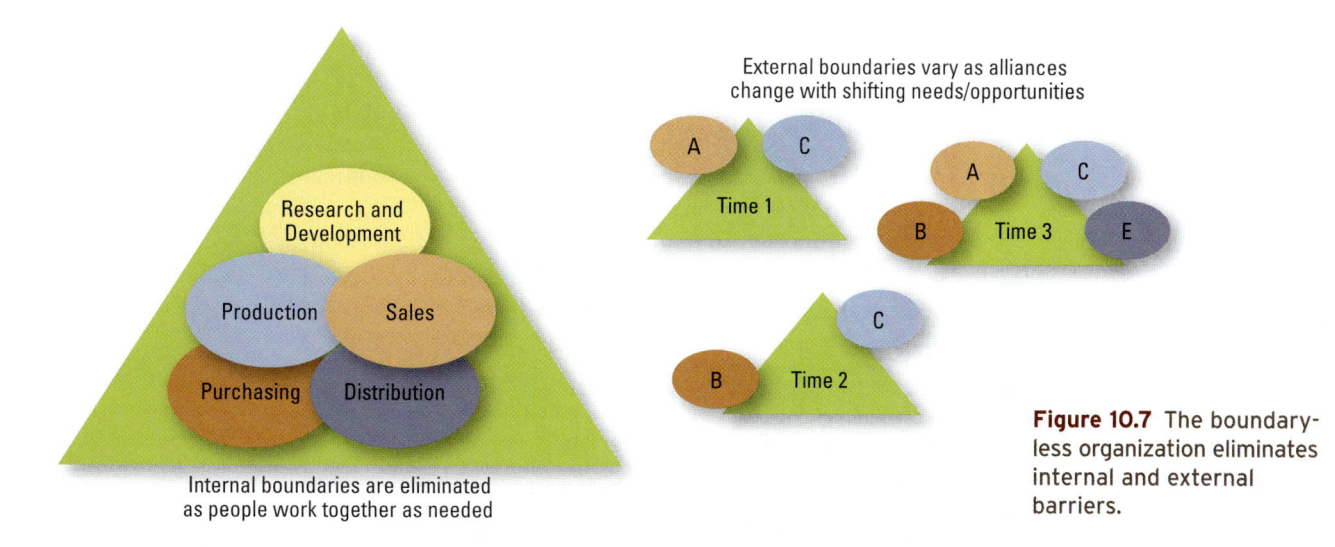

Figure 10.7 The boundaryless organization eliminates internal and external barriers.

supported in part by aggressive "digitization." The firm is moving more and more administrative work onto the Web—where it can be done faster and by persons directly involved. Intermediaries in the form of support personnel are not needed.[25]

Knowledge sharing is both a goal and an essential component of the boundaryless organization. One way to think of this is in the context of a very small organization, perhaps a start-up. In the small firm, everyone pitches in to help out as needed and when appropriate to get things done. There are no formal assignments, and there are no job titles or job descriptions standing in the way. People with talent work together as needed to get the job done. The boundaryless organization, in its pure form, is just like that. Even in the larger organizational context, meetings and spontaneous sharing are happening continuously; perhaps thousands of people working together in hundreds of teams form and disband as needed. At consulting giant PricewaterhouseCoopers, for example, knowledge sharing brings together 160,000 partners spread across 150 countries in a vast virtual learning and problem-solving network. Partners collaborate electronically through online databases where information is stored, problems posted, and questions asked and answered in real time by those with experience and knowledge relevant to the problem at hand. Technology makes collaboration instantaneous and always possible, breaking down boundaries that might otherwise slow or impede the firm's performance.[26]

In the organization/environment interface, boundaryless operations emerge in a special form that is sometimes called the **virtual organization**.[27] This is an organization that operates in a shifting network of external alliances that are engaged as needed using IT and the Internet. The boundaries that traditionally separate a firm from its suppliers, customers, and even competitors are largely eliminated. Virtual organizations come into being "as needed" when alliances are called into action to meet specific operating needs and objectives. When the work is complete, the alliance rests until next called into action. The virtual organization operates in this manner with the mix of mobilized alliances continuously shifting,

■ A **virtual organization** uses IT and the Internet to engage a shifting network of strategic alliances.

Canadian Managers

Decentralization from Head Office Leads to Quiet Success: Robert Ogilvie

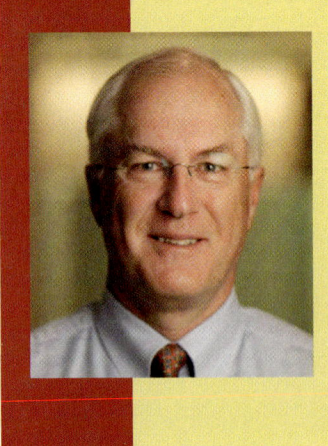

Robert Ogilvie, chairman of Toromont Industries Ltd., has been quietly managing one of the country's best performing companies. The Concord, Ontario-based operator of Caterpillar heavy-equipment dealerships actually operates two business segments: the Equipment Group, which includes the equipment rentals and dealerships, and the Compression Group, specializing in compression, process, and industrial and recreational refrigeration systems. According to Ogilvie, credit for Toromont's success goes to the company's business operators, who are given a lot of autonomy by head office. Each business unit is run by its own president. "Our job," says Ogilvie, "is to choose which businesses to invest in and set the culture and framework to motivate those guys." Ogilvie's vision of employee empowerment goes further. Soon after joining Toromont, Ogilvie overhauled the bonus calculation system, removing criteria that employees could not control, like stock performance. The company now measures and rewards employees based on absolute performance only.

Source: Jeff Sanford and John Gray, "Top CFO 2005," *Canadian Business*, April 25 – May 8, 2005.

and with an expansive pool of potential alliances always ready to be called upon as needed. Operating as a virtual organization, Athena Sustainable Materials Institute has earned itself an international reputation for its work on the sustainability of building materials. This small Canadian organization has done that without a large staff, fancy offices, or even laboratories. Athena brings specialists, primarily from universities, together to work on a specific project or contract. Once the project is completed, the specialists return to their regular work until Athena needs their skills again.[28]

> **BE SURE YOU CAN**
>
> - describe how organizations can include cross-functional teams and project teams in their structures
> - define the term network structure • illustrate how a new venture, such as a Web-based retailer, might use a network structure to organize its various operations • discuss the potential advantages and disadvantages of following a network approach • explain the concept of the boundaryless organization
>
> ✓ Learning check ❸

ORGANIZING TRENDS AND PRACTICES

When structures are modified, refined, and abandoned in the search for new ones, the organizing practices that create and implement them must change too. In Chapter 1 the concept of the **upside-down pyramid** was introduced as an example of the new directions in management. By putting customers on top, served by workers in the middle, who are in turn supported by managers at the bottom, this notion tries to refocus attention on the marketplace and customer needs. Although more of a concept than a depiction of an actual structure, such thinking is representative of forces shaping new directions in how the modern workplace is organized. Among the organizing trends to be discussed next, a common theme runs throughout—making the adjustments needed to streamline operations for cost efficiency, higher performance, and increased participation by workers.

■ The **upside-down pyramid** puts customers at the top, served by workers whose managers support them.

●●● SHORTER CHAINS OF COMMAND

A typical organization chart shows the **chain of command**, or the line of authority that vertically links each position with successively higher levels of management. The classical school of management suggests that the chain of command should operate according to the *scalar principle*: there should be a clear and unbroken chain of command linking every person in the organization with successively higher levels of authority, up to and including the top manager.

■ The **chain of command** links all persons with successively higher levels of authority.

When organizations grow in size they tend to get taller, as more and more levels of management are added to the chain of command. This increases overhead costs; it tends to decrease communication and access between top and bottom levels; it can greatly slow decision making; and it can lead to a loss of contact with the client or customer. These are all reasons why "tall" organizations with many levels of management are often criticized for inefficiencies and poor productivity. The current trend is toward shorter chains of command.

Trend. Organizations are being "streamlined" by cutting unnecessary levels of management; flatter, more horizontal structures are viewed as a competitive advantage.

take it to the case!

Nike
Spreading out to stay together

The next time you are looking for a company that uses outsourcing to capitalize on their core competencies, look no further than your feet. With one of the world's most recognized brands, their trademark "swoosh", Nike is among the most successful companies in North America. But how can a company that outsources most of their production remain connected to their products and their customers' needs? By focusing on what they do best! Nike adopted a decentralized structure in order to focus resources directly on their core competencies: comprehensive market research, advertising, and innovative research and design. As a result, Nike continues to dominate the highly competitive athletic market.

●●○ LESS UNITY OF COMMAND

Another classical management principle describes how the chain of command should operate in daily practice. The *unity-of-command principle* states that each person in an organization should report to one, and only one, supervisor. This notion of "one person–one boss" is a foundation of the traditional pyramid form of organization. It is intended to avoid the confusion potentially created when a person gets work directions from more than one source. Unity of command is supposed to ensure that everyone clearly understands assignments and does not get conflicting instructions. It is violated, for example, when a senior manager bypasses someone's immediate supervisor to give him or her orders. This can create confusion for the subordinate and also undermine the supervisor's authority.

The "two-boss" system of matrix structure is a clear violation of unity of command. Whereas the classical advice is to avoid creating multiple reporting relationships, the matrix concept creates them by design. It does so in an attempt to improve lateral relations and teamwork in special programs or projects. Unity of command is also less predominant in the team structure and in other arrangements that emphasize the use of cross-functional teams and task forces. The current trend is for less, not more, unity of command in organizations.

Trend. Organizations are using more cross-functional teams, task forces, and horizontal structures, and they are becoming more customer conscious; as they do so, employees often find themselves working for more than one "boss."

●●○ WIDER SPANS OF CONTROL

■ **Span of control** is the number of subordinates directly reporting to a manager.

The **span of control** is the number of persons directly reporting to a manager. When span of control is "narrow," only a few people are under a manager's immediate supervision; a "wide" span of control indicates that the manager supervises many

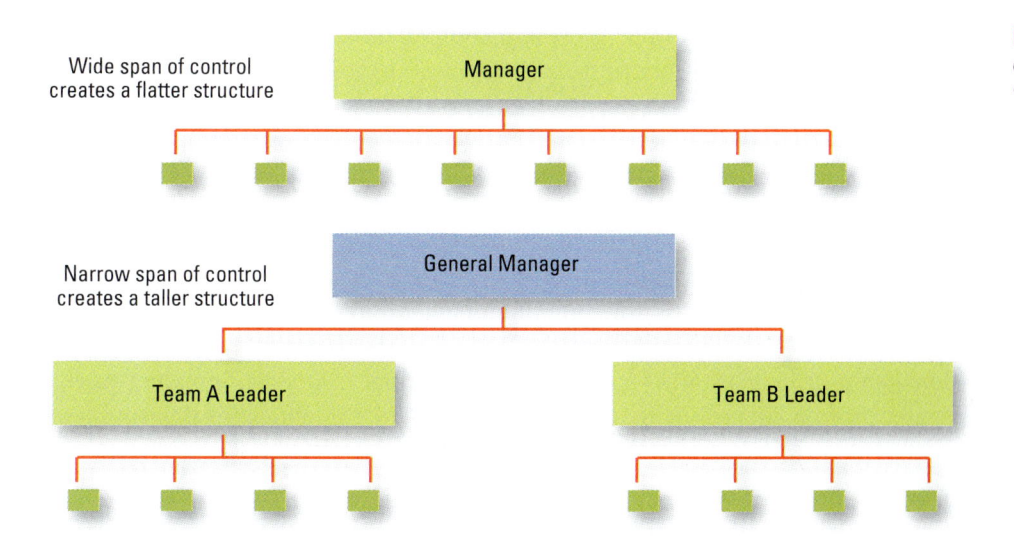

Figure 10.8 Spans of control in "flat" versus "tall" structures.

Wide span of control creates a flatter structure

Narrow span of control creates a taller structure

people. There was a time in the history of management thought when people searched for the ideal span of control. Although the magic number was never found, this *span-of-control principle* evolved: there is a limit to the number of people one manager can effectively supervise; care should be exercised to keep the span of control within manageable limits.

Figure 10.8 shows the relationship between span of control and the number of levels in the chain of command. *Flat structures* have wider spans of control and fewer levels of management; *tall structures* have narrow spans of control and many levels of management. Because tall organizations have more managers, they are more costly. They are also generally viewed as less efficient, less flexible, and less customer sensitive than flat organizations. Before making spans of control smaller, therefore, serious thought should always be given to both the cost of the added management overhead and the potential disadvantages of a taller chain of command. When spans of control are increased, by contrast, overhead costs are reduced. Workers with less direct supervision in flatter structures also benefit from more empowerment and independence.[29]

Trend. Many organizations are shifting to wider spans of control as levels of management are eliminated; managers are taking responsibility for larger numbers of subordinates who operate with less direct supervision.

●●● MORE DELEGATION AND EMPOWERMENT

All managers must decide what work they should do themselves and what should be left for others. At issue here is **delegation**—the process of entrusting work to others by giving them the right to make decisions and take action. There are three steps to delegation. In *step 1, the manager assigns responsibility* by carefully explaining the work or duties someone else is expected to do. This *responsibility* is an expectation for the other person to perform assigned tasks. In *step 2, the manager grants authority to act*. Along with the assigned task, the right to take

■ **Delegation** is the process of distributing and entrusting work to other persons.

necessary actions (for example, to spend money, direct the work of others, use resources) is given to the other person. *Authority* is a right to act in ways needed to carry out the assigned tasks. In *step 3, the manager creates accountability*. By accepting an assignment, the person takes on a direct obligation to the manager to complete the job as agreed upon. *Accountability*, originally defined in Chapter 1, is the requirement to answer to a supervisor for performance results.

A classical principle of organization warns managers not to delegate without giving the subordinate sufficient authority to perform. When insufficient authority is delegated, it will be very hard for someone to live up to performance expectations. They simply don't have the authority needed to get the job done. The *authority-and-responsibility principle* states—authority should equal responsibility when work is delegated from a supervisor to a subordinate. Useful guidelines for delegating are offered in *Manager's Notepad 10.3*.[30]

MANAGER'S Notepad 10.3
Useful guidelines for delegating

- Carefully choose the person to whom you delegate.
- Define the responsibility; make the assignment clear.
- Agree on performance objectives and standards.
- Agree on a performance timetable.
- Give authority; allow the other person to act independently.
- Show trust in the other person.
- Provide performance support.
- Give performance feedback.
- Recognize and reinforce progress.
- Help when things go wrong.
- Don't forget *your* accountability for performance results.

A common management failure is unwillingness to delegate. Whether due to a lack of trust in others or to a manager's inflexibility in the way things get done, failure to delegate can be damaging. It overloads the manager with work that could be done by others; it also denies others many opportunities to fully utilize their talents on the job. When well done, by contrast, delegation leads to empowerment, in that people have the freedom to contribute ideas and do their jobs in the best possible ways. This involvement can increase job satisfaction for the individual and frequently results in better job performance.

Trend. Managers in progressive organizations are delegating more; they are finding more ways to empower people at all levels to make more decisions affecting themselves and their work.

●●●DECENTRALIZATION WITH CENTRALIZATION

A question frequently asked is: "Should most decisions be made at the top levels of an organization, or should they be dispersed by extensive delegation throughout all levels of management?" The former approach is referred to as **centralization**; the latter is called **decentralization**. There is no classical principle on centralization and decentralization. The traditional pyramid form of organization may give the impression of being a highly centralized structure, while decentralization is characteristic of newer structures and many recent organizing trends. But the issue doesn't have to be framed as an either/or choice. Today's organizations can operate with greater decentralization without giving up centralized control. This is facilitated by developments in information technology.

With computer networks and advanced information systems, managers at higher levels can more easily stay informed about a wide range of day-to-day performance matters. Because they have information on results readily available, they can allow more decentralization in decision making.[31] If something goes wrong, presumably the information systems will sound an alarm and allow corrective action to be taken quickly. Using such a decentralized approach, Golder Associates has become one of the world's most successful engineering consulting firms. With the company president based in Calgary and over 70 offices worldwide, Golder relies on individual office and manager autonomy in order to respond to the unique needs of their international clientele. By decentralizing while at the same time stressing high levels of internal communication, coordination, and decision making, Golder ensures that management teams keep connected concerning the wants and needs of both the organization and its customers.[32]

Trend. Whereas delegation, empowerment, and horizontal structures are contributing to more decentralization in organizations, advances in information technology simultaneously allow for the retention of centralized control.

●●●REDUCED USE OF STAFF

When it comes to coordination and control in organizations, the issue of line-staff relationships is important. Chapter 1 described the role of staff as providing expert advice and guidance to line personnel. This can help ensure that performance

---

PERSONAL MANAGEMENT

It takes a lot of trust to be comfortable with **EMPOWERMENT**. But if you aren't willing and able to empower others, you'll not only compromise your own performance but also add to the stress of daily work. Empowerment involves allowing and helping others to do things, even things that you might be very good at doing yourself. The beauty of organizations is synergy—bringing together the contributions of many people to achieve something that is much greater than what any individual can accomplish alone. Empowerment gives synergy a chance. But many people, perhaps even you, suffer from control anxiety. They don't empower others because they fear losing control over a task or situation. In groups, they want or try to do everything by themselves; they are afraid to trust other team members with important tasks. Being "unwilling to let go," they try to do too much, with the risk of missed deadlines and even poor performance; they deny others opportunities to contribute, losing the benefits of their talents and often alienating them in the process. Does this description apply to you? Now is a good time to think seriously about your personal style—are you someone who empowers others, or do you suffer from control anxiety and an unwillingness to delegate?

Get to know yourself better

Complete Assessments #15—**Empowering Others**, and Exercise #15—**Leading Through Participation** from the Workbook and Personal Management Activity #10 on the companion website.

■ **Centralization** is the concentration of authority for most decisions at the top level of an organization.

■ **Decentralization** is the dispersion of authority to make decisions throughout all organization levels.

■ **Specialized staff** provide technical expertise for other parts of the organization.

standards are maintained in areas of staff expertise. **Specialized staff** perform a technical service or provide special problem-solving expertise for other parts of the organization. This could be a single person, such as a corporate safety director, or a complete unit, such as a corporate safety department. Many organizations rely on staff specialists to maintain coordination and control over a variety of matters. In a large retail chain, line managers in each store typically make daily operating decisions regarding direct sales of merchandise. But staff specialists at the corporate or regional levels provide direction and support so that all the stores operate with the same credit, purchasing, employment, and advertising procedures.

■ **Personal staff** are "assistant-to" positions that support senior managers.

Organizations may also employ **personal staff**, individuals appointed in "assistant-to" positions with the purpose of providing special support to higher-level managers. Such assistants help by following up on administrative details and performing other duties as assigned. They can benefit also in terms of career development, through the mentoring relationships that such assignments offer. An organization, for example, might select promising junior managers as temporary administrative assistants to senior managers. This helps them gain valuable experience at the same time that they are facilitating the work of executives.

Problems in line-staff distinctions can and do arise. In too many cases, organizations find that the staff grows to the point where it costs more in administrative overhead than it is worth. This is why staff cutbacks are common in downsizing and other turnaround efforts. There are also cases where conflicts in line-staff relationships cause difficulties. This often occurs when line and staff managers disagree over the extent of staff authority. At the one extreme, staff has purely *advisory authority* and can "suggest" but not "dictate." At the other extreme, it has *functional authority* to actually "require" that others do as requested within the boundaries of staff expertise. For example, a human resource department may advise line managers on the desired qualifications of new workers being hired (advisory authority); the department will likely require the managers to follow employment equity guidelines in the hiring process (functional authority).

There is no one best solution to the problem of how to divide work between line and staff responsibilities. What is best for any organization will be a cost-effective staff component that satisfies, but doesn't overreact to, needs for specialized technical assistance to line operations.

Trend. Organizations are reducing the size of staff; they are seeking lower costs and increased operating efficiency by employing fewer personnel and using smaller staff units.

✓ Learning check ❹

BE SURE YOU CAN
• define the terms chain of command, unity of command, span of control, delegation, empowerment, decentralization, centralization, and staff • describe the organizational trends that relate to each term • discuss the significance of these trends and practices for people and the new workplace

Chapter 10 STUDY GUIDE

WHERE WE'VE BEEN

Back to Edward Jones

The opening example of Edward Jones described the challenges of organizing to achieve competitive advantage. It suggests that any structure must meet the needs of the organization with respect to situational demands and opportunities. In this chapter you learned the traditional types of organizational structures—functional, divisional, and matrix. You learned about the new team, network, and boundaryless structures that are appearing. And you learned the current trends and practices that are changing the way people work together in today's organizations.

THE NEXT STEP
INTEGRATED LEARNING ACTIVITIES

Cases/Projects
- Nike Case
- Project 10—Service Learning in Management

Self-Assessments
- What Are Your Managerial Assumptions? (#4)
- Empowering Others (#15)
- Organizational Design Preference (#17)

Exercises in Teamwork
- What Managers Do (#2)
- Leading Through Participation (#16)
- The Future Workplace (#14)

STUDY QUESTION SUMMARY

1. What is organizing as a management function?
- Organizing is the process of arranging people and resources to work toward a common goal.
- Organizing decisions divide up the work that needs to be done, allocate people and resources to do it, and coordinate results to achieve productivity.
- Structure is the system of tasks, reporting relationships, and communication that links people and positions within an organization.
- The formal structure, such as shown on an organization chart, describes how an organization is supposed to work.
- The informal structure of organization consists of the unofficial relationships that develop among members.

2. What are the major types of organization structures?
- Departmentalization is the process of grouping people together in formal work units or teams.
- In functional structures, people with similar skills who perform similar activities are grouped together under a common manager.
- In divisional structures, people who work on a similar product, work in the same geographical region, serve the same customers, or participate in the same work process are grouped together under common managers.
- A matrix structure combines the functional and divisional approaches to create permanent cross-functional project teams.

3. **What are the new developments in organization structures?**
   - Increasing complexity and greater rates of change in the environment are challenging the performance capabilities of traditional organization structures.
   - New developments emphasize more horizontal structures that utilize teams and technology to best advantage.
   - Team structures use cross-functional teams and task forces to improve lateral relations and improve problem solving at all levels.
   - Network structures use contracted services and strategic alliances to support a core business or organizational centre.
   - Boundaryless organizations combine team and network structures with the advantages of technology to accomplish temporary tasks and projects.
   - Virtual organizations utilize IT and the Internet to mobilize a shifting mix of strategic alliances to accomplish specific tasks and projects.

4. **What organizing trends are changing the workplace?**
   - Traditional vertical command-and-control structures are giving way to more horizontal structures emphasizing employee involvement and flexibility.
   - Many organizations are now operating with shorter chains of command and less unity of command.
   - Many organizations are now operating with wider spans of control and fewer levels of management.
   - The emphasis in more organizations today is on effective delegation and empowerment.
   - Advances in information systems make it possible to operate with decentralization while still maintaining centralized control.
   - Reducing the size of staff is a trend in organizations seeking cost savings and greater efficiency.

KEY TERMS REVIEW

Boundaryless organization (p. 267)
Centralization (p. 273)
Chain of command (p. 269)
Cross-functional teams (p. 263)
Customer structure (p. 261)
Decentralization (p. 273)
Delegation (p. 271)
Departmentalization (p. 257)
Divisional structure (p. 259)
Formal structure (p. 256)

Functional chimneys problem (p. 258)
Functional structure (p. 257)
Geographical structure (p. 260)
Informal structure (p. 256)
Matrix structure (p. 261)
Network structure (p. 265)
Organization chart (p. 256)
Organization structure (p. 255)
Organizing (p. 255)
Outsourcing (p. 265)

Personal staff (p. 274)
Process structure (p. 261)
Product structure (p. 260)
Project teams (p. 263)
Span of control (p. 270)
Specialized staff (p. 274)
Team structure (p. 263)
Upside-down pyramid (p. 269)
Virtual organization (p. 268)

SELF-TEST 10

MULTIPLE-CHOICE QUESTIONS:

1. The main purpose of organizing as a management function is to _____.
   (a) make sure that results match plans (b) arrange people and resources to accomplish work (c) create enthusiasm for the work to be done (d) match strategies with operational plans

2. _____ is the system of tasks, reporting relationships, and communication that links together the various parts of an organization.
   (a) Structure (b) Staff (c) Decentralization (d) Differentiation

3. Transmission of rumours and resistance to change is a potential disadvantage often associated with _____.
   (a) virtual organizations (b) informal structures (c) delegation (d) specialized staff
4. An organization chart showing vice-presidents of marketing, finance, manufacturing, and purchasing all reporting to the president is depicting a _____ structure.
   (a) functional (b) matrix (c) network (d) product
5. The "two-boss" system of reporting relationships is found in the _____ structure.
   (a) functional (b) matrix (c) network (d) product
6. A manufacturing business with a functional structure has recently developed two new product lines. The president of the company might consider shifting to a/an _____ structure to gain a stronger focus on each product.
   (a) virtual (b) informal (c) divisional (d) network
7. Better lower-level teamwork and more top-level strategic management are among the expected advantages of a _____ structure.
   (a) divisional (b) matrix (c) geographical (d) product
8. "Tall" organizations tend to have long chains of command and _____ spans of control.
   (a) wide (b) narrow (c) informal (d) centralized
9. The unity-of-command principle is intentionally violated in the _____ structure.
   (a) network (b) matrix (c) geographical (d) product
10. In delegation, _____ is the right of a subordinate to act in ways needed to carry out the assigned tasks.
    (a) authority (b) responsibility (c) accountability (d) centrality
11. The functional chimneys problem occurs when people in different functions _____.
    (a) fail to communicate with one another (b) try to help each other work with customers (c) spend too much time coordinating decisions (d) focus on products rather than functions
12. A _____ structure tries to combine the best elements of the functional and divisional forms.
    (a) matrix (b) boundaryless (c) team (d) virtual
13. Outsourcing plays a central role in the _____ organization.
    (a) functional (b) divisional (c) network (d) team
14. A student volunteers to gather information on a company for a group case analysis project. The other members of the group agree and tell her that she can choose the information sources. This group is giving the student _____ to fulfill the agreed-upon task.
    (a) responsibility (b) accountability (c) authority (d) decentralization
15. The current trend in the use of staff in organizations is to _____.
    (a) give personnel more functional authority over line operations (b) reduce the number of personnel overall (c) better utilize IT to give staff more centralized control (d) combine all staff functions in one department

SHORT-RESPONSE QUESTIONS:

16. What is the difference between a product divisional structure and a geographical or area divisional structure?
17. What are symptoms that might indicate a functional structure is causing problems for the organization?
18. Explain by example the concept of a network organization structure.
19. What positive results might be expected when levels of management are reduced and the chain of command shortened in an organization?

APPLICATION QUESTION:

20. Faisal Sham supervises a group of seven project engineers. His unit is experiencing a heavy workload as the demand for different versions of one of his firm's computer components is growing. Faisal finds that he doesn't have time to follow up on all design details for each version. Up until now he has tried to do this all by himself. Two of the engineers have shown interest in helping him coordinate work on the various designs. As a consultant, what would you advise Faisal in terms of delegating work to them?

11 Organizational Design and Work Processes

CHAPTER 11 STUDY QUESTIONS

1. What are the essentials of organizational design?
2. How do contingency factors influence organizational design?
3. What are the major issues in subsystem design?
4. How can work processes be re-engineered?

Planning Ahead

After reading Chapter 11, you should be able to answer these questions in your own words.

KPMG INTERNATIONAL
DESIGN FOR INTEGRATION, EMPOWERMENT, AND FLEXIBILITY

After the technology sector, the changes that have taken place in the accounting profession over the past 15 years are unparalleled in any other industry. Accountants are now key members of the strategic planning team, and no longer the back-room bean counters of yesterday.

In Canada, KPMG International, a global firm providing tax, audit, and advisory services has worked hard to negotiate the changing accounting landscape. KPMG's roots date back to 1840; today, the company has offices in 35 communities across Canada, generating revenues of about $886 million. The professional staff number around 5,000; positions at the firm are highly sought after—not just in Canada, but in all the 148 countries it services.

To stay on top, KPMG organizes for high performance and staffs its business with talented professionals committed to excellence. KPMG's client services are organized into multidisciplinary teams, each team is focused on individual industry sectors designed to better serve every client's business. KPMG's organization is clearly a hybrid as it uses a client-centred industry sector while still providing key product services such as auditing, tax and consulting. For example, KPMG's audit practice helps clients manage risk by first thoroughly understanding their business and then converting that information into insights to improve client competence and performance.

Leadership at KPMG also recognizes the design challenges of matching the career opportunities of the new workplace with the diversity of today's generation of university graduates. Look under the career section at the KPMG Canadian website, and find the section for university students, "campus recruiting." The recruitment section also has a strong emphasis on the values of the company, stating, "What really sets KPMG apart is our shared set of values—our values define us as a firm and help to maintain our status as leaders in terms of the services we provide and the industries we serve." These values include, working together, bringing out the best in each other, respect, challenging assumptions, open and honest communication, a commitment to community, being a responsible corporate citizen, and acting with integrity.

KPMG knows that "one style doesn't fit all," and obviously values a good fit between its employees and the firm. By doing so, it keeps talent a main source of competitive advantage, and having good people allows KPMG to adapt to the changing times and to keep their clients satisfied.[1]

GET CONNECTED!

Could your career be in professional services? Find out more about KPMG and firms like it. Web surfing for career options can be time well spent.

Chapter 11 LEARNING PREVIEW

The example of KPMG shows how top organizations pay attention to the special interests of prospective employees. The message is that the firm will be adaptable and will do its best to fit work opportunities to the goals of talented persons. In this chapter you will learn about contingency factors in organizational design, including environment, strategy, technology, size and life cycle, and people. You will also learn the major design differences between bureaucratic and adaptive organizations, the dynamics of differentiation and integration in subsystems design, and the concept of process re-engineering as an approach to work process design.

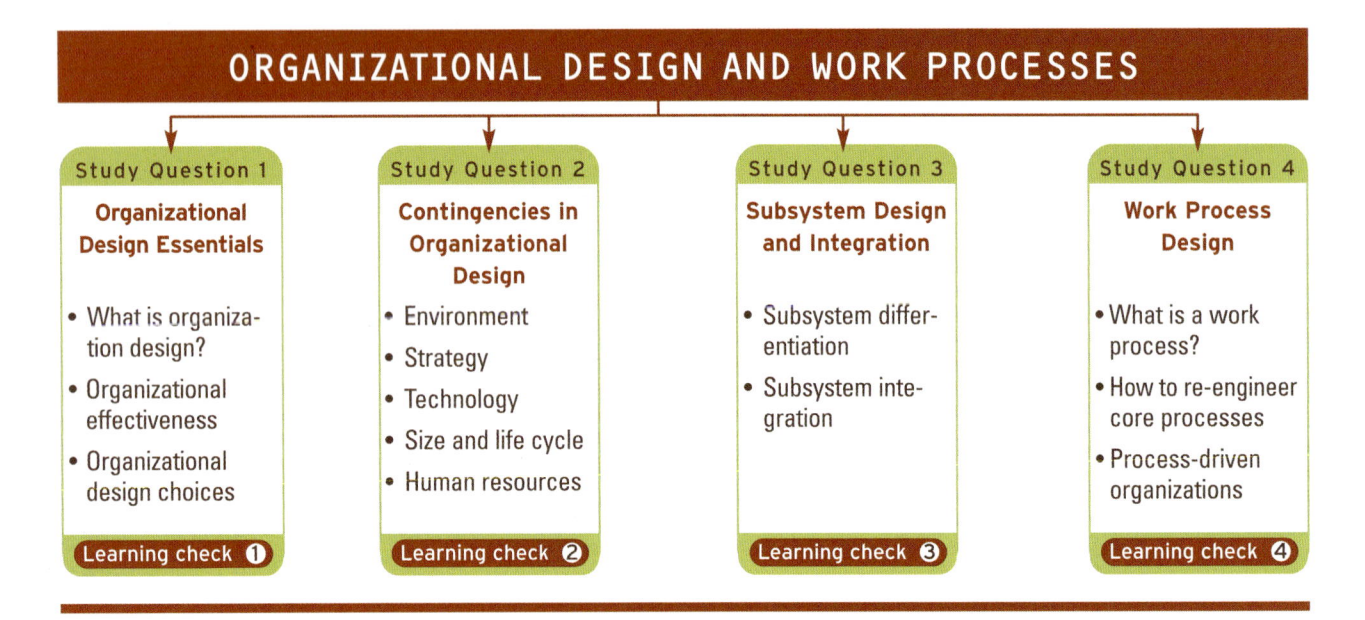

ORGANIZATIONAL DESIGN AND WORK PROCESSES

Study Question 1 — Organizational Design Essentials
- What is organization design?
- Organizational effectiveness
- Organizational design choices

Learning check 1

Study Question 2 — Contingencies in Organizational Design
- Environment
- Strategy
- Technology
- Size and life cycle
- Human resources

Learning check 2

Study Question 3 — Subsystem Design and Integration
- Subsystem differentiation
- Subsystem integration

Learning check 3

Study Question 4 — Work Process Design
- What is a work process?
- How to re-engineer core processes
- Process-driven organizations

Learning check 4

If you are in London, England, don't be surprised to find that St. Luke's isn't a church, it's an advertising agency. But it's also a unique one. Every employee is a part owner; a six-member board elected by staff members governs the company. Everyone's name is listed on the stationery—from the creative director to receptionist. The culture is informal, permeated by creativity. Workspaces are designed with common areas to maximize interaction and connectivity. Everyone focuses on great service to customers. One member of the firm describes working there as like "the difference between going to grade school and going to the university. At school the bell goes 'ding' and tells you what to do. We have no bell. Like the university, as long as you create great stuff, we don't care how you do it." You can expect this configuration—small in size and locally focused—to make St. Luke's quick, nimble, and creative.[2]

Now travel to Switzerland and visit the headquarters of Nestlé.[3] The global food giant has a product mix of beverages, ice cream, prepared foods, chocolates, pet care, and pharmaceuticals. It sells around the world—33 percent in the Americas, 32 percent in Europe, 17 percent in Asia and Africa, and 18 percent elsewhere. A stark contrast to St. Luke's in size and global reach, Nestlé might be described as one of the world's greatest organizational design challenges. CEO Peter Brabeck-Letmathe, a 35-year career veteran of the firm, recently reorganized in an attempt to boost profits and improve focus in its worldwide operations. In the past, the firm was decentralized into national companies. The new structure reconfigures them into three world regions, with the goal of gaining more co-operation and greater efficiencies. A corporate IT initiative supports the new structure, linking employees worldwide in a knowledge management and information system. In Nestlé's competitive environment, just as with St. Luke's, success depends on the ability to continuously achieve integration, empowerment, and flexibility.

Organizations everywhere are adjusting to best meet new competitive demands. Changing times require flexible and well-integrated organizations that can deliver high-quality products and services while still innovating for sustained future performance. Traditional structures are being flattened, networks are being developed, IT is being utilized, and decision making is being moved to the points where knowledge exists. The goals are clear—improved teamwork, more creativity, shorter product development cycles, better customer service, and higher performance overall. Yet, organizations still face widely varying problems and opportunities. There is no one best way to structure and manage them. The key to success is finding the best design to master the unique situational needs and challenges for each organization.[4]

ORGANIZATIONAL DESIGN ESSENTIALS

Just as organizations vary in size and type, so too do the variety of problems and opportunities that they face. This is why they use the different types of structures described in Chapter 10—from the traditional functional, divisional, and matrix structures, to the team and network structures, and even beyond to the boundaryless organization. It is why they change structures to try to best fit the demands of new circumstances in a dynamic environment. And it is why we see more and more organizations trying to operate in ways that improve problem solving and flexibility—more sharing of tasks, reduced emphasis on hierarchy, greater emphasis on lateral communication, more teamwork, and more decentralization of decision making and empowerment. An example of this organizational flexibility is DBG Canada Limited. DBG is a major supplier of automotive, heavy truck, and value-added metal assembly industries operating out of Mississauga, Ontario. The company has associates, not employees, who are building dynamic relationships with customers. Flexibility, problem solving, and effective empowerment has resulted in the company gaining the reputation as a company able to "turn on a dime."[5]

●●● WHAT IS ORGANIZATIONAL DESIGN?

Organizational design is the process of choosing and implementing structures that best arrange resources to accomplish the organization's mission and objectives.[6] Because every organization faces its own set of unique problems and opportunities, the best design at any moment is the one that achieves a good match between structure and situation. As shown in *Figure 11.1*, this includes taking into consideration the implications of environment, strategies, people, technology, and size.[7] The process of organizational design is thus a problem-solving activity, one that should be approached in a contingency fashion that takes all of these factors into account. There is no universal design that applies in all circumstances. The goal is to achieve a best fit between structure and the unique situation faced by each organization.

■ **Organizational design** is the process of creating structures that accomplish the organization's mission and objectives.

● ● ● ORGANIZATIONAL EFFECTIVENESS

■ **Organizational effectiveness** is sustainable high performance in accomplishing the mission and objectives.

The ultimate goal of organizational design should be to achieve **organizational effectiveness**—sustainable high performance in using resources to accomplish the mission and objectives. Theorists view and analyze organizational effectiveness from different perspectives.[8] The *systems resource approach* looks at the input side and defines effectiveness in terms of success in acquiring needed resources from the organization's environment. The *internal process approach* looks at the transformation process and examines how efficiently resources are utilized to produce goods and/or services. The *goal approach* looks at the output side to measure achievement of key operating objectives. And the *strategic constituencies approach* looks to the environment to analyze the impact of the organization on key stakeholders and their interests. Although they point in different directions, each of these approaches offers a framework for assessing how well an actual or proposed design is working.

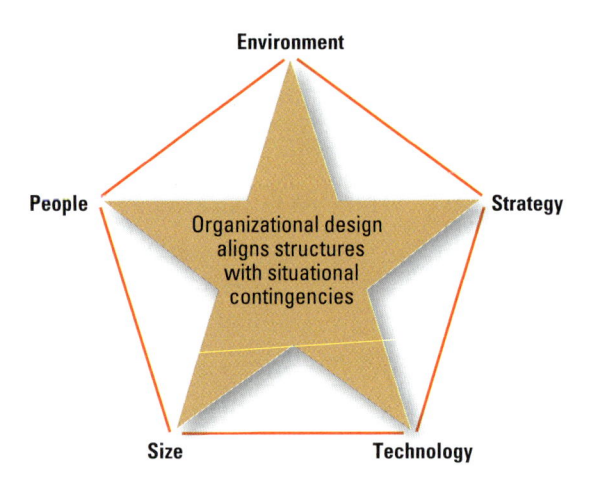

Figure 11.1 A framework for organizational design—aligning structures with situational contingencies.

Environment • Strategy • Technology • Size • People

Organizational design aligns structures with situational contingencies

Organizational effectiveness can also be evaluated according to specific criteria that set important performance benchmarks over time.[9] In the short run, the criteria focus on performance effectiveness in goal accomplishment and performance efficiency in resource utilization, as well as stakeholder satisfaction—including customers, employees, owners, and society at large. In the medium term, two more criteria become important: adaptability in the face of changing environments, and development of people and systems to meet new challenges. And in the long run, the effectiveness criterion is survival under conditions of uncertainty. For example, at the same time that Quebec-based Groupe Germain opened its first boutique hotel in Toronto, the tourist industry was hit by the unexpected SARS outbreak. Management recognized that their proposed strategy needed to change in order to adapt to the pressing environmental challenge. Rather than do things "in-house" with salaried employees, the company outsourced and made use of subcontractors for many necessary tasks. This internal process approach helped manage the company's cash flow with positive results; the family business survived and is now looking to expand its Ontario operations.[10]

Any organizational design should advance organizational effectiveness. Although there is no one universal design that applies in all circumstances, this does not mean that a given design—one in use or proposed—shouldn't be rigorously evaluated. In fact, quite the opposite applies. A design is a matter of choice, and that choice can be for the better or for the worse. Managers as decision makers need to make good organizational design choices; they need to make them with the goal of organizational effectiveness always in mind; and they need to make them with the assistance of an analytical framework that helps them sort through the many design alternatives that exist. In organization theory, these alternatives are broadly framed in the distinction between bureaucratic designs at one extreme and adaptive designs at the other.

ORGANIZATIONAL DESIGN CHOICES

As first introduced in the discussion on historical foundations of management in Chapter 2, a **bureaucracy** is a form of organization based on logic, order, and the legitimate use of formal authority. Its distinguishing features include a clear-cut division of labour, strict hierarchy of authority, formal rules and procedures, and promotion based on competency. According to sociologist Max Weber, bureaucracies were supposed to be orderly, fair, and highly efficient.[11] In short, they were a model form of organization. Yet if you use the term "bureaucracy" today, it may well be interpreted with a negative connotation. If you call someone a "bureaucrat," it may well be considered an insult. Instead of operating efficiently, the bureaucracies that we know are often associated with "red tape"; instead of being orderly and fair, they are often seen as cumbersome and impersonal to the point of insensitivity to customer or client needs. And the bureaucrats? Don't we assume that they work only according to rules, diligently following procedures and avoiding any opportunities to take initiative or demonstrate creativity?

Research recognizes that there are limits to bureaucracy, particularly in their tendencies to become unwieldy and rigid.[12] Instead of viewing all bureaucratic

■ A **bureaucracy** emphasizes formal authority, order, fairness, and efficiency.

take it to the case!

World-class entrepreneur places his "BET" on the future

It takes an entrepreneur to start a business, but it takes quality people and the right design to keep it running ... and growing. Robert Johnson, founder of BET Holdings II, Inc. knows that for sure and the company that he founded is the first American-African company to provide quality television programming, entertainment products, publishing, and Internet services specifically designed to appeal to African-American interests. The company owns and operates four television networks, including BET cable network, BET Films, a film production house, BET Event Productions and BET.com, the top African-American Internet portal. The company sold Arabesque Books, its line of African-American romance novels, to Harlequin, Inc. in 2005. In November 2000, Johnson sold BET Holdings to Viacom for $3 billion. He stayed on as chairman and CEO of BET till early 2006 when he officially ended his employment with the company that he founded more than 25 years ago.

Source: Information from "BET.com Ranked #1 in Unique Visitors Among African American Sites," PR Newswire (June 6, 2000); <www.Bet.com>, and <www.viacom.com>

structures as inevitably flawed, however, management theory asks the contingency questions: (1) When is a bureaucratic form a good choice for an organization? (2) What alternatives exist when it is not a good choice?

Pioneering research conducted in England during the early 1960s by Tom Burns and George Stalker helps answer these questions.[13] After investigating 20 manufacturing firms, they concluded that two quite different organizational forms could be successful, depending on the nature of a firm's external environment. A more bureaucratic form, which Burns and Stalker called *mechanistic*, thrived when the environment was stable. But it experienced difficulty when the environment was rapidly changing and uncertain. In these dynamic situations, a much less bureaucratic form, called *organic*, performed best. *Figure 11.2* portrays these two approaches as opposite extremes on a continuum of organizational design alternatives.

Mechanistic Designs

■ A **mechanistic design** is centralized with many rules and procedures, a clear-cut division of labour, narrow spans of control, and formal coordination.

Organizations with more **mechanistic designs** are highly bureaucratic in nature. As shown in the figure, they typically operate with more centralized authority, many rules and procedures, a precise division of labour, narrow spans of control, and formal means of coordination. Mechanistic designs are described as "tight" structures of the traditional vertical or pyramid form.[14] For a good example, visit your local fast-food restaurant. A relatively small operation, each store operates quite like others in the franchise chain and according to rules established by the corporate management. You will notice that service personnel work in orderly and disciplined ways, guided by training, rules and procedures, and close supervision by crew leaders who work alongside them. Even their appearances are carefully regulated, with everyone working in a standardized uniform. These restaurants perform well as they repetitively deliver items that are part of their standard

Figure 11.2 A continuum of organizational design alternatives—from bureaucratic to adaptive organizations.

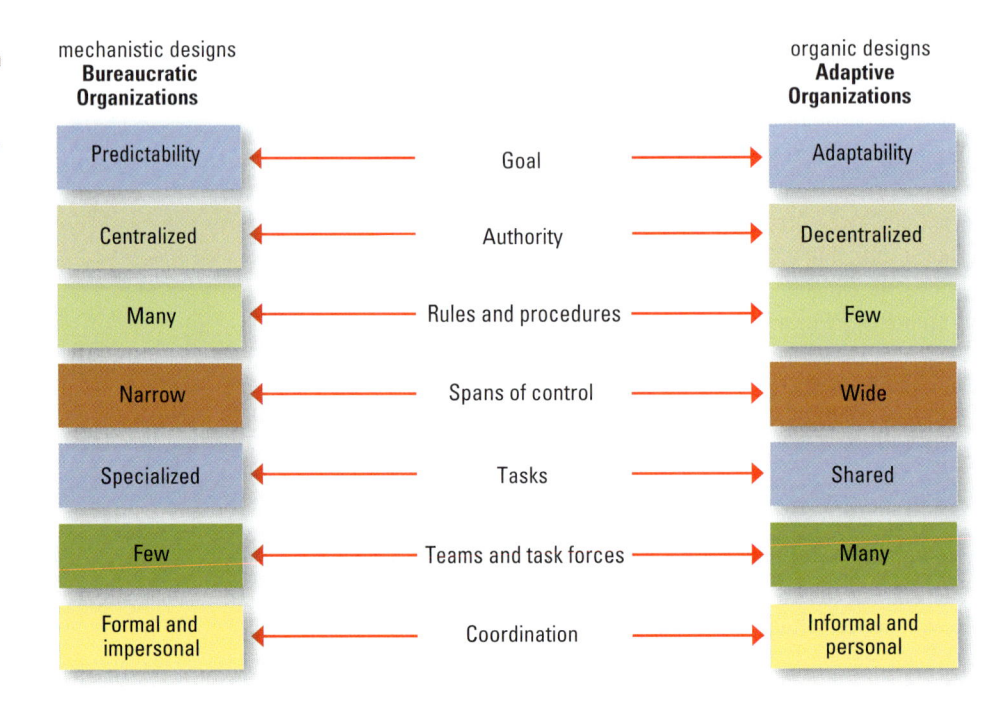

mechanistic designs **Bureaucratic Organizations**		organic designs **Adaptive Organizations**
Predictability	Goal	Adaptability
Centralized	Authority	Decentralized
Many	Rules and procedures	Few
Narrow	Spans of control	Wide
Specialized	Tasks	Shared
Few	Teams and task forces	Many
Formal and impersonal	Coordination	Informal and personal

menus. You quickly encounter the limits, however, if you try to order something not on the menu. The chains also encounter difficulty when consumer tastes change or take on regional preferences that are different from what the corporate menu provides. Adjustments to the system take a long time.

The limits of mechanistic designs and their tight vertical structures are especially apparent in organizations that must operate in dynamic, often uncertain, environments. It's hard, for example, to find a technology company, consumer products firm, financial services business, or dot.com retailer that isn't making continual adjustments in operations and organizational design. Things keep changing on them, and organizational effectiveness depends on being able to change with the times. Mechanistic designs find this hard to do.

Organic Designs

Dee Hock, the founder of Visa International, says: "We can't run 21st-century society with 17th-century notions of organization."[15] Harvard scholar and consultant Rosabeth Moss Kanter notes that the ability to respond quickly to shifting environmental challenges often distinguishes successful organizations from less successful ones:

> *The organizations now emerging as successful will be, above all, flexible; they will need to be able to bring particular resources together quickly, on the basis of short-term recognition of new requirements and the necessary capacities to deal with them…The balance between static plans—which appears to reduce the need for effective reaction—and structural flexibility needs to shift toward the latter.*[16]

The trend is toward **organic designs**, as portrayed in Figure 11.2, having more decentralized authority, fewer rules and procedures, less precise division of labour, wider spans of control, and more personal means of coordination. These create more **adaptive organizations** that operate with horizontal structures and with cultures that encourage worker empowerment and teamwork. They are described as relatively loose systems in which a lot of work gets done through informal structures

■ An **organic design** is decentralized with fewer rules and procedures, open divisions of labour, wide spans of control, and more personal coordination.

■ An **adaptive organization** operates with a minimum of bureaucratic features and encourages worker empowerment and teamwork.

Canadian Managers
Unique Artistry Becomes Booming Industry

By taking chances and staying true to his artistic vision, Guy Laliberté has transformed Cirque du Soleil from the group of street performers he founded in 1984 to an international business and cultural phenomenon. Under Laliberté's guidance as CEO, Cirque du Soleil has reinvented and revolutionized the circus arts. By 2006, it had five permanent and seven touring shows, including a Las Vegas premiere of its 13th production based on the music of the Beatles, and a show in Niagara Falls. The business employs more than 3,000 people worldwide, including 900 artists. Since 1984, the Cirque has performed for more than 50 million spectators. Its touring shows have made 250 stops in more than 100 cities. And, the business has branched out with Cirque du Soleil Images, a multimedia division, and Cirque du Soleil Musique, a recording company. It is also targetting another niche—merchandising and licensing.

Sources: Information from <www.cirquedusoleil.com>. Matthew Hays, "Goodbye big top, hello arena," *The Globe and Mail*, January 23, 2006. Brigitte Bélanger, Department of Foreign Affairs and International Trade, April 14, 1999.

and networks of interpersonal contacts.[17] Organic designs work well for organizations facing dynamic environments that demand flexibility in dealing with changing conditions. They are also increasingly popular in the new workplace, where the demands of total quality management and competitive advantage place more emphasis on internal teamwork and responsiveness to customers.

Above all, adaptive organizations are built upon a foundation of trust that people will do the right things on their own initiative. They move organizational design in the direction of what some might call *self-organization*, where the focus is on freeing otherwise capable people from unnecessarily centralized control and restrictions. Moving toward the adaptive form means letting workers take over production scheduling and problem solving; it means letting workers set up their own control systems; it means letting workers use their ideas to improve customer service. In the ultimately adaptive organizations, it means that members are given the freedom to do what they can do best—get the job done. This helps create what has been described in earlier chapters as a **learning organization**, one designed for continuous adaptation through problem solving, innovation, and learning.[18]

■ A **learning organization** is designed for continuous adaptation through problem solving, innovation, and learning.

✓ Learning check ❶

BE SURE YOU CAN
• define the terms organizational design and organizational effectiveness • explain alternative approaches and criteria for evaluating organizational effectiveness • differentiate the characteristics of bureaucratic designs and adaptive designs • discuss the implications of the Burns and Stalker study for organizational design • illustrate the types of situations in which the mechanistic design and the organic design work best

CONTINGENCIES IN ORGANIZATIONAL DESIGN

Good organizational design decisions should result in supportive structures that satisfy situational demands and advance organizational effectiveness. This is true contingency thinking. Among the contingency factors in the organizational design checklist featured in *Manager's Notepad 11.1* are the environment, strategy, technology, size and life cycle, and human resources.

●●● ENVIRONMENT

The organization's external environment and the degree of uncertainty it offers are of undeniable importance in organizational design.[19] A *certain environment* is composed of relatively stable and predictable elements. As a result, an organization can succeed with relatively few changes in the goods or services produced or in the manner of production over time. Bureaucratic organizations and mechanistic designs are quite adequate under such conditions. An *uncertain environment* will have more dynamic and less predictable elements. Changes occur frequently and may catch decision makers by surprise. As a result, organizations must be flexible and responsive over relatively short time horizons. This requires more adaptive organizations and organic designs. *Figure 11.3* summarizes these relationships, showing how increasing uncertainty in organizational environments calls for more horizontal and adaptive designs.

Due to uncertainty, especially around international tariffs, forestry is a tough industry to be in these days. Still, Hayes Forest Services Ltd., a full service forest services company operating from Duncan, B.C., is doing well and outperforming its competitors by "embracing the challenge of change." In an industry facing many

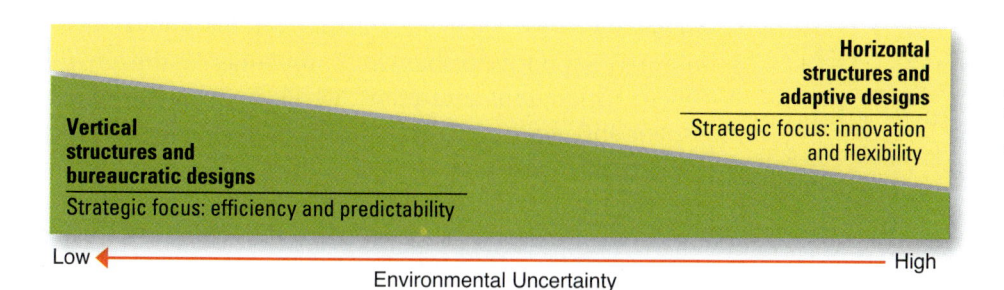

Figure 11.3 Environmental uncertainty and the performance of vertical and horizontal designs.

transformations, Hayes has become innovative by making the company a "one-stop" supplier, and by focusing on new approaches to doing old things, such as helicopter logging. Working successfully in an uncertain environment has helped make them one of the 50 best-managed companies in Canada.[20]

STRATEGY

The nature of organizational strategies and objectives is an important design contingency. Research on these contingency relationships is often traced to the pioneering work of Alfred Chandler Jr., who analyzed the histories of DuPont, General Motors, Sears, and Standard Oil.[21] Chandler's conclusion that "structure follows strategy" is a key element of organizational design. An organization's structure must support its strategy if the desired results are to be achieved.[22]

When strategy is stability oriented, the choice of organizational design is based on the premise that little significant change will be occurring in the external environment. This means that plans can be set and operations programmed to be routinely implemented. To best support this strategic approach, the organization should be structured to operate in well-defined and predictable ways. This is most characteristic of bureaucratic organizations that use more mechanistic design alternatives.

When strategy is growth oriented and when strategy is likely to change frequently, the situation as a whole becomes more complex, fluid, and uncertain. Operating

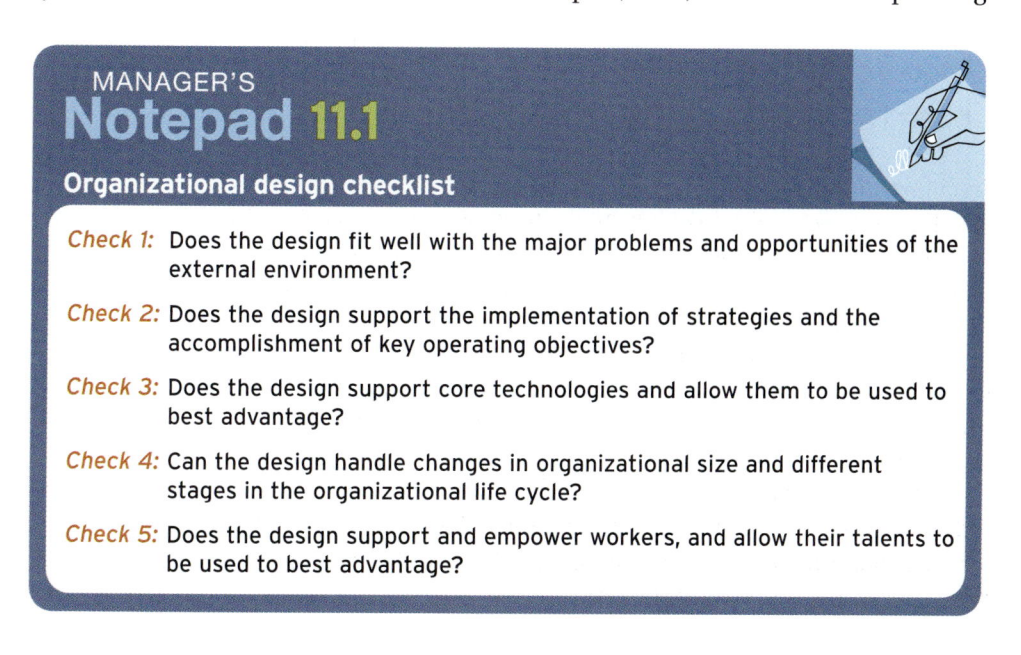

MANAGER'S Notepad 11.1

Organizational design checklist

Check 1: Does the design fit well with the major problems and opportunities of the external environment?

Check 2: Does the design support the implementation of strategies and the accomplishment of key operating objectives?

Check 3: Does the design support core technologies and allow them to be used to best advantage?

Check 4: Can the design handle changes in organizational size and different stages in the organizational life cycle?

Check 5: Does the design support and empower workers, and allow their talents to be used to best advantage?

> **PERSONAL MANAGEMENT**
>
> It is easy to make decisions when you have perfect information. But in the new world of work, you will often face unstructured problems and have to make decisions with incomplete information under uncertain conditions. Depending on your **TOLERANCE FOR AMBIGUITY**, you may be comfortable or uncomfortable dealing with these new realities. It takes personal flexibility and lots of confidence to cope well with unpredictability. Some people have a hard time dealing with the unfamiliar. They prefer to work with directions that minimize ambiguity and provide clear decision-making rules; they like the structure of mechanistic organizations with bureaucratic features. Other people are willing and able to perform in less structured settings that give them lots of flexibility in responding to changing situations; they like the freedom of organic organizations designed for adaptation. You must find a good fit between your personal preferences and the nature of the organizations in which you choose to work. To achieve this fit, you have to both know yourself and be able to read organizational cultures and structures. And whatever your tolerance for ambiguity may be, the best time to explore these issues of person–organization fit is now, before you take your first or next job.
>
> **Get to know yourself better**
> Complete Self-Assessments #16—**Turbulence Tolerance Test**, and #17—**Organizational Design Preferences**, from the Workbook and Personal Management Activity #11 from the companion website.

objectives are likely to include the need for innovation and flexible responses to changing competition in the environment. Operations and plans are likely to have short life spans and require frequent and even continuous modification over time. The most appropriate structure is one that allows for internal flexibility and freedom to create new ways of doing things. This is most characteristic of the empowerment found in adaptive organizations using more organic design alternatives.

SkyWave Mobile Communication Inc. is an organic organization that has revolutionized the tracking of ships and trucks with their DMR-200 series, the world's first D+ satellite terminal with an integrated antenna and scripting capability for fixed and mobile asset tracking, monitoring, and control. This innovative Canadian company is a market leader partially because they partner with other solution providers worldwide for mutual benefit. They are a flexible company.[23]

●●● TECHNOLOGY

Technology is the combination of knowledge, skills, equipment, computers, and work methods used to transform resource inputs into organizational outputs. It is the way tasks are accomplished using tools, machines, techniques, and human know-how. The availability of appropriate technology is a cornerstone of productivity, and the nature of the core technologies in use must be considered in organizational design.

In the early 1960s, Joan Woodward conducted a study of technology and structure in over 100 English manufacturing firms. She classified core *manufacturing technology* into three categories.[24] In **small-batch production**, such as a racing bicycle shop, a variety of custom products are tailor-made to order. Each item, or batch of items, is made somewhat differently to fit customer specifications. The equipment used may not be elaborate, but a high level of worker skill is often needed. In **mass production**, the organization produces a large number of uniform products in an assembly-line system. Workers are highly dependent on one another, as the product passes from stage to stage until completion. Equipment may be sophisticated, and workers often follow detailed instructions while performing simplified jobs. Organizations using continuous-process production are highly automated. They produce a few products by continuously feeding raw materials—such as liquids, solids, and gases—through a highly automated production system with largely computerized controls. Such systems are equipment intensive, but can often be operated by a relatively small labour force. Classic examples are automated chemical plants, steel mills, oil refineries, and power plants.

Woodward found that it was imperative to have the right combination of structure and technology to achieve organizational success. The best small-batch

■ **Technology** includes equipment, knowledge, and work methods that transform inputs into outputs.

■ **Small-batch production** manufactures a variety of products crafted to fit customer specifications.

■ **Mass production** manufactures a large number of uniform products with an assembly-line system.

and **continuous-process production** plants in her study had more flexible organic structures; the best mass-production operations had more rigid mechanistic structures. The implications of this research have become known as the *technological imperative*: technology is a major influence on organizational structure.

The importance of technology for organizational design applies in services as well as manufacturing, although the core *service technologies* are slightly different.[25] In health care, education, and related services, an **intensive technology** focuses the efforts of many people with special expertise on the needs of patients or clients. In banks, real-estate firms, insurance companies, employment agencies, and others like them, a **mediating technology** links together parties seeking a mutually beneficial exchange of values—typically a buyer and seller. Finally, a **long-linked technology** can function like mass production, where a client is passed from point to point for various aspects of service delivery.

■ In **continuous-process production** raw materials are continuously transformed by an automated system.

■ **Intensive technology** focuses the efforts and talents of many people to serve clients.

■ **Mediating technology** links together people in a beneficial exchange of values.

■ In **long-linked technology** a client moves from point to point during service delivery.

■ In the **organizational life cycle** an organization passes through different stages from birth to maturity.

●●● SIZE AND LIFE CYCLE

Typically measured by number of employees, organizational size is another contingency factor in organizational design.[26] Although research indicates that larger organizations tend to have more mechanistic structures than smaller ones, it is also clear that this is not always best for them.[27] In fact, a perplexing managerial concern is that organizations tend to become more bureaucratic as they grow in size, and consequently have more difficulty adapting to changing environments. It is especially important to understand the design implications of the **organizational life cycle**, or the evolution of an organization over time through different stages of growth.

The appeal of a biological life-cycle model is obvious. It explains that organizations are born, attempt to grow using many different forms, and eventually die. The theoretical underpinning of this model is primarily deterministic in that it describes organizations as passing from one stage to the next over time.

CANADIAN COMPANY IN THE NEWS | **Imperial Oil**

ORGANIZED GROWTH LEADS TO OIL RICHES

In 1880, the merging of 16 southwestern Ontario oil refiners led to the creation of the Imperial Oil Company Limited. Since that time, Imperial Oil has been a major contributor to the petroleum industry's growth. Its landmark discovery of oil at Leduc, Alberta signalled the beginning of the modern Canadian petroleum industry. The company also pioneered development of the Alberta oil sands through its role in the creation of Syncrude and the development of large-scale, in-situ bitumen recovery at Cold Lake. With initiatives like these, Imperial has become one of the largest producers of crude oil in Canada, a major producer of natural gas, the largest refiner and marketer of petroleum products, and a significant presence in the petrochemical industry. It distributes more than 700 products through a Canada-wide network of approximately 2,100 Esso service stations, 295 commercial bulk plants, and 30 distribution terminals. All of this could only be achieved through effective organizational design.

Source: Information from <www.imperialoil.ca>

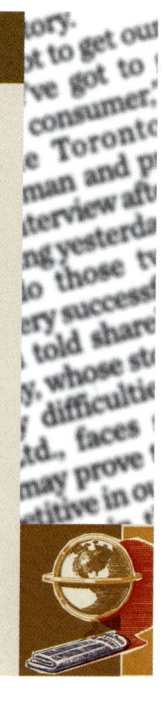

Larry Greiner's work provides the basic foundations for the life cycle of any organization. He looked at both evolutionary and revolutionary factors that influence organizational development. He proposed that growing organizations move through five distinct stages of development. Each phase is characterized by a relatively calm period of growth followed by a management crisis that, in turn, ushers in the next phase. The cycle is as follows:[28]

1. Growth through creativity, followed by a crisis of leadership;
2. Growth through direction, followed by a crisis of autonomy;
3. Growth through delegation, followed by a crisis of control;
4. Growth through coordination, followed by a crisis of red tape;
5. Growth through collaboration; followed by a crisis of psychological saturation among employees.

The last crisis may be resolved by using new structures and programs that allow employees the opportunity to periodically rest, reflect, and revitalize themselves.

Another approach to life cycle follows a four-staged model. The stages in the organizational life cycle can be described as follows:

1. *Birth stage*—when the organization is founded by an entrepreneur.
2. *Youth stage*—when the organization starts to grow rapidly.
3. *Mid-life stage*—when the organization has grown large with success.
4. *Maturity stage*—when the organization stabilizes at a large size.[29]

In its *birth stage* the founder usually runs the organization. It stays relatively small, and the structure is quite simple. The organization starts to grow rapidly during the *youth stage*, and management responsibilities extend among more people. Here, the simple structure begins to exhibit the stresses of change. An organization in the *mid-life stage* is even larger, with a more complex and increasingly formal structure. More levels appear in the chain of command, and the founder may have difficulty remaining in control. In the *maturity stage*, the organization stabilizes in size, typically with a mechanistic structure. It runs the risk of becoming complacent and slow in competitive markets. Bureaucratic tendencies toward stability may lead an organization at this stage toward decline. Steps must be taken to counteract these tendencies and provide for needed creativity and innovation.

One way of coping with the disadvantages of a large organization is *downsizing*; that is, taking actions to reduce the scope of operations and number of employees. This response is often used when top management is challenged to reduce costs quickly and increase productivity.[30] But, perhaps more significantly, good managers in many organizations find unique ways to overcome the disadvantages of large size before the crisis of downsizing hits. They are creative in fostering **intrapreneurship**, described in Chapter 6 as the pursuit of entrepreneurial behaviour by individuals and subunits within large organizations.[31] They also find ways for smaller entrepreneurial units to operate with freedom and autonomy within the larger organizational framework. **Simultaneous systems**, for example, are organizations that utilize both mechanistic and organic designs to meet the need for production efficiency and continued innovation. This "loose–tight" concept in organizational design is depicted in *Figure 11.4*.

■ **Intrapreneurship** is entrepreneurial behaviour by individuals and subunits within large organizations.

■ In **simultaneous systems** mechanistic and organic designs operate together in an organization.

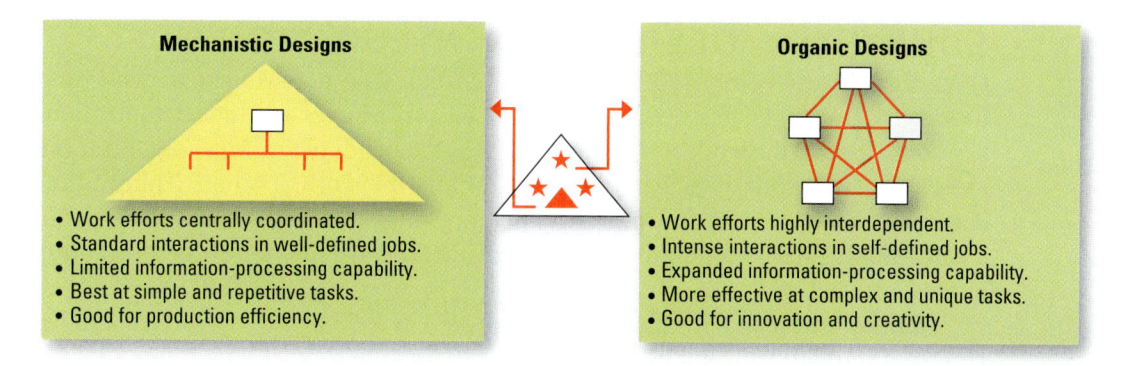

Mechanistic Designs
- Work efforts centrally coordinated.
- Standard interactions in well-defined jobs.
- Limited information-processing capability.
- Best at simple and repetitive tasks.
- Good for production efficiency.

Organic Designs
- Work efforts highly interdependent.
- Intense interactions in self-defined jobs.
- Expanded information-processing capability.
- More effective at complex and unique tasks.
- Good for innovation and creativity.

Figure 11.4 Simultaneous "loose-tight" properties of team structures support efficiency and innovation.

It is important to note that researchers have found that an opposite, or non-deterministic, life-cycle model of organizations also exists. With this model it is important to view the organization's development as a general growth and decline rather than a life cycle. Key to understanding organizational life cycles is an appreciation of how activities and structure will change over time as organizations try to match internal activities to changes in external conditions. A life cycles theory forms a road map, identifying critical transitional points for organizations and the pitfalls they should seek to avoid as they grow in size and complexity.

●●●● HUMAN RESOURCES

Another contingency factor in organizational design is people—the human resources that staff the organization for action. A good organizational design provides people with the supporting structures they need to achieve both high performance and satisfaction in their work. Modern management theory views people-structure relationships in a contingency fashion. The prevailing argument is that there should be a good "fit" between organizational structures and the human resources.[32]

An important human resource issue in organizational design is skill. Any design should allow the expertise and talents of organizational members to be unlocked and utilized to the fullest. Especially in the age of information and knowledge workers, high-involvement organic designs with their emphasis on empowerment are crucial. When IBM purchased the software firm Lotus, for example, the intention was to turn it into a building block for the firm's networking business. But Lotus was small, and IBM was huge. The whole thing had to be carefully handled or IBM might lose many of the talented people who created the popular LotusNotes and related products. The solution was to adapt the design to fit the people. IBM gave Lotus the space it needed to retain the characteristics of a creative software house. Said the firm's head of software at the time: "You have to keep the people, so you have to ask yourself why it is they like working there."[33]

> **BE SURE YOU CAN**
>
> • explain the contingency relationships between strategy and organizational design • differentiate among small-batch production, mass production, and continuous-process production • differentiate among intensive, mediating, and long-linked technologies in service industries • explain the concept of simultaneous systems and the loose–tight concept in organizational design
>
> ✓ Learning check ❷

SUBSYSTEM DESIGN AND INTEGRATION

■ A **subsystem** is a work unit or smaller component within a larger organization.

Organizations are composed of **subsystems**, such as a department or work unit headed by a manager, that operate as smaller parts of a larger and total organizational system. Ideally, the work of subsystems serves the needs of the larger organization. Ideally, too, the work of each subsystem supports the work of others. Things don't always work out this way, however. Another challenge of organizational design is to create subsystems and coordinate relationships so that the entire organization's interests are best met.

Important research in this area was reported in 1967 by Paul Lawrence and Jay Lorsch of Harvard University.[34] They studied 10 firms in three different industries—plastics, consumer goods, and containers. The firms were chosen because they differed in performance. The industries were chosen because they faced different levels of environmental uncertainty. The plastics industry was uncertain; the containers industry was more certain; the consumer goods industry was moderately uncertain. The results of the Lawrence and Lorsch study can be summarized as follows.

First, the total system structures of successful firms in each industry matched their respective environmental challenges. Successful plastics firms in uncertain environments had more organic designs; successful container firms in certain environments had more mechanistic designs. This result was consistent with the earlier research by Burns and Stalker already discussed in this chapter.[35] Second, Lawrence and Lorsch found that subsystem structures in the successful firms matched the challenges of their respective subenvironments. Subsystems within the successful firms assumed different structures to accommodate the special problems and opportunities of their operating situations. Third, the researchers found that subsystems in the successful firms worked well with one another, even though they were also very different from one another.

AROUND THE WORLD

Family firm builds a global future around customer service

In the competitive arena of business strategy, Enterprise Rent-a-Car has achieved success by pursuing a market that its rivals chose to ignore—renting cars to people whose cars are being serviced or out of commission because of accidents. Started in St. Louis by Jack Taylor in 1957, the privately held company is now bigger than Hertz and Avis. Its 500,000-vehicle fleet is run through some 5,000 offices by 50,000 employees spread around North America and now gaining ground in Europe as well. Current chairman and CEO Andy Taylor says his father built the company around a culture devoted to customer service and satisfaction. The culture is backed by staff selection and extensive training to put the right people in the field. And the Enterprise design ensures effectiveness by blending decentralization of operations with central control. Each branch gets a financial statement and customer satisfaction score every month. Says Taylor: "Our branch managers know exactly how well they did. They've got their bottom line."

Source: Information from Simon London, "Enterprise Drives Home the Service Ethic," *Financial Times* (June 2, 2003), p. 7.

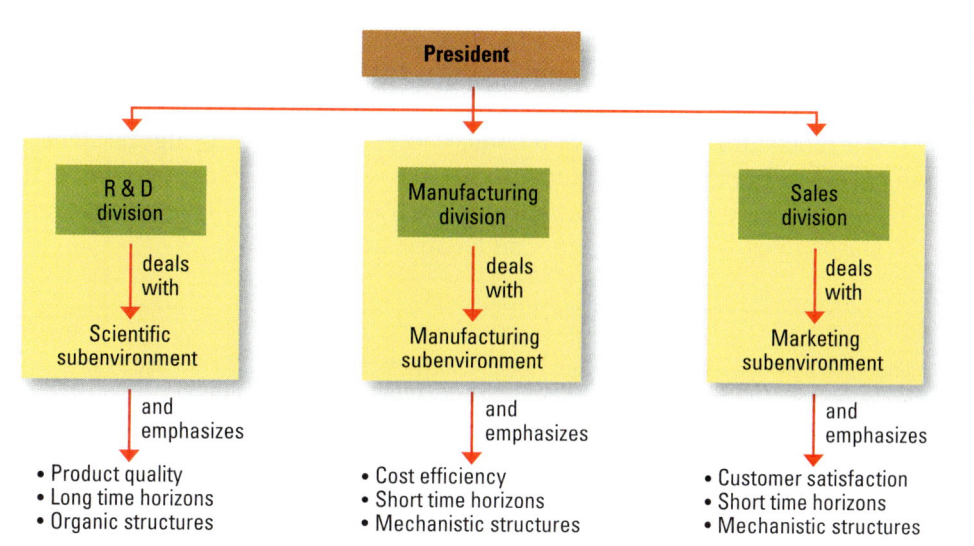

Figure 11.5 Subsystem differentiation among research and development (R&D), manufacturing, and sales divisions.

```
                        President
         ┌─────────────────┼─────────────────┐
         ▼                 ▼                 ▼
      R & D           Manufacturing         Sales
     division           division          division
       │                   │                  │
   deals with         deals with         deals with
       ▼                   ▼                  ▼
   Scientific         Manufacturing        Marketing
  subenvironment     subenvironment     subenvironment
       │                   │                  │
       and                 and                and
   emphasizes          emphasizes         emphasizes
       ▼                   ▼                  ▼
• Product quality    • Cost efficiency   • Customer satisfaction
• Long time horizons • Short time horizons • Short time horizons
• Organic structures • Mechanistic structures • Mechanistic structures
```

SUBSYSTEM DIFFERENTIATION

Figure 11.5 depicts operating differences among three divisions in one of the firms studied by Lawrence and Lorsch. It shows how research and development, manufacturing, and sales subunits operate differently in response to unique needs. This illustrates **differentiation**, which is the degree of difference that exists between the internal components of the organization.

There are four common *sources of subsystem differentiation*. First, the subsystems may have *differences in time orientation*. In a business firm, for example, the manufacturing subsystem may have a shorter-term outlook than does the research and development group. These differences can make it difficult for personnel from the two units to work well together. Second, the different tasks assigned to work units may also result in *differences in objectives*. For example, cost-conscious production managers and volume-conscious marketing managers may have difficulty agreeing on solutions to common problems. Third, *differences in interpersonal orientation* can affect subsystem relations. To the extent that patterns of communication, decision making, and social interaction vary, it may be harder for personnel from different subsystems to work together. And fourth, *differences in formal structure* can also affect subsystem behaviours. Someone who is used to flexible problem solving in an organic setting may find it very frustrating to work with a manager from a mechanistic setting who is used to strict rules.

■ **Differentiation** is the degree of difference between subsystems in an organization.

SUBSYSTEM INTEGRATION

The term **integration** in organization theory refers to the level of coordination achieved among an organization's internal components. Organizational design involves the creation of both differentiated structures and appropriate integrating mechanisms. A basic *organizational design paradox*, however, makes this a particularly challenging managerial task. Increased differentiation among organizational subsystems creates the need for greater integration; however, integration becomes harder to achieve as differentiation increases.

■ **Integration** is the level of coordination achieved between subsystems in an organization.

Manager's Notepad 11.2 identifies several mechanisms for achieving subsystem integration.[36] Integrating mechanisms that rely on vertical coordination and the use of authority relationships work best when differentiation is low. They include use of rules and procedures, hierarchical referral, and planning. Integrating mechanisms that emphasize horizontal coordination and improved lateral relations work better when differentiation is high.[37] They include the use of direct contact between managers, liaison roles, task forces, teams, and matrix structures.

> ✓ **Learning check 3**
>
> **BE SURE YOU CAN**
> • explain the difference between a system and a subsystem • define the terms differentiation and integration • discuss the implications of the Lawrence and Lorsch study for subsystem design • illustrate how subsystem differentiation might operate in a typical business • list several ways to improve subsystem integration in organizations

---

MANAGER'S Notepad 11.2

How to improve subsystem integration

- *Rules and procedures:* Clearly specify required activities.
- *Hierarchical referral:* Refer problems upward to a common superior.
- *Planning:* Set targets that keep everyone headed in the same direction.
- *Direct contact:* Have subunit managers coordinate directly.
- *Liaison roles:* Assign formal coordinators to link subunits together.
- *Task forces:* Form temporary task forces to coordinate activities and solve problems on a timetable.
- *Teams:* Form permanent teams with the authority to coordinate and solve problems over time.
- *Matrix organizations:* Create a matrix structure to improve coordination on specific programs.

WORK PROCESS DESIGN

From the emphasis on subsystems integration and more cross-functional collaboration in organizational design has come a popular development known as business **process re-engineering**.[38] This is defined by consultant Michael Hammer as the systematic and complete analysis of work processes and the design of new and better ones.[39] The goal of a re-engineering effort is to focus attention on the future, on customers, and on improved ways of doing things. It tries to break people and mindsets away from habits, preoccupation with past accomplishments, and tendencies to continue implementing old and outmoded ways of doing things. Simply put, re-engineering is a way of changing the way work is carried out in organizations.

■ **Process re-engineering** systematically analyzes work processes to design new and better ones.

WHAT IS A WORK PROCESS?

In his book *Beyond Reengineering*, Michael Hammer defines a **work process** as "a related group of tasks that together create a result of value for the customer."[40] They are the things people do to turn resource inputs into goods or services for customers. Hammer highlights the following key words in the implications of his definition: (1) *group*—tasks are viewed as part of a group rather than in isolation; (2) *together*—everyone must share a common goal; (3) *result*—the focus is on what is accomplished, not on activities; (4) *customer*—processes serve customers, and their perspectives are the ones that really count.

The concept of **workflow**, or the way work moves from one point to another in manufacturing or service delivery, is central to the understanding of processes.[41] The various parts of a work process must all be completed to achieve the desired results, and they must typically be completed in a given order. An important starting point for a re-engineering effort is to diagram or map these workflows as they actually take place. Then each step can be systematically analyzed to determine whether it is adding value, to consider ways of eliminating or combining steps, and to find ways to use technology to improve efficiency. At PeopleSoft, for example, paper forms are definitely out; the goal is to eliminate them as much as possible. Employees are even able to order their own supplies through a direct Web link to Office Depot. The firm's chief information officer once said: "Nobody jumps out of bed in the morning and says, 'I want to go to work and fill out forms.' We create systems that let people be brilliant rather than push paper."[42]

■ A **work process** is a related group of tasks that together create a value for the customer.

■ **Workflow** is the movement of work from one point to another in a system.

HOW TO RE-ENGINEER CORE PROCESSES

Given the mission, objectives, and strategies of an organization, business process re-engineering can be used to regularly assess and fine-tune work processes to ensure that they directly add value to operations. Through a technique called **process value analysis**, core processes are identified and carefully evaluated for their performance contributions. Each step in a workflow is examined. Unless a step is found to be important, useful, and contributing to the value added, it is eliminated. Process value analysis typically involves the following steps:[43]

■ **Process value analysis** identifies and evaluates core processes for their performance contributions.

1. Identify the core processes.
2. Map the core processes in respect to workflows.
3. Evaluate all tasks for the core processes.
4. Search for ways to eliminate unnecessary tasks or work.
5. Search for ways to eliminate delays, errors, and misunderstandings.
6. Search for efficiencies in how work is shared and transferred among people and departments.

Figure 11.6 shows an example of how re-engineering and better use of computer technology can streamline a purchasing operation. A purchase order should result in at least three value-added outcomes: order fulfillment, a paid bill, and a satisfied supplier. Work to be successfully accomplished includes such things as ordering, shipping, receiving, billing, and payment. A traditional business system might have

Figure 11.6 How re-engineering can streamline core business processes.

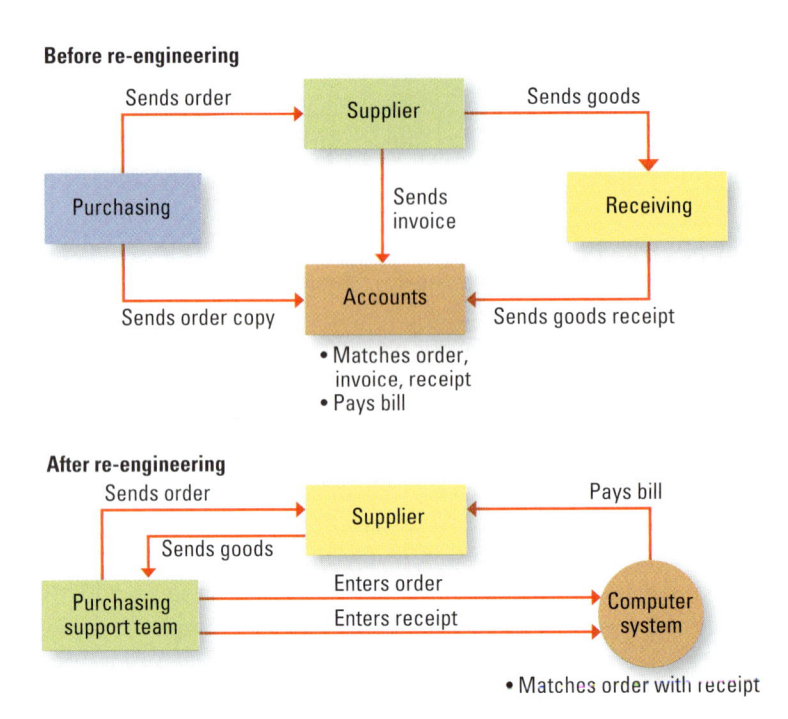

purchasing, receiving, and accounts payable as separate functions, with each communicating with each other and the supplier. Alternatively, process value analysis might result in re-engineering that designs a new purchasing support team whose members handle the same work more efficiently with the support of the latest computer technology.[44]

PROCESS-DRIVEN ORGANIZATIONS

Customers, teamwork, and efficiency are central to Hammer's notion of process re-engineering. He describes the case of Aetna Life & Casualty Company, where a complex system of tasks and processes once took as much as 28 days to accomplish.[45] Customer service requests were handled in step-by-step fashion by many different persons. After an analysis of workflows, the process was redesigned into a "one and done" format where a single customer service provider handled each request from start to finish. One of Aetna's customer account managers said after the change was made: "Now we can see the customers as individual people. It's no longer 'us' and 'them.'"[46]

Hammer also describes re-engineering at a unit of Verizon Communications. Before re-engineering, customer inquiries for telephone service and repairs required extensive consultation between technicians and their supervisors. After process value analysis, technicians were formed into geographical teams that handled their own scheduling, service delivery, and reporting. They were given cellular telephones and laptop computers to assist in managing their work, resulting in the elimination of a number of costly supervisory jobs. The technicians enthusiastically responded to the changes and opportunities. "The fact that you've got four or five people zoned in a certain geographical area," said one, "means that we get personally familiar with our customers' equipment and problems."[47]

The essence of process re-engineering is to locate control for processes with an identifiable group of people, and to focus each person and the entire system on meeting customer needs and expectations. It tries to eliminate duplication of work and systems bottlenecks to reduce costs, increase efficiency, and build capacity for change. Hammer describes the *process-driven organization* in the following words:

> *Its intrinsic customer focus and its commitment to outcome measurement make it vigilant and proactive in perceiving the need for change; the process owner, freed from other responsibilities and wielding the power of process design, is an institutionalized agent of change; and employees who have an appreciation for customers and who are measured on outcomes are flexible and adaptable.*[48]

BE SURE YOU CAN

• define the terms process re-engineering and work process • draw a map of the workflow in an organization familiar to you • explain how process value analysis can be used to streamline workflows and improve work performance

Learning check 4

Chapter 11 STUDY GUIDE

WHERE WE'VE BEEN

Back to KPMG

The opening example of KPMG International highlighted the importance of fitting organizational design with the people who intimately deliver high-performance outcomes. In Chapter 11 you learned the differences between bureaucratic and adaptive organizations, including the notions of mechanistic and organic designs. You also learned more about the concept of contingency thinking in management, with a special focus on how designs must successfully fit environment, strategy, technology, size and life cycle, and people. You also leaned about subsystem design and process re-engineering in organizations.

THE NEXT STEP
INTEGRATED LEARNING ACTIVITIES

Cases/Projects
- BET Holdings Case
- Project 10—Service Learning

Self-Assessments
- Turbulence Tolerance Test (#16)
- Organizational Design Preferences (#17)

Exercises in Teamwork
- Defining Quality (#3)
- What Would the Classics Say? (#4)
- Which Organization Culture Fits You? (#8)

STUDY QUESTION SUMMARY

1. What are the essentials of organizational design?
- Organizational design is the process of choosing and implementing structures that best use resources to serve the mission and purpose.
- Bureaucratic organizational designs are vertical and mechanistic; they work best for routine and predictable tasks.
- Adaptive organizational designs are horizontal and organic; they perform best in conditions requiring change and flexibility.

2. How do contingency factors influence organizational design?
- Environment, strategy, technology, size, and people are all contingency factors influencing organizational design.
- Certain environments lend themselves to vertical and mechanistic organizational designs; uncertain environments require more horizontal and adaptive organizational designs.
- Technology—including the use of knowledge, equipment, and work methods in the transformation process—is an important consideration in organizational design.
- Although organizations tend to become more mechanistic as they grow in size, design efforts must be used to allow for innovation and creativity in changing environments.

3. What are the major issues in subsystem design?
- Organizations are composed of multiple subsystems that must work well together.

- Differentiation is the degree of difference that exists between various subsystems; integration is the level of coordination achieved among them.
- As organizations become more highly differentiated, they have a greater need for integration, but as differentiation increases, integration is harder to accomplish.
- Low levels of differentiation can be integrated through authority relationships and vertical organizational designs.
- Greater differentiation requires more intense integration through horizontal designs, with an emphasis on cross-functional teams and lateral relations.

4. How can work processes be re-engineered?

- A work process is a related group of tasks that together create value for a customer.
- Business process engineering is the systematic and complete analysis of work processes and the design of new and better ones.
- In process value analysis all elements of a process and its workflows are examined to identify their exact contributions to key performance results.
- Re-engineering eliminates unnecessary work-steps, combines others, and uses technology to gain efficiency and reduce costs.

KEY TERMS REVIEW

Adaptive organization (p. 285)
Bureaucracy (p. 283)
Continuous-process production (p. 289)
Differentiation (p. 293)
Integration (p. 293)
Intensive technology (p. 289)
Intrapreneurship (p. 290)
Learning organization (p. 286)

Long-linked technology (p. 289)
Mass production (p. 288)
Mechanistic design (p. 284)
Mediating technology (p. 289)
Organic design (p. 285)
Organizational design (p. 281)
Organizational effectiveness (p. 282)
Organizational life cycle (p. 289)

Process re-engineering (p. 294)
Process value analysis (p. 295)
Simultaneous systems (p. 290)
Small-batch production (p. 288)
Subsystem (p. 292)
Technology (p. 288)
Work process (p. 295)
Workflow (p. 295)

SELF-TEST 11

MULTIPLE-CHOICE QUESTIONS:

1. The bureaucratic organization described by Max Weber is similar to the _____ organization described by Burns and Stalker.
   (a) adaptive (b) mechanistic (c) organic (d) adhocracy
2. Teamwork, task forces, and empowerment are common in organizations operating with _____.
   (a) mechanistic designs (b) strict bureaucracy (c) vertical structures (d) organic designs
3. The production method characteristic of an oil refinery is an example of what Woodward referred to as _____ technology.
   (a) intensive (b) continuous-process (c) mass-production (d) small-batch
4. As organizations grow in size, they tend to become more _____ in design, although this is not always best for them.
   (a) mechanistic (b) organic (c) adaptive (d) simultaneous
5. A basic paradox in subsystem design is that as differentiation increases, the need for _____ also increases but is harder to accomplish.
   (a) cost efficiency (b) innovation (c) integration (d) transformation
6. A(n) _____ organizational design works best in _____ environments.
   (a) flexible, stable (b) adaptive, uncertain (c) mechanistic, dynamic (d) organic, certain
7. A simple structure tends to work well when an organization is in the _____ stage of its life cycle.
   (a) birth (b) mid-life (c) maturity (d) decline

8. When the members of a marketing department pursue sales volume objectives and those in manufacturing pursue cost efficiency objectives, this is an example of _____.
   (a) simultaneous systems (b) subsystems differentiation (c) long-linked technology (d) small-batch production
9. A work process is defined as a related group of tasks that together create value for _____.
   (a) shareholders (b) customers (c) workers (d) society
10. The first step in process value analysis is to _____.
    (a) look for ways to eliminate unnecessary tasks (b) map or diagram the workflows (c) identify core processes (d) look for efficiencies in transferring work among people and departments
11. In the _____ approach to organizational effectiveness, the focus is on how well an organization satisfies customers and external stakeholders.
    (a) systems resource (b) strategic constituencies (c) process re-engineering (d) goal
12. After the short-term criteria of performance effectiveness and efficiency are met, an organizational design should next satisfy the organizational effectiveness criteria of _____.
    (a) cost and quality control (b) stability and survival (c) adaptability and development (d) shareholder value and profit maximization
13. A traditional vertical structure is the most appropriate choice when an organization is pursuing a strategic focus on _____.
    (a) intrapreneurship (b) innovation (c) stability (d) flexibility
14. A small Web-design firm that creates one-of-a-kind websites for customers is an example of a _____ technology in Woodward's classification scheme.
    (a) small-batch (b) continuous-process (c) long-linked (d) mediating
15. The major situational contingencies that affect the choice of organizational design include strategy, size, environment, technology, and _____.
    (a) performance (b) people (c) differentiation (d) workflow

SHORT-RESPONSE QUESTIONS:

16. Explain the practical significance of this statement: "Organizational design should always be addressed in contingency fashion."
17. What difference does environment make in organizational design?
18. Describe the relationship between differentiation and integration as issues in subsystem design.
19. If you were a re-engineering consultant, how would you describe the steps in a typical approach to process value analysis?

APPLICATION QUESTION:

20. Two business women, former university roommates, are discussing their jobs and careers over lunch. You overhear one saying to the other: "I work for a large corporation. It is bureaucratic and very authority driven. However, I have to say that it is also very successful. I like working there." Her friend responded: "My, I wouldn't like working there at all. In my organization things are very flexible and the structures are loose. We have a lot of freedom and the focus on operations is much more horizontal than vertical. And we, too, are very successful." After listening to the conversation and using insights from management theory, how can these two very different "success stories" be explained?

12 Human Resource Management

CHAPTER 12 STUDY QUESTIONS

Planning Ahead

After reading Chapter 12, you should be able to answer these questions in your own words.

1. Why do people make the difference?
2. What is strategic human resource management?
3. How do organizations attract a quality workforce?
4. How do organizations develop a quality workforce?
5. How do organizations maintain a quality workforce?

DOFASCO
"TAKE CARE OF PEOPLE, THEY'LL TAKE CARE OF BUSINESS"

This is an often used line, but in the case of Dofasco, a Canadian steel producer located in Hamilton, Ontario, it really is true. Featured yearly among the 50 "best companies to work for," Dofasco has developed a successful strategy of not only watching the financial measures, but of also monitoring its impact on the environment and ensuring employee productivity and job satisfaction.

Many initiatives help to ensure its employees remain satisfied. Decision making has been put in the hands of line workers with the removal of middle management and the development of cross-functional teams with responsibility for quality control. As John Mayberry, Dofasco's retired CEO, states, "People can make a phenomenal difference if you can tap into them, if you stop telling them to come to work, put their brains in a box, and do whatever the supervisor says."

Training and leadership are also important, and the company is preparing for the skills shortage expected as the baby boom generation begins to retire by, among other things, emphasizing its apprenticeship program. Dofasco spends about $13 million a year on training and development.

What about employee health and safety? Dofasco is number one according to Canada's National Quality Institute (NQI), which gives out Healthy Workplace awards. At Dofasco, volunteers run wellness initiatives including workshops in back care, nutrition, yoga, relaxation techniques, and Tai Chi. The company has also decreased its lost time due to injuries from 7 hours for every 200,000 hours worked in 1991, to 2.34 hours in 2001.

Employees are also proud of how Dofasco works to make the broader community better. "They see how we behave in the community, and they see that it's consistent with the way we behave with them," states Mayberry. He further notes that the Company has earned its employees trust, and that the deep values of the company are clearly being carried out, not just within the company, but also out into the community.

Though small by comparison, the company has continued to outperform its major competitors. It seems that Dofasco's motto, "Our product is steel, our strength is people," really does ring true.[1]

GET CONNECTED!

Working in an environment where you feel appreciated and valued is important. Dofasco puts its people as its primary strength. With all the opportunities for advancing your career, maintaining your health, and giving back to the community, Dofasco is an employer of choice.

Chapter 12 LEARNING PREVIEW

Dofasco has made its mark in a highly competitive industry not only by focusing on financial and environmental measures, but through a concentrated and innovative approach to motivating their employees. By empowering their employees to make decisions and providing training and leadership opportunities, Dofasco's competitive strength is their people. In this chapter you will learn about the process of human resource management through which managers attract, develop, and maintain a talented workforce. You will also learn about the complex legal environment within which such human resource management decisions are made.

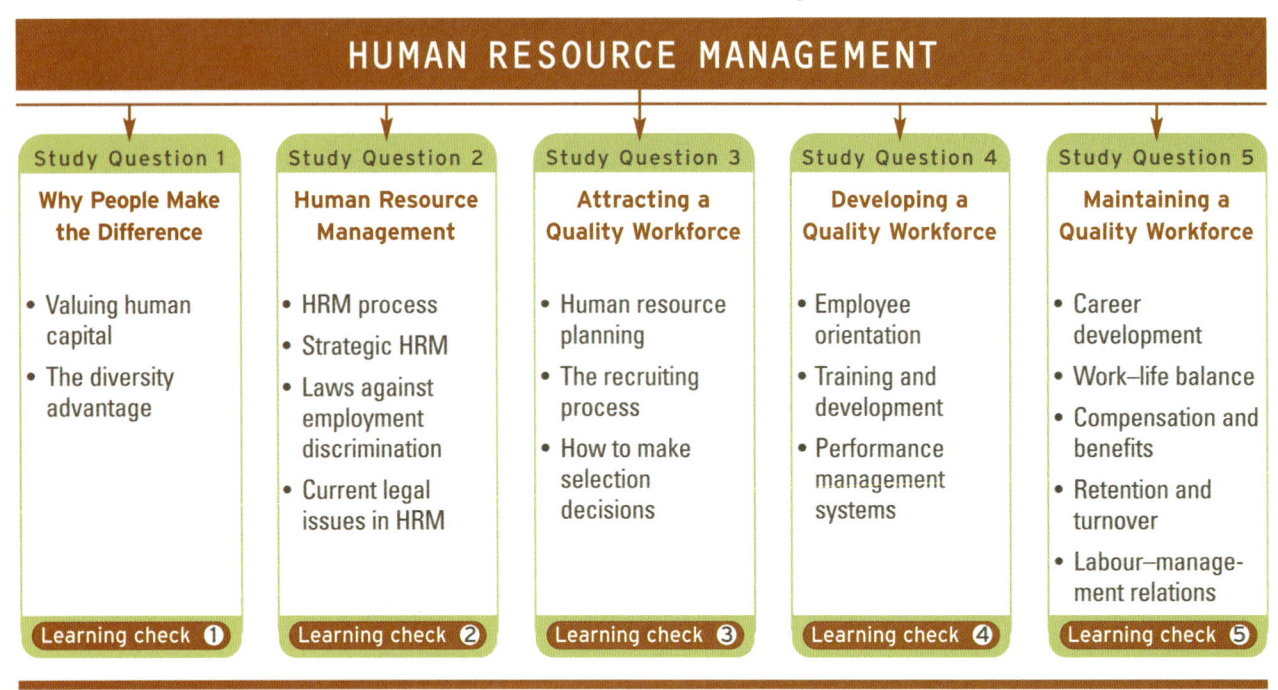

HUMAN RESOURCE MANAGEMENT

Study Question 1	Study Question 2	Study Question 3	Study Question 4	Study Question 5
Why People Make the Difference	**Human Resource Management**	**Attracting a Quality Workforce**	**Developing a Quality Workforce**	**Maintaining a Quality Workforce**
• Valuing human capital • The diversity advantage	• HRM process • Strategic HRM • Laws against employment discrimination • Current legal issues in HRM	• Human resource planning • The recruiting process • How to make selection decisions	• Employee orientation • Training and development • Performance management systems	• Career development • Work–life balance • Compensation and benefits • Retention and turnover • Labour–management relations
Learning check ❶	Learning check ❷	Learning check ❸	Learning check ❹	Learning check ❺

Today, perhaps more than ever before, the pressures of global competition and social change are influencing not just the organizations in which we work but the very nature of employment itself. In his book *The Future of Success*, Robert Reich calls this "the age of the terrific deal."[2] He also describes a shift away from a system in which people work loyally as traditional "employees" for "employers" who provide them career-long job and employment security.[3] In the emerging system we become sellers of our services (talents) to those buyers (employers) who are willing to pay for them. Those who do "buy" are looking for the very best people, whose capabilities and motivations match the demands of high-performance organizations. Reich is talking about changes to the **social contract**, or expectations of the employee-employer relationship. As today's organizations reconfigure around networks, teams, projects, flexibility, speed, and efficiency, the social contract is changing. For the individual, this means an emphasis on skills, responsibility, continuous learning, and mobility. For the organization, it means providing development opportunities, challenging work assignments, the best in resource support, and incentive compensation.[4]

■ The **social contract** reflects expectations in the employee-employer relationship.

All of this, of course, affects your future career. "Create a brand called 'You,'" "Build a portfolio of skills," "Protect your mobility," "Take charge of your destiny," "Add value to your organization," advise the career gurus.[5] The advice is on target, but the really tough question is, "Are you ready?" Test yourself by asking and answering these *career readiness questions*: Who am I? What do I want? What have I done? What do I know? What can I do? Why should someone hire me?

WHY PEOPLE MAKE THE DIFFERENCE

People have to be a top priority in any organization with high-performance aspirations. Testimonials like these say it all: "*People* are our most important asset"; "It's *people* who make the difference"; "It's the *people* who determine whether our company thrives or languishes." Found on websites, in annual reports, and in executive speeches, they communicate respect for people and the talents they bring to organizations.

VALUING HUMAN CAPITAL

A strong foundation of **human capital**—the economic value of people with job-relevant abilities, knowledge, experience, ideas, energies, and commitments—is essential to any organization's long-term performance success. Consider the strategic leadership implications of these comments made by Jeffrey Pfeffer in his book *The Human Equation: Building Profits by Putting People First*:[6]

■ **Human capital** is the economic value of people with job-relevant abilities, knowledge, ideas, energies, and commitments.

> *The key to managing people in ways that lead to profit, productivity, innovation, and real organizational learning ultimately lies in how you think about your organization and its people. ...When you look at your people, do you see costs to be reduced?...Or, when you look at your people do you see intelligent, motivated, trustworthy individuals—the most critical and valuable strategic assets your organization can have?*

In an *Academy of Management Executive* article entitled "Putting People First for Organizational Success," Jeffrey Pfeffer and John F. Veiga state: "There is a substantial and rapidly expanding body of evidence . . . that speaks to the strong connection between how firms manage their people and the economic results achieved."[7] They forcefully argue that organizations perform better when they treat their members better. The management practices associated with successful organizations are employment security, decentralization, use of teams, good compensation, extensive training, and information sharing.[8] James Baron and David Kreps also highlight the primacy of people in their book S*trategic Human Resources: Frameworks for General Managers*.[9] Stating that "human resources are key to organizational success or failure," they summarize empirical research showing a relationship between positive human resource policies and higher organizational performance.

THE DIVERSITY ADVANTAGE

The best employers and the best managers know that to succeed in today's challenging times they must place a primacy on people.[10] This means valuing diversity and being fully inclusive of all people with the talent and desire to do good work. Job-relevant talent is not restricted because of anyone's race, gender, religion, marital or parental status, sexual orientation, ethnicity, or other diversity characteristics. And anytime these characteristics interfere with finding, hiring, and utilizing the best employees, the loss will be someone else's gain.

Respect for people in all of their diversity is a major theme in the book *Proversity: Getting Past Face Value and Finding the Soul of People–A Manager's Journey,* by author and consultant Lawrence Otis Graham.[11] He suggests that managers committed to building high-performance work environments should take a simple test. The question is: which of the following qualities would you look for in anyone who works for you—work ethic, ambition and energy, knowledge, creativity, motivation, sincerity, outlook, collegiality and collaborativeness, curiosity, judgement and maturity, and integrity? In answering, you most likely selected all of these qualities, or at least you should have. The next test question is—where can you find people with these workplace qualities? The correct answer is, "everywhere."[12]

Canadian company Pelmorex Incorporated is known for being proactive in the field of equity and diversity. The company, which operates The Weather Network, won an Employment Equity Merit Award, presented by the Conference Board of Canada. The award recognizes "the importance of opening up the workplace to all our citizens, regardless of gender, race, culture or physical attributes."[13] Along with goals and policies, educational training, and outreach programs, many prominent on-air personalities form designated groups to deal with issues surrounding diversity in the workplace.

Diversity consultant and author R. Roosevelt Thomas puts the challenge this way: "Managers must find ways to get the highest level of contribution from their workers. And they will not be able to do that unless they are aware of the many ways that their understanding of diversity relates to how well, or how poorly, people contribute." Thomas goes further to identify what he calls the *diversity rationale* that must drive organizations today:

> To thrive in an increasingly unfriendly marketplace, companies must make it a priority to create the kind of environment that will attract the best new talent and will make it possible for employees to make their fullest contributions.[14]

Canadian Managers

Instilling Employee Pride

TD Bank Financial Group offers its employees an attractive compensation package, with competitive salaries and an employee stock purchase plan. But Teri Currie, executive vice-president of human resources, says that what makes TD's employees happiest is their pride in where they work, something she attributes to the bank's support of employee volunteerism. TD allows employees paid time off for volunteer activities. And, after volunteering with an organization for at least 40 hours in a year, employees can apply for a grant for the charity they support. "Our program allows them the flexibility in their schedule to be out in the community donating their time, and backing that activity up with corporate funding," says Currie. "Employees like to work for winning organizations, and winning organizations tend to create engaged employees, which produces results, which enhances shareholder value."

Source: Peter Evans, "Best Work Places 2006: Lessons from some of the best—TD Bank Financial Group," *Canadian Business,* April 10–23, 2006, p. 77.

> **BE SURE YOU CAN ✓ Learning check 1**
> • define the terms social contract and human capital • explain the logic behind this position: organizations perform better when they treat their people better • discuss how and why workforce diversity can be a source of performance advantage

HUMAN RESOURCE MANAGEMENT

A marketing manager at Ideo, an industrial design firm, once said: "If you hire the right people ... if you've got the right fit...then everything will take care of itself."[15] It really isn't quite that simple, but one fact of management remains very clear—if an organization doesn't have the right people available to do the required work, it has very little chance of long-term success.

●●● HUMAN RESOURCE MANAGEMENT PROCESS

The process of **human resource management**, or HRM, involves attracting, developing, and maintaining a talented and energetic workforce. The basic goal of human resource management is to build organizational performance capacity by raising human capital, and to ensure that highly capable and enthusiastic people are always available. The three major responsibilities of human resource management are as follows:

■ **Human resource management** is the process of attracting, developing, and maintaining a high-quality workforce.

1. *Attracting a quality workforce*—involves human resource planning as well as employee recruitment and selection.

2. *Developing a quality workforce*—involves employee orientation, training and development, and performance appraisal.

3. *Maintaining a quality workforce*—involves career development, work–life balance, compensation and benefits, retention and turnover, and labour–management relations.

The area of human resource management provides many career opportunities. HRM departments are common in most organizations. HRM specialists are increasingly important in an environment complicated by legal issues, labour shortages, economic turmoil, changing corporate strategies, changing personal values, new expectations, and more. As outsourcing of professional services becomes more popular, a growing number of firms provide specialized HRM services such as recruiting, compensation, outplacement, and the like. The Canadian Council of Human Resources Associations (CCHRA) is the result of the collaborative efforts of 10 provincial and specialist human resources associations that currently represent the interests of more than 30,000 professionals across Canada.[16] One of the more dynamic members is the Human Resources Professionals Association of Ontario (HRPAO). The mission of the organization is to set standards and enhance the profession while ensuring its membership is updated on the ever changing field of human resources.

●●● STRATEGIC HUMAN RESOURCE MANAGEMENT

All organizations, at all times, need to have the right people available to do the work required to achieve and sustain competitive advantage. Today, this challenge is increasingly addressed by making the human resources function an integral component of strategic management. **Strategic human resource management** mobilizes

■ **Strategic human resource management** mobilizes human capital to implement organizational strategies.

PERSONAL MANAGEMENT

PROFESSIONALISM! The code of ethics of the Human Resources Professionals Association of Ontario (www.hrpao.com) suggests the HR professional should meet the following requirements:

1. *Competence*   HR practitioners must maintain competence in carrying out professional responsibilities and ensure that services provided are within the limits of their knowledge, experience, and skill.
2. *Legal Requirements*   Adhere to any statutory acts, regulations, or by-laws that relate to the field of Human Resources Management as well as to all civil and criminal laws, regulations and statutes that apply in their jurisdiction.
3. *Dignity in the Workplace*   Support, promote, and apply the principles of human rights, equity, dignity, and respect in the workplace, within the profession, and in society as a whole.
4. *Balancing Interests*   Strive to balance organizational and employee needs and interests in the practice of their profession.
5. *Confidentiality*   Hold in strict confidence all confidential information acquired in the course of the performance of their duties and not divulge confidential information unless required by law.
6. *Conflict of Interest*   Avoid or disclose a potential conflict of interest that might influence or might be perceived to influence personal actions or judgements.
7. *Professional Growth and Support of Other Professionals*   Maintain personal and professional growth in Human Resources Management by engaging in activities that enhance the credibility and value of the profession.
8. *Enforcement*   The Canadian Council of Human Resources Associations works collaboratively with its Member Associations to develop and enforce high standards of ethical practice.

Get to know yourself better

Complete Self-Assessment #18—**Are You Cosmopolitan?**, and #19—**Performance Appraisal Assumptions**, from the Workbook and Personal Management Activity #12 on the companion website.

---

human capital through the HRM process to best implement organizational strategies.[17] One indicator that the HRM process is truly strategic to the organization is when the HRM function is headed by a senior executive reporting directly to the chief executive officer. When Robert Nardelli took over as CEO of Home Depot, for example, the first person he hired into the senior executive suite was Denis Donovan, who became the firm's executive vice-president for human resources. Donovan says, "CEOs and boards of directors are learning that human resources can be one of your biggest game-changers in terms of competitive advantage."[18] The strategic importance of HRM has been further accentuated by the spate of corporate ethics scandals. "It was a failure of people and that isn't lost on those in the executive suite," says Susan Meisinger, president of the Society for Human Resource Management.[19]

●●● LAWS AGAINST EMPLOYMENT DISCRIMINATION

Discrimination in employment occurs when someone is denied a job or a job assignment for reasons that are not job relevant. The *Canadian Human Rights Act* makes it illegal for employers to discriminate in hiring, promotion, and termination of employment based on prohibited grounds. A sample of major grounds on which discrimination is prohibited is provided in *Figure 12.1*. In Canada, federal legislation often provides the framework for provinces and municipalities when drafting their own legislation, which may vary slightly from province to province. These acts provide for the right to employment without regard to race, colour, national origin, religion, gender, age, or physical and mental ability. The intent is to ensure all citizens the right to gain and keep employment based only on their ability to do the job and their performance once on the job. Each provincial human rights commission has the power to impose remedies on organizations that do not provide a timely resolution to any discrimination charges brought against them. For example, the British Columbia Human Rights Tribunal has the power to order an organization to cease the discriminatory behaviour; make available the right, opportunity, or privilege that was denied; compensate for any wages lost or any expenses incurred; and provide damages for injury to feelings and self-respect.[20]

Figure 12.1 A sample of prohibited grounds of employment discrimination in Canadian provinces.

Prohibited Grounds for Discrimination	Provinces
Race or colour	All provinces
Religion	All provinces
Physical or mental disability	All provinces
Age if 18–64/65	All provinces except Ont., Que., and Man.
Sex (includes pregnancy and childbirth)	All provinces
Marital status	All provinces
Dependence on drugs/alcohol	All except Y.T. and N.W.T.
Family status	All except N.B. and N.L.
Sexual orientation	All except N.W.T.
National or ethnic origin	All except B.C. and Alta.
Ancestry or place of origin	Y.T., B.C., Alta., Man., Sask., N.W.T., Ont., N.B.
Language	Y.T., Ont., Que.
Social condition or origin	Que., N.L.
Source of income	Alta., Sask., Man., Que., P.E.I., N.S.
Political belief	Y.T., B.C., Man., Que., N.S., P.E.I., N.L.
Criminal conviction	Y.T., B.C., Que., P.E.I.
Pardoned conviction	B.C., N.W.T., Ont.

Source: <www.chrc-ccdp.ca>

Organizations are expected to show **employment equity** by giving preference in employment to four designated groups—Aboriginals, women, visible minorities, and people with physical/mental disability. The purpose of the *Employment Equity Act* is to "achieve equality in the workplace so that no person shall be denied employment opportunities or benefits for reasons unrelated to ability and, in the fulfillment of that goal, to correct the conditions of disadvantage in employment experienced by women, aboriginal peoples, persons with disabilities, and members of visible minorities by giving effect to the principle that employment equity means more than treating persons in the same way but also requires special measures and the accommodation of differences."[21] The *Employment Equity Act* applies to federal government departments and agencies, and to private sector employers that are governed by federal legislation, such as banks, broadcasters, and transportation companies, as well as Aboriginal band councils. Criticisms tend to focus on the use of group membership (e.g., female or minority status) as a criterion in employment decisions.[22] The issues raised include claims of reverse discrimination by members of majority populations. White males, for example, may claim that preferential treatment given to minorities in a particular situation interferes with their individual rights.

As a general rule, the *Canadian Human Rights Act* does not restrict an employer's right to establish **bona fide occupational** requirements. These are criteria for employment that can be clearly justified as being related to a person's capacity to perform a job. The use of bona fide occupational requirements based on race and colour is not allowed under any circumstances; those based on gender, religion, and age are very difficult to support.[23]

■ **Discrimination** occurs when someone is denied a job or job assignment for reasons not job relevant.

■ **Employment equity** is an effort to give preference in employment to Aboriginals, women, visible minorities, and people with physical/mental disability.

■ **Bona fide occupational requirements** are employment criteria justified by the capacity to perform a job.

●●● CURRENT LEGAL ISSUES IN HUMAN RESOURCE MANAGEMENT

All aspects of human resource management must be accomplished within the legal framework. Failure to do so is not only unjustified in a free society, it can also be a very expensive mistake resulting in fines and penalties. As a reminder, *Manager's Notepad 12.1* identifies questions that are considered illegal—or at least inappropriate—for an interviewer to ask during a job interview.[24] Of course, the Canadian legal and regulatory environment is constantly changing. A committed manager or human resource professional should always stay informed on the following and other issues of legal and ethical consequence.[25]

Sexual harassment occurs when people experience conduct or language of a sexual nature that affects their employment situation. Sexual harassment can be defined as behaviour that creates a hostile work environment, interferes with a person's ability to do a job, or interferes with their promotion potential. Organizations should have clear sexual harassment policies in place along with fair and equitable procedures for implementing them. Both the *Canadian Human Rights Act* and the Canada Labour Code protect employees from sexual harassment in the workplace.[26]

Pay equity provides that men and women in the same organization should be paid equally for doing equal work in terms of required skills, responsibilities, and

■ **Sexual harassment** is behaviour of a sexual nature that affects a person's employment situation.

MANAGER'S Notepad 12.1

Illegal, or inappropriate, (and acceptable questions) when interviewing a job candidate

- *Race:* No questions regarding race or colour are appropriate
- *Religion/creed:* No questions regarding religion or observance of religious holidays are appropriate. It is okay to ask if the shifts and days required will pose a problem.
- *National origin:* It is inappropriate to ask about ethnic origin or nationality. It is okay to ask if they are legally entitled to work in Canada.
- *Sex:* No questions regarding sexual orientation are appropriate.
- *Marital status:* May not ask about marital status or children. May ask if the travel and overtime expectations for the position will pose a problem.
- *Family planning:* No questions regarding present or future plans are allowed.
- *Age:* May not ask an applicant's age. May ask if they are between the ages of 18 and 65.
- *Arrest:* Inappropriate to ask if the applicant has ever been arrested. May ask if they have ever been convicted of a crime (relevant to job performance) for which they have not received a pardon.
- *Birthplace:* No questions regarding birthplace or the birthplace of parents or spouse.
- *Disability:* May not ask about specific disabilities. It is acceptable to ask if the applicant has any condition that could affect their ability to perform the major requirements of the job.

working conditions. But a lingering issue involving gender disparities in pay involves **comparable worth**, the notion that persons performing jobs of similar importance should be paid at comparable levels. Why should a long-distance truck driver, for example, be paid more than an elementary teacher in a public school? Does it make any difference that the former is a traditionally male occupation and the latter a traditionally female occupation? Advocates of comparable worth argue that such historical disparities are due to gender bias. They would like to have the issue legally resolved. Most provinces have three laws that address equal pay: a labour standards code, which applies to the private and public sectors; a human rights code addressing general discrimination; and a pay equity act, which applies to the broader civil service.[27]

> ■ **Comparable worth** holds that persons performing jobs of similar importance should be paid at comparable levels.

The legal status and employee entitlements of *part-time* workers and **independent contractors** are also being debated. In today's era of downsizing, outsourcing, and projects, more and more persons are hired as temporary workers who work under contract to an organization and do not become part of its permanent workforce. They work only "as needed." But, a problem occurs when they are engaged regularly by the same organization and become what many now call *permatemps*. Even though regularly employed, they work without benefits such as health coverage and pension eligibilities. A number of legal cases are now before the courts seeking to make such independent contractors eligible for benefits.

> ■ **Independent contractors** are hired on temporary contracts and are not part of the organization's permanent workforce, but they are also not covered under basic employment standards legislation.

Workplace privacy is the right of individuals to privacy on the job.[28] It is quite acceptable for employers to monitor the work performance and behaviour of their employees. But employer practices can become invasive and cross legal and ethical lines, especially with the capabilities of information technology. Computers can easily monitor emails and Internet searches to track personal and unauthorized usage; they can identify who is called by telephone and how long conversations last; they can document work performance moment to moment; and they can easily do more. All of this information, furthermore, can be stored in vast databases that make it available to others, even without the individual's permission. The legal status of such IT surveillance is being debated. Until things are cleared up, one consultant recommends the best approach for everyone is, "Assume you have no privacy at work."[29]

> ■ **Workplace privacy** is the right to privacy while at work.

> **BE SURE YOU CAN**
> • explain the human resource management process • define the terms discrimination, employment equity, and bona fide occupational requirement • explain arguments for and against employment equity • identify major laws that protect against discrimination in employment • discuss current legal issues of sexual harassment, comparable worth, and independent contractors

✓ Learning check ❷

ATTRACTING A QUALITY WORKFORCE

The first responsibility of human resource management is to attract to the organization a high-quality workforce. Lee Valley Tools, with stores in 11 Canadian cities, scrutinizes potential employees' belief systems before they are hired. Interviews at the company often consist of questions regarding character, respect, and trust. As founder Leonard Lee comments, "You can do almost anything with a person who has the right basic instincts, and you can do practically nothing with someone who doesn't."[30] To attract the right people to its workforce, an organization must first

HUMAN RESOURCE PLANNING

■ **Human resource planning** analyzes staffing needs and identifies actions to fill those needs.

Human resource planning is the process of analyzing an organization's human resource needs and determining how to best fill them. Effective and strategic human resource planning ensures that the best people are always in place when needed by the organization. The major elements in this process are shown in *Figure 12.2.*

Strategic human resource planning begins with a review of organizational mission, objectives, and strategies. This establishes a frame of reference for forecasting human resource needs and labour supplies. Ultimately, the planning process should help managers identify staffing requirements, assess the existing workforce, and determine what additions and/or replacements are required to meet future needs. GE Medical Systems uses a multi-generational staffing plan. For every new product plan there is a human resource plan associated with it—one that covers all generations of the product's anticipated life.[31]

■ **Job analysis** studies exactly what is done in a job, and why.

■ A **job description** details the duties and responsibilities of a job holder.

■ A **job specification** lists the qualifications required of a job holder.

The foundations for human resource planning are set by **job analysis**—the orderly study of job facts to determine just what is done, when, where, how, why, and by whom in existing or potential new jobs.[32] The job analysis provides useful information that can then be used to write and/or update **job descriptions.** These are written statements of job duties and responsibilities. The information in a job analysis can also be used to create **job specifications**. These are lists of the qualifications—such as education, prior experience, and skill requirements—needed by any person hired for, or placed in, a given job.

Figure 12.2 Steps in strategic human resource planning.

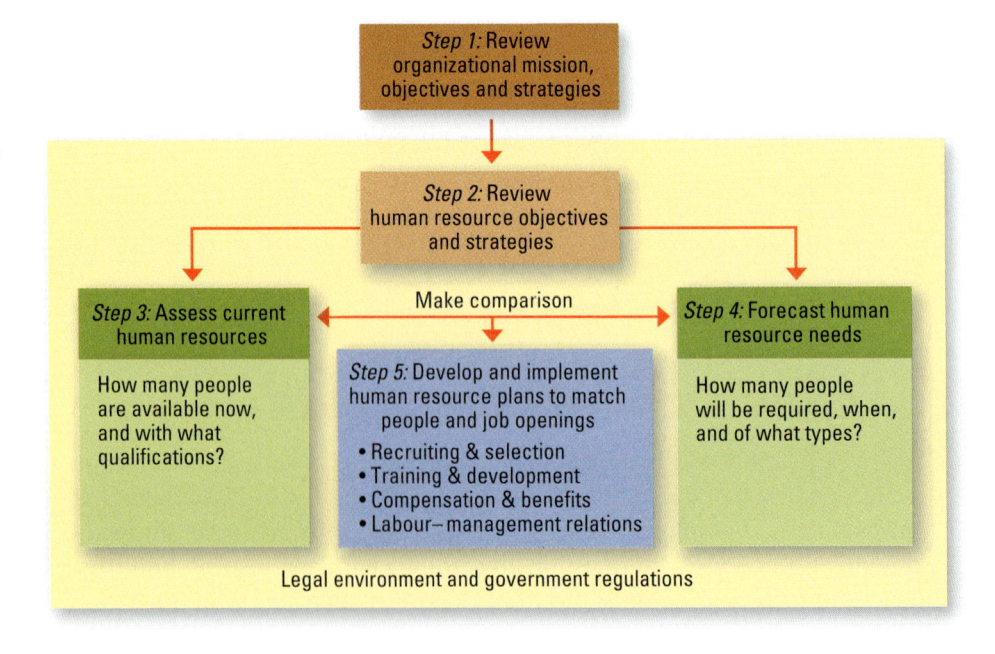

Step 1: Review organizational mission, objectives and strategies

Step 2: Review human resource objectives and strategies

Step 3: Assess current human resources
How many people are available now, and with what qualifications?

Make comparison

Step 4: Forecast human resource needs
How many people will be required, when, and of what types?

Step 5: Develop and implement human resource plans to match people and job openings
• Recruiting & selection
• Training & development
• Compensation & benefits
• Labour–management relations

Legal environment and government regulations

●●● THE RECRUITING PROCESS

Recruitment is a set of activities designed to attract a *qualified* pool of job applicants to an organization. Emphasis on the word "qualified" is important. Effective recruiting should bring employment opportunities to the attention of people whose abilities and skills meet job specifications. The three steps in a typical recruitment process are (1) advertisement of a job vacancy, (2) preliminary contact with potential job candidates, and (3) initial screening to create a pool of qualified applicants. In college and university recruiting, for example, advertising is done by the firm posting short job descriptions in print or online through campus placement centres. Preliminary contact involves a short 20- to 30-minute interview, during which the candidate presents a resumé and briefly explains his or her job qualifications. Successful candidates at this stage are usually invited for further interviews during a formal visit to the organization.

■ **Recruitment** is a set of activities designed to attract a qualified pool of job applicants.

External and Internal Recruitment

College and university recruiting is an example of *external recruitment* in which job candidates are sought from outside the hiring organization. Websites like workopolis.com and Monster.ca, newspapers, employment agencies, colleges, universities, technical training centres, personal contacts, walk-ins, employee referrals, and even persons in competing organizations are all sources of external recruits. Labour markets and recruiting are increasingly global in the new economy. When Nokia, the Finnish mobile-phone maker, needed high-tech talent, it posted all job openings on a website and received thousands of resumés from all over the world. The head of Nokia's recruiting strategy said, "There are no geographical boundaries anymore."[33]

Internal recruitment seeks applicants from inside the organization. For Pfizer Canada, the biggest recruiting challenge is finding individuals who fit in with the corporate culture. Pfizer emphasizes internal recruiting in order to identify candidates who not only have the technical skills required for the position, but who also have a demonstrated focus on performance and leadership flexibility that fits into their culture.[34] Most organizations have a procedure for announcing vacancies through newsletters, electronic bulletin boards, and the like. They also rely on managers to recommend subordinates as candidates for advancement. Internal recruitment creates opportunities for long-term career paths. Consider the story of Robert Goizueta, a former CEO of Coca-Cola. He made his way to the top over a 43-year career in the firm, an example of how loyalty and hard work can pay off.[35]

Both recruitment strategies offer potential advantages and disadvantages. External recruiting brings in outsiders with fresh perspectives. It also provides access to specialized expertise or work experience not otherwise available from insiders. Internal recruitment is usually less expensive. It also deals with persons whose performance records are well established. A history of serious internal recruitment also builds employees' loyalty and motivation, showing that one can advance by working hard and doing well when given responsibility.

Realistic Job Previews

In what may be called *traditional recruitment*, the emphasis is on selling the organization to job applicants. The emphasis is on the most positive features of the job and organization. Bias may even occur as the best features are exaggerated while negative features are avoided or even concealed. This form of recruitment may create unrealistic expectations that cause costly turnover when new hires become disillusioned and quit. The individual suffers a career disruption; the employer suffers lost productivity and the added costs of recruiting again.

The alternative is to provide **realistic job previews** that give candidates all the pertinent information about the job and organization without distortion and before the job is accepted.[36] Instead of "selling" only positive features, this approach tries to be open and balanced in describing the job and organization. Both favourable and unfavourable aspects are covered. The interviewer in a realistic job preview might use phrases such as: "Of course, there are some downsides…" "Things don't always go the way we hope…" "Something that you will want to be prepared for is…" "We have found that some new hires had difficulty with.…" This type of conversation helps the candidate establish "realistic" job expectations and better prepare for the inevitable "ups and downs" of a new job. Higher levels of early job satisfaction and less inclination to leave prematurely are among the expected benefits. At Prudential Grand Valley Realty in Kitchener, Ontario, Keith Church uses a job simulation to both attract quality applicants and make better hiring decisions. The online video-based assessment simulates the entire sales cycle, from building a rapport with the client all the way to closing the sale. The job simulation helps to evaluate the applicant on their ability to understand client needs, handle objections, and negotiate. It also allows the applicant to make a more informed decision, improving the fit between the candidate and the job.[37]

■ **Realistic job previews** provide job candidates with all pertinent information about a job and organization.

●●● HOW TO MAKE SELECTION DECISIONS

The process of **selection** involves choosing, from a pool of applicants, the person or persons who offer the greatest performance potential. Steps in a typical selection process are shown in *Figure 12.3*. They are (1) completion of a formal application form, (2) interviewing, (3) testing, (4) reference checks, (5) physical examination, and (6) final analysis and decision to hire or reject. The best employers exercise extreme care in making selection decisions, seeking the best fit between individual and organization.

■ **Selection** is choosing who to hire from a pool of qualified job applicants.

Application Forms

The application form declares the individual as a formal candidate for a job. It documents the applicant's personal history and qualifications. The personal resumé is often included with the job application. This important document should accurately summarize an applicant's special qualifications. As a job applicant, you should exercise great care in preparing your resumé for job searches. See the Student Portfolio section in the end-of-text *Management Learning Workbook* for advice. As a recruiter, you should also learn how to screen applications and resumés for insights that can help you make good selection decisions.

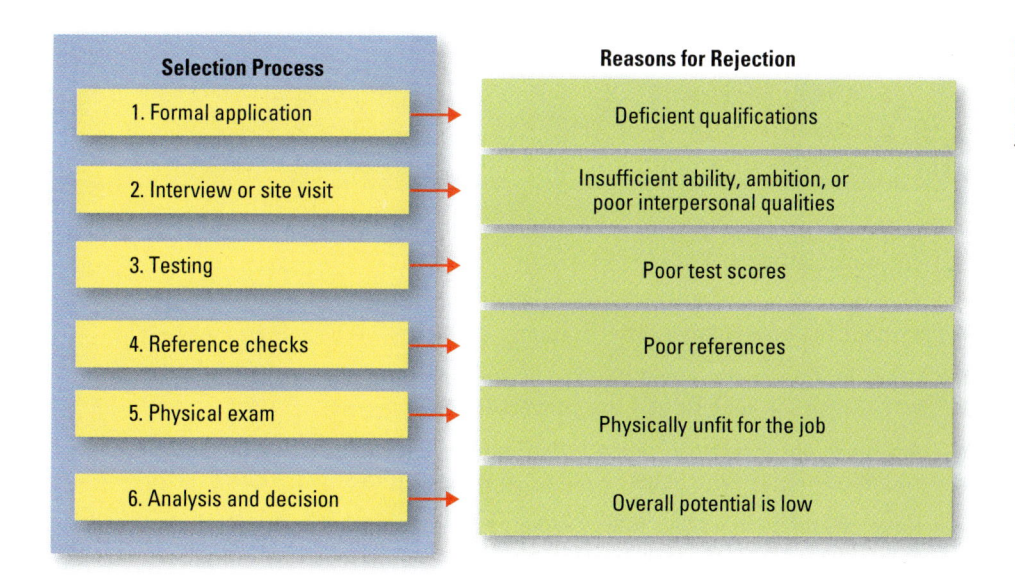

Figure 12.3 Steps in the selection process: the case of a rejected job applicant.

Selection Process	Reasons for Rejection
1. Formal application	Deficient qualifications
2. Interview or site visit	Insufficient ability, ambition, or poor interpersonal qualities
3. Testing	Poor test scores
4. Reference checks	Poor references
5. Physical exam	Physically unfit for the job
6. Analysis and decision	Overall potential is low

Interviews

Interviews are times in the selection process when both the job applicant and potential employer can learn a lot about one another. However, they can be difficult for both parties. Sometimes interviewers ask the wrong things, sometimes they talk too much, sometimes the wrong people do the interviewing, and sometimes their personal biases prevent an applicant's capabilities from being fully considered. Interviewees fail, too. They may be unprepared, they may be poor communicators, or they may lack interpersonal skills. An increasingly common and challenging interview setting for job applicants is highlighted in *Manager's Notepad 12.2*—the telephone interview.

Employment Tests

Testing is often used in the screening of job applicants. Some of the common employment tests are designed to identify intelligence, aptitudes, personality, and interests. Whenever tests are used, the goal should be to gather information that will help predict the applicant's eventual performance success. Like any selection device, tests should meet the criteria of reliability and validity. **Reliability** means that the device is consistent in measurement; it returns the same results time after time. **Validity** means that there is a demonstrable relationship between a person's score or rating on a selection device and his or her eventual job performance. In simple terms, validity means that a good test score really does predict good performance.

New developments in testing extend the process into actual demonstrations of job-relevant skills and personal characteristics. An **assessment centre** evaluates a person's potential by observing his or her performance in experiential activities designed to simulate daily work. A related approach is **work sampling**, which asks applicants to work on actual job tasks while being graded by observers on their performance. When Mercedes opened a new plant, it set up job-specific exercises to determine who had the best of the required skills and attitudes.[38] One was a

■ **Reliability** means a selection device gives consistent results over repeated measures.

■ **Validity** means scores on a selection device have demonstrated links with future job performance.

■ An **assessment centre** examines how job candidates handle simulated work situations.

■ In **work sampling** applicants are evaluated while performing actual work tasks.

> **MANAGER'S Notepad 12.2**
>
> **How to succeed in a telephone interview**
>
> - Be prepared ahead of time—study the organization, carefully list your strengths and capabilities.
> - Take the call in private—make sure you are in a quiet room, with privacy and without the possibility of interruptions.
> - Dress professionally—don't be casual; dressing right increases confidence and sets a tone for your side of the conversation.
> - Practise your interview "voice"—your impression will be made quickly; how you sound counts; it even helps to stand up while you talk.
> - Have reference materials handy—your resumé and other supporting documents should be within easy reach.
> - Have a list of questions ready—don't be caught hesitating; intersperse your best questions during the interview.
> - Ask what happens next—find out how to follow up by telephone, email, etc.; ask what other information you can provide.

tire-changing test, with colour-coded bolts and a set of instructions. As Charlene Paige took the test, she went slowly and carefully followed directions; two men with her changed the tires really fast. Charlene got the job and soon worked into a team leader position.[39]

Reference and Background Checks

Reference checks are inquiries to previous employers, academic advisors, co-workers, and/or acquaintances regarding the qualifications, experience, and past work records of a job applicant. Although they may be biased if friends are prearranged "to say the right things if called," reference checks are important. The Society for Human Resource Management estimates that 25 percent of job applications and resumés contain errors.[40] Infocheck Ltd., in their second annual resumé fraud study, found that 33 percent of final candidates had purposefully embellished their resumé.[41] Reference checks can better inform the potential employer. They can also help add credibility to the candidate if they back up what is said in an application.

Physical Examinations

Most organizations that do require medical/physical examinations are required to make it a post-offer condition of employment and justify this requirement. Under the Human Rights Code, employers cannot discriminate based on an assumption of physical disability. The same goes for drug testing, where the onus is on the employer to prove it is relevant to the position. This is often difficult to do, and also a significant privacy issue.

Final Decisions to Hire or Reject

The best selection decisions are most likely to be those involving extensive consultation among an applicant, future manager, or team leader and co-workers, as well as the human resource staff. Importantly, the emphasis in selection should be comprehensive and should focus on the person's capacity to perform well. Just as a "good fit" can produce long-term advantage, a "bad fit" can be the source of many long-term problems.

> **BE SURE YOU CAN**
> • explain the difference between internal recruitment and external recruitment • discuss the value of realistic job previews to employers and job candidates • differentiate reliability and validity as two criteria of selection devices • illustrate the operation of an assessment centre • discuss the importance of conducting background and reference checks
>
> ✓ Learning check ❸

DEVELOPING A QUALITY WORKFORCE

When people join an organization, they must "learn the ropes" and become familiar with "the way things are done." It is important to help newcomers fit into the work environment in a way that furthers their development and performance potential. **Socialization** is the process of influencing the expectations, behaviour, and attitudes of a new employee in a desirable way.[42]

■ **Socialization** systematically influences the expectations, behaviour, and attitudes of new employees.

●●● EMPLOYEE ORIENTATION

Socialization of newcomers begins with **orientation**—a set of activities designed to familiarize new employees with their jobs, co-workers, and key aspects of the organization as a whole. This includes clarifying mission and culture, explaining operating objectives and job expectations, and communicating policies and procedures. At the Disney World Resort in Buena Vista, Florida, each employee is carefully selected and trained to provide high-quality customer service as a "cast member." During orientation, newly hired employees are taught the corporate culture. They learn that everyone employed by the company, regardless of her or his specific job—be it entertainer, ticket seller, or groundskeeper—is there "to make the customer happy." The company's interviewers say that they place a premium on personality. "We can train for skills," says an HRM specialist. "We want people who are enthusiastic, who have pride in their work, who can take charge of a situation without supervision."[43]

■ **Orientation** familiarizes new employees with jobs, co-workers, and organizational policies and services.

The first six months of employment are often crucial in determining how well someone is going to fit in and perform over the long run. It is a time when the original expectations are tested and patterns are set for future relationships between an individual and employer. Unfortunately, orientation is sometimes neglected and newcomers are often left to fend for themselves. They may learn job and organizational routines on their own or through casual interactions with co-workers, and they may acquire job attitudes the same way.[44] The result is that otherwise well-intentioned and capable persons may learn the wrong things and pick up bad attitudes and habits. A good orientation, like Disney's, can set the stage for high performance, job satisfaction, and work enthusiasm.

●●● TRAINING AND DEVELOPMENT

■ **Training** provides learning opportunities to acquire and improve job-related skills.

Training is a set of activities that helps people acquire and improve job-related skills. This applies both to initial training of an employee and to upgrading or improving skills to meet changing job requirements. Progressive organizations invest in extensive training and development programs to ensure that their workers always have the capabilities needed to perform well.

On-the-Job Training

On-the-job training takes place in the work setting while someone is doing a job. A common approach is job rotation that allows people to spend time working in different jobs and thus expanding the range of their job capabilities. Another is **coaching**, in which an experienced person provides performance advice to someone else. In 2003, the Campbell Soup Company of Canada brought in a formal coaching strategy that started at the executive level and filtered down through the organization. A five-month Inspired Growth leadership program, just one of the four pillars of the initiative, has helped employees create a higher sense of awareness of their own values and strengths, and has re-engaged them in the organization. As a result Campbell's can better nurture and retain top talent, improve business, and encourage innovation.[45] One form of coaching is **mentoring**, in which early-career employees are formally assigned as proteges to senior persons. The mentoring relationship gives them regular access to advice on developing skills and becoming better informed about the organization. **Modelling** is an informal type of coaching. It occurs when someone demonstrates, through day-to-day personal behaviour, that which is expected of others. One way to learn managerial skills, for example, is to observe and practise the techniques displayed by good managers. Modelling is a very important influence on behaviour in organizations. A good example is how the behaviours of senior managers help set the ethical culture and standards for other employees.

■ **Coaching** occurs as an experienced person offers performance advice to a less-experienced person.

■ **Mentoring** assigns early career employees as proteges to more senior ones.

■ **Modelling** uses personal behaviour to demonstrate performance expected of others.

Off-the-Job Training

■ **Management development** is training to improve knowledge and skills in the management process.

Off-the-job training is accomplished outside the work setting. An important form is **management development**, designed to improve a person's knowledge and skill in the fundamentals of management. For example, *beginning managers* often benefit from training that emphasizes team leadership and communication; *middle managers* may benefit from training to better understand multi-functional viewpoints; *top managers* may benefit from advanced management training to sharpen their decision-making and negotiating skills, and to expand their awareness of corporate strategy and direction. At the Center for Creative Leadership, managers learn by participating in the "looking glass" simulation that models the pressures of daily work. The simulation is followed by extensive debriefings and discussions in which participants give feedback to one another. One participant commented, "You can look in the mirror but you don't see yourself. People have to say how you look."[46]

AROUND THE WORLD

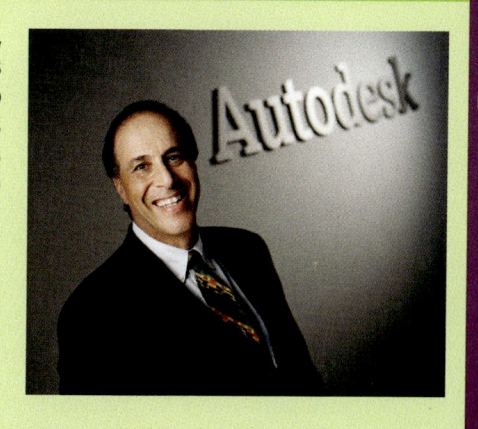

Software maker takes on the world with employee support

Family friendliness is valued at Autodesk, Inc., a 2D and 3D software company that serves every Fortune 100 firm and many of the world's top businesses. The company is rated highly by its employees in both external and internal surveys and is included in *Fortune's* 100 Best Companies to Work For and *Working Mother* magazine's Best Employers listing. An employee brochure states, "At Autodesk, we understand that a truly rewarding life is more than just a challenging, satisfying career—even one at Autodesk. You need time to relax and have fun with friends and family, flexibility and support for your personal needs, and opportunities to connect and contribute to your community." The company atmosphere is informal, employees and their managers often negotiate work schedules, and telecommuting can be an option. Employees in the United States can receive a six-week paid sabbatical for every four years of full-time employment, and can volunteer on company time up to four hours a month. The company's website says that its corporate strategy is advanced because of a special approach to "employee contentment—providing plenty of flexibility and freedom."

Source: Information from the corporate website: <www.autodesk.com>

●●● PERFORMANCE MANAGEMENT SYSTEMS

An important part of human resource management is design and implementation of a successful **performance management system**. This is a system that ensures that performance standards and objectives are set, that performance is regularly assessed for accomplishments, and that actions are taken to improve future performance.

■ A **performance management system** sets standards, assesses results, and plans for performance improvements.

Purpose of Performance Appraisal

The process of formally assessing someone's work accomplishments and providing feedback is **performance appraisal**. It serves both evaluation and development purposes. The *evaluation purpose* is intended to let people know where they stand relative to performance objectives and standards. The *development purpose* is intended to assist in their training and continued personal development.[47]

■ **Performance appraisal** is the process of formally evaluating performance and providing feedback to a job holder.

The evaluation purpose of performance appraisal focuses on past performance and measures results against standards. Performance is documented for the record and to establish a basis for allocating rewards. The manager acts in a *judgemental role* in which he or she gives a direct evaluation of another person's accomplishments. The development purpose of performance appraisal, by contrast, focuses on future performance and the clarification of success standards. It is a way of discovering performance obstacles and identifying training and development opportunities. Here the manager acts in a counselling role, focusing on the other person's developmental needs.

Like employment tests, any performance appraisal method can fulfill these purposes only when the criteria of *reliability* and *validity* are met. To be reliable, the method should consistently yield the same result, over time and/or for different raters; to be valid, it should be unbiased and measure only factors directly relevant to job performance. Both these criteria are especially important in today's complex legal environment. A manager who hires, fires, or promotes someone is increasingly called upon to defend such actions—sometimes in response to lawsuits alleging that the actions were discriminatory. At a minimum, written documentation of performance appraisals and a record of consistent past actions will be required to back up any contested evaluations.

Performance Appraisal Methods

■ A **graphic rating scale** uses a checklist of traits or characteristics to evaluate performance.

Organizations use a variety of performance appraisal methods.[48] One of the simplest is a **graphic rating scale** in which appraisers complete checklists of traits or performance characteristics. A manager rates the individual on each item using a numerical score. Although this approach is quick and easy to complete, its reliability and validity are questionable.

■ A **behaviourally anchored rating scale** uses specific descriptions of actual behaviours to rate various levels of performance.

A more advanced approach is the **behaviourally anchored rating scale** (BARS), which describes actual behaviours that exemplify various levels of performance achievement in a job. Look at the case of a customer service representative illustrated in *Figure 12.4*. "Extremely poor" performance is clearly defined as rude or disrespectful treatment of a customer. Because performance assessments are anchored to specific descriptions of work behaviour, a BARS is more reliable and valid than the graphic rating scale. The behavioural anchors can also be helpful in training people to master job skills of demonstrated performance importance.

■ The **critical-incident technique** keeps a log of someone's effective and ineffective job behaviours.

The **critical-incident technique** involves keeping a running log or inventory of effective and ineffective job behaviours. By creating a written record of positive and negative performance examples, this method documents success or failure patterns that can be specifically discussed with the individual. Using the case of the customer

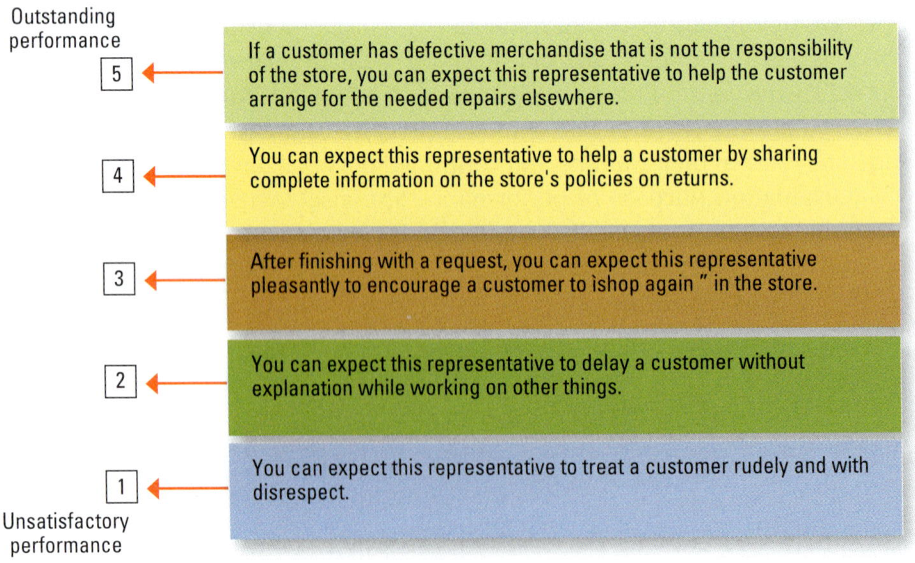

Figure 12.4 Sample behaviourally anchored rating scale for performance appraisal.

Outstanding performance

5 — If a customer has defective merchandise that is not the responsibility of the store, you can expect this representative to help the customer arrange for the needed repairs elsewhere.

4 — You can expect this representative to help a customer by sharing complete information on the store's policies on returns.

3 — After finishing with a request, you can expect this representative pleasantly to encourage a customer to ìshop again " in the store.

2 — You can expect this representative to delay a customer without explanation while working on other things.

1 — You can expect this representative to treat a customer rudely and with disrespect.

Unsatisfactory performance

service representative again, a critical-incidents log might contain the following types of entries: *Positive example*—"Took extraordinary care of a customer who had purchased a defective item from a company store in another city"; *negative example*—"Acted rudely in dismissing the complaint of a customer who felt that a sale item was erroneously advertised."

Some performance management systems use **multiperson comparisons**, which formally compare one person's performance with that of one or more others. Such comparisons can be used on their own or in combination with some other method. They can also be done in different ways. In *rank ordering*, all persons being rated are arranged in order of performance achievement. The best performer goes at the top of the list, the worst performer at the bottom; no ties are allowed. In *paired comparisons*, each person is formally compared with every other person and rated as either the superior or the weaker member of the pair. After all paired comparisons are made, each person is assigned a summary ranking based on the number of superior scores achieved. In *forced distribution*, each person is placed into a frequency distribution that requires that a certain percentage fall into specific performance classifications, such as top 10 percent, next 40 percent, next 40 percent, and bottom 10 percent.

■ A **multiperson comparison** compares one person's performance with that of others.

Not all performance appraisals are completed only by one's immediate boss. It is increasingly popular today to expand the role of a job's stakeholders in the appraisal process. The new workplace often involves use of *peer appraisal*, including in the process others who work regularly and directly with a job holder, and *upward appraisal*, including in the process subordinates reporting to the job holder. An even broader stakeholder approach is known as **360° feedback**, where superiors, subordinates, peers, and even internal and external customers are involved in the appraisal of a job holder's performance.[49]

■ **360° feedback** includes in the appraisal process superiors, subordinates, peers, and even customers.

> **BE SURE YOU CAN**
>
> • define the term socialization and describe its importance to organizations as part of the employee orientation process • differentiate coaching, mentoring, and modelling as on-the-job training approaches • explain the major types of performance appraisal methods—graphic rating scales, behaviourally anchored rating scales, critical-incident technique, and multiperson comparisons • discuss the strengths and weaknesses of each type

✓ Learning check ❹

MAINTAINING A QUALITY WORKFORCE

It is not enough to attract and develop workers with the talents to achieve high-performance results for the short term only. They must be successfully retained, nurtured, and managed for long-term effectiveness. When adverse turnover occurs and talented workers leave to pursue other opportunities, the resulting costs for the employer can be staggering. When the Society for Human Resource Management surveyed employers to identify the most effective tools for maintaining a quality workforce, they found the following: good benefits—especially health care, competitive salaries, flexible work schedules and personal time off, and opportunities for training and development.[50]

CAREER DEVELOPMENT

In his book *The Age of Unreason*, British scholar and consultant Charles Handy discusses dramatic new developments in the world of work and careers. Specifically, Handy says, "The times are changing and we must change with them."[51] A **career** is a sequence of jobs and work pursuits that constitutes what a person does for a living. For many of us, a career begins on an anticipatory basis with our formal education. From there it progresses into an initial job choice and any number of subsequent choices that may involve changes in task assignments, employing organizations, and even occupations. A *career path* is a sequence of jobs held over time during a career. Career paths vary between those that are pursued internally with the same employers and those pursued externally among various employers. Sobeys Inc., a national grocery retailer based in Stellarton, N.S., has developed career ladders to support its people, performance, and development strategy. With over 35,000 employees in more than 1,300 company stores and franchises across Canada, Sobeys's objective is to better define career paths for both store and office employees. Stephanie Curtis Sood, a HR advisor for the company, says, "We want to better position Sobeys as an organization where you can build a rewarding career."[52] Although many organizations place great emphasis on making long-term career opportunities available to their employees, Handy believes that external career paths will be increasingly important in the future.

Career planning is the process of systematically matching career goals and individual capabilities with opportunities for their fulfillment. It involves answering questions such as "Who am I?," "Where do I want to go?," and "How do I get there?" While some suggest that a career should be allowed to progress in a somewhat random but always opportunistic way, others view a career as something to be rationally planned and pursued in a logical step-by-step fashion. In fact, a well-managed

■ A **career** is a sequence of jobs that constitutes what a person does for a living.

■ **Career planning** is the process of matching career goals and individual capabilities with opportunities for their fulfillment.

---

take it to the case!

SAS Institute
Systems design for work-life balance makes a difference

SAS Institute, headquartered in Cary, North Carolina, is the world's largest privately held software company. Its 9,000-plus employees in some 50 countries help develop, refine, and market unique business intelligence software and services used by top firms worldwide to improve strategic management. Led by CEO Jim Goodnight, SAS has operated, since its founding, on the guiding principle, "If you treat employees as if they make a difference to the company, they will make a difference to the company . . . satisfied employees create satisfied customers." The firm is designed to allow employees to integrate their personal needs with the opportunities and demands of a SAS career. Work-life programs include child-care centres, eldercare support, health care clinics, wellness programs, fitness facilities, and more. SAS is well known for its repeat listings as one of *Fortune* magazine's "100 Best Companies to Work for in America."

Source: Information and quotes from corporate website: <www.sas.com>

career will probably include elements of each. The carefully thought-out plan can point you in a general career direction; an eye for opportunity can fill in the details along the way.

When you think about adult life stages or transitions, you should recognize that sooner or later most people's careers level off. A **career plateau** is a position from which someone is unlikely to move to a higher level of work responsibility.[53] Three common reasons for career plateaus are personal choice, limited abilities, and lack of opportunity. For some, the plateau may occur at a point in life when it suits their individual needs. For others, such as employees within 10 to 15 years of retirement age, plateaus can be very frustrating. Progressive employers seek ways to engage them with new opportunities in lateral moves, mentoring assignments, and even overseas jobs. Susan Peters, vice-president for executive development at GE, says: "Suddenly they come to a stage when they may have more flexibility to take a foreign assignment or do something they couldn't at a younger age."[54] She strongly believes in the value of broad experience and the willingness to pursue opportunities through lateral career moves.

■ A **career plateau** is a position from which someone is unlikely to move to a higher level of work responsibility.

WORK-LIFE BALANCE

"Hiring good people is tough," starts an article in the *Harvard Business Review*. The sentence finishes with, "keeping them can be even tougher."[55] A very important retention issue given today's fast-paced and complicated lifestyles is **work-life balance**—how people balance the demands of careers with their personal and family needs. "Family" in this context includes not just children but also elderly parents and other relatives in need of care. Human resource practices that support a healthy work-life balance are increasingly valued, with the chapter case on the SAS Institute a good example.

Included among work-life balance concerns are the unique needs of *single parents*, who must balance parenting responsibilities with a job, and *dual-career couples*, who must balance the career needs and opportunities of each partner. The special situations of both working mothers and working fathers are also being recognized.[56] Not surprisingly, the "family-friendliness" of an employer is now frequently and justifiably used as a screening criterion by job candidates. *Business Week*, *Maclean's*, and *Fortune* are among the magazines annually ranking employers on this criterion.

■ **Work-life balance** involves balancing career demands with personal and family needs.

COMPENSATION AND BENEFITS

Good compensation and benefit systems attract qualified people to the organization and help retain them. **Base compensation**, in the form of salary or hourly wages, can help get the right people into jobs to begin with and keep them there by making outside opportunities less attractive. Unless an organization's prevailing wage and salary structure is competitive in the relevant labour markets, it will be difficult to attract and retain a staff of highly competent workers. Also important are **fringe benefits**, the additional nonwage or nonsalary forms of compensation. Benefit packages can constitute some 30 percent or more of a typical worker's earnings. They usually include various options on disability protection, life insurance, and retirement plans.

The ever-rising cost of fringe benefits, particularly employee medical benefits, is a major worry for employers. Some are attempting to gain control over health

■ **Base compensation** is a salary or hourly wage paid to an individual.

■ **Fringe benefits** are nonmonetary forms of compensation such as life insurance and retirement plans.

Flexible benefits programs allow employees to choose from a range of benefit options.

Family-friendly benefits help employees achieve better work-life balance.

Employee assistance programs help employees cope with personal stresses and problems.

care costs by encouraging healthy lifestyles. An increasingly common approach, overall, is **flexible benefits**, sometimes known as *cafeteria benefits*, which lets the employee choose a set of benefits within a certain dollar amount. The growing significance of work-life balance in the new social contract is also reflected in a trend toward more **family-friendly benefits** that help employees better balance work and nonwork responsibilities. These include child care, eldercare, flexible schedules, parental leave, and part-time employment options, among others. The best employers also offer **employee assistance programs** that help employees deal with troublesome personal problems. EAPs may include assistance in dealing with stress, counselling on alcohol and substance abuse problems, referrals for domestic violence and sexual abuse, family and marital counselling, and advice on community resources.

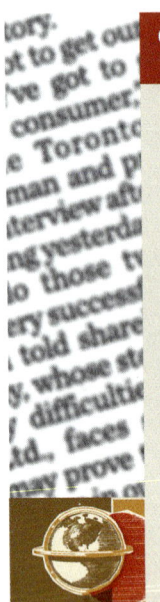

CANADIAN COMPANY IN THE NEWS — Pratt & Whitney Canada

PUTTING EMPLOYEES FIRST

In addition to having access to fitness centres, daycare, and recreation clubs, employees at Pratt & Whitney Canada can sign up for a variety of courses and academic programs, including flying lessons! P&WC was the first company in Canada to offer employees free first-aid training during work hours. The company has about 10 reward programs designed to recognize staff for personal and collective achievements. For example, the "Pioneers of Our Future" program rewards successful teams that have helped the company achieve its business objectives. P&WC also provides funding for staff members who want to become adoptive parents. And it encourages employees to commit to their communities through programs like matching gift, mini-grants, and volunteer team efforts.

Source: "An Employer of Choice," *Canadian Business*, Advertising Supplement, Nov. 21–Dec. 4, 2005.

●●● RETENTION AND TURNOVER

The several steps in the human resource management process both conclude and recycle with *replacement* decisions. These involve the management of promotions, transfers, terminations, layoffs, and retirements. Any replacement situation is an opportunity to review human resource plans, update job analyses, rewrite job descriptions and job specifications, and ensure that the best people are selected to perform the required tasks.

Some replacement decisions shift people between positions within the organization. *Promotion* is movement to a higher-level position; *transfer* is movement to a different job at a similar level of responsibility. Another set of replacement decisions relates to *retirement*, something most people look forward to…until it is close at hand. Then the prospect of being retired often raises fears and apprehensions. Many organizations offer special counselling and other forms of support for retiring employees, including advice on company benefits, money management, estate planning, and use of leisure time.

The most extreme replacement decisions involve *termination*, the involuntary and permanent dismissal of an employee. In some cases the termination is based on performance problems. The person involved is not meeting the requirements of the job or has violated key organizational policy. In other cases the termination may be due to financial conditions of the employer, such as those requiring downsizing or restructuring. The persons involved may be performing well but are being terminated as part of a workforce reduction. Where possible, organizations may provide outplacement services to help terminated employees find other jobs. In any and all cases, terminations should be handled fairly according to organizational policies and in full legal compliance. They should show respect for the person being dismissed, who may well find it hard to accept the decision.

LABOUR–MANAGEMENT RELATIONS

A final aspect of human resource management involves the role of organized labour. **Labour unions** are organizations, to which workers belong, that deal with employers on the workers' behalf.[57] Although they used to be associated primarily with industrial and business occupations, labour unions now represent such public-sector employees as teachers, university professors, police officers, and government workers. They are important forces in the modern workplace both in Canada and around the world. About 30 percent of Canadian workers belong to a union; the figures are around 13 percent for the United States and closer to 25 percent in Great Britain.[58]

Labour unions act as a collective "voice" for members in dealing with employers. They serve as bargaining agents that negotiate legal contracts affecting many aspects of the employment relationship. These **labour contracts**, for example, typically specify the rights and obligations of employees and management with respect to wages, work hours, work rules, seniority, hiring, grievances, and other conditions of employment. All of this has implications for management. In a unionized work setting, the labour contract and its legal implications must be considered when making human resource management decisions.

The foundation of any labour and management relationship is **collective bargaining**, which is the process of negotiating, administering, and interpreting labour contracts. Labour contracts and the collective bargaining process—from negotiating a new contract to resolving disputes under an existing one—are major influences on human resource management in unionized work settings. In Canada, national and international unions are closely governed by the Canadian Labour Congress, which promotes unionism and protection of member rights. In addition, the Canada Labour Code, provincial labour relations acts, and provincial acts like the *Trade Unions Act* in Saskatchewan or the *Labour Relations Act* in Ontario provides guidelines for employer and unions regarding certification, negotiation and management of collective agreements, and arbitration.[59]

■ A **labour union** is an organization that deals with employers on the workers' collective behalf.

■ A **labour contract** is a formal agreement between a union and employer about the terms of work for union members.

■ **Collective bargaining** is the process of negotiating, administering, and interpreting a labour contract.

The collective bargaining process typically occurs in face-to-face meetings between labour and management representatives. During this time, a variety of demands, proposals, and counter proposals are exchanged. Several rounds of bargaining may be required before a contract is reached or a dispute over a contract issue is resolved. And, as you might expect, the process can lead to problems. In *Figure 12.5*, labour and management are viewed as "win-lose" adversaries destined to be in opposition and possessed of certain weapons with which to fight one another. If labour–management relations take this form, a lot of energy on both sides can be expended in prolonged conflict. This adversarial approach is, to some extent, giving way to a new and more progressive era of greater co-operation. Each side seems more willing to understand the need for co-operation and mutual adjustment to new and challenging times.

Figure 12.5 The traditional adversarial view of labour–management relations.

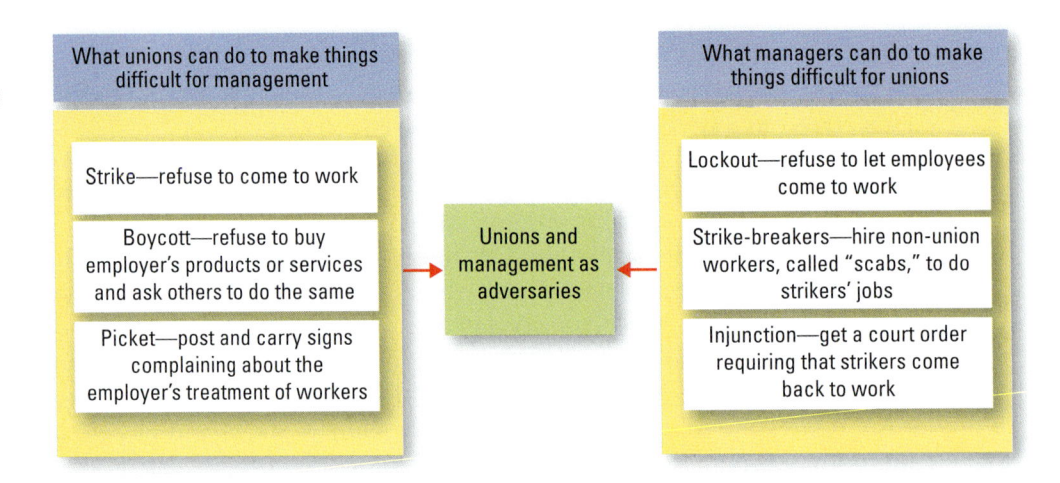

What unions can do to make things difficult for management
- Strike—refuse to come to work
- Boycott—refuse to buy employer's products or services and ask others to do the same
- Picket—post and carry signs complaining about the employer's treatment of workers

Unions and management as adversaries

What managers can do to make things difficult for unions
- Lockout—refuse to let employees come to work
- Strike-breakers—hire non-union workers, called "scabs," to do strikers' jobs
- Injunction—get a court order requiring that strikers come back to work

---

✓ **Learning check 5**

BE SURE YOU CAN

• define the terms career plateau and work-life balance • discuss the significance of each term for the human resource management process • explain why compensation and benefits are important elements in human resource management • define the terms labour union, labour contract, and collective bargaining • compare the adversarial and co-operative approaches to labour–management relations

Chapter 12 STUDY GUIDE

WHERE WE'VE BEEN

Back to Dofasco

The opening example of Dofasco introduced how organizations can outperform the competition by highlighting the importance of human resource activities within their strategic organizational goals. In this chapter you learned about the human resource management process, the legal environment that governs this process, and the managerial responsibilities through which decisions are made and actions taken to ensure that organizations always attract, develop, and maintain a talented workforce capable of creating high-performance results.

THE NEXT STEP
INTEGRATED LEARNING ACTIVITIES

Cases/Projects
- SAS Institute Case
- Project 5—Fringe Benefits Management
- Project 9—Management in Popular Culture

Self-Assessments
- Diversity Awareness (#7)
- Are You Cosmopolitan? (#18)
- Performance Appraisal Assumptions (#19)

Exercises in Teamwork
- Work vs. Family (#17)
- Compensation and Benefits Debate (#18)
- Case of the Contingency Workforce (#22)
- Upward Appraisal (#24)

STUDY QUESTION SUMMARY

1. Why do people make the difference?
- Even in this age of information, high technology, and globalization, people are irreplaceable assets that make organizations work.
- Organizations with positive human resource policies and practices are gaining significant performance advantages.
- The challenges of complexity and uncertainty in highly competitive environments are best met by a diverse and talented workforce.
- The diversity advantage is gained only when the talents of all persons, regardless of personal characteristics, are respected and given the opportunity to be displayed.

2. What is strategic human resource management?
- The human resource management process involves attracting, developing, and maintaining a quality workforce.
- Human resource management becomes strategic when it is integrated into the organization's strategic leadership.
- Human resource management is influenced by a complex and changing legal environment.
- Employment equity guarantees people the right to employment and advancement without discrimination.
- Current legal issues in HRM include sexual harassment, comparable worth, rights of independent contractors, and employee privacy.

3. How do organizations attract a quality workforce?
- Human resource planning is the process of analyzing staffing needs and identifying actions to satisfy these needs over time.
- The purpose of human resource planning is to make sure the organization always has people

with the right abilities available to do the required work.

- Recruitment is the process of attracting qualified job candidates to fill vacant positions.
- Realistic job previews provide candidates with accurate information on the job and organization.
- Managers use interviews, employment tests, and references to help make selection decisions; the use of assessment centres and work sampling is becoming more common.

4. How do organizations develop a quality workforce?
- Orientation is the process of formally introducing new employees to their jobs, performance expectations, and the organization.
- On-the-job training includes coaching, apprenticeship, modelling, and mentoring; off-the-job training includes formal programs, such as management development courses.
- Performance management systems establish work standards and the means for assessing performance results.
- Common performance appraisal methods are graphic rating scales, narratives, behaviourally anchored rating scales, and multiperson comparisons.

5. How do organizations maintain a quality workforce?
- Career planning systematically matches individual career goals and capabilities with opportunities for their fulfillment.
- Programs that address work-life balance and the complex demands of job and family responsibilities are increasingly important in human resource management.
- Compensation and benefits packages must be continually updated so that the organization stays competitive in labour markets.
- Whenever workers must be replaced through promotions, transfers, retirements, and/or terminations, the goal should be to treat everyone fairly while ensuring that remaining jobs are filled with the best personnel available.
- In collective bargaining situations, labour-management relations should be positively approached and handled with all due consideration of applicable laws.

KEY TERMS REVIEW

Assessment centre (p. 315)
Base compensation (p. 323)
Behaviourally anchored rating scale (p. 320)
Bona fide occupational requirements (p. 309)
Career (p. 322)
Career planning (p. 322)
Career plateau (p. 323)
Coaching (p. 318)
Collective bargaining (p. 325)
Comparable worth (p. 311)
Critical-incident technique (p. 320)
Discrimination (p. 309)
Employee assistance program (p. 324)
Employment equity (p. 309)
Family-friendly benefits (p. 324)
Flexible benefits (p. 324)

Fringe benefits (p. 323)
Graphic rating scale (p. 320)
Human capital (p. 305)
Human resource management (p. 307)
Human resource planning (p. 312)
Independent contractor (p. 311)
Job analysis (p. 312)
Job description (p. 312)
Job specification (p. 312)
Labour contract (p. 325)
Labour union (p. 325)
Management development (p. 318)
Mentoring (p. 318)
Modelling (p. 318)
Multiperson comparison (p. 321)
Orientation (p. 317)
Performance appraisal (p. 319)

Performance management system (p. 319)
Realistic job preview (p. 314)
Recruitment (p. 313)
Reliability (p. 315)
Selection (p. 314)
Sexual harassment (p. 310)
Social contract (p. 304)
Socialization (p. 317)
Strategic human resource management (p. 307)
360° feedback (p. 321)
Training (p. 318)
Validity (p. 315)
Work sampling (p. 315)
Work-life balance (p. 323)
Workplace privacy (p. 311)

SELF-TEST 12

MULTIPLE-CHOICE QUESTIONS:

1. Human resource management is the process of _____, developing, and maintaining a high-quality workforce.
   (a) attracting (b) compensating (c) appraising (d) selecting

2. A _____ is a criterion that can be legally justified for use in screening candidates for employment.
   (a) job description (b) bona fide occupational requirement (c) job specification (d) BARS
3. _____ programs are designed to ensure employment equity for persons historically unrepresented in the workforce.
   (a) Realistic recruiting (b) External recruiting (c) Employment equity (d) Employee assistance
4. An employment test that yields different results over time when taken by the same person should be replaced because it lacks _____.
   (a) validity (b) specificity (c) realism (d) reliability
5. The assessment centre approach to employee selection relies heavily on _____.
   (a) pencil-and-paper tests (b) simulations and experiential exercises (c) 360° feedback (d) formal one-on-one interviews
6. _____ is a form of on-the-job training wherein an individual learns by observing others who demonstrate desirable job behaviours.
   (a) Case study (b) Work sampling (c) Modelling (d) Simulation
7. The first step in human resource planning is to _____.
   (a) forecast human resource needs (b) forecast labour supplies (c) assess the existing workforce (d) review organizational mission, objectives, and strategies
8. Socialization of newcomers occurs during the _____ step of the staffing process.
   (a) recruiting (b) orientation (c) selecting (d) training
9. In human resource planning, a/an _____ is used to determine exactly what is done in an existing job.
   (a) critical-incident technique (b) assessment centre (c) job analysis (d) multiperson comparison
10. In what is called the new "social contract" between employers and employees, the implications for the individual include accepting more personal responsibility for _____.
    (a) learning and mobility (b) salary negotiation (c) labour–management relations (d) socialization
11. The _____ purpose of performance appraisal is being addressed when a manager describes training options that might help an employee improve future performance.
    (a) development (b) evaluation (c) judgemental (d) legal
12. When a team leader is required to rate 10 percent of team members as "superior," 80 percent as "good," and 10 percent as "unacceptable" for their performance on a project, this is an example of the _____ approach to performance appraisal.
    (a) graphic (b) forced distribution (c) behaviourally anchored rating scale (d) realistic
13. An employee with family problems that are starting to interfere with work would be pleased to learn that his employer had a(n) _____ plan to help on such matters.
    (a) employee assistance (b) cafeteria benefits (c) comparable worth (d) collective bargaining
14. A manager who _____ is displaying a commitment to valuing human capital.
    (a) believes payroll costs should be reduced wherever possible (b) is always looking for new ways to replace people with machines (c) protects workers from stress by withholding from them information about the organization's performance (d) views people as assets to be nurtured and developed over time

SHORT-RESPONSE QUESTIONS:

15. How do internal recruitment and external recruitment compare in terms of advantages and disadvantages for the employer?
16. Why is orientation an important part of the staffing process?
17. What is the difference between the graphic rating scale and the BARS as performance appraisal methods?
18. How does mentoring work as a form of on-the-job training?

APPLICATION QUESTION:

19. Sy Smith is not doing well in his job. The problems began to appear shortly after Sy's job was changed from a manual to a computer-based operation. He has tried hard, but is just not doing well in learning to use the computer and meet performance expectations. As a 55-year-old employee with over 30 years with the company, Sy is both popular and influential among his work peers. Along with his performance problems, you have also noticed the appearance of some negative attitudes, including a tendency for Sy to sometimes "badmouth" the firm. As Sy's manager, what options would you consider in terms of dealing with the issue of his retention in the job and in the company? What would you do and why?

13 Leading

CHAPTER 13 STUDY QUESTIONS

1. What is the nature of leadership?
2. What are the important leadership traits and behaviours?
3. What are the contingency theories of leadership?
4. What is transformational leadership?
5. What are current issues in leadership development?

Planning Ahead

After reading Chapter 13, you should be able to answer these questions in your own words.

LEADING WITH VISION,
CORDON BLEU, AND SPIRITUALITY

J.-Robert Ouimet of Ouimet-Cordon Bleu Foods is a leader with the unique vision of "reconciling human happiness with business profitability." As a strategic leader, Ouimet's accomplishments have earned him the Order of Quebec, the Order of Canada, and directorships on the boards of a number of organizations. He has expanded his small family business to become one of the top 50 food companies in Canada. Ouimet is quoted as saying, "I have only four competitors: Campbell's, Heinz, Maple Leaf, and Chef Boyardee.... They are Goliaths, we are David."

Ouimet isn't known only for his strategic leadership, but more for the personal vision that has always been a part of his business career. Personal faith is important to Ouimet, and he has sought the advice of spiritual leaders such as the Dalai Lama and Mother Teresa, who made a private visit to one of his plants in 1988. Spiritual principles have led Ouimet in developing a number of the management tools he advocates, including silence or meditation rooms, gestures of reconciliation, time set aside for reflection and/or prayer, and authentic communication. Ouimet believes these tools are an important way to "increase not only human happiness and well-being, but company profitability." To prove his theories, Ouimet tested them while writing his Ph.D. thesis. He has taken his ideas on the road, speaking to other companies and leaders and also to more than 167 public conferences and presentations in North America, Europe, the Middle East, the Far East, and Asia.

It is not just his 400 employees who benefit from Ouimet's strong belief and vision, his customers do as well. He notes, "[our] experience reconciling human happiness with business profitability has influenced the content of our product, the packaging, the pricing, and the promotion." The logo on the beef gravy states, "Cordon Bleu has you at heart." This packaging reflects that the product is low in fat and salt content, but also that the company combines the goal of profitability with efforts to provide information that satisfies the needs of the consumer. "That's the process that will lead to further transformation," notes Ouimet.

While not everyone is accepting of Ouimet's philosophy, there can be no doubt about his success. By seeing "consumers as individual human beings—very precious, one by one" and not only as potential profits, and perhaps by advising business leaders to "seek guidance from on high, not just from the bottom line," Ouimet has created a leadership profile that is all his own.[1]

GET CONNECTED!

There are many different styles of leadership. Good leaders aren't born, they are made. J.-Robert Ouimet has developed his own, very individualized leadership vision and profile. Use the many resources in the *Management Learning Workbook* to get in touch with your leadership skills.

Chapter 13 LEARNING PREVIEW

J.-Robert Ouimet exemplifies the importance of leadership through unique personal vision and values, and commitment to his employees and customers. Ouimet is an example of a leader who invests himself fully in the responsibilities of leadership. In this chapter you will learn about leadership concepts and the various approaches taken by scholars to understand leadership effectiveness. You will learn about the current issues in leadership development, and you will also be asked to reflect on your personal capacities to lead with excellence.

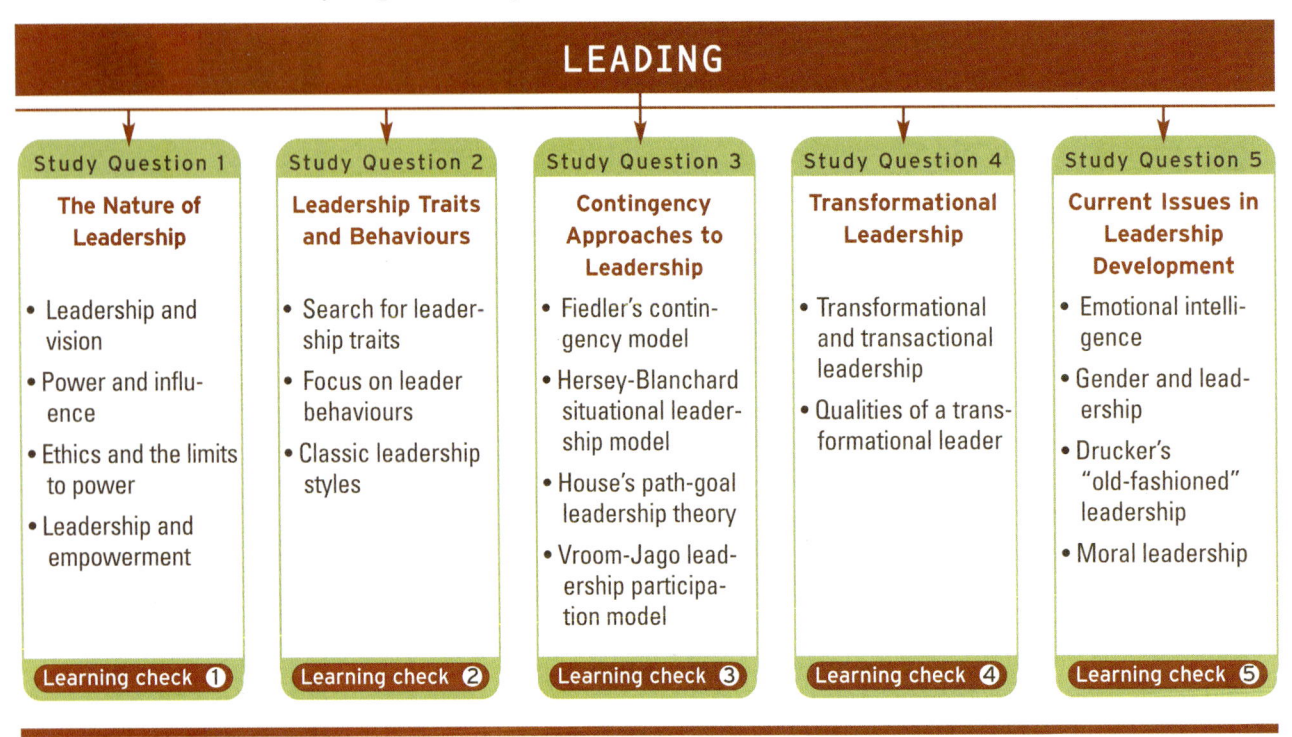

LEADING

Study Question 1

The Nature of Leadership

- Leadership and vision
- Power and influence
- Ethics and the limits to power
- Leadership and empowerment

Learning check 1

Study Question 2

Leadership Traits and Behaviours

- Search for leadership traits
- Focus on leader behaviours
- Classic leadership styles

Learning check 2

Study Question 3

Contingency Approaches to Leadership

- Fiedler's contingency model
- Hersey-Blanchard situational leadership model
- House's path-goal leadership theory
- Vroom-Jago leadership participation model

Learning check 3

Study Question 4

Transformational Leadership

- Transformational and transactional leadership
- Qualities of a transformational leader

Learning check 4

Study Question 5

Current Issues in Leadership Development

- Emotional intelligence
- Gender and leadership
- Drucker's "old-fashioned" leadership
- Moral leadership

Learning check 5

Rob McEwen, a former CEO and Chairman of Goldcorp Inc., described his leadership style by saying, "Challenge the NORM! I have pushed all of Goldcorp's employees to test the validity of entrenched assumptions within our mining industry. My goal is to engage the collective wisdom of Goldcorp's workforce to identify and implement alternative methods that are faster, more productive and more profitable. When achieved, this hard-earned success perpetuates growth. When we recognize the unique qualities of others, we become less inclined to believe that we alone know what is best."[2] Under his leadership, Goldcorp Inc., headquartered in Vancouver, has become a gold producer with one of the lowest production costs in the world. By valuing and respecting people, we learn how to provide them with meaningful work and opportunities. This leadership lesson extends to all types and sizes of organizations. Great leaders bring out the best in people. Consultant and author Tom Peters says that the leader is "rarely—possibly never?—the best performer."[3] They don't have to be; they thrive through, and by, the successes of others.

THE NATURE OF LEADERSHIP

Warren Bennis, a respected scholar and consultant, claims that too many North American corporations are "over-managed and under-led." The late Grace Hopper, a computer scientist and the first female admiral in the U.S. Navy, said, "You manage things; you lead people."[4] A glance at the shelves in your local bookstore will quickly confirm that **leadership**, the process of inspiring others to work hard to accomplish important tasks, is one of the most popular management topics. As shown in *Figure 13.1*, it is also one of the four functions that constitutes the management process. Planning sets the direction and objectives; organizing brings the resources together to turn plans into action; *leading* builds the commitments and enthusiasm for people to apply their talents to help accomplish plans; controlling makes sure things turn out right.

Managers today must lead under new and difficult conditions. The time frames for getting things accomplished are becoming shorter; leaders are expected to get things right the first time, with second chances few and far between; the problems to be resolved through leadership are complex, ambiguous, and multi-dimensional; leaders are expected to be long-term oriented even while meeting demands for short-term performance results.[5] Anyone aspiring to career success in leadership must rise to these challenges, and more, becoming good at communication, interpersonal relations, motivation, teamwork, and change—all topics in this final part of *Management*.

■ **Leadership** is the process of inspiring others to work hard to accomplish important tasks.

●●● LEADERSHIP AND VISION

"Great leaders," it is said, "get extraordinary things done in organizations by inspiring and motivating others toward a common purpose."[6] Frequently today, leadership is associated with **vision**—a future that one hopes to create or achieve in order to improve upon the present state of affairs. The term **visionary leadership** describes a leader who brings to the situation a clear and compelling sense of the future as well as an understanding of the actions needed to get there successfully.[7] But simply having the vision of a desirable future is not enough. Truly great leaders are extraordinarily good at turning their visions into accomplishments. This involves the ability to

■ A **vision** is a clear sense of the future.

■ **Visionary leadership** brings to the situation a clear sense of the future and an understanding of how to get there.

Figure 13.1 Leading viewed in relationship to the other management functions.

Leading—to inspire effort
- Communicate the vision
- Build enthusiasm
- Activate commitment, hard work

Planning—to set the direction

Organizing—to create structures

Controlling—to ensure results

communicate the vision in such a way that others are willing to work hard to achieve it. Visionary leaders, simply put, inspire others to take the actions necessary to turn vision into reality. At General Electric, for example, an "A" leader is considered to be someone "…with vision and the ability to articulate that vision to the team, so vividly and powerfully that it also becomes their vision."[8]

The five principles[9] for meeting the challenges of visionary leadership are:

- *Challenge the process:* Be a pioneer; encourage innovation and support people who have ideas.

- *Show enthusiasm:* Inspire others through personal enthusiasm to share in a common vision.

- *Help others to act:* Be a team player and support the efforts and talents of others.

- *Set the example:* Provide a consistent model of how others can and should act.

- *Celebrate achievements:* Bring emotion into the workplace and rally "hearts" as well as "minds."

The suggestions go beyond a manager's responsibilities for making long-term plans and drafting budgets, putting structures in place, assigning people to jobs, and making sure that results are consistent with plans. Leading with vision means doing all these things and more. It means having a clear vision, communicating that vision to all concerned, and getting people motivated and inspired to pursue the vision in their daily work. Visionary leadership means bringing meaning to people's work, making what they do worthy and valuable. Bonnie DuPont, a vice-president and high-ranking member of Enbridge's corporate leadership team, is a leader by example and one of the most senior women in the energy sector. Dupont believes that leadership involves setting a course, providing a vision, and motivating people by giving them objectives to achieve, the tools to do the job, and the incentives to succeed.[10]

●●● POWER AND INFLUENCE

The foundations of effective leadership lie in the way a manager uses power to influence the behaviour of other people. **Power** is the ability to get someone else to do something you want done. It is the ability to make things happen the way you want them to.[11] Research recognizes that a need for power is essential to executive success.[12] But this need for power is not a desire to control for the sake of personal satisfaction; it is a desire to influence and control others for the good of the group or organization as a whole. This "positive" face of power is the foundation of effective leadership. *Figure 13.2* shows that leaders gain power from both the positions they hold and from their personal qualities.[13]

Sources of Position Power

A manager's official status, or position, in the organization's hierarchy of authority is an important source of power. Although anyone holding a managerial position theoretically has this power, how well it is used will vary from one person to the next. Consequently, leadership success will vary as well. The three bases of *position power* are reward power, coercive power, and legitimate power.

■ **Power** is the ability to get someone else to do something you want done or to make things happen the way you want.

■ **Reward power** is the capacity to offer something of value as a means of influencing other people.

■ **Coercive power** is the capacity to punish or withhold positive outcomes as a means of influencing other people.

■ **Legitimate power** is the capacity to influence other people by virtue of formal authority, or the rights of office.

■ **Expert power** is the capacity to influence other people because of specialized knowledge.

Power of the POSITION: Based on things managers can offer to others.	**Power of the PERSON:** Based on how managers are viewed by others.
Rewards: "If you do what I ask, I'll give you a reward."	**Expertise** — as a source of special knowledge and information.
Coercion: "If you don't do what I ask, I'll punish you."	**Reference** — as a person with whom others like to identify.
Legitimacy: "Because I am the boss, you *must* do as I ask."	

Figure 13.2 Sources of position power and personal power used by managers.

Reward power is the ability to influence through rewards. It is the capability to offer something of value—a positive outcome—as a means of influencing the behaviour of other people. This involves the control of rewards or resources such as pay raises, bonuses, promotions, special assignments, and verbal or written compliments. To mobilize reward power, a manager says, in effect, "If you do what I ask, I'll give you a reward."

Coercive power is the ability to influence through punishment. It is the capacity to punish or withhold positive outcomes as a way to influence the behaviour of other people. A manager may attempt to coerce someone by threatening him or her with verbal reprimands, pay penalties, and even termination. To mobilize coercive power, a manager says, in effect, "If you don't do what I want, I'll punish you."

Legitimate power is the ability to influence through authority—the right, by virtue of one's organizational position or status, to exercise control over persons in subordinate positions. It is the capacity to influence the behaviour of other people by virtue of the rights of office. To mobilize legitimate power, a manager says, in effect, "I am the boss, therefore you are supposed to do as I ask."

Sources of Personal Power

The unique personal qualities of a manager are further sources of power. In fact, a truly successful leader is very good at building and using the two bases of *personal power*—expert power and referent power.

Expert power is the ability to influence through special expertise. It is the capacity to influence the behaviour of other people because of one's knowledge and skills. Expertise derives from the possession of technical understanding or information pertinent to the issue at hand. It is developed by acquiring relevant skills or competencies and by gaining a central position in relevant information networks. It is maintained by protecting one's credibility and not overstepping the boundaries of true expertise.

PERSONAL MANAGEMENT

Leadership is an interpersonal process. You either lead well or poorly in large part due to your ability to relate well to other people. Furthermore, in today's high-performance work settings, with their emphasis on horizontal structures, cross-functional teams, and projects, leading requires skillful **NETWORKING**. Within teams, across functions, and in day-to-day work encounters the best leaders get things done because they build and maintain positive working relationships with others. In the social context of organizations, there is very little you can do by yourself; the vast majority of work gets done because people in your networks help you out. For some of us, networking is as natural as walking down the street. For others, it is a big challenge in the intimidating realm of interpersonal relationships. But even if you fall into this last category, the fact remains: to be a successful leader you need networking skills. Don't underestimate the challenge; be prepared for leadership. Do you have confidence in these networking skills?

- *Network identification*—knowing and finding the right people to work with.
- *Network building*—engaging others and relating to them in positive ways.
- *Network maintenance*—actively nurturing and supporting others in their work.

Get to know yourself better

Complete Self-Assessment #20—**T-P Leadership Questionnaire**, and #22—**Least Preferred Co-Worker Scale**, from the Workbook and Personal Management Activity #13 on the companion website.

When a manager uses expert power, the implied message is, "You should do what I want because of my special expertise or information." Rose M. Patten, senior executive vice-president of Human Resources and head of Strategic Management for BMO Financial Group, is an example of an individual developing expert leadership power early in their career. She credits her significant volunteer activity at an early age as key in developing her leadership ability. These volunteer activities resulted in a number of leadership assignments and learning opportunities. While starting early provided the basis for leadership, Patten also believes that being in the right place at the right time is important. But, this holds true only if you are willing to tackle the challenge of change with courage and plunge yourself into uncharted waters. In 2005, she was named to the list of Canada's most powerful women, while the *Human Resource Executive's* "Honour Roll" recognized her leadership in establishing workforce diversity as an integral and strategic part of BMO.[14]

■ **Referent power** is the capacity to influence other people because of their desire to identify personally with you.

Referent power is the ability to influence through identification. It is the capacity to influence the behaviour of other people because they admire you and want to identify positively with you. Reference is a power derived from charisma or interpersonal attractiveness. It is developed and maintained through good interpersonal relations that encourage the admiration and respect of others. When a manager uses referent power, the implied message is, "You should do what I want in order to maintain a positive self-defined relationship with me."

Turning Power into Influence

To succeed at leadership, managers must both acquire all types of power and use them appropriately.[15] The best leaders understand that use of the various power bases results in quite different outcomes. When one relies on rewards and legitimacy to influence others, the likely outcome is temporary compliance. The follower will do what the leader requests, but only so long as the reward continues and/or the legitimacy persists. When one relies on coercion, compliance is also temporary and dependent on the continued threat of punishment. In this case, however, the compliance is often accompanied by resentment. The use of expert and reference power has the most enduring results, creating commitment rather than compliance. Followers respond positively because of internalized understanding or beliefs that create a long-lasting impact on behaviour.

Position power and the compliance it generates are often insufficient for managers to achieve and sustain needed influence. Personal power and the resulting commitment are what often make the difference between leadership success and mediocrity. This is particularly true in today's horizontal organizations with their emphasis on teamwork and co-operation. Four points to keep in mind when building your managerial power are as follows: (1) there is no substitute for expertise, (2) likable personal qualities are very important, (3) effort and hard work breed respect, and (4) personal behaviour must match expressed values.[16]

In organizations, power and influence are also linked to where one fits and how one acts in the structures and networks of the workplace.[17] *Centrality* is important. Managers gain power by establishing networks of interpersonal contacts and getting involved in the information flows within them. They avoid becoming isolated. *Criticality* is important. To gain power, managers must take good care of others who are dependent on them. They support them exceptionally well by doing things that add value to the work setting. *Visibility* is also important. It helps to become known as an influential person in the organization. Managers gain power by performing well in formal presentations, on key task forces or committees, and in special assignments that display their talents and capabilities.

ETHICS AND THE LIMITS TO POWER

On the issue of ethics and the limits to power, it is always helpful to remember Chester Barnard's *acceptance theory of authority*. He identifies four conditions that determine whether a leader's directives will be followed and true influence achieved:[18] the other person must (1) truly understand the directive, (2) feel capable of carrying out the directive, (3) believe that the directive is in the organization's best interests, and (4) believe that the directive is consistent with personal values.

In Chapter 3 it was noted that many ethical dilemmas begin when leaders and managers pressure followers to do questionable things. Using the acceptance theory of authority as a starting point, the ethical question a follower must always be prepared to ask is, "Where do I (or will I) draw the line; at what point do I (or will I) refuse to comply with requests?" Someday you may face a situation in which you are asked by someone in authority to do something that violates personal ethics and/or even the law. Can you…will you…when will you, say "no"? After all, as Barnard said, it is "acceptance" that establishes the limits of managerial power.

LEADERSHIP AND EMPOWERMENT

At many points in this book we have talked about **empowerment**, the process through which managers enable and help others to gain power and achieve influence within the organization. Effective leaders empower others by providing them with the information, responsibility, authority, and trust to make decisions and act independently. They know that when people feel empowered to act, they tend to

■ **Empowerment** enables others to gain and use decision-making power.

MANAGER'S Notepad 13.1
How to empower others

- Get others involved in selecting their work assignments and the methods for accomplishing tasks.
- Create an environment of co-operation, information sharing, discussion, and shared ownership of goals.
- Encourage others to take initiative, make decisions, and use their knowledge.
- When problems arise, find out what others think and let them help design the solutions.
- Stay out of the way; give others the freedom to put their ideas and solutions into practice.
- Maintain high morale and confidence by recognizing successes and encouraging high performance.

follow through with commitment and high-quality work. They also realize that power in organizations is not a "zero-sum" quantity; in order for someone to gain power, it isn't necessary for someone else to give it up. Indeed, today's high-performance organizations thrive by mobilizing power throughout all ranks of employees.

Derek Oland, CEO and chairman of Moosehead Breweries, has a management style that is collegial. He doesn't believe in the "one genius that leads the company" model. Rather, he strives to get the very best people around him, provides them with direction, and then lets them do their thing.[19] When asked how Suncor Energy came to be named as a "best in class" company, Darcie Park, the co-manager of the company's corporate sustainability report, said, "It starts at the top with leadership and commitment, and then every Suncor employee is expected to do his or her part."[20] Both are talking about leadership through empowerment—allowing and helping people to use their experience, knowledge, and judgement to make a real difference in daily workplace affairs. *Manager's Notepad 13.1* offers tips on how leaders can empower others.[21] Doing so requires respect for the talents and creativity of others. And it requires the confidence to let people work with initiative in responsible jobs, participate in decisions affecting their work, and make reasonable choices regarding their work-life balance.

> **Learning check 1**
>
> **BE SURE YOU CAN**
> • define the term vision • explain the concept of visionary leadership • define the term power • illustrate three types of position power and discuss how managers use each • illustrate two types of personal power and discuss how managers use each • explain the implications of Barnard's acceptance theory of authority for ethical behaviour in organizations • define the term empowerment • explain why managers benefit by empowering others

LEADERSHIP TRAITS AND BEHAVIOURS

For centuries, people have recognized that some persons perform very well as leaders, whereas others do not. The question still debated is, "Why?" Historically, the issue of leadership success has been studied from the perspective of the trait, behavioural, and contingency approaches. Each takes a slightly different tack in attempting to explain leadership effectiveness and identify the pathways to leadership development.

●●● SEARCH FOR LEADERSHIP TRAITS

An early direction in leadership research involved the search for universal traits or distinguishing personal characteristics that would separate effective and ineffective leaders.[22] Sometimes called the *great person theory*, the notion was to identify successful leaders and then determine what made them great.

Briefly, the results of many years of research in this direction can be summarized as follows. Physical characteristics such as a person's height, weight, and physique make no difference in determining leadership success. On the other hand, certain personal traits do seem to differentiate leaders, although they must always be considered along with situational factors. A study, by Jim Kouzes and Barry Posner, of over 3,400 managers, for example, found that followers rather consistently admired leaders who were honest, competent, forward-looking, inspiring, and credible.[23] In a comprehensive review of research to date, Shelley Kirkpatrick and Edwin Locke further identify these personal traits as being common among successful leaders.[24]

- *Drive:* Successful leaders have high energy, display initiative, and are tenacious.
- *Self-confidence:* Successful leaders trust themselves and have confidence in their abilities.
- *Creativity:* Successful leaders are creative and original in their thinking.
- *Cognitive ability:* Successful leaders have the intelligence to integrate and interpret information.
- *Business knowledge:* Successful leaders know their industry and its technical foundations.
- *Motivation:* Successful leaders enjoy influencing others to achieve shared goals.
- *Flexibility:* Successful leaders adapt to fit the needs of followers and demands of situations.
- *Honesty and integrity:* Successful leaders are trustworthy; they are honest, predictable, and dependable.

CANADIAN COMPANY IN THE NEWS — Inco Ltd.

GROOMING TOMORROW'S LEADERS

With today's aging workforce, companies need to consider who among their employees will lead the company in the future. Canada's largest nickel company, Inco Ltd., launched a Trailblazers program in 2001, to groom high-potential employees for leadership roles. Participants are given an individual development plan, as well as mentoring and coaching over 18 months as they work in a more demanding role. The goal is to prepare them for advanced positions in two to five years, rather than the usual eight to ten years. The program's success is evident in its expansion from an Ontario initiative to Inco's worldwide operations.

Source: "Developing Tomorrow's Leaders," *Canadian Business*, Advertising Supplement, Jan 17–30, 2005, Vol. 78, Iss. 2.

FOCUS ON LEADERSHIP BEHAVIOURS

Researchers next turned their attention toward how leaders behave when working with followers. Work in this tradition investigated **leadership styles**—the recurring patterns of behaviours exhibited by leaders.[25] If the best style could be identified, the implications were straightforward and practical—train leaders to become skilled at using it.

■ **Leadership style** is the recurring pattern of behaviours exhibited by a leader.

Most leader-behaviour research focused on two dimensions of leadership style: (1) concern for the task to be accomplished and (2) concern for the people doing the work. The terminology used to describe these dimensions varies among many studies. Concern for task is sometimes called "initiating structure," "job-centredness," and "task orientation"; concern for people is sometimes called "consideration," "employee centredness," and "relationship orientation." But, regardless of the terminology, the behaviours characteristic of each dimension are quite clear. A *leader high in concern for task* plans and defines work to be done, assigns task responsibilities, sets clear work standards, urges task completion, and monitors performance results.

Figure 13.3 Managerial styles in Blake and Mouton's Leadership Grid.

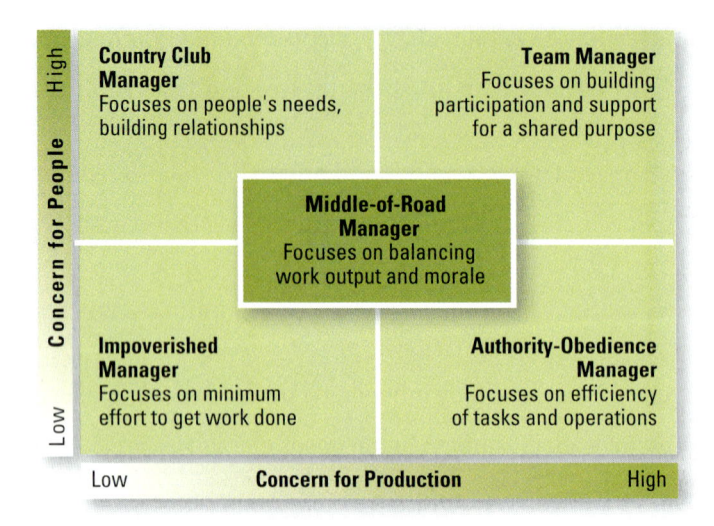

```
                    Concern for People
High │ Country Club Manager          │ Team Manager
     │ Focuses on people's needs,    │ Focuses on building
     │ building relationships        │ participation and support
     │                               │ for a shared purpose
     │        Middle-of-Road Manager
     │        Focuses on balancing
     │        work output and morale
     │ Impoverished Manager          │ Authority-Obedience Manager
     │ Focuses on minimum            │ Focuses on efficiency
Low  │ effort to get work done       │ of tasks and operations
     └───────────────────────────────┴───────────────────────────
       Low         Concern for Production          High
```

By contrast, a *leader high in concern for people* is warm and supportive toward followers, maintains good social relations with them, respects their feelings, is sensitive to their needs, and shows trust in them.

The results of leader behaviour research at first suggested that followers of people-oriented leaders would be more productive and satisfied than those working for more task-oriented leaders.[26] Later results, however, suggested that truly effective leaders were high in both concern for people and concern for task. *Figure 13.3* describes one of the popular versions of this conclusion—the Leadership Grid of Robert Blake and Jane Mouton.[27] This grid describes alternative leadership styles that managers display. It is designed to assist in the process of leadership development. The approach uses assessments (such as #20 in the *Management Learning Workbook*) to first determine where someone falls with respect to people and task concerns. Then a training program is designed to help shift the person's style in the preferred direction of becoming strong on both dimensions. Blake and Mouton called this preferred style *team management*. This leader shares decisions with subordinates, encourages participation, and supports the teamwork needed for high levels of task accomplishment. Today, this would be a manager who "empowers" others.

CLASSIC LEADERSHIP STYLES

■ A leader with an **autocratic style** acts in unilateral command-and-control fashion.

■ A leader with a **laissez-faire style** displays a "do the best you can and don't bother me" attitude.

■ A leader with a **democratic style** encourages participation with an emphasis on both task accomplishment and development of people.

Even today, when people describe the leaders with whom they work, their vocabulary includes three classic styles of leadership from the behavioural leadership theories.[28] A leader with an **autocratic style** emphasizes task over people, keeps authority and information to himself or herself, and acts in unilateral command-and-control fashion. A leader with a **laissez-faire style** does just the opposite, showing little concern for task, letting the group make decisions, and acting with a "do the best you can and don't bother me" attitude. In contrast to both, a leader with a **democratic style** is committed to task and people, getting things done while sharing information, encouraging participation in decision making, and otherwise helping others develop their skills and capabilities. You might wonder which style works best. The answer is debatable. Under the leadership styles of former CEOs Cedric Ritchie and Peter Godsoe, Scotiabank didn't just climb from being the smallest of Canada's "big five," it grew to be the second largest of the banks. But throughout the process, these two CEOs left managers in the dark about what was going on. Scotiabank's current CEO, Richard Waugh, has a leadership style that is much more democratic. "My style is, and will be, different than theirs," he says. "I'm broadening it out. We're more diverse, with a great team of people." Waugh's style has already brought a relaxed atmosphere and greater dialogue to board meetings. But others, watching Waugh, say his style may jar with Scotia's culture. "Somebody has to be the boss," says one fund manager with a stake in the bank. "Waugh is a very solid guy, but I don't believe he has the kind of force of presence that Ritchie and Godsoe had."[29] An important personal question, of course, is, "What type of leader are you?" And perhaps even more importantly, "How would the people with whom you work and study describe your style—autocratic, laissez-faire, or democratic?"

> **BE SURE YOU CAN**
> • contrast the trait and leader behaviour approaches to leadership research • identify five personal traits common among successful leaders • illustrate leader behaviours consistent with a high concern for task • illustrate leader behaviours consistent with a high concern for people • explain the leadership development implications of Blake and Mouton's Leadership Grid • describe three classic leadership styles

✓ Learning check ❷

CONTINGENCY APPROACHES TO LEADERSHIP

As leadership research continued, scholars recognized the need to probe beyond leader behaviours and examine yet another question: "When and under what circumstances is a particular leadership style preferable to others?" They developed the following *contingency approaches*, which share the goal of understanding the conditions for leadership success in different situations.

FIEDLER'S CONTINGENCY MODEL

An early contingency leadership model developed by Fred Fiedler proposed that good leadership depends on a match between leadership style and situational demands.[30] Leadership style in Fiedler's model is measured on the *least-preferred co-worker scale*, known as the LPC scale. It describes tendencies to behave either as a task-motivated (low LPC score) or relationship-motivated (high LPC score) leader. This "either/or" concept is important. Fiedler believes that leadership style is part of one's personality; therefore, it is relatively enduring and difficult to change. He doesn't place much hope in trying to train a task-motivated leader to behave in a relationship-motivated manner, or vice versa. Rather, Fiedler believes that the key to leadership success is putting our existing styles to work in situations for which they are the best "fit." This is true contingency leadership thinking with the goal of successfully matching one's style with situational demands.

Understanding Leadership Situations

In Fiedler's model, the amount of control a situation allows the leader is a critical issue in determining the correct style-situation fit. Three contingency variables are used to diagnose situational control. The *quality of leader–member relations* (good or poor) measures the degree to which the group supports the leader. The *degree of task structure* (high or low) measures the extent to which task goals, procedures, and guidelines are clearly spelled out. The *amount of position power* (strong or

Figure 13.4 Matching leadership style and situation—summary predictions from Fiedler's contingency theory.

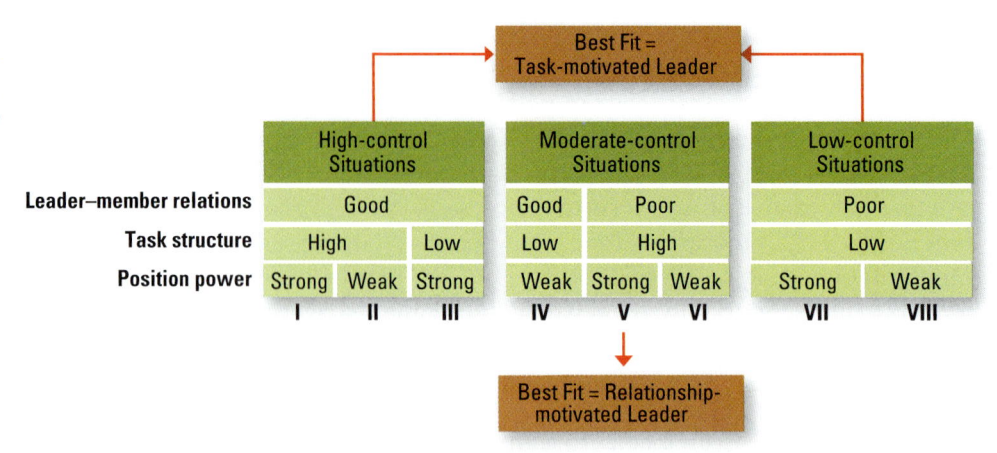

weak) measures the degree to which the position gives the leader power to reward and punish subordinates. *Figure 13.4* shows eight leadership situations that result from different combinations of these variables. They range from the most favourable situation of high control (good leader–member relations, high task structure, strong position power) to the least favourable situation of low control (poor leader–member relations, low task structure, weak position power).

Matching Leadership Style and Situation

Figure 13.4 also summarizes Fiedler's extensive research on the contingency relationships between situation control, leadership style, and leader effectiveness. Note that neither the task-oriented nor the relationship-oriented leadership style is effective all the time. Instead, each style appears to work best when used in the right situation. The results can be stated as two propositions. *Proposition 1* is that a task-oriented leader will be most successful in either very favourable (high-control) or very unfavourable (low-control) situations. *Proposition 2* is that a relationship-oriented leader will be most successful in situations of moderate control.

Assume, for example, that you are the leader of a team of bank tellers. The tellers seem highly supportive of you, and their job is clearly defined regarding what needs to be done. You have the authority to evaluate their performance and to make pay and promotion recommendations. This is a high-control situation consisting of good leader–member relations, high task structure, and strong position power. Figure 13.4 shows that a task-motivated leader would be most effective in this situation.

Now take another example. Suppose that you are chairperson of a committee asked to improve labour–management relations in a manufacturing plant. Although the goal is clear, no one can say for sure how to accomplish it. Task structure is low. Because committee members are free to quit any time they want, the chairperson has little position power. Because not all members believe the committee is necessary, poor leader–member relations are apparent. According to the figure, this low-control situation also calls for a task-motivated leader.

Finally, assume that you are the new head of a retail section in a large department store. Because you were selected over one of the popular sales clerks you now supervise, leader–member relations are poor. Task structure is high since the clerk's job is well defined. Your position power is low because the clerks work under a seniority system and fixed wage schedule. The figure shows that this moderate-control situation requires a relationship-motivated leader.

●●● HERSEY-BLANCHARD SITUATIONAL LEADERSHIP MODEL

In contrast to Fiedler's notion that leadership style is hard to change, the Hersey-Blanchard situational leadership model suggests that successful leaders do adjust their styles. And they do so based on the *maturity* of followers, indicated by their readiness to perform in a given situation.[31] "Readiness," in this sense, is based on how able and willing or confident followers are to perform required tasks. As shown in *Figure 13.5*, the possible leadership styles that result from different combinations of task-oriented and relationship-oriented behaviours are as follows:

- *Delegating*—allowing the group to take responsibility for task decisions; a low-task, low-relationship style.
- *Participating*—emphasizing shared ideas and participative decisions on task directions; a low-task, high-relationship style.
- *Selling*—explaining task directions in a supportive and persuasive way; a high-task, high-relationship style.
- *Telling*—giving specific task directions and closely supervising work; a high-task, low-relationship style.

Managers using this model must be able to implement the alternative leadership styles as needed. The *delegating style* works best in high-readiness situations of able and willing or confident followers; the *telling style* works best at the other extreme of low readiness, where followers are unable and unwilling or insecure. The *participating style* is recommended for low-to-moderate readiness (followers able but unwilling or insecure) and the *selling style* for moderate-to-high readiness (followers unable but willing or confident). Hersey and Blanchard further believe that leadership styles should be adjusted as followers change over time. The model also implies that if the correct styles are used in lower-readiness situations, followers will "mature" and grow in ability, willingness, and confidence. This allows the leader to become less directive as followers mature. Although the Hersey-Blanchard model is intuitively appealing, limited research has been accomplished on it to date.[32]

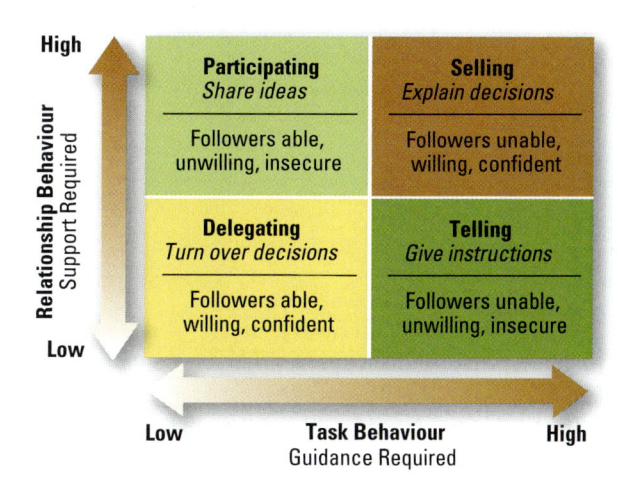

Figure 13.5 Leadership implications of the Hersey-Blanchard situational leadership model.

●●● HOUSE'S PATH-GOAL LEADERSHIP THEORY

A third contingency leadership approach is the path-goal theory advanced by Robert House.[33] This theory suggests that an effective leader is one who clarifies paths through which followers can achieve both task-related and personal goals. The best leaders raise motivation and help followers move along these paths. They remove any barriers that stand in the way and provide appropriate rewards for task accomplishment. Path-goal theorists believe leaders should be flexible and move back and forth among four leadership styles to create positive "path-goal" linkages.

- *Directive leadership*—letting subordinates know what is expected; giving directions on what to do and how; scheduling work to be done; maintaining definite standards of performance; clarifying the leader's role in the group.

- *Supportive leadership*—doing things to make work more pleasant; treating group members as equals; being friendly and approachable; showing concern for the well-being of subordinates.

- *Achievement-oriented leadership*—setting challenging goals; expecting the highest levels of performance; emphasizing continuous improvement in performance; displaying confidence in meeting high standards.

- *Participative leadership*—involving subordinates in decision making; consulting with subordinates; asking for suggestions from subordinates; using these suggestions when making a decision.

Path-Goal Predictions and Managerial Implications

The path-goal theory, summarized in *Figure 13.6*, advises managers to use leadership styles that fit situational needs. This means that the leader adds value by contributing things that are missing from the situation or that need strengthening; she or he specifically avoids redundant behaviours. For example, when team members are expert and competent at their tasks, it is unnecessary and even dysfunctional for the leader to tell them how to do things.

Figure 13.6 Contingency relationships in the path-goal leadership theory.

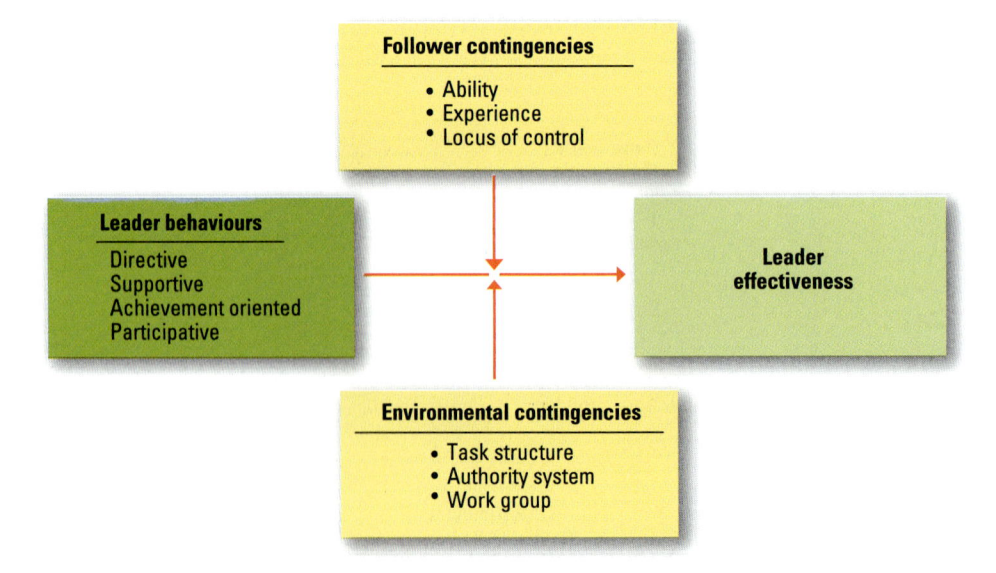

Follower contingencies
- Ability
- Experience
- Locus of control

Leader behaviours
Directive
Supportive
Achievement oriented
Participative

Leader effectiveness

Environmental contingencies
- Task structure
- Authority system
- Work group

The important contingencies for making good path-goal leadership choices include follower characteristics (ability, experience, and locus of control) and work environment characteristics (task structure, authority system, and work group). For example, the match of leader behaviours and situation might take the following forms.[34] When *job assignments* are unclear, directive leadership is appropriate to clarify task objectives and expected rewards. When *worker self-confidence* is low, supportive leadership is appropriate to increase confidence by emphasizing individual abilities and offering needed assistance. When *performance incentives* are poor, participative leadership is appropriate to clarify individual needs and identify appropriate rewards. When *task challenge* is insufficient in a job, achievement-oriented leadership is appropriate to set goals and raise performance aspirations.

Substitutes for Leadership

Path-goal theory has also contributed to the recognition of what are called **substitutes for leadership**.[35] These are aspects of the work setting and the people involved that can reduce the need for a leader's personal involvement. In effect, they make leadership from the "outside" unnecessary because leadership is already provided from within the situation. Possible substitutes for leadership include *subordinate characteristics* such as ability, experience, and independence; *task characteristics* such as routineness and availability of feedback; and *organizational characteristics* such as clarity of plans and formalization of rules and procedures. When these substitutes are present, managers should avoid duplicating them. Instead, they should concentrate on other and more important things.

■ **Substitutes for leadership** are factors in the work setting that direct work efforts without the involvement of a leader.

●●● VROOM-JAGO LEADER-PARTICIPATION MODEL

The Vroom-Jago leader-participation model is designed to help a leader choose the decision-making method that best fits the problem being faced.[36] The key issue is on the amount of decision-making participation allowed followers. The broad choices are for the leader to make an **authority, consultative**, or **group decision**.[37] In its current version, the model views a manager as leading effectively when making the right selection from among the following decision-making options:

- *Decide alone*—this is an authority decision; the manager decides how to solve the problem and communicates the decision to the group.
- *Consult individually*—the manager makes the decision after sharing the problem and consulting individually with group members to get their suggestions.
- *Consult with group*—the manager makes the decision after convening the group, sharing the problem, and consulting with everyone to get their suggestions.
- *Facilitate*—the manager convenes the group, shares the problem, and then facilitates group discussion to make a decision.
- *Delegate*—the manager convenes the group and delegates to group members the authority to define the problem and make a decision.

■ An **authority decision** is made by the leader and then communicated to the group.

■ A **consultative decision** is made by a leader after receiving information, advice, or opinions from group members.

■ A **group decision** is made by group members themselves.

In true contingency fashion, no one decision method is considered by the Vroom-Jago model as universally superior to any others. Each of the five decision methods is appropriate in certain situations, and each has its advantages and disadvantages.[38] Leadership success results when the decision type correctly matches the characteristics of the problem to be solved. The key rules guiding the choice relate to (1) *decision quality*—based on who has the information needed for problem solving; (2) *decision acceptance*—based on the importance of subordinate acceptance of the decision to its eventual implementation; and (3) *decision time*—based on the time available to make and implement the decision.

As shown in *Figure 13.7*, the more authority-oriented decisions work best when leaders personally have the expertise needed to solve the problem, they are confident and capable of acting alone, others are likely to accept and implement the decision they make, and little or no time is available for discussion. By contrast, in the following situations the more group-oriented and participative decision methods are recommended:

- The leader lacks sufficient expertise and information to solve this problem alone.
- The problem is unclear and help is needed to clarify the situation.
- Acceptance of the decision and commitment by others are necessary for implementation.
- Adequate time is available to allow for true participation.

Figure 13.7 Leadership implications of Vroom-Jago leader-participation model.

The more participative decision methods offer important benefits.[39] They help improve decision quality by bringing more information to bear on the problem. They help improve decision acceptance as participants gain understanding and become committed to the process. They also contribute to the development of leadership potential in others through the experience gained by active participation in the problem-solving process. However, there is a potential cost of lost efficiency. The greater the participation, the more time required for the decision process. Leaders do not always have sufficient time available; some problems must be resolved immediately. In such cases the authority decision may be the only option.[40]

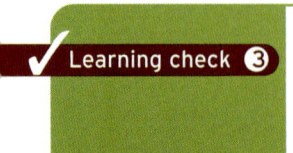

Learning check ③

BE SURE YOU CAN
• contrast the leader behaviour and contingency approaches to leadership research • explain the relationship between leadership style and a person's score on Fiedler's least-preferred co-worker scale • explain Fiedler's contingency thinking on matching leadership style and situation • identify the four leadership styles in the Hersey-Blanchard situational model • explain House's path-goal theory • illustrate the behaviours of directive, supportive, achievement-oriented, and participative leadership styles • define the term substitutes for leadership • contrast the authority, consultative, and group decisions in the Vroom-Jago model • explain when more participative decisions work best

TRANSFORMATIONAL LEADERSHIP

There is a great deal of interest today in "superleaders," persons whose visions and strong personalities have an extraordinary impact on others. They are often called **charismatic leaders** because of their special powers to inspire others in exceptional ways. Charisma was traditionally thought of as being limited to a few lucky persons who were born with it. Today, it is considered part of a broader set of special personal leadership that can be developed with foresight and practice.

■ A **charismatic leader** develops special leader–follower relationships and inspires followers in extraordinary ways.

●●● TRANSFORMATIONAL AND TRANSACTIONAL LEADERSHIP

Leadership scholars James MacGregor Burns and Bernard Bass suggest that the research and models we have discussed so far tend toward **transactional leadership**.[41] The impression is that if you learn the frameworks you can then apply them systematically to keep others moving forward to implement plans and achieve performance goals. Managers with this approach to leadership change styles, adjust tasks, and allocate rewards to achieve positive influence. Notably absent from this description is any evidence of "enthusiasm" and "inspiration," more emotional qualities that are characteristic of superleaders having charismatic appeal. Importantly, these are the very qualities that Burns and Bass associate with **transformational leadership**. This describes someone who is truly inspirational as a leader, who is personally excited about what they are doing, and who arouses others to seek extraordinary performance accomplishments. A transformational leader uses charisma and related qualities to raise aspirations and shift people and organizational systems into new high-performance patterns. The presence of transformational leadership is reflected in followers who are enthusiastic about the leader and his or her ideas, who work very hard to support them, who remain loyal and devoted, and who strive for superior performance accomplishments.

■ **Transactional leadership** directs the efforts of others through tasks, rewards, and structures.

■ **Transformational leadership** is inspirational and arouses extraordinary effort and performance.

take it to the case!

Southwest Airlines
It takes a leader to make the leadership difference

Herb Kelleher led Southwest Airlines from a small start-up in 1971 to become one of America's premier airlines. And he did it with a difference—low fares, on-time performance, and…fun! It wasn't just a winning airline industry strategy—finding a market niche and sticking with it—that Kelleher's leadership brought to the firm. It was also a leadership style focused on building and sustaining a positive organizational culture. Kelleher's personal style has been described as "dynamic" and based on "humour and friendliness." Colleen Barrett, his successor as CEO, follows the model. Under her leadership the firm is still tops in maintaining employee loyalty. What is Kelleher's advice to Barrett and other would-be leaders? "Ask your employees what's important to them. Ask your customers what is important to them. Then do it."

Source: Information from "We Weren't Just Airborne Yesterday," <www.swamedia.com/about_swa/airborne.html>

The transactional and transformational leadership approaches are not mutually exclusive. On its own, transactional leadership is probably insufficient to meet fully the leadership challenges and demands of today's dynamic work environments. Rather, it is a foundation or building block for solid day-to-day leadership. But in a context of continuous and often large-scale change, the additional and inspirational impact of transformational leadership becomes essential. One way to describe this in a classroom situation is the following. Skill at transactional leadership will earn you a B, allowing you to routinely lead people quite well. Moving from B to A leadership however, requires additional excellence in transformational leadership.

●●● QUALITIES OF A TRANSFORMATIONAL LEADER

The goal of excellence in transformational leadership offers a distinct management challenge, with important personal development implications. It is not enough to possess leadership traits, know the leadership behaviours, and understand leadership contingencies. Any manager must also be prepared to lead in an inspirational way and with a compelling personality. The transformational leader provides a strong sense of vision and a contagious enthusiasm that substantially raises the confidence, aspirations, and performance commitments of followers. The special qualities characteristic of transformational leaders include the following:[42]

- *Vision*—having ideas and a clear sense of direction; communicating them to others; developing excitement about accomplishing shared "dreams."

- *Charisma*—using the power of personal reference and emotion to arouse others' enthusiasm, faith, loyalty, pride, and trust in themselves.

- *Symbolism*—identifying "heroes" and holding spontaneous and planned ceremonies to celebrate excellence and high achievement.

- *Empowerment*—helping others develop by removing performance obstacles, sharing responsibilities, and delegating truly challenging work.

- *Intellectual stimulation*—gaining the involvement of others by creating awareness of problems and stirring their imaginations.

- *Integrity*—being honest and credible, acting consistently out of personal conviction, and following through on commitments.

> **Learning check 4**
>
> **BE SURE YOU CAN**
> • define the terms transformational leadership and transactional leadership • explain when transformational leadership becomes essential • identify the special personal qualities of transformational leaders

CURRENT ISSUES IN LEADERSHIP DEVELOPMENT

A number of issues and themes related to leadership development add further context to the many insights of this chapter. Of particular interest are research on both emotional intelligence and the relationship between gender and leadership, as well as practical discussions of the everyday work of a leader and the importance of ethical leadership in our society.

EMOTIONAL INTELLIGENCE

An area of leadership development that is currently very popular is **emotional intelligence**, first discussed in Chapter 1 as part of the essential human skills of managers. Popularized by the work of Daniel Goleman, "EI" is defined as "the ability to manage ourselves and our relationships effectively."[43] According to his research, emotional intelligence is an important influence on leadership effectiveness, especially in more senior management positions. In Goleman's words, "the higher the rank of the person considered to be a star performer, the more emotional intelligence capabilities showed up as the reason for his or her effectiveness."[44] This is a strong endorsement for considering whether or not EI is one of your leadership assets. Important too is Goleman's belief that emotional intelligence skills can be learned.

Emotional intelligence is the ability to manage our emotions in social relationships.

For purposes of research and training, Goleman breaks emotional intelligence down into five critical components.[45] He argues that each of us should strive for competency in each component and thereby maximize our ability to work well in relationships with others. The critical components of EI are the following:

- *Self-awareness*—understanding our own moods and emotions, and understanding their impact on our work and on others.

- *Self-regulation*—thinking before we act and controlling otherwise disruptive impulses.

- *Motivation*—working hard with persistence and for reasons other than money and status.

- *Empathy*—understanding the emotions of others and using this understanding to better relate to them.

- *Social skill*—establishing rapport with others and building good relationships and networks.

GENDER AND LEADERSHIP

One of the leadership themes of continuing interest deals with the question of whether gender influences leadership styles and/or effectiveness. Sara Levinson, president of NFL Properties Inc., for example, once asked the all-male members of her management team, "Is my leadership style different from a man's?" "Yes," they replied, suggesting that the very fact that she was asking the question was evidence of the difference. They also indicated that her leadership style emphasized communication, and gathering ideas and opinions from others. When Levinson probed further by asking, "Is this a distinctly 'female' trait?", they said that they thought it was.[46]

The evidence clearly supports the fact that both women and men can be effective leaders.[47] As suggested in the prior example, however, they may tend toward somewhat different styles.[48] Victor Vroom and his colleagues have investigated gender differences in respect to the leader-participation model discussed earlier.[49] They find women managers to be significantly more participative than their male counterparts. Other studies report that peers, subordinates, and supervisors of female leaders rate them higher than men on motivating others, fostering communication, listening to others, and producing high-quality work.[50] This style has been called *interactive leadership*.[51] Leaders with this style display behaviours typically considered democratic and participative—showing respect for others, caring for others, and sharing power and information with others. They focus on building consensus and good interpersonal relations through communication and involvement. The interactive style has qualities in common with the transformational leadership just discussed.[52] An interactive leader tends to use personal power, gaining influence over others through support, and interpersonal relationships. Men, by contrast, may tend toward more transactional approaches, relying more on directive and assertive behaviours, and using position power in a traditional "command and control" way.

Given the emphasis on shared power, communication, co-operation, and participation in the new-form organizations of today, these results are provocative. The interactive leadership style seems to be an excellent fit with the demands of a diverse workforce and the new workplace. As Harvard professor and consultant Rosabeth Moss Kanter says, "Women get high ratings on exactly those skills required to succeed in the Global Information Age, where teamwork and partnering are so important."[53] Gender issues aside, it seems clear that future leadership success for anyone will rest on one's capacity to lead through openness, positive relationships, support, and empowerment.

Canadian Managers
Leading through Innovation

David Patchell-Evans, founder and CEO of London, Ontario-based GoodLife Fitness Clubs, has built Canada's largest fitness chain by doing things differently. "In my business, people don't want a typical CEO," says Patchell-Evans, who prefers to be called "Patch." Innovation is the hallmark of his leadership style. He has acquired exclusive Canadian rights to Visual Fitness Planner, a software tool that allows clients to picture themselves before and after they've met their fitness goals. Other new ways to attract and retain customers Patchell-Evans has implemented include free DVD rentals, babysitting and tanning services, women-only fitness facilities, and a Web-based nutrition program to be launched in the fall of 2006. He's also planning to recycle energy from hot water, which he estimates will save $6,000 to $20,000 per year at seven locations retrofitted with the technology.

Source: Erin Pooley, "Most innovative CEO 2005: David Patchell-Evans, GoodLife Fitness Clubs," *Canadian Business*, April 25–May 8, 2005.

●●● DRUCKER'S "OLD-FASHIONED" LEADERSHIP

Peter Drucker offered a time-tested and very pragmatic view of leadership. It is based on what he referred to as a "good old-fashioned" look at the plain hard work it takes to be a successful leader. Consider, for example, his description of a telephone conversation with a potential consulting client. "We'd want you to run a seminar for us on how one acquires charisma," she said. Drucker's response was not what she expected. He advised her that there was more to leadership than the popular emphasis on personal "dash" or charisma. In fact, he said that "leadership…is work."[54]

Drucker's observations remind us that leadership effectiveness must have strong foundations. First, he believed that the basic building block of effective leadership is *defining and establishing a sense of mission*. A good leader sets the goals, priorities, and standards. A good leader keeps them all clear and visible, and maintains them. In Drucker's words, "The leader's first task is to be the trumpet that sounds a clear sound." Second, he believed in *accepting leadership as a responsibility rather than a rank*. Good leaders surround themselves with talented people. They are not afraid to develop strong and capable subordinates. And, they do not blame others when things go wrong. As Drucker said, "The buck stops here" is still a good adage to remember. Third, he stressed the importance of *earning and keeping the trust of others*. The key here is the leader's personal integrity. The followers of good leaders trust them. This means that they believe the leader means what he or she says and that his or her actions will be consistent with what is said. In Drucker's words again, "Effective leadership… is not based on being clever; it is based primarily on being consistent."

MORAL LEADERSHIP

As discussed in Chapter 3, society today is unforgiving in its demands that organizations be run with **ethical leadership**—that is, leadership by moral standards that meet the ethical test of being "good" and not "bad," of being "right" and not "wrong."[55] The expectation is that anyone in a leadership position will practise high ethical standards of behaviour, help to build and maintain an ethical organizational culture, and both help and require others to behave ethically in their work. *Management* has communicated throughout an essential belief about success in work and in life—long-term, sustainable success can only be built upon a foundation

■ **Ethical leadership** is always "good" and "right" by moral standards.

AROUND THE WORLD

In his book *Transforming Leadership: A New Pursuit of Happiness*, James MacGregor Burns explains that transformational leadership creates significant, even revolutionary, change in social systems. But he dissociates certain historical figures from this definition: Napoleon is out—too much order-and-obey in his style; Hitler is out—no moral foundations; Mao is out, too—no true empowerment of followers. Among Burns's positive role models from history are Gandhi, George Washington, and Eleanor Roosevelt. He firmly believes that great leaders follow agendas true to the wishes of followers. He gives the example of Franklin Delano Roosevelt, who said: "If we do not have the courage to lead the American people where they want to go, someone else will." Burns also says that wherever in the world great leadership is found it will always have a moral anchor point.

Source: James MacGregor Burns, *Transforming Leadership: A New Pursuit of Happiness* (New York: Atlantic Monthly Press, 2003); information from Christopher Caldwell, book review, *International Herald Tribune*, April 29, 2003, p. 18.

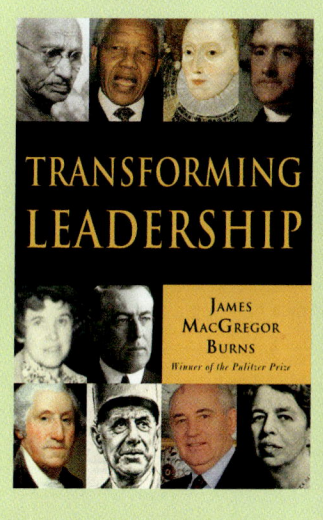

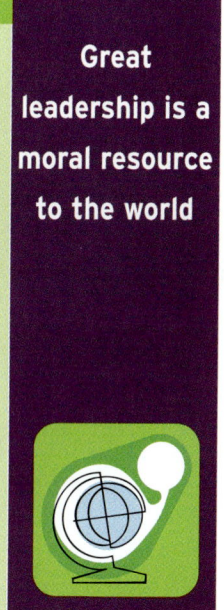

Great leadership is a moral resource to the world

of solid ethical behaviour. As a leader, you should not try to be ethical out of fear of being caught doing something wrong; you should want to be ethical because of the freedom and success that it brings. Ethical leaders have little to fear when the inevitable problems and traumas of daily work appear. They can act with confidence, always knowing that their actions are beyond reproach.

Ethical leadership begins with personal integrity, a concept fundamental to the notions of both transformational and good old-fashioned leadership. A leader with **integrity** is honest, credible, and consistent in putting values into action. When a leader has integrity, he or she earns the trust of followers. And when followers believe leaders are trustworthy, they are willing to commit themselves to behave in ways that live up to the leader's expectations. For managers in our high-pressure and competitive work environments, nothing can substitute for leadership strongly anchored in personal integrity. When viewed through the lens of what is truly the right thing to do, even the most difficult decisions become easier.

John W. Gardner talks with great insight about further "moral aspects" of leadership.[56] He does so with great respect for people and the talents that they bring with them to the workplace. "Most people in most organizations most of the time," Gardner writes, "are more stale than they know, more bored than they care to admit." Leaders, according to Gardner, have a moral obligation to build performance capacities by awakening the potential of each individual—to urge each person "to take the initiative in performing leader-like acts." He points out that high expectations tend to generate high performance. It is the leader's job to remove "obstacles to our effective functioning—to help individuals see and pursue shared purposes."

The concept of **authentic leadership** advanced by Fred Luthans and Bruce Avolio is relevant in this same context.[57] Authentic leadership activates performance through the positive psychological states of confidence, hope, optimism, and resilience. It enhances self-awareness and self-development by the leader and by her or his associates. The resulting positive self-regulation helps authentic leaders to clearly frame moral dilemmas, transparently respond to them, and serve as ethical role models.[58] There is no doubt that ethical leadership has such authenticity and is also strongly anchored in a true commitment to people. Pat Daniel, President and Chief Executive Officer of Enbridge Inc., is considered an authentic leader. He is known to have high integrity, a deep sense of service to his employees, the community, the environment, and a view that each of Enbridge's 4,000 employees has the potential to be a leader.[59]

■ **Integrity** in leadership is honesty, credibility, and consistency in putting values into action.

■ **Authentic leadership** activates positive psychological states to achieve self-awareness and positive self-regulation.

Learning check 5

BE SURE YOU CAN

• explain how emotional intelligence contributes to leadership success • discuss alternative views of the relationship between gender and leadership • list Drucker's three essentials of good old-fashioned leadership • define the term integrity and discuss it as a foundation for moral leadership

Chapter 13 STUDY GUIDE

WHERE WE'VE BEEN

Back to J.-Robert Ouimet

The opening example of J.-Robert Ouimet illustrates that leadership is a competitive tool that provides support for meaningful personal and organizational performance. In this chapter you learned about the trait and leader behaviour approaches to leadership, as well as important contingency models as developed by Fiedler, Hersey-Blanchard, House, and Vroom-Jago. You also learned the difference between transformational and transactional leadership, and were introduced to current issues in leadership development, including emotional intelligence, gender differences, and moral foundations.

THE NEXT STEP
INTEGRATED LEARNING ACTIVITIES

Cases/Projects
- Southwest Airlines Case
- Project 7—Gender and Leadership
- Project 9—Management in Popular Culture

Self-Assessments
- Emotional Intelligence (#2)
- "T-P" Leadership Questionnaire (#20)
- "T-T" Leadership Style (#21)
- Least-Preferred Co-Worker Scale (#22)

Exercises in Teamwork
- My Best Manager (#1)
- The Future Workplace (#14)
- Leading through Participation (#16)
- Sources and Uses of Power (#19)

STUDY QUESTION SUMMARY

1. What is the nature of leadership?
- Leadership is the process of inspiring others to work hard to accomplish important tasks.
- The ability to communicate a vision, a clear sense of the future, is increasingly considered to be an essential ingredient of effective leadership.
- Power is the ability to get others to do what you want them to do through leadership.
- Managerial power equals position power plus personal power.
- Sources of position power include rewards, coercion, and legitimacy or formal authority; sources of personal power include expertise and reference.
- Effective leaders empower others—that is, they help and allow others to make job-related decisions on their own.

2. What are the important leadership traits and behaviours?
- Early leadership research searched unsuccessfully for a set of personal traits that would always differentiate successful and unsuccessful leaders.
- Traits that do seem to have a positive impact on leadership include drive, integrity, and self-confidence.
- Research on leader behaviours focused on alternative leadership styles based on concerns for task and concerns for people.
- One suggestion of leader-behaviour researchers is that effective leaders will be good at team-based or participative leadership that is high in both task and people concerns.

3. What are the contingency theories of leadership?
- Contingency leadership approaches point out that no one leadership style always works best; the best style is one that properly matches the demands of each unique situation.

- Fiedler's contingency model describes how situational differences in task structure, position power, and leader–member relations may influence which leadership style works best.
- House's path-goal theory points out that leaders should add value to situations by responding with supportive, directive, achievement-oriented, and/or participative styles as needed.
- The Hersey-Blanchard situational model recommends using task-oriented and people-oriented behaviours, depending on the "maturity" levels of followers.
- The Vroom-Jago leader-participation theory advises leaders to choose decision-making methods—individual, consultative, group—that best fit the problems they are trying to solve.

4. What is transformational leadership?
- Charismatic leadership creates a truly inspirational relationship between leader and followers.
- Transactional leadership focuses on tasks, rewards, and structures to influence follower behaviour.
- Transformational leaders use charisma and emotion to inspire others toward extraordinary efforts in support of change and performance excellence.

5. What are current issues in leadership development?
- Emotional intelligence, the ability to manage our relationships and ourselves effectively, is an important leadership capability.
- The interactive leadership style often associated with women emphasizes communication, involvement, and interpersonal respect, all things consistent with the demands of the new workplace.
- Drucker and others remind us that leadership is "hard work" that always requires a personal commitment to consistently meeting high ethical and moral standards.

KEY TERMS REVIEW

Authentic leadership (p. 352)
Authority decision (p. 345)
Autocratic style (p. 340)
Charismatic leader (p. 347)
Coercive power (p. 334)
Consultative decision (p. 345)
Democratic style (p. 340)
Emotional intelligence (p. 349)
Empowerment (p. 337)

Ethical leadership (p. 351)
Expert power (p. 334)
Group decision (p. 345)
Integrity (p. 352)
Laissez-faire style (p. 340)
Leadership (p. 333)
Leadership style (p. 339)
Legitimate power (p. 334)
Power (p. 334)

Referent power (p. 336)
Reward power (p. 334)
Substitutes for leadership (p. 345)
Transactional leadership (p. 347)
Transformational leadership (p. 347)
Vision (p. 333)
Visionary leadership (p. 333)

SELF-TEST 13

MULTIPLE-CHOICE QUESTIONS:

1. Someone with a clear sense of the future and the actions needed to get there is considered a _____ leader.
   (a) task-oriented (b) people-oriented (c) transactional (d) visionary
2. Managerial power = _____ power × _____ power.
   (a) reward, punishment (b) reward, expert (c) legitimate, position (d) position, personal
3. A manager who says "Because I am the boss, you must do what I ask" is relying on _____ power.
   (a) reward (b) legitimate (c) expert (d) referent
4. The personal traits now considered important for managerial success include _____.
   (a) self-confidence (b) gender (c) age (d) personality
5. According to the Blake and Mouton model of leader behaviours, the most successful leader is one who acts with _____.
   (a) high initiating structure (b) high consideration (c) high concern for task and high concern for people (d) low job stress and high task goals

6. In Fiedler's contingency model, both highly favourable and highly unfavourable leadership situations are best dealt with by a _____ leader.
   (a) task-oriented (b) laissez-faire (c) participative (d) relationship-oriented
7. Directive leadership and achievement-oriented leadership are among the options in House's _____ theory of leadership.
   (a) trait (b) path-goal (c) transformational (d) life-cycle
8. Vision, charisma, integrity, and symbolism are all on the list of attributes typically associated with _____ leaders.
   (a) contingency (b) informal (c) transformational (d) transactional
9. _____ leadership theory suggests that leadership success is achieved by correctly matching leadership style with situations.
   (a) Trait (b) Fiedler's (c) Transformational (d) Blake and Mouton's
10. In the leader-behaviour approaches to leadership, someone who does a very good job of planning work, setting standards, and monitoring results would be considered a(n) _____ leader.
    (a) task-oriented (b) control-oriented (c) achievement-oriented (d) employee-centred
11. When a leader assumes that others will do as she asks because they want to positively identify with her, she is relying on _____ power to influence their behaviour.
    (a) expert (b) reference (c) legitimate (d) reward
12. The interactive leadership style often associated with women is characterized by _____.
    (a) inclusion and information sharing (b) use of rewards and punishments (c) command and control (d) emphasis on position power
13. A leader whose actions indicate an attitude of "do as you want and don't bother me" would be described as having a(n) _____ leadership style.
    (a) autocratic (b) country club (c) democratic (d) laissez-faire
14. The critical contingency variable in the Hersey-Blanchard situational model of leadership is _____.
    (a) followers' maturity (b) LPC (c) task structure (d) emotional intelligence
15. A leader who _____ would be described as achievement oriented in the path-goal theory.
    (a) works hard to achieve high performance (b) sets challenging goals for others (c) gives directions and monitors results (d) builds commitment through participation

SHORT-RESPONSE QUESTIONS:

16. Why does a person need both position power and personal power to achieve long-term managerial effectiveness?
17. What is the major insight offered by the Vroom-Jago leader-participation model?
18. What are the three variables that Fiedler's contingency model uses to diagnose the favourability of leadership situations, and what does each mean?
19. How does Peter Drucker's view of "good old-fashioned leadership" differ from the popular concept of transformational leadership?

APPLICATION QUESTION:

20. When Marcel Henry took over as leader of a new product development team, he was both excited and apprehensive. "I wonder," he said to himself on the first day in his new assignment, "if I can meet the challenges of leadership." Later that day, Marcel shares this concern with you during a coffee break. Based on the insights of this chapter, how would you describe to him the implications for his personal leadership development of current thinking on transformational leadership and moral leadership?

14 Motivation—Theory and Practice

CHAPTER 14 STUDY QUESTIONS

1. What is motivation?
2. What are the different types of individual needs?
3. What are the process theories of motivation?
4. What role does reinforcement play in motivation?
5. What are the challenges of motivation in the new workplace?

Planning Ahead
After reading Chapter 14, you should be able to answer these questions in your own words.

GENENTECH

PASSION FOR SCIENCE AND PEOPLE

What does it take to make it to the top of the "best companies to work for" lists produced by publications such as *Fortune*, *Science*, *Scientist*, and *Essence*, and the *San Francisco Business Times*? Genentech did it by attracting and keeping an energized and motivated staff.

Founded in 1976, Genentech's motivational culture has been its competitive advantage. Founders Bob Swanson and Herb Boyer knew the success of their venture depended on luring and keeping big-brain bioscience talent. Art Levinson continued this tradition when he became CEO in 1995. Levinson maintained the focus on championing the science, creating a stream of new drugs, and winning over employees. This focus has paid off. Genentech is not just the very first biotechnology company, it is the brightest star in the industry with year-end revenues approaching $6.6 billion in 2006—three times higher than four years ago.

Genentech pours a tremendous amount of energy into creating a culture that motivates and supports people with passion. The atmosphere is casual and collegial, and employees don't get assignments—they receive "appointments." They traverse the grounds by shuttle bus and bicycles provided by the company. Employees can visit the on-site libraries and a bank, use company subsidized daycare and cafeterias, or draw on the concierge service to help with personal errands. At Genentech, every milestone calls for celebration—and on very big occasions, very big celebrity bands. After an unusual run of drug approvals, the parking lot in front of Building 9 became the site of a rock concert featuring Elton John, Mary J. Blige, and Matchbox 20.

Genentech looks for people like Ellen Filvaroff, a senior scientist in molecular oncology. Her walls are decorated with pictures of her patients and her toddler. The perks she likes most are little things—like being able to purchase and mail birthday cards from the company store. But the biggest perk by far, she says, is having colleagues who can help crack the science. Collaboration at Genentech is easy and encouraged; sabbaticals keep creativity alive and stave off burnout; and scientists and engineers are encouraged to pursue pet projects.

While Genentech offers flexible medical benefits, long-term disability, and life insurance, they recognize that different things motivate different people. They provide employee recognition through a corporate bonus program, as well as cash bonuses when extraordinary milestones are reached. They offer stock purchase plans, flexible-spending accounts, discounts for cellular phones, vacations to Disneyland, legal services, and even pet insurance.

With all that Genentech has to offer it is no wonder it has been on many "100 Best Companies to Work For" lists for the past seven consecutive years.[1]

GET CONNECTED!

What do you want from work? Don't settle for anything less than the best fit between opportunities in your work environment and personal goals.

Chapter 14 LEARNING PREVIEW

The chapter opening example of Genentech demonstrates how management commitment to employees shown through the development of a supportive culture, the celebration of successes, an appreciation of individuality, and recognition that different things motivate different people pays off. In this chapter you will learn about the concept of motivation. You will examine the main content, process, and reinforcement theories that help to explain motivation to work. You will also gain an understanding of their practical implications.

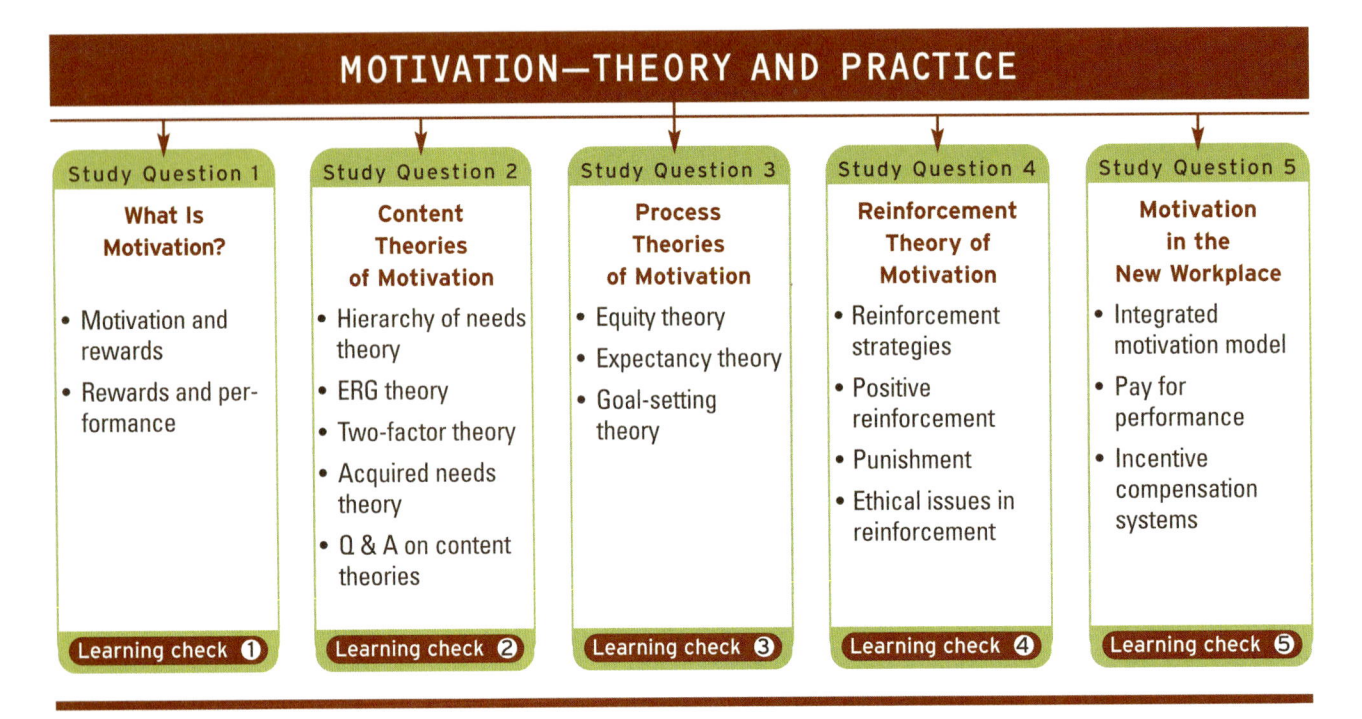

MOTIVATION—THEORY AND PRACTICE

Study Question 1
What Is Motivation?
- Motivation and rewards
- Rewards and performance

Learning check 1

Study Question 2
Content Theories of Motivation
- Hierarchy of needs theory
- ERG theory
- Two-factor theory
- Acquired needs theory
- Q & A on content theories

Learning check 2

Study Question 3
Process Theories of Motivation
- Equity theory
- Expectancy theory
- Goal-setting theory

Learning check 3

Study Question 4
Reinforcement Theory of Motivation
- Reinforcement strategies
- Positive reinforcement
- Punishment
- Ethical issues in reinforcement

Learning check 4

Study Question 5
Motivation in the New Workplace
- Integrated motivation model
- Pay for performance
- Incentive compensation systems

Learning check 5

Why do some people work enthusiastically, often doing more than required to turn out an extraordinary performance? Why do others hold back and do the minimum needed to avoid reprimand or termination? How can a team leader or manager build a high-performance work setting? What can be done to ensure that the highest possible performance is achieved by every person in every job on every workday? These questions are, or should be, asked by managers in all work settings. Good answers begin with a true respect for people, with all of their talents and diversity, as the human capital of organizations. The best managers already know this. Like the opening example of Genentech, the work cultures they create invariably reflect an awareness that "productivity through people" is an irreplaceable foundation for long-term success. Consider these comments by those who know what it means to lead a high-performance organization.[2]

> *When people feel connected to something with a purpose greater than themselves, it inspires them to reach for levels they might not otherwise obtain…Our business is based on human potential.*
>
> George Zimmer, founder and CEO of Men's Warehouse

No business goal is worth sacrificing your values. If you have to treat people poorly, or cut corners in your dealings with customers, forget it…You can build an organization based on mutual loyalty…but you can't do it if you treat people as disposable.

Patrick Kelly, CEO of PSS/World Medical, Inc.

In an increasingly competitive environment, it is vitally important that organizations take full advantage of the considerable potential inherent in their people.

Graham Dodd, Canadian practice leader at Watson Wyatt Canada

It is easy to say as a leader, or write in a mission statement, that "people are our most important asset." But the proof comes when actions back up the words. This means consistently demonstrating that one's organization is committed to people, that it offers a truly "motivational" work environment. Realistically, however, this task isn't always easy. The workplace often becomes complicated as the intricacies of human psychology come to play in daily events and situations. Sometimes a great employee who was motivated and energized turns into a dead-weight, pulling the company down. His ideas have dried up, he mopes around, and his only contribution to organizational functioning is relaying last night's hockey scores. Chances are he's checked out mentally from the company—something human-resource practitioners call "disengagement." Many would fire this slacker—or maybe not, says Jocelyn Bérard, managing director of DDI Canada, a human-resource consulting firm in Toronto. "Letting somebody go is not pleasant, and it can be very costly as well," says Bérard. "If you lose the person, you lose the expertise and sometimes even a client, and that's worse." Bérard suggests a better strategy would be to figure why the employee has changed and start working on getting the employee back psychologically.[3]

WHAT IS MOTIVATION?

The term **motivation** is used in management theory to describe forces within the individual that account for the level, direction, and persistence of effort expended at work. Simply put, a highly motivated person works hard at a job; an unmotivated person does not. A manager who leads through motivation does so by creating conditions under which other people feel consistently inspired to work hard. Obviously, a highly motivated workforce is indispensable to the achievement of sustained high-performance results.

■ **Motivation** accounts for the level, direction, and persistence of effort expended at work.

●●● MOTIVATION AND REWARDS

A *reward* is a work outcome of positive value to the individual. A motivational work setting is rich in rewards for people whose performance accomplishments help meet organizational objectives. In management, it is useful to distinguish between two types of rewards, extrinsic and intrinsic. **Extrinsic rewards** are externally administered. They are valued outcomes given to someone by another person, typically, a supervisor or higher-level manager. Common workplace examples are pay bonuses, promotions, time off, special assignments, office fixtures, awards, verbal praise, and recognition. The motivational stimulus of these extrinsic rewards originates outside of the individual; the rewards are made available by another person or by the organizational system.[4]

■ An **extrinsic reward** is provided by someone else.

take it to the case!

Nucor
A case for less management

Can a focus on delivering superior employee relations contribute to a company's success? Nucor thinks so! The highly successful steel company maintains an extremely streamlined management structure and limits executive perks, choosing instead to focus on recognizing performance at all levels of the organization. Nucor believes that empowering employees to make decisions results in their employees making creative and beneficial contributions to the organization. By emphasising the innovative potential of its people, Nucor continues to lead the highly competitive steel industry.

Located in Midland, Ontario, Baytech Plastics engineers, manufactures, finishes, and assembles high-quality, custom-molded plastic components for both domestic and international markets. The company has remained successful through periods of rapid change by retaining and motivating its high-quality workforce. How does this company minimize employee turnover while maximizing productivity? It places a priority on a number of extrinsic initiatives, including competitive wages, pension plan, and health and dental benefits; as well as an innovative pay-for-performance system developed in co-operation with the union. The result is happy employees and a turnover rate of about 1.2 percent.[5]

■ An **intrinsic reward** occurs naturally during job performance.

Intrinsic rewards, by contrast, are self-administered. They occur "naturally" as a person performs a task, and are, in this sense, built directly into the job itself. The major sources of intrinsic rewards are the feelings of competency, personal development, and self-control people experience in their work.[6] In contrast to extrinsic rewards, the motivational stimulus of intrinsic rewards is internal and does not depend on the actions of some other person. Being self-administered, they offer the great advantage and power of "motivating from within." An air traffic controller, for example, says: "I don't know of anything I'd rather be doing. I love working the airplanes."[7]

●●● REWARDS AND PERFORMANCE

Starbucks seems to have the recipe right—not just for coffee, but also for rewards and performance. The company offers a stock option plan to all its employees. Called "bean stock," the incentive plan offers employees stock options linked to their base pay. This means they can buy the company's stock at a fixed price in the future; if the market value is higher than the price of their option, they gain. Thus, they should be motivated to do things that help the firm perform best. CEO Howard Schultz says the plan has had a positive impact on attitudes and performance. The phrase "bean-stocking it" is even used by employees when they find ways to reduce costs or increase sales. Schultz is committed to the motivational value of this innovative reward plan.[8]

There are many possible ways to creatively and directly link rewards and performance in the new workplace, that is, to establish *performance-contingent rewards*. To take full advantage of the possibilities, however, managers must (1) respect diversity and individual differences in order to best understand what people want from work, and (2) allocate rewards in ways that satisfy the interests of both individuals and the organization. A variety of motivation theories provide insights into this complex process. The *content theories of motivation* help us to understand human needs and how people with different needs may respond to different work situations. The *process theories of motivation* describe how people give meaning to rewards and then make decisions on various work-related behaviours. The *reinforcement theory of motivation* focuses on the environment as a major source of rewards that influence human behaviour.

> **BE SURE YOU CAN**
>
> • define the term motivation • differentiate extrinsic and intrinsic rewards • explain the concept of performance-contingent rewards • differentiate the basic approaches of the content, process, and reinforcement theories
>
> ✓ Learning check ❶

CONTENT THEORIES OF MOTIVATION

Most discussions of motivation begin with the concept of individual **needs**—the unfulfilled physiological or psychological desires of an individual. Content theories of motivation use individual needs to explain the behaviours and attitudes of people at work. Although each of the following theories discusses a slightly different set of needs, all agree that needs cause tensions that influence attitudes and behaviour. Good managers and leaders establish conditions in which people are able to satisfy important needs through their work. They also eliminate work obstacles that interfere with the satisfaction of important needs.

■ A **need** is an unfulfilled physiological or psychological desire.

●●● HIERARCHY OF NEEDS THEORY

The theory of human needs developed by Abraham Maslow was introduced in Chapter 2 as an important foundation of the history of management thought. According to his hierarchy of human needs, **lower-order needs** include physiological, safety, and social concerns, and **higher-order needs** include esteem and self-actualization concerns.[9] Whereas lower-order needs are desires for social and physical well-being, the higher-order needs are desires for psychological development and growth.

Maslow uses two principles to describe how these needs affect human behaviour. The *deficit principle* states that a satisfied need is not a motivator of behaviour. People are expected to act in ways that satisfy deprived needs—that is, needs for which a "deficit" exists. The *progression principle* states that a need at one level does not become activated until the next lower-level need is already satisfied. People are expected to advance step-by-step up the hierarchy in their search for need satisfactions. At the level of self-actualization, the more these needs are satisfied, the stronger they are supposed to grow. According to Maslow, a person should continue

■ **Lower-order needs** are physiological, safety, and social needs in Maslow's hierarchy.

■ **Higher-order needs** are esteem and self-actualization needs in Maslow's hierarchy.

to be motivated by opportunities for self-fulfillment as long as the other needs remain satisfied. Although research has not verified the strict deficit and progression principles, Maslow's ideas are very helpful for understanding the needs of people at work and considering what can be done to satisfy them. His theory advises managers to recognize that deprived needs may result in negative attitudes and behaviours. By the same token, opportunities for need satisfaction may have positive motivational consequences. *Figure 14.1* illustrates how managers can use Maslow's ideas to better meet the needs of the people with whom they work. Notice that the higher-order self-actualization needs are served entirely by intrinsic rewards. The esteem needs are served by both intrinsic and extrinsic rewards. Lower-order needs are served solely by extrinsic rewards.

Figure 14.1 Opportunities for satisfaction in Maslow's hierarchy of human needs.

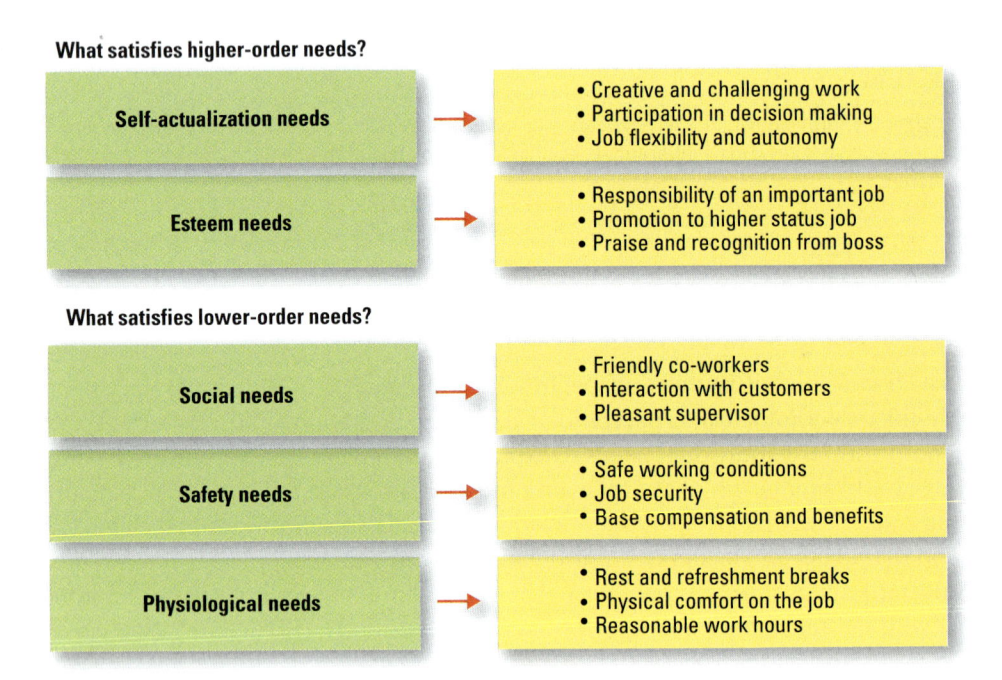

What satisfies higher-order needs?

Self-actualization needs →
- Creative and challenging work
- Participation in decision making
- Job flexibility and autonomy

Esteem needs →
- Responsibility of an important job
- Promotion to higher status job
- Praise and recognition from boss

What satisfies lower-order needs?

Social needs →
- Friendly co-workers
- Interaction with customers
- Pleasant supervisor

Safety needs →
- Safe working conditions
- Job security
- Base compensation and benefits

Physiological needs →
- Rest and refreshment breaks
- Physical comfort on the job
- Reasonable work hours

●●● ERG THEORY

One of the most promising efforts to build on Maslow's work is the ERG theory proposed by Clayton Alderfer.[10] This theory collapses Maslow's five needs categories into three. *Existence needs* are desires for physiological and material well-being. *Relatedness needs* are desires for satisfying interpersonal relationships. *Growth needs* are desires for continued psychological growth and development. Alderfer's ERG theory also differs from Maslow's theory in other respects. ERG does not assume that lower-level needs must be satisfied before higher-level needs become activated; any or all types of needs can influence individual behaviour at a given time. Alderfer also does not assume that satisfied needs lose their motivational impact. ERG theory contains a *frustration-regression principle*, according to which an already-satisfied lower-level need can become reactivated and influence behaviour when a higher-level need cannot be satisfied. Alderfer's approach offers an additional means for understanding human needs and their influence on people at work.

●●● TWO-FACTOR THEORY

The two-factor theory of Frederick Herzberg was developed from a pattern identified in the responses of almost 4,000 people to questions about their work.[11] When questioned about what "turned them on," they tended to identify things relating to the nature of the job itself. Herzberg calls these **satisfier factors**. When questioned about what "turned them off," they tended to identify things relating more to the work setting. Herzberg calls these **hygiene factors**.

As shown in *Figure 14.2*, the two-factor theory associates hygiene factors, or sources of *job dissatisfaction*, with aspects of *job context*. The *hygiene factors* include such things as working conditions, interpersonal relations, organizational policies and administration, technical quality of supervision, and base wage or salary. These factors contribute to more or less job dissatisfaction. Herzberg argues that improving them, such as by adding piped in music or implementing a no-smoking policy, can make people less dissatisfied with these aspects of their work. But this will not increase job satisfaction. That requires attention to an entirely different set of factors and managerial initiatives.

To improve motivation, Herzberg advises managers to focus on the satisfier factors. By making improvements in *job content* he believes that job satisfaction and performance can be raised. The important *satisfier factors* include such things as a sense of achievement, feelings of recognition, a sense of responsibility, the opportunity for advancement, and feelings of personal growth.

Scholars have criticized Herzberg's theory as being method-bound and difficult to replicate.[12] For his part, Herzberg reports confirming studies in countries located in Europe, Africa, the Middle East, and Asia.[13] At the very least, the two-factor theory remains a useful reminder that there are two important aspects of all jobs: *job content*, what people do in terms of job tasks; and *job context*, the work setting in which they do it. Herzberg's advice to managers is still timely: (1) always correct poor context to eliminate actual or potential sources of job dissatisfaction; and (2) be sure to build satisfier factors into job content to maximize opportunities for job satisfaction. The two-factor theory also cautions managers not to expect too much by way of motivational improvements from investments in things like special office fixtures, attractive lounges for breaks, and even high base salaries. Instead, it focuses attention on the nature of the job itself and on such things as responsibility and personal growth as opportunities for higher-order need satisfaction.

■ A **satisfier factor** is found in job content, such as a sense of achievement, recognition, responsibility, advancement, or personal growth.

■ A **hygiene factor** is found in the job context, such as working conditions, interpersonal relations, organizational policies, and salary.

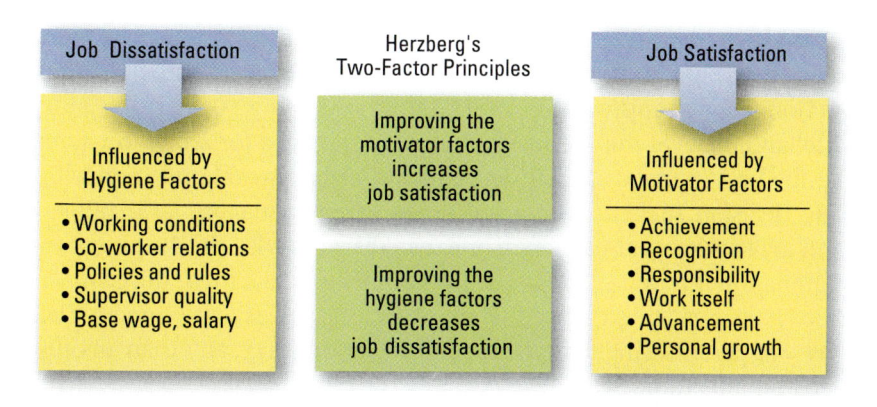

Figure 14.2 Herzberg's two-factor theory.

Job Dissatisfaction
Influenced by Hygiene Factors
- Working conditions
- Co-worker relations
- Policies and rules
- Supervisor quality
- Base wage, salary

Herzberg's Two-Factor Principles
Improving the motivator factors increases job satisfaction

Improving the hygiene factors decreases job dissatisfaction

Job Satisfaction
Influenced by Motivator Factors
- Achievement
- Recognition
- Responsibility
- Work itself
- Advancement
- Personal growth

●●● ACQUIRED NEEDS THEORY

In the late 1940s, David McClelland and his colleagues began experimenting with the Thematic Apperception Test (TAT) as a way of examining human needs. The TAT asks people to view pictures and write stories about what they see. The stories are then content analyzed for themes that display individual needs.[14] From this research, McClelland identified three needs that are central to his approach to motivation. **Need for Achievement** is the desire to do something better or more efficiently, to solve problems, or to master complex tasks. **Need for Power** is the desire to control other people, to influence their behaviour, or to be responsible for them. **Need for Affiliation** is the desire to establish and maintain friendly and warm relations with other people.

According to McClelland, people acquire or develop these needs over time as a result of individual life experiences. He also associates each need with a distinct set of work preferences. Managers are encouraged to recognize the strength of each need in themselves and in other people. Attempts can then be made to create work environments responsive to them. People high in the need for achievement, for example, like to put their competencies to work, they take moderate risks in competitive situations, and they are willing to work alone. As a result, the work preferences of high-need achievers include (1) individual responsibility for results, (2) achievable but challenging goals, and (3) feedback on performance.

Through his research, McClelland concludes that success in top management is not based on a concern for individual achievement alone. It requires broader interests that also relate to the needs for power and affiliation. People high in the need for power are motivated to behave in ways that have a clear impact on other people and events. They enjoy being in control of a situation and being recognized for this responsibility. A person with a high need for power prefers work that involves control over other persons, has an impact on people and events, and brings public recognition and attention.

Importantly, McClelland distinguishes between two forms of the power need. The *need for "personal" power* is exploitative and involves manipulation for the pure sake of personal gratification. This type of power need is not successful in management. By contrast, the *need for "social" power* is the positive face of power. It involves the use of power in a socially responsible way, one that is directed toward group or organizational objectives rather than personal ones. This need for social power is essential to managerial leadership.

People high in the need for affiliation seek companionship, social approval, and satisfying interpersonal relationships. They take a special interest in work that involves interpersonal relationships, work that provides for companionship, and work that brings social approval.

McClelland believes that people very high in the need for affiliation alone may not make the best managers; their desires for social approval and friendship may complicate decision making. There are times when managers and leaders must decide and act in ways that other persons may disagree with. To the extent that the need for affiliation interferes with someone's ability to make these decisions, managerial effectiveness will be sacrificed. Thus, the successful executive, in McClelland's view, is likely to possess a high need for social power that is greater than an otherwise strong need for affiliation.

■ **Need for Achievement** is the desire to do something better, to solve problems, or to master complex tasks.

■ **Need for Power** is the desire to control, influence, or be responsible for other people.

■ **Need for Affiliation** is the desire to establish and maintain good relations with people.

●●● QUESTIONS AND ANSWERS ON CONTENT THEORIES

Figure 14.3 shows how the human needs identified by Maslow, Alderfer, Herzberg, and McClelland compare with one another. Although the terminology varies, there is a lot of common ground. The insights of the theories can and should be used together to add to our understanding of human needs in the workplace. By way of summary, the following questions and answers further clarify the content theories and their managerial implications.[15]

"How many different individual needs are there?" Research has not yet identified a perfect list of individual needs at work. But, as a manager, you can use the ideas of Maslow, Alderfer, Herzberg, and McClelland to better understand the various needs that people may bring with them to the work setting. *"Can a work outcome or reward satisfy more than one need?"* Yes, work outcomes or rewards can satisfy more than one need. Pay is a good example. It is a source of performance feedback for the high need achiever. It can be a source of personal security for someone with strong existence needs. It can also be used indirectly to obtain things that satisfy social and ego needs. *"Is there a hierarchy of needs?"* Research does not support the precise five-step hierarchy of needs postulated by Maslow. It seems more legitimate to view human needs as operating in a flexible hierarchy, such as the one in Alderfer's ERG theory. However, it is useful to distinguish between the motivational properties of lower-order and higher-order needs. *"How important are the various needs?"* Research is inconclusive as to the importance of different needs. Individuals vary widely in this regard. They may also value needs differently at different times and at different ages or career stages. This is another reason why managers should use the insights of all the content theories to understand the differing needs of people at work.

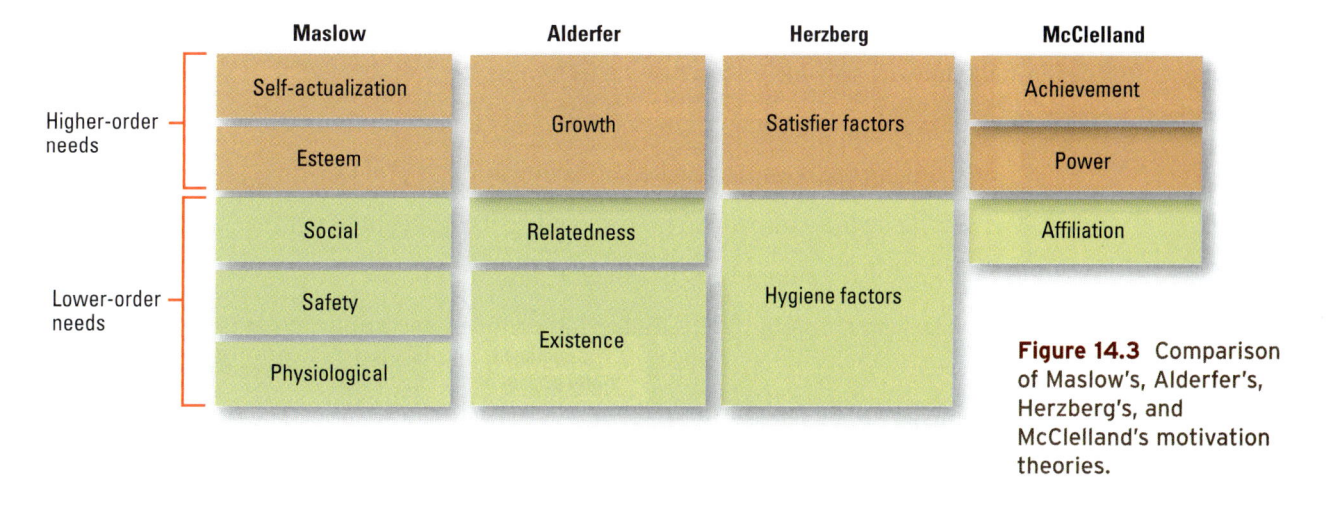

	Maslow	Alderfer	Herzberg	McClelland
Higher-order needs	Self-actualization	Growth	Satisfier factors	Achievement
	Esteem			Power
Lower-order needs	Social	Relatedness	Hygiene factors	Affiliation
	Safety	Existence		
	Physiological			

Figure 14.3 Comparison of Maslow's, Alderfer's, Herzberg's, and McClelland's motivation theories.

BE SURE YOU CAN

• define the term need • describe work practices that satisfy higher-order and lower-order needs in Maslow's hierarchy • contrast Maslow's hierarchy with ERG theory • describe work practices that influence hygiene factors and satisfier factors in Herzberg's two-factor theory • define needs for achievement, affiliation, and power in McClelland's theory • differentiate the needs for personal and social power • describe work practices that satisfy a person with a high need for achievement • compare the common ground among the content theories of Maslow, Alderfer, Herzberg, and McClelland

✓ Learning check ❷

PROCESS THEORIES OF MOTIVATION

Although the details vary, each of the content theories can help managers better understand individual differences and deal positively with them. The process theories add to this understanding. The equity, expectancy, and goal-setting theories offer advice and insight on how people actually make choices to work hard or not, based on their individual preferences, the available rewards, and possible work outcomes.

●●● EQUITY THEORY

The equity theory of motivation is best known in management through the work of J. Stacy Adams.[16] It is based on the logic of social comparisons and the notion that perceived inequity is a motivating state. That is, when people believe that they have been unfairly treated in comparison to others, they will be motivated to eliminate the discomfort and restore a sense of perceived equity to the situation. The classic example is pay. The equity question is, "In comparison with others, how fairly am I being compensated for the work that I do?" According to the equity theory, an individual who perceives that she or he is being treated unfairly in comparison to others will be motivated to act in ways that reduce the perceived inequity.

Figure 14.4 shows how the equity dynamic works in the form of input-to-outcome comparisons. These equity comparisons are especially common whenever managers allocate extrinsic rewards, things like compensation, benefits, preferred job assignments, and work privileges. The comparison points may be co-workers in the group, workers elsewhere in the organization, and even persons employed by other organizations. Perceived inequities occur whenever people feel that the rewards received for their work efforts are unfair given the rewards others appear to be getting. Adams predicts that people will try to deal with perceived negative inequity by any one or more of the following:

- Changing their work inputs by putting less effort into their jobs.
- Changing the rewards received by asking for better treatment.
- Changing the comparison points to make things seem better.
- Changing the situation by leaving the job.

Research on equity theory has largely been accomplished in the laboratory. It is most conclusive with respect to perceived negative inequity. People who feel

Figure 14.4 Equity theory and the role of social comparison.

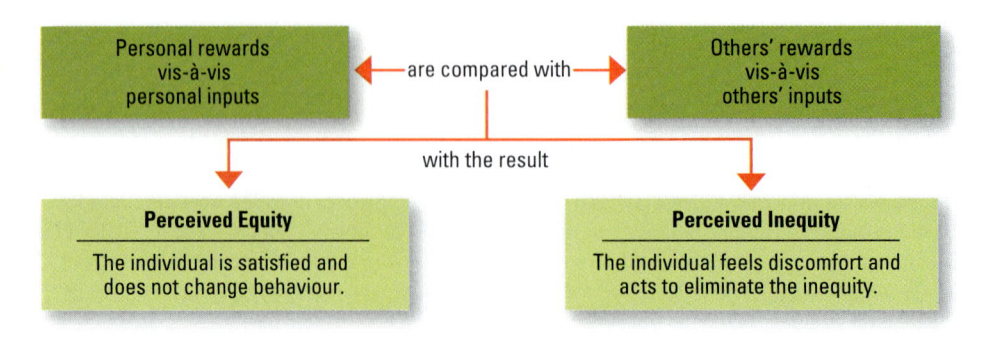

underpaid, for example, experience a sense of anger. This causes them to try to restore perceived equity to the situation by pursuing one or more of the actions described in the above list, such as reducing current work efforts to compensate for the missing rewards or even quitting the job.[17] There is also evidence that the equity dynamic occurs among people who feel overpaid. This time the perceived inequity is associated with a sense of guilt. The attempt to restore perceived equity may involve, for example, increasing the quantity or quality of work, taking on more difficult assignments, or working overtime.

A key point in the equity theory is that people behave according to their perceptions. What influences individual behaviour is not the reward's absolute value or the manager's intentions; the recipient's perceptions determine the motivational outcomes. Rewards perceived as equitable should have a positive result on satisfaction and performance; those perceived as inequitable may create dissatisfaction and cause performance problems.

Informed managers anticipate perceived negative inequities whenever especially visible rewards such as pay or promotions are allocated. Instead of letting equity dynamics get out of hand, they try to manage the perceptions. They carefully communicate the intended value of rewards being given, clarify the performance appraisals upon which they are based, and suggest appropriate comparison points.

In respect to pay, two equity situations mentioned earlier in the book are worth remembering. First is *gender equity*. It is well established that women, on the average, earn less than men. This difference is most evident in occupations traditionally dominated by men, such as the legal professions, but it also includes ones where females have traditionally held most jobs, such as teaching. Second is *comparable worth*. This is the concept that people doing jobs of similar value based on required education, training, and skills (such as nursing and accounting) should receive similar pay. Advocates of comparable worth claim that it corrects historical pay inequities and is a natural extension of the "equal-pay-for-equal-work" concept. Critics claim that "similar value" is too difficult to define and that the dramatic restructuring of wage scales would have a negative economic impact on society.

●●● EXPECTANCY THEORY

Victor Vroom's expectancy theory of motivation asks a central question: what determines the willingness of an individual to work hard at tasks important to the organization?[18] In response, the theory indicates that "people will do what they can do when they want to do it." More

---

PERSONAL MANAGEMENT

It is very difficult to say that someone completely lacks **INITIATIVE**. Each of us has to display a certain amount of initiative just to survive each day. But the initiative of people at work varies greatly, just as it does among students. For you the issue is: do you have the self-initiative to work hard and apply your talents to achieve high performance in school, in a job, on an assigned task? Don't hide from the answer. The way you work now in school or in a job is a good predictor of the future.

Part of the key to initiative lies in a good person–job fit; that is, finding the right job in the right career field. The rest, however, is all up to you. Only you can decide that you want to work really hard. Look at the following criteria for someone high in self-initiative. Consider how you behave as a student or in a job. Can you honestly say that each statement accurately describes you?

- Looks for problems, and fixes them.
- Does more than required; works beyond expectations.
- Helps others when they are stuck or overwhelmed.
- Tries to do things better; is not comfortable with the status quo.
- Thinks ahead; crafts ideas and makes plans for the future.

Get to know yourself better

Complete Self-Assessment #23—**Student Engagement Survey,** and #24—**Job Design Choices,** and #23—**Best Job Design,** from the Workbook and Personal Management Activity #14 on the companion website.

specifically, Vroom suggests that the motivation to work depends on the relationships among the *three expectancy factors*, depicted in *Figure 14.5* and described here:

- **Expectancy**—a person's belief that working hard will result in a desired level of task performance being achieved (this is sometimes called effort-performance expectancy).
- **Instrumentality**—a person's belief that successful performance will be followed by rewards and other potential outcomes (this is sometimes called performance-outcome expectancy).
- **Valence**—the value a person assigns to the possible rewards and other work-related outcomes.

In the expectancy theory, motivation *(M)*, expectancy *(E)*, instrumentality *(I)*, and valence *(V)* are related to one another in a multiplicative fashion: $M = E \times I \times V$. In other words, motivation is determined by expectancy times instrumentality times valence. This multiplier effect has important managerial implications.

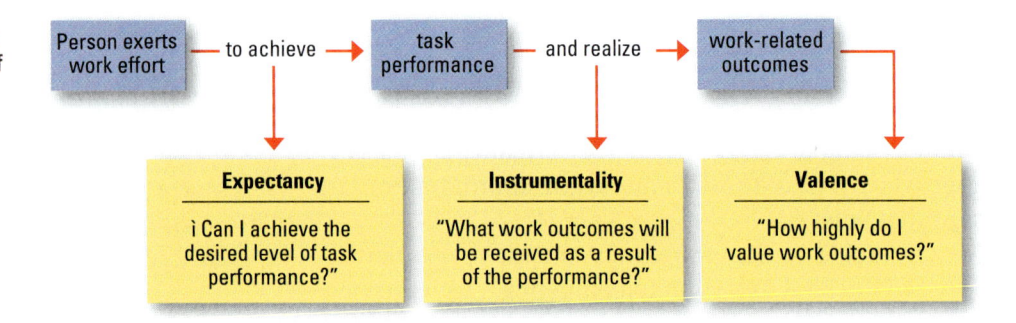

■ **Expectancy** is a person's belief that working hard will result in high task performance.

■ **Instrumentality** is a person's belief that various outcomes will occur as a result of task performance.

■ **Valence** is the value a person assigns to work-related outcomes.

Figure 14.5 Elements in the expectancy theory of motivation.

Person exerts work effort → to achieve → task performance → and realize → work-related outcomes

Expectancy: "Can I achieve the desired level of task performance?"

Instrumentality: "What work outcomes will be received as a result of the performance?"

Valence: "How highly do I value work outcomes?"

Mathematically speaking, a zero at any location on the right side of the equation (that is, for *E*, *I*, or *V*) will result in zero motivation. Managers are thus advised to act in ways that (1) maximize expectancy—people must believe that if they try, they can perform; (2) maximize instrumentality—people must perceive that high performance will be followed by certain outcomes; and (3) maximize valence—people must value the outcomes. Not one of these factors can be left unattended.

Suppose, for example, that a manager is wondering whether or not the prospect of earning a promotion will be motivational to a subordinate. A typical assumption is that people will work hard to earn a promotion. But is this necessarily true? Expectancy theory predicts that a person's motivation to work hard for a promotion will be low if any one or more of the following three conditions apply. First, *if expectancy is low, motivation will suffer*. The person may feel that he or she cannot achieve the performance level necessary to get promoted. So why try? Second, *if instrumentality is low, motivation will suffer*. The person may lack confidence that a high level of task performance will result in being promoted. So why try? Third, *if valence is low, motivation will suffer*. The person may place little value on receiving a promotion. It simply isn't much of a reward. So, once again, why try?

As shown in *Figure 14.6*, the management implications of expectancy theory include being willing to work with each individual to maximize his or her expectancies, instrumentalities, and valences in ways that support organizational objectives.

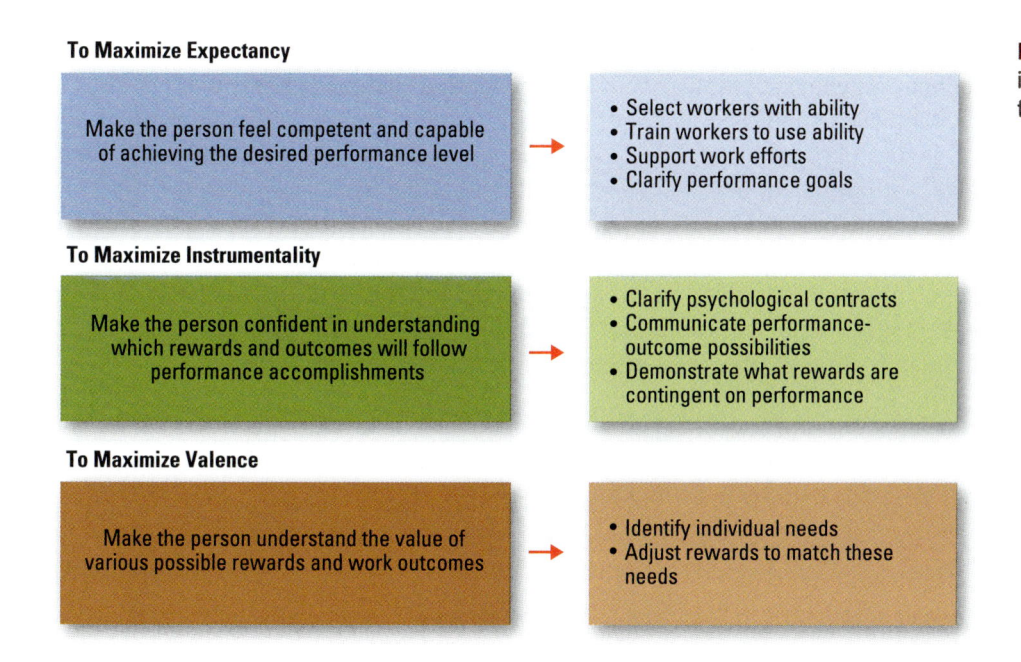

Figure 14.6 Managerial implications of expectancy theory.

To Maximize Expectancy

Make the person feel competent and capable of achieving the desired performance level →
- Select workers with ability
- Train workers to use ability
- Support work efforts
- Clarify performance goals

To Maximize Instrumentality

Make the person confident in understanding which rewards and outcomes will follow performance accomplishments →
- Clarify psychological contracts
- Communicate performance-outcome possibilities
- Demonstrate what rewards are contingent on performance

To Maximize Valence

Make the person understand the value of various possible rewards and work outcomes →
- Identify individual needs
- Adjust rewards to match these needs

The theory reminds managers that different people answer the question "Why should I work hard today?" in different ways. The implication is that every person must be respected as an individual with unique needs, preferences, and concerns regarding work. Knowing this, a manager can try to customize work environments to best fit individual needs and preferences.

GOAL-SETTING THEORY

The goal-setting theory described by Edwin Locke focuses on the motivational properties of task goals.[19] The basic premise is that task goals can be highly motivating *if* they are properly set and *if* they are well managed. Goals give direction to people in their work. Goals clarify the performance expectations between a supervisor and subordinate, between co-workers, and across subunits in an organization. Goals establish a frame of reference for task feedback. Goals also provide a foundation for behavioural self-management.[20] In these and related ways, Locke believes goal setting can enhance individual work performance and job satisfaction.

To achieve the motivational benefits of goal setting, research by Locke and his associates indicates that managers and team leaders must work with others to set the right goals in the right ways. The keys in this respect largely relate to *goal specificity, goal difficulty, goal acceptance,* and *goal commitment.* These are among the goal-setting recommendations provided in *Manager's Notepad 14.1*. Participation is a major element in applying these concepts to unlock the motivational value of task goals. The concept of management by objectives (MBO), described in Chapter 8 on planning and controlling, is a good example. When done well, MBO brings supervisors and subordinates together in a joint and participative process of goal setting and performance review. Research indicates that a positive impact is most likely to occur when the participation in MBO (1) allows for increased understanding of specific and difficult goals and (2) provides for greater acceptance of the goals and a sense of commitment to them. Along with participation, the opportunity to receive feedback on goal accomplishment is also essential to motivation.

Managers should be aware of the participation options in goal setting. It may not always be possible to allow participation when selecting exactly which goals need to be pursued, but it may be possible to allow participation in the decisions about how to best pursue them. Furthermore, the constraints of time and other factors operating in some situations may not allow for participation. In these settings, Locke's research suggests that workers will respond positively to externally imposed goals if supervisors assigning them are trusted and if workers believe they will be adequately supported in their attempts to achieve them.

> **MANAGER'S Notepad 14.1**
> **How to make goal setting work for you**
>
> - *Set specific goals:* They lead to higher performance than more generally stated ones, such as "Do your best."
> - *Set challenging goals:* When viewed as realistic and attainable, more difficult goals lead to higher performance than do easy goals.
> - *Build goal acceptance and commitment:* People work harder for goals they accept and believe in; they resist goals forced upon them.
> - *Clarify goal priorities:* Make sure that expectations are clear as to which goals should be accomplished first, and why.
> - *Provide feedback on goal accomplishment:* Make sure that people know how well they are doing in respect to goal accomplishment.
> - *Reward goal accomplishment:* Don't let positive accomplishments pass unnoticed; reward people for doing what they set out to do.

✓ Learning check 3

BE SURE YOU CAN
- explain the role of social comparison in Adams's equity theory • apply the equity theory to explain how people with felt negative inequity behave • define the terms expectancy, instrumentality, valence • explain the implications of Vroom's expectancy theory: $M = E \times I \times V$ • explain Locke's goal-setting theory • describe the fit between goal-setting theory and MBO

REINFORCEMENT THEORY OF MOTIVATION

■ The **law of effect** states that behaviour followed by pleasant consequences is likely to be repeated; behaviour followed by unpleasant consequences is not.

The content and process theories are concerned with explaining "why" people do things in terms of satisfying needs, resolving felt inequities, and/or pursuing positive expectancies and task goals. Reinforcement theory, by contrast, views human behaviour as determined by its environmental consequences. Instead of looking within the individual to explain motivation, it focuses on the external environment and the consequences it holds for the individual. The basic premises of reinforcement theory are based on what E. L. Thorndike called the **law of effect**: behaviour that results in a pleasant outcome is likely to be repeated; behaviour that results in an unpleasant outcome is not likely to be repeated.[21]

●●● REINFORCEMENT STRATEGIES

Psychologist B. F. Skinner popularized the concept of **operant conditioning** as the process of applying the law of effect to control behaviour by manipulating its consequences.[22] You may think of operant conditioning as learning by reinforcement. In management, the goal is to use reinforcement principles to systematically reinforce desirable work behaviour and discourage undesirable work behaviour.[23]

Four strategies of reinforcement are used in operant conditioning. **Positive reinforcement** strengthens or increases the frequency of desirable behaviour by making a pleasant consequence contingent on its occurrence. *Example:* A manager nods to express approval to someone who makes a useful comment during a staff meeting. **Negative reinforcement** increases the frequency of or strengthens desirable behaviour by making the avoidance of an unpleasant consequence contingent on its occurrence. *Example:* A manager who has been nagging a worker every day about tardiness does not nag when the worker comes to work on time. **Punishment** decreases the frequency of or eliminates an undesirable behaviour by making an unpleasant consequence contingent on its occurrence. *Example:* A manager issues a written reprimand to an employee whose careless work creates quality problems. **Extinction** decreases the frequency of, or eliminates, an undesirable behaviour by making the removal of a pleasant consequence contingent on its occurrence. *Example:* A manager observes that a disruptive employee is receiving social approval from co-workers; the manager counsels co-workers to stop giving this approval.

Figure 14.7 shows how these four reinforcement strategies can be applied in management. The supervisor's goal in the example is to improve work quality as part of a TQM program. Notice how the supervisor can use each of the strategies to influence continuous improvement practices among employees. Note, too, that both positive and negative reinforcement strategies strengthen desirable behaviour when it occurs. The punishment and extinction strategies weaken or eliminate undesirable behaviours.

■ **Operant conditioning** is the control of behaviour by manipulating its consequences.

■ **Positive reinforcement** strengthens a behaviour by making a desirable consequence contingent on its occurrence.

■ **Negative reinforcement** strengthens a behaviour by making the avoidance of an undesirable consequence contingent on its occurrence.

■ **Punishment** discourages a behaviour by making an unpleasant consequence contingent on its occurrence.

■ **Extinction** discourages a behaviour by making the removal of a desirable consequence contingent on its occurrence.

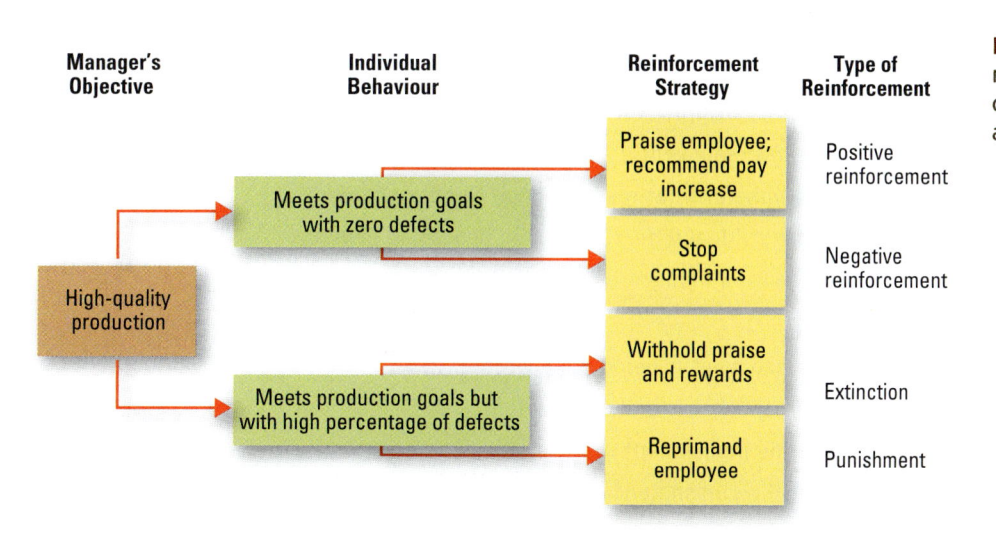

Figure 14.7 Applying reinforcement strategies: case of total quality management.

●●● WHAT IS AN EFFECTIVE TEAM?

An **effective team** is one that achieves and maintains high levels of task performance, member satisfaction, and viability for future action.[36] *Figure 16.3* shows how any team can be viewed as an open system that transforms various resource inputs into these outcomes. Among the important inputs are such things as the organizational setting, the nature of the task, the team size, and the membership characteristics.[37] Each of these factors influences the group process and helps set the stage for the accomplishment of group outcomes.

■ An **effective team** achieves high levels of task performance, membership satisfaction, and future viability.

Group Inputs

The *nature of the task* is always important. It affects how well a team can focus its efforts and how intense the group process needs to be to get the job done. Clearly defined tasks make it easier for team members to combine their work efforts. Complex tasks require more information exchange and intense interaction than do simpler tasks. The *organizational setting* can also affect how team members relate to one another and apply their skills toward task accomplishment. A key issue is the amount of support provided in terms of information, material resources, technology, organization structures, available rewards, and spatial arrangements. Increasingly, for example, organizations are being architecturally designed to directly facilitate teamwork. At SEI Investments, employees work in a large, open space without cubicles or dividers; each has a private set of office furniture and fixtures—but all on wheels; all technology easily plugs and unplugs from suspended power beams that run overhead. Project teams convene and disband as needed, and people easily meet and converse intensely, with the ebb and flow of work, all day.[38]

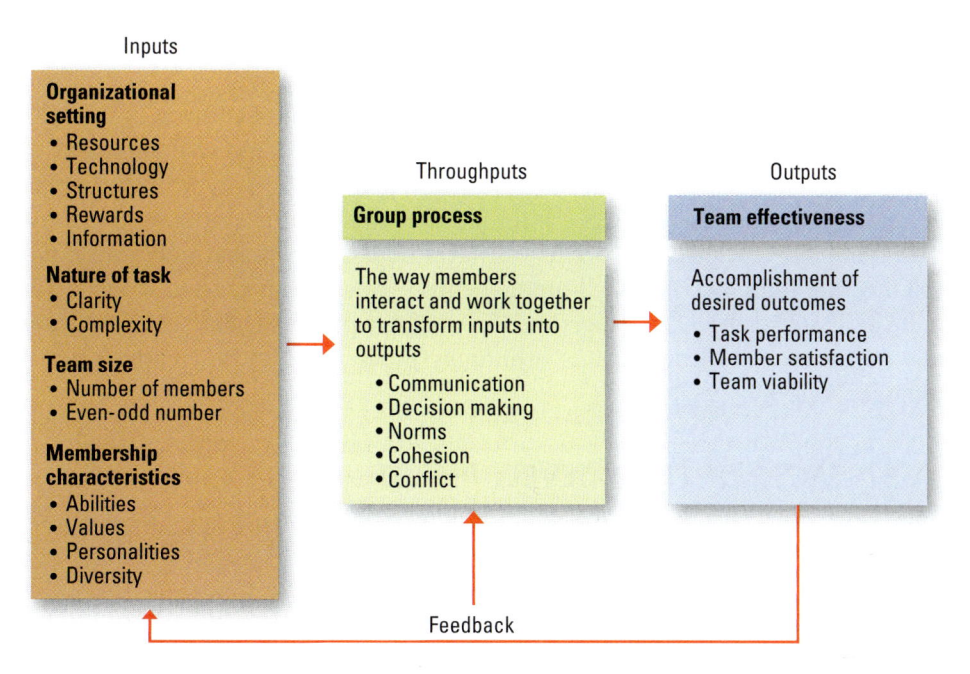

Figure 16.3 An open-systems model of work team effectiveness.

Inputs

Organizational setting
- Resources
- Technology
- Structures
- Rewards
- Information

Nature of task
- Clarity
- Complexity

Team size
- Number of members
- Even-odd number

Membership characteristics
- Abilities
- Values
- Personalities
- Diversity

Throughputs

Group process

The way members interact and work together to transform inputs into outputs
- Communication
- Decision making
- Norms
- Cohesion
- Conflict

Outputs

Team effectiveness

Accomplishment of desired outcomes
- Task performance
- Member satisfaction
- Team viability

Feedback

Team size affects how members work together, handle disagreements, and reach agreements. The number of potential interactions increases geometrically as teams increase in size, and communications become more congested. Teams larger than about six or seven members can be difficult to manage for the purpose of creative problem solving. When voting is required, teams with odd numbers of members help prevent "ties." In all teams, the *membership characteristics* are also important. Teams must have members with the right abilities, or skill mix, to master and perform tasks well. They must also have values and personalities that are sufficiently compatible for everyone to work well together.

Group Process

■ **Group process** is the way team members work together to accomplish tasks.

Although having the right inputs available to a team is important, it is not a guarantee of effectiveness. **Group process** counts too. This is the way the members of any team actually work together as they transform inputs into outputs. Also called *group dynamics*, the process aspects of any group or team include how members communicate with one another, make decisions, and handle conflicts, among other things. When the process breaks down and the internal dynamics fail in any way, team effectiveness can suffer. This *Team Effectiveness Equation* is a helpful reminder: Team effectiveness = quality of inputs + (process gains − process losses).

Team Diversity

Team diversity, in the form of different values, personalities, experiences, demographics, and cultures among the membership, can present significant group process challenges. The more homogeneous the team—the more similar the members are to one another—the easier it is to manage relationships. As team diversity increases, so too does the complexity of interpersonal relationships among members. But with the complications also come special opportunities. The more heterogeneous the team—the more diversity among members—the greater the variety of available ideas, perspectives, and experiences that can add value to problem solving and task performance.

In teamwork, as with organizations at large, the diversity lesson is very clear. There is a lot to gain when membership diversity is valued and well managed. The process challenge is to maximize the advantages of team diversity while minimizing its potential disadvantages. In the international arena, for example, research indicates that culturally diverse work teams have more difficulty learning how to work well together than do culturally homogeneous teams.[39] They tend to struggle more in the early stages of working together. But once the process challenges are successfully mastered, the diverse teams eventually prove to be more creative than the homogeneous ones.

●●● STAGES OF TEAM DEVELOPMENT

A synthesis of research on small groups suggests that there are five distinct phases in the life cycle of any team:[40]

1. *Forming*—a stage of initial orientation and interpersonal testing.

2. *Storming*—a stage of conflict over tasks and working as a team.

3. *Norming*—a stage of consolidation around task and operating agendas.
4. *Performing*—a stage of teamwork and focused task performance.
5. *Adjourning*—a stage of task completion and disengagement.

Forming Stage

The forming stage involves the first entry of individual members into a team. This is a stage of initial task orientation and interpersonal testing. As individuals come together for the first time or two, they ask a number of questions: "What can or does the team offer me?" "What will I be asked to contribute?" "Can my needs be met while my efforts serve the task needs of the team?"

In the forming stage, people begin to identify with other members and with the team itself. They are concerned about getting acquainted, establishing interpersonal relationships, discovering what is considered acceptable behaviour, and learning how others perceive the team's task. This may also be a time when some members rely on, or become temporarily dependent on, another member who appears "powerful" or especially "knowledgeable." Such things as prior experience with team members in other contexts and individual impressions of organization philosophies, goals, and policies may also affect member relationships in new work teams. Difficulties in the forming stage tend to be greater in more culturally and demographically diverse teams.

Storming Stage

The storming stage of team development is a period of high emotionality. Tension often emerges between members over tasks and interpersonal concerns. There may be periods of outright hostility and infighting. Coalitions or cliques may form around personalities or interests. Subteams form around areas of agreement and disagreement involving group tasks and/or the manner of operations. Conflict may develop as individuals compete to impose their preferences on others and to become influential in the group's status structure.

Important changes occur in the storming stage as task agendas become clarified and members begin to understand one another's interpersonal styles. Here attention begins to shift toward obstacles that may stand in the way of task accomplishment. Efforts are made to find ways to meet team goals while also satisfying individual needs. Failure in the storming stage can be a lasting liability, whereas success in the storming stage can set a strong foundation for later team effectiveness.

Norming Stage

Co-operation is an important issue for teams in the norming stage. At this point, members of the team begin to become coordinated as a working unit and tend to operate with shared rules of conduct. The team feels a sense of leadership, with each member starting to play useful roles. Most interpersonal hostilities give way to a precarious balancing of forces as norming builds initial integration. Harmony is emphasized, but minority viewpoints may be discouraged.

Canadian Managers
Supporting a Volunteer Team for Better Health Services

Running a charitable foundation takes lots of organization and teamwork. Just ask Bill Hallett. As President and CEO of the Niagara Health Systems Foundation, Hallett is responsible for designing and managing the major fundraising campaign "It's our Time" in support of a number of health care initiatives in the Niagara region of Ontario.

With any aggressive campaign seeking to raise large amounts of money, Hallett believes that the key to success is commitment to relationship building. In order to establish relationships that are critical to the success of the Foundation's initiatives, he has worked with the Niagara Health System Board of Trustees, volunteers, and staff at local hospital boards to recruit a team of community leaders to serve as the Foundation's board of directors. In addition, Hallett focuses on supporting strong partnerships with individual donors, local hospital foundations, auxiliaries, and municipal governments. Bill Hallett recognizes that fundraising involves both "friend raising" and getting the right team together.

Source: With information from the corporate website www.niagarahealth.on.ca and from 'Great Expectations,' *Philanthropic Trends*, Spring 2005.

In the norming stage, members are likely to develop initial feelings of closeness, a plan for the division of labour, and a sense of shared expectations. This helps protect the team from disintegration. Holding the team together may become even more important than successful task accomplishment.

Performing Stage

Teams in the performing stage are more mature, organized, and well functioning. This is a stage of total integration in which team members are able to deal in creative ways with both complex tasks and any interpersonal conflicts. The team operates with a clear and stable structure, and members are motivated by team goals.

The primary challenges of teams in the performing stage are to continue refining the operations and relationships essential to working as an integrated unit. Such teams need to remain coordinated with the larger organization and adapt successfully to changing conditions over time. A team that has achieved total integration will score high on the criteria of team maturity shown in *Figure 16.4*.[41]

Adjourning Stage

The final stage of team development is adjourning, when team members prepare to achieve closure and disband. Ideally, temporary committees, task forces, and project teams disband with a sense that important goals have been accomplished. This may be an emotional time, and disbandment should be managed with this possibility in mind. For members who have worked together intensely for a period of time, breaking up the close relationships may be painful. In all cases, the team would like to disband with members feeling they would work with one another again sometime in the future. Members should be acknowledged for their contributions and praised for the group's overall success.

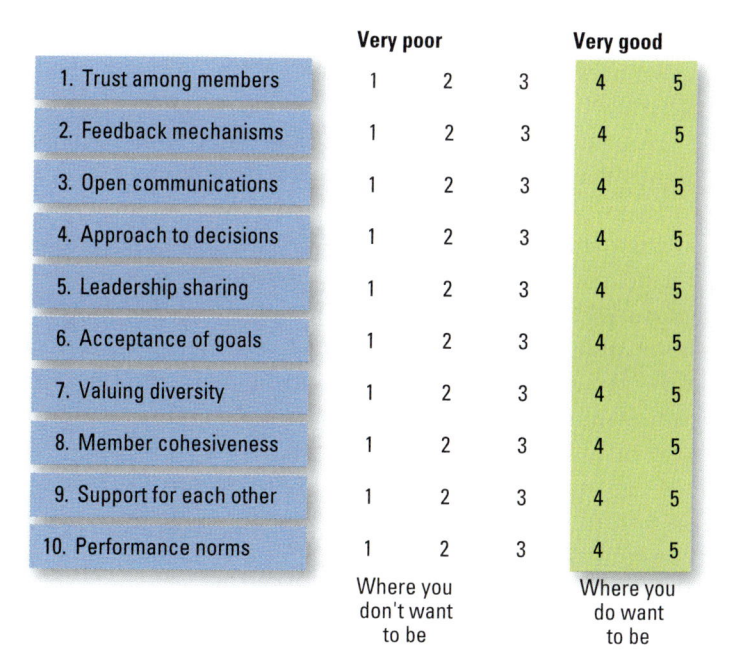

Figure 16.4 Criteria for assessing the maturity of a team.

	Very poor			Very good	
1. Trust among members	1	2	3	4	5
2. Feedback mechanisms	1	2	3	4	5
3. Open communications	1	2	3	4	5
4. Approach to decisions	1	2	3	4	5
5. Leadership sharing	1	2	3	4	5
6. Acceptance of goals	1	2	3	4	5
7. Valuing diversity	1	2	3	4	5
8. Member cohesiveness	1	2	3	4	5
9. Support for each other	1	2	3	4	5
10. Performance norms	1	2	3	4	5
	Where you don't want to be			Where you do want to be	

●●● NORMS AND COHESIVENESS

A **norm** is a behaviour expected of team members.[42] It is a "rule" or "standard" that guides their behaviour. When violated, a norm may be enforced with reprimands and other sanctions. In the extreme, violation of a norm can result in a member being expelled from a team or socially ostracized by other members. The *performance norm*, which defines the level of work effort and performance that team members are expected to contribute, is extremely important. In general, work groups and teams with positive performance norms are more successful in accomplishing task objectives than are teams with negative performance norms. Other important team norms relate to such things as helpfulness, participation, timeliness, quality, and innovation.

■ A **norm** is a behaviour, rule, or standard expected to be followed by team members.

Team leaders should help and encourage members to develop norms that support organizational objectives. During the forming and storming steps of development, for example, norms relating to membership issues such as expected attendance and levels of commitment are important. By the time the stage of performing is reached, norms relating to adaptability and change become most relevant. The following are guidelines for *how to build positive group norms*:[43]

- Act as a positive role model.
- Reinforce the desired behaviours with rewards.
- Control results by performance reviews and regular feedback.
- Train and orient new members to adopt desired behaviours.
- Recruit and select new members who exhibit the desired behaviours.
- Hold regular meetings to discuss progress and ways of improvement.
- Use team decision-making methods to reach agreement.

Cohesiveness is the degree to which members are attracted to and motivated to remain part of a team.

Team members vary in the degree to which they accept and adhere to group norms. Conformity to norms is largely determined by the strength of group **cohesiveness**, the degree to which members are attracted to be, and motivated to remain, part of a team.[44] Persons in a highly cohesive team value their membership and strive to maintain positive relationships with other team members. They experience satisfaction from team identification and interpersonal relationships. Because of this they tend to conform to the norms. Importantly, this can be good or bad for organizations; it depends on whether or not the performance norm is positive.

Look at *Figure 16.5*. When the performance norm of a team is positive, high cohesion and the resulting conformity to norms has a beneficial effect on overall team performance. This is a "best-case" scenario for both the manager and the organization. Competent team members work hard and reinforce one another's task accomplishments while experiencing satisfaction with the team. But when the performance norm is negative in a cohesive team, high conformity to the norm can have undesirable results. The figure shows this as a "worst-case" scenario where team performance suffers from restricted work efforts by members. Between these two extremes are mixed situations of moderate to low performance. To ensure employee buy-in and participation into their team philosophy and development, TELUS implemented their Team Machine. This web-based program allows employees to "recognize the outstanding performance, extraordinary efforts, and exceptional results that support our TELUS Values." Put forth by fellow employees, each individual or team member receives Team Machine Points that can either be redeemed or accumulated from the Team Machine Reward Selection.[45] The program has been successful in improving employee buy-in, motivation, and satisfaction.

Figure 16.5 How cohesiveness and norms influence team performance.

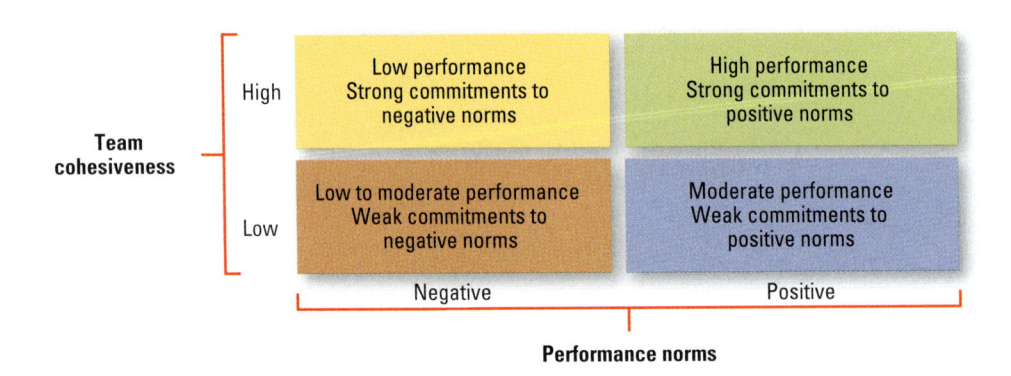

Team cohesiveness	Negative performance norms	Positive performance norms
High	Low performance — Strong commitments to negative norms	High performance — Strong commitments to positive norms
Low	Low to moderate performance — Weak commitments to negative norms	Moderate performance — Weak commitments to positive norms

To achieve and maintain the best-case scenario shown in *Figure 16.5*, managers should be skilled at influencing both the norms and cohesiveness of any team. They will want to build and maintain high cohesiveness in teams whose performance norms are positive. Guidelines on *how to increase cohesion* include the following:

- Induce agreement on team goals.
- Increase membership homogeneity.
- Increase interactions among members.
- Decrease team size.

- Introduce competition with other teams.
- Reward team rather than individual results.
- Provide physical isolation from other teams.

●●● TASK AND MAINTENANCE NEEDS

Research on the social psychology of groups identifies two types of activities that are essential if team members are to work well together over time.[46] **Task activities** contribute directly to the team's performance purpose, and **maintenance activities** support the emotional life of the team as an ongoing social system. Although the team leader or supervisor will often handle them, the responsibility for both types of activities should be shared and distributed among all team members. Anyone can help lead a team by acting in ways that satisfy its task and maintenance needs. This concept of *distributed leadership in teams* makes every member continually responsible for both recognizing when task or maintenance activities are needed and taking actions to provide them.

Figure 16.6 offers useful insights on distributed leadership in teams. Leading through task activities involves making an effort to define and solve problems and advance work toward performance results. Without the relevant task activities, such as initiating agendas, sharing information, and others listed in the figure, teams will have difficulty accomplishing their objectives. Leading through maintenance activities, by contrast, helps strengthen and perpetuate the team as a social system. When maintenance activities such as encouraging others and reducing tensions are performed well, good interpersonal relationships are achieved and the ability of the team to stay together over the longer term is ensured.

Both team task and maintenance activities stand in distinct contrast to the *dysfunctional activities* also described in *Figure 16.6*. Activities such as withdrawing and horsing around are usually self-serving to the individual member. They detract from, rather than enhance, team effectiveness. Unfortunately, very few teams are immune to dysfunctional behaviour by members. Everyone shares in the responsibility for minimizing its occurrence and meeting the distributed leadership needs of a team by contributing functional task and maintenance behaviours.

■ A **task activity** is an action taken by a team member that directly contributes to the group's performance purpose.

■ A **maintenance activity** is an action taken by a team member that supports the emotional life of the group.

Distributed leadership roles in teams

Team leaders provide task activities
- Initiating
- Information sharing
- Summarizing
- Elaborating
- Opinion giving

Team leaders provide maintenance activities
- Gatekeeping
- Encouraging
- Following
- Harmonizing
- Reducing tension

Team leaders avoid disruptive activities
- Being aggressive
- Blocking
- Self-confessing
- Seeking sympathy
- Competing
- Withdrawal
- Horsing around
- Seeking recognition

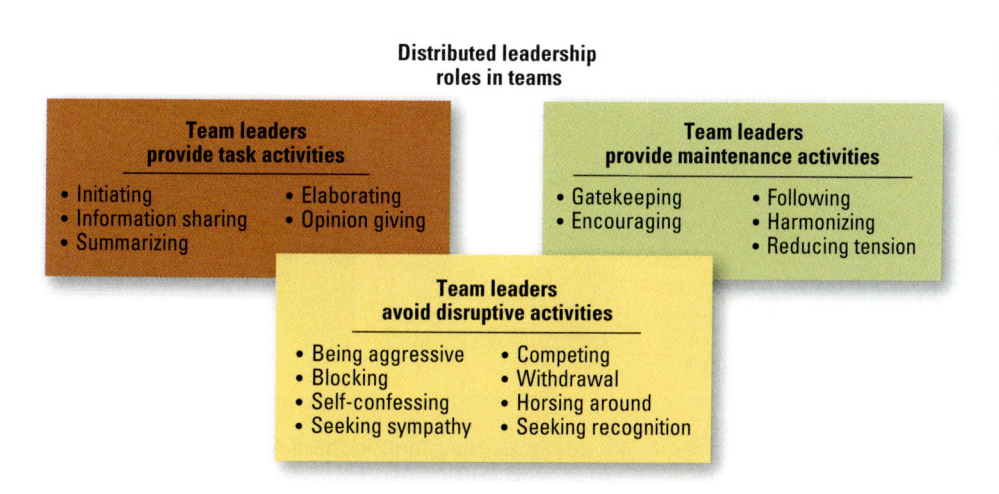

Figure 16.6 Distributed leadership helps teams meet task and maintenance needs.

COMMUNICATION NETWORKS

Figure 16.7 depicts three interaction patterns and communication networks that are common in teams.[47] When teams are interacting intensively and their members are working closely together on tasks, close coordination of activities is needed. This need is best met by a **decentralized communication network** in which all members communicate directly with one another. Sometimes this is called the *all-channel* or *star communication network*. At other times and in other situations team members work on tasks independently, with the required work being divided up among them. Activities are coordinated and results pooled by a central point of control. Most communication flows back and forth between individual members and this hub or centre point. This creates a **centralized communication network** as shown in the figure. Sometimes this is called a *wheel* or *chain communication structure*. When teams are composed of subgroups experiencing issue-specific disagreements, such as a temporary debate over the best means to achieve a goal, the resulting interaction pattern often involves a *restricted communication network*. Here, polarized subgroups contest one another and may even engage in antagonistic relations. Communication between the subgroups is limited and biased, with negative consequences for group process and effectiveness.

The best teams use communication networks in the right ways, at the right times, and for the right tasks. Centralized communication networks seem to work

- A **decentralized communication network** allows all members to communicate directly with one another.

- In a **centralized communication network**, communication flows only between individual members and a hub or centre point.

Figure 16.7 Interaction patterns and communication networks in teams.

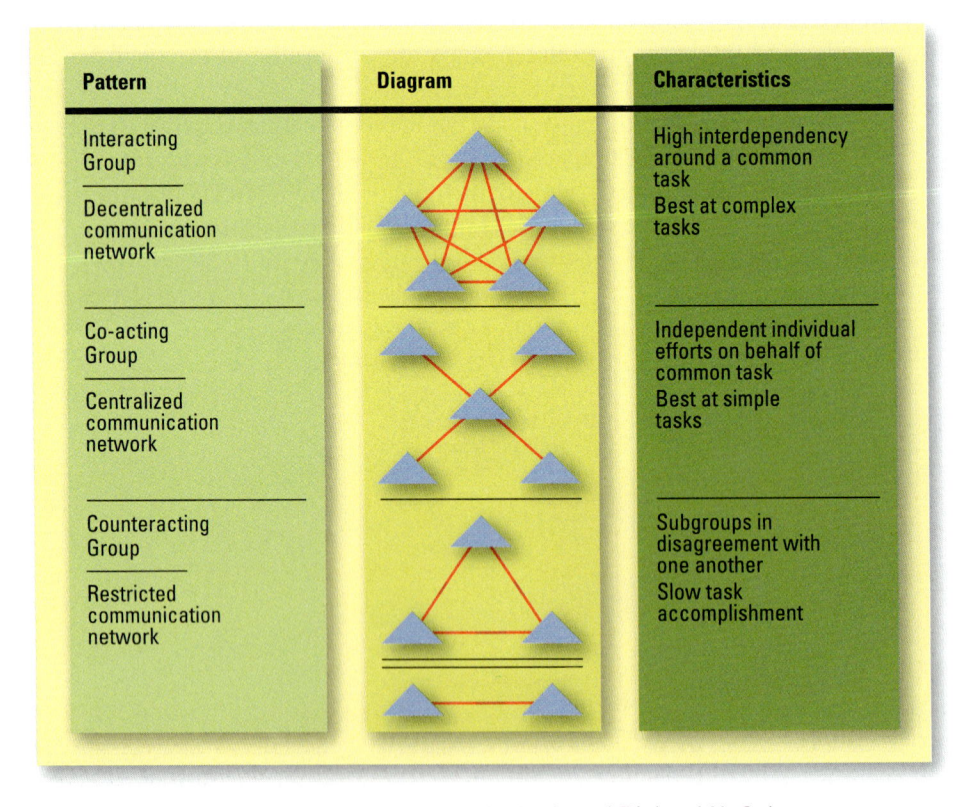

Pattern	Diagram	Characteristics
Interacting Group — Decentralized communication network		High interdependency around a common task. Best at complex tasks
Co-acting Group — Centralized communication network		Independent individual efforts on behalf of common task. Best at simple tasks
Counteracting Group — Restricted communication network		Subgroups in disagreement with one another. Slow task accomplishment

Source: John R. Schermerhorn, Jr., James G. Hunt, and Richard N. Osborn, *Organizational Behavior*, 8th ed. (New York: Wiley, 2003), p. 347. Used by permission.

better on simple tasks.[48] These tasks require little creativity, information processing, and problem solving and lend themselves to more centralized control. The reverse is true for more complex tasks, where interacting groups do better. Here, the decentralized networks work well since they are able to support the more intense interactions and information sharing required to perform complicated tasks. When teams get complacent, the conflict among co-acting groups can be a source of creativity and critical evaluation. But when subgroups have difficulty communicating with one another, task accomplishment typically suffers for the short run at least.

> **BE SURE YOU CAN**
>
> • define the term group effectiveness • identify inputs that influence group effectiveness • define the term group process, and explain its influence on team effectiveness • discuss how membership diversity influences team effectiveness • list five stages of group development • illustrate how group members act in each stage • define the term group norm and list ways to build positive group norms • define the term cohesiveness and list ways to increase and decrease group cohesion • explain how norms and cohesiveness interact to influence group performance • differentiate task, maintenance, and disruptive activities by group members • describe how and when groups should use decentralized and centralized communication networks
>
> ✓ Learning check ❸

DECISION MAKING IN TEAMS

Decision making, discussed extensively in Chapter 7, is the process of making choices among alternative possible courses of action. It is one of the most important group processes. It is also complicated by the fact that decisions in teams can be made in several different ways.

■ **Decision making** is the process of making choices among alternative courses of action.

●●● HOW TEAMS MAKE DECISIONS

Edgar Schein, a respected scholar and consultant, notes that teams make decisions by at least six methods: lack of response, authority rule, minority rule, majority rule, consensus, and unanimity.[49] In *decision by lack of response*, one idea after another is suggested without any discussion taking place. When the team finally accepts an idea, all others have been bypassed and discarded by simple lack of response rather than by critical evaluation. In *decision by authority rule*, the leader, manager, committee head, or some other authority figure makes a decision for the team. This can be done with or without discussion and is very time efficient. Whether the decision is a good one or a bad one, however, depends on whether the authority figure has the necessary information and on how well this approach is accepted by other team members. In *decision by minority rule*, two or three people are able to dominate or "railroad" the team into making a mutually agreeable decision. This is often done by providing a suggestion and then forcing quick agreement by challenging the team with such statements as "Does anyone object?...Let's go ahead, then."

One of the most common ways teams make decisions, especially when early signs of disagreement arise, is *decision by majority rule*. Here, formal voting may take place, or members may be polled to find the majority viewpoint. This method parallels the democratic political system and is often used without awareness of its potential problems. The very process of voting can create coalitions; that is, some people will be "winners" and others will be "losers" when the final vote is tallied. Those in the minority—the "losers"—may feel left out or discarded without having had a fair say. They may be unenthusiastic about implementing the decision of the "majority," and lingering resentments may impair team effectiveness in the future.

Teams are often encouraged to follow *decision by consensus*. This is where full discussion leads to one alternative being favoured by most members and the other members agree to support it. When a consensus is reached, even those who may have opposed the chosen course of action know that they have been heard and have had an opportunity to influence the decision outcome. Such consensus does not require unanimity. But it does require that team members be able to argue, engage in reasonable conflict, and still get along with and respect one another.[50] And it requires that there be the opportunity for any dissenting members to know that they have been able to speak and that they have been listened to. At the student-run and -funded Alberta Public Interest Research Group (APIRG), decisions are made by consensus. APIRG believes that consensus does not mean everyone thinks that the decision made is necessarily the best one possible or even that everyone is sure it will work. What it does believe is that, in making decisions, no one should feel that their position on the matter was misunderstood or that it wasn't given a proper hearing.[51]

A *decision by unanimity* may be the ideal state of affairs. Here, all team members agree on the course of action to be taken. This is a logically perfect method for decision making in teams, but it is also extremely difficult to attain in actual practice. One of the reasons that teams sometimes turn to authority decisions, majority voting, or even minority decisions, in fact, is the difficulty of managing the team process to achieve consensus or unanimity.

●●● ASSETS AND LIABILITIES OF GROUP DECISIONS

The best teams don't limit themselves to just one decision-making method. Instead, they vary methods to best fit the problems at hand, in true contingency management fashion. A very important team leadership skill is the ability to help a team choose the "best" decision method—one that provides for a timely and quality decision and one to which the members are highly committed. This reasoning is consistent with the Vroom-Jago leader-participation model discussed in Chapter 13.[52] You should recall that this model describes how leaders should utilize the full range of individual, consultative, and group decision methods as they resolve daily problems. To do this well, however, team leaders must understand the potential assets and potential liabilities of group decisions.[53]

The potential *advantages of group decision making* are significant. Because of this, the general argument is that team decisions should be sought whenever time and other circumstances permit. Team decisions make greater amounts of information, knowledge, and expertise available to solve problems. They expand the number of action alternatives that are examined; they help groups to avoid tunnel vision and tendencies to consider only a limited range of options. Team decisions increase the understanding and acceptance of outcomes by members. And importantly, team decisions increase the commitments of members to follow through to implement the decision once made. Simply put, team decisions can result in quality decisions that all members work hard to make successful.

The potential *disadvantages of group decision making* largely trace to the difficulties that can be experienced in group process. In a team decision there may be social pressure to conform. Individual members may feel intimidated or compelled

AROUND THE WORLD

Teams of all types are "in" at Motorola plants around the world. In Penang, Malaysia, a team spirit rallies workers, who in one year submitted 41,000 suggestions for improvement and saved the firm some $2 million. The Malaysian practices have been exported to other Motorola locations. Says one manager who spent three years working there, "The whole plant in Penang had this craving for learning." Motorola's Total Customer Satisfaction Teams bring together diverse members to address a specific goal, such as reduction in cycle time, quality improvement, profit improvement, environmental leadership, or process improvement. Teams also are critical to outreach and community. A Workforce & Education Team in Arizona links Motorola workers with educators in the community in an attempt to strengthen the educational system so that graduates have the skills and capabilities needed to compete in tomorrow's workplace.

Source: Information from "Importing Enthusiasm," *Business Week* (November 7, 1994); and corporate web site: <www.Motorola.com/General/inside.html>

High-tech runs with the support of teams

to go along with the apparent wishes of others. There may be minority domination, where some members feel forced or "railroaded" to accept a decision advocated by one vocal individual or small coalition. Also, the time required to make team decisions can sometimes be a disadvantage. As more people are involved in the dialogue and discussion, decision making takes longer. This added time may be costly, even prohibitively so, in certain circumstances.[54]

●●● GROUPTHINK

A high level of cohesiveness can sometimes be a disadvantage during decision making. Members of very cohesive teams feel so strongly about the group that they may not want to do anything that might detract from feelings of goodwill. This may cause them to publicly agree with actual or suggested courses of action, while privately having serious doubts about them. Strong feelings of team loyalty can make it hard for members to criticize and evaluate one another's ideas and suggestions. Unfortunately, there are times when desires to hold the team together at all costs and avoid disagreements may result in poor decisions.

Psychologist Irving Janis calls this phenomenon **groupthink**, the tendency for highly cohesive groups to lose their critical evaluative capabilities.[55] You should be alert to spot the following *symptoms of groupthink* when they occur in your decision-making teams:

- *Illusions of invulnerability:* Members assume that the team is too good for criticism or beyond attack.

- *Rationalizing unpleasant and disconfirming data:* Members refuse to accept contradictory data or to thoroughly consider alternatives.

- *Belief in inherent group morality:* Members act as though the group is inherently right and above reproach.

■ **Groupthink** is a tendency for highly cohesive teams to lose their evaluative capabilities.

> **MANAGER'S Notepad 16.3**
>
> **How to avoid groupthink**
>
> - Assign the role of critical evaluator to each team member; encourage a sharing of viewpoints.
> - Don't, as a leader, seem partial to one course of action; do absent yourself from meetings at times to allow free discussion.
> - Create subteams to work on the same problems and then share their proposed solutions.
> - Have team members discuss issues with outsiders and report back on their reactions.
> - Invite outside experts to observe team activities and react to team processes and decisions.
> - Assign one member to play a "devil's advocate" role at each team meeting.
> - Hold a "second-chance" meeting after consensus is apparently achieved to review the decision.

- *Stereotyping competitors as weak, evil, and stupid:* Members refuse to look realistically at other groups.
- *Applying direct pressure to deviants to conform to group wishes:* Members refuse to tolerate anyone who suggests the team may be wrong.
- *Self-censorship by members:* Members refuse to communicate personal concerns to the whole team.
- *Illusions of unanimity*: Members accept consensus prematurely, without testing its completeness.
- *Mind guarding*: Members protect the team from hearing disturbing ideas or outside viewpoints.

Groupthink can occur anywhere. On January 28, 1986, the space shuttle Challenger exploded in mid-air, killing all seven astronauts on board. The disaster resulted in one of the most in-depth aviation accident investigations in history. One of the most damning indictments to emerge was the extent to which a groupthink mentality by senior project leaders contributed to the disaster.[56] When and if you encounter groupthink, Janis suggests taking action along the lines shown in *Manager's Notepad 16.3*.

●●● CREATIVITY IN TEAM DECISION MAKING

Among the potential benefits that teams can bring to organizations is increased creativity. Two techniques that are particularly helpful for creativity in decision making are brainstorming and the nominal group technique.[57] Both can now be pursued in computer-mediated or virtual team discussions, as well as in face-to-face formats.

In **brainstorming,** teams of 5 to 10 members meet to generate ideas. Brainstorming teams typically operate within these guidelines. *All criticism is ruled*

■ **Brainstorming** engages group members in an open, spontaneous discussion of problems and ideas.

out—judgement or evaluation of ideas must be withheld until the idea-generation process has been completed. "*Freewheeling" is welcomed*—the wilder or more radical the idea, the better. *Quantity is important*—the greater the number of ideas, the greater the likelihood of obtaining a superior idea. *Building on one another's ideas is encouraged*—participants should suggest how ideas of others can be turned into better ideas, or how two or more ideas can be joined into still another hybrid idea.

By prohibiting criticism, the brainstorming method reduces fears of ridicule or failure on the part of individuals. Ideally, this results in more enthusiasm, involvement, and a freer flow of ideas among members. But there are times when team members have very different opinions and goals. The differences may be so extreme that a brainstorming meeting might deteriorate into antagonistic arguments and harmful conflicts. In such cases, a **nominal group technique** could help. This approach uses a highly structured meeting agenda to allow everyone to contribute ideas without the interference of evaluative comments by others. Participants are first asked to work alone and respond in writing with possible solutions to a stated problem. Ideas are then shared in round-robin fashion without any criticism or discussion; all ideas are recorded as they are presented. Ideas are next discussed and clarified in round-robin sequence, with no evaluative comments allowed. Next, members individually and silently follow a written voting procedure that allows for all alternatives to be rated or ranked in priority order. Finally, the last two steps are repeated as needed to further clarify the process.

■ The **nominal group technique** structures interaction among team members discussing problems and ideas.

> **BE SURE YOU CAN**
> • illustrate how groups make decisions by authority rule, minority rule, majority rule, consensus, and unanimity • list advantages and disadvantages of group decision making • define the term groupthink • identify the symptoms of groupthink • illustrate how brainstorming and the nominal group techniques can improve creativity in decision making

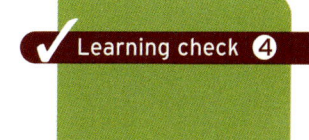

✓ Learning check ❹

LEADING HIGH-PERFORMANCE TEAMS

When we think of the word "team," sporting teams often come to mind. And we know these teams certainly have their share of problems. Members slack off or become disgruntled; even world-champion teams have losing streaks; and, the most highly talented players sometimes lose motivation, quibble with other team members, and lapse into performance slumps. When these things happen, the owners, managers, and players are apt to take corrective action to "rebuild the team" and restore what we have called team effectiveness. Work teams are teams in a similar sense. Even the most mature work team is likely to experience problems over time. When such difficulties arise, structured efforts at team building can help.

●●● THE TEAM-BUILDING PROCESS

Team building is a sequence of planned activities used to gather and analyze data on the functioning of a team, and to implement constructive changes to increase its operating effectiveness.[58] Most systematic approaches to team building follow the steps described in *Figure 16.8*. The cycle begins with awareness that a problem may exist or may develop within the team. Members then work together to gather and analyze data so that the problem is fully understood. Action plans are made by

■ **Team building** is a sequence of collaborative activities to gather and analyze data on a team and make changes to increase its effectiveness.

members and collectively implemented. Results are evaluated by team members working together. Any difficulties or new problems that are discovered serve to recycle the team-building process. Consider this added detail to the case featured in *Figure 16.8*.

> The consultant received a call from the hospital's director of personnel. He indicated that a new hospital president felt the top management team lacked cohesiveness and was not working well together as a team. The consultant agreed to facilitate a team-building activity that would include a day-long retreat at a nearby resort hotel. The process began when the consultant conducted interviews with the president and other members of the executive team. During the retreat, the consultant reported these results to the team as a whole. He indicated that the hospital's goals were generally understood by all but that they weren't clear enough to allow agreement on action priorities. Furthermore, he reported that interpersonal problems between the director of nursing services and the director of administration were making it difficult for the team to work together comfortably. These and other issues were addressed by the team at the retreat. Working sometimes in small subteams, and at other times together as a whole, they agreed first of all that action should be taken to clarify the hospital's overall mission and create a priority list of objectives for the current year. Led by the president, activity on this task would involve all team members and was targeted for completion within a month. The president asked that progress on the action plans be reviewed at each of the next three monthly executive staff meetings. Everyone agreed.

Figure 16.8 Steps in the team-building process: case of the hospital top management team.

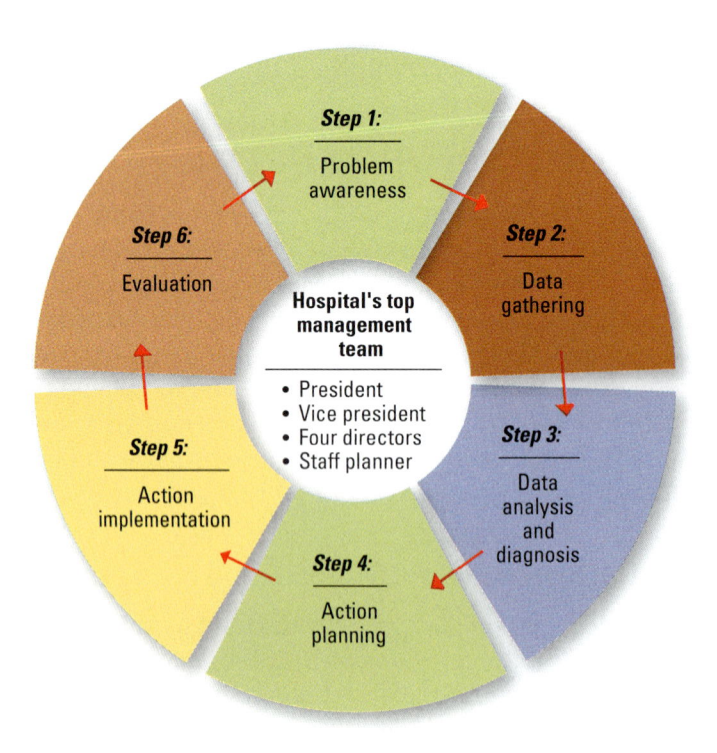

This example introduces team building as a way to assess a work team's functioning and take corrective action to improve its effectiveness. It can and should become a regular work routine. There are many ways to gather data on team functioning, including structured and unstructured interviews, questionnaires, and team meetings. Regardless of the method used, the basic principle of team building remains the same. The process requires that a careful and collaborative assessment of the team's inputs, processes, and results be made. All members should participate in data gathering, assist in data analysis, and collectively decide on actions to be taken.

Sometimes teamwork can be improved when people share the challenges of unusual and even physically demanding experiences. Outward Bound is famous for hands-on action learning, in a wilderness setting. More than a million people from companies that include Gulf Canada, Wood Gundy, and Maple Leaf Foods have taken part in its intensive outdoor education programs. Year-round, Outward Bound offers courses across Canada and tailors each course to meet individual company goals—perhaps to energize a stale team or help build trust between budding business partners.[59]

take it to the case!

Big Bertha's team hits a long ball

He has been described as "a man of vision, yet very focused with the willingness to undertake challenges others couldn't—or wouldn't—with a work-hard ethic that inspired us all." Ely Callaway, founder of Callaway Golf, maker of the famous "Big Bertha" driver, certainly was special. The goal he infused in his firm is continuous improvement, doing better than competitors and the firm's own past work. Callaway remains self-described as committed to producing golf products that are "Demonstrably Superior and Pleasingly Different," and to providing golfers with "A better game by design." Even as the firm has grown from a group of 5 in 1982 to over 3,000 employees today, it strives for a family atmosphere and a comfortable, enjoyable culture. New members of the Callaway Golf team are expected to have integrity, be honest and daring, and to work hard, with enthusiasm and a sense of personal accountability.

Source: Information from <www.callawaygolf.com>

●●●● SUCCESS FACTORS IN TEAMS

Among the many developments in the workplace today, the continuing effort to refine and apply creative team concepts is high on most executives' action agendas. But whether the group or team is working at the top, bottom, cross-functionally, or in direct customer service, high-performance results can't be left to chance. There are too many forces in the environment and group dynamics that can lead teams astray. Team success is only achieved through the special efforts of leaders and members alike. We know, for example, that high-performance teams generally share these characteristics:[60]

- a clear and elevating goal,
- a task-driven and results-oriented structure,

- competent and committed members who work hard,
- a collaborative climate,
- high standards of excellence,
- external support and recognition, and
- strong, principled leadership.

CANADIAN COMPANY IN THE NEWS: Blast Radius

WHAT IT TAKES TO BE THE BEST

Blast Radius, a global technology firm with Canadian headquarters in Vancouver, realized that service excellence and teamwork were critical to achieving corporate goals. To reinforce this message the CEO and the HR department defined these behaviours and included them in the performance management process. In addition, project managers provided feedback on these behaviours at the end of each project and provided cash rewards to teams of employees who demonstrated high levels of performance. To further support integrated recognition messages, employees nominated their peers and teams for awards in these areas.

Source: Natalie Michael, "Ring a bell and employees will deliver." *Canadian HR Reporter*, Aug 14, 2006. Vol.19, Iss. 14; pp 17-18.

TEAM LEADERSHIP CHALLENGES

The last point on this list—the need for strong and principled leadership—may be the key to them all. In their book, *Teamwork: What Can Go Right/What Can Go Wrong,* Carl Larson and Frank LaFasto state: "The right person in a leadership role can add tremendous value to any collective effort, even to the point of sparking the outcome with an intangible kind of magic."[61] They further point out that leaders of high-performing teams share many characteristics with the "transformational leader" examined in Chapter 13.

Successful team leaders *establish a clear vision of the future*. This vision serves as a goal that inspires hard work and the quest for performance excellence; it creates a sense of shared purpose. Successful team leaders help to *create change*. They are dissatisfied with the status quo, influence team members toward similar dissatisfaction, and infuse the team with the motivation to change in order to become better. Finally, successful team leaders *unleash talent*. They make sure the team is staffed with members who have the right skills and abilities. And they make sure these people are highly motivated to use their talents to achieve the group's performance objectives.

The best leaders know that teams are hard work, but that they are also worth it. You don't get a high-performing team by just bringing a group of people together and giving them a shared name or title. Leaders of high-performance teams create supportive climates in which team members know what to expect from the leader and each other, and know what the leader expects from them. They empower team members. By personal example they demonstrate the importance of setting aside self-interests to support the team's goals. And, they view team building as an ongoing leadership responsibility. An important aspect of this responsibility is developing future leaders for the team. Joe Liemandt, founder and CEO of the software firm Trilogy, Inc., says: "As Trilogy grew, one of the most important lessons we learned is that hiring for raw talent isn't enough. We had to build leaders. I believe you should always work to replace yourself."[62]

BE SURE YOU CAN
• define the term team building • illustrate how managers can use team building to improve group effectiveness • list three things that successful leaders do to create and maintain high-performance teams

✓ Learning check 5

Chapter 16 STUDY GUIDE

WHERE WE'VE BEEN

Back to C.O.R.E

The opening example of C.O.R.E. Digital Pictures showed talented individuals working together in a highly creative setting. It is also indicated that high performance by an organization depends on more than the involvement of talented individuals; it requires that they be blended together into effective teams. In this chapter you learned about the nature of teams and different types of teams found in organizations. You learned about group effectiveness, the stages of team development, and the input factors that influence team performance. You also learned about group processes and how leaders build high-performing teams that sustain themselves with satisfied members.

THE NEXT STEP
INTEGRATED LEARNING ACTIVITIES

Cases/Projects
- Callaway Golf Case
- Project 8—Superstars on the Team
- Project 9—Management in Popular Culture

Self-Assessments
- Emotional Intelligence (#2)
- T-T Leadership Style (#21)
- Team Leader Skills (#27)

Exercises in Teamwork
- Leading through Participation (#16)
- Lost at Sea (#26)
- Work Team Dynamics (#27)

STUDY QUESTION SUMMARY

1. How do teams contribute to organizations?
- A team is a collection of people working together to accomplish a common goal.
- Organizations operate as interlocking networks of formal work groups, which offer many benefits to the organizations and to their members.
- Teams help organizations through synergy in task performance, the creation of a whole that is greater than the sum of its parts.
- Teams help satisfy important needs for their members, providing various types of job support and social satisfactions.
- Social loafing and other problems can limit the performance of teams.

2. What are current trends in the use of teams?
- Teams are important mechanisms of empowerment and participation in the workplace.
- Committees and task forces are used to facilitate operations and allow special projects to be completed with creativity.
- Cross-functional teams bring members together from different departments and help improve lateral relations and integration in organizations.
- Employee involvement teams, such as the quality circle, allow employees to provide important insights into daily problem solving.
- New developments in information technology are making virtual teams, or computer-mediated teams, more commonplace.
- Self-managing teams are changing organizations by allowing team members to perform many tasks previously reserved for their supervisors.

3. How do teams work?
- An effective team achieves high levels of task performance, member satisfaction, and team viability.
- Important team input factors include the organizational setting, nature of the task, size, and membership characteristics.

- A team matures through various stages of development, including forming, storming, norming, performing, and adjourning.
- Norms are the standards or rules of conduct that influence the behaviour of team members; cohesion is the attractiveness of the team to its members.
- In highly cohesive teams, members tend to conform to norms; the best situation for a manager or leader is a team with positive performance norms and high cohesiveness.
- Distributed leadership in serving a team's task and maintenance needs helps in achieving long-term effectiveness.
- Effective teams make use of alternative communication networks to best complete tasks.

4. **How do teams make decisions?**
- Teams can make decisions by lack of response, authority rule, minority rule, majority rule, consensus, and unanimity.
- The potential advantages of group decision making include having more information available and generating more understanding and commitment.
- The potential liabilities to group decision making include social pressures to conform and greater time requirements.
- Groupthink is a tendency of members of highly cohesive teams to lose their critical evaluative capabilities and make poor decisions.
- Techniques for improving creativity in teams include brainstorming and the nominal group technique.

5. **What are the challenges of leading high-performance teams?**
- Team building helps team members develop action plans for improving the way they work together and the results they accomplish.
- The team-building process should be data based and collaborative, involving a high level of participation by all team members.
- High-performance work teams have a clear and shared sense of purpose as well as a strong internal commitment to its accomplishment.

KEY TERMS REVIEW

Brainstorming (p. 430)
Centralized communication network (p. 426)
Cohesiveness (p. 424)
Committee (p. 415)
Cross-functional team (p. 415)
Decentralized communication network (p. 426)
Decision making (p. 427)
Effective team (p. 419)
Employee involvement team (p. 416)

Formal group (p. 414)
Group process (p. 420)
Groupthink (p. 429)
Informal group (p. 414)
Maintenance activity (p. 425)
Nominal group technique (p. 431)
Norm (p. 423)
Project team (p. 415)
Quality circle (p. 416)
Self-managing work team (p. 417)

Social loafing (p. 411)
Synergy (p. 412)
Task activity (p. 425)
Task force (p. 415)
Team (p. 411)
Team building (p. 431)
Teamwork (p. 411)
Virtual team (p. 416)

SELF-TEST 16

MULTIPLE-CHOICE QUESTIONS:

1. When a group of people is able to achieve more than what its members could by working individually, this is called _____.
   (a) social loafing (b) consensus (c) viability (d) synergy

2. In an organization operating with self-managing teams, the traditional role of _____ is replaced by the role of team leader.
   (a) chief executive officer (b) first-line supervisor (c) middle manager (d) general manager

3. An effective team is defined as one that achieves high levels of task performance, member satisfaction, and _____.
   (a) resource efficiency (b) team viability (c) consensus (d) creativity
4. In the open-systems model of teams, the _____ is an important input factor.
   (a) communication network (b) decision-making method (c) performance norm (d) set of membership characteristics
5. A basic rule of team dynamics states that the greater the _____ in a team, the greater the conformity to norms.
   (a) membership diversity (b) cohesiveness (c) task structure (d) competition among members
6. Groupthink is most likely to occur in teams that are _____.
   (a) large in size (b) diverse in membership (c) high performing (d) highly cohesive
7. Gatekeeping is an example of a _____ activity that can help teams work effectively over time.
   (a) task (b) maintenance (c) team-building (d) decision-making
8. Members of a team tend to become more motivated and able to deal with conflict during the _____ stage of team development.
   (a) forming (b) norming (c) performing (d) adjourning
9. One way for a manager to build positive norms within a team is to _____.
   (a) act as a positive role model (b) increase group size (c) introduce groupthink (d) isolate the team from others
10. When teams are highly cohesive, _____.
    (a) members are high performers (b) members tend to be satisfied with their team membership (c) members have positive norms (d) the group achieves its goals
11. A "quality circle" is an example of how organizations try to use _____ teams for performance advantage.
    (a) virtual (b) informal (c) employee involvement (d) self-managing
12. It would be common to find members of self-managing work teams engaged in _____.
    (a) social loafing (b) multi-tasking (c) centralized communication (d) decision by authority rule
13. The "team effectiveness equation" states: Team effectiveness = quality of inputs + (_____ − process losses).
    (a) process gains (b) leadership impact (c) membership ability (d) problem complexity
14. A _____ decision is one in which all members agree on the course of action to be taken.
    (a) consensus (b) unanimity (c) majority (d) synergy
15. To increase the cohesiveness of a group, a manager would be best off _____.
    (a) starting competition with other groups (b) increasing the group size (c) acting as a positive role model (d) introducing a new member

Short-Response Questions:

16. How can a manager improve team effectiveness by modifying inputs?
17. What is the relationship among a team's cohesiveness, performance norms, and performance results?
18. How would a manager know that a team is suffering from groupthink (give two symptoms) and what could the manager do about it (give two responses)?
19. What makes a self-managing team different from a traditional work team?

Application Question:

20. Marcos Martinez has just been appointed manager of a production team operating the 11 p.m. to 7 a.m. shift in a large manufacturing firm. An experienced manager, Marcos is concerned that the team members really like and get along well with one another, but they also appear to be restricting their task outputs to the minimum acceptable levels. What could Marcos do to improve things in this situation and why should he do them?

17 Communication and Interpersonal Skills

CHAPTER 17 STUDY QUESTIONS

1. What is the communication process?
2. How can communication be improved?
3. How does perception influence communication?
4. How can we deal positively with conflict?
5. How can we negotiate successful agreements?

Planning Ahead

After reading Chapter 17, you should be able to answer these questions in your own words.

CENTER FOR CREATIVE LEADERSHIP

LEAD THE WAY WITH COMMUNICATION

The importance of communication and interpersonal skills in leadership development is mainstream at the internationally regarded Center for Creative Leadership. The Center's mission is to "advance the understanding, practice and development of leadership for the benefit of society worldwide." Branches in North America, Asia, Europe, as well as network associates—such as the Niagara Institute in Ontario—expand the Center's reach to managers worldwide and contribute to its global reputation for excellence. Leaders need to be able to communicate effectively and use interpersonal skills to engage others in their work. The Center for Creative Leadership helps managers gain better insights into their interpersonal styles and build leadership skills for personal and organizational success.

After 23 years with his organization, Dean Marion, a plant manager with BGF Industries, realized that his entire career had been driven by the goal of becoming plant manager. He recognizes that "because I was always focused on that, I had high expectations of myself and I put pressure on everybody around me to live up to those same expectations." Through personal coaching, Marion's focus turned to improving relationships with his peers and supervisors, and helping others to succeed. "I'm still a performance-driven person who looks at the bottom line," he emphasizes, "but the difference is that I'm not out there hammering at people." Similarly, The Women's Leadership Program offered Ellen Magnis an experience that gained her some much needed balance between her job and her personal life, and that at the same time gave her staff new opportunities to stand up and take charge and shine. She explains, "I come to work now and know I'm making a difference to them."

The Center for Creative Leadership was founded on the initiative of H. Smith Richardson, Jr., a successful executive. He believed, "what organizations needed was not just leadership for the present and the near future, but a kind of innovative leadership with a broader focus and a longer view. Such leadership would be concerned not with profits, markets, and business strategies alone, but with the place of business in society."[1]

GET CONNECTED!

Are you fully prepared to meet the leadership challenges of the future? Just how good are your communication skills? Are you comfortable dealing with conflict and negotiations?

Chapter 17 LEARNING PREVIEW

The chapter opening example of the Center for Creative Leadership introduced an organization devoted to leadership training that makes a difference—a real difference in the behaviour of leaders. The Center uses a variety of learning approaches to help participants better understand themselves and their behaviour when working with other persons. In this chapter you will learn about the communication process, communication barriers, and ways to become effective in interpersonal communication. You will learn about perception and how it influences communication through stereotypes and other perceptual distortions. You will also learn about the processes of conflict and negotiation, and how they can be engaged in positive and successful ways.

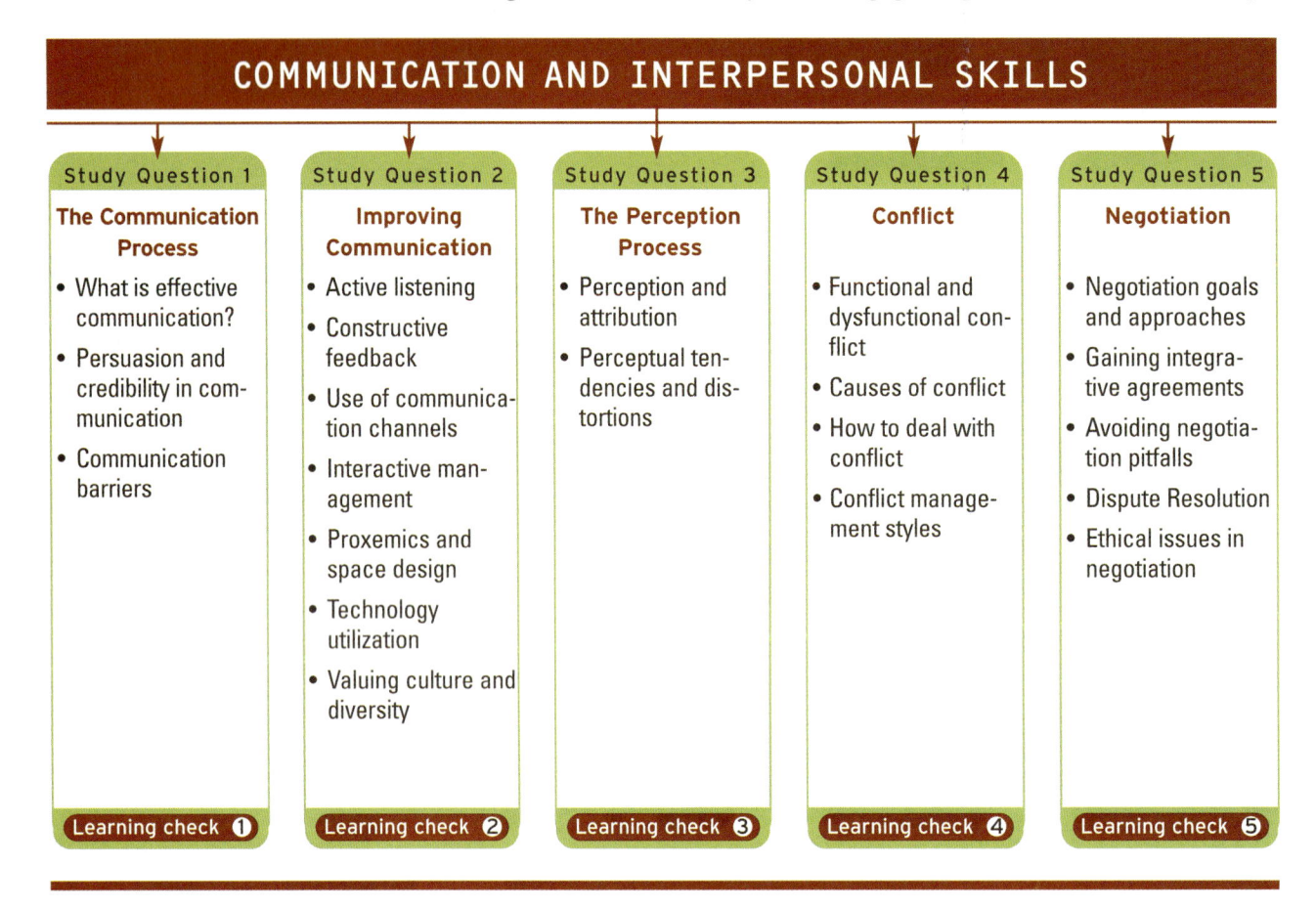

COMMUNICATION AND INTERPERSONAL SKILLS

Study Question 1	Study Question 2	Study Question 3	Study Question 4	Study Question 5
The Communication Process	**Improving Communication**	**The Perception Process**	**Conflict**	**Negotiation**
• What is effective communication?	• Active listening	• Perception and attribution	• Functional and dysfunctional conflict	• Negotiation goals and approaches
• Persuasion and credibility in communication	• Constructive feedback	• Perceptual tendencies and distortions	• Causes of conflict	• Gaining integrative agreements
• Communication barriers	• Use of communication channels		• How to deal with conflict	• Avoiding negotiation pitfalls
	• Interactive management		• Conflict management styles	• Dispute Resolution
	• Proxemics and space design			• Ethical issues in negotiation
	• Technology utilization			
	• Valuing culture and diversity			
Learning check ❶	Learning check ❷	Learning check ❸	Learning check ❹	Learning check ❺

Anyone heading into the new workplace must understand that the work of managers and team leaders is highly interpersonal and communication intensive. Whether you work at the top, building support for strategies and organizational goals, or at lower levels, interacting with others to support their work efforts and your own, communication and interpersonal skills are essential to your personal toolkit. Think back to the descriptions of managerial work by Henry Mintzberg, John Kotter, and others as discussed in Chapter 1. For Mintzberg, managerial success involves performing well as an information "nerve centre," gathering information from and disseminating information to internal and external sources.[2] For Kotter, it depends largely on one's ability to build and maintain a complex web of interpersonal networks with insiders and outsiders so as to implement work priorities and agendas.[3] Says Pam Alexander, CEO of Alexander Ogilvy Public Relations Worldwide: "Relationships are the most powerful form of media. Ideas will only get you so far these days. Count on personal relationships to carry you further."[4]

The ability to communicate well both orally and in writing is a critical managerial skill and the foundation of effective leadership.[5] Through communication, people exchange and share information with one another and influence one another's attitudes, behaviours, and understandings. Communication allows managers to establish and maintain interpersonal relationships, listen to others, and otherwise gain the information needed to create an inspirational workplace. No manager can handle conflict, negotiate successfully, and succeed at leadership without being a good communicator. Any student portfolio should include adequate testimony to one's abilities to communicate well in interpersonal relationships, in various forms of writing and public speaking, and increasingly through the electronic medium of the computer.

THE COMMUNICATION PROCESS

Communication is an interpersonal process of sending and receiving symbols with messages attached to them. In more practical terms, the key elements in the communication process are shown in *Figure 17.1*. They include a *sender*, who is responsible for encoding an intended *message* into meaningful symbols, both verbal and non-verbal. The message is sent through a *communication channel* to a *receiver*, who then decodes or interprets its *meaning*. This interpretation, importantly, may or may not match the sender's original intentions. *Feedback*, when present, reverses the process and conveys the receiver's response back to the sender. Another way to view the communication process is as a series of questions. "Who?" (sender) "says what?" (message) "in what way?" (channel) "to whom?" (receiver) "with what result?" (interpreted meaning).

■ **Communication** is the process of sending and receiving symbols with meanings attached.

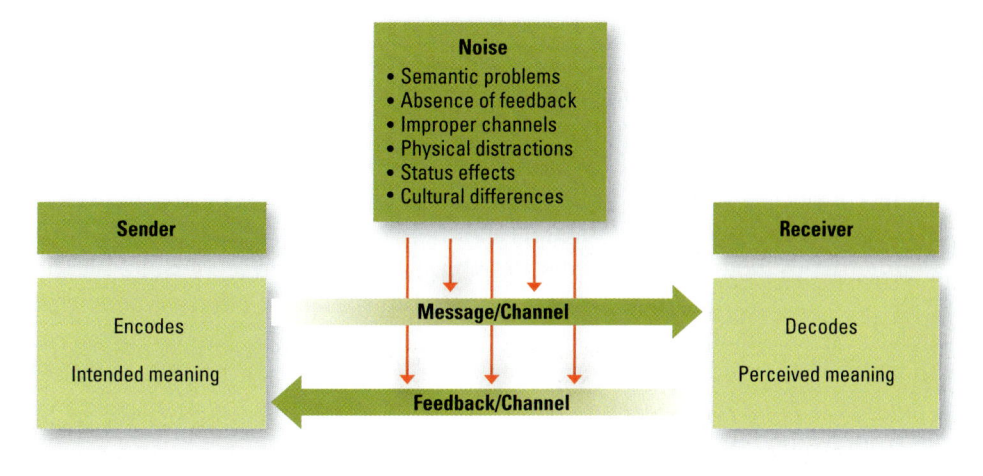

Figure 17.1 The interactive two-way process of interpersonal communication.

WHAT IS EFFECTIVE COMMUNICATION?

■ In **effective communication** the intended meaning is fully understood by the receiver.

■ **Efficient communication** occurs at minimum cost.

Effective communication occurs when the message is fully understood. The intended meaning of the sender and the interpreted meaning of the receiver are one and the same. However, the goal in communication—effectiveness—is not always achieved. **Efficient communication** occurs at minimum cost in terms of resources expended. Time, in particular, is an important resource in the communication process. Picture your instructor taking the time to communicate individually with each student about this chapter. It would be virtually impossible. Even if it were possible, it would be costly. This is why managers often leave voicemail messages and interact by email rather than visit their subordinates personally. Simply put, these alternatives are more efficient ways to communicate than through one-on-one and face-to-face communications. With the goal of transforming TELUS from a regional, western Canada-based company into a national telecommunications products and services provider, CEO Daren Entwistle focused on establishing an effective communication system. The process began with a weekly e-letter to employees, and, over the course of a two-year period, a CEO mailbox was established so that all company employees now have the opportunity to communicate directly with the CEO's office.[6]

One problem is that efficient communications are not always effective. A low-cost approach such as an email note to a distribution list may save time, but it does not always result in everyone getting the same meaning from the message. Without opportunities to ask questions and clarify the message, erroneous interpretations are possible. By the same token, an effective communication may not always be efficient. If a work team leader visits each team member individually to explain a new change in procedures, this may guarantee that everyone truly understands the change. But it may also be very costly in the demands it makes on the leader's time. A team meeting would be more efficient. In these and other ways, potential trade-offs between effectiveness and efficiency must be recognized in communication.

■ **Persuasion** is presenting a message in a manner that causes the other person to support it.

PERSUASION AND CREDIBILITY IN COMMUNICATION

Communication is not always just about sharing information or being "heard"; it often includes the desire of one party to influence or motivate the other in a desired way. Especially in management, one of the most important purposes of communication is **persuasion**, getting someone else to support the message being presented.[7]

■ **Credibility** is trust, respect, and integrity in the eyes of others.

Much of what happens in today's horizontal structures and organic designs is outside of the formal supervisor–subordinate relationship, and much of what happens within it is in the context of empowerment. Managers get things done by working with and persuading others who are their peers, teammates, co-workers. They get things done more by convincing than by order-giving. Furthermore, they must be able to persuade others over and over again in the dynamic and complex workplace; once is not enough.

■ **Noise** is anything that interferes with the communication process.

■ A **communication channel** is a medium through which the sender conveys a message to the receiver.

In terms of the power bases discussed in Chapter 13 on leadership, personal powers of expertise and reference are essential to the art of effective persuasion. Scholar and consultant Jay Conger says that many managers "confuse persuasion with taking bold stands and aggressive arguing." He points out that this often leads to "counter persuasion" responses and to questions regarding the manager's credibility.[8] And without **credibility**—trust, respect, and integrity in the eyes of others—he sees little chance that persuasion can be successful. Conger's advice is to build credibility for persuasive communication through expertise and relationships.

To build *credibility through expertise*, you must be knowledgeable about the issue in question and/or have a successful track record in dealing with similar issues in the past. In a hiring situation where you are trying to persuade team members to select candidate A rather than B, for example, you had better be able to defend your reasons. And it will always be better if your past recommendations turned out to be good ones. To build *credibility through relationships*, you must have a good working relationship with the person to be persuaded. The iron rule of reference power should be remembered: it is always easier to get someone to do what you want if they like you. To return to the prior example, if you have to persuade your boss to support a special bonus package to attract candidates, a good relationship will add credibility to your request.

COMMUNICATION BARRIERS

Communication is a shared and two-way process that requires effort and skill on the part of both the sender and the receiver. **Noise**, as previously shown in *Figure 17.1*, is anything that interferes with the effectiveness of the communication process. For example, when Yoshihiro Wada was president of Mazda Corporation, he once met with representatives of the firm's American joint-venture partner, Ford. But he had to use an interpreter. He estimated that 20 percent of his intended meaning was lost in the exchange between himself and the interpreter, and another 20 percent was lost between the interpreter and the Americans, with whom he was ultimately trying to communicate.[9] In addition to the obvious problems when different languages are involved, common sources of noise in communication include poor choice of channels, poor written or oral expression, failure to recognize non-verbal signals, physical distractions, and status effects.

Poor Choice of Channels

A **communication channel** is the medium through which a message is conveyed from sender to receiver. Good managers choose the right communication channel, or combination of channels, to accomplish their intended purpose in a given situation.[10] In general, *written channels* are acceptable for simple messages that are easy to convey and for those that require extensive dissemination quickly. They are also important as documentation when formal policies or directives are being conveyed. *Spoken channels* work best for messages that are complex and difficult to convey, and where immediate feedback to the sender is

---

PERSONAL MANAGEMENT

COMMUNICATION and **INTERPERSONAL SKILLS** top the lists of characteristics looked for in employment candidates by corporate recruiters today. Yet there are some worrisome statistics out there. An amazing 81 percent of university professors in one survey rated high school graduates as "fair" or "poor" in writing clearly; 78 percent rated students the same in spelling and use of grammar. In an American Management Association survey, managers rated their bosses only slightly above average (3.51 on a 5-point scale) on these important dimensions of communication—transforming ideas into words, credibility, listening and asking questions, and written and oral presentations.[11] There is no doubt that we are in very challenging times when it comes to finding internships and full-time jobs in a streamlined economy. Strong communication and interpersonal skills could differentiate you from others wanting the same job. What about it? Can you convince a recruiter that you have the skills you need to run effective meetings, write informative reports, use email correctly, deliver persuasive presentations, conduct job interviews, work well with others on a team, keep conflicts constructive and negotiations positive, network with peers and mentors, and otherwise communicate enthusiasm to the people with whom you work?

[Diagram: Your communication and interpersonal skills — Plan meetings, Write good reports, Use email well, Work well in teams, Network with peers & members, Give persuasive presentations, Negotiate deals, Conduct job interviews]

Get to know yourself better

Complete Self-Assessments #12—**Assertiveness**, and #28—**Conflict Management Styles** from the Workbook and Personal Management Activity #17 on the companion website.

valuable. They are also more personal and can create a supportive, even inspirational, emotional climate.

Poor Written or Oral Expression

Communication will be effective only to the extent that the sender expresses a message in a way that can be clearly understood by the receiver. This means that words must be well chosen and properly used to express the sender's intentions. Consider the following "bafflegab" found among some executive communications.

A business report said: "Consumer elements are continuing to stress the fundamental necessity of a stabilization of the price structure at a lower level than exists at the present time." (*Translation:* Consumers keep saying that prices must go down and stay down.)

A manager said: "Substantial economies were effected in this division by increasing the time interval between distribution of data-eliciting forms to business entities." (*Translation:* The division saved money by sending out fewer questionnaires.)

Both written and oral communication require skill. It isn't easy, for example, to write a concise letter or to express one's thoughts in an email report. Any such message can easily be misunderstood. It takes practice and hard work to express yourself well. The same holds true for oral communication that takes place in telephone calls, face-to-face meetings, formal briefings, video conferences, and the like. *Manager's*

MANAGER'S Notepad 17.1

How to make a successful presentation

- *Be prepared:* Know what you want to say; know how you want to say it; rehearse saying it.
- *Set the right tone:* Act audience centred; make eye contact; be pleasant and confident.
- *Sequence points:* State your purpose; make important points; follow with details; then summarize.
- *Support your points:* Give specific reasons for your points; state them in understandable terms.
- *Accent the presentation:* Use good visual aids; provide supporting "handouts" when possible.
- *Add the right amount of polish:* Attend to details; have room, materials, and arrangements ready to go.
- *Check your technology:* Check everything ahead of time; make sure it works and know how to use it.
- *Don't bet on the Internet:* Beware of plans to make real-time Internet visits; save sites on a disk and use a browser to open the file.
- *Be professional:* Be on time; wear appropriate attire; act organized, confident, and enthusiastic.

Notepad 17.1 identifies guidelines for an important communication situation—the executive briefing or formal presentation.[12]

Failure to Recognize Non-verbal Signals

Non-verbal communication takes place through such things as hand movements, facial expressions, body posture, eye contact, and the use of interpersonal space. It can be a powerful means of transmitting messages. Eye contact or voice intonation can be used intentionally to accent special parts of an oral communication. The astute observer notes the "body language" expressed by other persons. At times our body may be "talking" for us even as we otherwise maintain silence. And when we do speak, our body may sometimes "say" different things than our words convey. A **mixed message** occurs when a person's words communicate one message while his or her actions, body language, appearance, or use of interpersonal space communicate something else. Watch how people behave in a meeting. A person who feels under attack may move back in a chair or lean away from the presumed antagonist, even while expressing verbal agreement. All of this is done quite unconsciously, but it sends a message to those alert enough to pick it up.

Non-verbal channels probably play a more important part in communication than most people recognize. One researcher indicates that gestures alone may make up as much as 70 percent of communication.[13] In fact, a potential side effect of the growing use of electronic mail, computer networking, and other communication technologies is that gestures and other non-verbal signals that may add important meaning to the communication event are lost.

■ **Non-verbal communication** takes place through gestures and body language.

■ A **mixed message** results when words communicate one message, while actions, body language, or appearance communicate something else.

Physical Distractions

Any number of physical distractions can interfere with the effectiveness of a communication attempt. Some of these distractions, such as telephone interruptions,

---

Canadian Managers

Canadian's Communication Skills Put Her on Top Internationally

Ann Godbehere has the communications skills critical for today's style of CFO, says Simone Lauper, media relations officer at Swiss Reinsurance Co., the 140-year-old Zurich-based reinsurance giant. Godbehere is a core member of the Swiss Reinsurance management team that, in mid-2006, expected to finalize a $6.8-billion takeover of General Electric Co.'s Insurance Solutions unit. Her communications skills will be crucial in navigating the regulatory and integration hurdles involved with this takeover.

Godbehere was rated by *Institutional Investor* magazine as the leading CFO in the European insurance sector in 2004, an award she says reflects the team she has assembled. "I encourage people to say openly if they don't understand something," she says. "I'm not afraid to say 'I don't get it.'" This self-effacing but direct, inclusive, and tough-minded style represents traits of effective communications skills found in a good manager.

Sources: Gordon Pitts, "Canadians find influence, top careers in foreign lands," *The Globe and Mail*, January 16, 2006.

drop-in visitors, and lack of privacy, are evident in the following conversation between an employee, George, and his manager:

> *Okay, George*, let's hear your problem [phone rings, boss picks it up, promises to deliver a report "just as soon as I can get it done"]. Uh, now, where were we—oh, you're having a problem with your technician. She's [manager's secretary brings in some papers that need his immediate signature; secretary leaves] . . . you say she's overstressed lately, wants to leave…I tell you what, George, why don't you [phone rings again, lunch partner drops by]…uh, take a stab at handling it yourself…I've got to go now.[14]

Besides what may have been poor intentions in the first place, the manager in this example did not do a good job of communicating with George. This problem could be easily corrected. If George has something important to say, the manager should set aside adequate time for the meeting. Additional interruptions such as telephone calls and drop-in visitors could be eliminated by issuing appropriate instructions to the secretary. Many communication distractions can be avoided or at least minimized through proper planning.

Status Effects

"Criticize my boss? I don't have the right to." "I'd get fired." "It's her company, not mine." As suggested in these comments, the hierarchy of authority in organizations creates another potential barrier to effective communications. Consider the "corporate cover-up" once discovered at an electronics company. Product shipments were being predated and papers falsified to meet unrealistic sales targets set by the president. His managers knew the targets were impossible to attain, but at least 20 persons in the organization co-operated in the deception. It was months before the top found out. What happened in this case is **filtering**—the intentional distortion of information to make it appear favourable to the recipient.

■ **Filtering** is the intentional distortion of information to make it appear most favourable to the recipient.

The presence of such information filtering is often found in communications between lower and higher levels in organizations. Tom Peters, the popular management author and consultant, has called such information distortion "Management Enemy Number 1."[15] Simply put, it most often involves someone "telling the boss what he or she wants to hear." Whether the reason behind this is a fear of retribution for bringing bad news, an unwillingness to identify personal mistakes, or just a general desire to please, the end result is the same. The person receiving filtered communications can end up making poor decisions because of a biased and inaccurate information base.

> **BE SURE YOU CAN**
>
> • describe the communication process and identify its key components • differentiate effective and efficient communication • explain the role of credibility in persuasive communication • list the common sources of noise that create barriers to effective communication • illustrate how the barriers might affect communication between a team leader and team members • explain how mixed messages and filtering can interfere with communication in organizations

IMPROVING COMMUNICATION

A number of things can be done to overcome barriers and improve the process of communication. They include active listening, making constructive use of feedback, opening upward communication channels, understanding proxemics and the use of space, utilizing technology, and valuing diversity.

●●● ACTIVE LISTENING

Managers must be very good at listening. When people "talk," they are trying to communicate something. That "something" may or may not be what they are saying. **Active listening** is the process of taking action to help someone say exactly what he or she really means. It involves being sincere in listening to find the full meaning of what is being said. It also involves being disciplined in controlling emotions and withholding premature evaluations or interpretations. There are five rules for becoming an active listener:[16]

■ **Active listening** helps the source of a message say what he or she really means.

1. *Listen for message content:* Try to hear exactly what content is being conveyed in the message.
2. *Listen for feelings:* Try to identify how the source feels about the content in the message.
3. *Respond to feelings:* Let the source know that her or his feelings are being recognized.
4. *Note all cues:* Be sensitive to non-verbal and verbal messages; be alert for mixed messages.
5. *Paraphrase and restate:* State back to the source what you think you are hearing.

Different responses to the following two questions contrast how a "passive" listener and an "active" listener might act in real workplace conversations. Question 1: "Don't you think employees should be promoted on the basis of seniority?" *Passive listener's response:* "No, I don't!" *Active listener's response:* "It seems to you that they should, I take it?" Question 2: "What does the supervisor expect us to do about these out-of-date computers?" *Passive listener's response:* "Do the best you can, I guess."

MANAGER'S
Notepad 17.2

Ten steps to good listening

1. Stop talking.
2. Put the other person at ease.
3. Show that you want to listen.
4. Remove any potential distractions.
5. Empathize with the other person.
6. Don't respond too quickly; be patient.
7. Don't get mad; hold your temper.
8. Go easy on argument and criticism.
9. Ask questions.
10. Stop talking.

Active listener's response: "You're pretty disgusted with those machines, aren't you?" These examples show how active listening can facilitate communication in difficult circumstances, rather than discourage it. *Manager's Notepad 17.2* offers more guidelines for good listening.

●●● CONSTRUCTIVE FEEDBACK

■ **Feedback** is the process of telling someone else how you feel about something that person did or said.

The process of telling other people how you feel about something they did or said, or about the situation in general, is called **feedback.** The art of giving feedback is an indispensable skill, particularly for managers who must regularly give feedback to other people. Often this takes the form of performance feedback given as evaluations and appraisals. When poorly done, such feedback can be threatening to the recipient and cause resentment. When properly done, feedback—even performance criticism—can be listened to, accepted, and used to good advantage by the receiver.[17]

There are ways to help ensure that feedback is useful and constructive rather than harmful. To begin with, the sender must learn to recognize when the feedback he or she is about to offer will really benefit the receiver and when it will mainly satisfy some personal need. A supervisor who berates a computer programmer for errors, for example, actually may be angry about personally failing to give clear instruction in the first place. Also, a manager should make sure that any feedback is considered by the recipient as understandable, acceptable, and plausible. *Guidelines for giving "constructive" feedback* include the following:[18]

- Give feedback directly, and with real feeling, based on trust between you and the receiver.

- Make sure that feedback is specific rather than general; use good, clear, and preferably recent examples to make your points.

- Give feedback at a time when the receiver seems most willing or able to accept it.

- Make sure the feedback is valid; limit it to things the receiver can be expected to do something about.

- Give feedback in small doses; never give more than the receiver can handle at any particular time.

●●● USE OF COMMUNICATION CHANNELS

■ **Channel richness** is the capacity of a communication channel to effectively carry information.

Channel richness is the capacity of a communication channel to carry information in an effective manner.[19] *Figure 17.2* shows that face-to-face communication is very high in richness, enabling two-way interaction and real-time feedback. Formal reports and memos are very low in richness, due to impersonal one-way interaction with limited opportunity for feedback. Managers need to understand the limits of the possible channels and choose wisely when using them for communication.

●●● INTERACTIVE MANAGEMENT

■ In **management by wandering around** (MBWA) managers spend time outside of their offices to meet and talk with workers at all levels.

Interactive management approaches use a variety of means to keep communication channels open between organizational levels. A popular choice is **management by wandering around** (MBWA)—dealing directly with subordinates by regularly

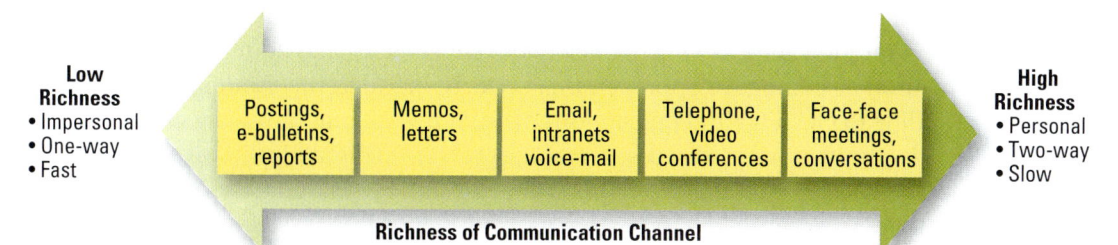

Figure 17.2 Channel richness and the use of communication media.

Low Richness
- Impersonal
- One-way
- Fast

Postings, e-bulletins, reports | Memos, letters | Email, intranets voice-mail | Telephone, video conferences | Face-face meetings, conversations

Richness of Communication Channel

High Richness
- Personal
- Two-way
- Slow

spending time walking around and talking with them about work-related matters. MBWA involves finding out for yourself what is going on in face-to-face communications. The basic objectives are to break down status barriers, increase the frequency of interpersonal contact, and get more and better information from lower-level sources. Of course, this requires a trusting relationship. Terry Curtis, president of EION Inc., believes in MBWA. In one of his previous positions as head of the IT department, he would take one day a month and shadow one of his employees. He would go where his employee went and do what they did. He said that "I would find out more stuff that day than all the other days of the month."[20]

Management practices designed to open channels and improve upward communications have traditionally involved *open office hours*, whereby busy senior executives like Patricia Gallup, CEO of PC Connection Inc., set aside time in their calendars to welcome walk-in visits during certain hours each week.[21] Today this approach can be expanded to include *online discussion forums* and "chat rooms" that are open at certain hours. Programs of regular *employee group meetings* are also helpful. Here, a rotating schedule of "shirtsleeve" meetings brings top managers into face-to-face contact with mixed employee groups throughout an organization. The face-to-face groups can be supplemented by *computer-mediated meetings* and *video conferences*, which serve similar purposes, overcoming time and distance limitations to communication. In some cases, a comprehensive communications program includes an *employee advisory council* composed of members elected by their fellow employees. Such councils meet with management on a regular schedule to discuss and react to new policies and programs that will affect employees.

At Vancity, Canada's largest credit union, the opportunity to take part in the television program, *Back to the Floor*, was looked upon as a chance to accomplish two goals—first, to connect the CEO with employees through a non-corporate program, and second, to gain a higher external profile by showing why the company was a great place to work. Paula Martin, vice-president of Public Affairs and Corporate Communications notes, "It was a perfect opportunity to help employees understand the business through the program's storyline. It wasn't part of the business plan for the employee communication program, but we saw an opportunity to do something spontaneous to support the company culture." Valuing communication as a key part of the company's culture has helped Vancity be named "Best employer in Canada for 2005" by *Maclean's* magazine.[22]

When executives suspect that they are having communication problems, *communication consultants* can be hired to conduct interviews and surveys of employees on their behalf. Productivity was chronically low at Rodebec, a copper rod manufacturing plant based in Saint-Romuald, Quebec, despite significant investment in capital improvements and training. Outside consultants were brought in to assess the problem and found there was a direct correlation between the low productivity and poor communication among management, supervisors, and employees.[23]

Another interactive approach that seeks to broaden the awareness of "bosses" regarding the feelings and perceptions of other people that they work closely with is **360-degree feedback**, discussed in Chapter 12.[24] This typically involves upward appraisals done by a manager's subordinates as well as additional feedback from peers, internal and external customers, and higher-ups. A self-assessment is also part of the process. The goal of 360-degree feedback is to provide the manager with information that can be used for constructive improvement. Managers who have participated in the process often express surprise at what they learn. Some have found themselves perceived as lacking vision, having bad tempers, being bad listeners, and lacking flexibility.[25] Eric Djukastein, co-founder and president of Victoria, B.C.-based Contech Electronics, found 360-degree feedback helpful. "It was illuminating and scary looking at the results—when your staff say you don't follow through on your commitments, that hurts," he says. "I was terrible at delivering so many things that a conscientious worker needs, such as regular performance reviews and wage reviews. I had a bad habit of doing things impulsively." Djukastein does see a bright side: "The good news is that it enabled me to open my eyes to things that were instrumental in changing my mental attitude."[26]

■ **360º feedback** includes views of bosses, peers, and subordinates in performance appraisals.

PROXEMICS AND SPACE DESIGN

An important but sometimes neglected part of communication involves proxemics, or the use of space.[27] The distance between people conveys varying intentions in terms of intimacy, openness, and status. And the physical layout of an office is an often-overlooked form of non-verbal communication. Check it out. Offices with chairs available for side-by-side seating convey different messages from those where the manager's chair sits behind the desk and those for visitors sit facing it in front.

Office or workspace architecture is an important influence on communication and behaviour. Architects and consultants specializing in *organizational ecology* are helping executives build offices conducive to the intense communication needed today. When Sun Microsystems built its San Jose, California facility, public spaces were designed to encourage communication among persons from different departments. Many meeting areas have no walls, and most of the walls that exist are glass. As manager of planning and research, Ann Bamesberger said: "We were creating a way to get these people to communicate with each other more." Importantly, the Sun project involved not only the assistance of expert architectural consultants, but also extensive inputs and suggestions from the employees themselves. The results seem to justify the effort. A senior technical writer, Terry Davidson, commented: "This is the most productive workspace I have ever been in."[28]

TECHNOLOGY UTILIZATION

When IBM surveyed employees to find out how they learned what was going on at the company, executives were not surprised that co-workers were perceived as credible and useful sources. But they were surprised that the firm's intranet ranked equally high. IBM's internal websites were ranked higher than news briefs, company memos, and information from managers.[29] The new age of communication is one of email, voice mail, instant messaging, teleconferencing, online discussions, videoconferencing, virtual or computer-mediated meetings, intranets, and Web portals. And the many implications of technology utilization must be understood.

Technology offers the power of the *electronic grapevine*, speeding messages and information from person-to-person. When the members of a Grade 6 class in Taylorsville, North Carolina (population 1,566), sent out the email message, "Hi!...We are curious to see where in the world our email will travel," they were surprised. Over a half-million replies flooded in, overwhelming not only the students but the school's computer system also.[30] Messages fly with equal speed and intensity around organizations. The results can be both functional—when the information is accurate and useful; and dysfunctional—when the information is false, distorted, or simply based on rumour. Managers should be quick to correct misimpressions and inaccuracies; they should also positively utilize the electronic grapevines as ways to quickly transfer factual and relevant information among organizational members.

Knowing how and when to use email may well be the biggest communication issue for people in organizations today. Purpose and privacy are two concerns. Employers are concerned that too much work time gets spent handling personal email; employees are concerned that employers are eavesdropping on their email messages. The best advice comes down to this: (1) find out the employer's policy on personal email and follow it; (2) don't assume that you ever have email privacy at work. Another major concern is email workload, which can be overwhelming. At Intel, for example, managers discovered that some employees faced up to 300 email messages a day and spent some two and one-half hours per day dealing with them. The firm initiated a training program to improve email utilization and efficiency.[31] Tips on managing your email include the following:[32]

- Read items only once.
- Take action immediately to answer, move to folders, or delete.
- Purge folders regularly of useless messages.
- Send group mail and use "reply to all" only when really necessary.
- Get off distribution lists without value to your work.
- Send short messages in the subject line, avoiding a full-text message.
- Put large files on websites, instead of sending as attachments.
- Use IM, instant messaging, as an email alternative.
- Don't forget the basic rule of email privacy: there isn't any.

●●●● VALUING CULTURE AND DIVERSITY

Workforce diversity and globalization are two of the most talked-about trends in modern society. Communicating under conditions of diversity, where the sender and receiver are part of different cultures, is certainly a significant challenge. Cross-cultural communication was first discussed in Chapter 5 on the global dimensions of management. It is useful to recall that a major source of difficulty is **ethnocentrism**, the tendency to consider one's culture superior to any and all others. Ethnocentrism can adversely affect communication in at least three major ways: (1) it may cause someone to not listen well to what others have to say; (2) it may cause someone to address

■ **Ethnocentrism** is the tendency to consider one's culture superior to any and all others.

or speak with others in ways that alienate them; and (3) it may lead to the use of inappropriate stereotypes when dealing with persons from another culture.[33]

For years, cultural challenges have been recognized by international travellers and executives. But as we know, you don't have to travel abroad to come face to face with communication and cultural diversity. The importance of cross-cultural communication skills applies at home just as much as it does in a foreign country. Just going to work is a cross-cultural journey for most of us today. The workplace abounds with subcultures based on gender, age, ethnicity, race, and other factors. All are a source of different perspectives, experiences, values, and expectations that can complicate the communication process. When the sender and receiver are unable to empathize with one another's cultures they will have difficulties understanding when and why certain words, gestures, and messages are misinterpreted.

Adept managers recognize the challenges surrounding communications. When Janet Plante, CEO of Davco Machine Ltd., was faced with a shortage of skilled journeymen labourers she knew she had to expand her recruiting strategy. As part of that new strategy, Davco took part in the Government of Alberta's Foreign Worker Readiness Program, travelling to Germany to hire skilled workers willing to work in Canada. Plante recognized that successfully incorporating global workers into the existing workforce would require some understanding of cultural differences. To ease the transition, Davco managers went through a significant amount of cultural sensitivity training: "We're trying to train our leaders to make the environment comfortable for everybody."[34]

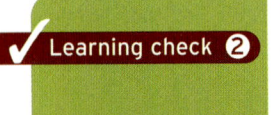

> **Learning check 2**
>
> **BE SURE YOU CAN**
> • define the term active listening • list the rules for active listening • illustrate how the guidelines for constructive feedback can be used when dealing with a subordinate having performance problems • explain how MBWA can improve upward communication • explain how proxemics and space design influence communication • discuss the influence of technology utilization on communication • explain the impact of ethnocentrism on communication

THE PERCEPTION PROCESS

■ **Perception** is the process through which people receive, organize, and interpret information from the environment.

Perception is the process through which people receive and interpret information from the environment. It is the way we form impressions about ourselves, other people, and daily life experiences. And it is the way we process information to make the decisions that ultimately guide our actions.[35] As shown in *Figure 17.3*, perception acts as a screen or filter through which information passes before it has an impact on

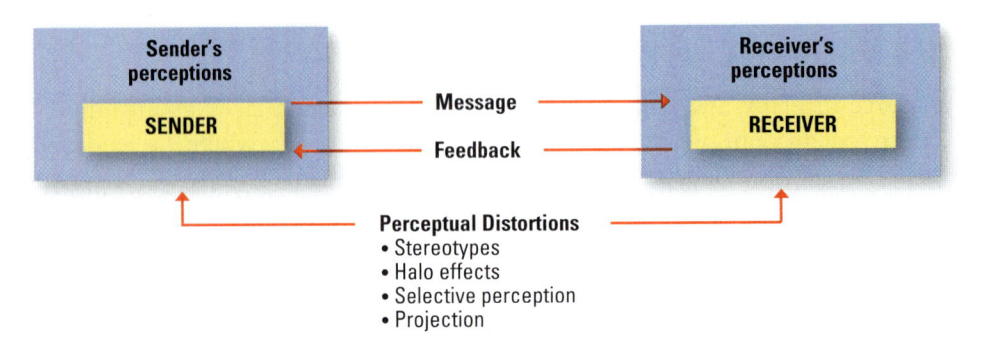

Figure 17.3 Perception and communication.

Sender's perceptions — SENDER — Message → Receiver's perceptions — RECEIVER
← Feedback

Perceptual Distortions
• Stereotypes
• Halo effects
• Selective perception
• Projection

communication, decision making, and action. Because perceptions are influenced by such things as cultural background, values, and other personal and situational circumstances, people can and do perceive the same things or situations differently. And importantly, people behave according to their perceptions.

●●● PERCEPTION AND ATTRIBUTION

One of the ways in which perception exerts its influence is through *attribution*, the process of developing explanations for events. It is natural for people to try to explain what they observe and the things that happen to them. The fact that people can perceive the same things quite differently has an important influence on attributions and their ultimate influence on behaviour.

In social psychology, attribution theory describes how people try to explain their own behaviour and that of others.[36] One of its significant applications is in the context of people's performance at work. Fundamental **attribution error** occurs when observers blame another person's performance failures more on internal factors relating to the individual than on external factors relating to the environment. In the case of someone who is producing poor-quality work, for example, a supervisor might blame a lack of job skills or laziness—an unwillingness to work hard enough. In response, the supervisor is likely to try to resolve the problem through training, motivation, or even replacement. The attribution error leads to the neglect of possible external explanations, for example, that the poor-quality work was caused by unrealistic time pressures or substandard technology. Opportunities to improve upon these factors through managerial action will thus be missed.

■ Fundamental **attribution error** overestimates internal factors and underestimates external factors as influences on someone's behaviour.

Another confounding aspect of perception and attribution occurs as a **self-serving bias**. This happens when individuals blame their personal failures or problems on external causes and attribute their successes to internal causes. You might think of this tendency the next time you "blame" your instructor for a poor course grade. The self-serving bias is harmful when it causes us to give insufficient attention to the need for personal change and development. While readily taking credit for successes, we are often too quick to focus on the environment to explain away our failures.

■ **Self-serving bias** explains personal success by internal causes and personal failures by external causes.

●●● PERCEPTUAL TENDENCIES AND DISTORTIONS

In addition to the attribution errors just discussed, a variety of perceptual tendencies and distortions can also influence communication and workplace behaviour. Of particular interest are the use of stereotypes, halo effects, selective perception, and projection.

Stereotypes

A **stereotype** occurs when someone is identified with a group or category, and then oversimplified attributes associated with the group or category are used to describe the individual. We all use stereotypes and they are not always negative or ill-intended. But those based on such factors as gender, age, and race can, and unfortunately still do, bias the perceptions of people in some work settings.

■ A **stereotype** is when attributes commonly associated with a group are assigned to an individual.

The *glass ceiling*, mentioned in Chapter 1 as an invisible barrier to career advancement, still exists. Legitimate questions can be asked about *racial and ethnic stereotypes* and about the slow progress of minority managers within corporate North America.

or develop skills for new positions.[15]

By 1993, Tom's of Maine was successfully moving beyond supplying products to health food stores and into supermarkets and drugstores, where most personal care products are purchased. Even as Tom's product distribution has expanded nationwide, the company's marketing strategy remains low key. Katie Shisler, vice-president of marketing, says, "We just tell them our story. We tell them why we have such a loyal base of consumers who vote with their dollars every day. A number of trade accounts appreciate our social responsibility and are willing to go out on a limb with us."[16] Tom Chappell agrees: "We're selling a lot more than toothpaste; we're selling a point of view—that nature is worth protecting."[17]

By the mid-1990s, Tom's of Maine was facing increasing competition. Its prices for baking soda toothpaste were similar to those of its competitors, but the prices of their deodorant and mouthwash were 20 to 40 percent higher. Tom Chappell didn't worry, however. He believes that "you have to understand from the outset that they have more in the marketing war chest than you. That's not the way you're going to get market share, you're going to get it by being who you are."[18] He explains his philosophy: "A small business obviously needs to distinguish itself from the commodities. If we try to act like commodities, act like a toothpaste, we give up our souls. Instead, we have to be peculiarly authentic in everything we do."[19] This authenticity is applied both to ingredients and to advertising decisions. "When you start doing that, customers are very aware of your difference. And they like the difference."[20]

Following the trend of other natural health care product companies, including Burt's Bees, in 2006 Tom's of Maine was purchased by a conglomerate, the Colgate-Palmolive Company. For approximately US$100 million—84 percent of outstanding shares—Colgate now has the opportunity to compete in the "natural" category of oral care products. Tom's leads in that niche, holding 60 percent of the market share. Tom Chappell remains on board to lead the company, which continues to be based in Kennebunk, Maine.[21]

A DIFFERENT KIND OF COMPANY?

Tom's of Maine distinguishes itself from other companies by stressing the "common good" in all of its endeavours. Not only concerned with corporate success, the company is passionately concerned about the wellness of its customers, employees, community, and the environment. In late 2000, the company launched Tom's Online Wellness Store to make its full product line available to customers around the globe. Among other customer-oriented activities, Tom's utilizes the services of a wellness advisory council and provides wellness education. The company also practises stewardship through its ongoing commitment to natural, sustainable, and responsible ingredients, products, and packaging. In embracing the philosophy of "doing well by doing good," Tom's has continued to produce impressive business results, with annual sales exceeding US$50 million, attesting to continued corporate wellness.[22]

Throughout the 1990s, Tom's of Maine was repeatedly recognized for providing a model of ethical business standards for others to follow. Among other awards, Tom and Kate Chappell have received the Corporate Conscience Award for Charitable Contributions from the Council of Economic Priorities, the New England Environmental Leadership Award, and the Governor's Award for Business Excellence.[23] Clearly, Tom's of Maine demonstrates that "common-good capitalism" can work so that businesses can simultaneously earn a profit and serve the common good. In an effort to pass these lessons on to other business people, Tom Chappell has authored two books, *The Soul of a Business: Managing for Profit and the Common Good* and *Managing Upside Down: Seven Intentions for Values-Centered Leadership*, and he has created the Saltwater Institute, a non-profit organization that provides training in the Seven Intentions.[24]

Chappell's Seven Intentions for seeking and achieving a values–profits balance are as follows:

1. Connect with goodness. Non-work discussions with an upbeat spin usually draw people to common ground, away from hierarchical titles.

2. Know thyself; be thyself. Discovering and tapping people's passions, gifts, and strengths generates creative energy.

3. Envision your destiny. The company is better served if its efforts are steered by strengths instead of following market whims.

4. **Seek counsel.** The journey is long, and assistance from others is absolutely necessary.
5. **Venture out.** The success of any business hinges on pushing value-enhanced products into the market.
6. **Assess.** Any idea must be regularly reviewed and refined if necessary.
7. **Pass it on.** Since developing and incorporating values is a trial-and-error process, sharing ideas and soliciting feedback allows for future growth.[25]

Tom's of Maine is a rare instance of a company that has found continued financial success by sticking to its principles and ethics, even in the face of pessimistic analysts and naysayers. What others might call idealism, Tom Chappell has put to work as simple pragmatism. But has acquisition by Colgate-Palmolive tainted the company's commitment to environmental and ethical standards and placed it in conflict with a large corporation's quest for profits? Or can a little company from Maine teach a cosmetics giant a thing or two about corporate responsibility? Take a trip down the aisles of your local grocery store to see what becomes of Tom's of Maine.

REVIEW QUESTIONS

1. Which way of thinking about ethical behaviour best describes Tom's of Maine and its founder, Tom Chappell?
2. How important were Tom Chappell's personal views in helping Tom's of Maine to be successful?
3. Define which "strategy" for social responsibility Tom Chappell seems to follow. Explain your answer.

YOU DO THE RESEARCH

1. Should Tom's stay independent, or should it merge with a larger firm?
2. Can Chappell's approach to ethical management work at larger firms?
3. Find five Internet sites that discuss ethics and social responsibility, and identify an important ethical lesson or insight that is provided on each site.

---

[1] Laura Zinn, "Tom Chappell: Sweet Success from Unsweetened Toothpaste," *Business Week* (September 2, 1991), p. 52.
[2] Janet Bamford, "Changing Business as Usual," *Working Women*, vol. 18 (November, 1993), p. 106.
[3] Craig Cox, "Interview: Tom Chappell, Minister of Commerce," *Business Ethics*, vol. 8 (January 1994), p. 42.
[4] Judy Quinn, "Tom's of Maine," *Incentive* (December 1993), p. A4.
[5] Ibid.
[6] Mary Martin, "Toothpaste and Theology," *Boston Globe* (October 10, 1993), p. A4.
[7] Craig Cox, op. cit.
[8] Mary Martin, "A 'Nuisance' to Rivals," *Boston Globe* (October 10, 1993), p. A4.
[9] Craig Cox, op. cit.
[10] Ibid.
[11] "The Tom's of Maine Mission," on the Web, <www.tomsofmaine.com>.
[12] Judy Quinn, op. cit.
[13] Ellyn E. Spragins, "Paying Employees to Work Elsewhere," *Inc.* (February 1993) p. 29.
[14] Judy Quinn, op. cit.
[15] Ibid.
[16] Martin Everett, "Profiles in Marketing: Katie Shisler," *Sales and Marketing Management* (March 1993) p. 12.
[17] Judy Quinn, op. cit.
[18] Craig Cox, op. cit.
[19] Ibid.
[20] Ibid.
[21] "Colgate Purchasing Tom's of Maine," press release on the Web, March 21, 2006, <www.tomsofmaine.com>. (December 2006).
[22] "Colgate Expands Reach of Quirky Toothpaste," *USA Today*, on the Web, March 21, 2006, <www.usatoday.com>.
[23] Tom's of Maine on the Web, <www.tomsofmaine.com>.
[24] Ibid.
[25] K. W. Meyers, "Tom's of Maine Business Plan Includes People," *Denver Rocky Mountain News* (October 5, 2000), p. 3B.

CASE 4

United Parcel Service: Where Technology Rules a Total Quality Road

United Parcel Service (UPS), the world's largest package distribution company, transports more than 3.75 billion parcels and documents annually. With more than 427,000 employees worldwide, 1,788 operating facilities, 1,838 daily flights, 91,700 vehicles, and the world's largest private communications system, UPS provides service in more than 200 countries.[1] How does UPS control such a vast and extended enterprise and still fulfill its commitment to serving the needs of the global marketplace?

CORPORATE HISTORY

In 1907, there was a great need for private messenger and delivery services. Only a few homes had private telephones, and luggage, packages, and personal messages had to be carried by hand. The U.S. Postal Service did not yet have the parcel post system. To help meet this need, an enterprising 19-year-old, James E. "Jim" Casey, borrowed $100 from a friend and established the American Messenger Company in Seattle, Washington. Despite stiff competition, the company did well, largely because of Jim Casey's strict policies on customer courtesy, reliability, round-the-clock service, and low rates. These principles, which guide UPS even today, are summarized by Jim's slogan: "Best Service and Lowest Rates."[2]

Obsessed with efficiency from the beginning, the company pioneered the concept of consolidated delivery—combining packages addressed to certain neighbourhoods onto one delivery vehicle. In this way, manpower and motorized equipment could be used more efficiently. The 1930s brought more growth. By this time, UPS provided delivery services in all major American West Coast cities, and a foothold had been established on the other coast with a consolidated delivery service in the New York City area. Many innovations were adopted, including the first mechanical system for package sorting. During this time, accountant George D. Smith joined the firm and helped make financial cost control the cornerstone of all planning decisions. The name United Parcel Service was adopted—"United" to emphasize the unity of the company's operations in each city, "Parcel" to identify the nature of the business, and "Service" to indicate what was provided to customers.[3] In 1975, Toronto was Canada's first city to enjoy UPS services and UPS's first international location.

In 1953, UPS resumed air service, which it had discontinued during the Depression, offering two-day service to major cities on the east and west coasts. Packages flew in the cargo holds of regularly scheduled airlines. Called UPS Blue Label Air, the service grew and by 1978 it was available in every state of the U.S., including Alaska and Hawaii. The demand for air parcel delivery increased in the 1980s at the same time that federal deregulation of the airline industry created new opportunities for UPS. Deregulation resulted in the established airlines reducing the number of flights being offered or abandoning routes altogether. To ensure dependability, UPS began to assemble its own jet cargo fleet, the largest in the industry. With growing demand for faster service, UPS entered the overnight air delivery business, and by 1985 UPS Next Day Air service was available in continental U.S. and Puerto Rico; Alaska and Hawaii were added later. That same year, UPS entered a new era, adding international air package and document service, linking the United States and six European nations.

UPS TODAY

In 1988, UPS received authorization from the U.S. Federal Aviation Administration (FAA) to operate its own aircraft, thus officially becoming an airline. Recruiting the best people available, UPS merged a number of different organizational cultures and procedures into a seamless operation called UPS Airline. UPS Airline was the fastest-growing airline in FAA history, formed in little more than one year with all the necessary technology and support systems. UPS Airline features some of the most advanced information systems in the world to support flight planning, scheduling, and load handling.[4]

Today, the UPS system moves more than 14 million

packages and documents daily around the globe. Packages are processed using advanced information technology and are transported by the company's own aircraft, chartered aircraft, and a fleet of delivery vehicles. While international package delivery operations constitute a substantial part of UPS's business, an important segment of the business is providing supply chain solutions for UPS customers.[5] In 2003, the company introduced a new brand logo representing a new, evolved UPS and adopted the acronym UPS as its formal name, indicating its broad range of capabilities and services beyond package delivery.[6] Today, UPS emphasizes its customer service orientation with the advertising slogan: "What can brown do for you?"

INNOVATIONS AT UPS

Known for its technological innovations, UPS keeps its package delivery and non-package operations on the cutting edge. Technology at UPS spans an incredible range, from specially designed package delivery vehicles to global computer and communications systems. UPS Worldport is the latest example of technology being used to increase efficiency and quality in the company's package operations. Located in Louisville, Kentucky, Worldport is a 360,000 square metre facility outfitted with overhead cameras to read smart labels and process documents, small packages, and irregular-shaped objects at a rate of over 300,000 packages per hour as they move along conveyors with astounding speed. Worldport also allows UPS to consolidate volume at a single location, thereby enabling the company to use larger and more efficient aircraft and streamlining the sorting at regional hubs throughout the world. UPS has planned a one billion dollar expansion of Worldport to be completed by 2010, building an additional 90,000 million square metres of space and increasing the number of conveyers to more than 32,000.[7]

UPS Supply Chain Solutions, the company's non-package operation, targets a variety of supply chain challenges faced by its customers, including helping them manage overseas suppliers, the logistics of post-sales parts and servicing, and order processing. This operation also coordinates transportation, vendors, contracts, and shipments, and simplifies international trade and regulatory compliance. UPS Supply Chain Solutions relies on a physical and virtual infrastructure for managing the flow of goods, information, and funds for different customers.[8] For example, through UPS Trade Direct Cross Border, Canadian company G3 was able to boost efficiency and reduce costs in the shipment of high-end backcountry ski equipment from Canada to hundreds of specialty shops and resorts throughout the United States. UPS consolidated shipments in Canada before moving them through customs, then repacked individual orders in the U.S. and shipped them at domestic rates. This streamlined G3's supply chain, enhanced customer service, and greatly reduced the company's costs.[9] Another supply chain solution was provided to TeddyCrafters, enabling that company to better manage the transportation and distribution of supplies from Asian and North American vendors. UPS designed a comprehensive inbound distribution system for TeddyCrafters that improved inventory management and provided for weekly restocking of the chain's retail stores. In each of these cases, and many others, UPS uses its own technological expertise in the transportation and distribution of documents and packages to help other companies achieve efficient, rapid, and low-cost solutions for all stages of their supply chains.[10]

THREE TRENDS DRIVING THE INDUSTRY

Frederick Smith of FedEx, a UPS competitor, identifies three trends driving the package delivery business: globalization, cost cutting, and Internet commerce.[11] *Globalization* will cause the world express-transportation market to explode to more than US$150 billion in value. While DHL Worldwide Express is a major player in the international market, UPS and FedEx are expanding at a rapid pace. Lee Hibbets of Air Cargo Management Group in Seattle states, "FedEx is seen as more aggressive, whereas UPS is a little bit more methodical and long term."[12] *Cost cutting* among customer firms, primarily by cutting inventory, fits into the package-firms' delivery systems. Technology plays a significant part in a delivery company's ability to assist customers in cutting their inventories. UPS and FedEx are competing fiercely in using technology to facilitate cost-cutting efforts. *Internet commerce*, the third trend, generates a huge need for shipping. Package delivery companies hope to capture the lion's share of the Internet commerce shipping business.

It remains to be seen who will win out in the package delivery wars, but UPS is a leader in the market. Its ability to track packages around the world is a testament to the value of technology in the workplace. With technological innovations generating higher productivity, the future for package delivery remains bright. Moreover, with attention being given to the challenges of supply chain management, package delivery companies like UPS can apply their technological expertise in developing additional business opportunities.

REVIEW QUESTIONS

1. Describe UPS's competitive advantage.
2. How does UPS approach customer relationship management?
3. How does technology enable UPS to be a quality-driven organization?

YOU DO THE RESEARCH

1. Describe the general environmental factors that affect UPS and its competitors in the package delivery industry.
2. Identify the stakeholders for UPS, and explain how those stakeholders potentially influence the company.
3. Describe the organizational culture at UPS and the role that it plays in the company's success.

---

[1] "UPS Fact Sheet," Media Kits on the Web, <www.pressroom.ups.com>
[2] United Parcel Service homepage, <www.ups.com>
[3] Rachael, Kamuf. "UPS Upping Employment as well as Technology," *Business First*, March 9, 1998.
[4] Information on the history of UPS services taken from the company website, <www.ups.com>.
[5] "Company History," About UPS on the Web, op. cit.
[6] "The UPS Logo: A Brief History," Fact Sheet on the Web, op. cit.
[7] "UPS Worldport Expansion Project," Fact Sheet on the Web, op. cit.
[8] UPS Supply Chain Solutions on the Web, op. cit.
[9] Consumer Goods and Retail Case Studies, on the Web, <www.ups-scs.com/solutions/case_consumer.html>.
[10] Ibid.
[11] Karen Walker, "Brown is Beautiful," *Airline Business* (November 1997), p. 46.
[12] Ibid.

CASE 5

Harley-Davidson: Where Style and Strategy Travel the Globe

With a celebration of almost legendary proportions, Harley-Davidson marked a century in business with a year-long International Road Tour. The party culminated in hometown Milwaukee.[1] Brought back from near bankruptcy, Harley-Davidson represents a true success story. Reacting to global competition, Harley has been able to re-establish itself as the dominant maker of big bikes in the United States. However, success often breeds imitation, and Harley faces a mixture of domestic and foreign competitors encroaching on its market. Can it meet the challenge?

HARLEY-DAVIDSON

When Harley-Davidson was founded in 1903, it was one of more than 100 firms producing motorcycles in the United States. The U.S. government became an important customer for the company's high-powered bikes with a reputation for reliability, using them in both world wars. By the 1950s, Harley-Davidson was the only remaining American manufacturer of motorcycles.[2]

But British competitors were beginning to enter the market with faster, lighter-weight bikes. Honda Motor Company of Japan began marketing lightweight bikes in the United States, moving into the production of middleweight vehicles in the 1960s. Harley initially tried to compete by manufacturing smaller bikes but had difficulty making them profitably. The company even purchased an Italian motorcycle firm, Aermacchi, but many Harley dealers were reluctant to sell the small Aermacchi Harleys.[3]

American Machine and Foundry Co. (AMF) took over Harley in 1969, and increased production from 14,000 to 50,000 bikes per year. This rapid expansion led to significant problems with quality, and better-built Japanese motorcycles began to take over the market. Harley's share of its major U.S. market—heavyweight motorcycles—fell to 23 percent.[4]

With the rallying cry "The Eagle Soars Alone," a group of 13 managers bought Harley-Davidson back from AMF in 1981 and began working to turn the company around. As Richard Teerlink, former CEO of Harley-Davidson, explained, "The solution was to get back to detail. The key was to know the business, know the customer, and pay attention to detail."[5] The key elements in this process were increasing quality and improving service to customers and dealers. Management kept the classic Harley-Davidson style and focused on the company's traditional strength, heavyweight and super-heavyweight bikes.

In 1983, Harley-Davidson asked the International Trade Commission (ITC) for tariff relief on the basis that Japanese manufacturers were stockpiling inventory in the United States and providing unfair competition. The tariff relief was granted on April 1, 1983, and a tariff was placed on all imported Japanese motorcycles that were 700cc or larger, for a five-year period. In 1987, Harley petitioned the ITC to have the tariff lifted because the company felt capable and confident of its ability to compete with foreign imports.

Once Harley's quality image had been restored, the company slowly began to increase production. In January of 1992 the company made only 280 bikes per day, increasing output to 345 bikes per day by the end of that year. Despite growing demand, production was scheduled to reach only 420 per day, approximately 100,000 per year, by 1996.[6] However, in 1996 Harley recognized the overwhelming demand and accomplished the first of many grand expansion plans with the opening of a new distribution centre in Wisconsin. In 1997, Harley began production in three separate, new facilities in Wisconsin and Missouri, and in 1998 opened a new assembly plant in Brazil. Expansions were announced for Wisconsin and Pennsylvania plants in 2001.[7]

As indicated by these expansions, the popularity of the motorcycles continued to increase throughout the 1980s. In 1983, the Harley Owners Group (H.O.G.) was formed. Membership numbers for the Harley owners' social club soared to almost 100,000 by the end of the decade, and today the group exceeds 1 million members.[8] When H.O.G. was formed, the average Harley purchaser was in his late thirties, with an average household income of over US$40,000. Teerlink didn't like the description of his customers as "aging" baby boomers: "Our customers want the sense of adventure that they get on our bikes. . . . Harley-Davidson doesn't sell transportation, we sell transformation. We sell excitement, a way of life."[9] However, the average age and income of Harley riders has continued to increase. As of late, the median age of a Harley rider was 47 and the median income was just under US$80,000.[10]

Although the company had been exporting motorcycles ever since it was founded, it was not until the late 1980s that Harley-Davidson management began to consider international markets. In 1987, the company acknowledged its ability to compete with foreign imports and started to seriously plan for the international market. Traditionally, the company's ads had been translated word for word into foreign languages. Now, ads were developed specifically for different markets, and motor cycle rallies were adapted to fit local customs.[11] The company also began to actively recruit and develop dealers in Europe and Japan. It purchased a Japanese distribution company and built a large parts warehouse in Germany to support its European operations. Harley-Davidson continued to look for ways to expand its activities. Recognizing that German motorcyclists rode at high speeds—often more than 160 kph—the company began to study ways to give Harleys a smoother ride. It also began to develop and market accessories that would give riders more protection.[12]

The company also created a line of Harley items, available through dealers or by catalogue, adorned with the Harley-Davidson logo. These jackets, caps, T-shirts, and other items became popular with non-bikers as well. In fact, the clothing and parts had a higher profit margin than the motorcycles; non-bike products made up as much as half of sales at some dealers.

INTERNATIONAL EFFORTS

Harley-Davidson continues to make inroads in overseas markets. At one time, the company held 30 percent of the worldwide market for heavyweight motorcycles—chrome-laden cruisers, aerodynamic rocket bikes, and oversize touring motorcycles. In the United States, Harley had 46.4 percent of the market, the largest share, followed by Honda with 20.2 percent. In Europe, Harley ranked sixth behind Honda, Yamaha, BMW, Suzuki, and Kawasaki, with only 6.6 percent of the market share. However, in the Asia/Pacific market, where it might be expected that Japanese bikes would dominate, Harley held 21.3 percent of the market compared with 19.2 percent for Honda in the early part of the twenty-first century.[13]

Now Harley-Davidson motorcycles are among America's fastest-growing exports to Japan. Harley's Japanese subsidiary adapted the company's marketing approach to Japanese tastes, even producing shinier and more complete tool kits than are available in the United States. Built in Japan by a licensed Japanese manufacturer before the Second World War already, Harley bikes have long been considered symbols of prestige there. Consistent with their U.S. counterparts, many Japanese enthusiasts see themselves as rebels on wheels.[14]

More recently, Harley has made inroads to the previously elusive Chinese market. Hoping to enter a country on the cusp of an economic revolution, the first official Chinese Harley-Davidson dealer opened its doors just outside downtown Beijing in 2006. Like other Harley stores, the Chinese outlet will stock bikes, parts and accessories, branded merchandise, and offer post-sale service. Despite China's growing middle class with disposable income, the new store has several hurdles ahead of it, including government imposed riding restrictions in urban areas. And, although its international sales grew 15 percent in recent years, the U.S. still represents more than 80 percent of Harley's total sales.[15]

Harley-Davidson continues to develop new products in order to increase its market share. Another recent effort by Harley to expand its buyer base involves the development of its Blast motorcycle from its Buell division. Fifty percent of Blast sales are to women, raising the overall percentage of women buying Harleys from 2 percent in 1987 to 9 percent by 1999. That 9 percent figure has remained constant for several years in a row. With 17 consecutive years of increased production, as well as record revenues and earnings, Harley's future appears bright.[16]

REVIEW QUESTIONS

1. Do you feel that Harley-Davidson's expansion into China came at the right time? Why or why not?
2. Harley appears to have moved from providing a product (motorcycles) to providing a service (a way of life). Discuss how this movement from products to services may have affected the company.
3. Suggest a manufacturer in a European or Asian country with which Harley could form an advantageous joint venture.

YOU DO THE RESEARCH

1. How have other motorcycle companies reacted to Harley-Davidson becoming more of an international player?
2. Should Harley alter its image as the North American population ages?

---

[1] Harley-Davidson on the Web, <www.harley-davidson.com>.
[2] Malia Boyd, "Harley-Davidson Motor Company," *Incentive* (September 1993), pp. 26–27.
[3] Shrader, et al., "Harley-Davidson, Inc.—1991," in Fred David, ed., *Strategic Management*, 4th ed. (New York: Macmillan, 1993), p. 655.
[4] Ibid.
[5] Martha H. Peak, "Harley-Davidson: Going Whole Hog to Provide Stakeholder Satisfaction," *Management Review*, vol. 82 (June 1993), p. 53.
[6] Harley-Davidson, 1992, Form 10K, p. 33.
[7] Harley-Davidson, op. cit.
[8] Ibid.
[9] Peak, op. cit.
[10] Harley-Davidson, op. cit.
[11] Kevin Kelly and Karen Miller, "The Rumble Heard Round the World: Harleys," *Business Week* (May 24, 1993) p. 60.
[12] Ibid.
[13] Harley-Davidson, op. cit.
[14] Sandra Dallas and Emily Thornton, "Japan's Bikers: The Tame Ones," *Business Week* (October 20, 1997), p. 159.
[15] "H-D Cautiously Upbeat Over Beijing Dealer," *Dealer News* (May 2006), p. 67.
[16] Harley-Davidson, op. cit.

CASE 6

Domino's Pizza: Customer-Driven Strategy Brings Pizzas to Your Door

Domino's Pizza has more than 8,000 company-owned and franchised stores in more than 50 countries. With sales of more than 400 million pizzas and revenues of nearly US$5 billion, it represents an impressive success story. Starting in 1960 with one store in Ypsilanti, Michigan, Tom Monaghan redefined the pizza industry and, in so doing, built a corporate powerhouse. It entered the international market in 1983 with the opening of its first store outside of the United States, in Winnipeg. Today more than 2,500 of the stores are international and revenue generated in those stores exceeds US$1 billion.[1] Given the chance, could you be another Tom Monaghan?

THE DOMINO STORY

In 1960, Tom Monaghan and his brother, James, borrowed US$500 to purchase "Domi-Nick's," a pizza store in Ypsilanti, Michigan. The following year Tom bought out his brother's half interest for a used Volkswagen Beetle. In 1965, Tom changed the name of the establishment to "Domino's Pizza." Two years later, he opened the first franchise location in Ypsilanti.[2]

Growing up in orphanages, Tom dreamed of succeeding in a big way. In his first 13 years in the business, he worked 100-hour weeks. He took only one vacation, and that was for six days when he married his wife, Margie.[3] The following quote exhibits his strong need to be the best at whatever he does: "I was distracted by some of the rewards of success, which was hurting my business. I put all of those distractions aside, and focused solely on Domino's Pizza. I decided to take a 'millionaire's vow of poverty'. I am focusing on God, family and Domino's Pizza."[4]

The pizza industry is highly fragmented, with nearly 70,000 pizzerias and US$35 billion in sales per year. More than three billion pizzas are sold each year in the United States, representing annual consumption of over 10 kilograms of pizza per person.[5] The issue for any pizzeria is how to gain an advantage and make its product stand out from the many others. Monaghan decided to concentrate only on pizzas, and developed the strategy of delivering a hot pie within 30 minutes. He chose to locate his early franchises in university towns and near military bases, both places where a lot of pizza is eaten. This strategy proved to be very successful, and by the late 1970s Domino's had more than 200 locations.[6]

Monaghan is credited with developing many of the pizza practices now taken for granted within the industry, including dough trays, corrugated pizza boxes, insulated bags to transport pizzas, and a unique system of internal franchising. "Tom Monaghan made pizza delivery what it is today," says Eric Marcus, owner of 46 Domino's locations in Ohio. "The one thing about Tom is that he knew what he wanted, and he knew how to stay focused on what he wanted. He had a vision that pizza should be delivered in 30 minutes or less."[7]

The 1980s proved to be a time of tremendous growth for Domino's, as it closed out the decade with more than 5,000 locations and US$2 billion in sales.[8] During that time, Monaghan purchased the Detroit Tigers baseball team and developed significant philanthropic activities in various Domino's communities.

However, the road to success was not entirely smooth, and Domino's did have to face hurdles and challenges along the way. In 1968, the firm's commissary and company headquarters were destroyed by fire. In 1976, Amstar Corp., maker of Domino Sugar, filed a trademark infringement lawsuit against the firm that was settled, in Domino's favour, in 1980. In 1993, responding to concerns for drivers' safety, the firm discontinued the "30-minute guarantee" and replaced it with a total satisfaction guarantee: "If for any reason you are dissatisfied with your Domino's Pizza dining experience, we will remake your pizza or refund your money."[9]

In 1998, Monaghan sold "a significant" portion of his ownership in Domino's to Bain Capital Inc., a Massachusetts investment firm. While he remained on the board of directors, he was no longer engaged in the day-to-day activities of the firm. Instead, he wanted to devote his time to religious pursuits, including the development of a planned Catholic community—Ave Maria,

Florida—and a Catholic university by the same name.[10]

David Brandon, formerly of Procter & Gamble and Valassis Communications, was hired as president. In his first full year as president, Domino's achieved a 4.4 percent growth in sales. Now chairman and CEO, Brandon has been recognized as the visionary who led Domino's to its 2003 win of the coveted "Chain of the Year" award given by *Pizza Today*. Jeremy White, editor-in-chief of the monthly trade publication, observed, "Domino's had an impressive year. Between solid product introductions, savvy advertising, and a 'people first' mentality that has trickled down from chairman and CEO Dave Brandon to store employees, the chain managed to post positive financial results in a time of economic instability."[11] *Pizza Today* honoured the company for outstanding sales, strong leadership, innovation, brand image, and customer satisfaction.[12]

DOMINO'S FUTURE

With a history of innovations in the pizza industry, Domino's leadership continues to look for new ways to enhance customer value. In Domino's early years, Tom Monaghan set the stage for the company's later successes with his innovations and brand development strategies. He even recognized how important it was to adapt to local culture in order to achieve success overseas. "Culture comes first. Some early attempts to open Domino's stores internationally faltered because the company tried to establish in markets that had cultures unaccustomed to pizza or the convenience of home delivery. Understanding cultures and adapting to them was the first step in the process of global expansion."[13] For example, Brandon notes that although delivery service has proven very popular in Japan and Taiwan, customers in China seem to want to leave their home to enjoy their pizza. Consequently, the company is experimenting with larger stores featuring sit-down areas.

Monaghan displayed the drive and determination representative of many entrepreneurs in today's dynamic market. He had what it took to succeed. Could you do what Tom Monaghan did?

REVIEW QUESTIONS

1. What allowed Tom Monaghan to develop Domino's into a worldwide enterprise?
2. How do you think the characters of Tom Monaghan and David Brandon differ? How are they similar? Why was each the right person for the company at the time?
3. If Tom Monaghan decided to develop the Domino's franchise in the present day, what advantages might he have as an entrepreneur in today's climate? What disadvantages might he face?

YOU DO THE RESEARCH

1. What are pizza parlours presently doing to differentiate their products?
2. Look at the profiles of other successful entrepreneurs. Do they have some character attributes in common?

---

[1] Domino's Pizza on the Web, <www.dominos.com>.
[2] Ibid.
[3] "Tom Monaghan," The American Dreams Collection, March 1, 2001, on the Web, <www.usdreams.com/Monaghan7677.html>.
[4] Ibid.
[5] Domino's Pizza on the Web, op. cit.
[6] "Tom Monaghan," op. cit.
[7] Amy Zuber, "Tom Monaghan," *Nation's Restaurant News* (September 13, 1999), pp. 139–141.
[8] "Tom Monaghan," op. cit.
[9] Domino's Pizza on the Web, op. cit.
[10] "Pizza Magnate Backs Off Catholic Town Plan." *Church & State* (May 2006), p. 21.
[11] "Top Honors," on the Web, <www.pizzatoday.com>.
[12] Ibid.
[13] Domino's Pizza on the Web, op. cit.

CASE 7

Kate Spade Turns Risk Into Opportunities

After graduating from college in 1986, Katherine (Kate) Noel Brosnahan was employed by *Mademoiselle* magazine, working her way up to senior fashion editor/head of accessories before her departure in 1991. During this time, Kate concluded that the women's fashion accessories market lacked stylish, practical handbags. Kate, along with her then boyfriend and now husband, Andy Spade, saw an opportunity and capitalized on it.[1] How did Kate and Andy capitalize on this opportunity?

THE START-UP

Kate and Andy set out "to develop a well-edited line of fashionable, but not 'trendy' handbags."[2] Kate developed design sketches for six handbags with simple shapes that emphasized utility, colour, and fabric. Kate also investigated production costs. Andy contributed the marketing expertise, drawing on his experience at several advertising agencies. In January 1993, Kate and Andy launched Kate Spade Handbags.[3]

Kate worked full-time to get the new company firmly established while Andy initially was involved only part-time. From January 1993 until September 1996, Andy worked nights and weekends on behalf of the new company while he continued to work full-time for an advertising agency. Andy became full-time president and creative director with Kate Spade Handbags in September 1996.

Early on, Kate and Andy recognized the crucial need for recruiting talented people to help them grow the business. In late 1993, Pamela Simotas joined the company to assist Kate with the sourcing of materials and the manufacturing of the handbags. In 1994, Elyce Arons joined the company to focus on sales and public relations. The addition of Simotas and Arons led to the creation of a partnership that now numbers seven persons, each of whom brings special expertise and talents to the company.[4]

GROWING INTO THE FUTURE

Kate Spade's vision focused on developing product lines and appropriately positioning the company in both the domestic and global marketplace. Kate Spade's original design philosophy relied on simplicity, elegance, and enduring quality "to create products that combined great personal style with long-lasting utility."[5] This design philosophy has been consistently applied to growing the company's product lines. In addition to the original six nylon tote bags, Kate Spade's product lines now include leather handbags and accessories, evening bags, baby bags, a luggage collection, shoes, glasses, paper products (e.g., personal organizers, address books, and journals), beauty products, and home accessories.[6] In 1999, Jack Spade, an accessories line for men, was launched under Andy's tutelage. Jack Spade products include messenger bags, briefcases, and utility bags, among other items.[7]

In mid-1996, Kate Spade opened its first retail shop in New York City's Soho neighbourhood. Expansion of the retail operation soon followed, with stores being opened in Boston, Los Angeles, San Francisco, and Chicago. Numerous Kate Spade outlets now exist in several Japanese cities, including Tokyo, Kyoto, and Osaka. International distribution of Kate Spade products has also expanded to Canada, Australia, the Bahamas, Bermuda, England, Guam, Hong Kong, Ireland, Korea, the Philippines, Puerto Rico, Saipan, Singapore, and Taiwan, just to name a few.[8] Kate Spade also launched an e-commerce operation in 2005.

With increased competition from rivals such as Coach, Tommy Hilfiger, Ralph Lauren, and Michael Kors, Kate Spade was faced with increasing pressure to rapidly expand both in product offerings and retail store locations.[9] In 1999, Neiman Marcus Group purchased a 56 percent stake in Kate Spade, although Kate and Andy Spade and their partners remained with the firm and continued to run the company on a day-to-day basis.[10]

An increased focus on growth brings with it the possibility of growing too much, too quickly. Analysts agree that over the years Kate Spade has fallen off the radar to some extent, due in part to its rapid expansion into non-core categories that detracted from its handbag business.[11] While the company experienced a 25 percent increase in retail sales in 2004,[12] in 2005 Neiman Marcus announced that it would begin to explore strategic options including a possible sale of Kate Spade.[13] Marybeth Schmitt, spokeswomen for Kate Spade, said, "This next move for Kate Spade is an important one, and they want to make sure it is in the best interest of the brands. Kate and Andy Spade and their partners are not in a hurry to negotiate the future of their company, but are only interested in finding the right strategic partners."[14] Andy Spade commented, "At this stage of our growth, it makes good business sense for the company to explore all options available. We are very excited and optimistic about the future of Kate Spade."[15]

In 2006, Kate and Andy Spade and partners Elyce Arons and Pamela Bell sold their remaining 44 percent of Kate Spade to Neiman Marcus.[16] Later that year, Liz Claiborne acquired Kate Spade from Neiman Marcus. "Our job now is to maintain the essence of Kate Spade while driving it to the next level, something we have done quite successfully with other acquired brands in our portfolio," said Trudy Sullivan, president of Liz Claiborne.[17] Liz Claiborne plans include an expanded Kate Spade with up to 200 international and domestic boutiques.[18]

In just over a decade, Kate Spade has grown from the germ of an idea about how to fill a void in the women's fashion accessories market into a business with multi-product lines and distribution in several North American and international locations. So what's next for the Spades? It is still unclear how long Kate and Andy Spade will remain with the company following the merger. Sources for Liz Claiborne have indicated that the pair, along with Elyce Arons and Pamela Bell, have service agreements through mid-2007, and that the firm is in discussions to extend those contracts.[19] Whatever happens next, it's clear that entrepreneurs Kate and Andy Spade have no intention of slowing down.

REVIEW QUESTIONS

1. Describe the key decisions that Kate and Andy faced in the start-up of their company.
2. What were the key elements of Kate Spade's growth in the first decade of its operations? What specific business decisions were made in implementing these key elements of growth?
3. What key decisions will Kate Spade need to make during the second decade of its operations?

YOU DO THE RESEARCH

1. How did Kate Spade develop its e-commerce operation?
2. How might Kate Spade further utilize information technology to help fuel continuing global expansion?

---

[1] Company website, <www.katespade.com>.
[2] Ibid.
[3] Ibid
[4] Ibid
[5] Ibid.
[6] Ibid
[7] Ibid
[8] L. McCauley, "Next Stop—The 21st Century," *Fast Company* (September 1999).
[9] Linda Tischler, "Power Couple," *Fast Company* (March 2005), p. 44.
[10] "Neiman Buys Kate Spade Stake," *Wall Street Journal* (February 5, 1999), p. 1.
[11] Eric Newman, "Analysts Laud Liz's Spade Buy," *Footwear News*, vol. 62 (November 13, 2006).
[12] Sophia Chabbott, "Kate Spade Negotiations: slow and steady," *WWD*, vol. 192 (July 11, 2006), p. 8.
[13] Sophia Chabbott with contributions from Vicki M. Young, "Kate Spade on the Block: NMG eyes strategic options," *WWD*, vol. 190 (September 19, 2005), p. 4.
[14] "Kate Spade Negotiations: slow and steady," op. cit.
[15] "Kate Spade on the Block: NMG eyes strategic options," op. cit.
[16] Sophia Chabbott with contributions from Jeanine Poggi, "Neiman's to Buy Rest of Spade," *WWD* (November 3, 2006), p. 2.
[17] "Liz Claiborne to Acquire Kate Spade," *Home Textiles Today* (November 13, 2006).
[18] Whitney Beckett, "Liz Claiborne's New Leader," *WWD*, vol. 192 (December 6, 2006), p. 11.
[19] "Analysts Laud Liz's Spade Buy," op. cit.

CASE 8

Wal-Mart: Self-Management Works at the Number-One Retailer

Wal-Mart, first opened in 1962 by Sam Walton in Rogers, Arkansas, has become the largest retailer in the world, with more than 6,500 store locations and approximately 1.8 million associates worldwide.[1] Despite the death of Sam Walton in 1992, Wal-Mart continues to be successful, reaching record annual sales of US$312.4 billion and earnings of US$11.2 billion.[2] Maintaining this phenomenal growth presents a significant challenge to Wal-Mart's current leadership.

CARRYING ON SAM WALTON'S LEGACY

In his 1990 letter to Wal-Mart stockholders, then-CEO David Glass laid out the company's philosophy: "We approach this new, exciting decade of the '90s much as we did in the '80s—focused on only two main objectives: (a) providing the customers what they want, when they want it, all at a value; and (b) treating each other as we would hope to be treated, acknowledging our total dependency on our associate partners to sustain our success."[3] Following in Sam Walton's footsteps, Glass believed that the traditional format of organization—employee commitment, cost control, carefully planned locations for new stores, and attention to customer needs and desires—would enable Wal-Mart to enjoy continued success.

Wal-Mart's success came through paying careful attention to its market niche: customers looking for quality at a bargain price. Customers did not have to wait for a sale to realize savings at Wal-Mart. As Glass looked ahead to the 1990s, he recognized the opportunities and threats that confronted Wal-Mart. Many of its stores were located in smaller towns, primarily throughout the American south and midwestern states. While the traditional geographical markets served by Wal-Mart were not saturated, growth in these areas was limited. Any strategy to achieve continuing growth would have to include expansion into additional geographical regions. In 1993, the company added the 91-store Pace Membership Warehouse chain, which it purchased from Kmart.[4] Competition was increasing as smaller regional chains such as Costco and Price Club merged and opened stores in many of the same markets as Wal-Mart.[5] Glass recognized that existing stores might have to introduce new product lines and higher-priced products in order to achieve year-to-year sales growth.

Wal-Mart has experimented with numerous retail formats over the years. Today, the company is made up of five retail divisions and five specialty divisions. The retail divisions include Wal-Mart Stores; SAM's Clubs, a membership warehouse; Neighborhood Markets, selling groceries, pharmaceuticals, and general merchandise; International Division; and Wal-mart.com, an online version of the neighbourhood Wal-Mart store. There are also three specialty divisions, Tire & Lube Express, Wal-Mart Optical, and Wal-Mart Pharmacy, that typically operated within the Wal-Mart stores, supercentres, and SAM'S Club outlets.

Wal-Mart has also worked to develop internationally. In March 1994, the company bought 122 Canadian Woolco stores, formerly owned by Woolworth Corp., the largest single purchase Wal-Mart had made.[6] This international expansion continued, and in 2003, Wal-Mart's international division was the second largest of the five with respect to sales and earnings. Today, the almost 2,600 international locations have reported US$62.7 billion in sales and an operating profit of US$3.3 billion.[7]

Wal-Mart subscribes to the corporate policy "buy American whenever possible." Nonetheless, it has a global purchasing system that allows it to effectively coordinate its entire worldwide supply chain and to share its buying power and merchandise network with all its operations throughout the world.[8] The company has set up an inventory control procedure based on a satellite communication system that links all stores with the Bentonville, Arkansas, headquarters. The satellite system is also used to transmit messages and training materials from headquarters, facilitate communications among stores, and can even be used to track the company's delivery trucks. In addition, Wal-Mart has an online system that links the company's computer systems with its suppliers. Because of its use of innovative technology, Wal-Mart has gained a competitive advantage in the speed with which it delivers goods to its customers.

While each new Wal-Mart brings jobs into communities, there are also other, negative, effects. A 1991 *Wall Street Journal* article noted that many small retailers are forced to close after a Wal-Mart opens nearby.[9] In one Wisconsin town, the large department store J. C. Penney lost 50 percent of its Christmas sales and closed down when Wal-Mart opened. In an Iowa town, four clothing and shoe stores, a hardware store, a drug store, and a dime store all went out of business as a result of Wal-Mart's arrival. Citizens of many communities across North America have successfully worked together to delay or change Wal-Mart's plans, or even prevented the retail giant from locating in the area all together.

Wal-Mart has faced considerable cultural resistance for its low-paying, part-time jobs and the disproportionately small number of its employees who qualify for full-time benefits, such as insurance. In response, Wal-Mart has made an inexpensive, "value plan" health insurance available to its employees. For about $25 a month, the plan covers a limited number of prescriptions before a deductible applies, but it also includes some negative cost-sharing features.[10]

Even Wal-Mart's "Bring it home to the USA" buying program produced controversy when an NBC news program found clothing that had been made overseas hanging under a "Made in the USA" sign in 11 Wal-Mart stores. In addition, a buying program video showed children sewing at a Wal-Mart supplier's factory in Bangladesh. Wal-Mart insisted that its supplier was obeying local labour laws, which allowed 14-year-olds to work. A company official had also paid a surprise visit to the factory and not found any problems. Then-CEO David Glass stated, "I can't tell you today that illegal child labour hasn't happened someplace, somewhere. All we can do is try our best to prevent it."[11]

SAM'S CULTURAL LEGACY

Wal-Mart's success is built upon its culture. Rob Walton, the company's current chairman of the board, says, "Although Wal-Mart has grown large, we still focus daily on the culture and values established by my father, Sam Walton."[12] Sam Walton founded and built Wal-Mart around three basic beliefs: *respect for the individual, service to our customers, and striving for excellence*. Wal-Mart's slogan that "our people make the difference" reflects the company's respect for, and commitment to, its employees. Diversity is also highly valued. Wal-Mart's philosophy of customer service emphasizes the lowest possible prices along with the best possible service to each and every customer. Lee Scott, Wal-Mart's current president and CEO, observes, "Sam was never satisfied that prices were as low as they needed to be or that our product's quality was as high as they deserved—he believed in the concept of striving for excellence before it became a fashionable concept."[13]

Three critical elements in Wal-Mart's approach to customer service are the *sundown rule*, the *ten-foot rule*, and *every day low prices*. The *sundown rule* means Wal-Mart sets a standard of accomplishing tasks on the same day that the need arises—in short, responding to requests by sundown on the day it receives them. The *ten-foot rule* promises that if an employee comes within ten feet or three metres of a customer, the employee must look the customer in the eye and ask if the person would like to be helped. *Every day low prices* is another important operating philosophy. Wal-Mart believes that by lowering markup, it will earn more because of increased volume, thereby bringing consumers added value for the dollar every day.[14]

Although Wal-Mart has enjoyed phenomenal success, there is no guarantee that it will continue to do so in the future. As the company's annual report points out, preserving and advancing the *every day low prices* concept and helping thousands of new associates to embrace the customer-centred Wal-Mart culture are essential for the company's continued growth.[15] But given the ever-increasing pressures of business, as well as a growing tide of resistance to Wal-Mart's competitive practices, how long can the company stay on top? Chances are there's a Wal-Mart nearby, so stop in and see what you think.

REVIEW QUESTIONS

1. What are Wal-Mart's key objectives? How have Wal-Mart's managerial philosophies and principles enabled it to pursue these key objectives?

2. How do planning and controlling seem to be linked at Wal-Mart?

3. In what ways does Wal-Mart save money through purchasing control?

YOU DO THE RESEARCH

1. Walmart's expansion into the grocery business has caused some problems for Canadian grocers. What has Loblaws or Sobeys done from a planning or control perspective to better compete with Walmart?

2. How might Walmart use scenario planning to assist them as they look to expand into other countries?

---

[1] "The Wal-Mart Story," on the Web, September 28, 2006, <www.walmartfacts.com>.
[2] "Financial Results," op. cit.
[3] "Wal-Mart Picks Up the PACE," *Business Week* (November 15, 1993), p. 45.
[4] Ibid.
[5] Wendy Zellner, "Warehouse Clubs Butt Heads—and Reach for the Ice Pack," *Business Week* (April 19, 1993), p. 68.
[6] William C. Symonds, "Invasion of the Retail Snatchers," *Business Week* (May 9, 1994), pp. 72–73.
[7] "International Operations," on the Web, <www.walmartstores.com>.
[8] 2003 Annual Report, op. cit., p. 3.
[9] Barbara Marsh, "Merchants Mobilize to Battle Wal-Mart in a Small Community," *Wall Street Journal* (June 5, 1991), p. A1.
[10] Victoria Colliver, "Health insurance for $25: Wal-Mart offers various lower-cost coverage plans for workers," *San Francisco Chronicle* (October 25, 2005).
[11] Bill Saporito, "David Glass Won't Crack Under Fire," *Fortune* (February 8, 1993), pp. 75, 78.
[12] 2003 Annual Report, <www.walmartstores.com>.
[13] Wal-Mart website, op. cit.
[14] Ibid.
[15] 2003 Annual Report, op. cit.

CASE 9

Skype: Making the Case For Free Calls

Look out phone companies; there's a new kid on the block who's aiming to take a bite out of your customer base. In its brief time in business, Skype has amassed more than 75 million customers around the world—from savvy teens, to Internet moguls, to businesses of all sizes.[1] Skype's peer-to-peer phone service allows users to make crystal-clear, computer-to-computer calls anywhere in the world. And Skype users pay long-distance and international rates that are comparable to traditional phone plans but without the overhead of a land line or regulatory fees. Why are customers in such a rush to sign up with Skype? And what's next for Skype's creators, the entrepreneurial Luxembourg duo?

A HISTORY OF BRINGING PEOPLE TOGETHER

Skype founders Niklas Zennstrom and Janus Friis are familiar to the business of connecting computer users worldwide, having previously created KaZaA—the well-known file-sharing network. Before its sale to Sharman Networks, KaZaA was one of the most popular peer-to-peer networking programs. Creating a network consisting entirely of users' computers, KaZaA allowed people to share videos and music to their hearts' content and much to the ire of the entertainment industry.[2]

Using the peer-to-peer knowledge they acquired from creating KaZaA, Zennstrom and Friis turned their energies toward making a dent in the burgeoning Voice over Internet Protocol (VoIP) movement, a technology that encodes voice signals into data packets that can be sent along high-speed Internet lines. In 2003, the two entrepreneurs launched Skype, a system that, at that time, connected users to the computers of other Skype members. Twenty-seven languages and four supported operating systems later, Skype users can now have text and video chats, as well as make outgoing calls to land line and mobile phones around the world. Windows to Mac, Mac to Linux, Linux to Windows Mobile—Skype users are not bound by the inter-operating system limitations that characterize other voice chat systems. And, like other messaging services, Skype can let other users know if you're free to take a call, busy "on the other line," or entirely away from your computer.[3]

CASHING IN ON YOUR CALLS

A bare-bones Skype setup of a computer, a high-speed Internet connection, and a combination headset/microphone will enable you to join the fun. But, as with any tech trend, many retailers have created add-on products to enhance the VoIP experience. A number of companies make feather-weight headsets for callers who plan to spend hours upon hours on the "phone". Users whose Internet devices support Bluetooth—as most modern laptops and BlackBerry-style organizers do—can use one of the many wireless Bluetooth headsets for a truly "mobile" experience. And to get their piece of the pie, gear vendors like Netgear and Belkin offer a new take on the traditional mobile phone: a phone that, without the aid of a computer, can place Skype calls from any open Wi-Fi source.[4]

LEAVING BEHIND DINOSAURS OF THE INTERNET AGE

With more customers than ever turning to computer-based telephony as an alternative, or complement, to traditional phone service, it should come as no surprise that the biggest names in Web services are scrambling to offer something similar in an effort to preserve brand allegiance. Yahoo!, Google, and MSN all have competing VoIP services, though none are currently as fully functioned as Skype. Yahoo! Messenger only supports PC to PC calls. GoogleTalk is similar: a proprietary messenger service that also connects via voice. Like so many of Google's other services, it's still in beta mode. However, recent U.S. Securities and Exchange Commission (SEC) filings indicate that Google will be using VoIP Inc.'s VoiceOne Communications to get into the VoIP business. VoiceOne will handle peering services for Google VoIP. And Microsoft jump-started the "tech rumour mill" in August 2005 when it purchased Teleo, a provider of PC to PC calling services. Much like the rest of the competition, Microsoft plans to integrate voice services into its Messenger and mail services.[5]

CAN IT TURN A PROFIT?

KaZaA's rampant adware became the bane of many PC users' existence, clogging the systems of its most devout enthusiasts. This time around Zennstrom and Friis seem determined to keep Skype's reputation squeaky clean at all costs. They plan to build Skype's profits through its SkypeOut service, which lets users make worldwide calls for very reasonable rates, and by offering value-added services to businesses. Knowing how much of the awareness of Skype is passed electronically from one Internet user to another, Zennstrom concedes that "if we had adware in Skype, it would kind of be counterproductive to our business model." He acknowledges that for a virally marketed product to succeed, "you need to gain trust of end users. . . . If there is a bunch of adware in the software, you probably don't recommend it to friends and family."[6]

IN BUSINESS FOR BUSINESS

With the advent of feasible VoIP providers like Skype, many businesses are thinking twice about their outdated PBX phone systems. New businesses see the cost and maintenance advantage of only laying one cable network. And while larger businesses can currently make calls within the same building or across a campus for free, VoIP service brings that same cost savings to calls to off-site employees or contractors.[7] This would bring freelancers or work-at-home parents even closer to the office. And since broadband tends to be a fixed expense per month, businesses would no longer have to worry about the length or frequency of the thousands of calls they make.

None of this is lost on Skype, which has made special marketing efforts to attract businesses to its service. Businesses using

Skype can conference with up to five callers at a time, regardless of whether all or just one of them are Skype users. Companies with toll-free numbers can be sure that Skype users can call them for free because Skype supports toll-free calling.[8] And to soothe the security concerns of any reasonable company, Skype has a specific security protocol in place to protect both the callers and their content.[9]

EBAY'S TURN TO PLACE A BID

Like so many Internet innovators before them, the founders of Skype eventually received an offer they couldn't refuse. In 2005 the startup was acquired by eBay for US$2.6 billion in cash and stock, with the offer of an additional US$1.5 billion in bonuses that could be paid by 2009.[10] And the online bidding giant wasted no time integrating Skype's services into its business plan. Sellers can now add the option of contact with purchasers who are Skype users by text chat or voice, assuming they are Skype users themselves. This gives unsure buyers the opportunity to converse with eBay sellers of expensive or complex items, and allows sellers to build trust with prospective clients by making themselves available for discussion.[11]

WATCH OUT, YOUTUBE

While Skype shows no signs of slowing down and its founders are maintaining their commitment to eBay, Zennstrom and Friis nevertheless have yet another venture up their sleeves. Working under the code name "The Venice Project," they assembled top programmers in a handful of cities around the world to develop software for distributing TV shows and other video files over the Web.[12] Deals with TV networks are in place, and users have been invited to test the new venture under its new name, Joost.[13]

MORE THAN JUST HYPE

Building on the experiences of the earlier peer-to-peer phenomena, Skype has charmed millions of users around the world by providing free, high-quality voice and video conversations. And by making it easy and affordable for Skype users to interact with more traditional phone users, the company has ensured that its ranks of users will be filled with more than just technology geeks and long-distance sweethearts. Whether actively soliciting businesses or opening its technology to third-party gear vendors, Skype is staying quick and mobile, reaching out in all directions to make new friends and customers.

But is there really the demand for video chatting that Skype predicts? And could the competing Internet portal brands harness the sheer size of its user bases to mount a formidable challenge? Stay tuned and see!

REVIEW QUESTIONS

1. What are the advantages for Skype of its acquisition by eBay? What are some possible disadvantages?
2. Might there ever come a time when Skype should begin charging users for Skype-to-Skype calls? If so, under what circumstances?
3. Does Skype demonstrate the characteristics of an adaptive organization? Why or why not?

YOU DO THE RESEARCH

1. How fast is the VoIP segment growing? Is Skype continuing to get its share of the market?
2. How crowded is the VoIP landscape? How does Skype differentiate itself from the other players?

---

[1] Jennifer LeClaire, "Skype Calls on EMI, Sony, Warner in Ringtone Deal," *TechNewsWorld* (April 27, 2006); on the Web, <www.technewsworld.com>. (August 2006).
[2] Steve Rosenbush, "Kazaa, Skype, and now 'The Venice Project'," *Business Week Online* (July 24, 2006).
[3] Skype website, <www.skype.com>.
[4] Skype website, op. cit.
[5] Olga Kharif, "Voice over Microsoft Protocol?" *Business Week Online* (February 1, 2006).
[6] Trevor Zion Bauknight, "Speaking Freely," *Business & Economic Review* (July–September 2006).
[7] Ron Condon, "Should You Switch to VoIP?" *Management Today* (July 2006).
[8] Skype website, op. cit.
[9] Ibid.
[10] Venice Project website, <www.theveniceproject.com>.
[11] Skype website, op. cit.
[12] Steve Rosenbush, "Kazaa, Skype, and now 'The Venice Project'," on the Web, July 24, 2006, <www.businessweek.com>. (December 2006).
[13] Joost website, <www.joost.com>.

CASE 10

Nike: Spreading Out to Stay Together

Nike is, indisputably, a giant in the athletics industry. Yet the Portland, Oregon, company has grown so large precisely because it knows how to stay small. By focusing on its core competencies, and outsourcing the rest, Nike has managed to become a sharply focused industry leader. But can it keep the lead?

WHAT DO YOU CALL A COMPANY OF THINKERS?

It's not a joke or a riddle. Rather, it's a conundrum that applies to one of the most successful companies in the United States. Nike is known worldwide for its products, none of which it actually makes. This begs two questions: if you don't make anything, what do you actually do, and if you outsource everything, what's left?

For starters, what's left is a whole lot of brand recognition. Nike, know by its trademark "swoosh", is still among the most recognized brands in the world and an industry leader in the US$57 billion sports footwear and apparel market. And with a 33 percent market share it dominates the global athletic shoe market.[1]

Since captivating the shoe-buying public in the early 1980s with indomitable spokesperson Michael Jordan, Nike continues to outpace the athletic shoe competition while branding an ever-widening universe of sports equipment, apparel, and paraphernalia. The omnipresent swoosh graces everything from bumper stickers, to sunglasses, to high school sports uniforms.

Not long after the introduction of its hit shoe, Air Jordans, the first strains of the "Just Do It" ad campaign sealed Nike's reputation as a megabrand. Nike made the strategic image shift from simply selling products to embodying love of sport, self-discipline, ambition, and other desirable traits of athleticism. It was also among the first in a long line of brands to latch on to the strategy of representing, in its advertising, the freedom of self-expression that can be had through the use of its products.

Advertising has played no small part in Nike's continued success. In the United States alone, Nike recently spent US$85 million annually on advertising,[2] with a recent combined total of US$213 million in measured media, according to TNS Media Intelligence.[3] By comparison, Adidas spent US$47 million and Reebok spent US$26 million.[4]

Portland ad agency Wieden + Kennedy has been instrumental in creating and perpetuating Nike's image, so much so that the agency has a large division, in-house, at Nike headquarters. This intimate relationship allows the ad designers to focus solely on Nike work, and it gives them unparalleled access to executives, researchers, and anyone else who might provide the inspiration for the next successful advertisement.

WHAT'S LEFT, THEN?

Although Nike has cleverly kept its ad agency close to home, it has relied on outsourcing for many of the non-executive responsibilities in order to reduce overhead. Actually, Nike took outsourcing to a new level, now barely producing any of its products in its own factories. All of its shoes, for instance, are made by subcontractors. Although this allocation of production hasn't had a negative impact on the quality of the shoes, it has harmed Nike's reputation among fair-trade critics.

After initial allegations of sweatshop labour conditions surfaced at Nike-sponsored factories, the company tried to reach out and reason with its more moderate critics. But this approach failed, and Nike found itself in the unenviable position of trying to defend its outsourcing practices while at the same time keeping details of the locations of its favoured production shops from the competition. In a bold move designed to convert the critics, Nike announced that it would post information on its website about all of the approximately 750 factories it uses to make the shoes, apparel, and other sporting goods that it sells. It released this data alongside a comprehensive new corporate responsibility report summarizing the environmental and labour situations of its contract factories.[5]

"This is a significant step that will blow away the myth that companies can't release their factory names because it's proprietary information," said Charles Kernaghan, executive director of the National Labor Committee, a New York-based anti-sweatshop group that has been no friend to Nike over the years. "If Nike can do it, so can Wal-Mart and all the rest."[6]

JORDAN ISN'T FOREVER

Knowing that shoe sales alone wouldn't be enough to sustain continued growth, Nike made the lateral move to learn more about its customers' involvement in sports and what needs it might be able to fill. Banking on the star power of the swoosh, Nike has successfully branded apparel, sporting goods, sunglasses, and even an MP3 player made by Philips. Like many large companies that have found themselves dealing with the limitations of their brands, Nike realized that it would have to successfully identify new needs in the market and also be able to supply creative and desirable solutions.

To achieve this, Nike has branched into merchandising arenas previously unexplored by the company. Taking up the company's original name once again, it quietly launched the Blue Ribbon Sports line of urban-themed apparel. Sold only at high-end shops, the line seeks to fill a niche only recently discovered by the Adidas–Stella McCartney collaboration.[7]

In keeping with the times, John R. Hoke III, head of Nike's design team, is encouraging his designers to develop environmentally sustainable designs. This may come as a surprise to anyone who has ever thought about how much foam and plastic goes into the average Nike sneaker, but a corporate-wide mission called "Considered" has designers rethinking the toxic materials used to put the spring in millions of steps. "I'm very passionate about this idea," Hoke said. "We are going to challenge ourselves to think a little bit differently about the way we create products."[8]

NIPPING AT NIKE'S HEELS

But despite its success, it hasn't been all roses for Nike recently. Feeling the need to step down, Phil Knight handed the reins to Bill Perez, former CEO of SC Johnson, who became the first outsider recruited for the executive tier since Nike's founding in 1968. But after barely a year on the job, Knight, who stayed close as chairman of the board, decided Perez couldn't "get his arms around the company." Citing numerous other conflicts, Knight accepted Perez's resignation and promoted Mark Parker, a 27-year veteran who was co-president of the Nike brand, as a replacement.[9]

Pressures are mounting from outside its Beaverton, Oregon, headquarters as well. German rival Adidas drew a few strides closer to Nike with the purchase of Reebok for approximately US$3.8 billion.[10] Joining forces will collectively now help the two brands negotiate shelf space and other sales issues in North American stores, as well as give them a size advantage in price discussion with Asian manufacturers. With recent combined global sales of US$12 billion, the new, combined company isn't far behind Nike's US$14 billion in sales.[11] According to Jon Hickey, senior vice-president of sports and entertainment marketing for the ad agency Mullen, Nike now has its "first real, legitimate threat since the '80s. There's no way either one would even approach Nike, much less overtake them, on their own," he said. "But now, Nike has to respond. This new, combined entity has a chance to make a run. Now, it's game on."[12]

But when faced with a challenge, Nike simply knocks its bat against its cleats and steps up to the plate. "Our focus is on growing our own business," said Nike spokesperson Alan Marks. "Of course we're in a competitive business, but we win by staying focused on our strategies and our consumers. And from that perspective nothing has changed."[13]

PUTTING IT ALL TOGETHER

Nike has balanced its immense size and the tremendous pressures for success by attaining a decentralized corporate structure. Individual business centres—such as research, production, and marketing—are free to focus on their core competencies, free the effects of being such a large company. Similarly, Nike has found continued success in the marketplace by moving away from being viewed simply as a huge sneaker company, instead positioning itself as a brand meeting the evolving needs of athletes. Will Nike continue to profit from an increasingly decentralized business model, or will it spread itself so thin that the competition will overtake it?

REVIEW QUESTIONS

1. If a sporting good can be used in a sporting event, and especially if that event can be televised, Nike has likely made such a product and added a swoosh to it. But in this day and age, are there any sporting products that Nike would do better not to produce? Explain your reasoning.

2. Nike's long-running "Just Do It" tagline establishes the brand—and therefore its products—as a means of self-expression, implying that "Our products help you be you." This has worked thus far for Nike, but this strategy is ubiquitous in the marketplace and is used to sell everything from yogurt to plastic surgery. Select and defend one of the following positions:

   a) This is an advantageous strategy for Nike because it adequately represents customers' perceptions of the Nike brand and its products.

   b) This strategy works against Nike's best interests and prevents customers from forming their own associations with Nike products.

   Whichever you choose, you may not cite the length of the "Just Do It" campaign as evidence for your point.

3. If you were charged today with the task of creating an athletics company comparable to Nike and were given the budget to do so, would you adopt the same decentralized structure as Nike? Why or why not?

YOU DO THE RESEARCH

1. Nike's reputation was marred by allegations that they were running "sweat shops" — what did they do to overcome this problem?

2. Do other shoe manufacturing companies organize themselves similar to Nike?

---

[1] "Adidas-Reebok Merger Lets Rivals Nip at Nike's Heels," *USA Today* (August 4, 2005).
[2] Ibid.
[3] Rich Thomaselli, "Deal Sets Stage for Full-Scale War with Nike," *Advertising Age*, vol. 76 (August 8, 2005).
[4] "Adidas-Reebok Merger," op. cit.
[5] Aaron Bernstein, "Nike Names Names," *Business Week Online* (April 13, 2005).
[6] Ibid.
[7] Rich Thomaselli, "Nike Launches Upscale Urban Street Wear Line," *Advertising Age*, vol. 76 (August 1, 2005).
[8] Stanley Holmes, "Green Foot Forward," *Business Week* (November 28, 2005).
[9] "Nike Replaces CEO After 13 Months," *USA Today* (January 24, 2006).
[10] "Just Doing It," *Economist*, vol. 376 (August 6, 2005).
[11] "Adidas-Reebok Merger," op. cit.
[12] "Deal Sets Stage," op. cit.
[13] "Adidas-Reebok Merger," op. cit.

CASE 11

BET Holdings: World-Class Entrepreneur Places BET on Future

Robert Johnson, born the ninth in a family of ten children in Hickory, Mississippi, is a true rags-to-riches success story. His father, Archie, chopped wood while his mother taught school. Ultimately, their search for a better life led them to Freeport, Illinois, a predominantly white working-class neighbourhood. Archie supplemented his factory jobs by operating his own junkyard on the predominantly black east side of town. Edna Johnson got a job at Burgess Battery, and although she eventually secured a job for Robert at the battery firm, he knew it wasn't for him.[1]

ROBERT JOHNSON'S JOURNEY TO BECOMING AN ENTREPRENEUR

Bob Johnson showed an enterprising nature at an early age, delivering papers, mowing lawns, and cleaning out tents at local fairs. At Freeport High School, he was an honours student and entered the University of Illinois upon graduation. Virgil Hemphill, his freshman roommate, commented: "He was not overly slick, overly smooth. He was kind of innocent and naïve. His strength was being able to talk to different types of people. I went to Freeport with him, and he could communicate with the regular people and with the suit-and-tie people."[2]

Johnson did well at university, studying history, holding several work-study jobs, and participating in Kappa Alpha Psi, a black fraternity. After graduation in 1968, he was admitted to a two-year program at Princeton University's Woodrow Wilson School of Public and International Affairs. He had a full scholarship plus expenses but dropped out after the first semester to marry his college sweetheart, Sheila Crump, a former cheerleader and a gifted violinist. He eventually returned to Princeton to earn his Master's degree in public administration in 1972.[3]

He moved on to Washington, D.C., to first work at the Corporation for Public Broadcasting and then at the Washington Urban League, where the director, Sterling Tucker, appreciated Johnson's ability to think both "micro-ly and macro-ly" while still "thinking like a visionary" in pursuing larger goals.[4] Moving on to work for the Congressional Black Caucus, Johnson became impressed with the possibilities for black power that lay in television—cable in particular. In 1976, he began working as a lobbyist for the National Cable Television Association (NCTA), where he gained valuable insight into the cable industry.

At the NCTA's 1979 convention, Johnson met Bob Rosencrans, president of UA-Columbia Cablevision. While Bob Johnson had a strong idea for providing cable programming to minority audiences, he had no satellite time. Rosencrans, on the other hand, was looking for programs to support his local franchises and to fill some unused slots on one of the cable TV satellites. According to Rosencrans, "I just said, 'Bob, you're on. Let's go.' I don't think we even charged him. We knew he couldn't afford much, and for us, it was a plus because it gave us more ammunition to sell cable. The industry was not attracting minority customers."[5]

With US$15,000 from a consulting contract that he received upon his departure from NCTA, Robert Johnson launched Black Entertainment Television (BET) at 11:00 p.m. on January 8, 1980. The first BET show was a 1974 African safari movie, *Visit to a Chief's Son*. Initially, BET aired for only two hours on Friday nights. The shows bounced off an RCA satellite and into 3.8 million homes served by Rosencrans's franchises. Johnson received his first crucial financing from John Malone of TCI in the form of a US$380,000 loan plus US$120,000 for a 20 percent ownership in BET.[6]

To raise capital in the 1980s, Johnson sold off pieces of BET to Time Inc. and Taft Broadcasting for more than US$10 million. However, from the start, controversy over programming followed Johnson with his heavy reliance on music videos (60 percent of total programming), gospel and religious programs, infomercials, and reruns of older shows such as *Sanford and Son* and *227*.[7]

THE GROWTH OF BET HOLDINGS

Robert Johnson had grand plans for BET, seeking to turn the enterprise into what marketers call an umbrella brand.[8] The firm published two national magazines that reached 250,000 readers: *Young Sisters and Brothers* for teens and *Emerge* for affluent adults. BET also had interests in film production, electronic retailing, and radio. The first BET Sound Stage restaurant opened in suburban Washington and another in Disney World in Orlando. With the Hilton hotel chain as a partner, Johnson explored opening a casino in Las Vegas, Nevada. Johnson wanted to capture a share of black consumers' disposable income, valued at US$425 billion annually. To do this, he partnered primarily with big names as such Disney, Hilton, Blockbuster, Microsoft, and others. "You simply cannot get big anymore by being 100 percent black-owned anything," Johnson claimed.[9] His Black Entertainment Television cable station provided the perfect medium to target this increasingly affluent black audience.

BET Inc. aims to become the leading African-American multi-media entertainment company and is committed to establishing the most valued consumer brand within the African-American marketplace."[10]

Black Entertainment Television, aimed toward serving the African-American community, remains at the core of the BET business empire. As of late 2005, Black Entertainment Television has reached more than 80 million cable subscribers in the United States.[11] Included among this subscriber base are more than 90 percent of all black households that have cable hookups. BET's related digital cable businesses include BET on Jazz, BET Gospel, BET Classic Soul, BET International, and BET Hip Hop. BET Books publishes literature with African-American themes written by African-American authors. BET Pictures produces documentaries on African-American themes and made-for-TV movies. BET Interactive, a partnership between BET, Microsoft, Liberty Digital Media, News Corporation, and USA Networks created the Internet portal BET.com, the leading online site for African-Americans.[12]

The company grew into such a success story that Viacom Inc. purchased it for US$3 billion in November 2001. Until his retirement in 2005, Robert Johnson remained chairman and CEO of the Viacom subsidiary, reporting to Viacom's then president and chief operating officer, Mel Karmazin.[13] Debra Lee, former president and COO, took control of BET in 2006. Johnson stated, "I could not have chosen a better chief executive and outstanding leader to succeed me at BET than Debra Lee. I am convinced that BET's legacy is in great hands."[14] Karmazin described the acquisition of BET Holdings as "a strategically perfect fit. . . . Viacom is home to the industry's most creative and distinctive branded programming, the perfect environment for BET's television and online business to grow and prosper."[15]

REVIEW QUESTIONS

1. Is a mechanistic organizational design or an organic organizational design more appropriate for BET? Explain your answer.
2. How might environment and strategy influence BET's organizational design?
3. As a multi-faceted, multimedia entertainment company, what challenges regarding differentiation and integration does BET likely face?

YOU DO THE RESEARCH

1. Was Robert Johnson correct in selling his BET Holdings to Viacom?
2. Will BET Interactive become a major force on the Web?
3. What's next for Robert Johnson?

---

[1] Peter Perl, "His Way," *Washington Post* (December 14, 1997), Magazine Section, W08.
[2] Ibid.
[3] Ibid.
[4] Ibid.
[5] Ibid.
[6] Ibid.
[7] Ibid.
[8] Adam Zagorin, "BET's Too Hot a Property," *Time* (October 20, 1997), p. 80.
[9] Perl, op. cit.
[10] "The Facts," Viacom Website, <www.viacom.com/thefacts>.
[11] Ibid.
[12] Robert L. Johnson, Founder, on the Web, <www.bet.com/articles>.
[13] Joe Flint, "Viacom Changes Leadership at BET and Spike TV," *Wall Street Journal* (January 31, 2005), p. B4.
[14] "Debra Lee Assumes Helm of Black America's Network," on the Web, <www.bet.com/News/debra_lee.htm>.
[15] Carol King, "Viacom Acquires BET Holdings," on the Web, <www.internetnews.com/bus-news>.

CASE 12

SAS Institute: Systems Help People Make a Difference

Founded in 1976 by Dr. James Goodnight and Dr. John Sall, SAS Institute Inc. provides business intelligence software and services at more than 40,000 customer sites around the world, including 96 percent of the companies on the 2006 *Fortune* "Global 500" list. SAS, which stands for statistical analysis software, is headquartered in Cary, North Carolina. It is the world's largest privately held software company, having more than 400 offices worldwide with more than 10,000 employees. With an unbroken record of growth and profitability, SAS had revenue of US$1.68 billion in 2005 and invested about 24 percent of that into research and development.[1] The phenomenal success story of SAS is, in no small part, due to its human resources (HR) strategy, policies, and practices. How do their HR strategy, policies, and practices contribute so much to the success of SAS?

HUMAN RESOURCES POLICIES AND PRACTICES AT SAS

Fast Company metaphorically describes the SAS Institute as a modern company that is like a kingdom in a fairy-tale land. "Although this company is thoroughly modern (endowed with advanced computers, the best child care, art on almost every wall, and athletic facilities that would make an NBA trainer drool), there is something fairy-tale-like about the place. The inhabitants are happy, productive, and well rounded—in short, content in a way that's almost unheard of today. They are loyal to the kingdom and to its king, who in turn is the model of a benevolent leader. The king, almost unbelievably, goes by the name Goodnight."[2]

SAS is strongly committed to its employees. The company strives to hire talented people and goes to extraordinarily lengths to ensure that they are satisfied. James Goodnight, the CEO of SAS, explains, "We've made a conscious effort to ensure that we're hiring and keeping the right talent to improve our products and better serve our customers. To attract and retain that talent, it's essential that we maintain our high standards in regards to employee relations."[3]

SAS has been widely recognized for its work-life programs and emphasis on employee satisfaction. The company's various honours include being recognized by *Working Mothers* magazine as one of the "100 Best Companies for Working Mothers" and by *Fortune* magazine as one of the "100 Best Companies to Work for in America." The recognition from *Working Mothers* has been received fewer than 13 times, and the *Fortune* recognition has occurred for nine consecutive years, with six of these being top-10 rankings.[4]

SAS pays its employees competitively, with salaries targeted at the average for the software industry.[5] It does not provide stock options like other companies in the industry. Instead of relying on high salaries and stock options to attract and retain workers like many software companies do, SAS takes a very different approach. It focuses on providing meaningful and challenging work, and it encourages teamwork. SAS also provides a host of benefits that appeal to the employees and helps to keep them satisfied. As one employee, who took a 10 percent pay cut to join SAS, said, "It's better to be happy than to have a little more money."[6] Employees are given the freedom, flexibility, responsibility, and resources to do their jobs, and they are also held accountable for results. Managers know what employees are doing and they work, writing computer code, alongside them.[7] "The company employs very few external contractors and very few part-time staff, so there is a strong sense of teamwork throughout the organization."[8] SAS employees are clearly involved in their work. One employee notes, "When you walk down the halls here, it's rare that you hear people talking about anything but work."[9]

Included among the various employee benefits and services that SAS provides for free, or at greatly reduced costs, are health care by two doctors and eight nurse practitioners on-site, a recreation centre, dry cleaning, car washing, a credit union, a farmers' market, on-site child care, and a heavily subsidized employee cafeteria.[10] All of these benefits are geared toward employees having a better work experience and a better balance between their work lives and their personal lives.[11] The company's commitment to work-life balance is evident in SAS's 35-hour workweek, which clearly recognizes the importance of employees' personal lives.[11] Jeff Chambers, SAS vice-president of human resources explains, "It's acceptable to go home at 4 p.m. for your kid's soccer game. You get hard-driving people who want to work all hours—they won't like it here. They'll be working alone."[12] In reflecting on the company's generous benefits package, David Russo, a former head of human resources, said, "To some people, this looks like the Good Ship Lollipop, floating down the stream. It's not. It's part of a soundly designed strategy." That strategy is intended "to make it impossible for people not to do their work."[13]

EXTRAORDINARY EMPLOYEE BENEFITS: AT WHAT COST?

While SAS goes to extraordinary lengths to ensure that employees are satisfied, the company expects and demands productivity and performance results in return. The owners of SAS want employees to be satisfied because they believe satisfied employees will be excellent performers and will provide exceptional service to the company's customers. The company philosophy is, "If you treat employees as if they make a difference to the company, they will make a difference to the company.... Satisfied employees create satisfied customers."[14] This viewpoint might be described as a form of enlightened realism and also enlightened self interest on the part of the company. Satisfied employees make for satisfied customers, and satisfied customers make for an ongoing stream of revenue and profits for SAS.

SAS's leaders recognize both the benefits and costs associated with keeping employees satisfied. One of the most significant benefits for SAS is a very low annual turnover rate, which recently was just over 6 percent, compared with approximately 25 percent for the industry as a whole.[15] This low turnover saves the company about US$50–70 million annually in employee replacement costs.[16] On the cost side, of course, is the company's monetary outlay for the various programs. Jeff Chambers argues, however, that the savings in employee replacement expenses more than pays for the company's generous benefits: "If you set these things up right, they pay for themselves."[17]

Perhaps of more concern on the "cost side" is the potential for employees to fail to perform to the company's standards. In commenting on the company's performance expectations for employees, Goodnight says, "I like to be around happy people, but if they don't get that next release out, they're not going to be very happy."[18] Pondering the likelihood that SAS employees would take advantage of the company's relaxed atmosphere, John Sall, executive vice-president and co-founder of SAS, observes, "I can't imagine that playing Ping-Pong would be more interesting than work."[19]

Clearly, human resource management at SAS is a two-way street. SAS has an HR strategy and related policies and practices that attract, motivate, and retain highly capable workers who make significant contributions to the ongoing success of the company. Goodnight and the other SAS leaders expect nothing less than superior performance from the employees, and they continue to get it. The employees are loyal and committed to the company, and they are productive—so loyal, committed, and productive, in fact, that only a small percentage of the employees ever leave once they have been hired at SAS. Having quality employees who want to stay—isn't this the human resources goal that should challenge all companies?

REVIEW QUESTIONS

1. What is the basic management philosophy that governs employee relationship management at SAS Institute?

2. Explain how the SAS human resources strategy, policies, and practices affect the company's ability to attract, develop, and maintain a quality workforce.

3. What impact have the SAS human resources strategy, policies, and practices had on the company's financial success?

YOU DO THE RESEARCH

1. Compare SAS with Trilogy Software, a competitor in the computer software industry, in terms of approaches to attracting, developing, and maintaining a quality workforce.

2. Why does Trilogy take the approach that it does? Why does SAS take the approach that it does?

3. Would the SAS approach to attracting, developing, and maintaining a quality workforce be adaptable to any company in any industry? Why or why not?

[1] SAS corporate statistics, on the Web, <www.sas.com/presscenter>.
[2] Charles Fishman, "Sanity Inc.," *Fast Company* (January 1999).
[3] "SAS Marks 6th Straight Year on *Fortune* List of '100 Best Companies to Work For'," on the Web, <www.sas.com/news/preleases>.
[4] "SAS Cracks Fortune's 100 Best Companies to Work For List Again," on the Web, January 11, 2006, <www.sas.com/news/mediacoverage>.
[5] Workforce Stability Institute, "Keeping Employees Without Breaking the Bank," on the Web, <www.employee.org>.
[6] Charles Fishman, op. cit.
[7] Ibid.
[8] Workforce Stability Institute, op. cit.
[9] Charles Fishman, op. cit.
[10] Kim Nash, "To Have, And to Hold," *Computerworld* on the Web, <www.computerworld.com/printthis/2000/0,4814,45742,00.html>, (January 7, 2007).
[11] Workforce Stability Institute, op. cit.
[12] Kim Nash, op. cit.
[13] Charles Fishman, op. cit.
[14] Information on the Web, <www.sas.com/corporate/worklife/>.
[15] Fay Hansen, "The Turnover Myth," *Workforce Management*, vol. 84 (June 2005), p. 34.
[16] Ibid.
[17] "Why Work Life Balance is Essential to Good Business," Trapper Woods International on the Web, <www.trapperwoods.com/timemanagement/>, (January, 2007).
[18] Diane Brady, "Rethinking the Rat Race," *Business Week* (August 26, 2002), p. 142.
[19] Charles Fishman, op. cit.

CASE 13

Southwest Airlines: How Herb Kelleher Led the Way

The U.S. airline industry experienced problems in the early 1990s. From 1989 through 1993, the largest airlines, including American, United, Delta, and USAir, lost billions of dollars. Only Southwest Airlines remained profitable throughout that period. Herb Kelleher, who co-founded Southwest in 1971 and was its CEO until 2001, pointed out that "we didn't make much for a while there. It was like being the tallest guy in a tribe of dwarfs."[1] Nevertheless, Southwest Airlines has grown to the point of having operating revenues of US$7.6 billion. This is particularly noteworthy because Southwest flies to only 62 cities in 32 states, and its average flight length is only 864 kilometres. How did a little airline get to be so big? Its success is due to its core values, developed by Kelleher and carried out daily by the company's 32,000 employees.[2] These core values are humour, altruism, and "luv"—the company's stock ticker symbol.[3]

SOUTHWEST AIRLINES' UNIQUE CHARACTER AND SUCCESS

Besides its short-haul focus, some of the things that make Southwest Airlines so unique in the industry are the fact that the airline does not assign seats or sell tickets through the reservation systems used by travel agents. Many passengers buy tickets at the gate. The only foods served are peanuts, pretzels, and similar snacks, but passengers don't seem to mind. In fact, serving Customers (always written with a capital C at Southwest) is the focus of the company's employees. When Colleen Barrett, currently Southwest's president, was the executive vice-president for Customers, she said, "We will never jump on employees for leaning too far toward the customer, but we come down on them hard for not using common sense."[4] Southwest's core values produce employees who are highly motivated and who care about the customers, and also about one another.

One way in which Southwest carries out this philosophy is by treating employees and their ideas with respect. While executive vice-president, Colleen Barrett formed a "culture committee" made up of employees from different functional areas and levels of the company. The committee meets quarterly to come up with ideas for maintaining Southwest's corporate spirit and image. Also, all managers, officers, and directors are expected to "get out in the field," to meet and get to know the other employees and the jobs they do. Employees are encouraged to use their creativity and sense of humour to make their jobs and the customers' experiences more enjoyable. Gate agents, for example, are given a book of games to play with waiting passengers when a flight is delayed. Flight agents might do an imitation of Elvis or Mr. Rogers while making announcements. Others have jumped out of the overhead luggage bins to surprise boarding passengers.[5]

Kelleher, currently chairman of the executive committee, knows that not everyone would be happy as a Southwest employee: "What we are looking for, first and foremost, is a sense of humour. Then we are looking for people who have to excel to satisfy themselves and who work well in a collegial environment." He feels that the company can teach specific skills but that a compatible attitude is most important. When asked to prove that she had a sense of humour, Mary Ann Adams, hired in 1997 as a finance executive, recounted a practical joke in which she turned an unflattering picture of her boss into a screen saver for her department.[6]

To encourage employees to treat one another as well as they treat their customers, departments examine linkages within Southwest to see what their "internal customers" need. The provisioning department, for example, whose responsibility is to provide the snacks and drinks for each flight, selects a flight attendant as "customer of the month." The provisioning department's own "board of directors" makes the selection decision. Other departments have sent pizza and ice cream to their chosen internal customers. Employees write letters commending the work of other employees or departments, and these letters are valued as much as those from external customers. When problems do occur between departments, the employees themselves work out solutions in supervised meetings.

Employees exhibit the same attitude of altruism and "luv," Southwest's term for its relationship with its customers, toward external groups as well. A significant number of Southwest employees volunteer their time at Ronald McDonald Houses throughout Southwest's service territory. When the company purchased a small regional airline, employees personally sent cards and company T-shirts to their new colleagues to welcome them to the Southwest family. They demonstrate similar caring toward the company itself. As gasoline prices rose during the period of the Gulf War in the early 1990s, many of the employees created the "Fuel from the Heart" program, donating fuel to the company by deducting the cost of one or more gallons from their paycheques.

Acting in the company's best interests is also directly in the interest of the employees. Southwest has a profit-sharing plan for all eligible employees, and, unlike many of its competitors, Southwest consistently has profits to share. Employees can also purchase Southwest stock at 90 percent of market value; at least 13 percent of Southwest's employees have taken advantage of this. Approximately 81 percent of employees are unionized, and the company has a history of good labour relations.[7]

Southwest Airlines is a low-cost operator. According to Harvard University professor John Kotter, setting the standard for low costs in the airline industry does not mean Southwest is *cheap*. "Cheap is trying to get your prices down by nibbling costs off everything . . . [firms like Southwest Airlines] are thinking 'efficient', which is very different. . . . They recognize that you don't necessarily have to take a few pennies off of everything. Sometimes you might even spend more."[8] By buying one type of plane—the Boeing 737—Southwest saves on both pilot training and maintenance costs; the *cheap* paradigm would favour used planes. As a result of its "cost-saving" approach, Southwest has the youngest fleet of airplanes in the industry.

Southwest currently operates a fleet of 453 Boeing 737 jets.[9] By using each plane an average of 12 hours per day, Southwest is able to make more trips with fewer planes than any other airline. Since May

1988, Southwest Airlines has won the monthly "Triple Crown" distinction of airline service—Best On-Time Record, Best Baggage Handling, and Fewest Customer Complaints—more than 30 times. From 1992 through 1996, Southwest won the annual "Triple Crown" each year.[10]

SOUTHWEST'S ONGOING CHALLENGES

Despite its impressive record of success, Southwest Airlines has pressing concerns to address. Management worries about the effects on employee morale of the limited opportunities for promotion. The company has created "job families", with each having various grade levels so that employees can work their way up within their job category. However, within five or six years employees will begin to achieve the maximum compensation level for their job category.

Another issue is that of maintaining the culture of caring and fun while at the same expanding rapidly into new markets. Southwest's success has been built with the enthusiasm and hard work of its employees; as Kelleher said, "The people who work here don't think of Southwest as a business. They think of it as a crusade."[11] Cultivating that crusading atmosphere is a continuing priority for the company.

As Herb Kelleher prepared to relinquish his role as Southwest's CEO, a major concern for investors was whether the company's success, so much of it attributable to Kelleher's unique management and leadership style, could be maintained. Recent events, however, seem to demonstrate that Kelleher's successors, longtime Southwest employees Gary Kelly (currently vice-chairman of the board and CEO) and Colleen Barrett (currently the company president), were well prepared to handle the challenges of maintaining Southwest's culture and level of success. As Barrett wrote in the company's *Spirit* magazine, "Air travel changed forever two years ago, but our steadfast determination remains unbroken to provide the high-spirited Customer Service, low fares, and frequent non-stop flights that Americans want and need."[12] Not even terrorist attacks can derail the company that Herb Kelleher led to success. Southwest Airlines continues to be recognized by *Fortune* magazine as America's most admired airline as well as one of the most admired companies in the United States. In 2003, *Air Transport World* magazine selected Southwest as the "Airline for the Year" for its 30 consecutive years of profitability, while at the same time providing affordable fares for millions of passengers. Other recognitions of Southwest culture and success continue to pile up.

SOMETIMES THE VOYAGE IS BETTER THAN THE DESTINATION

From its roots as a regional carrier in Texas, Southwest Airlines grew to become one of the most profitable—and arguably the most beloved—airlines in American history through careful of attention to efficiency and value in its expenditures. At the same time, the company has managed to maintain high levels of employee satisfaction by focusing on its internal customers above all else, who, in turn, are positively motivated to show that same degree of concern for external customers. But as fuel prices continue to climb and airlines consolidate for security, can Southwest hang on as that rare breed—an independent, domestic airline? All signs indicate clear skies ahead.

REVIEW QUESTIONS

1. What role has leadership played in the success of Southwest Airlines?
2. What is the key to Southwest's continued success under leaders other than Herb Kelleher?
3. In what ways has Herb Kelleher exemplified Peter Drucker's notion of "old-fashioned" leadership?

YOU DO THE RESEARCH

1. Which of the leadership theories in Chapter 13 seem to provide the most useful explanation of Herb Kelleher's success in leading Southwest Airlines?
2. How does Southwest Airlines develop its "leadership pool" so that there is no shortage of future leaders in the organization?

[1] Kenneth Lablich, "Is Herb Kelleher America's Best CEO?" *Fortune* (May 2, 1994), p. 45.
[2] "Little Giant," *Southwest Airlines Spirit* (June 2006), p. 154.
[3] James Campbell Quick, "Crafting an Organizational Culture: Herb's Hand at Southwest Airlines," *Organizational Dynamics*, vol. 21 (August 1992), p. 47.
[4] Richard S. Teitelbaum, "Where Service Flies Right," *Fortune* (August 24, 1992), p. 115.
[5] Colleen Barrett, "Pampering Customers on a Budget," *Working Woman* (April 1993), pp. 19–22.
[6] Justin Martin, "So, You Want to Work for the Best ….," *Fortune* (January 12, 1998), p. 77.
[7] See the company website, <www.southwest.com>.
[8] J. P. Kotter quoted in Mark Ballon, "The Cheapest CEO in America," *Inc.* (October 1997), p. 60.
[9] "Little Giant," op. cit.
[10] Southwest Airlines website, op. cit.
[11] Teitelbaum, op. cit., p. 116.
[12] "Colleen's Corner," on the Web, June 27, 2003, <www.southwest.com>.

CASE 14

Nucor: A Case for Less Management

Unlike many industry competitors, North Carolina-based Nucor has achieved both financial success and a satisfied, productive workforce. As its mission statement affirms, Nucor is "the safest, highest quality, lowest cost, most productive and most profitable steel and steel products company in the world."[1] For much of this, Nucor credits the quality of its employees, who enjoy some of the most immediate access to upper management in the business world. But can superior employee relations really build a US$12.7 billion company?[2]

A HISTORY OF HEAVY METAL

Nucor's roots lie with auto entrepreneur Ransom E. Olds, founder of the venerable Oldsmobile brand and later Reo Motor Cars. As technology evolved and ownership changed hands, the company ultimately became the Nuclear Corporation of America, doing business in the nuclear instrument and electronics sectors through the mid-twentieth century.[3]

After facing several lean years, and near bankruptcy in 1964, then newly installed president F. Kenneth Iverson and vice-president of finance Samuel Siegel led the company through a major restructuring. They chose, logically, to reorganize the company around its primary profit centres—a steel joist business named Vulcraft, based out of South Carolina and Nebraska. The reshaped company pulled up its Arizonan roots and moved to Charlotte, North Carolina just two years later, expanding its joist business into Alabama and Texas.[4]

Four years after rebuilding the company, management made another pivotal decision: to integrate backward through the supply chain by building a steel mill—its first—in South Carolina. Four years later, the company changed its name again, this time to Nucor Corporation. It spent the remainder of the 1970s supplementing its Vulcraft facilities with additional joist plants and steel bar mills.[5]

The 1980s saw Nucor pioneering within the field of steel production. At its Crawfordsville, Indiana, plant Nucor developed a process called thin slab casting, which dramatically reduced the investment and operating costs necessary to produce sheet steel. Through this process, Nucor could expand its business into growing markets, like the domestic auto assembly industry, achieving record profits while keeping expenditures to a minimum. Clients and critics were equally impressed, and *Forbes* magazine described

Nucor's achievement as "the most substantial, technological, industrial innovation in the past 50 years."[6]

Since the 1990s, Nucor has continued a series of record-setting strategic expansions. Through a partnership with Yamato Kogyo, a Japanese steelmaker, Nucor added two mills to a site in Arkansas that has grown to be the largest structural beam facility in the western hemisphere. Adding two mills to a site in Berkeley County, South Carolina, resulted in the creation of the largest mini-mill in the world, which produces more than 2.7 million tons of steel a year.[7]

These days, Nucor is the largest steel producer in the United States. Having recycled approximately 15.4 million tonnes of scrap steel (4.5 million of those tonnes being made up of scrap automobiles) in a recent year, Nucor is also the nation's largest recycler. The company plans to continue its growth by means of a four-part expansion strategy, the first part of which is to optimize existing operations. The second part is to pursue strategic acquisitions, which Nucor has done with its purchase of both the Auburn Steel Company and ITEC Steel Inc., in 2001. A year later, Nucor absorbed the assets of Birmingham Steel Corporation, continuing its trend of consolidating the playing field. And most recently, the company purchased the assets of Connecticut Steel Corporation.[8] To complete its four-part strategy, Nucor seeks to commercialize new technologies and grow internationally through joint ventures. To fulfill this last plan, Nucor has partnered with Chinese and Japanese companies on an Australian plant, as well as a joint pig iron venture in northern Brazil.[9]

KEEPING EQUAL COMPANY

Worldwide, there are approximately 11,500 Nucor employees, most of whom would rather not work anywhere else. And Nucor management has worked hard to make it so. The company is divided into operational divisions, each of which sports an extremely streamlined management structure that keeps each division light, nimble, and able to adjust quickly to market fluctuations. A typical Nucor division has only three levels of management between hourly employees and the company president.[10]

Like the Japanese manufacturing giants before it, Nucor empowers its workers to make decisions as necessary to keep operations running smoothly. As long as Nucor's goals and measurables are understood by everyone, there exist firm guidelines by which employees may judge their responses.

Much of this is owed to the egalitarian philosophies of former president Ken Iverson, who promoted the idea of equality among all his employees and firmly believed that associates of every level could make creative and beneficial contributions if given the opportunity. Typical of his style was his decision to do away with coloured hardhats in the plants, as they had become status symbols that kept "distance" between functional areas. Not everyone immediately appreciated the benefits of doing away with this system. "I got all kinds of flack from our foremen," Iverson recalled in a 1998 interview. "They said, 'You can't do that!' So we held training programs to explain that their authority didn't come from the colour of the hat that they wore."[11] True to his own philosophies, Iverson was later convinced to revise his idea when it was discovered that maintenance personnel couldn't be located quickly enough in an emergency, so they eventually donned yellow hardhats.

And in business culture fraught with executive perks, Nucor's rather modest appointment offerings are a refreshing alternative to CEO compensation packages gone wild. Not only do executives *not* enjoy top perks such as better vacation schedules or insurance programs, Nucor officers also aren't even eligible for certain benefits like profit sharing or the employee stock purchase plan. All executives fly coach, and they eat in the same dining halls as line workers when working on-site. There are no company cars or executive parking places, either.[12]

All Nucor employees are eligible for bonus earnings based on the company's performance. And for upper executives, performance goal rewards may account for up to 80 percent of their total compensation. Employees at all levels understand that the company's success—and thus their earnings—are tied to their collective performance.[13]

MAKING STEEL, MAKING PROFITS

From teetering on the brink of bankruptcy in the 60s, Nucor has moved on to become a manufacturing success story through a reorganization that emphasized the business's core talents and the innovative potential of its employees. By valuing individual contributions and creating an atmosphere in which employees are inclined to take ownership, Nucor has persuaded its associates to take a big-picture view of their roles in the company, which in turn has led to substantial year-on-year profits and growth. But, in an era of continued consolidation in the steel industry and rising material prices, can Nucor continue to innovate and lead the pack? Where could this manufacturing leader go next?

REVIEW QUESTIONS:

1. Why do you think that Nucor has chosen to adopt a streamlined management structure?
2. In setting performance goal rewards for upper executives at up to 80 percent of their total compensation, how do you think that Nucor motivates its top management?
3. How does Nucor's method of employee compensation satisfy both workers' lower-order needs and their higher-order needs?

YOU DO THE RESEARCH

1. How do Canadian steel companies compare to Nucor's approach to motivating employees – are they creating employee centred organizations like Nucor?
2. Are other manufacturing organizations decreasing the status differences between management and employee (i.e. no company cars, same lunch rooms, all fly coach) as Nucor has done?

---

[1] "About Us," on the Web, <www.nucor.com>.
[2] Nanette Byrnes and Michael Arndt, "The Art of Motivation," *Businessweek* on the Web, May 1, 2006, <www.businessweek.com>. (August 2006).
[3] "About Us," op. cit.
[4] Ibid.
[5] Ibid.
[6] Ibid.
[7] Ibid.
[8] Ibid.
[9] Ibid.
[10] Ibid.
[11] Tom Terez, "The Soft Side of a Steel Company," on the Web, <www.betterworkplacenow.com/iverson.html>. (August, 2006).
[12] "About Us," op. cit.
[13] Ibid.

CASE 15

Steinway & Sons: Craftwork, Tradition, and Time Build Grand Pianos

Steinway & Sons remains one of the best-known producers of concert pianos in the world. Throughout its great history, the company has shown a distinctive talent for innovation, as evidenced by its more than 100 patents, and is known for quality workmanship. In an age of mass production, Steinway continues to manufacture a limited number of handmade pianos in a unique testament to individual craftsmanship. However, some rival piano makers have tried to challenge Steinway's dominance of the concert piano market.[1] Can Steinway continue its cherished ways, or will it need to adjust to new circumstances?

A LONG AND GOLDEN HISTORY

German immigrant Heinrich "Henry" Steinway founded Steinway & Sons in 1853. Henry was a master cabinetmaker who built his first piano in the kitchen of his home in Seesen, Germany. He had built 482 pianos by the time he established Steinway & Sons. The first piano produced by the company, number 483, was sold to a New York family for $500. It is now displayed at New York City's Metropolitan Museum of Art.

Steinway & Son's unique quality became obvious early in the history of the firm, as the company won a number of gold medals in several American and European exhibitions in 1855. The company gained further international recognition in 1867 at the Paris Exhibition when it was awarded the prestigious "Grand Gold Medal of Honor" for excellence in manufacturing and engineering. Henry Steinway developed his pianos using emerging technical and scientific research, including the acoustical theories of the renowned physicist Hermann von Helmhotz. The Steinway factory today still uses many of the craftsmanship techniques handed down from previous generations.[2]

As a result of two world wars, the Depression, and the emergence of radio and television, there was a decline in demand for pianos from the 1920s onward.[3] Steinway & Sons was sold to CBS in 1968. Many concert artists complained that the quality of the pianos had suffered as a result of that ownership. Pianists talked of the "Teflon controversy" when Steinway replaced some fabric innards with Teflon (it now coats the Teflon with fabric). Steinway was sold by CBS to a group of private investors in 1985, and many experts voiced the opinion that Steinway's legendary quality was returning. By this time Yamaha Corporation was also selling concert pianos in direct competition to Steinway. Larry Fine, a piano expert, argued that "a Steinway has a kind of sustained, singing tone that a Yamaha doesn't have. Yamaha has a more brittle tone in the treble that some jazz pianists prefer."[4]

THE STEINWAY FACTORY

Today, even with increased competition, the making of a Steinway piano follows the Steinway tradition. Every grand piano takes more than a year to complete and incorporates more than 1,000 details that set a Steinway apart from its competitors. A tour of the Steinway factory is a trip back through time, as the key steps in the process of crafting a piano and many of the manufacturing techniques have not been changed since 1853.[5]

Using a method that was patented in 1878, the piano manufacturing process begins with the creation of the inner and outer piano rims that give a grand piano its distinctive shape; this is known as the piano case. Eighteen layers of rock maple, each 6.7 metres in length, are laminated together and then formed into the piano shape on a giant vise. The rim-bending team centres the wood on the vise and forces it into place with the aid of wood clamps.

Meanwhile, the soundboard is carefully hand formed by an expert craftsman. It must be slightly thinner at the edges so that it can vibrate properly once it is glued to the piano's inner rim. The bridge of the soundboard is notched for the piano strings before the soundboard can be placed into the piano case. A highly skilled craftsman, with years of training, performs this operation because precision is so essential to the quality of the piano's sound.

A wooden brace assembly is crafted to fit inside the piano

case to help support the 155 kilogram cast-iron plate that provides the rigid and stable foundation for approximately 18,000 kilograms of tension from the piano strings. This brace is secured to the rim of the piano with fine carpentry joinery and maple dowels, and any necessary adjustments are made before final installation of the plate.

After the soundboard and cast-iron plate are properly fitted in the piano case, the piano wires are installed, using both a machine-guided stringer and appropriate hand tools. Next, the felt hammers are formed using glue and a copper forming tool. The felt hammers are then put on the hammer shanks and dampers are installed to prevent unintentional vibration of the piano strings. A master technician, using mirrors to see while reaching underneath the piano, painstakingly matches the damper felts to the strings and then adjusts the levers that control each of the dampers.

Next, the keyboard is calibrated by inserting lead weights into the body of each key so that the pressure required to push a key down is the same for every key. Subsequently, a master "voicer" will adjust the tone quality of each key. This is done by sticking the hammer's felt with a small row of needles to reduce the stiffness of the felt to achieve a more mellow tone, or by applying a small amount of lacquer to the felt for the opposite effect. Finally, a technician regulates the tone by turning the tuning pins to adjust string tension.

Steinway's process of making a grand piano is complex, requiring numerous steps and procedures that must be performed by highly skilled craftsmen. True craftsmen produce the world's finest quality concert pianos. However, not everyone wants or can afford a Steinway piano. What has Steinway & Sons done to reach other markets while maintaining the Steinway reputation for product quality?

EXPANSION BEYOND THE CLASSIC STEINWAY PIANOS

In recent years, Steinway developed the Boston Piano in an attempt to broaden its market. Steinway & Sons designed Boston Pianos using the latest computer technology and then outsourced the manufacturing to Kawai, the second-largest Japanese piano maker. By transferring its quality and knowledge of building pianos to the Boston Piano operation, Steinway was able to open up a whole new market. The Boston Piano venture demonstrated that Steinway's core competence of hand craftsmanship could be applied in a newer, high-technology manner to a lower-priced market niche.[6] In early 2001, Steinway & Sons introduced a third line of pianos, called the Essex, to complement its Steinway and Boston lines. The Essex line now offers eight grand and 18 upright models ranging in price from US$5,200 to $17,800. With the Essex, Steinway now provides pianos for every level of musical ability and budget.[7]

Having been sold again in 1995, Steinway & Sons was then merged with the Selmer Company, a manufacturer of woodwind, stringed, and percussion instruments.[8] With this merger, Steinway & Sons is now a stronger and more diversified firm. The question remains, however, can the company continue to operate in the way that has proved successful over the past 150 years?

REVIEW QUESTIONS

1. The equation specifying that Performance = Ability × Support × Effort is known as the individual performance equation. Using this equation, explain the exceptional performance that is required of, and exhibited by, the craftsmen at Steinway.

2. Use the core job characteristics model to explain the implications of Steinway's piano manufacturing process for work motivation and behaviour.

3. How does Steinway's piano manufacturing process exhibit the need for teamwork? How does this relate to job enrichment?

YOU DO THE RESEARCH

1. How does Steinway continue its emphasis on craftsmanship in this age of mass production?

2. Can any of Steinway's processes be transferred to other companies?

3. What other consumer products appear to be using a Steinway approach to producing its products?

[1] M. Cox, "Steinway Faces Yamaha Push in Piano Market," *Wall Street Journal* (January 19, 1988).
[2] Steinway & Sons on the Web, <www.steinway.com>.
[3] Steinway Musical Properties Inc. company history on the Web, <www.fundinguniverse.com>.
[4] M. Cox, op. cit.
[5] "Factory Tour," on the web, <www.steinway.com>.
[6] "Boston Piano," on the web, op. cit.
[7] "Steinway Unveils Essex Piano," Business Wire (January 23, 2001) and Steinway & Sons website, op. cit.
[8] Steinway Musical Properties Inc. company history, op. cit.

CASE 16

Callaway Golf: Big Bertha's Team Hits a Long Ball

Callaway Golf Company designs, creates, builds, and sells what founder Ely Callaway would have called "Demonstrably Superior and Pleasingly Different" golf products. Today, for Callaway Golf this means "any club, ball, or putter in the Callaway Golf family must be a significant improvement not only upon the products of our competitors, but also our own."[1] How does the company achieve its goals of manufacturing and distributing demonstrably superior and pleasingly different golf products?

CALLAWAY'S DSPD PHILOSOPHY

In 1982, after a long business career in textiles and wine making, Ely Callaway bought a 50 percent interest in Hickory Stick USA, a small pitching wedge and putter manufacturing operation. Callaway's goal was to bring his philosophy of making demonstrably superior and pleasingly different (DSPD) products, to golfing.

The DSPD philosophy was based on his previous business experiences and served as the primary guiding principle for Callaway Golf, the company that grew out of Hickory Stick USA.[2] This philosophy provides an important foundation for Callaway Golf's corporate mission: "Callaway Golf Company is driven to be a world class organization that designs, develops, makes, and delivers demonstrably superior and pleasingly different golf products that incorporate breakthrough technologies and backs those products with noticeably superior customer service. We share every golfer's passion for the game, and commit our talents and technology to increasing the satisfaction and enjoyment all golfers derive from pursuing that passion."[3]

IMPLEMENTING THE DSPD PHILOSOPHY

Callaway Golf's numerous innovations "revolutionized the industry with friendly clubs that helped golfers of all abilities find more enjoyment and a few more great shots in their game."[4] These innovations included the 2-Ball putter and the HX aerodynamic cover pattern on golf balls. Perhaps the company's most publicized innovation was the Big Bertha driver with its large, forgiving stainless steel head.

Capitalizing on the design and manufacturing of "demonstrably superior and pleasingly different golf products," Callaway Golf continued to grow. It went public with its stock in 1992, also the year it acquired Odyssey Putters. Callaway entered the golf ball market in 2000.[5] In 2003, Calloway further expanded with the purchase of the Top-Flite Golf Company.[6] According to George Fellows, company president and CEO, in 2006 the company experienced "gains in woods, balls, and accessories and we were able to maintain our number one market position in irons and putters."[7]

Callaway Golf operates in 107 countries, building on Ely Callaway's vision of helping the average golfer find more enjoyment in the game. Ely Callaway, now deceased, retired from the company in 2001. His vision continues at Callaway Golf, first through the leadership of his hand-picked successor Ron Drapeu, and then with George Fellows, who took over as CEO in 2005.

TEAMWORK AT CALLAWAY GOLF

Teamwork at Callaway Golf is built around five different areas: research and development, information systems, manufacturing, sales, and general/administrative services. The *research and development team*—responsible for designing, building prototypes, and testing the company's innovative, premium golf equipment—draws on the engineering, analytical, and computer skills of people trained in a wide range of industries. The *information systems team* supplies the company's information needs around the clock using various computer applications. The *manufacturing team* achieves levels of efficiency, innovation, and safety that are at the top of the golf industry, using the latest manufacturing and assembly techniques. The manufacturing team members have backgrounds in industrial, mechanical, electrical, and process engineering, as well as in chemistry and aerodynamics, among other fields. The *sales team* spans the world, providing golf retailers with the latest innovations in golf equipment and the highest quality service. The *general/administrative team*—helping to build and grow the company by supporting the activities of the other teams—consists of accountants, legal experts, artists, human resource generalists, receptionists, writers, and others.[8]

While the backgrounds of the members of these teams reflect considerable diversity, all of the team members share some common characteristics. Callaway Golf looks for "integrity, honesty, daring, enthusiasm, accountability and hard work" in its employees. In addition, the company seeks to keep a "healthy balance between career and play," recognizing that this results in "happier people who are more productive in every aspect of their lives."[9] Thus far, Callaway Golf has used both similarities and differences among it employees to forge five very effective teams. Will Callaway be able to maintain this balance in the future, or will diversity be sacrificed for commonality, or commonality for diversity?

REVIEW QUESTIONS

1. What is the DSPD philosophy? Explain how the operations of the different teams reflect the DSPD philosophy.
2. What team member characteristics does Callaway Golf consider to be important? Why do these characteristics seem to be important?
3. Consider the question at the very end of the case: "Will Callaway be able to maintain this balance in the future, or will diversity be sacrificed for commonality, or commonality for diversity?" What is the most reasonable answer to this question? Why?

YOU DO THE RESEARCH

1. Identify a competitor of Callaway Golf. How does Callaway Golf's DSPD philosophy compare with the fundamental management philosophy of the competitor? What managerial insights do you gain from making this comparison?
2. Use the Callaway Golf competitor that you identified for the previous question. How does Callaway Golf's emphasis on teamwork compare with the competitor's approach to organizing and utilizing the talents of its employees? What insights about teamwork does this comparison provide?

---

[1] "Our Founder," on the Web, <www.callawaygolf.com>.

[2] "History," op. cit

[3] "Investor Relations," op. cit.

[4] "History," op. cit.

[5] Ibid.

[6] "Business Brief—Callaway Golf: Bankruptcy Court Approval Is Given to Acquire Top-Flite," *Wall Street Journal* (September 5, 2003), p. 1.

[7] "Callaway Golf Releases Preliminary," on the Web, <www.callawaygolf.com>.

[8] "Callaway Golf Teams," op. cit.

[9] "Careers," op. cit.

CASE 17

The United Nations: Conflict and Negotiation in the Global Community

The United Nations (UN),[1] like its precursor the League of Nations, was established after a devastating world war in order to promote co-operation, peace, and security among its member countries. With 51 countries participating, the UN officially came into existence on October 24, 1945. Now, with over 192 members, it includes most countries in the world. Member countries accept the obligations of the UN Charter, an international treaty that sets out basic principles of international relations. It is an organization that truly embraces the concepts of diversity, co-operation, and conflict resolution and prevention. However, the UN does much more than resolve conflict. Looking at the major headings on its home page you find, in addition to peace and security, emphases on economic and social development, human rights, humanitarian affairs, and international law.[2]

A WORLD ORDER—HOW DOES IT WORK?

The United Nations is made up of six main branches:

- General Assembly—This body considers critical international problems.

    Each member country has one vote and key decisions require a two-thirds majority, while for lesser matters a simple majority is sufficient. In recent years there has been a striving for consensus decision making, in an effort to promote harmony.

- Security Council—The 15-member council has primary responsibility for maintaining international peace and security. Five of the member countries—China, France, the Russian Federation, the United Kingdom, and the United States—are permanent members; the other ten are elected for two-year terms. Under the UN Charter, members are obligated to follow the Security Council's directives. Decisions require nine "yes" votes, and any permanent member can veto a decision. The Security Council tries to exhaust all possibilities for resolution prior to authorizing the use of force. The possibilities short of force include negotiation, mediation, reference to the International Court of Justice, and economic pressure.

- Economic and Social Council—The 54-member council coordinates the economic and social work of the UN system. Members are elected for three-year terms.

- Trusteeship Council—This council was formed to administer 11 trust territories. When the final territory became self-governing in 1994, the rules of procedure were changed. The current council is composed of the five permanent members of the Security Council and meets only if needed.

- International Court of Justice—Often called the World Court, this body is responsible for deciding disputes between countries, when the countries involved agree to participate. The 15 judges, elected jointly by the General Assembly and Security Council, make decisions that those appearing before them are obligated to accept.

- Secretariat—Headed by the elected Secretary-General, the staff of the Secretariat handles the administrative work of the United Nations.

In addition to these branches, there are a number of other agencies and programs, such as the International Monetary Fund and the World Health Organization, that are linked to the UN through co-operative agreements. These organizations, along with the UN's six branches, subunits, programs, and funds, form the UN system. The UN system promotes human rights, protects the environment, fights disease, fosters economic development, and reduces poverty, in addition to preserving world peace and security.[3]

The UN's greatest opportunity for impact lies in its ability to influence international public opinion. Through the UN, world conflicts are discussed on a world stage with a world audience. However, that does not guarantee that conflict can be prevented or that peacekeeping is a simple exercise. In fact, one of the organization's most inclusive experiences to date involved engaging in conflict. The UN served as a focal point in arranging a coalition of nations to counter Iraq's invasion and occupation of Kuwait in the early 1990s. Under the auspices of the Security Council, 34 nations provided the military forces necessary for Operation Desert Storm and drove Saddam Hussein's forces out of Kuwait. Former U.S. President George H. W. Bush's claim of a "New World Order" as a result of the outcome did not come to pass.

Peacekeeping, sometimes a very dangerous enterprise, can be of short duration or last for decades. As many as 2,312 peacekeepers have died since the inception of the UN, with more UN peacekeepers dying in 2005 than in any other year of the past decade.[4] In that year there were seventeen peacekeeping missions in operation, including two in Asia, three in the Middle East, three in Europe, and six in Africa.[5] Two of those have been in operation for decades; the mission at the India–Pakistan border began in 1949, and UN peacekeepers have been in Cyprus since 1964. It seems that the goal of durable peace may be difficult to achieve.

OTHER CONFLICTS

While the Security Council has the primary responsibility for maintaining international peace and security, the Security Council itself is not always at peace. After the September 11, 2001, terrorist attacks on the World Trade Center and the Pentagon, the Security Council speedily adopted a resolution that obligated member countries to ensure that terrorists would be brought to justice. However, the dissension among Security Council members regarding the appropriate action to take against Iraq subsequent to September 11 was newsworthy and unresolved. Some members wished to continue trying to settle the matter peacefully through diplomatic means but, in the end, the United States and its allies took non-sanctioned action against Saddam Hussein. In December 2006, in his final speech as outgoing Secretary-General for the United Nations, Kofi Annan remained critical of the U.S. involvement in the Iraq war.[6] It remains to be seen, under the leadership of the new Secretary-General Ban Ki-Moon, whether there will any lasting breach in relations among members or damage to the power and prestige of the UN. The UN Security Council has implicitly accepted the situation by adopting resolutions indicating their willingness to continue to be involved in the process of stabilizing a postwar Iraq.

The structure of the Security Council, its funding, and its priorities are also a source of conflict within the UN. While the UN provides an infrastructure that transcends national borders, thereby encouraging international solutions to world problems, many smaller countries argue against domination by the larger nations, particularly by the Security Council's permanent membership.

In reaction to pressure from a number of nations, including the United States, the UN launched a reform movement in the late 1990s. Discussions on financing, operations, and Security Council makeup continue, but often to the frustration of the smaller countries. These frustrations are best expressed by quotations taken from the speeches made during the General Assembly's September 22 to October 7, 1997 debate on UN reform.[7] The following quotes illustrate the frustration felt over the power of the Security Council and the lack of transparency in its actions:

If reform of the [Security] Council is to be truly comprehensive and consistent with the spirit and realities of our time, then we must seek to remove—or at least, as a first step, restrict—the use of the veto power. Democracy in the United Nations is a mockery if the voice of the majority is rendered meaningless by the narrow interests of the dominant few. (Minister for Foreign Affairs of Malaysia, HE Dato' Seri Abdullah bin Haji Ahmad Badawi)

We also believe that real reform of the Security Council should aim above all at ensuring that the decision-making machinery and processes have the transparency, effectiveness and pluralism that must characterize every democratic institution. This includes, among other specific measures, the limitation of the veto power of the Council's permanent members, and for timelier and more effective action to prevent international conflicts at the request of any State Member of the Organization. (President of the Republic of Ecuador, HE Mr. Fabian Alarcon Rivera)

We would similarly like to see certain restrictions placed on the use of the veto. We understand that all efforts at restructuring and reform in the United Nations, however, should be focused on economic growth and development. In addition, my country is calling for a reversal in the diminishing role of the General Assembly. The accountability of the Security Council to the General Assembly must be re-emphasized, and the General Assembly should more actively assert its role in the maintenance of international peace and security. (Chair of the delegation of Antigua and Barbuda, HE Mr. Patrick Albert Lewis)

Another source of dissension among UN members is the direction of the UN toward goals that are not immediately related to maintaining peace and security. The United States withheld its dues, for a number of years, in protest against certain UN policies and the level administrative waste within its programs. The disagreement concerning the funding and priorities of the UN is illustrated in the following quotes drawn from the same debate, in which implicit reference also is made to the withholding of funds by United States and other member countries:[8]

The situation of the United Nations social sphere is the most worrisome. The greatest burden of the Organization's budgetary crisis has fallen upon the bodies involved whose financing has dropped by many millions of dollars during the present decade.... In a world where 1.3 billion people still survive on less than a dollar a day, in a world where, for the price of one combat plane, 57,000 children in Africa can be fed for a year, it is impossible to conceive of a reform of the United Nations whose priority is not to strengthen the work of its institutions and programmes dedicated to social issues. (President of the Republic of Colombia, HE Mr. Ernesto Samper Pisano, also Chair of the Non-Aligned Movement)

While we are deeply engaged in this process of reform we must not lose sight of the fundamental goals that impelled us to undertake it in the first place: to enhance the organization's ability to foster development and to address the root causes of poverty and conflict. Reform should not become a euphemism for budget slashing or an excuse for certain Member States to renege on their financial obligations to the Organization. (Minister for Foreign Affairs of Indonesia, HE Mr. Ali Alatas)

Jamaica also endorses the need for measures to improve efficiency, and we have no quarrel with reform to streamline and rationalize the system. In welcoming these steps, we must however emphasize that reform is not synonymous with cost cutting. Reform is not about doing less; it is about doing better. (Prime Minister of Jamaica, The Right Honourable Percival James Patterson)

If the United Nations is to be reformed and made effective, then adequate financing is a matter of top priority. We therefore appeal to all Member States to pay their dues in full, on time, and without conditions. (First Deputy Prime Minister and Minister for Foreign Affairs of Uganda, HE The Honourable Iriya Kategaya)

It is apparent that considerable concern exists over the funding, the organization, and the role of the UN. But does that mean that the UN has failed?

THE FUTURE

Even in the face of frustration, it appears that most members continue to believe that the UN still represents the world's best opportunity to create a climate of communication and dispute resolution across national borders and to promote worldwide well-being. They recognize that the UN has had notable success in a variety of areas, including both the Nuclear Non-Proliferation Treaty (1968) and the Comprehensive Nuclear-Test-Ban Treaty (1996), the promotion of democracy, the improvement of world health, and the resolution of conflicts within and between member nations.

In response to the Programme for Reform launched in 1997, there have been three phases of reform spearheaded by the Secretary-General. The first, *Strengthening of the United Nations: an agenda for further change* focuses on the aim of adapting the internal structures and culture of the United Nations to new expectations and new challenges. Since then, there have been some important achievements—not least of these being the Millennium Declaration itself. This document contains a clear set of priorities, including precise, time-bound development goals in key areas—such as peace, security and disarmament, economic development and poverty eradication, environmental protection, and human rights, among others—that serve as a common policy framework for the entire

United Nations system.[9]

The second phase of reform began in 2005 with the document *In Larger Freedom: Towards Development, Security, and Human Rights for all,* which reviewed the progress to date toward the goals of Millennium Declaration and attempted to revitalize consensus on key challenges and priorities in converting ideas into collective action. Target areas for reform are found under four headings: *Freedom from want, Freedom from fear, Freedom to live in dignity, and Strengthening the United Nations.*[10]

The final phase, *Investing in the United Nations,* responded to requests for change made at the 2005 World Summit. While generating some improvements, previous reforms have primarily addressed the symptoms rather than the causes of the United Nations weaknesses, leading this report to recommend a massive restructuring of the United Nations Secretariat.[11]

Despite the focus on reform, crisis and scandal continue to plague the United Nations. In 2003, the UN was badly divided because of the U.S.-led action in Iraq. Mr. Annan came under savage criticism both from the U.S., for his opposition to the war, and from the rest of the world, for failing to oppose it enough. In August 2003, the UN office in Baghdad was bombed, killing many of its brightest stars.[12] In 2004, evidence came to light of UN mismanagement over Iraq's oil-for-food program, resulting in investigations of bribery and other charges against eight senior UN procurement officials. In the same year, the head of the UN budget oversight committee was indicted on money-laundering charges, and another official pleaded guilty to skimming nearly US$1 million off UN contracts. The UN's own office of Internal Oversight found that UN peacekeeping operations had mismanaged some US$300 million in expenditures.[13] Critics continue to claim that the reforms and recommendations made by the Secretary-General in response to its internal difficulties will make no difference as they would not resolve the fundamental problems of the United Nations.[14]

Will the member countries, under the new leadership of Ban Ki-Moon, continue to support the UN, to join forces, and to seize the opportunities to revitalize the organization? Will Ban Ki-Moon be able to achieve a United Nations that is, in Kofi Annan's words, a "unique and universal instrument for concerted action in pursuit of the betterment of humankind"?[15] Or has the United Nations been irreparably damaged—and destined to go the way of the League of Nations?

REVIEW QUESTIONS

1. What is the difference between mediation and negotiation? Can you find an effective use of each by the UN?
2. Based on the quotes given, how would you classify the *General Debate on Reform* in terms of conflict management styles?
3. If reform does occur, how do you think the reform will be perceived: lose–lose, win–lose, or win–win?
4. What suggestions might you make to the UN to improve communication and conflict resolution?

YOU DO THE RESEARCH

1. What does the most recent Security Council resolution about Iraq indicate regarding the UN's involvement in that area?
2. In how many peacekeeping operations is the UN currently involved?
3. How many member countries are currently in arrears in their payments to the UN?
4. What are the current issues on the UN agenda?

---

[1] "About the United Nations," on the Web, <www.un.org>.
[2] Ibid.
[3] Ibid.
[4] "Message by the Secretary-General: 2006 International Day of United Nations Peacekeepers," on the Web, <www.un.org/Depts/dpko/peacekeepers06/SG_message06.pdf>.
[5] "Peacekeeping," on the Web, <www.un.org/peace/>.
[6] Steven Edwards, "Annan uses swan song to dump on Bush," CanWest News Service on the Web, December 12, 2006.
[7] "Selected Quotations on the Subject of UN Reform," <www.globalpolicy.org/reform/quotes.htm>.
[8] Ibid.
[9] "Millennium Declaration," on the Web, <www.un.org/millenniumgoals/background.html>.

[10] "In Larger Freedom," on the Web, <www.un.org/largerfreedom/summary.html>.
[11] "Investing in the United Nations," on the Web, <www.un.org/reform/investinginun/summary.shtml>.
[12] Mark Turner, "In the Spotlight Kofi Annan: Gamble of a peacemaker," *Financial Times*, (August 28, 2006), p. 32.
[13] "Kofi and UN 'Ideals'," *Wall Street Journal* (December 14, 2006). p. A.20.
[14] Ryan Gawn, "A Year of Bold Decision? What UN Reform Would Have Looked Like," *Peace Magazine*, vol. 21 (Oct-Dec 2005), p. 16.
[15] "Selected Quotations on the Subject of UN Reform," on the Web, <www.globalpolicy.org/reform/quotes.htm>.

CASE 18

The Walt Disney Company: The Art of Brand Building Keeps Disney Centre Stage

The Walt Disney Company has evolved from a wholesome family-oriented entertainment company into a massive multimedia conglomerate. Not only is it a producer of media, but Disney also distributes its own and others' media products through a variety of channels; operates theme parks and resorts; and produces, sells, and licenses consumer products based on Disney characters and other intellectual property. CEO Michael Eisner and his successor, Robert Iger, have been instrumental in many of these developments. How can such extensive changes occur while trying to maintain the Disney brand?

DISNEY THROUGH THE YEARS

After his first film business failed, artist Walt Disney and his brother, Roy, started a film studio in Hollywood in 1923. The first Mickey Mouse cartoon, *Plane Crazy*, was completed in 1928. *Steamboat Willie*, the first cartoon with a soundtrack, was the third production. The studio's first animated feature film was *Snow White* in 1937, followed by *Fantasia* and *Pinocchio* in the 1940s. Disneyland, the theme park developed largely by Walt, opened in 1955 in Anaheim, California. The television series *Mickey Mouse Club* was produced from 1955 to 1959, and, under a number of different names, including *The Wonderful World of Disney*, a Disney weekly television series ran for 29 years.[1]

Walt Disney died in 1966 of lung cancer, and in 1971 Roy Disney died. His son, Roy E., took over the organization, but the creative leadership of brothers Walt and Roy Disney was noticeably absent. Walt's son-in-law, Ron Miller, became president in 1980, but many industry watchers felt that Disney had lost its creative energy and sense of direction because of lacklustre corporate leadership and nepotism. In 1984, the Bass family, in alliance with Roy E. Disney, bought a controlling interest in the company. Their decision to bring in a new CEO, Michael Eisner from Paramount, and a new president, Frank Wells from Warner Bros., ushered in a new era in the history of Disney.[2]

WORK THE BRAND

Before putting on his mouse ears, Michael Eisner had been involved in the entertainment industry from the beginning, starting his career at ABC television in the 1960s. He exhibited a knack for taking organizations from last place to first through a combination of hard work and timely decisions. For example, when he arrived at Paramount Pictures in 1976, that company was dead last among the six major motion picture studios. During his time as the company's president, Paramount moved into first place with blockbusters such as *Raiders of the Lost Ark*, *Trading Places*, *Beverly Hills Cop*, and *Airplane*, along with other megahits. By applying the lessons on keeping costs down that he learned in television at ABC, he kept the average cost of a Paramount movie at US$8.5 million during his tenure, while the industry average was US$12 million.[3]

Eisner viewed Disney as a greatly underutilized franchise identifiable by millions throughout the world. In addition to re-energizing film production, Eisner wanted to extend the brand recognition of Disney products through a number of new avenues. Examples of his efforts over the years include the cable Disney Channel, Tokyo Disneyland, video distribution, Disney stores, Broadway shows such as *Beauty and the Beast*, and additional licensing arrangements for the Disney characters. However, in the early 1990s problems began emerging for Disney. EuroDisney, the firm's theme park in France, was responsible for over US$500 million in losses for Disney due to miscalculations on attendance and concessions. In 1994, Eisner underwent emergency open-heart bypass surgery, and Frank Wells, always working in the shadow of his boss but increasingly viewed as integral to the success of Disney, died in a helicopter crash. Eisner's choice to succeed Wells, Michael Ovitz from Creative Artists Agency, did not work out, and Ovitz soon left. Stories of Eisner's dictatorial management style brought succession worries to shareholders.

CAPITAL CITIES/ABC

Once again, Eisner ushered in a new era at Disney by announcing the US$19 billion takeover of Capital Cities/ABC on July 31, 1995, changing its corporate name back to ABC. The deal came in the same week as Westinghouse Electric Corporation's US$5.4 billion offer for CBS Inc. Disney's move represented one of several consolidations of the media conglomerates that increasingly control the distribution of entertainment programming in the United States. Disney ranked as the third-largest media conglomerate behind AOL Time Warner and Viacom.

One of the biggest questions arising from the ABC deal is whether Disney paid too dearly for a declining network asset. Viewership among all the major networks was declining and the networks were squeezed by having to pay extravagantly for programming while attracting an audience of older viewers who were scorned by advertisers. However, networks could be viewed as the lifeblood of the global entertainment giants that own them and as loss leaders that act to promote their parent company's more lucrative operations. In this scenario, ABC would act as Disney's megaphone to tell the masses about Disney movies, theme parks, Disney-made shows, and toys. Another financial advantage occurs when the network owns and syndicates a hit show, one that can be sold to other networks at a good profit.[4]

Eisner appreciated the importance of both programming content and the distribution assets needed to deliver it.[5] As a result of many of Eisner's decisions, the Walt Disney Company has been transformed from a sleepy film production studio into a major entertainment giant, with its revenues of US$2 billion in 1987 increasing to over US$34 billion in 2006.[6] Its stock price has multiplied more than 15 times, creating enormous wealth for both stockholders and executives of Disney.

HARD TIMES AND BRAND INVESTMENT

Not everything Disney touches turns to gold. For example, in early 2001, the company was forced to downscale its go.com Internet site as it continued to lose hundreds of millions of dollars.[7] Moreover, in the period from fiscal 1998 through 2000, net income declined by half, from US$1.85 billion to US$920 million, while operating revenue grew from US$22.98 billion to US$25.4 billion.[8] However, after a net loss of US$158 million in 2001, Disney's financial situation improved showing a steady increase in both net income and operating revenues well into 2006.[9]

Disney remained committed to integrating its various operations into the greater Disney picture and to developing its brands. As Michael Eisner said in the late 1990s: "It sounds funny, but I am thinking about the millennium change. I've got to protect the Disney brand well into the future."[10]

DISNEY'S FUTURE

Like his predecessor Michael Eisner, Robert Iger began his career at ABC where he held a series of increasingly responsible senior management positions including serving as president and COO of Capital Cities/ABC at the time of the ABC merger with the Walt Disney Company. He became chairman of the Disney-owned ABC Group and then president of Walt Disney International in 1999. In 2000, he was named president and COO of the Walt Disney Company and assumed the role of president and CEO when Michael Eisner retired in 2005.[11]

Focusing on developing a path for long-term growth, Iger thinks Disney is ready for a change. "Not that there was necessarily anything wrong with Michael's approach, but he'd been there for a while, and change is something the company could use and wants."[12] Despite criticisms surrounding his selection to the post of CEO, Iger wasted no time in making his mark at Disney. When asked for the motivation behind the deal to sell episodes of shows on the video iPod, Iger stated, "I really wanted to use it as a catalyst to get the company thinking about breaking with tradition and following the consumer."[13]

Iger has had to make some unpopular decisions to get Disney ready for a new, more competitive, market. In 2006, to combat rising costs and boost profitability in its film division, Disney announced plans to slash 20 percent of its studio staff and cut annual production in half, focusing more on animated or Disney branded films. Igar also plans to cut the production budget at Mirimax, Disney's art house label.[14] Under Iger's leadership Disney is also branching out into unprecedented territory in announcing a US$100 million program for its video game unit, launching a line of Disney and ESPN cell phones, and actively looking for more deals to distribute films and TV programming on demand.[15] In January 2006, Disney acquired its long-time animation partner Pixar, reviving Disney's fading animation department.[16]

Today, the Walt Disney Company's businesses include media networks, studio entertainment, parks and resorts, and consumer products.[17] In all of these business segments, the Walt Disney Company has been very careful in maintaining its brand identity and family-values image. However, the company recognizes that not everything is a Disney cartoon. For example, when the company goes outside its tradition, it produces its films under the Pixar or Buena Vista labels. Such movies are still family oriented in a broadly defined manner but are not the typical Disney film. The company's competitive advantage is rooted in maintaining strong and differentiated brands, most notably the Disney and ESPN brands. These brands are powerful from a business perspective because they are unique, thereby differentiating the products, and they are relevant to consumers.[18] This competitive advantage has helped return the Walt Disney Company to financial success. Continuing that trend depends on finding a path for long-term growth against the backdrop of a fast-evolving digital landscape, while at the same time maintaining its creative culture.[19]

REVIEW QUESTIONS

1. Examine the internal and external forces for change faced by Disney.
2. How have external forces in the entertainment industry affected Disney's need for change?
3. What changes do you foresee in the entertainment industry in the next five years?

YOU DO THE RESEARCH

1. Disney has apparently turned it fortunes around. What are the prospects that the company will maintain this success in the future?
2. Has the Walt Disney Company really moved past its reputation as a children's movie and theme park provider?
3. Are media conglomerates headed for trouble?

---

[1] "Disney," *Hoover's Handbook of American Business*, (Texas: Hoover's Business Press, 1997).
[2] Ibid.
[3] "Michael Eisner's Biography," Academy of Achievement Lobby on the Web, <www.achievement.org>.
[4] Marc Gunther, "What's Wrong with This Picture?" *Fortune* (January 12, 1998), pp. 106-114.
[5] Michael Oneal, "Disney's Kingdom," *Business Week* (August 14, 1995), pp. 30-34.
[6] "Letter from Michael Eisner," News for the Disney Board on the Web, March 13, 2005, <http://corporate.disney.go.com/corporate/board_news/2004/index0.html>.
[7] Ibid.
[8] "2000 Fact Book," Investor Relations on the Web, <corporate.disney.go.com>.
[9] "2006 Annual Report," op. cit.
[10] Barry Shlachter and Jim Fuquay, "Disney Holds Annual Shareholders Meeting in Fort Worth, Texas," *Fort Worth Star-Telegram* (March 7, 2001).
[11] "Robert A. Iger Executive Biography," Management Team on the Web, <corporate.disney.go.com>.
[12] Merissa Marr, "Boss Talk: Redirecting Disney; CEO Iger's Push for Change Goes Far Beyond iPod Deal; Fewer Films, Evolving Parks," *Wall Street Journal* (December 5, 2005), pg. B.
[13] Ibid.
[14] Joshua Chaffin, "Disney changes focus in shake-up," *Financial Times* (July 20, 2006), p. 24.
[15] "Buzzmakers," Business Week (December 19, 2005), p. 64.
[16] Joshua Chaffin, "Tough decisions for Walt Disney after deal," *Financial Times* (January 25, 2006), p. 1.
[17] "2006 Annual Report," op. cit.
[18] "2002 Annual Report," op. cit.
[19] Merissa Marr, op. cit.

ACTIVE LEARNING PROJECTS

PROJECT 1

Diversity Lessons—"What Have We Learned?"

QUESTION

What are the current "facts" in terms of progress for visible minorities, the disabled, Aboriginals, and women in the workplace? What lessons of diversity have been learned? What are the "best" employers doing?

Possible Research Directions

- Examine case studies of employers reported as having strong diversity programs. What do they have in common? What do they do differently?
- Find out what we know about how well people of different racial, ethnic, gender, lifestyle, physical abilities, and generational groups work together. What are the common problems, if any? What concerns do managers and workers have?
- Get specific data on how the "glass ceiling" affects the careers of women and members of diverse groups in various occupational settings. Analyze the data and develop the implications.
- Take a critical look at the substance of diversity training programs. What do these programs try to accomplish, and how? Are they working or not, and how do we know?

PROJECT 2

Corporate Social Responsibility—"What's the Status?"

QUESTION

Where do businesses stand today with respect to the criteria for evaluating social responsibility discussed in the textbook?

Possible Research Directions

- Create a scale that could be used to measure the social responsibility performance of an organization. Review the scholarly research in this area, but also include your own ideas and expectations.
- Use your scale to research and evaluate the "status" of major organizations and local ones on social responsibility performance. How well are they doing? Would you use them as models of social responsibility for others to follow, or not?
- Conduct research to identify current examples of the "best" and the "worst" organizations in terms of performance or social responsibility criteria. Pursue this investigation on an (a) international, (b) national, and/or (c) local scale.

PROJECT 3

Globalization—"What Are the Pros and Cons?"

QUESTION

"Globalization" is frequently in the news. You can easily read or listen to both advocates and opponents. What is the bottom line? Is globalization good or bad, and for whom?

Possible Research Directions

- What does the term "globalization" mean? Review various definitions and find the common ground.
- Read and study the scholarly arguments about globalization. Summarize what the scholars say about the forces and consequences of globalization in the past, present, and future.
- Examine current events relating to globalization. Summarize the issues and arguments. What is the positive side of globalization? What are the negatives that some might call its "dark" side?
- Consider globalization from the perspective of your local community or one of its major employers. Is globalization a threat or an opportunity, and why?
- Take a position on globalization. State what you believe to be the best course for government and business leaders to take. Justify your position.

PROJECT 4

Diversity Management—"Where Do We Go from Here?"

QUESTION

Organizational researchers argue that it is time to move beyond employment equity and learn how to "manage diversity." There are a lot of issues that may be raised in this context—issues of equal employment opportunity, hiring quotas, reverse discrimination, and others. What is the status of managing diversity today?

Possible Research Directions

- Read articles on the subject of managing diversity. Make sure you are clear on the term "employment equity" and its legal underpinnings. Research the topic, identify the relevant laws, and make a history line to chart its development over time.
- Examine current debates on employment equity. What are the issues? How are the "for" and "against" positions being argued?
- Identify legal cases where reverse discrimination has been charged. How have they been resolved and with what apparent human resource management implications?
- Look at actual organizational policies on diversity. Analyze them and identify the common ground. Prepare a policy development guideline for use by human resource managers.
- As you ponder these issues and controversies be sure to engage different perspectives. Talk to and read about people of different "majority" and "minority" groups. Find out how they view these things—and why.

PROJECT 5

Fringe Benefits—"How Can They Be Managed?"

QUESTION

Employers complain that the rising cost of "fringe benefits" is a major concern. Is this concern legitimate? If so, how can fringe benefits be best managed?

Possible Research Directions

- Find out exactly what constitutes "fringe benefits" as part of the typical compensation package. Look in the literature and also talk to local employers. Find out what percentage of a typical salary is represented in fringe benefits.
- Find and interview two or three human resource managers in your community. Ask them to describe their fringe benefits programs and how they manage fringe benefits costs. What do they see happening in the future? What do they recommend? Talk to two or three workers from different employers in your community. Find out how things look to them and what they recommend.

- Pick a specific benefit such as dental benefits. What are the facts? How are employers trying to manage the rising cost? What are the implications for workers?
- Examine the union positions on fringe benefits. How is this issue reflected in major labour negotiations? What are the results of major recent negotiations?
- Look at fringe benefits from the perspective of temporary, part-time, or contingent workers. What do they get? What do they want? How are they affected by rising costs?

PROJECT 6

CEO Pay—"Is It Too High?"

QUESTION

What is happening in the area of executive compensation? Are CEOs paid too much? Are they paid for "performance," or are they paid for something else?

Possible Research Directions

- Check the latest reports on CEO pay. Get the facts and prepare a briefing report as if you were writing a short informative article for *Canadian Business* magazine. The title of your article should be "Status Report: Where We Stand Today on CEO Pay."
- Address the pay-for-performance issue. Do corporate CEOs get paid for performance or for something else? What do the researchers say? What do the business periodicals say? Find some examples to explain and defend your answers to these questions.
- Take a position: Should a limit be set on CEO pay? If no, why not? If yes, what type of limit do we set? Who, if anyone, should set these limits—company boards of directors, or someone else?
- Examine the same issues in the government setting. Are premiers and prime ministers paid too much?

PROJECT 7

Gender and Leadership—"Is There a Difference?"

QUESTION

Do men and women lead differently?

Possible Research Directions

- Review the discussion on gender and leadership in the textbook, Chapter 13. Find and read the articles cited in the endnotes. Then, update this literature by finding and reading the most recent scholarly findings and reports.
- Interview managers from organizations in your local community. Ask them whether men and women lead differently. Ask them to give you specific examples to justify their answers. Look for patterns and differences. Do male managers and female managers answer the question similarly?

- Interview workers from organizations in your local community. Ask them the question. Ask them to give you specific examples to justify their answers. Look for patterns and differences. Do male workers and female workers answer the question similarly? Do the same for students—pressing them to share insights and examples from their experiences in course study groups and student organizations.
- Summarize your findings. Describe the implications of your findings in terms of leadership development for both men and women.

PROJECT 8

Superstars on the Team—"What Do They Mean?"

QUESTION

Do we want a "superstar" on our team?

Possible Research Directions

- Everywhere you look—in entertainment, in sports, and in business—a lot of attention these days goes to the superstars. What is the record of teams and groups with superstars? Do they really outperform the rest?
- What is the real impact of a superstar's presence on a team or in the workplace? What do they add? What do they cost? Consider the potential costs of having a superstar on a team in the equation: Benefits − Costs = Value. What is the bottom line of having a superstar on the team?
- Interview the athletic coaches on your campus. Ask them whether having a superstar means outperforming others. Compare and contrast their answers. Interview players from various teams. Do the same for them.
- Develop a set of guidelines for creating team effectiveness for a situation where a superstar is present. Be thorough and practical. Can you give advice good enough to ensure that a superstar always creates super performance for the team or work group or organization?

PROJECT 9

Management in Popular Culture—"Seeing Ourselves Through Our Pastimes"

QUESTION

What management insights are found in popular culture and reflected in our everyday living?

Possible Research Directions

- Listen to music. Pick out themes that reflect important management concepts and theories. Put them together in a multimedia report that presents your music choices and describes their messages about management and working today.

- Watch television. Look again for the management themes. In a report, describe what popular television programs have to say about management and working. Also consider TV advertisements. How do they use and present workplace themes to help communicate their messages?
- Read the comics, also looking for management themes. Compare and contrast management and working in two or three popular comic strips.
- Read a best-selling novel. Find examples of management and work themes in the novel. Report on what the author's characters and their experiences say about people at work.
- Watch a film or video. Again, find examples of management and work themes. In a report describe the message of the movie in respect to management and work today.

Note: These ideas are borrowed from the extensive work in this area by Dr. Robert (Lenie) Holbrook of Ohio University.

PROJECT 10

Service Learning in Management—"Learning from Volunteering"

QUESTION

What can you learn about management and leadership by working as a volunteer for a local community organization?

Possible Research Directions

- Explore service learning opportunities on your campus. Talk to your instructor about how to add a service learning component to your management course.
- List the nonprofit organizations in your community that might benefit from volunteers. Contact one or more of them and make inquiries as to how you might help them. Do it, and then report back on what you learned as a result of the experience that is relevant to management and leadership.
- Locate the primary schools in your community or region. Contact the school principals and ask how you might be able to help teachers working with students in Grades 1–6. Do it, and then report back on what you learned with respect to personal management and leadership development.
- For either the nonprofit organization or the primary school, form a group of students who share similar interests in service learning. Volunteer as a group to help the organization and prepare a team report on what you learned.
- Take the initiative. Create service learning ideas of your own—to be pursued individually or as part of a team. While working as a volunteer always keep your eyes and ears open for learning opportunities. Continually ask—"What is happening here in respect to: leadership, morale, motivation, teamwork, conflict, interpersonal dynamics, organization culture and structures, and more?"

EXERCISES IN TEAMWORK

EXERCISE 1

My Best Manager

PREPARATION

Working alone, make a list of the *behavioural attributes* that describe the best manager you have ever worked for. This could be someone you worked for in a full-time or part-time job, summer job, volunteer job, student organization, or whatever. If you have trouble identifying an actual manager, make a list of behavioural attributes of the type of manager you would most like to work for in your next job.

INSTRUCTIONS

Form into groups as assigned by your instructor, or work with a nearby classmate. Share your list of attributes and listen to the lists of others. Be sure to ask questions and make comments on items of special interest. Work together to create a master list that combines the unique attributes of the "best" managers experienced by members of your group. Have a spokesperson share that list with the rest of the class.

Source: Adapted from John R. Schermerhorn, Jr., James G. Hunt, and Richard N. Osborn, *Managing Organizational Behavior*, 3rd ed. (New York: Wiley, 1988), pp. 32–33. Used by permission.

EXERCISE 2

What Managers Do

PREPARATION

Think about the questions that follow. Record your answers in the spaces provided.

1. How much of a typical manager's time would you expect to be allocated to these relationships? (total should = 100%)

    ___% of time working with subordinates

    ___% of time working with boss

    ___% of time working with peers and outsiders

2. How many hours per week does the average manager work? ___ hours

3. What amount of a manager's time is typically spent in the following activities? (total should = 100%)

    ___% in scheduled meetings

    ___% in unscheduled meetings

    ___% doing desk work

    ___% talking on the telephone

    ___% walking around the organization/ work site

INSTRUCTIONS

Talk over your responses with a nearby classmate. Explore the similarities and differences in your answers. Be prepared to participate in a class discussion led by your instructor.

EXERCISE 3

Defining Quality

PREPARATION

Write your definition of the word quality here.
QUALITY =

INSTRUCTIONS

Form groups as assigned by your instructor. (1) Have each group member present a definition of the word "quality." After everyone has presented, come up with a consensus definition of *quality*. That is, determine and write down one definition of the word with which every member can agree. (2) Next, have the group assume the position of top manager in each of the following organizations. Use the group's *quality* definition to state for each a *quality objective* that can guide the behaviour of members in producing high-"quality" goods and/or services for customers or clients. Elect a spokesperson to share group results with the class as a whole.

Organizations:

   a. A college of business administration
   b. A community hospital
   c. A retail sporting goods store
   d. A fast-food franchise restaurant
   e. A Canada Post branch
   f. A full-service bank branch
   g. A student-apartment rental company
   h. A used textbook store
   i. A computer software firm

EXERCISE 4

What Would the Classics Say?

PREPARATION

Consider this situation:

Six months into his new job, Bob, a laboratory worker, is performing just well enough to avoid being fired. When hired he was carefully selected and had the abilities required to do the job really well. At first Bob was enthusiastic about his new job, but now he isn't performing up to this high potential. Fran, his supervisor, is concerned and wonders what can be done to improve this situation.

INSTRUCTIONS

Assume the identify of one of the following persons: Frederick Taylor, Henri Fayol, Max Weber, Abraham Maslow, Chris Argyris. Assume that *as this person* you have been asked by Fran for advice on the management situation just described. Answer these questions as you think your assumed identity would respond. Be prepared to share your answers in class and to defend them based on the text's discussion of this person's views.

1. As (*your assumed identity*), what are your basic beliefs about good management and organizational practices?
2. As (*your assumed identity*), what do you perceive may be wrong in this situation that would account for Bob's low performance?
3. As (*your assumed identity*), what could be done to improve Bob's future job performance?

EXERCISE 5

The Great Management History Debate

PREPARATION

Consider the question "What is the best thing a manager can do to improve productivity in her or his work unit?"

INSTRUCTIONS

The instructor will assign you, individually or in a group, to one of the following positions. Complete the missing information as if you were the management theorist referred to. Be prepared to argue and defend your position before the class.

- Position A: "Mary Parker Follett offers the best insight into the question. Her advice would be to … " (advice to be filled in by you or the group).
- Position B: "Max Weber's ideal bureaucracy offers the best insight into the question. His advice would be to …" (advice to be filled in by you or the group).
- Position C: "Henri Fayol offers the best insight into the question. His advice would be to . . . " (advice to be filled in by you or the group).
- Position D: "The Hawthorne studies offer the best insight into the question. Elton Mayo's advice would be to …" (advice to be filled in by you or the group).

EXERCISE 6

Confronting Ethical Dilemmas

PREPARATION

Read and indicate your response to each of the situations below.

a. Pierre Tremblay, vice president of a large construction firm, receives in the mail a large envelope marked "personal." It contains a competitor's cost data for a project that both firms will be bidding on shortly. The data are accompanied by a note from one of Pierre's subordinates saying: "This is the real thing!" Pierre knows that the data could be a major advantage to his firm in preparing a bid that can win the contract. *What should he do?*

b. Kay Smith is one of your top-performing subordinates. She has shared with you her desire to apply for promotion to a new position just announced in a different division of the company. This will be tough on you since recent budget cuts mean you will be unable to replace anyone who leaves, at least for quite some time. Kay knows this and in all fairness has asked your permission before she submits an application. It is rumoured that the son of a good friend of your boss is going to apply for the job. Although his credentials are less impressive than Kay's, the likelihood is that he will get the job if she doesn't apply. *What will you do?*

c. Marty Jose got caught in a bind. She was pleased to represent her firm as head of the local community development committee. In fact, her supervisor's boss once held this position and told her in a hallway conversation, "Do your best and give them every support possible." Going along with this, Marty agreed to pick up the bill (several hundred dollars) for a dinner meeting with local civic and business leaders. Shortly therafter, her supervisor informed everyone that the entertainment budget was being eliminated in a cost-saving effort. Marty, not wanting to renege on supporting the community development committee, was able to charge the dinner bill to an advertising budget. Eventually, an internal auditor discovered the mistake and reported it to you, the personnel director. Marty is scheduled to meet with you in a few minutes. *What will you do?*

INSTRUCTIONS

Working alone, make the requested decisions in each of these incidents. Think carefully about your justification for the decision. Meet in a group assigned by your instructor. Share your decisions and justifications in each case with other group members. Listen to theirs. Try to reach a group consensus on what to do in each situation and why. Be prepared to share the group decisions, and any dissenting views, in general class discussion.

EXERCISE 7

What Do You Value in Work?

PREPARATION

Rank order the nine items in terms of how important (9 = most important) they would be to you in a job.

How important is it to you to have a job that:

___ Is respected by other people?

___ Encourages continued development of knowledge and skills?

___ Provides job security?

___ Provides a feeling of accomplishment?

___ Provides the opportunity to earn a high income?

___ Is intellectually stimulating?
___ Rewards good performance with recognition?
___ Provides comfortable working conditions?
___ Permits advancement to high administrative responsibility?

INSTRUCTIONS

Form into groups as designated by your instructor. Within each group, the *men in the group* will meet to develop a consensus ranking of the items as they think the women in the survey ranked them. The reasons for the rankings should be shared and discussed so they are clear to everyone. The *women in the group* should not participate in this ranking task. They should listen to the discussion and be prepared to comment later in class discussions. A spokesperson for the men in the group should share the group's rankings with the class.

OPTIONAL INSTRUCTIONS

Form into groups as designated by your instructor but with each group consisting entirely of men or women. Each group should meet and decide which of the work values members of the opposite sex ranked first in the survey. Do this again for the work value ranked last. The reasons should be discussed, along with the reasons why each of the other values probably was not ranked first … or last. A spokesperson for each group should share group results with the rest of the class.

Source: Adapted from Roy J. Lewicki, Donald D. Bowen, Douglas T. Hall, and Francine S. Hall, *Experiences in Management and Organizational Behavior*, 3rd ed. (New York: Wiley, 1988), pp.23–26. Used by permission.

EXERCISE 8

Which Organizational Culture Fits You?

INSTRUCTIONS

Indicate which one of the following organizational cultures you feel most comfortable working in.

1. A culture that values talent, entrepreneurial activity, and performance over commitment; one that offers large financial rewards and individual recognition.

2. A culture that stresses loyalty, working for the good of the group, and getting to know the right people; one that believes in "generalists" and step-by-step career progress.

3. A culture that offers little job security; one that operates with a survival mentality, stresses that every individual can make a difference, and focuses attention on "turn-around" opportunities.

4. A culture that values long-term relationships; one that emphasizes systematic career development, regular training, and advancement based on gaining functional expertise.

INTERPRETATION

These labels identify the four different cultures: 1 = "the baseball team," 2 = "the club," 3 = "the fortress," and 4 = "the academy."

Discuss results in work groups assigned by your instructor. To some extent, your future career success may depend on working for an organization in which there is a good fit between you and the prevailing corporate culture. This exercise can help you learn how to recognize various cultures, evaluate how well they can serve your needs, and recognize how they may change with time. A risk taker, for example, may be out of place in a "club" but fit right in with a "baseball team." Someone who wants to seek opportunities wherever they may occur may be out of place in an "academy" but fit right in with a "fortress."

Source: Developed from Carol Hymowitz, "Which Corporate Culture Fits You?" *Wall Street Journal* (July 17, 1989), p. B1.

EXERCISE 9

Beating the Time Wasters

PREPARATION

1. Make a list of all the things you need to do tomorrow. Prioritize each item in terms of *how important it is to create outcomes that you can really value*. Use this classification scheme:

   (A) Most important, top priority

   (B) Important, not top priority

   (C) Least important, low priority

   Look again at all activities you have classified as B. Reclassify any that are really A's or C's. Look at your list of A's. Reclassify any that are really B's or C's. Double-check to make sure you are comfortable with your list of C's.

2. Make a list of all the "time wasters" that often interfere with your ability to accomplish everything you want to on any given day.

INSTRUCTIONS

Form into groups as assigned by the instructor. Have all group members share their lists and their priority classifications. Members should politely "challenge" each other's classifications to make sure that only truly "high-priority" items receive an A rating. They might also suggest that some C items are of such little consequence that they might not be worth doing at all. After each member of the group revises his or her "to do" list based on this advice, go back and discuss the time wasters identified by group members. Develop a master list of time wasters and what to do about them. Have a group spokesperson be prepared to share discussion highlights and tips on beating common time wasters with the rest of the class.

Source: Developed from Roy J. Lewicki, Donald D. Bowen, Douglas T. Hall, and Francine S. Hall, *Experiences in Management and Organizational Behavior*, 3rd ed. (New York: Wiley, 1988), pp. 314–16.

EXERCISE 10

Personal Career Planning

PREPARATION

Complete the following three activities, and bring the results to class. Your work should be in a written form suitable for your instructor's review.

Step 1: *Strengths and Weaknesses Inventory* Different occupations require special talents, abilities, and skills if people are to excel in their work. Each of us, you included, has a repertoire of existing strengths and weaknesses that are "raw materials" we presently offer a potential employer. Of course, actions can (and should!) be taken over time to further develop current strengths and to turn weaknesses into strengths. Make a list identifying your most important strengths and weaknesses at the moment in relation to the career direction you are most likely to pursue upon graduation. Place a * next to each item you consider most important to address in your courses and student activities *before* graduation.

Step 2. *Five-Year Career Objectives* Make a list of 3 to 5 career objectives that are appropriate given your list of personal strengths and weaknesses. Limit these objectives to ones that can be accomplished within 5 years of graduation.

Step 3. *Five-Year Career Action Plans* Write a specific action plan for accomplishing each of the 5 objectives. State exactly what you will do, and by when, in order to meet each objective. If you will need special support or assistance, identify it and state how you will obtain it. Remember, an outside observer should be able to read your action plan for each objective and end up feeling confident that (a) he or she knows exactly what you are going to do and (b) why.

INSTRUCTIONS

Form into groups as assigned by the instructor. Share your career-planning analysis with the group; listen to those of others. Participate in a discussion that examines any common patterns and major differences among group members. Take advantage of any opportunities to gather feedback and advice from others. Have one group member be prepared to summarize the group discussion for the class as a whole. Await further class discussion led by the instructor.

Source: Developed in part from Roy J. Lewicki, Donald D. Bowen, Douglas T. Hall, and Francine S. Hall, *Experiences in Management and Organizational Behavior*, 3rd ed. (New York: Wiley, 1988), pp. 261–67. Used by permission.

EXERCISE 11

Decision-Making Biases

INSTRUCTIONS

How good are you at avoiding potential decision-making biases? Test yourself by answering the following questions:

1. Which is riskier:
   (a) driving a car on a 800 km trip?
   (b) flying on a 800 km commercial airline flight?

2. Are there more words in the English language:
   (a) that begin with r?
   (b) that have r as the third letter?

3. Rajeev is finishing his MBA at a prestigious university. He is very interested in the arts and at one time considered a career as a musician. Is Rajeev more likely to take a job:
   (a) in the management of the arts?
   (b) with a management consulting firm?

4. You are about to hire a new central-region sales director for the fifth time this year. You predict that the next director should work out reasonably well since the last four were "lemons" and the odds favour hiring at least one good sales director in five tries. Is this thinking
   (a) correct?
   (b) incorrect?

5. A newly hired engineer for a computer firm in the Calgary area has 4 years' experience and good all-round qualifications. When asked to estimate the starting salary for this employee, a chemist with very little knowledge about the profession or industry guessed an annual salary of $35,000. What is your estimate?

   $ ___ per year

SCORING

Your instructor will provide answers and explanations for the assessment questions.

INTERPRETATION

Each of the preceding questions examines your tendency to use a different judgemental heuristic. In his book *Judgment in Managerial Decision Making*, 3rd ed. (New York: Wiley, 1994), pp. 6-7, Max Bazerman calls these heuristics "simplifying strategies, or rules of thumb" used in making decisions. He states, "In general, heuristics are helpful, but their use can sometimes lead to severe errors. … If we can make managers aware of the potential adverse impacts of using heuristics, they can then decide when and where to use them." This assessment offers an initial insight into your use of such heuristics. An informed decision maker understands the heuristics, is able to recognize when they appear, and eliminates any that may inappropriately bias decision making.

Test yourself further. Write next to each item the name of the judgemental heuristic that you think applies (see Chapter 7).

Source: Incidents from Max H. Bazerman, *Judgment in Managerial Decision Making*, 3rd ed. (New York: Wiley, 1994), pp. 13–14. Used by permission.

EXERCISE 12

Strategic Scenarios

PREPARATION

In today's turbulent environments, it is no longer safe to assume that an organization that was highly successful yesterday will continue to be so tomorrow—or that it will even be in existence. Changing times exact the best from strategic planners. Think about the situations currently facing the following well-known organizations. Think, too, about the futures they may face.

Tim Hortons

Apple Computer

Yahoo.com

The Bay

Air Canada

Canadian Broadcasting Corporation

INSTRUCTIONS

Form into groups as assigned by your instructor. Choose one or more organizations from the prior list (as assigned) and answer for the organization the following questions:

1. What in the future might seriously threaten the success, perhaps the very existence, of this organization? (As a group develop at least three such future scenarios.)
2. Estimate the probability (0 to 100 percent) of each future scenario occurring.
3. Develop a strategy for each scenario that will enable the organization to successfully deal with it.

Thoroughly discuss these questions within the group and arrive at your best possible consensus answers. Be prepared to share and defend your answers in general class discussion.

Source: From *The Dynamics of Organizational Theory: Gaining a Macro*, 2nd edition by Veiga/Yanouzas, 1984. Reprinted with permission of South-Western, a division of Thompson Learning: www.thomsonrights.com.

EXERCISE 13

The MBO Contract

Listed below are performance objectives from an MBO contract for a plant manager.

PREPARATION

a. To increase deliveries to 98% of all scheduled delivery dates

b. To reduce waste and spoilage to 3% of all raw materials used

c. To reduce lost time due to accidents to 100 work days/year

d. To reduce operating cost to 10% below budget

e. To install a quality-control system at a cost of less than $53,000

f. To improve production scheduling and increase machine utilization time to 95% capacity

g. To complete a management development program this year

h. To teach a community college course in human resource management

INSTRUCTIONS

1. Study this MBO contract. In the margin write one of the following symbols to identify each objective as an improvement, maintenance, or personal development objective.

    I = Improvement objective
    M = Maintenance objective
    P = Personal development objective

2. Assume that this MBO contract was actually developed and implemented under the following circumstances. After each statement, write "yes" if the statement reflects proper MBO procedures and write "no" if it reflects poor MBO procedures.

(a) The president drafted the 8 objectives and submitted them to Chang for review.

(b) The president and Chang thoroughly discussed the 8 objectives in proposal form before they were finalized.

(c) The president and Chang scheduled a meeting in 6 months to review Chang's progress on the objectives.

(d) The president didn't discuss the objectives with Chang again until the scheduled meeting was held.

(e) The president told Chang his annual raise would depend entirely on the extent to which these objectives were achieved.

3. Share and discuss your responses to parts 1 and 2 of the exercise with a nearby classmate. Reconcile any differences of opinion by referring back to the chapter discussion of MBO. Await further class discussion.

EXERCISE 14

The Future Workplace

INSTRUCTIONS

Form groups as assigned by the instructor. Brainstorm to develop a master list of the major characteristics you expect to find in the future workplace in the year 2020. Use this list as background for completing the following tasks:

1. Write a one-paragraph description of what the typical "Workplace 2020 manager's" workday will be like.
2. Draw a "picture" representing what the "Workplace 2020 organization" will look like.

Choose a spokesperson to share your results with the class as a whole and explain their implications for the class members.

EXERCISE 15

Dots and Squares Puzzle

INSTRUCTIONS

1. Shown here is a collection of 16 dots. Study the figure to determine how many "squares" can be created by connecting the dots.

2. Draw as many squares as you can find in the figure while making sure a dot is at every corner of every square. Count the squares and write this number in the margin to the right of the figure.

3. Share your results with those of a classmate sitting nearby. Indicate the location of squares missed by either one of you.

4. Based on this discussion, redraw your figure to show the maximum number of possible squares. Count them and write this number to the left of the figure.

5. Await further class discussion led by your instructor.

•　•　•　•

•　•　•　•

•　•　•　•

•　•　•　•

EXERCISE 16

Leading Through Participation

PREPARATION

Read each of the following vignettes. Write in the margin whether you think the leader should handle the situation with an individual decision (I), consultative decision (C), or group decision (G).

VIGNETTE I

You are a general supervisor in charge of a large team laying an oil pipeline. It is now necessary to estimate your expected rate of progress in order to schedule material deliveries to the next field site. You know the nature of the terrain you will be travelling and have the historical data needed to calculate the mean and variance in the rate of speed over the type of terrain. Given these two variables, it is a simple matter to calculate the earliest and latest times at which materials and support facilities will be needed at the next site. It is important that your estimate be reasonably accurate; underestimates result in idle supervisors and workers, and overestimates result in materials being tied up for a period of time before they are to be used. Progress has been good, and your 5 supervisors along with the other members of the gang stand to receive substantial bonuses if the project is completed ahead of schedule.

VIGNETTE II

You are supervising the work of 12 engineers. Their formal training and work experience are very similar, permitting you to use them interchangeably on projects. Yesterday, your manager informed you that a request had been received from an overseas affiliate for 4 engineers to go abroad on extended loan for a period of 6 to 8 months. He argued and you agreed that for a number of reasons this request should be filled from your group. All your engineers are capable of handling this assignment, and from the standpoint of present and future projects there is no particular reason that any one should be retained over any other. The problem is complicated by the fact that the overseas assignment is in what is generally regarded in the company as an undesirable location.

VIGNETTE III

You are the head of a staff unit reporting to the vice president of finance. He has asked you to provide a report on the firm's current portfolio including recommendations for changes in the selection criteria currently employed. Doubts have been raised about the efficiency of the existing system in the current market conditions, and there is considerable dissatisfaction with prevailing rates of return. You plan to write the report, but at the moment you are quite perplexed about the approach to take. Your own specialty is the bond market, and it is clear to you that a detailed knowledge of the equity market, which you lack, would greatly enhance the value of the report. Fortunately, 4 members of your staff are specialists in different segments of the equity market. Together, they possess a vast amount of knowledge about the intricacies of investment. However, they seldom agree on the best way to achieve anything when it comes to the stock market. Whereas they are obviously conscientious as well as knowlegeable, they have major differences when it comes to investment philosophy and strategy. The report is due in 6 weeks, You have already begun to familiarize yourself with the firm's current portfolio and have been provided by management with a specific set of constraints that any portfolio must satisfy. Your immediate problem is to come up with some alternatives to the firm's present practices and select the most promising ones for detailed analysis in your report.

VIGNETTE IV

You are on the division manager's staff and work on a wide variety of problems of both an administrative and technical nature. You have been given the assignment of developing a universal method to be used in each of the 5 plants in the division for manually reading equipment registers, recording the readings, and transmitting the scoring to a centralized information system. All plants are located in a relatively small geographical region. Until now there has been a high error rate in the reading and/or transmittal of the data. Some locations have considerably higher error rates than others, and the methods used to record and transmit the data vary between plants. It is probable, therefore, that part of the error variance is a function of specific local conditions rather than anything else, and this will complicate the establishment of any system common to all plants. You have the information on error rates but no information on the local practices that generate these errors or on the local conditions that necessitate the different practices. Everyone would benefit from an improvement in the quality of the data because they are used in a number of important decisions. Your contacts with the plants are through the quality control supervisors responsible for collecting the data. They are a conscientious group committed to doing their jobs well but are highly sensitive to interference on the part of higher management in their own operations. Any solution that does not receive the active support of the various plant supervisors is unlikely to reduce the error rate significantly.

INSTRUCTIONS

Form groups as assigned by the instructor. Share you choices with other group members and try to achieve a consensus on how the leader should best handle each situation. Refer back to the discussion of the Vroom-Jago "leader-participation" theory presented in Chapter 13. Analyze each vignette according to their ideas. Do you come to any different conclusions? If so, why? Nominate a spokesperson to share your results in general class discussion.

Source: Victor H. Vroom and Arthur G. Jago, *The New Leadership* (Englewood Cliffs, NJ: Prentice Hall, 1988).

EXERCISE 17

Work vs. Family—You Be the Judge

1. Read the following situation.

    Joanna, a single parent, was hired to work 8:15 a.m. to 5:30 p.m. weekdays selling computers for a firm. Her employer extended her workday until 6:30 p.m. on weekdays and added 8:15 a.m. to 2:30 p.m. on Saturday. Joanna refused to work the extra hours, saying that she had a six-year-old son and that so many work hours would lead to neglect. The employer said this was a special request during a difficult period and that all employees needed to share in helping out during the "crunch." Still refusing to work the extra hours, Joanna was fired.

2. You be the judge in this case. Take an individual position on the following questions:

    Should Joanna be allowed to work only the hours agreed to when she was hired? Or is the employer correct in asking all employees, regardless of family status, to work the extra hours? Why?

3. Form into groups as assigned by the instructor. Share your responses to the questions and try to develop a group consensus. Be sure to have a rationale for the position the group adopts. Appoint a spokesperson who can share results with the class. Be prepared to participate in open class discussion.

Source: This case scenario is from Sue Shellenbarger, "Employees Challenge Policies on Family and Get Hard Lessons," *Wall Street Journal* (December 17, 1997), p. B1.

EXERCISE 18

Compensation and Benefits Debate

PREPARATION

Consider the following quotations.

On compensation: "A basic rule of thumb should be—pay at least as much, and perhaps a bit more, in base wage or salary than what competitors are offering."

On benefits: "When benefits are attractive or at least adequate, the organization is in a better position to employ highly qualified people."

INSTRUCTIONS

Form groups as assigned by the instructor. Each will be given either one of the preceding position statements or one of the following alternatives.

On compensation: "Given the importance of controlling costs, organizations can benefit by paying as little as possible for labour."

On benefits: "Given the rising cost of health-care and other benefit programs and the increasing difficulty many organizations have staying in business, it is best to minimize paid benefits and let employees handle more of the cost on their own."

Each group should prepare to debate a counterpoint group on its assigned position. After time is allocated to prepare for the debate, each group will present its opening positions. Each will then be allowed one rebuttal period to respond to the other group. General class discussion on the role of compensation and benefits in the modern organization will follow.

EXERCISE 19

Sources and Uses of Power

PREPARATION

Consider *the way you have behaved* in each of the situations described below. They may be from a full-time or part-time job, student organization or class group, sports team, or whatever. If you do not have an experience of the type described, try to imagine yourself in one; think about how you would expect yourself to behave.

1. You needed to get a peer to do something you wanted that person to do but were worried he or she didn't want to do it.

2. You needed to get a subordinate to do something you wanted her or him to do but were worried the subordinate didn't want to do it.

3. You needed to get your boss to do something you wanted him or her to do but were worried the boss didn't want to do it.

INSTRUCTIONS

Form into groups as assigned by the instructor. Start with situation 1 and have all members of the group share their approaches. Determine what specific sources of power (see Chapter 13) were used. Note any patterns in group members' responses. Discuss what is required to be successful in this situation. Do the same for situations 2 and 3. Note any special differences in how situations 1, 2, and 3 should be or could be handled. Choose a spokesperson to share results in general class discussion.

EXERCISE 20

After Meeting/Project Review

PREPARATION

After participating in a meeting or a group project, complete the following assessment.

1. How satisfied are *you* with the outcome of the meeting project?

Not at all satisfied						Totally satisfied
1	2	3	4	5	6	7

2. How do you think *other members of the meeting/project group would rate you* in terms of your influence on what took place?

No influence						Very high influence
1	2	3	4	5	6	7

3. In your opinion, how *ethical* is any decision that was reached?

Highly unethical						Highly ethical
1	2	3	4	5	6	7

4. To what extent did you feel "*pushed into*" going along with the decision?

Not pushed into it at all						Very pushed into it
1	2	3	4	5	6	7

5. How *committed* are *you* to the agreements reached?

Not at all committed						Highly committed
1	2	3	4	5	6	7

6. Did you understand what was expected of you as a member of the meeting or project group?

Not at all clear						Perfectly clear
1	2	3	4	5	6	7

7. Were participants in the meeting/project group discussions listening to each other?

Never						Always
1	2	3	4	5	6	7

8. Were participants in the meeting/project group discussions honest and open in communicating with one another?

Never						Always
1	2	3	4	5	6	7

9. Was the meeting/project completed efficiently?

Not at all						Very much
1	2	3	4	5	6	7

10. Was the outcome of the meeting/project something that you felt proud to be a part of?

Not at all						Very much
1	2	3	4	5	6	7

INSTRUCTIONS

In groups (actual meeting/project group or as assigned by the instructor) share results and discuss their implications (a) for you, and (b) for the effectiveness of meetings and group project work in general.

Source: Developed from Roy J. Lewicki, Donald D. Bowen, Douglas T. Hall, and Francine S. Hall, *Experiences in Management and Organizational Behavior*, 4th ed. (New York: Wiley, 1997), pp. 195–197.

EXERCISE 21

Why Do We Work?

PREPARATION

Read the following "ancient story."

In days of old a wandering youth happened upon a group of men working in a quarry. Stopping by the first man, he said, "What are you doing?" The worker grimaced and groaned as he replied, "I am trying to shape this stone, and it is back-breaking work." Moving to the next man, he repeated the question. This man showed little emotion as he answered, "I am shaping a stone for a building." Moving to the third man, our traveller heard him singing as he worked. "What are you doing?" asked the youth. "I am helping to build a cathedral," the man proudly replied.

INSTRUCTIONS

In groups assigned by your instructor, discuss this short story. Ask and answer the question: "What are the lessons of this ancient story for (a) workers and (b) managers of today?" Ask members of the group to role-play each of the stonecutters, respectively, while they answer a second question asked by the youth: "Why are you working?" Have someone in the group be prepared to report and share the group's responses with the class as a whole.

Source: Developed from Brian Dumaine, "Why Do We Work," *Fortune* (December 26, 1994), pp. 196–204.

EXERCISE 22

The Case of the Contingency Workforce

PREPARATION

Part-time and contingency work is a rising percentage of the total employment in Canada. Go to the library and read about the current use of part-time and contingency workers in business and industry. Ideally, go to the Internet, enter a government website, like "Statistics Canada" and locate some current statistics on the size of the contingent labour force, the proportion that is self-employed and part-time, and the proportion of part-timers who are voluntary and involuntary.

INSTRUCTIONS

In your assigned work group, pool the available information on the contingency workforce. Discuss the information. Discuss one another's viewpoints on the subject as well as its personal and social implications. Be prepared to participate in a classroom "dialogue session" in which your group will be asked to role-play one of the following positions:

a. Vice president for human resources of a large discount retailer hiring contingency workers.

b. Owner of a local specialty music shop hiring contingency workers.

c. Recent graduate of your college or university working as a contingency employee at the discount retailer in (a).

d. Single parent with two children in elementary school, working as a contingency employee of the music shop in (b).

The question to be answered by the (a) and (b) groups is "What does the contingency workforce mean to me?" The question to be answered by the (c) and (d) groups is "What does being a contingency worker mean to me?"

EXERCISE 23

The "Best" Job Design

PREPARATION

Use the left-hand column to rank the following job characteristics in the order most important *to you* (1 = highest to 10 = lowest). Then use the right-hand column to rank them in the order in which you think they are most important *to others*.

___ Variety of tasks ___
___ Performance feedback ___
___ Autonomy/freedom in work ___
___ Working on a team ___
___ Having responsibility ___
___ Making friends on the job ___
___ Doing all of a job, not part ___
___ Importance of job to others ___
___ Having resources to do well ___
___ Flexible work schedule ___

INSTRUCTIONS

Form work groups as assigned by your instructor. Share your rankings with other group members. Discuss where you have different individual preferences and where your impressions differ from the preferences of others. Are there any major patterns in your group—for either the "personal" or the "other" rankings? Develop group consensus rankings for each column. Designate a spokesperson to share the group rankings and results of any discussion with the rest of the class.

Source: Developed from John M. Ivancevich and Michael T. Matteson, *Organizational Behavior and Management*, 2nd ed. (Homewood, IL: BPI/Irwin, 1990), p. 500.

EXERCISE 24

Upward Appraisal

INSTRUCTIONS

Form into work groups as assigned by the instructor. The instructor will then leave the room. As a group, complete the following tasks:

1. Within each group create a master list of comments, problems, issues, and concerns about the course experience to date that members would like to communicate with the instructor.

2. Select one person from the group to act as spokesperson and give your feedback to the instructor when he or she returns to the classroom.

3. The spokespersons from all the groups should meet to decide how the room should be physically arranged (placement of tables, chairs, etc.) for the feedback session. This should allow the spokespersons and instructor to communicate while they are being observed by other class members.

4. While the spokespersons are meeting, members remaining in the groups should discuss what they expect to observe during the feedback session.

5. The classroom should be rearranged. The instructor should be invited in.

6. Spokespersons should deliver feedback to the instructor while observers make notes.

7. After the feedback session is complete, the instructor will call on observers for comments, ask the spokespersons for their reactions, and engage the class in general discussion about the exercise and its implications.

Source: Developed from Eugene Owens, "Upward Appraisal: An Exercise in Subordinate's Critique of Superior's Performance," *Exchange: The Organizational Behavior Teaching Journal*, vol. 3 (1978), pp. 41–42.

EXERCISE 25

How to Give, and Take, Criticism

PREPARATION

The "criticism session" may well be the toughest test of a manager's communication skills. Picture Setting 1—you and a subordinate meeting to review a problem with the subordinate's performance. Now picture Setting 2—you and your boss meeting to review a problem with *your* performance. Both situations require communication skills in giving and receiving feedback. Even the most experienced person can have difficulty, and the situations can end as futile gripe sessions that cause hard feelings. The question is "How can such 'criticism sessions' be handled in a positive manner that encourages improved performance … and good feelings?"

INSTRUCTIONS

Form into groups as assigned by the instructor. Focus on either Setting 1 or Setting 2, or both as also assigned by the instructor. First, answer the question from the perspective assigned. Second, develop a series of action guidelines that could best be used to handle situations of this type. Third, prepare and present a mini-management training session to demonstrate the (a) unsuccessful and (b) successful use of these guidelines.

If time permits, outside of class prepare a more extensive management training session that includes a videotape demonstration of your assigned criticism setting being handled first poorly and then very well. Support the videotape with additional written handouts and an oral presentation to help your classmates better understand the communication skills needed to successfully give and take criticism in work settings.

EXERCISE 26

Lost at Sea

CONSIDER THIS SITUATION

You are adrift on a private yacht in the South Pacific when a fire of unknown origin destroys the yacht and most of its contents. You and a small group of survivors are now in a large raft with oars. Your location is unclear, but you estimate that you are about 1,500 km south-southwest of the nearest land. One person has just found in her pockets 5 $1 coins and a packet of matches. Everyone else's pockets are empty. The items at the right are available to you on the raft.

INSTRUCTIONS

1. *Working alone*, rank in Column **A** the 15 items in order of their importance to your survival ("1" is most important and "15" is least important).

2. *Working in an assigned group*, arrive at a "team" ranking of the 15 items and record this ranking in Column **B**. Appoint one person as group spokesperson to report your group rankings to the class.

3. *Do not write in Column* **C** until further instructions are provided by your instructor.

Source: Adapted from "Lost at Sea: A Consensus-Seeking Task," in *The 1975 Handbook for Group Facilitators*, University Associates, Inc.

	A	B	C
Sextant	___	___	___
Shaving mirror	___	___	___
25 litres water	___	___	___
Mosquito netting	___	___	___
1 survival meal	___	___	___
Maps of Pacific Ocean	___	___	___
Flotable seat cushion	___	___	___
10 litres oil-gas mix	___	___	___
Small transistor radio	___	___	___
Shark repellent	___	___	___
2 square metres black plastic	___	___	___
1 litre 20-proof rum	___	___	___
5 metres nylon rope	___	___	___
24 chocolate bars	___	___	___
Fishing kit	___	___	___

EXERCISE 27

Work Team Dynamics

PREPARATION

Think about your course work group, a work group you are involved in for another course, or any other group suggested by the instructor. Indicate how often each of the following statements accurately reflects your experience in the group. Use this scale:

1 = Always   2 = Frequently   3 = Sometimes
4 = Never

___ 1. My ideas get a fair hearing.

___ 2. I am encouraged to give innovative ideas and take risks.

___ 3. Diverse opinions within the group are encouraged.

___ 4. I have all the responsibility I want.

___ 5. There is a lot of favouritism shown in the group.

___ 6. Members trust one another to do their assigned work.

___ 7. The group sets high standards of performance excellence.

___ 8. People share and change jobs a lot in the group.

___ 9. You can make mistakes and learn from them in this group.

___ 10. This group has good operating rules.

INSTRUCTIONS

Form groups as assigned by your instructor. Ideally, this will be the group you have just rated. Have all group members share their ratings, and make one master rating for the group as a whole. Circle the items over which there are the biggest differences of opinion. Discuss those items and try to find out why they exist. In general, the better a group scores on this instrument, the higher its creative potential. If everyone has rated the same group, make a list of the five most important things members can do to improve its operations in the future. Nominate a spokesperson to summarize the group discussion for the class as a whole.

Source: Adapted from William Dyer, *Team Building*, 2nd ed. (Reading, MA: Addison-Wesley, 1987), pp. 123–125.

EXERCISE 28

Feedback and Assertiveness

INSTRUCTIONS

Indicate the degree of discomfort you would feel in each situation below by circling the appropriate number:

1. high discomfort
2. some discomfort
3. undecided
4. very little discomfort
5. no discomfort

1 2 3 4 5   1. Telling an employee who is also a friend that she or he must stop coming to work late.

1 2 3 4 5   2. Talking to an employee about his or her performance on the job.

1 2 3 4 5   3. Asking an employee if she or he has any comments about your rating of her or his performance.

1 2 3 4 5   4. Telling an employee who has problems in dealing with other employees that he or she should do something about it.

1 2 3 4 5   5. Responding to an employee who is upset over your rating of his or her performance.

EXERCISES IN TEAMWORK

1 2 3 4 5   **6.** An employee's becoming emotional and defensive when you tell her or him about mistakes on the job.

1 2 3 4 5   **7.** Giving a rating that indicates improvement is needed to an employee who has failed to meet minimum requirements of the job.

1 2 3 4 5   **8.** Letting a subordinate talk during an appraisal interview.

1 2 3 4 5   **9.** An employee's challenging you to justify your evaluation in the middle of an appraisal interview.

1 2 3 4 5   **10.** Recommending that an employee be discharged.

1 2 3 4 5   **11.** Telling an employee that you are uncomfortable with the role of having to judge his or her performance.

1 2 3 4 5   **12.** Telling an employee that her or his performance can be improved.

1 2 3 4 5   **13.** Telling an employee that you will not tolerate his or her taking extended coffee breaks.

1 2 3 4 5   **14.** Telling an employee that you will not tolerate her or his making personal telephone calls on company time.

INSTRUCTIONS

Form three-person teams as assigned by the instructor. Identify the 3 behaviours with which they indicate the most discomfort. Then each team member should practise performing these behaviours with another member, while the third member acts as an observer. Be direct, but try to perform the behaviour in an appropriate way. Listen to feedback from the observer and try the behaviours again, perhaps with different members of the group. When finished, discuss the exercise overall. Be prepared to participate in further class discussion.

Source: Adapted from Judith R. Gordan, *A Diagnostic Approach to Organizational Behavior*, 3rd edition. (Boston: Allyn & Bacon, 1991).

EXERCISE 29

Creative Solutions

INSTRUCTIONS

Complete these 5 tasks while working alone. Be prepared to present and explain your responses in class.

1. Divide the following shape into four pieces of exactly the same size.

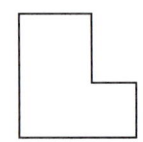

2. Without lifting your pencil from the paper, draw no more than 4 lines that cross through all of the following dots.

3. Draw the design for a machine that will turn the pages of your textbook so you can eat a snack while studying.

4. Why would a wheelbarrow ever be designed this way?

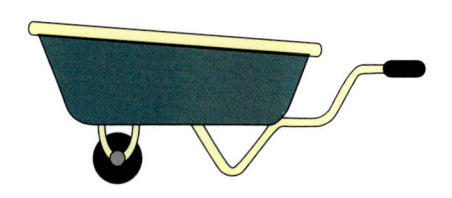

5. Turn the following into words.
   (a) ___ program
   (b) r\e\a\d\i\n\g
   (c) ECNALG
   (d) j
       u
       yousme
       t
   (e) stand
       i

OPTIONAL INSTRUCTIONS

After working alone, share your responses with a nearby classmate or with a group. See if you can develop different and/or better solutions based on this exchange of ideas.

Source: Ideas 2 and 5 found in Russell L. Ackoff, *The Art of Problem Solving* (New York: Wiley, 1978); ideas 1 and 4 found in Edward De Bono, *Lateral Thinking: Creativity Step by Step* (New York: Harper & Row, 1970); source for 5 is unknown.

EXERCISE 30

Force-Field Analysis

INSTRUCTIONS

1. Form into your class discussion groups.
2. Review the concept of force-field analysis—the consideration of forces driving in support of a planned change and forces resisting the change.

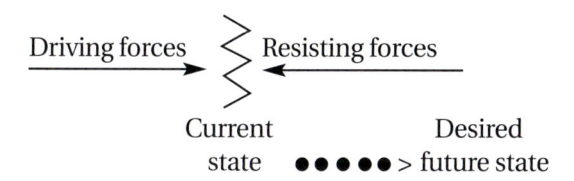

Driving forces → ⋛ ← Resisting forces

Current state ●●●●● > Desired future state

3. Use this force-field analysis worksheet in the assignment:

   List of Driving Forces (those supporting the change)

   _____
   _____ … list as many as you can think of

   List of Resisting Forces (those working against the change)

   _____
   _____ … list as many as you can think of

4. Apply force-field analysis and make your lists of driving and resisting forces for one of the following situations:

(a) Due to rapid advances in Web-based computer technologies, the possibility exists that the course you are presently taking could be in part offered online. This would mean a reduction in the number of required class sessions but an increase in students' responsibility for completing learning activities and assignments through computer mediation.

(b) A new owner has just taken over a small walk-in-and-buy-by-the-slice pizza shop in a college town. There are eight employees, three of whom are full-time and five of whom are part-timers. The shop is open seven days a week from 10:30 a.m. to 10:30 p.m. each day. The new owner believes there is a market niche available for late-night pizza and would like to stay open each night until 2 a.m.

(c) A situation assigned by the instructor.

5. Choose the three driving forces that are most significant to the proposed change. For each force develop ideas on how it could be further increased or mobilized in support of the change.

6. Choose the three resisting forces that are most significant to the proposed change. For each force develop ideas on how it could be reduced or turned into a driving force.

7. Be prepared to participate in a class discussion led by the instructor.

SELF-ASSESSMENTS

ASSESSMENT 1

A 21st-Century Manager?

INSTRUCTIONS

Rate yourself on the following personal characteristics. Use this scale.

S = Strong, I am very confident with this one.

G = Good, but I still have room to grow.

W = Weak, I really need work on this one.

U = Unsure, I just don't know.

1. *Resistance to stress:* The ability to get work done even under stressful conditions.
2. *Tolerance for uncertainty:* The ability to get work done even under ambiguous and uncertain conditions.
3. *Social objectivity:* The ability to act free of racial, ethnic, gender, and other prejudices or biases.
4. *Inner work standards:* The ability to personally set and work to high performance standards.
5. *Stamina:* The ability to sustain long work hours.
6. *Adaptability:* The ability to be flexible and adapt to changes.

7. *Self-confidence:* The ability to be consistently decisive and display one's personal presence.

8. *Self-objectivity:* The ability to evaluate personal strengths and weaknesses and to understand one's motives and skills relative to a job.

9. *Introspection:* The ability to learn from experience, awareness, and self-study.

10. *Entrepreneurism:* The ability to address problems and take advantage of opportunities for constructive change.

SCORING

Give yourself 1 point for each S, and 1/2 point for each G. Do not give yourself points for W and U responses. Total your points and enter the result here [PMF = ___].

INTERPRETATION

This assessment offers a self-described *profile of your management foundations* (PMF). Are you a perfect 10, or is your PMF score something less than that? There shouldn't be too many 10s around. Ask someone who knows you to assess you on this instrument. You may be surprised at the differences between your PMF score as you described it and your PMF score as described by someone else. Most of us, realistically speaking, must work hard to grow and develop continually in these and related management foundations. This list is a good starting point as you consider where and how to further pursue the development of your managerial skills and competencies. The items on the list are recommended by the American Assembly of Collegiate Schools of Business (AACSB) as the skills and personal characteristics that should be nurtured in college and university students of business administration. Their success—and yours—as 21st-century managers may well rest on (1) an initial awareness of the importance of these basic management foundations and (2) a willingness to strive continually to strengthen them throughout the work career.

Source: See *Outcome Measurement Project*, Phase I and Phase II Reports (St. Louis: American Assembly of Collegiate Schools of Business, 1986 and 1987).

ASSESSMENT 2

Emotional Intelligence

INSTRUCTIONS

Rate yourself on how well you are able to display the abilities for each item listed below. As you score each item, try to think of actual situations in which you have been called upon to use the ability. Use the following scale.

1	2	3	4	5	6	7
Low Ability			Neutral			High Ability

1 2 3 4 5 6 7 **1.** Identify changes in physiological arousal.

1 2 3 4 5 6 7 **2.** Relax when under pressure in situations.

1 2 3 4 5 6 7 **3.** Act productively when angry.

1 2 3 4 5 6 7 **4.** Act productively in situations that arouse anxiety.

1 2 3 4 5 6 7 **5.** Calm yourself quickly when angry.

1 2 3 4 5 6 7 **6.** Associate different physical cues with different emotions.

1 2 3 4 5 6 7 **7.** Use internal "talk" to affect your emotional states.

1 2 3 4 5 6 7 **8.** Communicate your feelings effectively.

1 2 3 4 5 6 7 **9.** Reflect on negative feelings without being distressed.

1 2 3 4 5 6 7 **10.** Stay calm when you are the target of anger from others.

1 2 3 4 5 6 7 **11.** Know when you are thinking negatively.

1 2 3 4 5 6 7 **12.** Know when your "self-talk" is instructional.

1 2 3 4 5 6 7   13. Know when you are becoming angry.
1 2 3 4 5 6 7   14. Know how you interpret events you encounter.
1 2 3 4 5 6 7   15. Know what senses you are currently using.
1 2 3 4 5 6 7   16. Accurately communicate what you experience.
1 2 3 4 5 6 7   17. Identify what information influences your interpretations.
1 2 3 4 5 6 7   18. Identify when you experience mood shifts.
1 2 3 4 5 6 7   19. Know when you become defensive.
1 2 3 4 5 6 7   20. Know the impact your behaviour has on others.
1 2 3 4 5 6 7   21. Know when you communicate incongruently.
1 2 3 4 5 6 7   22. "Gear up" at will.
1 2 3 4 5 6 7   23. Regroup quickly after a setback.
1 2 3 4 5 6 7   24. Complete long-term tasks in designated time frames.
1 2 3 4 5 6 7   25. Produce high energy when doing uninteresting work.
1 2 3 4 5 6 7   26. Stop or change ineffective habits.
1 2 3 4 5 6 7   27. Develop new and more productive patterns of behaviour.
1 2 3 4 5 6 7   28. Follow words with actions.
1 2 3 4 5 6 7   29. Work out conflicts.
1 2 3 4 5 6 7   30. Develop consensus with others.
1 2 3 4 5 6 7   31. Mediate conflict between others.
1 2 3 4 5 6 7   32. Exhibit effective interpersonal communication skills.
1 2 3 4 5 6 7   33. Articulate the thoughts of a group.
1 2 3 4 5 6 7   34. Influence others, directly or indirectly.
1 2 3 4 5 6 7   35. Build trust with others.
1 2 3 4 5 6 7   36. Build support teams.
1 2 3 4 5 6 7   37. Make others feel good.
1 2 3 4 5 6 7   38. Provide advice and support to others, as needed.
1 2 3 4 5 6 7   39. Accurately reflect people's feelings back to them.
1 2 3 4 5 6 7   40. Recognize when others are distressed.
1 2 3 4 5 6 7   41. Help others manage their emotions.
1 2 3 4 5 6 7   42. Show empathy to others.
1 2 3 4 5 6 7   43. Engage in intimate conversations with others.
1 2 3 4 5 6 7   44. Help a group to manage emotions.
1 2 3 4 5 6 7   45. Detect incongruence between others' emotions or feelings and their behaviours.

SCORING

This instrument measures six dimensions of your emotional intelligence. Find your scores as follows.

Self-awareness—Add scores for items 1, 6, 11, 12, 13, 14, 15, 16, 17, 18, 19, 20, 21

Managing emotions—Add scores for items 1, 2, 3, 4, 5, 7, 9, 10, 13, 27

Self-motivation—Add scores for items 7, 22, 23, 25, 26, 27, 28

Relating well—Add scores for items 8, 10, 16, 19, 20, 29, 30, 31, 32, 33, 34, 35, 36, 37, 38, 39, 42, 43, 44, 45

Emotional mentoring—Add scores for items 8, 10, 16, 18, 34, 35, 37, 38, 39, 40, 41, 44, 45

INTERPRETATION

The prior scoring indicates your self-perceived abilities in these dimensions of emotional intelligence. To further examine your tendencies, go back for each dimension and sum the number of responses you had that were 4 and lower (suggesting lower ability), and sum the number of responses you had that were 5 or better (suggesting higher ability). This gives you an indication by dimension of where you may have room to grow and develop your emotional intelligence abilities.

Source: Scale from Hendrie Weisinger, *Emotional Intelligence at Work* (San Francisco: Jossey-Bass, 1998), pp. 214–15. Used by permission.

ASSESSMENT 3

Learning Tendencies

INSTRUCTIONS

In each of the following pairs, distribute 10 points between the two statements to best describe how you like to learn. For example:

_3_ (a) I like to read.

_7_ (b) I like to listen to lectures.

1. _____ (a) I like to learn through working with other people and being engaged in concrete experiences.

   _____ (b) I like to learn through logical analysis and systematic attempts to understand a situation.

2. _____ (a) I like to learn by observing things, viewing them from different perspectives, and finding meaning in situations.

   _____ (b) I like to learn by taking risks, getting things done, and influencing events through actions taken.

SCORING

Place "dots" on the following graph to record the above scores: "Doing" = 2b. "Watching" = 1b. "Feeling" = 1a. "Thinking" = 2a. Connect the dots to plot your learning tendencies.

INTERPRETATION

This activity provides a first impression of your learning tendencies or style. Four possible learning styles are identified on the graph—convergers, accommodators, divergers, and assimilators. Consider the following descriptions for their accuracy in describing you. For a truly good reading on your learning tendencies, ask several others to complete the Step 1 questions for you, and then assess how their results compare with your own perceptions.

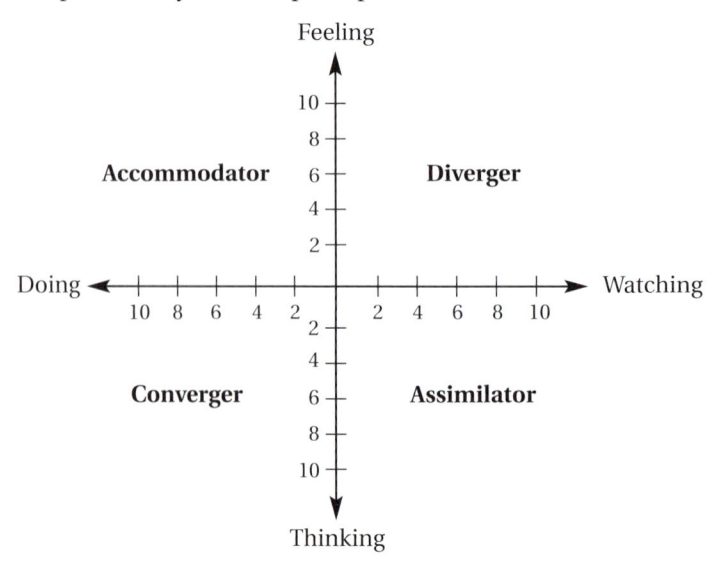

Convergers—combined tendencies toward abstract conceptualization (thinking) and active experimentation (doing). They like to learn in practical situations. They prefer to deal with technical issues and solve problems through systematic investigation of alternatives. Good at experimentation, finding new ways of doing things, making decisions.

Accommodators—combine concrete experience (feeling) with active experimentation (doing). They like to learn from hands-on experience. They prefer "gut" responses to problems rather than systematic analysis of alternatives. Good at influencing others, committing to goals, seeking opportunities.

Divergers—combine concrete experience (feeling) with reflective observation (watching). They like to learn from observation. They prefer to participate in brainstorming and imaginative information gathering. Good at listening, imagining, and being sensitive to feelings.

Assimilators—combine abstract conceptualization (thinking) with reflective observation (watching). They like to learn through information. They prefer ideas and concepts to people and value logical reasoning. Good at organizing information, building models, and analyzing data.

Source: Developed from David A. Kolb, "Learning Style Inventory" (Boston, MA: McBer & Company, 1985); see also his article "On Management and the Learning Process," in David A. Kolb, Irwin M. Rubin, and James M. McIntyre, eds., *Organizational Psychology: A Book of Readings*, 2nd ed. (Englewood Cliffs, NJ: Prentice-Hall, 1974), pp. 27–42.

ASSESSMENT 4

What Are Your Managerial Assumptions?

INSTRUCTIONS

Read the following statements. Use the space in the margins to write "Yes" if you agree with the statement, or "No" if you disagree with it. Force yourself to take a "yes" or "no" position. Do this for every statement.

1. Are good pay and a secure job enough to satisfy most workers?
2. Should a manager help and coach subordinates in their work?
3. Do most people like real responsibility in their jobs?
4. Are most people afraid to learn new things in their jobs?
5. Should managers let subordinates control the quality of their work?
6. Do most people dislike work?
7. Are most people creative?
8. Should a manager closely supervise and direct the work of subordinates?
9. Do most people tend to resist change?
10. Do most people work only as hard as they have to?
11. Should workers be allowed to set their own job goals?
12. Are most people happiest off the job?
13. Do most workers really care about the organization they work for?
14. Should a manager help subordinates advance and grow in their jobs?

SCORING

Count the number of "yes" responses to items 1, 4, 6, 8, 9, 10, 12; write that number here as [X = ___]. Count the number of "yes" responses to items 2, 3, 5, 7, 11, 13, 14; write that score here [Y = ___].

INTERPRETATION

This assessment sheds insight into your orientation toward Douglas McGregor's Theory X (your "X" score) and Theory Y (your "Y" score) assumptions. You should review the discussion of McGregor's thinking in Chapter 2 and consider further the ways in which you are likely to behave toward other people at work. Think, in particular, about the types of "self-fulfilling prophecies" you are likely to create.

ASSESSMENT 5

Terminal Values Survey

INSTRUCTIONS

Rate each of the following values in terms of its importance to you. Think about each value *in terms of its importance as a guiding principle in your life.* As you work, consider each value in relation to all the other values listed in the survey.

TERMINAL VALUES

1. A comfortable life   1   2   3   4   5   6   7
   Of lesser importance — Of greater importance

2. An exciting life   1   2   3   4   5   6   7
   Of lesser importance — Of greater importance

3. A sense of accomplishment   1   2   3   4   5   6   7
   Of lesser importance — Of greater importance

4. A world at peace   1   2   3   4   5   6   7
   Of lesser importance — Of greater importance

5. A world of beauty   1   2   3   4   5   6   7
   Of lesser importance — Of greater importance

6. Equality   1   2   3   4   5   6   7
   Of lesser importance — Of greater importance

7. Family security   1   2   3   4   5   6   7
   Of lesser importance — Of greater importance

8. Freedom   1   2   3   4   5   6   7
   Of lesser importance — Of greater importance

9. Happiness	1	2	3	4	5	6	7	
	Of lesser importance						Of greater importance	
10. Inner harmony	1	2	3	4	5	6	7	
	Of lesser importance						Of greater importance	
11. Mature love	1	2	3	4	5	6	7	
	Of lesser importance						Of greater importance	
12. National security	1	2	3	4	5	6	7	
	Of lesser importance						Of greater importance	
13. Pleasure	1	2	3	4	5	6	7	
	Of lesser importance						Of greater importance	
14. Salvation	1	2	3	4	5	6	7	
	Of lesser importance						Of greater importance	
15. Self-respect	1	2	3	4	5	6	7	
	Of lesser importance						Of greater importance	
16. Social recognition	1	2	3	4	5	6	7	
	Of lesser importance						Of greater importance	
17. True friendship	1	2	3	4	5	6	7	
	Of lesser importance						Of greater importance	
18. Wisdom	1	2	3	4	5	6	7	
	Of lesser importance						Of greater importance	

SCORING

To score this instrument, you must multiply your score for each item times a "weight"—e.g. (#3 × 5) = your new question 3 score.

1. Calculate your Personal Values Score as: (#1 × 5) + (#2 × 4) + (#3 × 4) + (#7) + (#8) + (#9 × 4) + (#10 × 5) + (#11 × 4) + (#13 × 5) + (#14 × 3) + (#15 × 5) + (#16 × 3) + (#17 × 4) + (#18 × 5)
2. Calculate your Social Values Score as: (#4 × 5) + (#5 × 3) + (#6 × 5) + (#12 × 5)
3. Calculate your Terminal Values Score as: Personal Values − Social Values

INTERPRETATION

Terminal values reflect a person's preferences concerning the "ends" to be achieved. They are the goals individuals would like to achieve in their lifetimes.

Different value items receive different weights in this scale. (Example: "A comfortable life" receives a weight of "5" while "Freedom" receives a weight of "1.") Your score on Personal Values has your Social Values score subtracted from it to determine your Terminal Values score.

Source: Adapted from James Weber, "Management Value Orientations: A Typology and Assessment," *International Journal of Value Based Management*, vol. 3, no. 2 (1990), pp. 37–54.

ASSESSMENT 6

Instrumental Values Survey

INSTRUCTIONS

Rate each of the following values in terms of its importance to you. Think about each value in terms of its importance as a guiding principle in your life. As you work, consider each value in relation to all the other values listed in the survey.

INSTRUMENTAL VALUES

1. Ambitious — 1 2 3 4 5 6 7
   Of lesser importance — Of greater importance

2. Broadminded — 1 2 3 4 5 6 7
   Of lesser importance — Of greater importance

3. Capable — 1 2 3 4 5 6 7
   Of lesser importance — Of greater importance

4. Cheerful — 1 2 3 4 5 6 7
   Of lesser importance — Of greater importance

5. Clean — 1 2 3 4 5 6 7
   Of lesser importance — Of greater importance

6. Courageous — 1 2 3 4 5 6 7
   Of lesser importance — Of greater importance

7. Forgiving — 1 2 3 4 5 6 7
   Of lesser importance — Of greater importance

8. Helpful — 1 2 3 4 5 6 7
   Of lesser importance — Of greater importance

9. Honest   1   2   3   4   5   6   7
Of lesser importance   Of greater importance

10. Imaginative   1   2   3   4   5   6   7
Of lesser importance   Of greater importance

11. Independent   1   2   3   4   5   6   7
Of lesser importance   Of greater importance

12. Intellectual   1   2   3   4   5   6   7
Of lesser importance   Of greater importance

13. Logical   1   2   3   4   5   6   7
Of lesser importance   Of greater importance

14. Loving   1   2   3   4   5   6   7
Of lesser importance   Of greater importance

15. Obedient   1   2   3   4   5   6   7
Of lesser importance   Of greater importance

16. Polite   1   2   3   4   5   6   7
Of lesser importance   Of greater importance

17. Responsible   1   2   3   4   5   6   7
Of lesser importance   Of greater importance

18. Self-controlled   1   2   3   4   5   6   7
Of lesser importance   Of greater importance

SCORING

To score this instrument, you must multiply your score for each item times a "weight"—e.g. (#3 × 5) = your new question 3 score.

1. Calculate your Competence Values Score as: (#1 × 5) + (#2 × 2) + (#3 × 5) + (#10 × 5) + (#11 × 5) + (#12 × 5) + (#13 × 5) + (#17 × 4)

2. Calculate your Moral Values Score as: (#4 × 4) + (#5 × 3) + (#6 × 2) + (#7 × 5) + (#8 × 5) + (#9 × 2) + (#14 × 5) + (#15) + (#16 × 3)

3. Calculate your Instrumental Values Score as: Competence Values − Moral Values

INTERPRETATION

Instrumental Values are defined as the "means" for achieving desired ends. They represent how you might go about achieving your important end states, depending on the relative importance you attach to the instrumental values.

Different value items receive different weights in this scale. (Example: "Ambitious" receives a weight of "5" while "Obedient" receives a weight of "1.") Your score on Competence Values has your Moral Values score subtracted from it to determine your Instrumental Values score.

Source: Adapted from James Weber, "Management Value Orientations: A Typology and Assessment," *International Journal of Value Based Management*, vol. 3, no. 2 (1990), pp. 37–54.

ASSESSMENT 7

Diversity Awareness

INSTRUCTIONS

Complete the following questionnaire.

DIVERSITY AWARENESS CHECKLIST

Consider where you work or go to school as the setting for the following questions. Indicate "O" for often, "S" for sometimes, and "N" for never in response to each of the following questions as they pertain to the setting.

___ 1. How often have you heard jokes or remarks about other people that you consider offensive?

___ 2. How often do you hear men "talk down" to women in an attempt to keep them in an inferior status?

___ 3. How often have you felt personal discomfort as the object of sexual harassment?

___ 4. How often do you work or study with Asians or black Canadians?

___ 5. How often have you felt disadvantaged because members of ethnic groups other than yours were given special treatment?

___ 6. How often have you seen a woman put in an uncomfortable situation because of unwelcome advances by a man?

___ 7. How often does it seem that Asians, francophones, Caucasians, women, men, and members of minority demographic groups seem to "stick together" during work breaks or other leisure situations?

___ 8. How often do you feel uncomfortable about something you did and/or said to someone of the opposite sex or a member of an ethnic or racial group other than yours?

___ 9. How often do you feel efforts are made in this setting to raise the level of cross-cultural understanding among people who work and/or study together?

___ 10. How often do you step in to communicate concerns to others when you feel actions and/or words are used to the disadvantage of minorities?

SCORING

There are no correct answers for the Diversity Awareness Checklist.

INTERPRETATION

In the diversity checklist, the key issue is the extent to which you are "sensitive" to diversity issues in the workplace or university. Are you comfortable with your responses? How do you think others in your class responded? Why not share your responses with others and examine different viewpoints on this important issue?

Source: Items for the WV Cultural Awareness Quiz selected from a longer version by James P. Morgan, Jr., and published by University Associates, 1987.

ASSESSMENT 8

Global Readiness Index

INSTRUCTIONS

Rate yourself on each of the following items to establish a baseline measurement of your readiness to participate in the global work environment.

RATING SCALE

1 = Very Poor
2 = Poor
3 = Acceptable
4 = Good
5 = Very Good

___ 1. I understand my own culture in terms of its expectations, values, and influence on communication and relationships.

___ 2. When someone presents me with a different point of view, I try to understand it rather than attack it.

___ 3. I am comfortable dealing with situations where the available information is incomplete and the outcomes unpredictable.

___ 4. I am open to new situations and am always looking for new information and learning opportunities.

___ 5. I have a good understanding of the attitudes and perceptions toward my culture as they are held by people from other cultures.

___ 6. I am always gathering information about other countries and cultures and trying to learn from them.

___ 7. I am well informed regarding the major differences in government, political, and economic systems around the world.

___ 8. I work hard to increase my understanding of people from other cultures.

___ 9. I am able to adjust my communication style to work effectively with people from different cultures.

___ 10. I can recognize when cultural differences are influencing working relationships and adjust my attitudes and behaviour accordingly.

SCORING

The goal is to score as close to a perfect "5" as possible on each of the three dimensions of global readiness. Develop your scores as follows.

Items (1 + 2 + 3 + 4)/4
= ___ Global Mindset Score

Items (5 + 6 + 7)/3
= ___ Global Knowledge Score

Items (8 + 9 + 10)/3
= ___ Global Work Skills Score

INTERPRETATION

To be successful in the 21st-century work environment, you must be comfortable with the global economy and the cultural diversity that it holds. This requires a *global mindset* that is receptive to and respectful of cultural differences, *global knowledge* that includes the continuing quest to know and learn more about other nations and cultures, and *global work skills* that allow you to work effectively across cultures.

Source: Developed from "Is Your Company Really Global?", *Business Week* (December 1, 1997).

ASSESSMENT 9

Time Orientation

INSTRUCTIONS

This instrument examines your tendencies to favour "monochronic" or "polychronic" time orientations. Rate your tendencies for each item below using the following scale.

RATING SCALE

1 = Almost never
2 = Seldom
3 = Sometimes
4 = Usually
5 = Almost always

___ 1. I like to do one thing at a time.
___ 2. I have a strong tendency to build lifetime relationships.
___ 3. I concentrate on the job at hand.
___ 4. I base the level of promptness on the particular relationship.
___ 5. I take time commitments (deadlines, schedules) seriously.
___ 6. I borrow and lend things often and easily.
___ 7. I am committed to the job.
___ 8. Intimacy with family and friends is more important than respecting their privacy.
___ 9. I adhere closely to plans.
___ 10. I put obligations to family and friends before work concerns.
___ 11. I am concerned about not disturbing others (follow rules of privacy).
___ 12. I change plans often and easily.
___ 13. I emphasize promptness in meetings.
___ 14. I am committed to people and human relationships.
___ 15. I show great respect for private property (seldom borrow or lend).
___ 16. I am highly distractible and frequently interrupt what I am doing.
___ 17. I am comfortable with short-term relationships.
___ 18. I like to do many things at once.

SCORING

To obtain your monochronic time orientation score, sum results for items 1, 3, 5, 7, 9, 11, 13, 15, 17. To obtain your polychronic time orientation score, sum results for items 2, 4, 6, 8, 10, 12, 14, 16, 18.

INTERPRETATION

A person high in monochronic time orientation approaches time in a linear fashion with things dealt with one at a time in an orderly fashion. Time is viewed as a precious commodity, not to be wasted; this person values punctuality and promptness.

A person high in polychronic time orientation tends to do a number of things at once, intertwining them together in a dynamic process that considers changing circumstances. Commitments are viewed as objectives, but capable of adjustment when necessary.

Cultural differences in orientations toward time can be observed. Tendencies toward monochronic time orientation are common to North America and northern European cultures. Tendencies toward polychronic time orientation are common in cultures of the Middle East, Asia, and Latin America.

Source: Adapted from J. Ned Seelye and Alan Seelye-James. *Culture Clash* (Lincolnwood, IL: NTC Business Books, 1996).

ASSESSMENT 10

Entrepreneurship Orientation

INSTRUCTIONS

Answer the following questions.

1. What portion of your university expenses did you earn (or are you earning)?
   (a) 50 percent or more
   (b) less than 50 percent
   (c) none

2. In university, your academic performance was/is
   (a) above average.
   (b) average.
   (c) below average.

3. What is your basic reason for considering opening a business?
   (a) I want to make money.
   (b) I want to control my own destiny.
   (c) I hate the frustration of working for someone else.

4. Which phrase best describes your attitude toward work?
   (a) I can keep going as long as I need to; I don't mind working for something I want.
   (b) I can work hard for a while, but when I've had enough, I quit.
   (c) Hard work really doesn't get you anywhere.

5. How would you rate your organizing skills?
   (a) superorganized
   (b) above average
   (c) average
   (d) I do well if I can find half the things I look for

6. You are primarily a(n)
   (a) optimist.
   (b) pessimist.
   (c) neither.

7. You are faced with a challenging problem. As you work, you realize you are stuck. You will most likely
   (a) give up.
   (b) ask for help.
   (c) keep plugging; you'll figure it out.

8. You are playing a game with a group of friends. You are most interested in
   (a) winning.
   (b) playing well.
   (c) making sure that everyone has a good time.
   (d) cheating as much as possible.

9. How would you describe your feelings toward failure?
   (a) Fear of failure paralyzes me.
   (b) Failure can be a good learning experience.
   (c) Knowing that I might fail motivates me to work even harder.
   (d) "Damn the torpedoes! Full speed ahead."

10. Which phrase best describes you?
    (a) I need constant encouragement to get anything done.
    (b) If someone gets me started, I can keep going.
    (c) I am energetic and hard-working—a self-starter.

11. Which bet would you most likely accept?
    (a) a wager on a dog race
    (b) a wager on a racquetball game in which you play an opponent
    (c) Neither. I never make wagers.

12. At the Kentucky Derby, you would bet on
    (a) the 100-to-1 long shot.
    (b) the odds-on favourite.
    (c) the 3-to-1 shot.

(d) none of the above.

SCORING

Give yourself 10 points for each of the following answers: 1a, 2a, 3c, 4a, 5a, 6a, 7c, 8a, 9c, 10c, 11b, 12c; total the scores and enter the results here [I = ___]. Give yourself 8 points for each of the following answers: 3b, 8b, 9b; total the scores and enter the results here [II = ___]. Give yourself 6 points for each of the following answers; 2b, 5b; total the scores and enter the results here [III = ___]. Give yourself 5 points for this answer: 1b; enter the result here [IV = ___]. Give yourself 4 points for this answer: 5c; enter the result here [V = ___]. Give yourself 2 points for each of the following answers: 2c, 3a, 4b, 6c, 9d, 10b, 11a, 12b; total the scores and enter the results here [VI = ___]. Any other scores are worth 0 points. Total your summary scores for I + II + III + IV + V + VI and enter the result here [EP = ___].

INTERPRETATION

This assessment offers an impression of your *entrepreneurial profile*, or EP. It compares your characteristics with those of typical entrepreneurs. Your instructor can provide further information on each question as well as some additional insights into the backgrounds of entrepreneurs. You may locate your EP score on the following grid.

100 +	= Entrepreneur extraordinaire
80–99	= Entrepreneur
60–79	= Potential entrepreneur
0–59	= Entrepreneur in the rough

Source: Instrument adapted from Norman M. Scarborough and Thomas W. Zimmerer, *Effective Small Business Management*, 3rd ed. (Columbus: Merrill, 1991), pp. 26–27.

ASSESSMENT 11

Your Intuitive Ability

INSTRUCTIONS

Complete this survey as quickly as you can. Be honest with yourself. For each question, select the response that most appeals to you.

1. When working on a project, do you prefer to
    (a) be told what the problem is but be left free to decide how to solve it?
    (b) get very clear instructions about how to go about solving the problem before you start?

2. When working on a project, do you prefer to work with colleagues who are
    (a) realistic?
    (b) imaginative?

3. Do you most admire people who are
    (a) creative?
    (b) careful?

4. Do the friends you choose tend to be
    (a) serious and hard working?
    (b) exciting and often emotional?

5. When you ask a colleague for advice on a problem you have, do you
    (a) seldom or never get upset if he or she questions your basic assumptions?
    (b) often get upset if he or she questions your basic assumptions?

6. When you start your day, do you
    (a) seldom make or follow a specific plan?
    (b) usually first make a plan to follow?

7. When working with numbers do you find that you
    (a) seldom or never make factual errors?
    (b) often make factual errors?

8. Do you find that you
    (a) seldom daydream during the day and really don't enjoy doing so when you do it?
    (b) frequently daydream during the day and enjoy doing so?

9. When working on a problem, do you
    (a) prefer to follow the instructions or rules when they are given to you?

(b) often enjoy circumventing the instructions or rules when they are given to you?

10. When you are trying to put something together, do you prefer to have

   (a) step-by-step written instructions on how to assemble the item?

   (b) a picture of how the item is supposed to look once assembled?

11. Do you find that the person who irritates you the most is the one who appears to be

   (a) disorganized?

   (b) organized?

12. When an unexpected crisis comes up that you have to deal with, do you

   (a) feel anxious about the situation?

   (b) feel excited by the challenge of the situation?

SCORING

Total the number of "a" responses circled for questions 1, 3, 5, 6, 11; enter the score here [A = ___]. Total the number of "b" responses for questions 2, 4, 7, 8, 9, 10, 12; enter the score here [B = ___]. Add your "a" and "b" scores and enter the sum here [A + B = ___]. This is your intuitive score. The highest possible intuitive score is 12; the lowest is 0.

INTERPRETATION

In his book *Intuition in Organizations* (Newbury Park, CA: Sage, 1989), pp. 10–11, Weston H. Agor states, "Traditional analytical techniques…are not as useful as they once were for guiding major decisions. … If you hope to be better prepared for tomorrow, then it only seems logical to pay some attention to the use and development of intuitive skills for decision making." Agor developed the preceding survey to help people assess their tendencies to use intuition in decision making. Your score offers a general impression of your strength in this area. It may also suggest a need to further develop your skill and comfort with more intuitive decision approaches.

Source: AIM Survey (El Paso, TX: ENFP Enterprises, 1989). Copyright ©1989 by Weston H. Agor.

ASSESSMENT 12

Assertiveness

INSTRUCTIONS

This instrument measures tendencies toward aggressive, passive, and assertive behaviours in work situations. For each statement below, decide which of the following answers best fits you.

1 = Never true
2 = Sometimes true
3 = Often true
4 = Always true

___ 1. I respond with more modesty than I really feel when my work is complimented.

___ 2. If people are rude, I will be rude right back.

___ 3. Other people find me interesting.

___ 4. I find it difficult to speak up in a group of strangers.

___ 5. I don't mind using sarcasm if it helps me make a point.

___ 6. I ask for a raise when I feel I really deserve it.

___ 7. If others interrupt me when I am talking, I suffer in silence.

___ 8. If people criticize my work, I find a way to make them back down.

___ 9. I can express pride in my accomplishments without being boastful.

___ 10. People take advantage of me.

___ 11. I tell people what they want to hear if it helps me get what I want.

___ 12. I find it easy to ask for help.

___ 13. I lend things to others even when I don't really want to.

___ 14. I win arguments by dominating the discussion.

___ 15. I can express my true feelings to someone I really care for.

___ 16. When I feel angry with other people, I bottle it up rather than express it.

___ 17. When I criticize someone else's work, they get mad.

___ 18. I feel confident in my ability to stand up for my rights.

SCORING

Obtain your scores as follows:

Aggressiveness tendency score—Add items 2, 5, 8, 11, 14, and 17

Passive tendency score—Add items 1, 4, 7, 10, 13, and 16

Assertiveness tendency score—Add items 3, 6, 9, 12, 15, and 18

INTERPRETATION

The maximum score in any single area is 24. The minimum score is 6. Try to find someone who knows you well. Have this person complete the instrument also as it relates to you. Compare his or her impression of you with your own score. What is this telling you about your behaviour tendencies in social situations?

Source: From Douglas T. Hall, Donald D. Bowen, Roy J. Lewicki, and Francine S. Hall, *Experiences in Management and Organizational Behaviour*, 2nd ed. (New York: Wiley, 1985). Used by permission.

ASSESSMENT 13

Time Management Profile

INSTRUCTIONS

Complete the following questionnaire by indicating "Y" (yes) or "N" (no) for each item. Force yourself to respond yes or no. Be frank and allow your responses to create an accurate picture of how you tend to respond to these kinds of situations.

___ 1. When confronted with several items of similar urgency and importance, I tend to do the easiest one first.

___ 2. I do the most important things during that part of the day when I know I perform best.

___ 3. Most of the time I don't do things someone else can do; I delegate this type of work to others.

___ 4. Even though meetings without a clear and useful purpose upset me, I put up with them.

___ 5. I skim documents before reading them and don't complete any that offer a low return on my time investment.

___ 6. I don't worry much if I don't accomplish at least one significant task each day.

___ 7. I save the most trivial tasks for that time of day when my creative energy is lowest.

___ 8. My workspace is neat and organized.

___ 9. My office door is always "open"; I never work in complete privacy.

___ 10. I schedule my time completely from start to finish every workday.

___ 11. I don't like "to do" lists, preferring to respond to daily events as they occur.

___ 12. I "block" a certain amount of time each day or week that is dedicated to high-priority activities.

SCORING

Count the number of "Y" responses to items 2, 3, 5, 7, 8, 12. [Enter that score here ___.] Count the number of "N" responses to items 1, 4, 6, 9, 10, 11. [Enter that score here ___.] Add together the two scores.

INTERPRETATION

The higher the total score, the closer your behaviour matches recommended time management guidelines. Reread those items where your response did not match the desired one. Why don't they match? Do you have reasons why your behaviour in this instance should be different from the recommended time management guideline? Think about what you can do (and how easily it can be done) to adjust your behaviour to be more consistent with these guidelines. For further reading, see Alan Lakein, *How to Control Your Time and Your Life* (New York: David McKay, no date), and William Oncken, *Managing Management Time* (Englewood Cliffs, NJ: Prentice Hall, 1984).

Source: Suggested by a discussion in Robert E. Quinn, Sue R. Faerman, Michael P. Thompson, and Michael R. McGrath, *Becoming a Master Manager: A Contemporary Framework* (New York: Wiley, 1990), pp. 75–76.

ASSESSMENT 14

Facts and Inferences

PREPARATION

Often, when we listen or speak, we don't distinguish between statements of fact and those of inference. Yet, there are great differences between the two. We create barriers to clear thinking when we treat inferences (guesses, opinions) as if they are facts. You may wish at this point to test your ability to distinguish facts from inferences by taking the accompanying fact-inference test based on those by Haney (1973).

INSTRUCTIONS

Carefully read the following report and the observations based on it. Indicate whether you think the observations are true, false, or doubtful on the basis of the information presented in the report. Write T if the observation is definitely true, F if the observation is definitely false, and ? if the observation may be either true or false. Judge each observation in order. Do not reread the observations after you have indicated your judgement, and do not change any of your answers.

A well-liked university instructor had just completed making up the final examinations and had turned off the lights in the office. Just then a tall, broad figure with dark glasses appeared and demanded the examination. The professor opened the drawer. Everything in the drawer was picked up, and the individual ran down the corridor. The president was notified immediately.

___ 1. The thief was tall, broad, and wore dark glasses.
___ 2. The professor turned off the lights.
___ 3. A tall figure demanded the examination.
___ 4. The examination was picked up by someone.
___ 5. The examination was picked up by the professor.
___ 6. A tall, broad figure appeared after the professor turned off the lights in the office.
___ 7. The man who opened the drawer was the professor.
___ 8. The professor ran down the corridor.
___ 9. The drawer was never actually opened.
___ 10. Three persons are referred to in this report.

When told to do so by your instructor, join a small work group. Now, help the group complete the same task by making a consensus decision on each item. Be sure to keep a separate record of the group's responses and your original individual responses.

SCORING

Your instructor will read the correct answers. Score both your individual and group responses.

INTERPRETATION

To begin, ask yourself if there was a difference between your answers and those of the group for each item. If so, why? Why do you think people, individually or in groups, may answer these questions incorrectly? Good planning depends on good decision making by the people doing the planning. Being able to distinguish "facts" and understand one's "inferences" are important steps toward improving the planning process. Involving others to help do the same can frequently assist in this process.

Source: From De Vito, Joseph A. *Messages: Building Interpersonal Communication Skills*, 6/e Published by Allyn and Bacon, Boston, MA. Copyright © 2005 by Pearson Education. Reprinted by permission of the publisher.

ASSESSMENT 15

Empowering Others

INSTRUCTIONS

Think of times when you have been in charge of a group—this could be a full-time or part-time work situation, a student work group, or whatever. Complete the following questionnaire by recording how you feel about each statement according to this scale:

1 = Strongly disagree 2 = Disagree 3 = Neutral
4 = Agree 5 = Strongly agree

When in charge of a group, I find that:

____ 1. Most of the time other people are too inexperienced to do things, so I prefer to do them myself.

____ 2. It often takes more time to explain things to others than to just do them myself.

____ 3. Mistakes made by others are costly, so I don't assign much work to them.

____ 4. Some things simply should not be delegated to others.

____ 5. I often get quicker action by doing a job myself.

____ 6. Many people are good only at very specific tasks and so can't be assigned additional responsibilities.

____ 7. Many people are too busy to take on additional work.

____ 8. Most people just aren't ready to handle additional responsibilities.

____ 9. In my position, I should be entitled to make my own decisions.

SCORING

Total your responses: enter the score here [____].

INTERPRETATION

This instrument gives an impression of your *willingness to delegate*. Possible scores range from 9 to 45. The higher your score, the more willing you appear to be to delegate to others. Willingness to delegate is an important managerial characteristic: It is essential if you—as a manager—are to "empower" others and give them opportunities to assume responsibility and exercise self-control in their work. With the growing importance of empowerment in the new workplace, your willingness to delegate is worth thinking about seriously. Be prepared to share your results and participate in general class discussion.

Source: Questionnaire adapted from L. Steinmetz and R. Todd, *First Line Management*, 4th ed. (Homewood, IL: BPI/Irwin, 1986), pp. 64–67.

ASSESSMENT 16

Turbulence Tolerance Test

INSTRUCTIONS

The following statements were made by a 37-year-old manager in a large, successful corporation. How would you like to have a job with these characteristics? Using the following scale, choose your response to the left of each statement.

0 = This feature would be very unpleasant for me.
1 = This feature would be somewhat unpleasant for me.
2 = I'd have no reaction to this feature one way or another.
3 = This would be enjoyable and acceptable most of the time.
4 = I would enjoy this very much; it's completely acceptable.

___ 1. I regularly spend 30 to 40 percent of my time in meetings.

___ 2. Eighteen months ago my job did not exist, and I have been essentially inventing it as I go along.

___ 3. The responsibilities I either assume or am assigned consistently exceed the authority I have for discharging them.

___ 4. At any given moment in my job, I have on the average about a dozen phone calls to be returned.

___ 5. There seems to be very little relation in my job between the quality of my performance and my actual pay and fringe benefits.

___ 6. About 2 weeks a year of formal management training is needed in my job just to stay current.

___ 7. Because we have very effective employment equity policies in my company and because it is thoroughly multinational, my job consistently brings me into close working contact at a professional level with people of many races, ethnic groups and nationalities, and of both sexes.

___ 8. There is no objective way to measure my effectiveness.

___ 9. I report to three different bosses for different aspects of my job, and each has an equal say in my performance appraisal.

___ 10. On average about a third of my time is spent dealing with unexpected emergencies that force all scheduled work to be postponed.

___ 11. When I have to have a meeting of the people who report to me, it takes my secretary most of a day to find a time when we are all available, and even then, I have yet to have a meeting where everyone is present for the entire meeting.

___ 12. The university degree I earned in preparation for this type of work is now obsolete, and I probably should go back for another degree.

___ 13. My job requires that I absorb 100–200 pages of technical materials per week.

___ 14. I am out of town overnight at least 1 night per week.

___ 15. My department is so interdependent with several other departments in the company that all distinctions about which departments are responsible for which tasks are quite arbitrary.

___ 16. In about a year I will probably get a promotion to a job in another division that has most of these same characteristics.

___ 17. During the period of my employment here, either the entire company or the division I worked in has been reorganized every year or so.

___ 18. While there are several possible promotions I can see ahead of me, I have no real career path in an objective sense.

___ 19. While there are several possible promotions I can see ahead of me, I think I

___ have no realistic chance of getting to the top levels of the company.

___ 20. While I have many ideas about how to make things work better, I have no direct influence on either the business policies or the personnel policies that govern my division.

___ 21. My company has recently put in an "assessment centre" where I and all other managers will be required to go through an extensive battery of psychological tests to assess our potential.

___ 22. My company is a defendant in an antitrust suit, and if the case comes to trial, I will probably have to testify about some decisions that were made a few years ago.

___ 23. Advanced computer and other electronic office technology is continually being introduced into my division, necessitating constant learning on my part.

___ 24. The computer terminal and screen I have in my office can be monitored in my bosses' offices without my knowledge.

SCORING

Add up all of your scores and then divide the total by 24. This is your "Turbulence Tolerance Test" (TTT) score.

INTERPRETATION

This instrument gives an impression of your tolerance for managing in turbulent times—something likely to characterize the world of work well into the new century. In general, the higher your TTT score, the more comfortable you seem to be with turbulence and change—a positive sign.

For comparison purposes, the average TTT scores for some 500 MBA students and young managers was 1.5-1.6. The test's author suggests TTT scores may be interpreted much like a grade point average in which 4.0 is a perfect "A". On this basis, a 1.5 is below a "C"! How did you do?

Source: Peter B. Vail, *Managing as a Performance Art: New Ideas for a World of Chaotic Change* (San Francisco: Jossey-Bass, 1989), pp. 8–9. Used by permission.

ASSESSMENT 17

Organizational Design Preference

INSTRUCTIONS

In the margin near each item, write the number from the following scale that shows the extent to which the statement accurately describes your views.

5 = strongly agree

4 = agree somewhat

3 = undecided

2 = disagree somewhat

1 = strongly disagree

I prefer to work in an organization where

1. goals are defined by those in higher levels.
2. work methods and procedures are specified.
3. top management makes important decisions.
4. my loyalty counts as much as my ability to do the job.
5. clear lines of authority and responsibility are established.
6. top management is decisive and firm.
7. my career is pretty well planned out for me.
8. I can specialize.
9. my length of service is almost as important as my level of performance.

10. management is able to provide the information I need to do my job well.
11. a chain of command is well established.
12. rules and procedures are adhered to equally by everyone.
13. people accept the authority of a leader's position.
14. people are loyal to their boss.
15. people do as they have been instructed.
16. people clear things with their boss before going over his or her head.

SCORING

Total your scores for all questions. Enter the score here [___].

INTERPRETATION

This assessment measures your preference for working in an organization designed along "organic" or "mechanistic" lines (see Chapter 11). The higher your score (above 64), the more comfortable you are with a mechanistic design; the lower your score (below 48), the more comfortable you are with an organic design. Scores between 48 and 64 can go either way. This organizational design preference represents an important issue in the new workplace. Indications are that today's organizations are taking on more and more organic characteristics. Presumably, those of us who work in them will need to be comfortable with such designs.

Source: From *The Dynamics of Organizational Theory: Gaining a Macro*, 2nd edition by Veiga/Yanouzas, 1984. Reprinted with permission of South-Western, a division of Thomson Learning: www.thomsonrights.com.

ASSESSMENT 18

Are You Cosmopolitan?

INSTRUCTIONS

Answer the following questions.

1. You believe it is the right of the professional to make his or her own decisions about what is to be done on the job.

   Strongly disagree 1 2 3 4 5 Strongly agree

2. You believe a professional should stay in an individual staff role regardless of the income sacrifice.

   Strongly disagree 1 2 3 4 5 Strongly agree

3. You have no interest in moving up to a top administrative post.

   Strongly disagree 1 2 3 4 5 Strongly agree

4. You believe that professionals are better evaluated by professional colleagues than by management.

   Strongly disagree 1 2 3 4 5 Strongly agree

5. Your friends tend to be members of your profession.

   Strongly disagree 1 2 3 4 5 Strongly agree

6. You would rather be known or get credit for your work outside rather than inside the company.

   Strongly disagree 1 2 3 4 5 Strongly agree

7. You would feel better making a contribution to society than to your organization.

   Strongly disagree 1 2 3 4 5 Strongly agree

8. Managers have no right to place time and cost schedules on professional contributors.

   Strongly disagree 1 2 3 4 5 Strongly agree

SCORING

Add your score for each item to get a total score between 8 and 40.

INTERPRETATION

A "cosmopolitan" identifies with the career profession, and a "local" identifies with the employing organization. A score of 30–40 suggests a "cosmopolitan" work orientation, 10–20 a "local" orientation, and 20–30 a "mixed" orientation.

Source: Developed from Joseph A. Raelin, *The Clash of Cultures, Managers and Professionals*, (Boston: Harvard Business School Press, 1986).

ASSESSMENT 19

Performance Appraisal Assumptions

INSTRUCTIONS

In each of the following pairs of statements, check off the statement that best reflects your assumptions about performance evaluation.

Performance evaluation is

1. (a) a formal process that is done annually.
   (b) an informal process done continuously.

2. (a) a process that is planned for subordinates.
   (b) a process that is planned with subordinates.

3. (a) a required organizational procedure.
   (b) a process done regardless of requirements.

4. (a) a time to evaluate subordinates' performance.
   (b) a time for subordinates to evaluate their manager.

5. (a) a time to clarify standards.
   (b) a time to clarify the subordinate's career needs.

6. (a) a time to confront poor performance.
   (b) a time to express appreciation.

7. (a) an opportunity to clarify issues and provide direction and control.
   (b) an opportunity to increase enthusiasm and commitment.

8. (a) only as good as the organization's forms.
   (b) only as good as the manager's coaching skills.

SCORING

There is no formal scoring for this assessment, but there may be a pattern to your responses. Check them again.

INTERPRETATION

In general, the "a" responses represent a more traditional approach to performance appraisal that emphasizes its *evaluation* function. This role largely puts the supervisor in the role of documenting a subordinate's performance for control and administrative purposes. The "b" responses represent a more progressive approach that includes a strong emphasis on the *counselling* or *development* role. Here, the supervisor is concerned with helping the subordinate do better and with learning from the subordinate what he or she needs to be able to do better. There is more of an element of reciprocity in this role. It is quite consistent with new directions and values emerging in today's organizations.

Source: Developed in part from Robert E. Quinn, Sue R. Faerman, Michael P. Thompson, and Michael R. McGrath, *Becoming a Master Manager: A Contemporary Framework* (New York: Wiley, 1990), p. 187. Used by permission.

ASSESSMENT 20

"T-P" Leadership Questionnaire

INSTRUCTIONS

The following items describe aspects of leadership behaviour. Respond to each item according to the way you would most likely act if you were the leader of a work group. Circle whether you would most likely behave in the described way: always (A), frequently (F), occasionally (O), seldom (S), or never (N).

A F O S N   1. I would most likely act as the spokesperson of the group.

A F O S N   2. I would encourage overtime work.

A F O S N   3. I would allow members complete freedom in their work.

A F O S N   4. I would encourage the use of uniform procedures.

A F O S N   5. I would permit the members to use their own judgement in solving problems.

A F O S N   6. I would stress being ahead of competing groups.

A F O S N   7. I would speak as a representative of the group.

A F O S N   8. I would push members for greater effort.

A F O S N   9. I would try out my ideas in the group.

A F O S N   10. I would let the members do their work the way they think best.

A F O S N   11. I would be working hard for a promotion.

A F O S N   12. I would tolerate postponement and uncertainty.

A F O S N   13. I would speak for the group if there were visitors present.

A F O S N   14. I would keep the work moving at a rapid pace.

A F O S N   15. I would turn the members loose on a job and let them go to it.

A F O S N   16. I would settle conflicts when they occur in the group.

A F O S N   17. I would get swamped by details.

A F O S N   18. I would represent the group at outside meetings.

A F O S N   19. I would be reluctant to allow the members any freedom of action.

A F O S N   20. I would decide what should be done and how it should be done.

A F O S N   21. I would push for increased performance.

A F O S N   22. I would let some members have authority, which I could otherwise keep.

A F O S N   23. Things would usually turn out as I had predicted.

A F O S N   24. I would allow the group a high degree of initiative.

A F O S N   25. I would assign group members to particular tasks.

A F O S N   26. I would be willing to make changes.

A F O S N   27. I would ask the members to work harder.

A F O S N   28. I would trust the group members to exercise good judgement.

A F O S N   29. I would schedule the work to be done.

A F O S N   30. I would refuse to explain my actions.

A F O S N   31. I would persuade others that my ideas are to their advantage.

A F O S N   32. I would permit the group to set

its own pace.

A F O S N 33. I would urge the group to beat its previous record.

A F O S N 34. I would act without consulting the group.

A F O S N 35. I would ask that group members follow standard rules and regulations.

SCORING/INTERPRETATION

Score the instrument as follows.

a. Write a "1" next to each of the following items if you scored them as S (seldom) or N (never).
8, 12, 17, 18, 19, 30, 34, 35

b. Write a "1" next to each of the following items if you scored them as A (always) or F (frequently).
1, 2, 3, 4, 5, 6, 7, 9, 10, 11, 13, 14, 15, 16, 20, 21, 22, 23, 24, 25, 26, 27, 28, 29, 31, 32, 33

c. Circle the "1" scores for the following items, and then add them up to get your TOTAL "P" SCORE = ___.
3, 5, 8, 10, 15, 18, 19, 22, 23, 26, 28, 30, 32, 34, 35

d. Circle the "1" scores for the following items, and then add them up to get your TOTAL "T" SCORE = ___.
1, 2, 4, 6, 7, 9, 11, 12, 13, 14, 16, 17, 20, 21, 23, 25, 27, 29, 31, 33

e. Record your scores on the following graph to develop an indication of your tendencies toward task-oriented leadership, people-oriented leadership, and shared leadership. Mark your T and P scores on the appropriate lines, then draw a line between these two points to determine your shared leadership score.

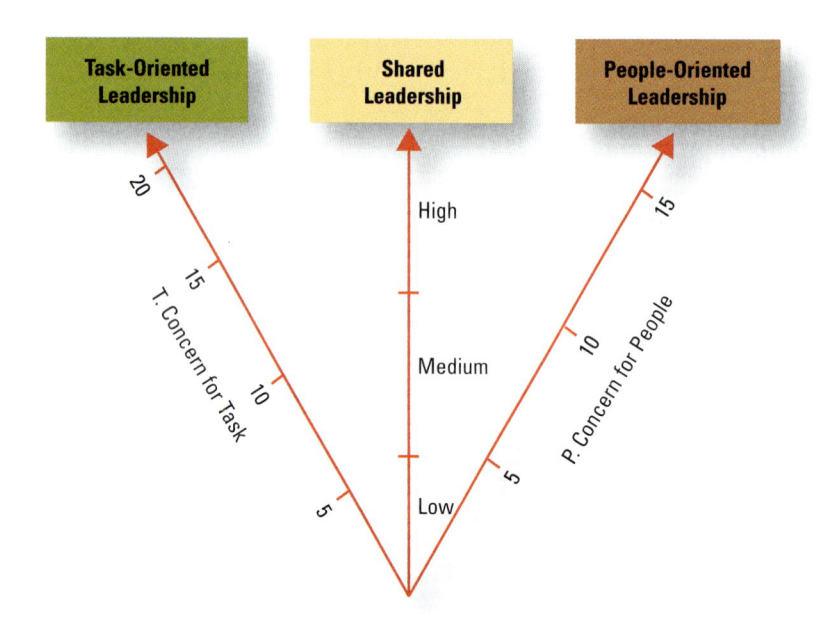

Source: Modified slightly from "T-P Leadership Questionnaire," University Associates, Inc., 1987.

ASSESSMENT 21

"T-T" Leadership Style

INSTRUCTIONS

For each of the following 10 pairs of statements, divide 5 points between the two according to your beliefs or perceptions of yourself or according to which of the two statements characterizes you better. The 5 points may be divided between the a and b statements in any one of the following ways: 5 for a, 0 for b; 4 for a, 1 for b; 3 for a, 2 for b; 1 for a, 4 for b; 0 for a, 5 for b, but not equally (2-1/2) between the two. Weigh your choices between the two according to which one characterizes you or your beliefs better.

1. (a) As leader I have a primary mission of maintaining stability.
   (b) As leader I have a primary mission of change.

2. (a) As leader I must cause events.
   (b) As leader I must facilitate events.

3. (a) I am concerned that my followers are rewarded equitably for their work.
   (b) I am concerned about what my followers want in life.

4. (a) My preference is to think long range: What might be.
   (b) My preference is to think short range: What is realistic.

5. (a) As a leader I spend considerable energy in managing separate but related goals.
   (b) As a leader I spend considerable energy in arousing hopes, expectations, and aspirations among my followers.

6. (a) Although not in a formal classroom sense, I believe that a significant part of my leadership is that of teacher.
   (b) I believe that a significant part of my leadership is that of facilitator.

7. (a) As leader I must engage with followers on an equal level of morality.
   (b) As leader I must represent a higher morality.

8. (a) I enjoy stimulating followers to want to do more.
   (b) I enjoy rewarding followers for a job well done.

9. (a) Leadership should be practical.
   (b) Leadership should be inspirational.

10. (a) What power I have to influence others comes primarily from my ability to get people to identify with me and my ideas.
    (b) What power I have to influence others comes primarily from my status and position.

SCORING

Circle your points for items 1b, 2a, 3b, 4a, 5b, 6a, 7b, 8a, 9b, 10a and add up the total points you allocated to these items; enter the score here [T = ___]. Next, add up the total points given to the uncircled items 1a, 2b, 3a, 4b, 5a, 6b, 7a, 8b, 9a, 10b; enter the score here [T = ___].

INTERPRETATION

This instrument gives an impression of your tendencies toward "transformational" leadership (your T score) and "transactional" leadership (your T score). You may want to refer to the discussion of these concepts in Chapter 13. Today, a lot of attention is being given to the transformational aspects of leadership—those personal qualities that inspire a sense of vision and the desire for extraordinary accomplishment in followers. The most successful leaders of the future will most likely be strong in both "T"s.

Source: Questionnaire by W. Warner Burke, Ph.D. Used by permission.

ASSESSMENT 22

Least-Preferred Co-worker Scale

INSTRUCTIONS

Think of all the different people with whom you have ever worked—in jobs, in social clubs, in student projects, or whatever. Next think of the one person with whom you could work least well—that is, the person with whom you had the most difficulty getting a job done. This is the one person—a peer, boss, or subordinate—with whom you would least want to work. Describe this person by circling numbers at the appropriate points on each of the following pairs of bipolar adjectives. Work rapidly. There are no right or wrong answers.

Pleasant	8 7 6 5 4 3 2 1	Unpleasant
Friendly	8 7 6 5 4 3 2 1	Unfriendly
Rejecting	1 2 3 4 5 6 7 8	Accepting
Tense	1 2 3 4 5 6 7 8	Relaxed
Distant	1 2 3 4 5 6 7 8	Close
Cold	1 2 3 4 5 6 7 8	Warm
Supportive	8 7 6 5 4 3 2 1	Hostile
Boring	1 2 3 4 5 6 7 8	Interesting
Quarrelsome	1 2 3 4 5 6 7 8	Harmonious
Gloomy	1 2 3 4 5 6 7 8	Cheerful
Open	8 7 6 5 4 3 2 1	Guarded
Backbiting	1 2 3 4 5 6 7 8	Loyal
Untrustworthy	1 2 3 4 5 6 7 8	Trustworthy
Considerate	8 7 6 5 4 3 2 1	Inconsiderate
Nasty	1 2 3 4 5 6 7 8	Nice
Agreeable	8 7 6 5 4 3 2 1	Disagreeable
Insincere	1 2 3 4 5 6 7 8	Sincere
Kind	8 7 6 5 4 3 2 1	Unkind

SCORING

This is called the "least-preferred coworker scale" (LPC). Compute your LPC score by totalling all the numbers you circled; enter that score here [LPC = ___].

INTERPRETATION

The LPC scale is used by Fred Fiedler to identify a person's dominant leadership style (see Chapter 13). Fiedler believes that this style is a relatively fixed part of one's personality and is therefore difficult to change. This leads Fiedler to his contingency views, which suggest that the key to leadership success is finding (or creating) good "matches" between style and situation. If your score is 73 or above, Fiedler considers you a "relationship-motivated" leader; if your score is 64 or below, he considers you a "task-motivated" leader. If your score is between 65 and 72, Fiedler leaves it up to you to determine which leadership style is most like yours.

Source: Fred E. Fiedler and Martin M. Chemers, *Improving Leadership Effectiveness: The Leader Match Concept*, 2nd ed. (New York: Wiley, 1984).

ASSESSMENT 23

Student Engagement Survey

INSTRUCTIONS

Use the following scale to indicate the degree to which you agree with the following statements:

1—No agreement

2—Weak agreement

3—Some agreement

4—Considerable agreement

5—Very strong agreement

1. Do you know what is expected of you in this course?
2. Do you have the resources and support you need to do your coursework correctly?
3. In this course, do you have the opportunity to do what you do best all the time?
4. In the last week, have you received recognition or praise for doing good work in this course?
5. Does your instructor seem to care about you as a person?
6. Is there someone in the course who encourages your development?
7. In this course, do your opinions seem to count?
8. Does the mission/purpose of the course make you feel your study is important?
9. Are other students in the course committed to doing quality work?
10. Do you have a best friend in the course?
11. In the last six sessions, has someone talked to you about your progress in the course?
12. In this course, have you had opportunities to learn and grow?

SCORING

Score the instrument by adding up all your responses. A score of 0–24 suggests you are "actively disengaged" from the learning experience; a score of 25–47 suggests you are "moderately engaged"; a score of 48–60 indicates you are "actively engaged."

INTERPRETATION

This instrument suggests the degree to which you are actively "engaged" or "disengaged" from the learning opportunities of your course. It is a counterpart to a survey used by the Gallup Organization to measure the "engagement" of American workers. The Gallup results are surprising—indicating that up to 19 percent of U.S. workers are actively disengaged, with the annual lost productivity estimated at some US $300 billion per year. One has to wonder: What are the costs of academic disengagement by students?

Source: This survey was developed from a set of "Gallup Engagement Questions" presented in John Thackray, "Feedback for Real," *Gallup Management Journal* (March 15, 2001), retrieved from http://gmj.gallup.com/management_articles/employee_engagement/article.asp?i 5 238&p 5 1, June 5, 2003; data reported from James K. Harter, "The Cost of Disengaged Workers," *Gallup Poll* (March 13, 2001).

ASSESSMENT 24

Job Design Choices

INSTRUCTIONS

People differ in what they like and dislike about their jobs. Listed below are 12 pairs of jobs. For each pair, indicate which job you would prefer. Assume that everything else about the jobs is the same—pay attention only to the characteristics actually listed for each pair of jobs. If you would prefer the job in Column A, indicate how much you prefer it by putting a check mark in a blank to the left of the Neutral point. If you prefer the job in Column B, check one of the blanks to the right of Neutral. Check the Neutral blank only if you find the two jobs equally attractive or unattractive. Try to use the Neutral blank sparingly.

COLUMN A   **COLUMN B**

1. A job that offers little or no challenge. |__|__|__|__|__|__|__| A job that requires you to be completely isolated from coworkers.
   Strongly prefer A — Neutral — Strongly prefer B

2. A job that pays well. |__|__|__|__|__|__|__| A job that allows considerable opportunity to be creative and innovative.
   Strongly prefer A — Neutral — Strongly prefer B

3. A job that often requires you to make important decisions. |__|__|__|__|__|__|__| A job in which there are many pleasant people to work with.
   Strongly prefer A — Neutral — Strongly prefer B

4. A job with little security in a somewhat unstable organization. |__|__|__|__|__|__|__| A job in which you have little or no opportunity to participate in decisions that affect your work.
   Strongly prefer A — Neutral — Strongly prefer B

5. A job in which greater responsibility is given to those who do the best work. |__|__|__|__|__|__|__| A job in which greater responsibility is given to loyal employees who have the most seniority.
   Strongly prefer A — Neutral — Strongly prefer B

6. A job with a supervisor who sometimes is highly critical. |__|__|__|__|__|__|__| A job that does not require you to use much of your talent.
   Strongly prefer A — Neutral — Strongly prefer B

7. A very routine job. |__|__|__|__|__|__|__| A job in which your coworkers are not very friendly.
   Strongly prefer A — Neutral — Strongly prefer B

8. A job with a supervisor who respects you and treats you fairly.

| Strongly prefer A | | Neutral | | Strongly prefer B | |

A job that provides constant opportunities for you to learn new and interesting things.

9. A job that gives you a real chance to develop yourself personally.

| Strongly prefer A | | Neutral | | Strongly prefer B | |

A job with excellent vacation and fringe benefits.

10. A job in which there is a real chance you could be laid off.

| Strongly prefer A | | Neutral | | Strongly prefer B | |

A job that offers very little chance to do challenging work.

11. A job that gives you little freedom and independence to do your work in the way you think best.

| Strongly prefer A | | Neutral | | Strongly prefer B | |

A job with poor working conditions.

12. A job with very satisfying teamwork.

| Strongly prefer A | | Neutral | | Strongly prefer B | |

A job that allows you to use your skills and abilities to the fullest extent.

SCORING/INTERPRETATION

People differ in their need for psychological growth at work. This instrument measures the degree to which you seek growth-need satisfaction. Score your responses as follows:

For items 1, 2, 7, 8, 11, and 12 give yourself the following points for each item:

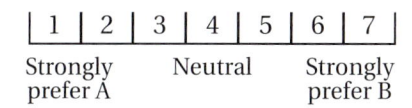

| 1 | 2 | 3 | 4 | 5 | 6 | 7 |
Strongly prefer A — Neutral — Strongly prefer B

For items 3, 4, 5, 6, 9, and 10 give yourself the following points for each item:

| 7 | 6 | 5 | 4 | 3 | 2 | 1 |
Strongly prefer A — Neutral — Strongly prefer B

Add up all of your scores and divide by 12 to find the average. If you score above 4.0, your desire for growth-need satisfaction through work tends to be high and you are likely to prefer an enriched job. If you score below 4.0, your desire for growth-need satisfaction through work tends to be low and you are likely to not be satisfied or motivated with an enriched job.

Source: Hackman, J.R./Oldham, G.R., WORK REDESIGN © 1980, pp. 275-294. Reprinted by permission of Pearson Education, Inc. Upper Saddle River, New Jersey.

ASSESSMENT 25

Cognitive Style

INSTRUCTIONS

This assessment is designed to get an impression of your cognitive style, based on the work of psychologist Carl Jung. For each of the following 12 pairs, place a "1" next to the statement that best describes you. Do this for each pair even though the description you chose may not be perfect.

1. ___ (a) I prefer to learn from experience.
   ___ (b) I prefer to find meanings in facts and how they fit together.

2. ___ (a) I prefer to use my eyes, ears, and other senses to find out what is going on.
   ___ (b) I prefer to use imagination to come up with new ways to do things.

3. ___ (a) I prefer to use standard ways to deal with routine problems.
   ___ (b) I prefer to use novel ways to deal with new problems.

4. ___ (a) I prefer to learn from experience.
   ___ (b) I prefer to find meanings in facts and how they fit together.

5. ___ (a) I am patient with details but get impatient when they get complicated.
   ___ (b) I am impatient and jump to conclusions but am also creative, imaginative, and inventive.

6. ___ (a) I enjoy using skills already mastered more than learning new ones.
   ___ (b) I like learning new skills more than practising old ones.

7. ___ (a) I prefer to decide things logically.
   ___ (b) I prefer to decide things based on feelings and values.

8. ___ (a) I like to be treated with justice and fairness.
   ___ (b) I like to be praised and to please other people.

9. ___ (a) I sometimes neglect or hurt other people's feelings without realizing it.
   ___ (b) I am aware of other people's feelings.

10. ___ (a) I give more attention to ideas and things than to human relationships.
    ___ (b) I can predict how others will feel.

11. ___ (a) I do not need harmony; arguments and conflicts don't bother me.
    ___ (b) I value harmony and get upset by arguments and conflicts.

12. ___ (a) I am often described as analytical, impersonal, unemotional, objective, critical, hard-nosed, rational.
    ___ (b) I am often described as sympathetic, people-oriented, unorganized, uncritical, understanding, ethical.

SCORING

Sum your scores as follows, and record them in the space provided. (Note that the Sensing and Feeling scores will be recorded as negatives.)

(−) *Sensing* (S Type) = 1a + 2a + 3a + 4a + 5a + 6a

(   ) *Intuitive* (N Type) = 1b + 2b + 3b + 4b + 5b + 6b

(   ) *Thinking* (T Type) = 7a + 8a + 9a + 10a + 11a + 12a

(−) *Feeling* (F Type) = 7b + 8b + 9b + 10b + 11b + 12b

Plot your scores on the following graph. Place an "X" at the point that indicates your suggested problem-solving style.

INTERPRETATION

This assessment examines cognitive style through the contrast of personal tendencies toward information gathering (sensation vs. intuition) and information evaluation (feeling vs. thinking) in one's approach to problem solving. The result is a classification of four master cognitive styles, with the following characteristics. Read the descriptions and consider the implications of your suggested style, including how well you might work with persons whose styles are very different.

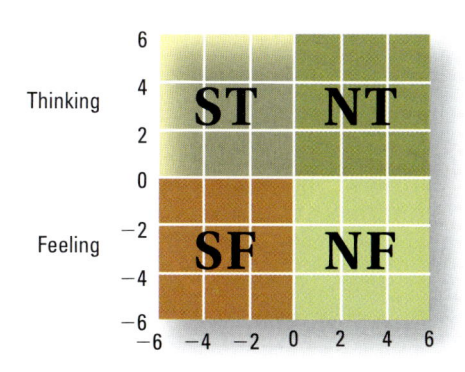

Sensation Thinkers: STs tend to emphasize the impersonal rather than the personal and take a realistic approach to problem solving. They like hard "facts," clear goals, certainty, and situations of high control.

Intuitive Thinkers: NTs are comfortable with abstraction and unstructured situations. They tend to be idealistic, prone toward intellectual and theoretical positions; they are logical and impersonal but also avoid details.

Intuitive Feelers: NFs prefer broad and global issues. They are insightful and tend to avoid details, being comfortable with intangibles; they value flexibility and human relationships.

Sensation Feelers: SFs tend to emphasize both analysis and human relations. They tend to be realistic and prefer facts; they are open communicators and sensitive to feelings and values.

Source: Developed from Donald Bowen, "Learning and Problem-Solving: You're Never Too Jung," in Donald D. Bowen, Roy J. Lewicki, Donald T. Hall, and Francine S. Hall, eds., *Experiences in Management and Organizational Behaviour*, 4th ed. (New York: Wiley, 1997), pp. 7–13; and John W. Slocum, Jr., "Cognitive Style in Learning and Problem Solving," ibid., pp. 349–353.

ASSESSMENT 26

Internal/External Control

INSTRUCTIONS

Circle either "a" or "b" to indicate the item you most agree with in each pair of the following statements.

1. (a) Promotions are earned through hard work and persistence.
   (b) Making a lot of money is largely a matter of breaks.

2. (a) Many times the reactions of teachers seem haphazard to me.
   (b) In my experience I have noticed that there is usually a direct connection between how hard I study and the grades I get.

3. (a) The number of divorces indicates that more and more people are not trying to make their marriages work.
   (b) Marriage is largely a gamble.

4. (a) It is silly to think that one can really change another person's basic attitudes.
   (b) When I am right I can convince others.

5. (a) Getting promoted is really a matter of being a little luckier than the next guy.
   (b) In our society an individual's future earning power is dependent upon his or her ability.

6. (a) If one knows how to deal with people, they are really quite easily led.
   (b) I have little influence over the way other people behave.

7. (a) In my case the grades I make are the results of my own efforts; luck has little or nothing to do with it.
   (b) Sometimes I feel that I have little to do with the grades I get.

8. (a) People like me can change the course of world affairs if we make ourselves heard.

(b) It is only wishful thinking to believe that one can really influence what happens in society at large.

9. (a) Much of what happens to me is probably a matter of chance.

   (b) I am the master of my fate.

10. (a) Getting along with people is a skill that must be practised.

    (b) It is almost impossible to figure out how to please some people.

SCORING

Give 1 point for 1b, 2a, 3a, 4b, 5b, 6a, 7a, 8a, 9b, 10a.

- 8–10 = high *internal* locus of control
- 6–7 = moderate *internal* locus of control
- 5 = mixed locus of control
- 3–4 = moderte *external* locus of control

INTERPRETATION

This instrument offers an impression of your tendency toward in *internal locus of control* or *external locus of control*. Persons with a high internal locus of control tend to believe they have control over their own destinies. They may be most responsive to opportunities for greater self-control in the workplace. Persons with a high external locus of control tend to believe that what happens to them is largely in the hands of external people or forces. They may be less comfortable with self-control and more responsive to external controls in the workplace.

Source: Instrument from Julian P. Rotter, "External Control and Internal Control," *Psychology Today* (June 1971), p. 42.

ASSESSMENT 27

Team Leader Skills

INSTRUCTIONS

Consider your experience in groups and work teams. Ask: "What skills do I bring to team leadership situations?" Then, complete the following inventory by rating yourself on each item using this scale.

1 = Almost Never
2 = Seldom
3 = Sometimes
4 = Usually
5 = Almost Always

1 2 3 4 5   **1.** I facilitate communications with and among team members between team meetings.

1 2 3 4 5   **2.** I provide feedback/coaching to individual team members on their performance.

1 2 3 4 5   **3.** I encourage creative and "out-of-the-box" thinking.

1 2 3 4 5   **4.** I continue to clarify stakeholder needs/expectations.

1 2 3 4 5   **5.** I keep team members' responsibilities and activities focused within the team's objectives and goals.

1 2 3 4 5   **6.** I organize and run effective and productive team meetings.

1 2 3 4 5   **7.** I demonstrate integrity and personal commitment.

1 2 3 4 5   **8.** I have excellent persuasive and influence skills.

1 2 3 4 5   **9.** I respect and leverage the team's cross-functional diversity.

1 2 3 4 5   10. I recognize and reward individual contributions to team performance.

1 2 3 4 5   11. I use the appropriate decision-making style for specific issues.

1 2 3 4 5   12. I facilitate and encourage broader management with the team's key stakeholders.

1 2 3 4 5   13. I ensure that the team meets its team commitments.

1 2 3 4 5   14. I bring team issues and problems to the team's attention and focus on constructive problem solving.

1 2 3 4 5   15. I provide a clear vision and direction for the team.

SCORING

The inventory measures seven dimensions of team leadership. Add your scores for the items listed next to each dimension below to get an indication of your potential strengths and weaknesses.

1,9   Building the Team
2,10   Developing People
3,11   Team Problem Solving/Decision Making
4,12   Stakeholder Relations
5,13   Team Performance
6,14   Team Process
7,8,15   Providing Personal Leadership

INTERPRETATION

The higher the score, the more confident you are on the particular skill and leadership capability. When considering the score, ask yourself if others would rate you the same way. Consider giving this inventory to people who have worked with you in teams and have them rate you. Compare the results to your self-assessment. Also, remember that it is doubtful that any one team leader is capable of exhibiting all the skills listed above. More and more, organizations are emphasizing "top-management teams" that blend a variety of skills, rather than depending on the vision of the single, heroic leader figure. As long as the necessary leadership skills are represented within the membership, it is more likely that the team will be healthy and achieve high performance. Of course, the more skills you bring with you to team leadership situations, the better.

Source: Developed from Lynda McDermott, Nolan Brawley, and William Waite, *World-Class Teams: Working across Borders* (New York: Wiley, 1998).

ASSESSMENT 28

Conflict Management Styles

INSTRUCTIONS

Think of how you behave in conflict situations in which your wishes differ from those of one or more other persons. In the space to the left of each of the following statements, write the number from the following scale that indicates how likely you are to respond that way in a conflict situation.

1 = very unlikely   2 = unlikely
3 = likely   4 = very likely

___ 1. I am usually firm in pursuing my goals.
___ 2. I try to win my position.
___ 3. I give up some points in exchange for others.
___ 4. I feel that differences are not always worth worrying about.
___ 5. I try to find a position that is intermediate between the other person's and mine.
___ 6. In approaching negotiations, I try to be considerate of the other person's wishes.
___ 7. I try to show the logic and benefits of my positions.

___ 8. I always lean toward a direct discussion of the problem.

___ 9. I try to find a fair combination of gains and losses for both of us.

___ 10. I attempt to work through our differences immediately.

___ 11. I try to avoid creating unpleasantness for myself.

___ 12. I try to soothe the other person's feelings and preserve our relationship.

___ 13. I attempt to get all conerns and issues immediately out in the open.

___ 14. I sometimes avoid taking positions that would create controversy.

___ 15. I try not to hurt others' feelings.

SCORING

Total your scores for items 1, 2, 7; enter that score here [*Competing* = ___]. Total your scores for items 8, 10, 13; enter that score here [*Collaborating* = ___]. Total your scores for items 3, 5, 9; enter that score here [*Compromising* = ___]. Total your scores for items 4, 11, 14; enter that score here [*Avoiding* = ___]. Total your scores for items 6, 12, 15; enter that score here [*Accommodating* = ___].

INTERPRETATION

Each of the scores above corresponds to one of the conflict management styles discussed in Chapter 16. Research indicates that each style has a role to play in management but that the best overall conflict management approach is collaboration; only it can lead to problem solving and true conflict resolution. You should consider any patterns that may be evident in your scores and think about how to best handle the conflict situations in which you become involved.

Source: Adapted from Thomas-Kilmann, *Conflict Mode Instrument.* Copyright © 1974, Xicom, Inc., Tuxedo, NY 10987.

ASSESSMENT 29

Stress Self-Test

INSTRUCTIONS

Complete the following questionnaire. Circle the number that best represents your tendency to behave on each bipolar dimension.

Am casual about appointments	1 2 3 4 5 6 7 8	Am never late
Am not competitive	1 2 3 4 5 6 7 8	Am very competitive
Never feel rushed	1 2 3 4 5 6 7 8	Always feel rushed
Take things one at a time	1 2 3 4 5 6 7 8	Try to do many things at once
Do things slowly	1 2 3 4 5 6 7 8	Do things fast
Express feelings	1 2 3 4 5 6 7 8	"Sit on" feelings
Have many interests	1 2 3 4 5 6 7 8	Have few interests but work

SCORING

Total the numbers circled for all items, and multiply this by 3; enter the result here [___].

INTERPRETATION

This scale is designed to measure your personality tendency toward Type A or Type B behaviours. As described in Chapter 16, a Type A personality is associated with high stress. Persons who are Type A tend to bring stress on themselves even in situations where others are relatively stress-free. This is an important characteristic to be able to identify in yourself and in others.

Points	Personality
120+	A+
106 – 119	A
100 – 105	A–
90 – 99	B+
below 90	B

Source: Adapted from R. W. Bortner. "A Short Rating Scale as a Potential Measure of Type A Behaviour," *Journal of Chronic Diseases*, vol. 22 (1966), pp. 87–91.

ASSESSMENT 30

Work-Life Balance

INSTRUCTIONS

Complete this inventory by circling the number that indicates the extent to which you agree or disagree with each of the following statements.

1. How much time do you spend on nonwork-related activities such as taking care of family, spending time with friends, participating in sports, enjoying leisure time?

   Almost none/never   1   2   3   4   5   Very much/always

2. How often do family duties and nonwork responsibilities make you feel tired out?

   Almost none/never   1   2   3   4   5   Very much/always

3. How often do you feel short of time for family-related and nonwork activities?

   Almost none/never   1   2   3   4   5   Very much/always

4. How difficult is it for you to do everything you should as a family member and friend to others?

   Almost none/never   1   2   3   4   5   Very much/always

5. I often feel that I am being run ragged, with not enough time in a day to do everything and do it well.

   Almost none/never   1   2   3   4   5   Very much/always

6. I am given entirely too much work to do.

   Almost none/never   1   2   3   4   5   Very much/always

7. How much conflict do you feel there is between the demands of your job and your family, and nonwork activities life?

   Almost none/never   1   2   3   4   5   Very much/always

8. How much does your job situation interfere with your family life?

   Almost none/never   1   2   3   4   5   Very much/always

9. How much does your family life and nonwork activities interfere with your job?

   Almost none/never   1   2   3   4   5   Very much/always

SCORING

1. Family Demand Score: Total items #1, #2, #3, #4 and divide by 4.
2. Work Demand Score: Total items #5, #6 and divide by 2.
3. Work-Family Conflict Score: Total items #7, #8, #9 and divide by 3.

Your responses to items 1–4 are totalled and divided by 4, giving you the Life Demand score. Your responses to items 5–6 are totalled and divided by 2, resulting in your Work Demand score. Responses to items 7–9 are summed and divided by 3, giving your Work-Life conflict score.

INTERPRETATION

Compare yourself with these scores from a sample of Chinese and American workers.

	U.S.	Chinese	Your Scores
Life Demand	3.53	2.58	4
Work Demand	2.83	2.98	4
Work-Life Conflict	2.53	2.30	4.67

Are there any suprises in this comparison?

Work-life conflict is defined as "a form of interrole conflict in which the role pressures from the work and family nonwork domains are mutually noncompatible in some respect." Demands of one role make it difficult to satisfy demands of the others.

Source: Based on Nini Yang, Chao. D. Chen, Jaepil Choi, and Yimin Zou, "Sources of Work-Family Conflict: A Sino–U.S. Comparison of the Effects of Work and Family Demands," *Academy of Management Journal*, vol. 43, no. 1, pp. 113–123.

STUDENT PORTFOLIO BUILDER

What Is a Student Portfolio?

A *Student Portfolio* is a paper or electronic collection of documents that summarizes your academic and personal accomplishments in a way that effectively communicates with academic advisors and potential employers.[1] At a minimum, your portfolio should include the following:

- an up-to-date professional résumé
- a listing of courses in your major and related fields of study
- a listing of your extracurricular activities and any leadership positions
- documentation of your career readiness in terms of skills and learning outcomes

The purpose of a Student Portfolio is twofold—academic assessment and career readiness.

---

[1] The value and use of Student Portfolios are described by David S. Chappell and John R. Schermerhorn, Jr., in "Using Electronic Student Portfolios in Management Education: A Stakeholder Perspective," *Journal of Management Education*, vol. 23 (1999), pp. 651–62; and "Electronic Student Portfolios in Management Education" in Robert deFelippi and Charles Wrankel (eds.), *Educating Managers with Tomorrow's Technology* (Information Age Press, 2003), pp. 101–129.

1. *Academic Assessment Goal* The Student Portfolio serves as an ongoing academic assessment tool that documents your learning and academic accomplishments. As you progress through a curriculum, the portfolio depicts the progress you are making in acquiring the skills and competencies necessary to be successful in lifelong career pursuits. Over time, your portfolio will become increasingly sophisticated in the range and depth of learning and accomplishments that are documented. A well-prepared Student Portfolio is a very effective way of summarizing your academic achievements in consultation with both faculty advisors and professors.

2. *Career Readiness Goal* The Student Portfolio serves as an important means of communicating your résumé and credentials to potential employers, as you search for both internship and full-time job opportunities. The portfolio is an effective career tool that offers value far beyond the standard résumé. Potential employers can readily examine multiple aspects of your accomplishments and skill sets in order to make a desired match. A professional and complete portfolio allows potential employers to easily review your background and range of skills and capabilities. It may convey your potential to a much greater depth and with a more positive impression than a traditional résumé. There is no doubt that a professional and substantive portfolio can help set you apart from the competition and attract the interest of employers.

PLANNING YOUR STUDENT PORTFOLIO

Your Student Portfolio should document, in a progressive and clear manner, your credentials and academic work. As you progress through the curriculum in your major and supplementary fields of study, the portfolio should be refined and materials added to display your most up-to-date skills, competencies, and accomplishments. Use of the *Management* **Skill and Outcome Assessment Framework**, described shortly, will help you to do this. Students should use the portfolio to store their coursework.

The closer you get to graduation, the entries in your portfolio should become more specific to your job and career goals. In this way, your portfolio becomes a dynamic and evolving career tool with value far beyond that of the standard résumé. We recommend that our students plan their portfolios to serve two immediate career purposes: (1) obtain a professional internship for the junior/senior year period while still a student, and (2) obtain their initial full-time job after graduation. A typical student of ours begins his or her portfolio as a sophomore in second year and then refines and adds to it throughout the program of study.

RÉSUMÉ WRITING GUIDE

The first thing that should go into your Student Portfolio is a professional résumé. Don't worry about how sophisticated or complete it is at first. The important things are to (1) get it started and (2) continue to build it as your experience grows. You will be surprised at how complete it will become with systematic attention and a personal commitment to take full advantage of the professional development opportunities available to you.

The following example should help get you started. It shows both a professional format and the types of things that can and should be included. I have also annotated the sample to show how an internship recruiter or potential employer might respond when reading the résumé for the first time. Wouldn't you like to have such positive reactions to the accomplishments and experiences documented in your résumé?

INTERVIEW PREPARATION GUIDE

You will know that your Student Portfolio was worthwhile and successful when it helps you land a preferred internship or your first-choice job. But the portfolio only helps get you to the point of a formal interview. The next step is doing well in it. In order to prepare for this step in the recruiting process, consider the following tips on job interviewing.[2]

- *Research the organization*—Make sure you read their recent literature, including annual reports; scan current news reports; and examine the industry and their major competitors.

- *Prepare to answer common interview questions*—Sample questions include: What do you really want to do in life? What do you consider your greatest strengths and weaknesses? How can you immediately contribute to our organization? Why did you choose your college or university? What are your interests outside of work? What was your most rewarding university experience? How would one of your professors describe you? What do you see yourself doing five years from now?

- *Dress for success*—Remember that impressions count, and first impressions often count the most. If you aren't sure what to wear or how to look, get advice from your professors and from career counsellors at your college or university.

- *Follow-up*—After the interview, send a "thank you" letter, ideally no longer than a week later. In the letter be sure to mention specific things about the organization that are important/insightful to you, and take the opportunity to clarify again where and how you believe you would fit as a valuable employee. Be prompt in providing any additional information requested during the interview.

SKILL AND OUTCOME ASSESSMENT FRAMEWORK

Skill and outcome assessment is an increasingly important part of management education. It allows you to document key academic accomplishments and career readiness for faculty review and for review by potential employers. Following guidelines of the AACSB, the International Association for Management Education, I suggest integrating into your portfolio specific documentation of your accomplishments in the following six areas of professional development.

---

[2] This section and the tips were recommended by Dr. Robert Lenie Holbrook of Ohio University.

RÉSUMÉ SAMPLE

■ Note: The annotations indicate positive reactions by a prospective employer to the information being provided.

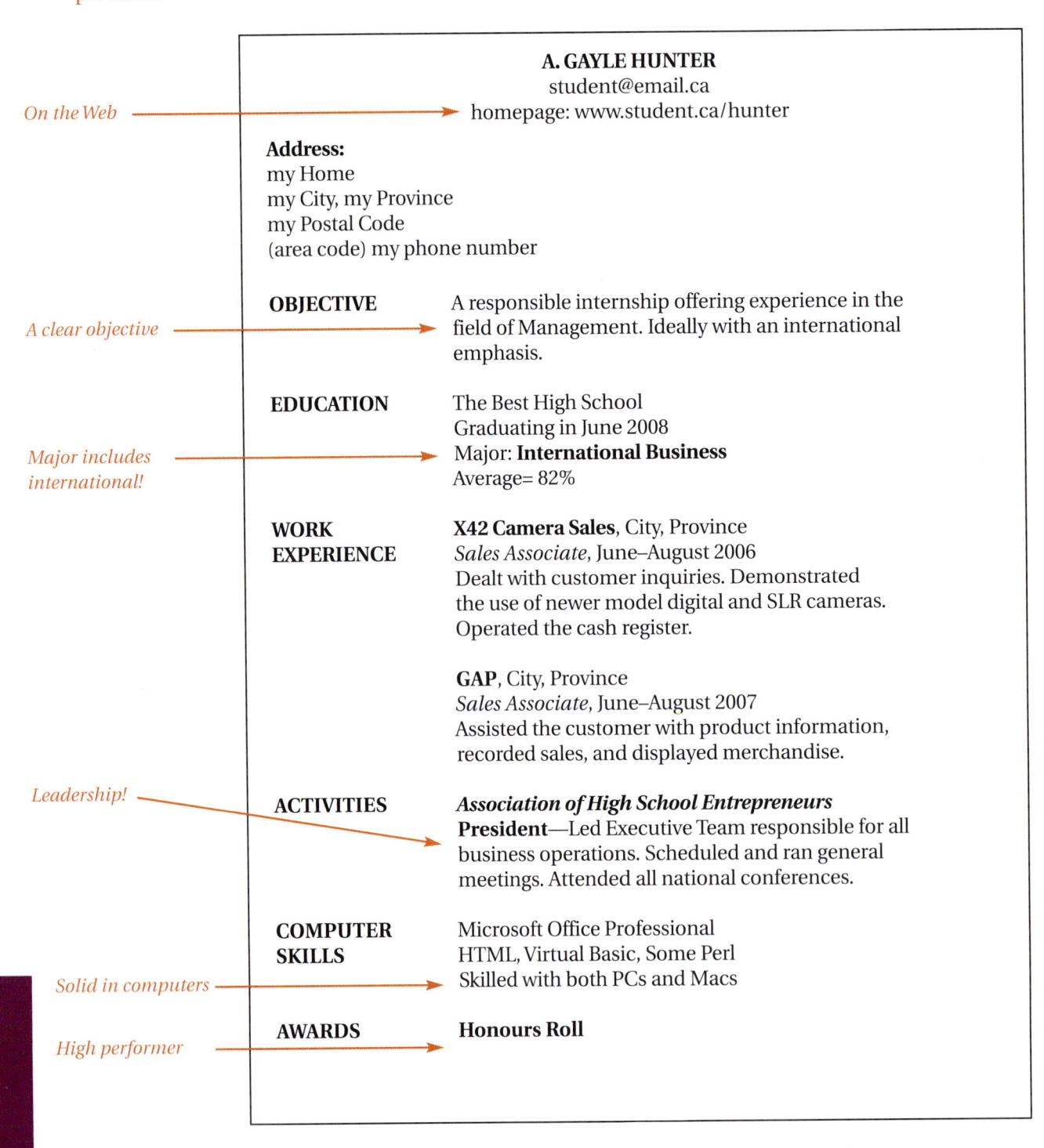

On the Web →

A. GAYLE HUNTER
student@email.ca
homepage: www.student.ca/hunter

Address:
my Home
my City, my Province
my Postal Code
(area code) my phone number

OBJECTIVE

A clear objective → A responsible internship offering experience in the field of Management. Ideally with an international emphasis.

EDUCATION

The Best High School
Graduating in June 2008
Major includes international! → Major: **International Business**
Average= 82%

WORK EXPERIENCE

X42 Camera Sales, City, Province
Sales Associate, June–August 2006
Dealt with customer inquiries. Demonstrated the use of newer model digital and SLR cameras. Operated the cash register.

GAP, City, Province
Sales Associate, June–August 2007
Assisted the customer with product information, recorded sales, and displayed merchandise.

ACTIVITIES

Leadership! → ***Association of High School Entrepreneurs***
President—Led Executive Team responsible for all business operations. Scheduled and ran general meetings. Attended all national conferences.

COMPUTER SKILLS

Microsoft Office Professional
HTML, Virtual Basic, Some Perl
Solid in computers → Skilled with both PCs and Macs

AWARDS

High performer → **Honours Roll**

1. *Communication*—Demonstrates ability to share ideas and findings clearly in written and oral expression, and with technology utilization.
2. *Leadership*—Demonstrates ability to influence and support others to perform complex and ambiguous tasks.
3. *Teamwork*—Demonstrates ability to work effectively as a team member and as a team leader.
4. *Critical Thinking*—Demonstrates ability to gather and analyze information for creative problem solving.
5. *Self-Management*—Demonstrates ability to evaluate oneself, modify behaviour, and meet obligations.
6. *Professionalism*—Demonstrates ability to sustain a positive impression, instill confidence, and advance in a career.

The many learning resources and activities in this Management Learning Workbook—cases, projects, exercises, and self-assessments—relate to these skills and outcome assessment areas. There is no better time than the present to start participating in the learning experiences and documenting your results and accomplishments in your student portfolio.

Getting Started with Your *Student Portfolio*

The basic Student Portfolio consists of (1) a professional résumé and (2) a compendium of coursework samples that displays your career readiness skills and capabilities.

PORTFOLIO FORMAT

The easiest way to organize a paper portfolio is with a three-ring binder. This binder should be professional in appearance and have an attractive cover page that clearly identifies it as your student portfolio. The binder should be indexed with dividers that allow a reader to easily browse the résumé and other materials to gain a complete view of your special credentials.

In today's age of information technology and electronic communication, it is also highly recommended that you develop an online or *electronic portfolio*. This format allows you to communicate easily and effectively through the Internet with employers offering potential internship and job placements. An online version of your student portfolio can be displayed either on your personal website or on one provided by your university. Once you have created an electronic portfolio, it is easy to maintain. It is also something that will impress reviewers and help set you apart from the competition. At the very least, the use of an electronic portfolio communicates to potential employers that you are a full participant in this age of information technology.

MANAGEMENT SKILL AND OUTCOME ASSESSMENT FRAMEWORK

Communication – Demonstrates ability to share ideas and findings clearly in written and oral expression.

- Writing
- Oral presentation
- Giving and receiving feedback
- Technology utilization

Leading – Demonstrates ability to influence and support others to perform complex and ambiguous tasks.

- Diversity awareness
- Global awareness
- Project management
- Strategic leadership

Teamwork – Demonstrates ability to work effectively as a team member and a team leader.

- Team contribution
- Team leadership
- Conflict management
- Negotiation and consensus building

Critical Thinking – Demonstrates ability to gather and analyze information for creative problem solving.

- Problem solving
- Judgement and decision making
- Information gathering/interpretation
- Creativity and innovation

Self-Management – Demonstrates ability to evaluate oneself, modify behaviour, and meet obligations.

- Ethical understanding/behaviour
- Personal flexibility
- Tolerance for ambiguity
- Performance responsibility

Professionalism – Demonstrates ability to sustain a positive impression, instill confidence, and advance in a career.

- Personal presence
- Personal initiative
- Career management
- Unique "value added"

CAREER DEVELOPMENT PLAN—A PORTFOLIO PROJECT

A very good way to enhance your Student Portfolio is by completing the following project as part of your introductory management course, or on your own initiative. Called the "Career Development Plan," the objective of this project is to identify professional development opportunities that you can take advantage of to advance your personal career readiness.

Deliverable: Write and file in your Student Portfolio a two-part career development memorandum that is written in professional format and addressed to your instructor or to "prospective employer." The memorandum should do the following:

- *Part A.* Answer the question: "What are my personal strengths and weaknesses as a potential manager?"

    It is recommended that you use the *Management* Skill and Outcome Assessment Framework in structuring your analysis. It is recommended that you support your answer in part by analysis of results from your work with a selection of experiential exercises and self-assessments from this workbook. You can also supplement the analysis with other relevant personal insights.

- *Part B.* Answer the question: "How can I best take advantage of available opportunities to improve my managerial potential?"

    Make this answer as specific as possible. Describe a clear plan of action that encompasses the time available to you between now and graduation. This plan should include summer activities, as well as academic and extracurricular experiences. Your goal should be to build a résumé and complete portfolio that will best present you as a skilled and valuable candidate for the entry-level job that you would like in your chosen career field.

Evaluation: Your career development memorandum should be professional and error-free, and meet the highest standards of effective written communication. It should be sufficiently analytical in Part A to show serious consideration of your personal strengths and weaknesses in managerial potential at this point in time. It should be sufficiently detailed and in-depth in Part B so that you can objectively evaluate your progress step-by-step between now and graduation. Overall, it should be a career development plan you can be proud to formally include in your Student Portfolio. It should serve as a positive indicator of your professionalism.

SAMPLE PORTFOLIO COMPONENTS

The following samples document a range of accomplishments and capabilities. As with the sample résumé presented earlier, they are shown here with illustrative comments (written in red) that indicate how a prospective employer might react when reading them in print or viewing them online. As you look at these samples, ask: "How can I best display my course and academic accomplishments to document my learning and career readiness?"

WRITTEN ASSIGNMENT IN FRENCH

Second language skill!

La Conception de L'Amour Pendant toute L'Histoire

La conception de l'amour pendant toute l'histoire est très intéressante, à voir. Pendant l'histoire, les formes de l'amour ont changé un peu, mais l'idée de base reste la même. Dans les ouvrages au XVIème siècle, on peut trouver des idées de l'amour qui sont semblables à la conception de l'amour dans notre société moderne. Avec une comparaison entre la poésie de Louise Labé et Ronsard au XVIème siècle, et le film Indochine, que Regis Wargnier a réalisé en 1992, on peut voir la conception de l'amour pendant l'histoire.

INTERNATIONAL VIRTUAL TEAMWORK PROJECT

Shows high initiative!

Experienced with virtual groups

Cross-cultural awareness!

Project Overview and Deliverables

In my high school management course I volunteered for a special assignment called the "International Virtual Teamwork Project." Through this experience I learned about cross-cultural issues in management and had the opportunity to experience the challenges of working as a member of a virtual team. The instructor's description of the project completed by my international virtual team follows.

This project requires extra effort to participate in an *international virtual team.* Students from each participating high school will form into 4–5 person teams. Each team will complete a "domestic" project (Part A) and then participate in an "international" comparison project working with a team from the other university (Part B). A final report will be created by each pair of teams working together. The same final report will be submitted for grading. The final report will also be posted on the course website.

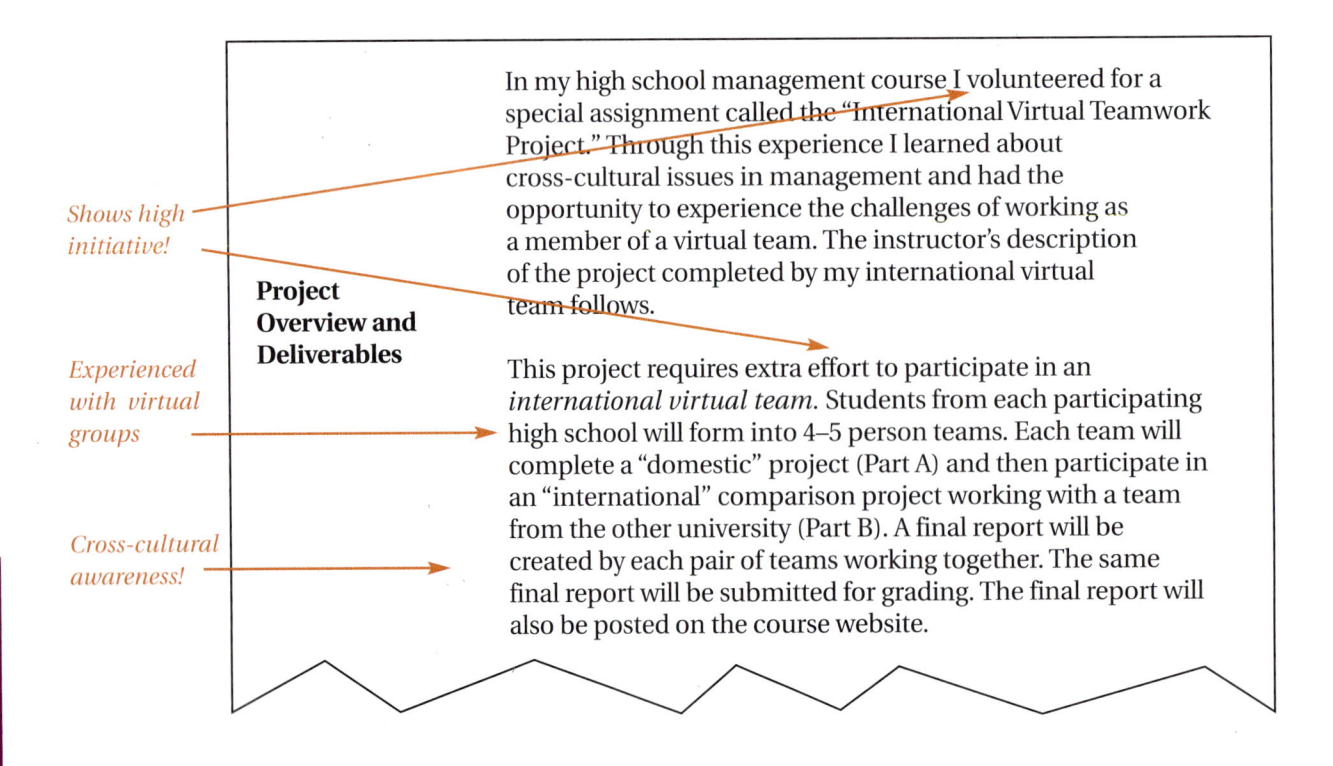

Self-Test Answers

CHAPTER 1

1. d
2. c
3. a
4. b
5. a
6. a
7. c
8. a
9. b
10. b
11. c
12. a
13. b
14. c
15. c
16. Managers must value people and respect subordinates as mature, responsible, adult human beings. This is part of their ethical and social responsibility as persons to whom others report at work. The work setting should be organized and managed to respect the rights of people and their human dignity. Included among the expectations for ethical behaviour would be actions to protect individual privacy, provide freedom from sexual harassment, and offer safe and healthy job conditions. Failure to do so is socially irresponsible. It may also cause productivity losses due to dissatisfaction and poor work commitments.
17. The manager is held accountable by her boss for performance results of her work unit. The manager must answer to her boss for unit performance. By the same token, the manager's subordinates must answer to her for their individual performance. They are accountable to her.
18. If the glass ceiling effect operates in a given situation, it would act as a hidden barrier to advancement beyond a certain level. Managers controlling promotions and advancement opportunities in the firm would not give them to female candidates, regardless of their capabilities. Although the newly hired graduates may progress for a while, sooner or later their upward progress in the firm would be halted by this invisible barrier.
19. Kenichi Ohmae uses the term "borderless world" to describe how more businesses are operating on a global scale. Globalization means that the countries and peoples of the world are increasingly interconnected and that business firms increasingly cross national boundaries in acquiring resources, getting work accomplished, and selling their products. This internationalization of work will affect most everyone in the new economy. People will be working with others from different countries, working in other countries, and certainly buying and using products and services produced in whole or in part in other countries. As countries become more interdependent economically, products are sold and resources purchased around the world, and business strategies increasingly target markets in more than one country.
20. One approach to this question is through the framework of essential management skills offered by Katz. At the first level of management, technical skills are important and I would feel capable in this respect. However, I would expect to learn and refine these skills through my work experiences. Human skills, the ability to work well with other people, will also be very important. Given the diversity anticipated for this team, I will need good human skills. Included here would be my emotional intelligence, or ability to understand my emotions and those of others when I am interacting with them. I will also have a leadership responsibility to help others on the team develop and utilize these skills so that the team itself can function effectively. Finally, I would expect opportunities to develop my conceptual or analytical skills in anticipation of higher-level appointments. In terms of personal development, I should recognize that the conceptual skills will increase in importance relative to the technical skills as I move upward in management responsibility. The fact that the members of the team will be diverse, with some of different demographic and cultural backgrounds from my own, will only increase the importance of my abilities in the human skills area. It will be a challenge to embrace and value differences to create the best work experience for everyone and to fully value everyone's potential contributions to the audits we will be doing. Conceptually I will need to understand the differences and try to utilize them to solve problems faced by the team, but in human relationships I will need to excel at keeping the team spirit alive and everyone committed to working well together over the life of our projects.

CHAPTER 2

1. d
2. b
3. b
4. a
5. c
6. a
7. a
8. b
9. c
10. c
11. a
12. d
13. c
14. c
15. a
16. Theory Y assumes that people are capable of taking responsibility and exercising self-direction and control in their work. The notion of self-fulfilling prophecies is that managers who hold these assumptions will act in ways that encourage workers to display these characteristics, thus confirming and reinforcing the original assumptions. The emphasis on greater participation and involvement in the modern workplace is an example of Theory Y assumptions in practice. Presumably, by valuing participation and involvement, managers will create self-fulfilling prophecies in which workers behave this way in response to being treated with respect. The result is a positive setting where everyone gains.

17. According to the deficit principle, a satisfied need is not a motivator of behaviour. The social need will only motivate if it is deprived or in deficit. According to the progression principle, people move step-by-step up Maslow's hierarchy as they strive to satisfy needs. For example, once the social need is satisfied, the esteem need will be activated.

18. Contingency thinking takes an "if–then" approach to situations. It seeks to modify or adapt management approaches to fit the needs of each situation. An example would be to give more customer contact responsibility to workers who want to satisfy social needs at work, while giving more supervisory responsibilities to those who want to satisfy their esteem or ego needs.

19. The external environment is the source of the resources an organization needs to operate. In order to continue to obtain these resources, the organization must be successful in selling its goods and services to customers. If customer feedback is negative, the organization must make adjustments or risk losing the support needed to obtain important resources.

20. A bureaucracy operates with a strict hierarchy of authority, promotion based on competency and performance, formal rules and procedures, and written documentation. Enrique can do all of these things in his store, since the situation is probably quite stable and most work requirements are routine and predictable. However, bureaucracies are quite rigid and may deny employees the opportunity to make decisions on their own. Enrique must be careful to meet the needs of the workers and not to make the mistake—identified by Argyris—of failing to treat them as mature adults. While remaining well organized, the store manager should still be able to help workers meet higher-order esteem and self-fulfillment needs as well as assume responsibility as would be consistent with McGregor's Theory Y assumptions.

CHAPTER 3

1. b
2. a
3. d
4. c
5. c
6. d
7. b
8. a
9. c
10. b
11. d
12. c
13. c
14. d
15. b

16. The individualism view is that ethical behaviour is that which best serves long-term interests. The justice view is that ethical behaviour is fair and equitable in its treatment of people.

17. The rationalizations are believing that: (1) the behaviour is not really illegal, (2) the behaviour is really in everyone's best interests, (3) no one will find out, and (4) the organization will protect you.

18. The socio-economic view of corporate social responsibility argues that socially responsible behaviour is in a firm's long-run best interests. It should be good for profits, it creates a positive public image, it helps avoid government regulation, it meets public expectations, and it is an ethical obligation.

19. Government agencies implement and enforce laws that are passed to regulate business activities. They act on the public's behalf to ensure compliance with laws on such matters as occupational safety and health, consumer protection, and environmental protection.

20. The manager could make a decision based on any one of the strategies. As an obstructionist, the manager may assume that Bangladesh needs the business and that it is a local matter as to who will be employed to make the gloves. As a defensive strategy, the manager may decide to require the supplier to meet the minimum employment requirements under Bangladeshi law. Both of these approaches represent cultural relativism. As an accommodation strategy, the manager may require that the supplier go beyond local laws and meet standards set by equivalent laws in Canada. A proactive strategy would involve the manager in trying to set an example by operating in Bangladesh only with suppliers who not only meet local standards but also actively support the education of children in the communities in which they operate. These latter two approaches would be examples of universalism.

CHAPTER 4

1. a
2. c
3. b
4. b
5. d
6. c
7. c
8. a
9. b
10. a
11. a
12. b
13. a
14. d
15. b

16. Possible operating objectives reflecting a commitment to competitive advantage through customer service include: (1) providing high-quality goods and services, (2) producing at low cost so that goods and services can be sold at low prices, (3) providing short waiting times for goods and services, and (4) providing goods and services meeting unique customer needs.

17. External customers are the consumers or clients in the specific environment who buy the organization's goods or use its services. Internal customers are found internally in the workflows among people and subsystems in the organization. They are individuals or groups within the organization who utilize goods and

services produced by others also inside the organization.

18. The core culture of the organization consists of the values that shape and direct the behaviour of members. Examples would be "honesty" and "quality" in everything that people do. Value-based management actively models such core values, communicates them, and encourages others to live up to them in their work. Responsibility for value-based management is shared by all managers, from senior executives to first-level supervisors and team leaders.

19. Subcultures are important in organizations because of the many aspects of diversity found in the workforce. Although working in the same organization and sharing the same organizational culture, members differ in subculture affiliations based on such aspects as gender, age, and ethnic differences, as well as in respect to occupational and functional affiliations. It is important to understand how subculture differences may influence working relationships. For example, a 40-year-old manager of 20-year-old workers must understand that the values and behaviours of the younger workforce may not be totally consistent with what she or he believes in, and vice versa.

20. I disagree with this statement since a strong organizational or corporate culture can be a positive influence on any organization, large or small. Also, issues of diversity, inclusiveness, and multiculturalism apply as well. In fact, such things as a commitment to pluralism and respect for diversity should be part of the core values and distinguishing features of the organization's culture. The woman working for the large company is mistaken in thinking that the concepts do not apply to her friend's small business. In fact, the friend as owner and perhaps founder of the business should be working hard to establish the values and other elements that will create a strong and continuing culture and respect for diversity. Employees of any organization should have core organizational values to serve as reference points for their attitudes and behaviour. The rites and rituals of everyday organizational life are also important ways to recognize positive accomplishments and add meaning to the employment relationships. It may even be that the friend's roles as creator and sponsor of the corporate culture and diversity leader are more magnified in the small-business setting. As the owner and manager, she is visible every day to all employees. How she acts will have a great impact on any "culture" that is established in her business.

CHAPTER 5

1. c
2. b
3. b
4. d
5. b
6. a
7. a
8. c
9. a
10. d
11. d
12. a
13. c
14. d
15. c

16. The North American Free Trade Agreement, NAFTA, provides the framework for Mexico, the United States, and Canada to free the flows of investments, products, and workers across their borders. This agreement creates a large consumer market and is an opportunity for business in all three countries to take full advantage of the entire North American region as a resource and customer base.

17. The relationship between an MNC and a host country should be mutually beneficial. Sometimes, however, host countries complain that MNCs take unfair advantage of them and do not include them in the benefits of their international operations. The complaints against MNCs include taking excessive profits out of the host country, hiring the best local labour, not respecting local laws and customs, and dominating the local economy. Engaging in corrupt practices is another important concern.

18. The power-distance dimension of national culture reflects the degree to which members of a society accept status and authority inequalities. Since organizations are hierarchies with power varying from top to bottom, the way power differences are viewed from one setting to the next is an important management issue. Relations between managers and subordinates or team leaders and team members will be very different in high power-distance cultures than in low power-distance ones. The significance of these differences is most evident in international operations when a manager from a high power-distance culture has to perform in a low power-distance one, or vice versa. In both cases, the cultural differences can cause problems as the manager deals with local workers.

19. For each region of the world you should identify a major economic theme or issue or element. For example: Europe—the European Union should be discussed for its economic significance to member countries and to outsiders; the Americas—NAFTA should be discussed for its current implications as well as potential significance once Chile and other nations join; Asia—the Asia-Pacific Economic Forum should be identified as a platform for growing regional economic co-operation among a very economically powerful group of countries; Africa—the new non-racial democracy in South Africa should be cited as a stimulus to broader outside investor interest in Africa.

20. Kim must recognize that the cultural differences between Canada and Japan may affect the success of group-oriented work practices such as quality circles and work teams. Canada was one of the most individualistic cultures in Hofstede's study of national cultures; Japan is much more collectivist. Group practices such as the quality circle and teams are natural and consistent with the Japanese culture. When introduced into a more individualistic culture, these same practices might cause difficulties or require some time for workers to get used to. At the very least, Kim should

CHAPTER 6

1. d
2. a
3. b
4. b
5. b
6. a
7. d
8. a
9. b
10. a
11. b
12. d
13. c
14. b
15. a

16. Entrepreneurship is rich with diversity. It is an avenue for business entry and career success that is pursued by many women and members of minority groups. Data show almost one third of Canadian businesses are owned by women. Many report leaving other employment because they had limited opportunities. For them, entrepreneurship made available the opportunities for career success that they lacked. Minority-owned businesses are one of the fastest-growing sectors. Visible minorities are entering the SME marketplace at one and a half times the rate per year of other entrepreneurs.

17. The three stages in the life cycle of an entrepreneurial firm are birth, breakthrough, and maturity. In the birth stage, the leader is challenged to get customers, establish a market, and find the money needed to keep the business going. In the breakthrough stage, the challenges shift to becoming and staying profitable, and managing growth. In the maturity stage, a leader is more focused on revising/maintaining a good business strategy and more generally managing the firm for continued success and possibly more future growth.

18. The limited partnership form of small business ownership consists of a general partner and one or more "limited partners." The general partner(s) play an active role in managing and operating the business; the limited partners do not. All contribute resources of some value to the partnership for the conduct of the business. The advantage of any partnership form is that the partners may share in profits, but their potential for losses is limited by the size of their original investments.

19. This is the realm of "intrapreneurship," or entrepreneurship that takes place within the context of a large organization. One of the ways to stimulate entrepreneurship in such settings is to make it a valued part of the culture—in other words, to reward entrepreneurial behaviour, not discourage it. Another way is to set up entrepreneurial units, sometimes called skunkworks, that are allowed to operate free from any constraints of the larger organization. The creative teamwork in these units can be a major force for entrepreneurship.

20. My friend is right—it takes a lot of forethought and planning to prepare the launch of a new business venture. In response to the question of how to ensure that I am really being customer-focused, I would ask and answer for myself the following questions. In all cases I would try to frame my business model so that the answers are realistic but still push my business toward a strong customer orientation. The "customer" questions might include: "Who are my potential customers? What market niche am I shooting for? What do the customers in this market really want? How do these customers make purchase decisions? How much will it cost to produce and distribute my product/service to these customers? How much will it cost to attract and retain customers?" Following an overall executive summary, which includes a commitment to this customer orientation, I would address the following areas in writing up my initial business plan. The plan would address such areas as company description—mission, owners, and legal form—as well as an industry analysis, product and services description, marketing description and strategy, staffing model, financial projections with cash flows, and capital needs.

CHAPTER 7

1. c
2. a
3. c
4. c
5. c
6. a
7. c
8. b
9. a
10. b
11. a
12. c
13. a
14. d
15. a

16. An optimizing decision is one that represents the absolute "best" choice of alternatives. It is selected from a set of all known alternatives. A satisficing decision selects the first alternative that offers a "satisfactory" choice, not necessarily the absolute best choice. It is selected from a limited or incomplete set of alternatives.

17. The ethics of a decision can be checked with the "spotlight" question: "How would you feel if your family found out?" "How would you feel if this were published in the local newspaper?" Also, one can test the decision by evaluating it on four criteria. (1) Utility—does it satisfy all stakeholders? (2) Rights—does it respect everyone's rights? (3) Justice—is it consistent with fairness and justice? (4) Caring—does it meet responsibilities for caring?

18. A manager using systematic thinking is going to approach problem solving in a

logical and rational fashion. The tendency will be to proceed in a linear step-by-step fashion, handling one issue at a time. A manager using intuitive thinking will be more spontaneous and open in problem solving. He or she may jump from one stage in the process to the other and deal with many different things at once.

19. It almost seems contradictory to say that one can prepare for crisis, but it is possible. The concept of crisis management is used to describe how managers and others prepare for unexpected high-impact events that threaten an organization's health and well-being. Crisis management involves both anticipating possible crises and preparing teams and plans ahead of time for how to handle them if they do occur. Many organizations today, for example, are developing crisis management plans to deal with terrorism and computer "hacking" attacks.

20. This is what I would say: Continuing developments in information technology are changing the work setting for most employees. An important development for the traditional white-collar worker falls in the area of office automation—the use of computers and related technologies to facilitate everyday office work. In the "electronic office" of today and tomorrow, you should be prepared to work with and take full advantage of the following: smart workstations supported by desktop computers; voice messaging systems whereby computers take dictation, answer the telephone, and relay messages; database and word processing software systems that allow storage, access, and manipulation of data as well as the preparation of reports; electronic mail systems that send mail and data computer to computer; electronic bulletin boards for posting messages; and computer conferencing and video conferencing that allow people to work with one another every day over great distances. These are among the capabilities of the new workplace. To function effectively, you must be prepared not only to use these systems to full advantage but also to stay abreast of new developments as they become available.

CHAPTER 8

1. d
2. a
3. b
4. d
5. b
6. d
7. c
8. c
9. c
10. d
11. a
12. d
13. d
14. d
15. a

16. The five steps in the formal planning process are: (1) define your objectives, (2) determine where you stand relative to objectives, (3) develop premises about future conditions, (4) identify and choose among action alternatives to accomplish objectives, and (5) implement action plans and evaluate results.

17. Benchmarking is the use of external standards to help evaluate one's own situation and develop ideas and directions for improvement. The bookstore owner/manager might visit other bookstores in other towns that are known for their success. By observing and studying the operations of those stores and then comparing her store with them, the owner/manager can develop plans for future action.

18. Douglas McGregor's concept of Theory Y involves the assumption that people can be trusted to exercise self-control in their work. This is the essence of internal control—people controlling their own work by taking personal responsibility for results. If managers approach work with McGregor's Theory Y assumptions, they will, according to him, promote more self-control or internal control by people at work.

19. A progressive discipline system works by adjusting the discipline to fit the severity and frequency of the inappropriate behaviour. In the case of a person who comes late to work, for example, progressive discipline might involve a verbal warning after 3 late arrivals, a written warning after 5, and a pay-loss penalty after 7. In the case of a person who steals money from the business, there would be immediate dismissal after the first such infraction.

20. I would begin the speech by describing MBO as an integrated planning and control approach. I would also clarify that the key elements in MBO are objectives and participation. Any objectives should be clear, measurable, and time-defined. In addition, these objectives should be set with the full involvement and participation of the employees; they should not be set by the manager and then told to the employees. Given this, I would describe how each business manager should jointly set objectives with each of his or her employees and jointly review progress toward their accomplishment. I would suggest that the employees should work on the required activities while staying in communication with their managers. The managers, in turn, should provide any needed support or assistance to their employees. This whole process could be formally recycled at least twice per year.

CHAPTER 9

1. a
2. b
3. c
4. c
5. d
6. b
7. c
8. a
9. b
10. c
11. d

12. b

13. d

14. a

15. c

16. A corporate strategy sets long-term direction for an enterprise as a whole. Functional strategies set directions so that business functions such as marketing and manufacturing support the overall corporate strategy.

17. A SWOT analysis is useful during strategic planning. It involves the analysis of organizational strengths and weaknesses, and of environmental opportunities and threats.

18. An e-business strategy uses the Internet to help achieve sustainable competitive advantage. This can be done through B2B strategies that link businesses electronically with one another in business-to-business relationships. A good example is B2B in supply chain management, where suppliers are linked by the Internet and extranets to customers' information systems. They follow sales and track inventories in real time and ship new orders as needed. The B2C approach is more of a retailing model linking businesses to customers. An example is Amazon.com, which uses on-line sales and on-line customer interaction to sell its products.

19. Strategic leadership is the ability to enthuse people to participate in continuous change, performance enhancement, and the implementation of organizational strategies. The special qualities of the successful strategic leader include the ability to make trade-offs, create a sense of urgency, communicate the strategy, and engage others in continuous learning about the strategy and its performance responsibilities.

20. Porter's competitive strategy model involves the possible use of three alternative strategies: differentiation, cost leadership, and focus. In this situation, the larger department store seems better positioned to follow the cost leadership strategy. This means that Kim may want to consider the other two alternatives. A differentiation strategy would involve trying to distinguish Kim's products from those of the larger store.

This might involve a "made in Canada" theme or an emphasis on leather or canvas or some other type of clothing material. A focus strategy might specifically target university students and try to respond to their tastes and needs rather than those of the larger community. This might involve special orders and other types of individualized service for the student market.

CHAPTER 10

1. b

2. a

3. b

4. a

5. b

6. c

7. b

8. b

9. b

10. a

11. a

12. a

13. c

14. c

15. b

16. The product structure organizes work around a product; the division or unit would be headed by a product manager or executive. The geographical structure organizes work by area or location; different geographical regions would be headed by regional managers or executives.

17. The functional structure is prone to problems of internal coordination. One symptom may be that the different functional areas, such as marketing and manufacturing, are not working well together. This structure is also slow in responding to changing environmental trends and challenges. If the firm finds that its competitors are getting to market faster with new and better products, this is another potential indicator that the functional structure is not supporting operations properly.

18. A network structure often involves one organization "contracting out" aspects of its operations to other organizations that specialize in them. The example used in the text was of a company that contracted out its mailroom services. Through the formation of networks of contracts, the organization is reduced to a core of essential employees whose expertise is concentrated in the primary business areas. The contracts are monitored and maintained in the network to allow the overall operations of the organization to continue even though they are not directly accomplished by full-time employees.

19. By reducing levels of management, the organization may benefit from lower overhead costs. It can also benefit as lower levels find they are in closer and more frequent contact with higher levels, and vice versa. Communication should flow more readily and quickly up and down the chain of command, as there are fewer levels to pass through. This should also mean that decisions are made more quickly.

20. Faisal must first have confidence in the two engineers—he must trust them and respect their capabilities. Second, he must have confidence in himself—trusting his own judgement to give up some work and allow these others to do it. Third, he should follow the rules of effective delegation. These include being very clear on what must be accomplished by each engineer. Their responsibilities should be clearly understood. He must also give them the authority to act in order to fulfill their responsibility, especially in relationship to the other engineers. And he must not forget his own final accountability for the results. He should remain in control and, through communication, make sure that work proceeds as planned.

CHAPTER 11

1. b

2. d

3. b

4. a

5. c

6. b
7. a
8. b
9. b
10. c
11. b
12. c
13. c
14. a
15. b
16. The term "contingency" is used in management to indicate that management strategies and practices should be tailored to fit the unique needs of individual situations. There is no universal solution that fits all problems and circumstances. Thus, in organizational design, contingency thinking must be used to identify and implement particular organizational points in time. What works well at one point in time may not work well in another as the environment and other conditions change.
17. The environment is an important influence on organizational design. The more complex, variable, and uncertain the elements in the general and specific environments, the more difficult it is for the organization to operate. This calls for more organic designs. In general, stable and more certain environments allow for mechanistic designs since operations can be more routine and predictable.
18. Differentiation and integration are somewhat conflicting in organizational design. As differentiation increases—that is, as more differences are present in the complexity of the organization—more integration is needed to ensure that everything functions together to the betterment of the whole organization. However, the greater the differentiation, the harder it is to achieve integration. Thus, when differentiation is high, organization design tends to shift toward the use of more complex horizontal approaches to integration and away from the vertical ones such as formal authority and rules or policies. In horizontal integration, the focus is on such things as cross-functional teams and matrix structures.

19. The focus of process re-engineering is on reducing costs and streamlining operations efficiency while improving customer service. This is accomplished by closely examining core business processes through the following sequence of activities: (1) identify the core processes; (2) map them in a workflows diagram; (3) evaluate all tasks involved; (4) seek ways to eliminate unnecessary tasks; (5) seek ways to eliminate delays, errors, and misunderstandings in the workflows; and (6) seek efficiencies in how work is shared and transferred among people and departments.

20. This situation involves the basic contingency notion of organizational design. There is no one best way to design an organiztion, and different designs serve organizations well under different circumstances. The first person is most likely working for an organization facing rather routine and known environmental demands. This allows for the organizational design to become more vertical and mechanistic, focusing as it does on predictable problems and outcomes. The individuals who remain in such a design are probably compatible with the internal climate of such an organization and thus find it a good "fit," resulting in reasonable levels of job satisfaction. By contrast, the second person probably works for an organization facing uncertain challenges in a dynamic environment, with the result that it is by design a more adaptive or flexible structure emphasizing horizontal rather than vertical operations. In this case, the design fits the demands of the environment, and it is also most likely to satisfy those individuals who remain with it over time. Thus we have a good demonstration of two aspects of contingency factors in organizational design: the environment-structure-performance fit and the structure-individual fit.

CHAPTER 12

1. a
2. b
3. c
4. d

5. b
6. c
7. d
8. b
9. c
10. a
11. a
12. b
13. a
14. d

15. Internal recruitment deals with job candidates who already know the organization well. It is also a strong motivator because it communicates to everyone the opportunity to advance in the organization through hard work. External recruitment may allow the organization to obtain expertise not available internally. It also brings in employees with new and fresh viewpoints who are not biased by previous experience in the organization.

16. Orientation activities introduce a new employee to the organization and the work environment. This is a time when the individual may develop key attitudes and when performance expectations will also be established. Good orientation communicates positive attitudes and expectations and reinforces the desired organizational culture. It formally introduces the individual to important policies and procedures that everyone is expected to follow.

17. The graphic rating scale simply asks a supervisor to rate an employee on an established set of criteria, such as quantity of work or attitude toward work. This leaves a lot of room for subjectivity and debate. The behaviourally anchored rating scale asks the supervisor to rate the employee on specific behaviours that had been identified as positively or negatively affecting performance in a given job. This is a more specific appraisal approach and leaves less room for debate and disagreement.

18. Mentoring is when a senior and experienced individual adopts a newcomer or more junior person with the goal of helping him or her develop into a successful worker. The mentor may or may

not be the individual's immediate supervisor. The mentor meets with the individual and discusses problems, shares advice, and generally supports the individual's attempts to grow and perform. Mentors are considered very useful for persons newly appointed to management positions.

19. As Sy's supervisor, you face a difficult but perhaps expected human resource management problem. Not only is Sy influential as an informal leader, he also has considerable experience on the job and in the company. Even though he is experiencing performance problems using the new computer system, there is no indication that he doesn't want to work hard and continue to perform for the company. Although retirement is an option, Sy may also be transferred, promoted, or simply terminated. The latter response seems unjustified and may cause legal problems. Transferring Sy, with his agreement, to another position could be a positive move; promoting Sy to a supervisory position in which his experience and networks would be useful is another possibility. The key in this situation seems to be moving Sy out so that a computer-literate person can take over the job, while continuing to utilize Sy in a job that better fits his talents. Transfer and/or promotion should be actively considered both in his and in the company's interest.

CHAPTER 13

1. d
2. d
3. b
4. a
5. c
6. a
7. b
8. c
9. b
10. a
11. b
12. a
13. d
14. a
15. b
16. Position power is based on reward, coercion or punishment, and legitimacy or formal authority. Managers, however, need to have more power than that made available to them by the position alone. Thus, they have to develop personal power through expertise and reference. This personal power is essential in helping managers to get things done beyond the scope of their position power alone.
17. Leader-participation theory suggests that leadership effectiveness is determined in part by how well managers or leaders handle the many different problem or decision situations that they face every day. Decisions can be made through individual or authority, consultative, or group-consensus approaches. No one of these decision methods is always the best; each is a good fit for certain types of situations. A good manager or leader is able to use each of these approaches and knows when each is the best approach to use in various situations.
18. (1) Position power—how much power the leader has in terms of rewards, punishments, and legitimacy. (2) Leader–member relations—the quality of relationships between the leader and followers. (3) Task structure—the degree to which the task is clear and well defined, or open ended and more ambiguous.
19. Drucker said that good leaders have more than the "charisma" or "personality" being popularized in the concept of transformational leadership. He reminded us that good leaders work hard to accomplish some basic things in their everyday activities. These include: (1) establishing a clear sense of mission, (2) accepting leadership as a responsibility, not a rank, and (3) earning and keeping the respect of others.
20. In his new position, Marcel must understand that the transactional aspects of leadership are not sufficient to guarantee him long-term leadership effectiveness. He must move beyond the effective use of task-oriented and people-oriented behaviours and demonstrate through his personal qualities the capacity to inspire others. A charismatic leader develops a unique relationship with followers in which they become enthusiastic, highly loyal, and high achievers. Marcel needs to work very hard to develop positive relationships with the team members. He must emphasize in those relationships high aspirations for performance accomplishments, enthusiasm, ethical behaviour, integrity and honesty in all dealings, and a clear vision of the future. By working hard with this agenda and by allowing his personality to positively express itself in the team setting, Marcel should make continuous progress as an effective and moral leader.

CHAPTER 14

1. c
2. d
3. d
4. b
5. b
6. d
7. c
8. b
9. d
10. a
11. b
12. a
13. b
14. c
15. a
16. People high in need for achievement will prefer work settings and jobs in which they have (1) challenging but achievable goals, (2) individual responsibility, and (3) performance feedback.
17. Participation is important to goal-setting theory because, in general, people tend to be more committed to the accomplishment of goals they have helped to set. When people participate in the setting of goals, they also understand them better. Participation in goal setting improves goal acceptance and understanding.
18. Motivation is formally defined as the forces within an individual that account for the level, direction, and persistence

of effort expended at work. Thus a person who is highly motivated will work hard. This does not necessarily mean that person will be a high performer. High performance also depends on ability and support, not just effort due to high motivation.

19. Herzberg suggests that job content factors are the satisfiers or motivators. Based in the job itself, they represent such things as responsibility, sense of achievement, and feelings of growth. Job context factors are considered sources of dissatisfaction. They are found in the job environment and include such things as base pay, technical quality of supervision, and working conditions. Whereas improvements in job context make people less dissatisfied, improvements in job content are considered necessary to motivate them to high-performance levels.

20. It has already been pointed out in the answer to question 16 that a person with a high need for achievement likes moderately challenging goals and performance feedback. Participation of both manager and subordinate in goal setting offers an opportunity to choose goals to which the subordinate will respond and which also will serve the organization. Furthermore, through goal setting, the manager and individual subordinates can identify performance standards or targets. Progress toward these targets can be positively reinforced by the manager. Such reinforcements can serve as indicators of progress to someone with high need for achievement, thus responding to their desires for performance feedback.

CHAPTER 15

1. a
2. c
3. c
4. c
5. a
6. b
7. b
8. a
9. b

10. b
11. d
12. c
13. a
14. b
15. c

16. A psychological contract is the individual's view of the inducements he or she expects to receive from the organization in return for his or her work contributions. The contract is healthy when the individual perceives that the inducements and contributions are fair and in a state of balance.

17. Growth-need strength helps determine which individuals are good candidates for job enrichment. A person high in growth-need strength seeks higher-order satisfaction of ego and self-fulfillment needs at work. These are needs to which job enrichment can positively respond. A person low in growth-need strength may not respond well to the demands and responsibilities of an enriched job.

18. All the Big Five personality traits are relevant to the workplace. To give some basic examples, consider the following. Extroversion suggests whether or not a person will reach out to relate and work well with others. Agreeableness suggests whether or not a person is open to the ideas of others and willing to go along with group decisions. Conscientiousness suggests whether someone can be depended on to meet commitments and perform agreed-upon tasks. Emotional stability suggests whether or not someone will be relaxed and secure, or uptight and tense, in work situations. Openness suggests whether someone will be open to new ideas or resistant to change.

19. The compressed workweek, or 4–40 schedule, offers employees the advantage of a three-day weekend. However, it can cause problems for the employer in terms of ensuring that operations are covered adequately during the normal five workdays of the week. Labour unions may resist, and the compressed workweek will entail more complicated work scheduling. In addition, some employees find that the schedule is tiring and can cause family adjustment problems.

20. The high-performance equation states: Performance = Ability × Support × Effort. The multiplication signs are important. They indicate that each of the performance factors must be high and positive in order for high performance to occur. That is, neither ability nor effort can be neglected by Kurt or any of the managers or team leaders in his plant. Furthermore, the factors are straightforward in their managerial implications. Ability is an issue of proper selection, training, and development of all employees. Support involves providing capable employees with such things as clear goals, appropriate technology, helpful structures, and an absence of performance obstacles such as poor rules and procedures. Effort involves making sure that the environment is motivating and offers varied intrinsic as well as extrinsic rewards. Only by giving direct and serious attention to each of these factors can Kurt and his management team take full advantage of the insights of the high-performance equation.

CHAPTER 16

1. d
2. b
3. b
4. d
5. b
6. d
7. b
8. c
9. a
10. b
11. c
12. b
13. a
14. b
15. a

16. Input factors can have a major impact on group effectiveness. In order to best prepare a group to perform effectively, a manager should make sure that the right people are put in the group (maximize

available talents and abilities), that these people are capable of working well together (membership characteristics should promote good relationships), that the tasks are clear, and that the group has the resources and environment needed to perform up to expectations.

17. A group's performance can be analyzed according to the interaction between cohesiveness and performance norms. In a highly cohesive group, members tend to conform to group norms. Thus, when the performance norm is positive and cohesion is high, we can expect everyone to work hard to support the norm—high performance is likely. By the same token, high cohesion and a low performance norm will act similarly—low performance is likely. With other combinations of norms and cohesion, the performance results will be more mixed.

18. The textbook lists several symptoms of groupthink along with various strategies for avoiding groupthink (see Manager's Notepad 16.3). For example, a group whose members censure themselves from contributing "contrary" or "different" opinions and/or whose members keep talking about outsiders as "weak" or the "enemy" may be suffering from groupthink. This may be avoided or corrected, for example by asking someone to be the "devil's advocate" for a meeting and by inviting an outside observer to help gather different viewpoints.

19. In a traditional work group, the manager or supervisor directs the group. In a self-managing team, the members of the team provide self-direction. They plan, organize, and evaluate their work, share tasks, and help one another develop skills; they may even make hiring decisions. A true self-managing team does not need the traditional "boss" or supervisor, since the team as a whole takes on the supervisory responsibilities.

20. Marcos is faced with a highly cohesive group whose members conform to a negative or low-performance norm. This is a difficult situation that ideally resolved by changing the performance norm. In order to gain the group's commitment to a high-performance norm, Marcos should act as a positive role model for the norm. He must communicate the norm clearly and positively to the group. He should not assume that everyone knows what he expects of them. He may also talk to the informal leader and gain his or her commitment to the norm. He might carefully reward high-performance behaviours within the group. He may introduce new members with high-performance records and commitments. And he might hold group meetings in which performance standards and expectations are discussed, with an emphasis on committing to new high-performance directions. If his attempts to introduce a high-performance norm fail, Marcos may have to take steps to reduce group cohesiveness so that individual members can pursue higher-performance results without feeling bound by group pressures to restrict their performance.

CHAPTER 17

1. b
2. a
3. c
4. b
5. c
6. b
7. b
8. d
9. c
10. a
11. d
12. a
13. b
14. b
15. d

16. The manager's goal in active listening is to help the subordinate say what he or she really means. To do this, the manager should carefully listen for the content of what someone is saying, paraphrase or reflect back what the person appears to be saying, remain sensitive to non-verbal cues and feelings, and not be evaluative.

17. The halo effect occurs when a single attribute of a person, such as the way he or she dresses, is used to evaluate or form an overall impression of the person. Selective perception occurs when someone focuses in a situation on those aspects that reinforce or are most consistent with his or her existing values, beliefs, or experiences.

18. Win-lose outcomes are likely when conflict is managed through high-assertiveness and low-co-operativeness styles. In this situation of competition, the conflict is resolved by one person or group dominating another. Lose-lose outcomes occur when conflict is managed through avoidance (where nothing is resolved) and possibly when it is managed through compromise (where each party gives up something to the other). Win-win outcomes are associated mainly with problem solving and collaboration in conflict management, which is a result of high assertiveness and high co-operativeness.

19. In a negotiation, both substance and relationship goals are important. Substance goals relate to the content of the negotiation. A substance goal, for example, may relate to the final salary agreement between a job candidate and a prospective employer. Relationship goals relate to the quality of the interpersonal relationships among the negotiating parties. Relationship goals are important because the negotiating parties most likely have to work together in the future. For example, if relationships are poor after a labour–management negotiation, the likelihood is that future problems will occur.

20. Harold can do a number of things to establish and maintain a system of upward communication for his department store branch. To begin, he should, as much as possible, try to establish a highly interactive style of management based upon credibility and trust. Credibility is earned through building personal power through expertise and reference. With credibility, he might set the tone for the department managers by using MBWA—"managing by wandering around." Once this pattern is established, trust will build between him and other store employees, and he

should find that he learns a lot from interacting directly with them. Harold should also set up a formal communication structure, such as bimonthly store meetings, where he communicates store goals, results, and other issues to the staff, and in which he listens to them in return. An e-mail system whereby Harold and his staff could send messages to one another from their workstation computers would also be beneficial.

CHAPTER 18

1. b
2. a
3. b
4. c
5. c
6. b
7. c
8. a
9. d
10. a
11. a
12. d
13. c
14. a
15. c

16. Lewin's three phases of planned change are: Unfreezing—preparing a system for change; changing—moving or creating change in a system; and refreezing—stabilizing and reinforcing change once it has occurred.

17. In general, managers can expect that others will be more committed and loyal to changes that are brought about through shared power strategies. Rational persuasion strategies can also create enduring effects if they are accepted. Force-coercion strategies tend to have temporary effects only.

18. The statement that "OD equals planned change plus" basically refers to the fact that OD tries both to create change in an organization and to make the organization members capable of creating such change for themselves in the future.

19. The Type A personality is characteristic of people who bring stress on themselves by virtue of personal characteristics. These tend to be compulsive individuals who are uncomfortable waiting for things to happen, who try to do many things at once, and who generally move fast and have difficulty slowing down. Type A personalities can be stressful for both the individuals and the people around them. Managers must be aware of Type A personality tendencies in their own behaviour and among others with whom they work. Ideally, this awareness will help the manager take precautionary steps to best manage the stress caused by this personality type.

20. In any change situation, it is important to remember that successful planned change occurs only when all three phases of change—unfreezing, changing, and refreezing—have been taken care of. Thus, I would not rush into the changing phase. Rather, I would work with the people involved to develop a felt need for change based on their ideas and inputs as well as mine. Then I would proceed by supporting the changes and helping to stabilize them into everyday routines. I would also be sensitive to any resistance and respect that resistance as a signal that something important is being threatened. By listening to resistance, I would be in a position to better modify the change to achieve a better fit with the people and the situation. Finally, I would want to take maximum advantage of the shared power strategy, supported by rational persuasion, and with limited use of force-coercion (if it is used at all). By doing all of this, I would like my staff to feel empowered and committed to constructive improvement through planned change.

Glossary

A

Above-average returns exceed what could be earned from alternative investments of equivalent risk.

Accommodation or **smoothing** plays down differences and highlights similarities to reduce conflict.

An **accommodative strategy** of social responsibility tries to satisfy prevailing economic, legal, and ethical performance criteria.

Accountability is the requirement to show performance results to a supervisor.

Action research is a collaborative process of collecting data, using it for action planning, and evaluating the results.

Active listening involves taking action to help the source of a message say what he or she really means.

An **adaptive organization** operates with a minimum of bureaucratic features and encourages worker empowerment and teamwork.

The **administrative decision model** describes how managers act in situations of limited information and bounded rationality.

An **administrator** is a manager who works in a public or nonprofit organization.

An **after-action review** formally reviews results to identify lessons learned in a completed project, task force, or special operation.

Agreeableness is being good-natured, co-operative, and trusting.

An **analyzer strategy** seeks the stability of a core business while selectively responding to opportunities for innovation and change.

An **angel investor** is a wealthy individual willing to invest in return for equity in a new venture.

APEC, Asia-Pacific Economic Cooperation is a platform for regional economic alliances among Asian and Pacific Rim countries.

Applications software allows the user to perform a variety of information-based tasks without writing unique computer programs.

An **apprenticeship** is a special form of training that involves a formal assignment to serve as understudy or assistant to a person who already has the desired job skills.

Arbitration is the process by which parties to a dispute agree to abide by the decision of a neutral and independent third party, called an arbitrator.

Asia-Pacific Economic Cooperation (APEC) is a platform for regional economic co-operation among Asian and Pacific Rim countries.

An **assessment centre** is a selection technique that engages job candidates in a series of experimental activities over a 1- or 2-day period.

An **attitude** is a predisposition to act in a certain way.

Attribution error overestimates internal factors and underestimates external factors as influences on someone's behaviour.

Authentic leadership activates high self-awareness and self-regulated positive behaviour in one's self and others.

Authoritarianism is the degree to which a person tends to defer to authority.

Authority is the right to assign tasks and direct the activities of subordinates in ways that support accomplishment of the organization's purpose.

An **authority decision** is a decision made by the leader and then communicated to the group.

A leader with an **autocratic style** acts in unilateral command-and-control fashion.

Automation is the total mechanization of a job.

Avoidance involves pretending that a conflict doesn't really exist or hoping that a conflict will simply go away.

B

A **B2C business strategy** uses IT to link businesses with consumers.

A **bargaining zone** is the area between one party's minimum reservation point and the other party's maximum reservation point.

Base compensation is a salary or hourly wage paid to an individual.

BATNA is the "best alternative to a negotiated agreement," or what can be done if an agreement cannot be reached.

The **BCG matrix** ties strategy formulation to an analysis of business opportunities according to market growth rate and market share.

The **behavioural decision model** describes decision making with limited information and bounded rationality.

A **behaviourally anchored rating scale (BARS)** is a performance appraisal method that uses specific descriptions of actual behaviours to rate various levels of performance.

Benchmarking is a process of comparing operations and performance with other organizations known for excellence.

Best practices are things that lead to superior performance.

Bona fide occupational qualifications are exceptions to employment equity justified by individual capacity to perform a job.

A **bonus pay plan** provides cash bonuses to employees based on the achievement of specific performance targets.

In **bottom-up change**, change initiatives come from all levels in the organization.

Bottom-up planning begins with ideas developed at lower management levels, which are modified as they are passed up the hierarchy to top management.

A **boundaryless organization** eliminates internal boundaries among parts and external boundaries with the external environment.

Brainstorming is a group technique for generating a large quantity of ideas by free-wheeling contributions made without criticism.

Break-even analysis calculates where sales revenues cover costs.

A **budget** is a plan that commits resources to projects or programs; a formalized way of allocating resources to specific activities.

Bureaucracy is a rational and efficient form of organization founded on logic, order, and legitimate authority.

Business incubators offer space, shared services, and advice to help small businesses get started.

A **business plan** describes the direction for a new business and the financing needed to operate it.

A **business strategy** identifies the intentions of a division or strategic business unit to compete in its special product and/or service domain.

C

A **career** is a sequence of jobs that constitute what a person does for a living.

Career planning is the process of systematically matching career goals and individual capabilities with opportunities for their fulfillment.

A **career plateau** is a position from which someone is unlikely to move to a higher level of work responsibility.

A **career portfolio** documents academic and personal accomplishments for external review.

Centralization is the concentration of authority for most decisions at the top level of an organization.

In a **centralized communication network**, communication flows only between individual members and a hub or centre point.

A **certain environment** offers complete information on possible action alternatives and their consequences.

The **chain of command** links all persons with successively higher levels of authority.

A **change agent** is a person or group that takes leadership responsibility for changing the existing pattern of behaviour of another person or social system.

Changing is the central phase in the planned change process in which a planned change actually takes place.

Channel richness is the capacity of a communication channel to effectively carry information.

A **charismatic leader** is a leader who develops special leader-follower relationships and inspires followers in extraordinary ways.

Child labour is the full-time employment of children for work otherwise done by adults.

A **CIO** is a senior executive responsible for IT and its utilization throughout an organization.

The **classical decision model** describes how managers ideally make decisions using complete information.

Coaching is the communication of specific technical advice to an individual.

A **code of ethics** is a written document that states values and ethical standards intended to guide the behaviour of employees.

Coercive power is the capacity to punish or withhold positive outcomes as a means of influencing other people.

Cognitive dissonance is discomfort felt when attitude and behaviour are inconsistent.

Cohesiveness is the degree to which members are attracted to and motivated to remain part of a team.

Collaboration or **problem solving** involves working through conflict differences and solving problems so everyone wins.

Collective bargaining is the process of negotiating, administering, and interpreting a labour contract.

A **combination strategy** involves stability, growth, and retrenchment in one or more combinations.

Commercializing innovation turns ideas into economic value added.

A **committee** is a formal team designated to work on a special task on a continuing basis.

Communication is the process of sending and receiving symbols with meanings attached.

A **communication channel** is the medium through which a message is sent.

Comparable worth holds that persons performing jobs of similar importance should be paid at comparable levels.

Comparative management is the study of how management practices differ systematically from one country and/or culture to the next.

Competition or **authoritative command** uses force, superior skill, or domination to "win" a conflict.

A **competitive advantage** is a special edge that allows an organization to deal with market and environmental forces better than its competitors.

A **compressed workweek** is any work schedule that allows a full-time job to be completed in less than the standard 5 days of 8-hour shifts.

Compromise occurs when each party to the conflict gives up something of value to the other.

Computer competency is the ability to understand and use computers to advantage.

Growth through **concentration** is within the same business area.

A **conceptual skill** is the ability to think analytically and solve complex problems to the benefit of everyone involved.

A **concurrent control** or *steering control* is a control that acts in anticipation of problems and focuses primarily on what happens during the work process.

Conflict is a disagreement over issues of substance and/or an emotional antagonism.

Conflict resolution is the removal of the reasons—substantial and/or emotional—for a conflict.

Conscientiousness is being responsible, dependable, and careful in work.

Constructive stress acts in a positive way to increase effort, stimulate creativity, and encourage diligence in one's work.

A **consultative decision** is a decision made by a leader after receiving information, advice, or opinions from group members.

Contingency planning identifies alternative courses of action that can be taken if and when circumstances change with time.

Contingency thinking maintains that there is no one best way to manage; what is best depends on the situation.

Contingency workers are employed on a part-time and temporary basis to supplement a permanent workforce.

Continuous improvement involves always searching for new ways to improve operations quality and performance.

In **continuous-process production**, raw production materials continuously move through an automated system.

A **control chart** is a method for quality control in which work results are displayed on a graph that clearly delineates upper control limits and lower control limits.

Controlling is the process of measuring performance and taking action to ensure desired results.

A **core competency** is a special strength that gives an organization a competitive advantage.

Core values are underlying beliefs shared by members of the organization and that influence their behaviour.

Corporate culture is the predominant value system for the organization as a whole.

Corporate governance is the system of control and performance monitoring of top management.

Corporate social responsibility is an obligation of an organization to act in ways that serve both its own interests and the interests of its many external publics.

A **corporate strategy** sets long-term direction for the total enterprise.

A **corporation** is a legal entity that exists separately from its owners.

Corruption involves illegal practices to further one's business interests.

Cost-benefit analysis involves comparing the costs and benefits of each potential course of action.

A **cost leadership strategy** is a corporate competitive strategy that seeks to achieve lower costs than competitors by improving efficiency of production, distribution, and other organizational systems.

Creativity is the generation of a novel idea or unique approach that solves a problem or crafts an opportunity.

Credibility is trust and respect in the eyes of others.

A **crisis** is an unexpected problem that can lead to disaster if not resolved quickly and appropriately.

Crisis management is preparation for the management of crises that threaten an organization's health and well-being.

A **critical-incident technique** is a performance appraisal method that involves a running log of effective and ineffective job behaviours.

A **cross-functional team** is a team structure in which members from different functional departments work together as needed to solve problems and explore opportunities.

Cultural relativism suggests there is no one right way to behave; ethical behaviour is determined by its cultural context.

Culture is a shared set of beliefs, values, and patterns of behaviour common to a group of people.

Culture shock is the confusion and discomfort a person experiences when in an unfamiliar culture.

Currency risk is possible loss because of fluctuating exchange rates.

Customer relationship management strategically tries to build lasting relationships and add value to customers.

A **customer structure** is a divisional structure that groups together jobs and activities that serve the same customers or clients.

A **cybernetic control system** is a control system that is entirely self-contained in its performance monitoring and correction capabilities.

Cycle time is the elapsed time between the receipt of an order and the delivery of a finished good or service.

D

Data are raw facts and observations.

Debt financing involves borrowing money that must be repaid over time with interest.

Decentralization is the dispersion of authority to make decisions throughout all levels of the organization.

A **decentralized communication network** allows all members to communicate directly with one another.

A **decision** is a choice among alternative courses of action for dealing with a "problem."

Decision making is the process of making choices among alternative possible courses of action.

The **decision-making process** begins with identification of a problem and ends with evaluation of implemented solutions.

A **decision support system** allows managers to interact with a computer to utilize information for solving structured and semistructured problems.

A **defender strategy** is a corporate competitive strategy that emphasizes existing products and current market share without seeking growth.

A **defensive strategy** of social responsibility seeks to protect the organization by doing the minimum legally required to satisfy social expectations.

Delegation is the process of distributing and entrusting work to other persons.

Departmentalization is the process of grouping together people and jobs under common supervisors to form various work units or departments.

Design for disassembly is the design of products with attention to how their component parts will be used when product life ends.

Design for manufacturing is creating a design that lowers production costs and improves quality in all stages of production.

Destructive stress impairs the performance of an individual.

Differentiation is the degree of differences that exist among people, departments, or other internal components of an organization.

A **differentiation strategy** is a corporate strategy that seeks competitive advantage through uniqueness, by developing goods and/or services that are clearly different from those offered by the competition.

Discipline is the act of influencing behaviour through reprimand.

Discrimination is an active form of prejudice that disadvantages people by denying them full benefits of organizational membership.

A **distinctive competence** is a special strength that gives an organization a competitive advantage in its operating domain.

Distributive justice concerns the degree to which people are treated the same regardless of individual characteristics such as ethnicity, race, gender, or age.

Distributive negotiation focuses on "win-lose" claims made by each party for certain preferred outcomes.

Growth through **diversification** is by acquisition of or investment in new and different business areas.

The term **diversity** describes race, gender, age, and other individual differences.

Divestiture sells off parts of the organization to focus attention and resources on core business areas.

A **divisional structure** groups together people who work on the same product, work with similar customers, or work in the same area or processes.

Downsizing decreases the size of operations with the intent to become more streamlined.

A **dual-career couple** is one in which both adult partners are employed.

Dysfunctional conflict is destructive and hurts task performance.

E

An **e-business strategy** strategically uses the Internet to gain competitive advantage.

The **economic order quantity (EOQ)** method orders a fixed number of items every time an inventory level falls to a predetermined point.

Effective communication occurs when the intended meaning of the source and the perceived meaning of the receiver are identical.

An **effective group** is a group that achieves and maintains high levels of both task performance and membership satisfaction over time.

Effective negotiation occurs when issues of substance and working relationships among the negotiating parties are maintained or even improved in the process.

An **effective team** achieves high levels of both task performance and membership satisfaction.

Efficient communication is communication that occurs at minimum cost in terms of resources expended.

Electronic commerce or e-business uses information technology to support on-line commercial transactions.

An **emergent strategy** develops over time as managers learn from and respond to experience.

Emotional conflict results from feelings of anger, distrust, dislike, fear, and resentment as well as from personality clashes.

Emotional intelligence is the ability to manage ourselves and our relationships effectively.

Emotional stability is being relaxed, secure, and unworried.

Employee assistance programs help employees cope with personal stresses and problems.

An **employee involvement team** meets on a regular basis to use its talents to help solve problems and achieve continuous improvement.

An **employee stock ownership plan (ESOP)** allows employees to share ownership of their employing organization through the purchase of stock.

Employment discrimination occurs when non-job relevant criteria are used for hiring and job placements.

Empowerment distributes decision-making power throughout an organization.

Employment equity is an effort to give preference in employment to Aboriginals, women, visible minorities, and people with physical/mental disability.

An **enterprise-wide network** is a set of computer-communication links that connects a diverse set of activities throughout an organization.

An **entrepreneur** is willing to pursue opportunities in situations others view as problems or threats.

Entrepreneurship is dynamic, risk-taking, creative, and growth-oriented behaviour.

Environmental uncertainty is a lack of complete information about the environment.

Environmentalism is the expression and demonstration of public concern for conditions of the natural or physical environment.

Equity financing involves exchanging ownership shares for outside investment monies.

Escalating commitment is the tendency to continue to pursue a course of action even though it is not working.

Ethical behaviour is accepted as "right" or "good" in the context of a governing moral code.

An **ethical dilemma** is a situation with a potential course of action that, although offering potential benefit or gain, is also unethical.

The attempt to externally impose one's ethical standards on other cultures is criticized as a form of **ethical imperialism**.

Ethical leadership is always "good" and "right" by moral standards.

Ethics set moral standards as to what is good or bad, or right or wrong in one's conduct.

Ethics training seeks to help people better understand the ethical aspects of decision making and to incorporate high ethical standards into their daily behaviour.

Ethnocentric attitudes consider practices of the home country as the best.

Ethnocentrism is the tendency to consider one's culture as superior to all others.

The **euro** is the new common European currency.

The **European Union (EU)** is a political and economic alliance of European countries that have agreed to support mutual economic growth and to lift barriers that previously limited cross-border trade and business development.

Eustress is stress that is constructive for an individual and helps her or him achieve a positive balance with the external environment.

An **expatriate** lives and works in a foreign country.

Expectancy is a person's belief that working hard will result in high task performance.

Expert power is the capability to influence other people because of specialized knowledge.

An **expert system** is a computer program designed to analyze and solve problems at the level of the human expert.

Exporting is the process of producing products locally and selling them abroad in foreign markets.

External control is control that occurs through direct supervision or administrative systems, such as rules and procedures.

An **external customer** is a customer or client who buys or uses the organization's goods and/or services.

Extinction discourages a behaviour by making the removal of a desirable consequence contingent on the occurrence of the behaviour.

Extranets are computer networks that use the public Internet for communication between the organization and its environment.

An **extrinsic reward** is a reward given as a motivational stimulus to a person, usually by a superior.

Extroversion is being outgoing, sociable, and assertive.

F

A **family business** is owned and controlled by members of a family.

Family-friendly benefits help employees achieve better work-life balance.

Feedback is the process of telling someone else how you feel about something that person did or said or about the situation in general.

A **feedback control** or *post-action control* is a control that takes place after an action is completed.

A **feedforward control** or *preliminary control* ensures that proper directions are set and that the right resources are available to accomplish them before the work activity begins.

Filtering is the intentional distortion of information to make it appear most favourable to the recipient.

First-line managers oversee single units and pursue short-term performance objectives consistent with the plans of middle- and top-management levels.

A **first-mover advantage** comes from being first to exploit a niche or enter a market.

A **flexible benefits** program allows employees to choose from a range of benefit options within certain dollar limits.

A **flexible budget** allows the allocation of resources to vary in proportion with various levels of activity.

Flexible manufacturing involves the ability to change manufacturing processes quickly and efficiently to produce different products or modifications of existing ones.

Flexible working hours are work schedules that give employees some choice in the pattern of daily work hours.

A **focus strategy** is a corporate competitive strategy that concentrates attention on a special market segment to serve its needs better than the competition.

A **focused cost leadership strategy** seeks the lowest costs of operations within a special market segment.

A **focused differentiation strategy** offers a unique product to a special market segment.

A **force-coercion strategy** attempts to bring about change through formal authority and/or the use of rewards or punishments.

Forecasting attempts to predict outcomes; it involves a projection into the future based on historical data combined in some scientific manner.

A **formal group** is created by the formal authority within the organization.

Formal structure is the structure of the organization in its pure or ideal state.

Framing error occurs when a problem is solved in the context in which it is perceived or presented.

A **franchise** is when one business owner sells to another the right to operate the same business in another location.

Fringe benefits are additional nonmonetary forms of compensation (e.g., health plans, retirement plans) provided to an organization's workforce.

The **functional chimneys problem** is a lack of communication and coordination across functions.

Functional conflict is constructive and helps task performance.

A **functional group** is a formally designated work group consisting of a manager and subordinates.

Functional managers are responsible for one area of activity, such as finance, marketing, production, personnel, accounting, or sales.

A **functional strategy** guides activities within one specific area of operations.

A **functional structure** is an organizational structure that groups together people with similar skills who perform similar tasks.

A **functional team** is a formally designated work team with a manager or team leader.

G

A **gain-sharing plan** allows employees to share in any savings or "gains" realized through their efforts to reduce costs and increase productivity.

In the **General Agreement on Tariffs and Trade (GATT)** and **World Trade Organization (WTO)**, member nations agree to ongoing negotiations and reducing tariffs and trade restrictions.

The **general environment** is composed of the cultural, economic, legal–political, and educational conditions in the locality in which an organizational operates.

General managers are responsible for complex organizational units that include many areas of functional activity.

Geocentric attitudes value talent and best practices from all over the world.

A **geographical structure** is a divisional structure that groups together jobs and activities being performed in the same location or geographical region.

The **glass ceiling effect** is an invisible barrier that limits the advancement of women and minorities to higher-level responsibilities in organizations.

The **global economy** is an economic perspective based on worldwide interdependence of resource supplies, product markets, and business competition.

A **global manager** works successfully across international boundaries.

Global sourcing is a process of purchasing materials or components in various parts of the world and then assembling them at home into a final product.

Globalization is the worldwide interdependence of resource flows, product markets, and business competition.

A **globalization strategy** adopts standardized products and advertising for use worldwide.

A **grapevine** is a common informal communication network.

A **graphic rating scale** is a performance appraisal method that uses a checklist of traits or characteristics thought to be related to high-performance outcomes in a given job.

A **group** is a collection of people who regularly interact with one another over time in respect to the pursuit of one or more common goals.

Group cohesiveness is the degree to which members are attracted to and motivated to remain part of a group.

A **group decision** is a decision made with the full participation of all group members.

A **group decision-support system** facilitates group efforts at solving complex problems while utilizing computerized information systems.

Group dynamics are forces operating in groups that affect task performance and membership satisfaction.

A **group norm** is a behaviour, rule, or standard expected to be followed by group members.

Group process is the way team members work together to accomplish tasks.

Groupthink is a tendency for highly cohesive teams to lose their evaluative capabilities.

Groupware is a software system that allows people from different locations to work together in computer-mediated collaboration.

A **growth strategy** involves expansion of the organization's current operations.

Growth-need strength is an individual's desire to achieve a sense of psychological growth in her or his work.

H

A **halo effect** occurs when one attribute is used to develop an overall impression of a person or situation.

The **Hawthorne effect** is the tendency of persons singled out for special attention to perform as expected.

Heuristics are strategies for simplifying decision making.

High-context cultures rely on non-verbal and situational cues as well as spoken or written words in communication.

Higher-order needs, in Maslow's hierarchy, are esteem and self-actualization needs.

Human capital is the economic value of people with job-relevant abilities, knowledge, ideas, energies, and commitments.

The **human relations movement** is based on the viewpoint that managers who use good human relations in the workplace will achieve productivity.

Human resource maintenance is a team's ability to maintain its social fabric so that members work well together.

Human resource management is the process of attracting, developing, and maintaining a talented and energetic workforce.

Human resource planning is the process of analyzing staffing needs and identifying actions to fill those needs over time.

Human resources are the people, individuals, and groups that help organizations produce goods or services.

A **human skill** is the ability to work well in co-operation with other people.

A **hygiene factor** is a factor in the work setting, such as working conditions, interpersonal relations, organizational policies, and administration, supervision, and salary.

I

Importing is the process of acquiring products abroad and selling them in domestic markets.

Incremental change bends and adjusts existing ways to improve performance.

Independent contractors are hired on temporary contracts and are not part of the organization's official workforce.

An **individual decision** is made when a manager chooses a preferred course of action without consulting others.

The **individualism view** is a view of ethical behaviour based on the belief that one's primary commitment is to the advancement of long-term self-interests.

An **informal group** is not offically created and emerges based on relationships and shared interests among members.

Informal learning occurs as people interact informally throughout the workday.

Informal structure is the undocumented and officially unrecognized structure that coexists with the formal structure of an organization.

Information is data made useful for decision making.

Information competency is the ability to utilize computers and information technology to locate, retrieve, evaluate, organize, and analyze information for decision making.

An **information system** collects, organizes, and distributes data regarding activities occurring inside and outside an organization.

Information technology is the use of electronic devices that aid in the creation, management, and use of information.

Innovation is the process of taking a new idea and putting it into practice as part of the organization's normal operating routines.

An **input standard** is a standard that measures work efforts that go into a performance task.

Inside-out planning focuses planning on internal strengths and trying to do better than what one already does.

Instant messaging is instantaneous communication between people on-line at the same time.

Instrumental values are preferences regarding the means for accomplishing desired ends.

Instrumentality is a person's belief that various work-related outcomes will occur as a result of task performance.

Integration is the level of coordination achieved among subsystems in an organization.

Integrity in leadership is honesty, credibility, and consistency in putting values into action.

Intellectual capital is the collective brainpower or shared knowledge of a workforce.

Intensive technology focuses the efforts and talents of many people with high interdependence to serve clients.

Interactional justice is the degree to which others are treated with dignity and respect.

Internal control is self-control that occurs through self-discipline and the personal exercise of individual or group responsibility.

An **internal customer** is someone who uses or depends on the work of another person or group within the organization.

An **international business** conducts commercial transactions across national boundaries.

International management involves the conduct of business or other operations in foreign countries.

Intranets are computer networks that allow persons within an organization to share databases and communicate electronically.

Intrapreneurship is entrepreneurial behaviour displayed by people or subunits within large organizations.

An **intrinsic** or **natural reward** is a reward that occurs naturally as a person performs a task or job.

Intuitive thinking occurs when someone approaches problems in a flexible and spontaneous fashion.

Inventory consists of materials or products kept in storage.

An **IPO** is an initial selling of shares of stock to the public and for trading on a stock exchange.

ISO certification is granted by the International Organization for Standardization to indicate that a business meets a rigorous set of quality standards.

ISO 14000 offers a set of certification standards for responsible environmental policies.

J

A **job** is the collection of tasks a person performs in support of organizational objectives.

Job analysis is an orderly study of job requirements and facets that can influence performance results.

Job burnout is physical and mental exhaustion that can be incapacitating personally and in respect to work.

A **job description** is a written statement that details the duties and responsibilities of any person holding a particular job.

Job design is the allocation of specific work tasks to individuals and groups.

Job enlargement is a job-design strategy that increases task variety by combining into one job two or more tasks that were previously assigned to separate workers.

Job enrichment is a job-design strategy that increases job depth by adding to a job some of the planning and evaluating duties normally performed by the supervisor.

Job involvement is the extent to which an individual is dedicated to a job.

Job performance is the quantity and quality of task accomplishment by an individual or group.

Job rotation is a job-design strategy that increases task variety by periodically shifting workers among jobs involving different tasks.

Job satisfaction is the degree to which an individual feels positively or negatively about various aspects of the job, including assigned tasks, work setting, and relationships with co-workers.

Job scope is the number and combination of tasks an individual or group is asked to perform.

Job sharing is an arrangement that splits one job between two people.

Job simplification is a job-design strategy that involves standardizing work procedures and employing people in clearly defined and very specialized tasks.

A **job specification** is a list of the qualifications required of any job occupant.

A **joint venture** is a form of international business that establishes operations in a foreign country through joint ownership with local partners.

The **justice view** considers ethical behaviour as that which treats people impartially and fairly according to guiding rules and standards.

Just-in-time scheduling (JIT) schedules materials to arrive at a workstation or facility "just in time" to be used.

K

Keiretsu is a Japanese term describing alliances or business groups that link together manufacturers, suppliers, and finance companies with common interests.

Knowledge management is the process of utilizing organizational knowledge to achieve competitive advantage.

A **knowledge worker** is someone whose knowledge is a critical asset to employers.

L

A **labour contract** is a formal agreement between a union and the employing organization that specifies the rights and obligations of each party with respect to wages, work hours, work rules, and other conditions of employment.

A **labour union** is an organization to which workers belong and that deals with employers on their collective behalf.

Thorndike's **law of effect** states that behaviour followed by pleasant consequences is likely to be repeated, whereas behaviour followed by unpleasant consequences is not likely to be repeated.

Leadership is the process of inspiring others to work hard to accomplish important tasks.

Leadership style is the recurring pattern of behaviours exhibited by a leader.

Leading is the process of arousing enthusiasm and directing human resource efforts toward organizational goals.

Lean production involves streamlining systems and implementing new technologies to allow work to be performed with fewer workers and smaller inventories.

Learning is any change in behaviour that occurs as a result of experience.

A **learning organization** utilizes people, values, and systems to continuously change and improve its performance based on the lessons of experience.

Legitimate power is the capability to influence other people by virtue of formal authority or the rights of office.

A **licensing agreement** occurs when a firm pays a fee for the rights to make or sell another company's products.

Lifelong learning is continuous learning from daily experiences and opportunities.

Line managers have direct responsibility for activities making direct contributions to the production of the organization's basic goods or services.

Lobbying expresses opinions and preferences to government officials.

Locus of control is the extent to which one believes that what happens is in one's control.

In **long-linked technology** a client moves from point to point during service delivery.

In **lose-lose conflict** no one achieves his or her true desires and the underlying reasons for conflict remain unaffected.

Low-context cultures emphasize communication via spoken or written words.

Lower-order needs, in Maslow's hierarchy, are physiological, safety, and social needs.

M

Machiavellianism is the extent to which someone is manipulative in using power to achieve goals.

A **maintenance activity** is an action taken by a team member that supports the emotional life of the group.

Management is the process of planning, organizing, leading, and controlling the use of resources to accomplish performance goals.

Management by exception focuses managerial attention on substantial differences between actual and desired performance.

Management by objectives (MBO) is a process of joint objective setting between a superior and subordinate.

In **management by wandering around (MBWA)**, workers at all levels talk with bosses about a variety of work-related matters.

Management development is training to improve knowledge and skills in the fundamentals of management.

A **management information system (MIS)** collects, organizes, and distributes data in such a way that the information meets managers' needs.

Management science or **operations research** is a scientific approach to management that uses mathematical techniques to analyze and solve problems.

A **manager** is a person who supports and is responsible for the work of others.

Managerial competency is a skill or personal characteristic that contributes to high performance in a management job.

Managing diversity is building an inclusive work environment that allows everyone to reach their full potential.

Maquiladoras are foreign manufacturing plants that operate in Mexico with special privileges.

Mass customization involves manufacturing individualized products quickly and with the production efficiencies once only associated with mass production of uniform products.

Mass production manufactures a large number of uniform products with an assembly-line type of system.

A **master budget** is a comprehensive short-term budget for an organization as a whole.

A **matrix structure** combines functional and divisional approaches to emphasize project or program teams.

A **mechanistic design** is highly bureaucratic, with centralized authority, many rules and procedures, a clearcut division of labour, narrow spans of controls, and formal coordination.

Mediating technology links together parties seeking a mutually beneficial exchange of values.

In **mediation** a neutral party engages in substantive discussions with conflicting parties in the hope that the dispute can be resolved.

Mentoring is the act of sharing experiences and insights between a seasoned and a junior manager.

Merit pay is a system of awarding pay increases in proportion to performance contributions.

Middle managers report to top-level management, oversee the work of several units, and implement plans consistent with higher-level objectives.

The **mission** of an organization is its reason for existing as a supplier of goods and/or services to society.

A **mixed message** results when a person's words communicate one message while actions, body language, or appearance communicate something else.

Modelling demonstrates through personal behaviour that which is expected of others.

In a **monochronic culture** people tend to do one thing at a time.

The **moral-rights view** is a view of ethical behaviour that seeks to respect and protect the fundamental rights of people.

Most favoured nation status gives a trading partner most favourable treatment for imports and exports.

Motion study is the science of reducing a task to its basic physical motions.

Motivation is a term used in management theory to describe forces within the individual that account for the level, direction, and persistence of effort expended at work.

A **multicultural organization** is based on pluralism and operates with respect for diversity in the workplace.

Multi-dimensional thinking is the capacity to view many problems at once, in relationship to one another, and across long and short time horizons.

A **multidomestic strategy** customizes products and advertising to best fit local needs.

A **multinational corporation (MNC)** is a business firm with extensive international operations in more than one foreign country.

A **multiperson comparison** is a performance appraisal method that involves comparing one person's performance with that of one or more other persons.

N

NAFTA is the **North American Free Trade Agreement** linking Canada, the United States, and Mexico in a regional economic alliance.

A **narrative approach** to performance appraisal method uses a written essay description of a person's job performance.

Nationalization is when a government seizes ownership of foreign assets.

A **need** is a physiological or psychological deficiency that a person wants to satisfy.

Need for Achievement (nAch) is the desire to do something better or more efficiently, to solve problems, or to master complex tasks.

Need for Affiliation (nAff) is the desire to establish and maintain good relations with people.

Need for Power (nPower) is the desire to control, influence, or be responsible for other people.

Negative reinforcement strengthens a behaviour by making the avoidance of an undesirable consequence contingent on the occurrence of the behaviour.

Negotiation is the process of making joint decisions when the parties involved have different preferences.

A **network** is a system of computers that are linked together to allow users to easily transfer and share information.

A **network structure** is an organizational structure that consists of a central core with "networks" of outside suppliers of essential business services.

Noise is anything that interferes with the effectiveness of the communication process.

The **nominal group technique** is a group technique for generating ideas by following a structured format of individual response, group sharing without criticism, and written balloting.

A **nonprogrammed decision** is unique and specifically tailored to a problem at hand.

Nonverbal communication is communication that takes place through channels such as body language and the use of interpersonal space.

A **norm** is a behaviour, rule, or standard expected to be followed by team members.

O

Objectives are the specific results or desired end states that one wishes to achieve.

An **obstructionist strategy** avoids social responsibility and reflects mainly economic priorities.

An **OD intervention** is a structured activity initiated by consultants or managers that directly assists in a comprehensive organizational development program.

An **open system** interacts with its environment and transforms resource inputs into outputs.

Openness is being curious, receptive to new ideas, and imaginative.

Operant conditioning is the process of controlling behaviour by manipulating its consequences.

An **operating budget** is a budget that assigns resources to a responsibility centre on a short-term basis.

Operating objectives are specific results that organizations try to accomplish.

An **operational plan** is a plan of limited scope that addresses those activities and resources required to implement strategic plans.

Operations management is a branch of management theory that studies how organizations transform resource inputs into product and service outputs.

An **optimizing decision** results when a manager chooses an alternative that gives the absolute best solution to a problem.

An **organic design** is decentralized with fewer rules and procedures, more open divisions of labour, wide spans of control, and more personal coordination.

An **organization** is a collection of people working together in a division of labour to achieve a common purpose.

An **organization chart** is a diagram that describes the basic arrangement of work positions within an organization.

Organization development (OD) is the application of behavioural science knowledge in a long-range effort to improve an organization's ability to cope with change in its external environment and increase its internal problem-solving capabilities.

Organization structure is the system of tasks, reporting relationships, and communication that links people and groups together to accomplish tasks that serve the organizational purpose.

Organizational behaviour is the study of individuals and groups in organizations.

Organizational commitment is defined as the loyalty of an individual to the organization.

Organizational communication is the process through which information is exchanged through interactions among people inside an organization.

Organizational culture is the system of shared beliefs and values that develops within an organization and guides the behaviour of its members.

Organizational design is the process of creating structures that best organize resources to serve mission and objectives.

Organizational ecology is the study of how building design may influence communication and productivity.

Organizational effectiveness is sustainable high performance in accomplishing mission and objectives.

The **organizational life cycle** is the evolution of an organization over time through different stages of growth.

Organizational stakeholders are directly affected by the behaviour of the organization and hold a stake in its performance.

Organizing is the process of arranging people and resources to work toward a common purpose.

Orientation consists of activities through which new employees are made familiar with their jobs, their co-workers, and the policies, rules, objectives, and services of the organization as a whole.

An **output standard** is a standard that measures performance results in terms of quantity, quality, cost, or time.

Outside-in planning uses analysis of the external environment and makes plans to take advantage of opportunities and avoid problems.

Outsourcing is when a business function is contracted to an outside supplier.

P

Participatory planning is the inclusion in the planning process of as many people as possible from among those who will be affected by plans and/or asked to help implement them.

A **partnership** is when two or more people agree to contribute resources to start and operate a business together.

Part-time work is work done on a basis that classifies the employee as "temporary" and requires less than the standard 40-hour workweek.

Peer-to-peer file sharing connects PCs directly to one another over the Internet without the support of a central server.

Perception is the process through which people receive, organize, and interpret information from the environment.

Performance appraisal is a process of formally evaluating performance and providing feedback on which performance adjustments can be made.

Performance effectiveness is an output measure of a task or goal accomplishment.

Performance efficiency is a measure of the resource cost associated with goal accomplishment.

A **performance gap** is a discrepancy between the desired and actual state of affairs.

A **performance management system** sets standards, assesses results, and plans actions to improve future performance.

A **performance norm** identifies the level of work effort and performance expected of group members.

Personal staff are "assistant-to" positions that provide special administrative support to higher-level positions.

Personal wellness is the pursuit of one's physical and mental potential through a personal-health promotion program.

Personality is the profile of characteristics making a person unique from others.

Persuasion is presenting a message in a manner that causes the other person to support it.

A **plan** is a statement of the intended means for accomplishing a desired result.

Planned change involves action to align the organization with anticipated future challenges.

Planning is the process of setting objectives and determining what should be done to accomplish them.

A **policy** is a standing plan that communicates broad guidelines for making decisions and taking action.

Political action committees collect money for donation to political campaigns.

Political risk is the possible loss of investment or control over a foreign asset because of political changes in the host country.

Political-risk analysis forecasts how political events may impact foreign investments.

Polycentric attitudes assume locals know the best ways to manage in their countries.

In a **polychronic culture** time is used to accomplish many different things at once.

A **portfolio planning** approach seeks the best mix of investments among alternative business opportunities.

Positive reinforcement strengthens a behaviour by making a desirable consequence contingent on the occurrence of the behaviour.

Power is the ability to get someone else to do something you want done or to make things happen the way you want.

Prejudice is the holding of negative, irrational attitudes toward individuals because of their group identity.

Principled negotiation or **integrative negotiation** uses a "win-win" orientation to reach solutions acceptable to each party.

Privatization is the selling of state-owned enterprises into private ownership.

A **proactive strategy** meets all the criteria of social responsibility, including discretionary performance.

A **problem** is a difference between an actual situation and a desired situation.

Problem solving is the process of identifying a discrepancy between an actual and desired state of affairs and then taking action to resolve it.

Problem-solving style is the way people gather and evaluate information for decision making.

A **problem symptom** is a sign of the presence of a performance deficiency or opportunity that should trigger a manager to act.

Procedural justice concerns the degree to which policies and rules are fairly administered.

A **procedure** or **rule** is a standing plan that precisely describes what actions are to be taken in specific situations.

A **process** is a group of related tasks creating something of value to a customer.

Process innovations result in better ways of doing things.

Process re-engineering systematically analyzes work processes to design new and better ones.

A **process structure** groups jobs and activities that are part of the same processes.

Process value analysis identifies and evaluates core processes for their performance contributions.

Product innovations result in new or improved goods or services.

Product life cycle is the series of stages a product or service goes through in the "life" of its marketability.

A **product structure** is an organizational structure that groups together jobs and activities working on a single product or service.

Productivity is a summary measure of the quantity and quality of work performance with resource utilization considered.

A **profit-sharing plan** distributes a proportion of net profits to employees during a stated performance period.

The **program evaluation and review technique (PERT)** is a means for identifying and controlling the many separate events involved in the completion of projects.

A **programmed decision** applies a solution from past experience to the problem at hand.

Progressive discipline is the process of tying reprimands in the form of penalties or punishments to the severity of the employee's infractions.

Project management makes sure that activities required to complete a project are accomplished on time and correctly.

Project managers coordinate complex projects with task deadlines and people with many areas of expertise.

A **project schedule** is a single-use plan for accomplishing a specific set of tasks.

Project teams are convened for a particular task or project and disband once it is completed.

Projection is the assignment of personal attributes to other individuals.

Projects are one-time activities that have clear beginning and end points.

A **prospector strategy** is a corporate competitive strategy that involves pursuing innovation and new opportunities in the face of risk and with the prospects of growth.

Protectionism is a call for tariffs and favourable treatments to protect domestic firms from foreign competition.

Proxemics is the use of interpersonal space, such as in the process of interpersonal communication.

A **psychological contract** is the shared set of expectations held by an individual and the organization, specifying what each expects to give and receive from the other in the course of their working relationship.

Punishment discourages a behaviour by making an unpleasant consequence contingent on the occurrence of that behaviour.

Q

Quality is a degree of excellence, often defined as the ability to meet customer needs 100 percent of the time.

A **quality circle** is a group of employees who meet periodically to discuss ways of improving the quality of their products or services.

Quality control involves checking processes, material, products, or services to ensure that they meet high standards.

Quality of work life (QWL) is the overall quality of human experiences in the workplace.

R

A **rational persuasion strategy** attempts to bring about change through persuasion backed by special knowledge, empirical data, and rational argument.

Reactive change responds to events as or after they occur.

A **reactor strategy** is a corporate competitive strategy that involves simply responding to competitive pressures in order to survive.

Realistic job previews are attempts by the job interviewer to provide the job candidate with all pertinent information about a prospective job and the employing organization, without distortion and before a job offer is accepted.

A **reason strategy** of influence relies on personal power and persuasion based on data, needs, and/or values.

A **reciprocity strategy** of influence involves the mutual exchange of values and a search for shared positive outcomes.

Recruitment is a set of activities designed to attract a qualified pool of job applicants to an organization.

Referent power is the capability to influence other people because of their desires to identify personally and positively with the power source.

Refreezing is the final stage in the planned change process during which the manager is concerned with stabilizing the change and creating the conditions for its long-term continuity.

Reliability refers to the ability of an employment test to yield the same result over time if taken by the same person.

Replacement is the management of promotions, transfers, terminations, layoffs, and retirements.

Responsibility is the obligation to perform that results from accepting assigned tasks.

Restructuring changes the scale and/or mix of operations to gain efficiency and improve performance.

A **retrenchment strategy** involves slowing down, cutting back, and seeking performance improvement through greater efficiencies in operations.

A **retribution strategy** of influence relies on position power and results in feelings of coercion or intimidation.

A **reward** is a work outcome of positive value to the individual.

Reward power is the capability to offer something of value—a positive outcome—as a means of influencing other people.

A **risk environment** is a problem environment in which information is lacking, but some sense of the "probabilities" associated with action alternatives and their consequences exists.

Robotics is the use of computer-controlled machines to completely automate work tasks previously performed by hand.

A **role** is a set of activities expected of a person in a particular job or position within the organization.

Role ambiguity occurs when a person is uncertain about what others expect in terms of his or her behaviour.

Role conflict occurs when a role is unable to respond to the expectations held by others.

Role overload occurs when too many role expectations are being communicated to a person at a given time.

Role underload occurs when a person is underutilized or asked to do too little and/or to do things that fail to challenge her or his talents and capabilities.

S

A **satisficing decision** involves choosing the first satisfactory alternative that comes to your attention.

A **satisfier factor** is a factor in job content, such as a sense of achievement, recognition, responsibility, advancement, or personal growth, experienced as a result of task performance.

Scenario planning identifies alternative future "scenarios" and makes plans to deal with each.

Scientific management involves developing a science for every job, including rules of motion and standardized work instruments, careful selection and training of workers, and proper supervisory support for workers.

Selection is the process of choosing from a pool of applicants the person or persons who best meet job specifications.

Selective perception is the tendency to define problems from one's own point of view or to single out for attention things consistent with one's existing beliefs, values, or needs.

A **self-fulfilling prophecy** occurs when a person acts in ways that confirm another's expectations.

A **self-managing work team**, sometimes called an autonomous work group, is a group of workers whose jobs have been redesigned to create a high degree of task interdependence and who have been given authority to make decisions about how they go about the required work.

Self-monitoring is the degree to which someone is able to adjust behaviour in response to external factors.

Self-serving bias explains personal success by internal causes and personal failures by external causes.

Semantic barriers are verbal and nonverbal symbols that are poorly chosen and expressed, creating barriers to successful communication.

Sexual harassment occurs as behaviour of a sexual nature that affects a person's employment situation.

Shaping is positive reinforcement of successive approximations to the desired behaviour.

A **shared power strategy** is a participative change strategy that relies on involving others to examine values, needs, and goals in relationship to an issue at hand.

Simultaneous systems operate when mechanistic and organic designs operate together in an organization.

A **single-use plan** is used only once.

A **skill** is the ability to translate knowledge into action that results in the desired performance.

Skills-based pay is a system of paying workers according to the number of job-relevant skills they master.

Skunkworks are teams allowed to work creatively together, free of constraints from the larger organization.

Small-batch production is the production of a variety of custom products that are tailor-made, usually with considerable craftsmanship, to fit customer specifications.

Small Business Development Centres (SBDC) offer guidance and support to small business owners in how to set up and run a business operation.

The **social contract** reflects expectations in the employee-employer relationship.

Social loafing is the tendency of some people to avoid responsibility by "free-riding" in groups.

A **social responsibility audit** is a systematic assessment and reporting of an organization's commitments and accomplishments in areas of social responsibility.

Socialization is the process of systematically changing the expectations, behaviour, and attitudes of a new employee in a manner considered desirable by the organization.

A **sociotechnical system** designs jobs so that technology and human resources are well integrated in high-performance systems with maximum opportunities for individual satisfaction.

A **sole proprietorship** is an individual pursuing business for a profit.

Span of control is the number of subordinates reporting directly to a manager.

Specialized staff are positions that perform a technical service or provide special problem-solving expertise for other parts of the organization.

A **specific environment** is composed of the actual organizations and persons with whom the focal organization must interact in order to survive and prosper.

A **stability strategy** maintains the present course of action.

Staff managers use special technical expertise to advise and support the efforts of line workers.

Stakeholders are the persons, groups, and institutions directly affected by an organization's performance.

A **standing plan** is used more than once.

Statistical quality control is the use of statistical techniques to assist in the quality control process.

A **stereotype** results when an individual is assigned to a group or category and then the attributes commonly associated with the group or category are assigned to the individual in question.

In a **strategic alliance** organizations join together in partnership to pursue an area of mutual interest.

A **strategic business unit (SBU)** is a separate operating division that represents a major business area and operates with some autonomy vis-à-vis other similar units in the organization.

A **strategic constituencies analysis** is the review and analysis of the interests of external stakeholders of an organization.

Strategic human resource management mobilizes human capital to implement organizational strategies.

Strategic intent focuses and applies organizational energies on a unifying and compelling goal.

Strategic leadership enthuses people to continuously change, refine, and improve strategies and their implementation.

Strategic management is the managerial responsibility for leading the process of formulating and implementing strategies that lead to longer-term organizational success.

Strategic opportunism is the ability to remain focused on long-term objectives by being flexible in dealing with short-term problems and opportunities as they occur.

A **strategic plan** is comprehensive and addresses longer-term needs and directions of the organization.

A **strategy** is a comprehensive plan or action orientation that sets critical direction and guides the allocation of resources for an organization to achieve long-term objectives.

Strategy formulation is the process of creating strategies.

Strategy implementation is the process of putting strategies into action.

Stress is a state of tension experienced by individuals facing extraordinary demands, constraints, or opportunities.

A **stressor** is anything that causes stress.

A **structured problem** is familiar, straightforward, and clear in its information requirements.

Subcultures within organizations are common to groups of people with similar values and beliefs based upon shared personal characteristics.

Substantive conflict is disagreement over such things as goals; the allocation of resources; distribution of rewards, policies, and procedures; and job assignments.

Substitutes for leadership are factors in the work setting that move work efforts toward organizational objectives without the direct involvement of a leader.

A **subsystem** is a work unit or smaller component within a larger organization.

A **succession plan** describes how the leadership transition and related financial matters will be handled.

The **succession problem** is the issue of who will run the business when the current head leaves.

Supply chain management strategically links all operations dealing with resource supplies.

Survivor syndrome is the stress experienced by people who fear for their jobs after having "survived" large layoffs and staff cutbacks in an organization.

Sustainable career advantage is a combination of personal attributes that allows you to consistently outperform others in meeting needs of employers.

Sustainable development meets the needs of the present without hurting future generations.

Sweatshops employ workers at very low wages, for long hours, and in poor working conditions.

A **SWOT analysis** sets the stage for strategy formulation by analyzing organizational strengths and weaknesses and environmental opportunities and threats.

A **symbolic leader** uses symbols to establish and maintain a desired organizational culture.

Synergy is the creation of a whole that is greater than the sum of its individual parts.

A **system** is a collection of interrelated parts working together for a purpose.

Systematic thinking occurs when someone approaches problems in a rational and analytical fashion.

T

A **task activity** is an action taken by a group member that contributes directly to the group's performance purpose.

A **task force** is a formal team convened for a specific purpose and expected to disband when that purpose is achieved.

Task goals are performance targets for individuals and/or groups.

A **team** is a collection of people who regularly interact to pursue common goals.

Team building is a sequence of collaborative activities to gather and analyze data on a team and make changes to increase its effectiveness.

Team leaders and **supervisors** report to middle managers and directly supervise nonmanagerial workers.

A **team structure** is an organizational structure through which permanent and temporary teams are created to improve lateral relations and solve problems throughout an organization.

Teamwork is the process of people working together in groups to accomplish common goals.

A **technical skill** is the ability to use a special proficiency or expertise in one's work.

The **technological imperative** states that technology is a major influence on organizational structure.

Technology is the combination of equipment, knowledge, and work methods that allows an organization to transform inputs into outputs.

Telecommuting or **flexiplace** involves working at home or other places using computer links to the office.

Terminal values are preferences about desired end states.

Theory X is a set of managerial assumptions that people in general dislike work, lack ambition, are irresponsible and resistant to change, and prefer to be led than to lead.

Theory Y is a set of managerial assumptions that people in general are willing to work and accept responsibility and are capable of self-direction, self-control, and creativity.

Theory Z is a term that describes a management framework used by American firms following Japanese examples.

In **top-down change**, the change initiatives come from senior management.

Top-down planning begins with broad objectives set by top management.

Top managers are the highest-level managers and work to ensure that major plans and objectives are set and accomplished in accord with the organization's purpose.

Total quality management (TQM) is managing with an organization-wide commitment to continuous work improvement, product quality, and meeting customer needs completely.

Training involves a set of activities that provide learning opportunities through which people can acquire and improve job-related skills.

A **trait** is a relatively stable and enduring personal characteristic of an individual.

Transactional leadership is leadership that orchestrates and directs the efforts of others through tasks, rewards, and structures.

Transformational change results in a major and comprehensive redirection of the organization.

Transformational leadership is the ability of a leader to get people to do more than they originally expected to do in support of large-scale innovation and change.

A **transnational corporation** is an MNC that operates worldwide on a borderless basis.

A **transnational strategy** seeks efficiencies of global operations with attention to local markets.

A **Type A personality** is a person oriented toward extreme achievement, impatience, and perfectionism and who may find stress in circumstances others find relatively stress-free.

360-degree feedback is an upward communication approach that involves upward appraisals done by a manager's subordinates, as well as additional feedback from peers, internal and external customers, and higher-ups.

U

An **uncertain environment** is a problem environment in which information is so poor that it is difficult even to assign probabilities to the likely outcomes of known alternatives.

Unfreezing is the initial phase in the planned change process during which the manager prepares a situation for change.

Universalism suggests that ethical standards apply across all cultures.

Unplanned change occurs spontaneously or at random and without a change agent's direction.

An **unstructured problem** involves ambiguities and information deficiencies.

The **upside-down pyramid** puts customers at the top, served by workers whose managers support them.

The **utilitarian view** considers ethical behaviour as that which delivers the greatest good to the greatest number of people.

V

Valence is the value a person assigns to work-related outcomes.

Validity refers to the ability of an employment test to measure exactly what it is intended relative to the job specification.

A **value chain** is the sequence of activities that transform materials into finished products.

Value-based management actively develops, communicates, and enacts shared values in an organization.

Values are broad beliefs about what is or is not appropriate behaviour.

Venture capitalists make large investments in new ventures in return for an equity stake in the business.

Growth through **vertical integration** is by acquiring suppliers or distributors.

A **virtual meeting** is a meeting conducted by a computer-mediated process of information sharing and decision making.

The **virtual office** enables workers to "commute" via computer networks, fax machines, and express mail delivery service.

A **virtual organization** is a shifting network of strategic alliances that are engaged as needed.

A **virtual team** is a group of people who work together and solve problems through computer-based rather than face-to-face interactions.

Vision is a term used to describe a clear sense of the future.

Visionary leadership brings to the situation a clear sense of the future and an understanding of how to get there.

W

A **whistleblower** exposes the misdeeds of others in organizations.

A **wholly owned subsidiary** is a local operation completely owned by a foreign firm.

A **win-lose conflict** occurs when one party achieves its desires at the expense and exclusion of the other party's desires.

A **win-win conflict** occurs when conflict is resolved to the mutual benefit of all concerned parties.

A **work process** is a related group of tasks that together create a value for the customer.

Work-at-home involves accomplishing a job while spending all or part of one's work time in the home.

Work-life balance involves balancing career demands with personal and family needs.

Workflow is the movement of work from one point to another in a system.

Workforce diversity is a term used to describe demographic differences (age, gender, race and ethnicity, and able-bodiedness) among members of the workforce.

Workplace privacy is the right to privacy while at work.

Workplace rage is overtly aggressive behaviour toward co-workers or the work setting.

In the **World Trade Organization (WTO)**, member nations agree to negotiate and resolve disputes about tariffs and trade restrictions.

Z

A **zero-based budget** allocates resources to a project or activity as if it were brand new.

End Notes

CHAPTER 1 NOTES

1. Sources for the opening vignette:

   Patrick Sullivan, "Speech to CIPS," Toronto, November 13, 2003, on the Web, <www.cipstoronto.ca>.

   (November 2006). Information from the Workopolis website, <www.workopolis.com>.

TEXT NOTES

2. Information from the *Fast Company* website, <www.fastcompany.com>.

3. Charles O'Reilly III and Jeffrey Pfeffer, *Hidden Value: How Great Companies Achieve Extraordinary Results with Ordinary People* (Boston: Harvard Business School Press, 2000), p. 2.

4. For a research perspective see Denise M. Rousseau, "Organizational Behavior in the New Organizational Era," *Annual Review of Psychology*, vol. 48 (1997), pp. 515–46; for a consultant's perspective see Tom Peters, *The Circle of Innovation* (New York: Knopf, 1997); and Joan Magretta, *Managing in the New Economy* (Boston: Harvard Business School Press, 1999).

5. See Kevin Kelly, *New Rules for a New Economy: 10 Radical Strategies for a Connected World* (New York: Penguin, 1999).

6. Max DePree's books include *Leadership Is an Art* (New York: Dell, 1990) and *Leadership Jazz* (New York: Dell, 1993). See also Herman Miller's home page, <www.hermanmiller.com>.

7. Thomas A. Stewart, *Intellectual Capital: The Wealth of Organizations* (New York: Bantam, 1998).

8. See Peter F. Drucker, *The Changing World of the Executive* (New York: T.T. Times Books, 1982), and *The Profession of Management* (Cambridge, MA: Harvard Business School Press, 1997); and Francis Horibe, *Managing Knowledge Workers: New Skills and Attitudes to Unlock the Intellectual Capital in Your Organization* (New York: Wiley, 1999).

9. Kenichi Ohmae's books include *The Borderless World: Power and Strategy in the Interlinked Economy* (New York: Harper, 1989); *The End of the Nation State* (New York: Free Press, 1996); and *The Invisible Continent: Four Strategic Imperatives of the New Economy* (New York: Harper, 1999).

10. For information on Ballard Power Systems, see <www.ballard.com>.

11. For a discussion of globalization see Thomas L. Friedman, *The Lexus and the Olive Tree: Understanding Globalization* (New York: Bantam Doubleday Dell, 2000); and John Micklethwait and Adrian Woolridge, *A Future Perfect: The Challenges and Hidden Promise of Globalization* (New York: Crown, 2000).

12. Alfred E. Eckes, Jr., and Thomas W. Zeiler, *Globalization and the American Century* (Cambridge, UK: Cambridge University Press, 2003), pp. 1–2.

13. Michael E. Porter, *The Competitive Advantage of Nations: With a New Introduction* (New York: Free Press, 1998).

14. See, for example, Carl Shapiro and Hal R. Varian, *Information Rules: A Strategic Guide to the Network Economy* (Cambridge, MA: Harvard Business School Press, 1998).

15. *Workforce 2000: Work and Workers for the 21st Century* (Indianapolis: Towers Perrin/Hudson Institute, 1987).

16. Richard W. Judy and Carol D'Amico, eds., *Workforce 2020: Work and Workers for the 21st Century* (Indianapolis: Hudson Institute, 1997).

17. See Richard D. Bucher, *Diversity Consciousness: Opening Our Minds to People, Cultures, and Opportunities* (Upper Saddle River, NJ: Prentice-Hall, 2000).

18. View RS 1985, c H-6 of the Canadian Human Rights Act on the Web, <www.lois.justice.gc.ca>. (December 2006).

19. For a discussion of diversity issues, see R. Roosevelt Thomas, "From Affirmative Action to Affirming Diversity," *Harvard Business Review* (March–April 1990), pp. 107–17; and *Beyond Race and Gender: Unleashing the Power of Your Total Workforce by Managing Diversity* (New York: AMACOM, 1992).

20. Quotations from Thomas, op. cit. (1990); and *Business Week* (August 8, 1990), p. 50, emphasis added.

21. Survey results reported in Rebecca Gomez, "Women Execs Increasing in Number, Survey Finds," *Columbus Dispatch* (November 19, 2002), p. D12.

22. Sue Shellenbarger, "Number of Women Managers Rises," *Wall Street Journal* (September 30, 2003), p. D2; "Best Companies for Women of Color," Working Mother Media on the Web, <www.workingmother.com>. (December 2006).

23. Stephanie N. Mehta, "What Minority Employees Really Want," *Fortune* (July 10, 2000), pp. 181–86.

24. Information from "Racism in Hiring Remains, Study Says," *Columbus Dispatch* (January 17, 2003), p. B2.

25. For background see Taylor Cox, Jr., "The Multicultural Organization," *Academy of Management Executive*, vol. 5 (1991), pp. 34–47; and *Cultural Diversity in Organizations: Theory, Research and Practice* (San Francisco: Berrett-Koehler, 1993).

26. For discussions of the glass ceiling effect see Ann M. Morrison, Randall P. White, and Ellen Van Velso, *Breaking the Glass Ceiling* (Reading, MA: Addison-Wesley, 1987); Anne E. Weiss, *The Glass Ceiling: A Look at Women in the Workforce* (New York: Twenty First Century, 1999); and Debra E. Meyerson and Joyce K. Fletcher, "A Modest Manifesto for Shattering the Glass Ceiling," *Harvard Business Review* (January–February 2000).

27. Judith B. Rosener, "Women Make Good Managers, So What?" *Business Week* (December 11, 2000), p. 24.

28. Portions adapted from John W. Dienhart and Terry Thomas, "Ethical Leadership: A Primer on Ethical Responsibility in Management," in John R. Schermerhorn, Jr., ed., *Management, 7th ed.* (New York: Wiley, 2002).

29. Judy and D'Amico, op. cit.

30. Credo selection from <www.jnj.com>.

31. Charles Handy, *The Age of Unreason* (Cambridge, MA: Harvard Business School Press, 1990).

32. "Is Your Job Your Calling?" *Fast Company* (February–March 1998), p. 108.

33. Tom Peters, "The New Wired World of Work," *Business Week* (August 28, 2000), pp. 172–73.

34. Robert Reich, "The Company of the Future," *Fast Company* (November 1998), p. 124ff.

35. Developed from Peters, op. cit. (2000).

36. For an overview of organizations and organization theory see W. Richard Scott, *Organizations; Rational, Natural and Open Systems, 4th ed.* (Englewood Cliffs, NJ: Prentice-Hall, 1998).

37. Ronald B. Lieber, "Why Employees Love These Companies," *Fortune* (January 12, 1998), pp. 72–74; and David Whitford, "A Human Place to Work," *Fortune* (January 8, 2001), pp. 108–20. See also <www.medtronic.com>.

38. For a discussion of organizations as systems, see Scott, op. cit. and Lane Tracy, *The Living Organization* (New York: Quorum Books, 1994).

39. Developed in part from Jay A. Conger, *Winning 'em Over: A New Model for Managing in the Age of Persuasion* (New York: Simon & Schuster, 1998), pp. 180–81; Stewart D. Friedman, Perry Christensen, and Jessica De Groot, "Work and Life: The End of the Zero-Sum Game," *Harvard Business Review* (November–December 1998), pp. 119–29; Chris Argyris, "Empowerment: The Emperor's New Clothers," *Harvard Business Review* (May–June 1998), pp. 98–105, and John A. Byrne, "Management by Web," *Business Week* (August 28, 2000), pp. 84–98.

40. Philip B. Crosby, *Quality Is Still Free: Making Quality Certain in Uncertain Times* (New York: McGraw-Hill, 1995). For a comprehensive review see Robert E. Cole and W. Richard Scott, eds., *The Quality Movement & Organization Theory* (Thousand Oaks, CA: Sage, 2000).

41. Jeffrey Pfeffer and John F. Veiga, "Putting People First for Organizational Success," *Academy of Management Executive*, vol. 13 (May 1999), pp. 37–48; and Jeffrey Pfeffer, *The Human Equation: Building Profits by Putting People First* (Boston: Harvard Business School Press, 1998).

42. "Workweek," *Wall Street Journal* (January 9, 2001), p. 1.

43. Henry Mintzberg, "The Manager's Job: Folklore and Fact," *Harvard Business Review*, vol. 53 (July–August 1975), p. 61. See also his book *The Nature of Managerial Work* (New York: Harper & Row, 1973, and Harper-Collins, 1997).

44. Hal Lancaster, "Middle Managers Are Back—But Now They're 'High-Impact' Players," *Wall Street Journal* (April 14, 1998), p. B1.

45. Information from David Whitford, "A Human Place to Work," *Fortune* (January 8, 2001), pp. 108–20.

46. Lancaster, op. cit.

47. For a perspective on the first-level manager's job, see Leonard A. Schlesinger and Janice A. Klein, "The First-Line Supervisor: Past, Present and Future," pp. 370–82, in Jay W. Lorsch, ed., *Handbook of Organizational Behavior* (Englewood Cliffs, NJ: Prentice-Hall, 1987). Research reported in "Remember Us?," *Economist* (February 1, 1992), p. 71.

48. Whitford, op. cit.

49. Stewart D. Friedman, Perry Christensen, and Jessica De Groot, "Work and Life: The End of the Zero-Sum Game," *Harvard Business Review* (November–December 1998), pp. 119–29.

50. For a classic study see Thomas A. Mahoney, Thomas H. Jerdee, and Stephen J. Carroll, "The Job(s) of Management," *Industrial Relations*, vol. 4 (February 1965), pp. 97–110.

51. This running example is developed from information from "Accountants Have Lives, Too, You Know," *Business Week* (February 23, 1998), pp. 88–90, and the Ernst & Young website <www.ey.com>.

52. Mintzberg, op. cit. (1973/1997), p. 30.

53. See, for example, John R. Veiga and Kathleen Dechant, "Wired World Woes: www.help," *Academy of Management Executive*, vol. 11 (August 1997), pp. 73–79.

54. See Mintzberg, op. cit (1973/1997); and Henry Mintzberg, "Covert Leadership: The Art of Managing Professionals," *Harvard Business Review* (November–December 1998), pp. 140–47; and, Jonathan Gosling and Henry Mintzberg, "The Five Minds of a Manager," *Harvard Business Review* (November, 2003), pp. 1–9.

55. Mintzberg, op. cit. (1973/1997), p. 60.

56. For research on managerial work see Morgan W. McCall, Jr., Ann M. Morrison, and Robert L. Hannan, *Studies of Managerial Work: Results and Methods. Technical Report #9* (Greensboro, NC: Center for Creative Leadership, 1978), pp. 7–9. See also John P. Kotter, "What Effective General Managers Really Do," *Harvard Business Review* (November– December 1982), pp. 156–57.

57. Kotter, op. cit. p. 164. See also his book *The General Managers* (New York: Free Press, 1986); and David Barry, Catherine Durnell Crampton, and Stephen J. Carroll, "Navigating the Garbage Can: How Agendas Help Managers Cope with Job Realities," *Academy of Management Executive*, vol. 11 (May 1997), pp. 43–56.

58. To read more on the Johari Window, see R. P. Esposito, H. McAdoo, and L. Scher, "The Johari Window Test: A Research Note," *Journal of Humanistic Psychology*, vol. 18, no. 1 (1978), pp. 79–81.

59. Robert L. Katz, "Skills of an Effective Administrator," *Harvard Business Review* (September–October 1974), p. 94.

60. Hendrie Weisinger, *Emotional Intelligence at Work* (San Francisco: Jossey-Bass, 2000).

61. See Daniel Goleman's books *Emotional Intelligence* (New York: Bantam, 1995) and *Working with Emotional Intelligence* (New York: Bantam, 1998); and his articles "What Makes a Leader," *Harvard Business Review* (November–December 1998), pp. 93–102, and "Leadership That Makes a Difference," *Harvard Business Review* (March–April 2000), pp. 79–90, quote from p. 80.

62. Richard E. Boyatzis, *The Competent Manager: A Model for Effective Performance* (New York: Wiley, 1982). See also Jon P. Briscoe and Douglas T. Hall, "Grooming and Picking Leaders Using Competency Frameworks: Do They Work?", *Organizational Dynamics* (Autumn 1999), pp. 37–52.

CHAPTER 2 NOTES

1. Sources for the opening vignette:

   R. Alsop, "Ranking Corporate Reputations; Tech Companies Score High in Yearly Survey As Google Makes Its Debut in Third Place," *Wall Street Journal* (December 6, 2005).

   K.J. Delaney, "Google as—Get This—Value Play," *Wall Street Journal* (August 18, 2005).

   G. Robertson, "Yahoo's search for Net supremacy," *Globe and Mail* (December 10, 2005).

   "How Google's unsung hero won AOL deal," *Globe and Mail* (December 20, 2005).

TEXT NOTES

2. Pauline Graham, *Mary Parker Follett—Prophet of Management: A Celebration of Writings from the 1920s* (Boston: Harvard Business School Press, 1995).

3. For a timeline of twentieth-century management ideas see "75 Years of Management Ideas and Practices: 1922–1997," *Harvard Business Review,* supplement (September–October 1997).

4. A thorough review and critique of the history of management thought, including management in ancient civilizations, is provided by Daniel A. Wren, *The Evolution of Management Thought, 4th ed.* (New York: Wiley, 1993).

5. For a timeline of major people and themes see "75 Years of Management," op. cit.

6. For a sample of this work see Henry L. Gantt, *Industrial Leadership* (Easton, MD: Hive, 1921; Hive edition published in 1974); Henry C. Metcalfe and Lyndall Urwick, eds., *Dynamic Administration: The Collected Papers of Mary Parker Follett* (New York: Harper & Brothers, 1940); James D. Mooney, *The Principles of Administration, rev. ed.* (New York: Harper & Brothers, 1947); Lyndall Urwick, *The Elements of Administration* (New York: Harper & Brothers, 1943); and *The Golden Book of Management* (London: N. Neame, 1956).

7. References on Taylor's work are from Frederick W. Taylor, *The Principles of Scientific Management* (New York: W. W. Norton, 1967), originally published by Harper & Brothers in 1911. See Charles W. Wrege and Amedeo G. Perroni, "Taylor's Pig-Tale: A Historical Analysis of Frederick W. Taylor's Pig Iron Experiments," *Academy of Management Journal*, vol. 17 (March 1974), pp. 6–27 for a criticism. See Edwin A. Lock, "The Ideas of Frederick W. Taylor: An Evaluation," *Academy of Management Review*, vol. 7 (1982), p. 14 for an examination of the contemporary significance of Taylor's work. See also the biography, Robert Kanigel, *The One Best Way* (New York: Viking, 1997).

8. Kanigel, op. cit.

9. See Frank B. Gilbreth, *Motion Study* (New York: Van Nostrand, 1911).

10. Available in the English language as Henri Fayol, *General and Industrial Administration* (London: Pitman, 1949); subsequent discussion is based on M. B. Brodie, *Fayol on Administration* (London: Pitman, 1949).

11. M. P. Follett, *Freedom and Coordination* (London: Management Publications Trust, 1949).

12. Judith Garwood, "A Review of *Dynamic Administration: The Collected Papers of Mary Parker Follett,*" *New Management*, vol. 2 (1984), pp. 61–62; eulogy from Richard C. Cabot, "Follett, Mary Parker," *Encyclopaedia of Social Work, vol. 15*, p. 351.

13. Henderson and Talcott Parsons, eds. and trans., *Max Weber: The Theory of Social Economic Organization* (New York: Free Press, 1947).

14. Ibid., p. 337.

15. The Hawthorne studies are described in detail in F. J. Roethlisberger and William J. Dickson, *Management and the Worker* (Cambridge, MA: Harvard University Press, 1966); and G. Homans, *Fatigue of Workers* (New York: Reinhold, 1941). For an interview with three of the participants in the relay assembly test-room studies, see R. G. Greenwood, A. A. Bolton, and R. A. Greenwood, "Hawthorne a Half Century Later: 'Relay Assembly Participants Remember'," *Journal of Management*, vol. 9 (1983), pp. 217–31.

16. The criticisms of the Hawthorne studies are detailed in Alex Carey, "The Hawthorne Studies: A Radical Criticism," *American Sociological Review*, vol. 32 (1967), pp. 403–16; H. M. Parsons, "What Happened at Hawthorne?" *Science*, vol. 183 (1974), pp. 922–32; and B. Rice, "The Hawthorne Defect: Persistence of a Flawed Theory," *Psychology Today*, vol. 16 (1982), pp. 70–74. See also Wren, op. cit.

17. This discussion of Maslow's theory is based on Abraham H. Maslow, *Eupsychian Management* (Homewood, IL: Richard D. Irwin, 1965); and Abraham H. Maslow, *Motivation and Personality, 2nd ed*. (New York: Harper & Row, 1970).

18. Douglas McGregor, *The Human Side of Enterprise* (New York: McGraw-Hill, 1960).

19. See Gary Heil, Deborah F. Stevens, and Warren G. Bennis, *Douglas McGregor on Management: Revisiting the Human Side of Enterprise* (New York: Wiley, 2000).

20. Chris Argyris, *Personality and Organization* (New York: Harper & Row, 1957).

21. The ideas of Ludwig von Bertalanffy contributed to the emergence of this systems perspective on organizations. See his article, "The History and Status of General Systems Theory," *Academy of Management Journal*, vol. 15 (1972), pp. 407–26. This viewpoint is further developed by Daniel Katz and Robert L. Kahn in their classic book, *The Social Psychology of Organizations* (New York: Wiley, 1978). For an integrated systems view see Lane Tracy, *The Living Organization* (New York: Quorum Books, 1994). For an overview, see W. Richard Scott, *Organizations: Rational, Natural, and Open Systems, 4th ed.* (Upper Saddle River, NJ: Prentice-Hall, 1998).

22. Chester I. Barnard, *Functions of the Executive* (Cambridge, MA: Harvard University Press, 1938).

23. See discussion by Scott, op. cit., pp. 66–68.

24. Peter F. Drucker, "The Future That Has Already Happened," *Harvard Business Review*, vol. 75 (September–October

1997), pp. 20–24. See also Shaker A. Zahra, "An Interview with Peter Drucker," *Academy of Management Executive*, vol. 17 (2003), pp. 9–12.

25. For an overview, see Scott, op. cit., pp. 95–97.

26. For the classics see W. Edwards Deming, *Quality, Productivity, and Competitive Position* (Cambridge, MA: MIT Press, 1982); and Joseph M. Juran, *Quality Control Handbook, 3rd ed.* (New York: McGraw-Hill, 1979).

27. D. Wren, *The History of Management Thought* (Hoboken, NJ: Wiley, 2005).

28. Jay R. Gailbraith, "Designing the Networked Organization: Leveraging Size and Competencies" in Susan Albers Mohrman, Jay R. Galbraith, Edward E. Lawler III and Associates, *Tomorrow's Organization: Crafting Winning Capabilities in a Dynamic World* (San Francisco: Jossey-Bass, 1998), pp. 92–94.

29. Thomas J. Peters and Robert H. Waterman, Jr., *In Search of Excellence: Lessons from America's Best-Run Companies* (New York: Harper & Row, 1982). For a retrospective see William C. Bogner, "Tom Peters on the Real World of Business" and "Robert Waterman on Being Smart and Lucky," *Academy of Management Executive*, vol. 16 (2002), pp. 40–50.

30. William Ouchi, *Theory Z: How American Businesses Can Meet the Japanese Challenge* (Reading, MA: Addison-Wesley, 1981); and Richard Tanner Pascale and Anthony G. Athos, *The Art of Japanese Management: Applications for American Executives* (New York: Simon & Schuster, 1981).

31. Ouchi, op. cit.; see also the review by J. Bernard Keys, Luther Tray Denton, and Thomas R. Miller, "The Japanese Management Theory Jungle—Revisited," *Journal of Management*, vol. 20 (1994), pp. 373–402.

32. Peter Senge, *The Fifth Discipline* (New York: Harper, 1990).

33. John Gardner, *No Easy Victories* (New York: Harper & Row, 1968).

34. Peter F. Drucker, "Looking Ahead: Implications of the Present," *Harvard Business Review* (September–October, 1997), pp. 18–32.

35. Quote from Allan H. Church, Executive Commentary, *Academy of Management Executive* (February 2002), p. 74.

36. Quote from Ralph Z. Sorenson, "A Lifetime of Learning to Manage Effectively," *Wall Street Journal* (February 28, 1983), p. 18.

CHAPTER 3 NOTES

1. Sources for the opening vignette:

   J. Bagnall, "Well Healed," *Canadian Business Magazine* (December 5, 2005).

   Information from the Aldo website <www.aldoshoes.com>.

TEXT NOTES

2. Adapted from Terry Thomas, John W. Dienhart, and John R. Schermerhorn, Jr., "Leading Toward Ethical Behavior in Business," working paper (2003).

3. For more on the WorldCom debacle see Susan Pulliam, "A Staffer Ordered to Commit Fraud Balked, Then Caved," *Wall Street Journal* (June 23, 2003), pp. A1, A6; for more on the Andersen saga see Barbara Ley Toffler, *Final Accounting: Ambition, Greed and the Fall of Arthur Andersen* (New York: Broadway Books, 2003).

4. Mark Heinz, *Wall Street Journal*, (February 19, 1998), p. 1.

5. See the discussion by Lynn Sharpe Paine, "Managing for Organizational Integrity," *Harvard Business Review* (March–April 1994), pp. 106–117.

6. This quote is from an interview with Jana Matthews for the magazine of her alma mater, Earlham College. See "Business as an Ethical Activity," *Earlhamite* (Winter 2003), pp. 14–15.

7. Desmond Tutu, "Do More Than Win," *Fortune* (December 30, 1991), p. 59.

8. For an overview, see Linda K. Trevino and Katherine A. Nelson, *Managing Business Ethics, 3rd ed.* (New York: Wiley, 2003).

9. Ibid.

10. Milton Rokeach, *The Nature of Human Values* (New York: Free Press, 1973). See also W. C. Frederick and J. Weber, "The Values of Corporate Executives and Their Critics: An Empirical Description and Normative Implications," in W. C. Frederick and L. E. Preston, eds., *Business Ethics: Research Issues and Empirical Studies* (Greenwich, CT: JAI Press, 1990).

11. See Gerald F. Cavanagh, Dennis J. Moberg, and Manuel Velasquez, "The Ethics of Organizational Politics," *Academy of Management Review*, vol. 6 (1981), pp. 363–74; Justin G. Locknecker, Joseph A. McKinney, and Carlos W. Moore, "Egoism and Independence: Entrepreneurial Ethics," *Organizational Dynamics* (winter 1988), pp. 64–72; and Justin G. Locknecker, Joseph A. McKinney, and Carlos W. Moore, "The Generation Gap in Business Ethics," *Business Horizons* (September–October 1989), pp. 9–14.

12. Raymond L. Hilgert, "What Ever Happened to Ethics in Business and in Business Schools," *Diary of Alpha Kappa Psi* (April 1989), pp. 4–8.

13. Jerald Greenburg, "Organizational Justice: Yesterday, Today, and Tomorrow," *Journal of Management*, vol. 16, (1990) pp. 399–432; and Mary A. Konovsky, "Understanding Procedural Justice and Its Impact on Business Organizations," *Journal of Management*, vol. 26 (2000), pp. 489–511.

14. Interactional justice is described by Robert J. Bies, "The Predicament of Injustice: The Management of Moral Outrage," in L. L. Cummings & B. M. Staw, eds., *Research in Organizational Behavior*, vol. 9 (Greenwich, CT: JAI Press, 1987), pp. 289–319. The example is from Carol T. Kulik & Robert L. Holbrook, "Demographics in Service Encounters: Effects of Racial and Gender Congruence on Perceived Fairness," *Social Justice Research*, vol. 13 (2000), pp. 375–402.

15. Robert D. Haas, "Ethics—A Global Business Challenge," *Vital Speeches of the Day* (June 1, 1996), pp. 506–9.

16. Thomas Donaldson, "Values in Tension: Ethics Away from Home," *Harvard Business Review*, vol. 74 (September–October 1996), pp. 48–62.

17. Thomas Donaldson and Thomas W. Dunfee, "Towards a Unified Conception of Business Ethics: Integrative Social Contracts Theory," *Academy of Management Review*, vol. 19 (1994), pp. 252–85.

18. Developed from Donaldson, op. cit.

19. Reported in Barbara Ley Toffler, "Tough Choices: Managers Talk Ethics," *New Management*, vol. 4 (1987), pp. 34–39. See also Barbara Ley Toffler, *Tough Choices: Managers Talk Ethics* (New York: Wiley, 1986).

20. See discussion by Trevino and Nelson, op. cit., pp. 47–62.

21. Information from Steven N. Brenner and Earl A. Mollander, "Is the Ethics of Business Changing?" *Harvard Business Review*, vol. 55 (January–February 1977).

22. Saul W. Gellerman, "Why 'Good' Managers Make Bad Ethical Choices," *Harvard Business Review*, vol. 64 (July–August, 1986), pp. 85–90.

23. Reported in Adam Smith, "Wall Street's Outrageous Fortunes," *Esquire* (April 1987), p. 73.

24. The Body Shop came under scrutiny over the degree to which its business practices actually live up to this charter and the company's self-promoted green image. See, for example, John Entine, "Shattered Image," *Business Ethics* (September–October 1994), pp. 23–28.

25. Steve Maich, "Selling Ethics at Nortel," *Maclean's* (January 24, 2005).

26. Information on this case from William M. Carley, "Antitrust Chief Says CEOs Should Tape All Phone Calls to Each Other," *Wall Street Journal* (February 15, 1983), p. 23; "American Air, Chief End Antitrust Suit, Agree Not to Discuss Fares with Rivals," *Wall Street Journal* (July 15, 1985), p. 4; "American Airlines Loses Its Pilot," *Economist* (April 18, 1998), p. 58.

27. Alan L. Otten, "Ethics on the Job: Companies Alert Employees to Potential Dilemmas," *Wall Street Journal* (July 14, 1986), p. 17; and "The Business Ethics Debate," *Newsweek* (May 25, 1987), p. 36.

28. See "Whistle-Blowers on Trial," *Business Week* (March 24, 1997), pp. 172–78; and "NLRB Judge Rules for Massachusetts Nurses in Whistle-Blowing Case," *American Nurse* (January–February 1998), p. 7.

29. Greg Watson, "Auditor, ad man heroes of Adscam," *Ottawa Sun* (November 1, 2005).

30. For a review of whistle-blowing, see Marcia P. Micelli and Janet P. Near, *Blowing the Whistle* (Lexington, MA: Lexington Books, 1992); see also Micelli and Near, "Whistleblowing: Reaping the Benefits," *Academy of Management Executive*, vol. 8 (August 1994), pp. 65–72.

31. Information from James A. Waters, "Catch 20.5: Mortality as an Organizational Phenomenon," *Organizational Dynamics*, vol. 6 (spring 1978), pp. 3–15.

32. Information from Ethics Resource Center, "Major Survey of America's Workers Finds Substantial Improvements in Ethics," *Wall Street Journal* (May 21, 2003).

33. Robert D. Gilbreath, "The Hollow Executive," *New Management*, vol. 4 (1987), pp. 24–28.

34. Developed from recommendations of the Government Accountability Project reported in "Blowing the Whistle without Paying the Piper."

35. Quote taken from BCE's code of business conduct found on the company website, <www.bce.ca>. (December 2006).

36. Information from <www.josephsoninstitute.org/MED/MED-2sixpillars.htm>.

37. Information taken from the Social Responsibility page of the corporate website, <www.gapinc.com>. (December 2006).

38. For a good review see Robert H. Miles, *Managing the Corporate Social Environment* (Englewood Cliffs, NJ: Prentice-Hall, 1987).

39. See Thomas Donaldson and Lee Preston, "The Stakeholder Theory of the Corporation," *Academy of Management Review*, vol. 20 (January 1995), pp. 65–91.

40. Information from Sustainable Development page of Natural Resources Canada on the Web, <www.nrcan.gc.ca>. (December 2006).

41. See Joel Makower, *Putting Social Responsibility to Work for Your Business and the World* (New York: Simon & Schuster, 1994), pp. 17–18.

42. The historical framework of this discussion is developed from Keith Davis, "The Case for and against Business Assumption of Social Responsibility," *Academy of Management Journal* (June 1973), pp. 312–22; Keith Davis and William Frederick, *Business and Society: Management: Public Policy, Ethics*, 5th ed. (New York: McGraw-Hill, 1984). The debate is also discussed by Makower, op. cit., pp. 28–33. See also, "Civics 101," *Economist* (May 11, 1996), p. 61.

43. The Friedman quotation is from Milton Friedman, *Capitalism and Freedom* (Chicago: University of Chicago Press, 1962); the Samuelson quotation is from Paul A. Samuelson, "Love That Corporation," *Mountain Bell Magazine* (spring 1971). Both are cited in Davis, op. cit.

44. Davis and Frederick, quoted in op. cit.

45. See James K. Glassman, "When Ethics Meet Earnings," *International Herald Tribune* (May 24–25, 2003), p. 15.

46. See Makower, op. cit. (1994), pp. 71–75; and Sandra A. Waddock and Samuel B. Graves, "The Corporate Social Performance-Financial Performance Link," *Strategic Management Journal* (1997), pp. 303–19.

47. Davis, op. cit.

48. The "compliance–conviction" distinction is attributed to Mark Goyder in Martin Waller, "Much Corporate Responsibility Is Box-Ticking," *Times Business* (July 8, 2003), p. 21.

49. Archie B. Carroll, "A Three-Dimensional Model of Corporate Performance," *Academy of Management Review*, vol. 4 (1979), pp. 497–505. Carroll's continuing work in this area is most recently reported in Mark S. Schwartz and Archie B. Carroll, "Corporate Social Responsibility: A Three Domain Approach," *Business Ethics Quarterly*, vol. 13 (2003), pp. 503–530.

50. Elizabeth Gatewood and Archie B. Carroll, "The Anatomy of Corporate Social Response," *Business Horizons*, vol. 24 (September–October 1981), pp. 9–16.

51. David Bornstein, *How to Change the World: Social Entrepreneurs and the*

Power of New Ideas (New York: Oxford University Press, 2004).

52. Information taken from <www.ashoka.org>.

53. C. Leadbeater, *The Rise of the Social Entrepreneur* (London: Demos 1997).

54. Judith Burns, "Everything You Wanted to Know About Corporate Governance… But Didn't Know to Ask," *Wall Street Journal* (October 27, 2003), p. R6.

55. See for example "Pay for Performance Report," *Institute of Management and Administration* (December, 2003).

CHAPTER 4 NOTES

1. Sources for the opening vignette:

   With information from the corporate websites <www2.bmo.com> and <www4.bmo.com> (November 22, 2006).

TEXT NOTES

2. Robert Reich, *The Future of Success* (New York: Knopf, 2001), p. 7.

3. Quote from *The New Blue* (IBM Annual Report, 1997), p. 8.

4. Reich, op. cit.

5. See Michael E. Porter, *Competitive Strategy: Techniques for Analyzing Industries and Competitors* (New York: Free Press, 1980); and *Competitive Advantage: Creating and Sustaining Superior Performance* (New York: Free Press, 1986); also, Richard A. D'Aveni, *Hyper-Competition: Managing the Dynamics of Strategic Maneuvering* (New York: Free Press, 1994).

6. Joseph M. Juran, "Made in U.S.A.: A Renaissance in Quality," *Harvard Business Review* (July–August 1993), pp. 42–50.

7. Michael Porter, *The Competitive Advantage of Nations* (New York: Free Press, 1989).

8. See Richard D. Bucher, *Diversity Consciousness: Opening Our Minds to People, Cultures, and Opportunities* (Upper Saddle River, NJ: Prentice-Hall, 2000), p. 201.

9. James D. Thompson, *Organizations in Action* (New York: McGraw-Hill, 1967); and Robert B. Duncan, "Characteristics of Organizational Environments and Perceived Environmental Uncertainty," *Administrative Science Quarterly*, vol. 17 (1972), pp. 313–27. For discussion of the implications of uncertainty see Hugh Courtney, Jane Kirkland, and Patrick Viguerie, "Strategy Under Uncertainty," *Harvard Business Review* (November–December 1997), pp. 67–79.

10. Quotation from a discussion by Richard J. Shonberger and Edward M. Knod, Jr., *Operations Management: Serving the Customer, 3rd ed.* (Plano, TX: Business Publications, 1988), p. 4.

11. Rosabeth Moss Kanter, "Transcending Business Boundaries: 12,000 World Managers View Change," *Harvard Business Review* (May–June 1991), pp. 151–64.

12. Reported in Jennifer Steinhauer, "The Undercover Shoppers," *New York Times* (February 4, 1998), pp. C1, C2.

13. Information from "How Marriott Never Forgets a Guest," *Business Week* (February 21, 2000), p. 74.

14. Roger D. Blackwell and Kristina Blackwell, "The Century of the Consumer: Converting Supply Chains into Demand Chains," *Supply Chain Management Review* (fall 1999).

15. See Joseph M. Juran, *Quality Control Handbook, 3rd ed.* (New York: McGraw-Hill, 1979) and "The Quality Trilogy: A Universal Approach to Managing for Quality," in H. Costin, ed., *Total Quality Management* (New York: Dryden, 1994); W. Edwards Derning, *Out of Crisis* (Cambridge, MA: MIT Press, 1986); and "Deming's Quality Manifesto," *Best of Business Quarterly*, vol. 12 (winter 1990–1991), pp. 6–10. See also Howard S. Gitlow and Shelly J. Gitlow, *The Deming Guide to Quality and Competitive Position* (Englewood Cliffs, NJ: Prentice-Hall, 1987); and Juran, op. cit. (1993).

16. See information on the Malcolm Baldrige National Quality Award, on the Web, <www.quality.nist.gov>; see also, "Does the Baldrige Award Really Work?" *Harvard Business Review* (January–February 1992), pp. 126–47.

17. Philip B. Crosby, *Quality Is Free* (New York: McGraw-Hill, 1979); *The Eternally Successful Organization* (New York: McGraw-Hill, 1988); and *Quality Is Still Free: Making Quality Certain in Uncertain Times* (New York: McGraw-Hill, 1995).

18. Rafael Aguay, *Dr. Deming: The American Who Taught the Japanese About Quality* (New York: Free Press, 1997); and W. Edwards Deming, op. cit. (1986).

19. See Edward E. Lawler III, Susan Albers Mohrman, and Gerald E. Ledford, Jr., *Employee Involvement and Total Quality Management: Practices and Results in Fortune 1000 Companies* (San Francisco: Jossey-Bass, 1992).

20. Edward E. Lawler III and Susan Albers Mohrman, "Quality Circles After the Fad," *Harvard Business Review* (January–February 1985), pp. 65–71.

21. Quotes from Arnold Kanarick, "The Far Side of Quality Circles." *Management Review*, vol. 70 (October 1981), pp. 16–17.

22. See B. Joseph Pine II, Bart Victor, and Andrew C. Boynton, "Making Mass Customization Work," *Harvard Business Review* (September–October 1993), pp. 108–19; and "The Agile Factory: Custom-made, Direct from the Plant," *Business Week,* special report on "21st Century Capitalism" (January 23, 1995), pp. 158–59; and Justin Martin, "Give 'Em *Exactly* What They Want," *Fortune* (November 10, 1997), p. 283.

23. Edgar H. Schein, "Organizational Culture," *American Psychologist*, vol. 45 (1990), pp. 109–19. See also Schein's *Organizational Culture and Leadership, 2nd ed.* (San Francisco: Jossey-Bass, 1997); and *The Corporate Culture Survival Guide* (San Francisco: Jossey-Bass, 1999).

24. James Collins and Jerry Porras, *Built to Last* (New York: Harper Business, 1994).

25. Schein, op. cit. (1997); Terrence E. Deal and Alan A. Kennedy, *Corporate Cultures: The Rites and Rituals of Corporate Life* (Reading, MA: Addison-Wesley, 1982); and Ralph Kilmann, *Beyond the Quick Fix* (San Francisco: Jossey-Bass, 1984).

26. In their book *Corporate Culture and Performance* (New York: Macmillan, 1992), John P. Kotter and James L. Heskett make the point that strong

cultures have the desired effects over the long term only if they encourage adaptation to a changing environment. See also Collins and Porras, op. cit. (1994).

27. Andrew Wahl, "Stop the Rot: Advice for Turning Culture Around," *Canadian Business Magazine* (October 10–23, 2005).

28. Andrew Wahl, "Culture Shock: A Survey of Canadian Executives Reveals that Corporate Culture is in Need of Improvement," *Canadian Business Magazine* (October 10–23, 2005).

29. This is a simplified model developed from Schein, op. cit. (1997).

30. Andrew Wahl, op. cit.

31. James C. Collins and Jerry I. Porras, "Building Your Company's Vision," *Harvard Business Review* (September–October 1996), pp. 65–77.

32. Ralph H. Kilmann, Mary J. Saxton, and Roy Serpa, "Issues in Under-standing and Changing Corporate Culture," *California Management Review*, vol. 28 (1986), pp. 87–94.

33. See Mary Kay Ash, *Mary Kay: You Can Have It All* (New York: Roseville, CA: Prima Publishing, 1995).

34. Lee Gardenswartz and Anita Rowe, *Managing Diversity: A Complete Desk Reference and Planning Guide* (Chicago: Irwin, 1993).

35. R. Roosevelt Thomas, Jr., *Beyond Race and Gender* (New York: AMACOM, 1992), p. 10; see also R. Roosevelt Thomas, Jr., "From 'Affirmative Action' to 'Affirming Diversity,'" *Harvard Business Review* (November–December 1990), pp. 107–17; R. Roosevelt Thomas, Jr., with Marjorie I. Woodruff, *Building a House for Diversity* (New York: AMACOM, 1999).

36. Thomas Kochan, Katerina Bezrukova, Robin Ely, Susan Jackson, Aparna Joshi, Karen Jehn, Jonathan Leonard, David Levine, and David Thomas, "The Effects of Diversity on Business Performance: Report of the Diversity Research Network," reported in SHRM Foundation Research Findings, on the Web, <www.shrm.org/foundation>. (December 2006).

37. Gardenswartz and Rowe, op. cit., p. 220.

38. Taylor Cox, Jr., *Cultural Diversity in Organizations* (San Francisco: Berrett Koehler, 1994).

39. Joseph A. Raelin, *Clash of Cultures* (Cambridge, MA: Harvard Business School Press, 1986).

40. Geert Hofstede, *Culture's Consequences* (Beverly Hills: Sage, 1982).

41. See Anthony Robbins and Joseph McClendon III, *Unlimited Power: A Black Choice* (New York: Free Press, 1997); and Augusto Failde and William Doyle, *Latino Success: Insights from America's Most Powerful Latino Executives* (New York: Free Press, 1996).

42. See, for example, the discussion in Ron Zembke, Claire Raines, and Bob Filipczak, *Generations at Work: Managing the Clash of Veterans, Boomers, Xers, and Nexters in Your Workplace* (New York: AMACOM, 1999); and Brian O'Reilly, "Meet the Future: It's Your Kids," *Fortune* (July 24, 2000), pp. 144–64.

43. Barbara Benedict Bunker, "Appreciating Diversity and Modifying Organizational Cultures: Men and Women at Work," Chapter 5 in Suresh Srivastva and David L. Cooperrider, eds., *Appreciative Management and Leadership* (San Francisco: Jossey-Bass, 1990).

44. See Gary N. Powell, *Women & Men in Management* (Thousand Oaks, CA: Sage, 1993) and Cliff Cheng, ed., *Masculinities in Organizations* (Thousand Oaks, CA: Sage, 1996). For added background, see also Sally Helgesen, *Everyday Revolutionaries: Working Women and the Transformation of American Life* (New York: Doubleday, 1998).

45. Stephanie N. Mehta, "What Minority Employees Really Want," *Fortune* (July 10, 2000), pp. 181–86.

46. Information from "The Bugs in Microsoft Culture," *Fortune* (January 8, 2001), p. 128.

47. Data reported in "How to Enable the Disabled," *Business Week* (November 6, 2000), p. 36.

48. This section is based on ideas set forth by Thomas, op. cit. (1992); and Thomas and Woodruff, op. cit. (1999).

49. Thomas, op. cit. (1992), p. 17.

50. Thomas and Woodruff, op. cit. (1999), pp. 211–26.

51. Based on ibid., pp. 11–12.

52. Survey reported in "The Most Inclusive Workplaces Generate the Most Loyal Employees," *Gallup Management Journal*, December 2001, on the Web, <gmj.gallup.com>. (December 2006).

53. "Diversity Today: Corporate Recruiting Practices in Inclusive Workplaces," *Fortune* (June 12, 2000), p. S4.

CHAPTER 5 NOTES

1. Sources for the opening vignette.

   J. Sanford, "Beat China on Cost: Gildan taps other labour pool and trade pacts," *Canadian Business Magazine* (November 7, 2005).

   J. Sanford and J. Gray, "Top CFO 2005: Lawrence Sellyn, Gildan Activewear Inc.," *Canadian Business Magazine* (April 25, 2005).

   Additional information from the Gildan website, <www.gildan.com>.

TEXT NOTES

2. Information from Lindsay Whipp and Kae Inoue, "Japan Carmakers to Expand U.S. Output," *International Herald Tribune* (May 23, 2003), p. B3.

3. Robin Blumenthal and Vito J. Racanelli, "O, Canada, Expect Funds to Flow to You," *Barron's*, vol. 86 (January 2, 2006), p. 11.

4. See Kenichi Ohmae, *The Evolving Global Economy* (Cambridge, MA: Harvard Business School Press, 1995).

5. For a discussion of globalization see Thomas L. Friedman, *The Lexus and the Olive Tree: Understanding Globalization* (New York: Bantam Doubleday Dell, 2000); and John Micklethwait and Adrian Woodridge, *A Future Perfect: The Challenges and Hidden Promise of Globalization* (New York: Crown, 2000).

6. Rosabeth Moss Kanter, *World Class:*

Thinking Locally in the Global Economy (New York: Simon & Schuster, 1995), preface.

7. See the discussion by Alfred E. Eckes, Jr., and Thomas W. Zeiler, *Globalization and the American Century* (Cambridge, UK: Cambridge University Press, 2003).

8. Quote from Jeffrey E. Garten, "The Mind of the CEO," *Business Week* (February 5, 2001), p. 106.

9. The *Economist* on the Web, <www.economist.com>, is a good weekly source of information on Europe.

10. A monthly publication that covers the *maquiladora* industries is the *Twin Plant News* (El Paso, Texas) on the Web, <www.twin-plant-news.com>.

11. Warren Jestin, Mary Webb, Aron Gampel, Pablo Bréard, "Keeping Canada Competitive—The Importance of Being Earnest," *Global Outlook* (December 2005), pp. 1, 15.

12. For an overview of business in China see John Studdard and James G. Shiro, *The New Silk Road: Secrets of Business Success in China Today* (New York: Wiley, 2000). Export data from "Surviving the Onslaught," *Wall Street Journal* (October 6, 2003), p. B1.

13. Information from Hiawatha Bray, "Philippines Vies for 'Back-Office' Operations," *International Herald Tribune* (May 23, 2003), p. 14.

14. The *Economist* on the Web, <www.economist.com>, is a good weekly source of information on Africa.

15. Bray, op. cit.

16. James A. Austin and John G. McLean, "Pathways to Business Success in Sub-Saharan Africa," *Journal of African Finance and Economic Development*, vol. 2 (1996), pp. 57–76.

17. Information from "International Business: Consider Africa," *Harvard Business Review*, vol. 76 (January–February 1998), pp. 16–18.

18. Information taken from MBendi, Information for Africa on the Web, <www.mbendi.co.za/orsadc.htm>. (December 2006).

19. See "Inside View: South Africa," *New York Times* (September 18, 2000), pp. A15–A17.

20. Quote from John A. Byrne, "Visionary vs. Visionary," *Business Week* (August 28, 2000), p. 210.

21. With information from <www.statcan.ca>. (July 2006).

22. Developed from Anthony J. F. O'Reilly, "Establishing Successful Joint Ventures in Developing Nations: A CEO's Perspective," *Columbia Journal of World Business* (spring 1988), pp. 65–71; and "Best Practices for Global Competitiveness," *Fortune* (March 30, 1998), pp. S1–S3, special advertising section.

23. CBC News on the Web, <www.cbc.ca>.

24. Whipp and Inoue, op. cit.

25. Quoted from "Own Words: Percy Barnevik, ABB and Investor," *Financial Times Limited*, (1998).

26. Information from Karby Leggett, "U.S. Auto Makers Find Promise—and Peril—in China," *Wall Street Journal* (June 19, 2003), p. B1.

27. See Peter F. Drucker, "The Global Economy and the Nation-State," *Foreign Affairs*, vol. 76 (September–October 1997), pp. 159–71.

28. Adapted from R. Hall Mason. "Conflicts between Host Countries and Multinational Enterprise," *California Management Review*, vol. 17 (1974), pp. 6–7.

29. For a good overview, see Randall E. Stros, *Bulls in the China Shop and Other Sino-American Business Encounters* (New York: Pantheon, 1991); as well as Studdard and Shir, op. cit.

30. For an interesting discussion of one company's experience in China see Jim Mann, *Beijing Jeep: A Case Study of Western Business in China* (Boulder, CO: Westview Press, 1997).

31. Information from the corporate website, <www.nikeBiz.com/labor>. (December 2006).

32. "An Industry Monitors Child Labor," *New York Times* (October 16, 1997), pp. B1, B9; on the Web, <www.rugmark.de>. (December 2006).

33. Definition from World Commission on Environment and Development, *Our Common Future* (Oxford: Oxford University Press, 1987).

34. Examples reported in Neil Chesanow, *The World-Class Executive* (New York: Rawson Associates, 1985).

35. Based on Barbara Benedict Bunker, "Appreciating Diversity and Modifying Organizational Cultures: Men and Women at Work," in Suresh Srivastava and David L. Cooperrider, eds., *Appreciative Management and Leadership: The Power of Positive Thought and Action in Organizations* (San Francisco: Jossey-Bass, 1990), pp. 127–49.

36. For a good overview of the practical issues, see Richard D. Lewis, *The Cultural Imperative: Global Trends in the 21st Century* (Yarmouth, ME: Intercultural Press, 2002); and Martin J. Gannon, *Understanding Global Cultures* (Thousand Oaks, CA: Sage, 1994).

37. Information from Ronald B. Lieber, "Flying High, Going Global," *Fortune* (July 7, 1997), pp. 195–197.

38. See Gary P. Ferraro, "The Need for Linguistic Proficiency in Global Business," *Business Horizons* (May–June 1996), pp. 39–46; quote from Carol Hymowitz, "Companies Go Global, but Many Managers Just Don't Travel Well," *Wall Street Journal* (August 15, 2000), p. B1.

39. Edward T. Hall, *Beyond Culture* (New York: Doubleday, 1976).

40. Edward T. Hall, *The Silent Language* (New York: Anchor Books, 1959); *The Hidden Dimension* (New York: Anchor Books, 1969).

41. Hall, op. cit., (1959).

42. Lady Borton, "Learning to Work with Viet Nam," *The Academy of Management Executive*, vol. 14 (December 2000), pp. 20–31.

43. Edward T. Hall, *Hidden Differences* (New York: Doubleday, 1990).

44. Both examples from Hymowitz, op. cit.

45. Geert Hofstede, *Culture's Consequences* (Beverly Hills: Sage, 1984).

46. This dimension is explained more thoroughly by Geert Hofstede et al.,

Masculinity and Femininity: The Taboo Dimension of National Cultures (Thousand Oaks, CA.: Sage, 1998).

47. For an introduction to the fifth dimension, see Geert Hofstede and Michael H. Bond, "The Confucius Connection: From Cultural Roots to Economic Growth," *Organizational Dynamics*, vol. 16 (1988), pp. 4–21, which presents comparative data from Bond's "Chinese Values Survey."

48. With information from <http://www.geert-hofstede.com/hofstede_canada.shtml>. (November 2006).

49. Michael Schuman, "How Interbrew Blended Disparate Ingredients in Korean Beer Venture," *Wall Street Journal* (July 24, 2000), pp. A1, A6.

50. Fons Trompenaars, *Riding the Waves of Culture: Understanding Cultural Diversity in Business* (London: Nicholas Brealey Publishing, 1993).

51. See Robert B. Reich, "Who Is Them?" *Harvard Business Review* (March–April 1991), pp. 77–88.

52. "Going International: Willett Systems Limited," *Fortune* (February 16, 1998), p. S6, special advertising section.

53. Mark Clifford and Majeet Kripalani, "Different Countries, Adjoining Cubicles," *Business Week* (August 28, 2000), pp. 182–184.

54. For a perspective on the role of women in expatriate managerial assignments, see Marianne Jelinek and Nancy J. Adler, "Women: World-Class Managers for Global Competition" *Academy of Management Executive* (February 1988), pp. 11–19.

55. Geert Hofstede, "Motivation, Leadership, and Organization," p. 43. See also Hofstede's "Cultural Constraints in Management Theories," *Academy of Management Review*, vol. 7 (1993), pp. 81–94.

56. The classics are William Ouchi, *Theory Z: How American Businesses Can Meet the Japanese Challenge* (Reading, MA: Addison-Wesley, 1981), and Richard Tanner Pascale and Anthony G. Athos, *The Art of Japanese Management: Applications for American Executives* (New York: Simon & Schuster, 1981). See also J. Bernard Keys, Luther Tray Denton, and Thomas R. Miller, "The Japanese Management Theory Jungle—Revisited," *Journal of Management*, vol. 20 (1994), pp. 373–402.

57. For a good discussion, see Chapters 4 and 5 in Miriam Erez and P. Christopher Earley, *Culture, Self-Identity, and Work* (New York: Oxford University Press, 1993).

58. For a good discussion of the historical context of Japanese management practices see Makoto Ohtsu, *Inside Japanese Business: A Narrative History 1960–2000* (Armonk, NY: M.E. Sharpe, 2002), pp. 39–41.

59. Lewis, op. cit.

60. Information from Ohtsu, op. cit.

61. Quote from Kenichi Ohmae, "Japan's Admiration for U.S. Methods Is an Open Book," *Wall Street Journal* (October 10, 1983), p. 21. See also his book, *The Borderless World: Power and Strategy in the Interlinked Economy* (New York: Harper, 1989).

62. See, for example, Mzamo P. Mangaliso, "Building Competitive Advantage from *ubuntu:* Management lessons from South Africa," *Academy of Management Executive*, vol. 15 (2001), pp. 23–33.

63. Geert Hofstede, "A Reply to Goodstein and Hunt," *Organizational Dynamics*, vol. 10 (summer 1981), p. 68.

64. This discussion is based on Howard V. Perlmutter, "The Tortuous Evolution of the Multinational Corporation," *Columbia Journal of World Business*, vol. 4 (January–February, 1969).

CHAPTER 6 NOTES

1. Sources for the opening vignette:

    SIFE website, <www.sife.org/canada>.

    ACE website, <www.acecanada.ca>.

TEXT NOTES

2. Information from <www.acecanada.ca>. (November 2006)

3. Speech at the Lloyd Greif Center for Entrepreneurial Studies, Marshall School of Business, University of Southern California, 1996.

4. Information from the corporate websites.

5. Information on Frank Stronach found on the Web, <www.empireclubfoundation.com>. (December 2006).

6. Information from <www.chapters.indigo.ca>. (November 2006).

7. Information from Stephen Kimber, "Bag-boy calls," *Globe and Mail* (September 26, 2003), pp. 66 and <www.sobeys.com>.

8. Information from <www.lakeportbrewing.ca> and Sasha Nagy, "Teresa Cascioli: Creativity was spawned from pure desperation," *Globe and Mail* on the Web, September 21, 2005, <www.theglobeandmail.com>. (November 2006).

9. Information from <www.timhortons.com>.

10. For a review and discussion of the entrepreneurial mind see Jeffry A. Timmons, *New Venture Creation: Entrepreneurship for the 21st Century* (New York: Irwin/McGraw-Hill, 1999), pp. 219–25.

11. See the review by Robert D. Hisrich and Michael P. Peters, *Entrepreneurship*, 4th ed. (New York: Irwin/McGraw-Hill, 1998), pp. 67–70; and Paulette Thomas, "Entrepreneurs' Biggest Problems and How They Solve Them," *Wall Street Journal Reports* (March 17, 2003), pp. R1, R2.

12. Information from Janet Whitman, "How Do You Handle Extraordinary Growth?" *Wall Street Journal Reports* (March 17, 2003), p. R3.

13. Based on research summarized by Hisrich and Peters, op. cit., pp. 70–74.

14. Information from Jim Hopkins, "Serial Entrepreneur Strikes Again at Age 70," *USA Today* (August 15, 2000).

15. Timothy Butler and James Waldroop, "Job Sculpting: The Art of Retaining Your Best People," *Harvard Business Review* (September–October 1999), pp. 144–52.

16. Hopkins, op. cit.

17. Information from the Standing Committee on the Status of Women, "Parental Benefits for Self-employed Women," on the Web, June 13, 2005, <www.wec.ca/taskforce.html>. (December 2006).

18. Hopkins, op. cit.

19. National Foundation for Women Business Owners, *Women Business Owners of Color: Challenges and Accomplishments* (1998).

20. Information from Industry Canada, Small Business Policy Branch, "Visible Minority Entrepreneurs," SME Financing Data Initiative, Small Business Financing Profiles, on the Web, March 2005, <www.strategis.ic.gc.ca>. (October 2006).

21. This list is developed from Timmons, op. cit, pp. 47–48; and Hisrich and Peters, op. cit., pp. 67–70.

22. Information from Industry Canada, "Key Small Business Statistics," Small Business Research and Policy, on the Web, January 2006, <www.strategis.ic.gs.ca>. (November 2006).

23. John Case, "The Rewards: Is it worth it to run your own business?" *Inc.*, State of Small Business Issue 2001 (May 15, 2001), pp. 50–51.

24. Julia Angwin, "Used-Car Auctioneers, Dealers Meet Online," *Wall Street Journal* (November 20, 2003), pp. B1, B13; and "Renaissance in Cyberspace," *Wall Street Journal* (November 20, 2003), p. B1.

25. Conversation from the case "Am I My Uncle's Keeper?" by Paul I. Karofsky (Northeastern University Center for Family Business); on the Web, <www.fambiz.com>. (December 2006).

26. Arthur Andersen, *Survey of Small and Mid-Sized Businesses: Trends for 2000* (2000).

27. Ibid.

28. George Gendron, "The Failure Myth," *Inc.* (January 2001), p. 13.

29. Based on Norman M. Scarborough and Thomas W. Zimmerer, *Effective Small Business Management* (Englewood Cliffs, NJ: Prentice-Hall, 2000), pp. 25–30; and Scott Clark, "Most Small-Business Failures Tied to Poor Management," *Business Journal* (April 10, 2000).

30. See, for example, John L. Nesheim, *High Tech Start Up* (New York: Free Press, 2000).

31. Discussion based on "The Life Cycle of Entrepreneurial Firms," in Ricky Griffin, ed., *Management*, 6th ed. (New York: Houghton Mifflin, 1999), pp. 309–10; and Neil C. Churchill and Virginia L. Lewis, "The Five Stages of Small Business Growth," *Harvard Business Review* (May–June 1993), pp. 30–50.

32. Developed from William S. Sahlman, "How to Write a Great Business Plan," *Harvard Business Review* (July–August 1997), pp. 98–108.

33. Standard components of business plans are described in many text sources such as Linda Pinson and Jerry Jinnett, *Anatomy of a Business Plan: A Step-by-Step Guide to Starting Smart, Building the Business, and Securing Your Company's Future*, 4th ed. (Dearbern Trade, 1999); Scarborough and Zimmerer, op. cit.; and on websites such as <www.americanexpress.com>, <www.businesstown.com>, and <www.bizplanit.com>.

34. "You've Come a Long Way Baby," *Business Week Frontier* (July 10, 2000).

35. Gifford Pinchot III, *Intrapreneuring, or Why You Don't Have to Leave the Corporation to Become an Entrepreneur* (New York: Harper & Row, 1985).

36. Information from John A. Byrne, "Management by Web," *Business Week* (August 28, 2000), pp. 84–97.

CHAPTER 7 NOTES

1. Sources for the opening vignette.

   Information from company website, <www.chaptersindigo.ca>.

   Ken Mark, "Indigo Books Starts a New Chapter," *Chain Store Age* (October 2005), p. 22A–23A.

   Rebecca Harris, "Indigo gets its wish...list," *Marketing*, vol. 110 (November 28, 2005), p. 4.

   Patricia MacInnis and Jennifer Brown, "Outsourcing: The Dating Game," *Computing Canada*, vol. 30 (April 9, 2004), pp. 12–18.

   Leah Eichler, "Cautiously, Respectfully Bullish," *Publishers Weekly* (April 29, 2002).

   With information from <http://www.sap.com/industries/retail/pdf/CS_IBM-Indigo.pdf>. (January 2007)

TEXT NOTES

2. See Alvin Toffler, *Powershift: Knowledge, Wealth, and Violence at the Edge of the 21st Century* (New York: Bantam Books, 1990).

3. "E-Meetings Redefine Productivity," *Fortune*, Special Advertising Section (February 5, 2001), p. S2.

4. Peter F. Drucker, "Looking Ahead: Implications of the Present," *Harvard Business Review* (September–October 1997), pp. 18–32. See also Shaker A. Zahra, "An Interview with Peter Drucker," *Academy of Management Executive*, vol. 17 (August 2003), pp. 9–12.

5. Thomas A. Stewart, *Intellectual Capital: The Wealth of Organizations* (New York: Doubleday, 1997).

6. Information from Robert W. Bly, "Does Your 'Second Generation' Site Get a Passing Grade?" (September 8, 2000).

7. See Susan G. Cohen and Don Mankin, "The Changing Nature of Work: Managing the Impact of Information Technology," Chapter 6 in Susan Albers Mohrman, Jay R. Galbraith, Edward E. Lawler III and Associates, *Tomorrow's Organization: Crafting Winning Capabilities in a Dynamic World* (San Francisco: Jossey-Bass, 1988), pp. 154–78.

8. See "Technology: The Best Way to Go," *Wall Street Journal Reports* (September 15, 2003).

9. Gerry Blackwell, "Telework," *IT Business Edge* on the Web, May 25, 2006, <www.itbusiness.ca>. (June 24, 2006).

10. Drucker, op. cit., "Looking Ahead" (1997), p. 22.

11. Information from John A. Byrne, "Visionary vs. Visionary," *Business Week* (August 28, 2000), pp. 210–14.

12. Jaclyn Fierman, "Winning Ideas from Maverick Managers," *Fortune* (February 6, 1995), pp. 66–80.

13. Information from Pui-Wing Tam, ". . . Communication with Employees," *Wall*

Street Journal (September 15, 2003), pp. R4, R10.

14. Ann Zimmerman, "To Sell Goods to Wal-Mart, Get on the Net," *Wall Street Journal* (November 21, 2003), pp. B1, B6.

15. Henry Mintzberg, *The Nature of Managerial Work* (New York: HarperCollins, 1997).

16. For scholarly reviews, see Dean Tjosvold, "Effects of Crisis Orientation on Managers' Approach to Controversy in Decision Making," *Academy of Management Journal*, vol. 27 (1984), pp. 130–38; and Ian I. Mitroff, Paul Shrivastava, and Firdaus E. Udwadia, "Effective Crisis Management," *Academy of Management Executive*, vol. 1 (1987), pp. 283–92.

17. Allan Britnell, "Crisis? What crisis?" *Profit*, vol. 22 (November 2003), pg. 77.

18. Developed from Anna Muoio, "Where There's Smoke It Helps to Have a Smoke Jumper," *Fast Company*, vol. 33, p. 290.

19. See David Greisling, *I'd Like to Buy the World a Coke: The Life and Leadership of Roberto Goizueta* (New York: Wiley, 1998).

20. See Hugh Courtney, Jane Kirkland, and Patrick Viguerie, "Strategy Under Uncertainty," *Harvard Business Review* (November–December 1997), pp. 67–79.

21. For a good discussion, see Watson H. Agor, *Intuition in Organizations: Leading and Managing Productively* (Newbury Park, CA: Sage, 1989); Herbert A. Simon, "Making Management Decisions: The Role of Intuition and Emotion," *Academy of Management Executive*, vol. 1 (1987), pp. 57–64; Orlando Behling and Norman L. Eckel, "Making Sense Out of Intuition," *Academy of Management Executive*, vol. 5 (1991), pp. 46–54.

22. Daniel J. Isenberg, "How Senior Managers Think," *Harvard Business Review*, vol. 62 (November–December 1984), pp. 81–90.

23. Daniel J. Isenberg, "The Tactics of Strategic Opportunism," *Harvard Business Review*, vol. 65 (March–April 1987), pp. 92–97.

24. See George P. Huber, *Managerial Decision Making* (Glenview, IL: Scott, Foresman 1975). For a comparison, see the steps in Xerox's problem-solving process as described in David A. Garvin, "Building a Learning Organization," *Harvard Business Review* (July–August 1993), pp. 78–91; and the Josephson model for ethical decision making, on the Web, <www.josephsoninstitute.org>.

25. Peter F. Drucker, *Innovation and Entrepreneurship: Practice and Principles* (New York: Harper & Row, 1985).

26. For a sample of Simon's work see Herbert A. Simon, *Administrative Behavior* (New York: Free Press, 1947); James G. March and Herbert A. Simon, *Organizations* (New York: Wiley, 1958); Herbert A. Simon, *The New Science of Management Decision* (New York: Harper, 1960).

27. Information from Carol Hymowitz, "Independent Program Puts College Students on Leadership Paths," *Wall Street Journal* (January 14, 2003), p. B1.

28. This presentation is based on the work of R. H. Hogarth, D. Kahneman, A. Tversky, and others, as discussed in Max H. Bazerman, *Judgment in Managerial Decision Making*, 3rd ed. (New York: Wiley, 1994).

29. Barry M. Staw, "The Escalation of Commitment to a Course of Action," *Academy of Management Review*, vol. 6 (1981), pp. 577–87; and Barry M. Staw and Jerry Ross, "Knowing When to Pull the Plug," *Harvard Business Review*, vol. 65 (March–April 1987), pp. 68–74.

30. The classic work is Norman R. Maier, "Assets and Liabilities in Group Problem Solving," *Psychological Review*, vol. 74 (1967), pp. 239–49.

31. I. Janis, *Groupthink: Psychological Studies of Policy Decisions and Fiascoes*, 2nd ed. (Boston: Houghton Mifflin, 1982).

32. Maier, op. cit.

33. Josephson, op. cit.

34. Based on Gerald F. Cavanagh, *American Business Values*, 4th ed. (Upper Saddle River, NJ: Prentice-Hall, 1998).

35. Peter F. Drucker, "The Future That Has Already Happened," *Harvard Business Review*, vol. 75 (September–October 1997), pp. 20–24; and Peter F. Drucker, Esther Dyson, Charles Handy, Paul Daffo, and Peter M. Senge, "Looking Ahead: Implications of the Present," *Harvard Business Review*, vol. 75 (September–October, 1997).

36. See, for example, Thomas H. Davenport and Laurence Prusak, *Working Knowledge: How Organizations Manage What They Know* (Cambridge, MA: Harvard Business School Press, 1997).

37. Peter Senge, *The Fifth Discipline* (New York: Harper, 1990).

38. Steven E. Prokesch, "Unleashing the Power of Learning," *Harvard Business Review* (September–October 1997), pp. 147–68.

CHAPTER 8 NOTES

1. Sources for the opening vignette:

   Andrew Wahl, "A few modest proposals," *Canadian Business*, vol. 79 (December 26, 2005–January 15, 2006), p. 19.

   "BSG aligns with Cognos to help drive Middle East channel," *Al Bawaba* (November 20, 2005), p. 1.

   "Cognos ranked as a leader in performance management solutions," *Al Bawaba* (December 22, 2005), p. 1.

   "Cognos unveils new blueprints for initiative and strategic long range planning," *Al Bawaba* (October 19, 2005), p. 1.

   "Lufthansa Selects Cognos 8 Business Intelligence," news release on the Web, January 24, 2006 <www.cognos.com>. (December 2006).

TEXT NOTES

2. Gary Hamel, *Leading the Revolution* (Boston: Harvard Business School Press, 2000).

3. Quote from "Today's Companies Won't Make It, and Gary Hamel Knows Why," *Fortune* (September 4, 2000), pp. 386–87.

4. T. J. Rodgers, William Taylor, and Rick Foreman, "No Excuses Management," *World Executive's Digest* (May 1994) pp. 26–30.

5. Eaton Corporation Annual Report (1985).

6. Henry Mintzberg, "The Manager's Job: Folklore and Fact," *Harvard Business Review*, vol. 53 (July–August 1975), pp. 54–67; and Henry Mintzberg, "Planning on the Left Side and Managing on the Right," *Harvard Business Review*, vol. 54 (July–August 1976), pp. 46–55.

7. Carolyn Ryan, "The hunt for the no-telephone poll," Canada Votes, CBC on the Web, January 23, 2006, <www.cbc.ca>. (December 2006). With information from the corporate website <http://www.decima.com>.

8. Quote from Stephen Covey and Roger Merrill, "New Ways to Get Organized at Work," *USA Weekend* (February 6–8, 1998), p. 18. Books by Stephen R. Covey include *The 7 Habits of Highly Effective People: Powerful Lessons in Personal Change* (New York: Fireside, 1990); and Stephen R. Covey and Sandra Merril Covey, *The 7 Habits of Highly Effective Families: Building a Beautiful Family Culture in a Turbulent World* (New York: Golden Books, 1996).

9. Quotes from *Business Week* (August 8, 1994), pp. 78–86.

10. See William Oncken, Jr., and Donald L. Wass, "Management Time: Who's Got the Monkey?" *Harvard Business Review*, vol. 52 (September–October 1974), pp.75–80; and featured as an HBR classic, *Harvard Business Review* (November–December 1999).

11. Amitai Etzioni, "Mixed Scanning: A 'Third' Approach to Decision-making," (1967) in Andreas Faludi, *A Reader in Planning Theory* (Pergamon Press, 1973), pp. 219–20.

12. Based on information from David Macleod, "Planning and Environmental Information," on the Web, <www3.sympatico.ca/david.macleod/PTHRY.HTM>. (December 2006).

13. Survey results from "Hurry Up and Decide," *Business Week* (May 14, 2001), p. 16.

14. See Elliot Jaques, *The Form of Time* (New York: Russak & Co., 1982). For an executive commentary on his research, see Walter Kiechel III, "How Executives Think," *Fortune* (December 21, 1987), pp. 139–44.

15. See Henry Mintzberg, "Rounding Out the Manager's Job," *Sloan Management Review* (fall 1994), pp. 1–25.

16. Information from "Avoiding a Time Bomb: Sexual Harassment," *Business Week*, Enterprise issue (October 13, 1997), pp. ENT20–21.

17. For a thorough review of forecasting, see J. Scott Armstrong, *Long-Range Forecasting, 2nd ed.* (New York: Wiley, 1985).

18. The scenario-planning approach is described in Peter Schwartz, *The Art of the Long View* (New York: Doubleday/Currency, 1991); and Arie de Geus, *The Living Company: Habits for Survival in a Turbulent Business Environment* (Boston, MA: Harvard Business School Press, 1997).

19. Greg Williams, Joy Mabon, and Bev Heim-Myers, "Best Practice: Strategic planning in a complex environment: The health-care example," *Ivey Business Journal* on the Web, January–February 2006, < www.ivey-businessjournal.com>. (December 2006).

20. See, for example, Robert C. Camp, *Business Process Benchmarking* (Milwaukee: ASQ Quality Press 1994); Michael J. Spendolini, *The Benchmarking Book* (New York: AMACOM, 1992); and Christopher E. Bogan and Michael J. English, *Benchmarking for Best Practices: Winning Through Innovative Adaptation* (New York: McGraw-Hill, 1994).

21. "How Classy Can 7-Eleven Get?" *Business Week* (September 1, 1997), pp. 74–75; and Kellie B. Gormly, "7-Eleven Moving Up a Grade," *Columbus Dispatch* (August 3, 2000), pp. C1–C2.

22. "The Renewal Factor: Friendly Fact, Congenial Controls," *Business Week* (September 14, 1987), p. 105.

23. Rob Cross and Lloyd Baird, "Technology Is Not Enough: Improving Performance by Building Institutional Memory," *Sloan Management Review* (spring 2000), p. 73.

24. "Forging the link between diversity and business strategy," BMO Financial Group website <www2.bmo.com>. (August 2006).

25. Information from Raju Narisetti, "For IBM, a Groundbreaking Sales Chief," *Wall Street Journal* (January 19, 1998), pp. B1, B5.

26. Based on discussion by Harold Koontz and Cyril O'Donnell in *Essentials of Management* (New York: McGraw-Hill, 1974), pp. 362–65; see also Cross and Baird, op. cit.

27. Information from Louis Lee, "I'm Proud of What I've Made Myself Into—What I've Created," *Wall Street Journal* (August 27, 1997), pp. B1, B5; and Jim Collins, "Bigger, Better, Faster," *Fast Company*, vol. 71 (June 2003), p. 74; on the Web, June 2003, <www.fastcompany.com>. (December 2006).

28. See John F. Love, *McDonald's: Behind the Arches* (New York: Bantam Books, 1986); and Ray Kroc and Robert Anderson, *Grinding It Out: The Making of McDonald's* (New York: St. Martin's Press, 1990).

29. See Dale D. McConkey, *How to Manage by Results, 3rd ed.* (New York: AMACOM, 1976); Stephen J. Carroll, Jr., and Henry J. Tosi, Jr., *Management by Objectives: Applications and Research* (New York: Macmillan, 1973); and Anthony P. Raia, *Managing by Objectives* (Glenview, IL: Scott, Foresman, 1974).

30. For a discussion of research, see Carroll and Tosi, op. cit.; Raia, op. cit., and Steven Kerr, "Overcoming the Dysfunctions of MBO," *Management by Objectives*, vol. 5 (1976). Information in part from Dylan Loeb McClain, "Job Forecast: Internet's Still Hot," *New York Times* (January 30, 2001), p. 9.

31. McGregor, op. cit.

32. The work on goal setting and motivation is summarized in Edwin A. Locke and Gary P. Latham, *Goal Setting: A Motivational Technique That Works!* (Englewood Cliffs, NJ: Prentice-Hall, 1984).

33. The "hot stove rules" are developed from R. Bruce McAfee and William Poffenberger, *Productivity Strategies: Enhancing Employee Job Performance* (Englewood Cliffs, NJ: Prentice-Hall, 1982), pp. 54–55. They are originally attributed to Douglas McGregor, "Hot

Stove Rules of Discipline," in G. Strauss and L. Sayles, eds., *Personnel: The Human Problems of Management* (Englewood Cliffs, NJ: Prentice-Hall, 1967).

CHAPTER 9 NOTES

1. Sources for the opening vignette:

   Corporate website <www.taxi.ca>.

   Laura Bogomolny, "The Contenders," *Canadian Business*, vol. 77 (August 16–29, 2004), p. 55.

   Rae Ann Fera, "Splitting a Cab: Taxi Continues Canadian Dominance, Makes Splash in New York," *Boards* (January 2006), p. 32.

   Danny Kucharsky, "The long drive home," *Marketing* (November 22, 2004), p. 28.

   Paul-Mark Rendon, "New York story," *Marketing* (September 27, 2004), p. 7.

   Marcus Robinson, "Creative control: Zak Mroueh puts Taxi in the driver's seat," *Boards* (September 2005), p. 30.

   Natalia Williams, "Gold-Taxi Shocking Upset!" *Strategy* (December 2005), p. 39.

TEXT NOTES

2. Jim Collins, "Bigger, Better, Faster," *Fast Company*, vol. 71 (June 2003), p. 74; on the Web, <www.fastcompany.com>. (December 2006).

3. Keith H. Hammond, "Michael Porter's Big Ideas," *Fast Company* (March 2001), pp. 150–56; on the Web, <www.fastcompany.com>. (December 2006).

4. Jeff Sanford, "Want a piece of this?" *Canadian Business*, vol. 79 (February 13–26, 2006), p. 83.

5. Tara Perkins, "Investors to bet on Tim Hortons' growth prospects," *Canadian Press* (March 20, 2006); on the Web, <www.canada.com/topics/finance/story.html>. (December 2006).

6. Gary Hamel and C. K. Prahalad, "Strategic Intent," *Harvard Business Review* (May–June 1989), pp. 63–76.

7. Information and quotes from Marcia Stepanek, "How Fast Is Net Fast?" *Business Week E-Biz* (November 1, 1999), pp. EB52–EB54.

8. For research support, see Daniel H. Gray, "Uses and Misuses of Strategic Planning," *Harvard Business Review*, vol. 64 (January–February 1986), pp. 89–97.

9. Hammond, op. cit., p. 153.

10. Michael A. Hitt, R. Duane Ireland, and Robert E. Hoskisson, *Strategic Management: Competitiveness and Globalization* (Minneapolis: West, 1997), p. 5.

11. See Michael E. Porter, *Competitive Strategy: Techniques for Analyzing Industries and Competitors* (New York: Free Press, 1980), and *Competitive Advantage: Creating and Sustaining Superior Performance* (New York: Free Press, 1986); and Richard A. D'Aveni, *Hyper-Competition: Managing the Dynamics of Strategic Maneuvering* (New York: Free Press, 1994).

12. D'Aveni, op. cit.

13. Example from "Memorable Memo: McDonald's Sends Operators to War on Fries," *Wall Street Journal* (December 18, 1997), p. B1.

14. Peter F. Drucker, "Five Questions," *Executive Excellence* (November 6, 1994), pp. 6–7.

15. Peter F. Drucker, *Management: Tasks, Responsibilities, Practices* (New York: Harper & Row, 1973), p. 122.

16. Ibid.

17. See Laura Nash, "Mission Statements—Mirrors and Windows," *Harvard Business Review* (March–April 1988), pp. 155–6; James C. Collins and Jerry I. Porras, "Building Your Company's Vision," *Harvard Business Review* (September–October 1996), pp. 65–77; and James C. Collins and Jerry I. Porras, *Built to Last: Successful Habits of Visionary Companies* (New York: Harper Business, 1997).

18. Gary Hamel, *Leading the Revolution* (Boston, MA: Harvard Business School Press, 2000), pp. 72–73.

19. For a discussion of non-profit organization mission statements, see Peter F. Drucker, "Self-Assessment: The First Action Requirement of Leadership," Drucker Foundation Self-Assessment Tool, on the Web, <www.leader-toleader.org>. (December 2006)

20. Retrieved from <www.norpaccontrols.com/tcc>. (August 2006).

21. Terrence E. Deal and Allen A. Kennedy, *Corporate Cultures: The Rites and Rituals of Corporate Life* (Reading, MA: Addison-Wesley, 1982), p. 22. For more on organizational culture see Edgar H. Schein, *Organizational Culture and Leadership, 2nd ed.* (San Francisco: Jossey-Bass, 1997).

22. Peter F. Drucker's views on organizational objectives are expressed in his classic books *The Practice of Management* (New York: Harper & Row, 1954), and *Management: Tasks, Responsibilities, Practices* (New York: Harper & Row, 1973). For a more recent commentary, see his article, "Management: The Problems of Success," *Academy of Management Executive*, vol. 1 (1987), pp. 13–19.

23. C. K. Prahalad and Gary Hamel, "The Core Competencies of the Corporation," *Harvard Business Review* (May–June 1990), pp. 79–91; see also Hitt, et al., op. cit., pp. 99–103.

24. For a discussion of Michael Porter's approach to strategic planning, see his books *Competitive Strategy* and *Competitive Advantage*; his article, "What Is Strategy? *Harvard Business Review* (November–December, 1996), pp. 61–78; and Richard M. Hodgetts' interview, "A Conversation with Michael E. Porter: A Significant Extension Toward Operational Improvement and Positioning," *Organizational Dynamics* (summer 1999), pp. 24–33.

25. Based on information from a press release of February 3, 2006, on the Web, <www.ccithermal.com>. (December 2006).

26. David Finlayson, "Management kudos for CCI," *Edmonton Journal* (March 21, 2006); and on the Web, <www.ccithermal.com>. (December 2006).

27. The four grand strategies were originally described by William F. Glueck, *Business Policy: Strategy Formulation and Management Action, 2nd ed.* (New York: McGraw-Hill, 1976).

28. Hitt et al., op. cit., p. 197.

29. See William McKinley, Carol M. Sanchez, and A. G. Schick, "Organizational Downsizing: Constraining, Cloning, Learning," *Academy of Management Executive*, vol. 9 (August 1995), pp. 32–44.

30. Kim S. Cameron, Sara J. Freeman, and A. K. Mishra, "Best Practices in White-Collar Downsizing: Managing Contradictions," *Academy of Management Executive*, vol. 4 (August 1991), pp. 57–73.

31. This strategy classification is found in Hitt, et al., op. cit.; the attitudes are from a discussion by Howard V. Perlmutter, "The Tortuous Evolution of the Multinational Corporation," *Columbia Journal of World Business*, vol. 4 (January–February 1969).

32. See Michael E. Porter, "Strategy and the Internet," *Harvard Business Review* (March 2001), pp. 63–78.

33. Information from Michael Rappa, Business Models on the Web, <www.digitalenterprise.org>. (December 2006)

34. Hammond, op. cit.

35. D'Aveni, op. cit.

36. D'Aveni, op. cit.

37. Porter, op cit. (1980), (1986), (1996).

38. Information from <www.polo.com>.

39. David Knibb, "Service Formula," *Airline Business*, vol. 21 (December 2005), p. 68.

40. Richard G. Hammermesh, "Making Planning Strategic," *Harvard Business Review*, vol. 64 (July–August 1986), pp. 115–120; and Richard G. Hammermesh, *Making Strategy Work* (New York: Wiley, 1986).

41. See Gerald B. Allan, "A Note on the Boston Consulting Group Concept of Competitive Analysis and Corporate Strategy," Harvard Business School, Intercollegiate Case Clearing House, ICCH9-175-175 (Boston: Harvard Business School, June 1976).

42. The adaptive model is described in Raymond E. Miles and Charles C. Snow's book, *Organizational Strategy, Structure, and Process* (New York: McGraw-Hill, 1978); and their articles, "Designing Strategic Human Resources Systems," *Organizational Dynamics*, vol. 13 (summer 1984), pp. 36–52; and "Fit, Failure, and the Hall of Fame," *California Management Review*, vol. 26 (spring 1984), pp. 10–28.

43. James Brian Quinn, "Strategic Change: Logical Incrementalism," *Sloan Management Review*, vol. 20 (fall 1978), pp. 7–21.

44. Henry Mintzberg, *The Nature of Managerial Work* (New York: Harper & Row, 1973); and John R. P. Kotter, *The General Managers* (New York: Free Press, 1982).

45. Henry Mintzberg, "Planning on the Left Side and Managing on the Right," *Business Review*, vol. 54 (July–August 1976), pp. 46–55; Henry Mintzberg and James A. Waters, "Of Strategies, Deliberate and Emergent," *Strategic Management Journal*, vol. 6 (1985), pp. 257–72; Henry Mintzberg, "Crafting Strategy," *Harvard Business Review*, vol. 65 (July–August 1987), pp. 66–75.

46. For research support, see Daniel H. Gray, "Uses and Misuses of Strategic Planning," *Harvard Business Review*, vol. 64 (January–February 1986), pp. 89–97.

47. For a discussion of corporate governance issues, see Hugh Sherman and Rajeswararao Chaganti, *Corporate Governance and the Timeliness of Change* (Westport, CT: Quorum Books, 1998).

48. See Carol Hyowitz, "GE Chief Is Charting His Own Strategy, Focusing on Technology," *Wall Street Journal* (September 23, 2003), p. B1.

49. See R. Duane Ireland and Michael A. Hitt, "Achieving and Maintaining Strategic Competitiveness in the 21st Century," *Academy of Management Executive*, vol. 13 (1999), pp. 43–57.

50. Hammond, op. cit.

51. Michael Dell quotes from Matt Murray, "As Huge Companies Keep Growing, CEOs Struggle to Keep Pace," *Wall Street Journal* (February 8, 2001), pp. A1, A6.

52. Jon R. Katzenbach, "The Myth of the Top Management Team," *Harvard Business Review* (November–December 1997), pp. 82–91.

CHAPTER 10 NOTES

1. Sources for the opening vignette:

    From "Information and Statistics Fact Sheet" and "Edward Jones Again Named One of the '50 Best Employers in Canada'," on the Web, <www.edwardjones.com>. (November 2006).

TEXT NOTES

2. Henry Mintzberg and Ludo Van der Heyden, "Organigraphs: Drawing How Companies Really Work," *Harvard Business Review* (September–October 1999), pp. 87–94.

3. See, for example, Charles O'Reilly III and Jeffrey Pfeffer, *Hidden Value: How Great Companies Achieve Extraordinary Results with Ordinary People* (Boston: Harvard Business School Press, 2000); Jeffrey Pfeffer and John F. Veiga, "Putting People First for Organizational Success," *Academy of Management Executive*, vol. 13 (May 1999), pp. 37–48; Jeffrey Pfeffer, *The Human Equation: Building Profits by Putting People First* (Boston: Harvard Business School Press, 1998); Jeffrey Pfeffer, "When It Comes to 'Best Practices'—Why Do Smart Organizations Occasionally Do Dumb Things?" *Organizational Dynamics*, vol. 25 (summer 1996), pp. 33–44; and Michael Beer, "How to Develop an Organization Capable of Sustained High Performance: Embrace the Drive for Results—Capability Development Paradox," *Organizational Dynamics*, vol. 29 (spring 2001), pp. 233–247.

4. The classic work is Alfred D. Chandler's, *Strategy and Structure* (Cambridge, MA: MIT Press, 1962).

5. See Alfred D. Chandler, Jr., "Origins of the Organization Chart," *Harvard Business Review* (March–April 1988), pp. 156–57.

6. See David Krackhardt and Jeffrey R. Hanson, "Informal Networks: The Company Behind the Chart," *Harvard Business Review* (July–August 1993), pp. 104–11.

7. With information from George A. Neufeld, Peter A. Simeoni, and Marilyn A. Taylor, "High-performance research organization," *Research Technology Management*, vol. 44.

(November–December 2001), pp. 42–53.

8. See Kenneth Noble, "A Clash of Styles: Japanese Companies in the U.S." *New York Times* (January 25, 1988), p. 7.

9. For a discussion of departmentalization, see H. I. Ansoff and R. G. Bradenburg, "A Language for Organization Design," *Management Science*, vol. 17 (August 1971), pp. B705–B731; Mariann Jelinek, "Organization Structure: The Basic Conformations," in Mariann Jelinek, Joseph A. Litterer, and Raymond E. Miles, eds., *Organizations by Design: Theory and Practice* (Plano, TX: Business Publications, 1981), pp. 293–302; Henry Mintzberg, "The Structuring of Organizations," in James Brian Quinn, Henry Mintzberg, and Robert M. James, eds., *The Strategy Process: Concepts, Contexts, and Cases* (Englewood Cliffs, NJ: Prentice-Hall, 1988), pp. 276–304.

10. Robert L. Simison, "Jaguar Slowly Sheds Outmoded Habits," *Wall Street Journal* (July 26, 1991), p. A6; and Richard Stevenson, "Ford Helps Jaguar Get Back Old Sheen," *International Herald Tribune* (December 14, 1994), p. 11.

11. These alternatives are well described by Mintzberg, op. cit.

12. The focus on process is described in Michael Hammer, *Beyond Reengineering* (New York: Harper Business, 1996).

13. Ibid.

14. Excellent reviews of matrix concepts are found in Stanley M. Davis and Paul R. Lawrence, *Matrix* (Reading, MA: Addison-Wesley, 1977); Paul R. Lawrence, Harvey F. Kolodny, and Stanley M. Davis, "The Human Side of the Matrix," *Organizational Dynamics*, vol. 6 (1977), pp. 43–61; and Harvey F. Kolodny, "Evolution to a Matrix Organization," *Academy of Management Review*, vol. 4 (1979), pp. 543–53.

15. Davis and Lawrence, op. cit.

16. Developed from Frank Ostroff, *The Horizontal Organization: What the Organization of the Future Looks Like and How It Delivers Value to Customers* (New York: Oxford University Press, 1999).

17. The nature of teams and teamwork is described in Jon R. Katzenbach and Douglas K. Smith, "The Discipline of Teams," *Harvard Business Review* (March–April 1993), pp. 111–20.

18. Susan Albers Mohrman, Susan G. Cohen, and Allan M. Mohrman, Jr., *Designing Team-Based Organizations* (San Francisco: Jossey-Bass, 1996).

19. See Glenn M. Parker, *Cross-Functional Teams* (San Francisco: Jossey-Bass, 1995).

20. Information from William Bridges, "The End of the Job," *Fortune* (September 19, 1994), pp. 62–74; Alan Deutschman, "The Managing Wisdom of High-Tech Superstars," *Fortune* (October 17, 1994), pp. 197–206.

21. See the discussion by Jay R. Galbraith, "Designing the Networked Organization: Leveraging Size and Competencies," in Susan Albers Mohrman, Jay R. Galbraith, Edward E. Lawler III and Associates, *Tomorrow's Organizations: Crafting Winning Strategies in a Dynamic World* (San Francisco: Jossey-Bass, 1998), pp. 76–102. See also Rupert F. Chisholm, *Developing Network Organizations: Learning from Practice and Theory* (Reading, MA: Addison-Wesley, 1998).

22. With information from Yvon Bigras, "Transforming SMEs," *CMA Management*, vol.76 (September 2002), pp. 31–33.

23. See Jerome Barthelemy, "The Seven Deadly Sins of Outsourcing," *Academy of Management Executive*, vol. 17 (2003), pp. 87–98.

24. See Ron Ashkenas, Dave Ulrich, Todd Jick, and Steve Kerr, *The Boundaryless Organization: Breaking the Chains of Organizational Structure* (San Francisco: Jossey-Bass, 1996).

25. Robert Slater, *Jack Welch and the GE Way: Management Insights and Leadership Secrets from the Legendary CEO* (New York: 1998); and "Jack the Job-Killer Strikes Again," *Business Week* (February 12, 2001), p. 12.

26. Information from John A. Byrne, "Management by Web," *Business Week* (August 28, 2000), pp. 84–97.

27. See the collection of articles by Cary L. Cooper and Denise M. Rousseau, eds., *The Virtual Organization: Vol. 6, Trends in Organizational Behavior* (New York: Wiley, 2000).

28. See Korky Koroluk, "Canadian institute gains attention on world stage," *Daily Commercial News and Construction Record*, vol. 77 (September 17, 2004), p. GB1.

29. David Van Fleet, "Span of Management Research and Issues," *Academy of Management Journal*, vol. 26 (1983), pp. 546–52.

30. Developed from Roger Fritz, *Rate Your Executive Potential* (New York: Wiley, 1988), pp. 185–86; Roy J. Lewicki, Donald D. Bowen, Douglas T. Hall, and Francine S. Hall, *Experiences in Management and Organizational Behavior*, 3rd ed. (New York: Wiley, 1988), p. 144.

31. David North, "Is your head office a useless frill?", *Canadian Business*, vol. 70 (November 14, 1997), pp. 78–80.

32. See George P. Huber, "A Theory of Effects of Advanced Information Technologies on Organizational Design, Intelligence, and Decision Making," *Academy of Management Review*, vol. 15 (1990), pp. 67–71.

CHAPTER 11 NOTES

1. Sources for the opening vignette:

   Information from the company website, <www.kpmg.com> and <www.kpmg.ca >. (November 2006).

TEXT NOTES

2. Described by Andrew Ross Sorkin, "Gospel According to St. Luke's," *New York Times* (February 12, 1998), pp. C1, C7; see also the corporate website, <www.stlukes.co.uk>.

3. Information and quotes from corporate website and Judith Rehak, "A Swiss Giant Awakens with a Start," *International Herald Tribune* (May 3–4, 2003), pp. 13–14.

4. For a discussion of organization theory, see W. Richard Scott, *Organizations: Rational, Natural, and Open Systems*, 4th ed. (Upper Saddle River, NJ: Prentice-Hall, 1998).

5. Information taken from the corporate website, <www.dbgcanada.com>. (November 2006).

6. For a classic work see Jay R. Galbraith, *Organizational Design* (Reading, MA: Addison-Wesley, 1977).

7. This framework is based on Harold J. Leavitt, "Applied Organizational Change in Industry," in James G. March, *Handbook of Organizations* (New York: Rand-McNally, 1965), pp. 144–70; and Edward E. Lawler III, *From the Ground Up: Six Principles for the New Logic Corporation* (San Francisco: Jossey-Bass Publishers, 1996), pp. 44–50.

8. See the discussion in Gaerth Jones, *Organizaional Theory and Design*, 3rd ed. (Upper Saddle River, NJ: Prentice-Hall, 2001).

9. See the discussion in James L. Gibson, John M. Ivancevich, and James H. Donnelly, Jr., *Organizations: Behavior, Structure, Processes*, 5th ed. (Homewood, IL: Richard D. Irwin, 1991).

10. Peter Diekmeyer, "Hotelier Taps Demand for Quantity, Service," *National Post* (February 3, 2006).

11. Max Weber, *The Theory of Social and Economic Organization,* A. M. Henderson, trans., and H. T. Parsons (New York: Free Press, 1947).

12. For classic treatments of bureaucracy, see Alvin Gouldner, *Patterns of Industrial Bureaucracy* (New York: Free Press, 1954); and Robert K. Merton, *Social Theory and Social Structure* (New York: Free Press, 1957).

13. Tom Burns and George M. Stalker, *The Management of Innovation* (London: Tavistock, 1961; republished by Oxford University Press, London, 1994).

14. See Henry Mintzberg, *Structure in Fives: Designing Effective Organizations* (Englewood Cliffs, NJ: Prentice-Hall, 1983).

15. Information from Thomas Petzinger, Jr., "Self-Organization Will Free Employees to Act Like Bosses," *Wall Street Journal* (January 3, 1997), p. B1.

16. See Rosabeth Moss Kanter, *The Changing Masters* (New York: Simon & Schuster, 1983). Quotation from Rosabeth Moss Kanter and John D. Buck, "Reorganizing Part of Honeywell: From Strategy to Structure," *Organizational Dynamics*, vol. 13 (winter 1985), p. 6.

17. See for example, Jay R. Galbraith, Edward E. Lawler III and Associates, *Organizing for the Future* (San Francisco: Jossey-Bass Publishers, 1993); and Susan Albers Mohrman, Jay R. Galbraith, Edward E. Lawler III and Associates, *Tomorrow's Organizations: Crafting Winning Strategies in a Dynamic World* (San Francisco: Jossey-Bass, 1998).

18. Peter Senge, *The Fifth Discipline: The Art and Practice of the Learning Organization* (New York: Doubleday, 1994).

19. A classic treatment of environment and organizational design is found in James D. Thompson, *Organizations in Action* (New York: McGraw-Hill, 1967). See also Scott, op. cit., pp. 264–69.

20. Information and media release found on the corporate website, <www.hayes.bc.ca>.

21. Alfred D. Chandler, Jr., *Strategy and Structure: Chapter in the History of American Industrial Enterprise* (Cambridge, MA: MIT Press, 1962).

22. See, for example, Danny Miller, "Configurations of Strategy and Structure: Towards a Synthesis," *Strategic Management Journal*, vol. 7 (1986), pp. 233–49.

23. Information taken from the corporate website, <www.skywavemobile.com>. (November 2006).

24. Joan Woodward, *Industrial Organization: Theory and Practice* (London: Oxford University Press, 1965; republished by Oxford University Press, 1994).

25. This classification is from Thompson, op. cit.

26. See Peter M. Blau and Richard A. Schoennerr, *The Structure of Organizations* (New York: Basic Books, 1971); and Scott, op. cit., pp. 259–63.

27. D. E. Gumpert, "The Joys of Keeping the Company Small," *Harvard Business Review* (July–August 1986), pp. 6–8, 12–14.

28. L. Greiner, "Evolution and Revolution as Organizations Grow," *Harvard Business Review*, vol. 50 (1972), pp. 37–46.

29. John R. Kimberly and Robert H. Miles, *The Organizational Life Cycle* (San Francisco: Jossey-Bass, 1980).

30. Kim Cameron, Sarah J. Freeman, and Naneil K. Mishra, "Best Practices in White-Collar Downsizing: Managing Contradictions," *Academy of Management Executive*, vol. 5 (August 1991), pp. 57–73.

31. See Gifford Pinchot III, *Intrapreneuring: Or Why You Don't Have to Leave the Corporation to Become an Entrepreneur* (New York: Harper & Row, 1985).

32. See Jay Lorsch and John Morse, *Organizations and Their Members: A Contingency Approach* (New York: Harper & Row, 1974); and Scott, op. cit., pp. 263–64.

33. "The Rebirth of IBM," *Economist* (June 6, 1998), pp. 65–68.

34. Paul R. Lawrence and Jay W. Lorsch, *Organizations and Environment* (Boston: Division of Research, Graduate School of Business Administration, Harvard University, 1967).

35. Burns and Stalker, op. cit.

36. See Jay R. Galbraith, op. cit., and Susan Albers Mohrman, "Integrating Roles and Structure in the Lateral Organization," chapter 5 in Jay R. Galbraith, Edward E. Lawler III and Associates, *Organizing for the Future* (San Francisco: Jossey-Bass Publishers, 1993).

37. For a good discussion of coordination and integration approaches, see Scott, op. cit., pp. 231–39.

38. Michael Hammer and James Champy, *Reengineering the Corporation: A Manifesto for Business Revolution*, rev. ed. (New York: Harper Business, 1999).

39. Michael Hammer, *Beyond Reengineering* (New York: Harper Business, 1997).

40. Ibid., p. 5; see also the discussion of processes in Gary Hamel, *Leading the Revolution* (Boston, MA: Harvard Business School Press, 2000).

41. Thomas M. Koulopoulos, *The Workflow Imperative* (New York: Van Nostrand Reinhold, 1995); Hammer, *Beyond Reengineering,* op. cit. (1997).

42. Paul Roberts, "Humane Technology—PeopleSoft," *Fast Company*, vol. 14 (1998), p. 122.

43. Ronni T. Marshak, "Workflow Business Process Reengineering," special advertising section, *Fortune* (1997).

44. A similar example is found in Hammer, op. cit. (1997), pp. 9–10.

45. Ibid., pp. 28–30.

46. Ibid., p. 29.

47. Ibid., p. 27.

48. Quote from Hammer and Company website, <www.hammerandco.com>.

CHAPTER 12 NOTES

1. Sources for the opening vignette:

   Anonymous, "Employee Wellness," *Canadian HR Reporter*, vol. 17 (February 23, 2004), pp. 9ff.

   David Brown, "Success Starts at the Middle," *Canadian HR Reporter*, vol. 16 (June 2, 2003), pp.1ff.

   Cheryl Dahle, "A Steelmaker's Heart of Gold," *Fast Company* (June 2003), pp. 46ff.

   S. Mingail, "Tackling Workplace Literacy a No-Brainer," *Canadian HR Reporter*, vol. 17 (November 22, 2004), pp. G3, G11.

   Raizel Robin, "Taking Care of Business: Dofasco is now a national leader in workplace health," *Canadian Business*, vol. 76 (November 24–December 7, 2003).

   Marilyn Scales, "Canada's Top 40," *Canadian Mining Journal*, vol. 124 (September 2003).

   Cindy Waxer, "Steelmaker Revives Apprentice Program to Address Graying Workforce, Forge Next Leaders," *Workforce Management*, vol. 85, pp. 40ff.

TEXT NOTES

2. Robert B. Reich, *The Future of Success* (New York: Knopf, 2000).

3. Robert B. Reich, "The Company of the Future," *Fast Company* (November 1998), pp. 124ff.

4. See Jeffrey Pfeffer, *The Human Equation: Building Profits by Putting People First* (Boston: Harvard University Press, 1998).

5. See, for example, Charles Handy, *The Age of Unreason* (Cambridge, MA: Harvard Business School Press, 1990); and Tom Peters, "The Brand Called You," *Fast Company* (August 1997), pp. 83ff.

6. Pfeffer, op. cit., p. 292.

7. Jeffrey Pfeffer and John F. Veiga, "Putting People First for Organizational Success," *Academy of Management Executive*, vol. 13 (May 1999), pp. 37–48.

8. Ibid; and Pfeffer, op. cit.

9. James N. Baron and David M. Kreps, *Strategic Human Resources: Frameworks for General Managers* (New York: Wiley, 1999).

10. R. Roosevelt Thomas, Jr., *Beyond Race and Gender* (New York: AMACOM, 1992).

11. Lawrence Otis Graham, *Proversity: Getting Past Face Value and Finding the Soul of People* (New York: Wiley, 1997).

12. See also R. Roosevelt Thomas Jr.'s books, op. cit.; and (with Marjorie I. Woodruff) *Building a House for Diversity* (New York: AMACOM, 1999); and Richard D. Bucher, *Diversity Consciousness* (Englewood Cliffs, NJ: Prentice-Hall, 2000).

13. "IBM Canada and Pelmorex Incorporated honoured at the Employment Equity Merit Awards," on the Web, October 9, 2003, <http://www.hrsdc.gc.ca>. (December 2006).

14. Thomas, op. cit., p. 4.

15. Quote from William Bridges, "The End of the Job," *Fortune* (September 19, 1994), p. 68.

16. Message from the president, found on the Canadian Council of Human Resources Associations website, <www.cchra-ccarh.ca>. (December 2006).

17. See Baron and Kreps, op. cit.

18. Quotes from Kris Maher, "Human-Resources Directors Are Assuming Strategic Roles," *Wall Street Journal* (June 17, 2003), p. B8.

19. Ibid.

20. Human Rights Program Part IV: Measures Adopted by the Governments of the Provinces: British Columbia, on the Web, <www.pch.gc.ca/progs>. (November 2006).

21. Taken from the Employment Equity Act, on the Web, <http://laws.justice.gc.ca>. (November 2006).

22. See the discussion by David A. DeCenzo and Stephen P. Robbins, *Human Resource Management, 6th ed.* (New York: Wiley, 1999), pp. 66–68, 81–83.

23. Ibid., pp. 77–79.

24. Information from "There Are Questions You Shouldn't Answer," *New York Times* (January 30, 2001), p. 2.

25. See discussion by DeCenzo and Robbins, op. cit., pp. 79–90.

26. Canadian Human Rights Commission, "Anti-Harassment Policies for the Workplace: An Employer's Guide," on the Web, March 2006, <www.chrc-ccdp.ca>. (November 2006).

27. Information on pay equity found on the Web, <www.workrights.ca>. (November 2006).

28. See Frederick S. Lane, *The Naked Employee: How Technology is Compromising Workplace Privacy* (New York: AMACOM, 2003).

29. Quote from George Myers, "Bookshelf," *Columbus Dispatch* (June 9, 2003), p. E6.

30. Kristen Goff, "'Strong Belief System' Key Factor in Quality Workforce, Lee Says," *Ottawa Citizen* (October 24, 2006), p. B3.

31. Information from Thomas A. Stewart, "In Search of Elusive Tech Workers," *Fortune* (February 16, 1998), pp. 171–72.

32. See Ernest McCormick, "Job and Task Analysis," in Marvin Dunnette, ed., *Handbook of Industrial and*

Organizational Psychology (Chicago: Rand McNally, 1976), pp. 651–96.

33. Information from Gautam Naik, "India's Technology Whizzes Find Passage to Nokia," *Wall Street Journal* (August 1, 2000), p. B1.

34. Uyen Vu, "The drug sector's staffing remedies," *Canadian HR Reporter*, vol.16 (February 10, 2003), pp. 1ff.

35. See David Greising, *I'd Like to Buy the World a Coke: The Life and Leadership of Roberto Goizueta* (New York: Wiley, 1998).

36. See John P. Wanous, *Organizational Entry: Recruitment, Selection, and Socialization of Newcomers* (Reading, MA: Addison-Wesley, 1980), pp. 34–44.

37. Ravit Abelman and Igor Kotlyar, "Simulation Turns Recruitment into a Two-Way Street: Applicants can get a better sense of the job while the company gets a sampling of how the candidate will perform," *Canadian HR Reporter*, vol. 16 (December 1, 2003), p. G6.

38. Information from Justin Martin, "Mercedes: Made in Alabama," *Fortune* (July 7, 1997), pp. 150–58.

39. Information from Kemba J. Dunham, "The Jungle: Focus on Recruitment, Pay and Getting Ahead," *Wall Street Journal* (September 23, 2003), p. B8.

40. Reported in "Would You Hire This Person Again?" *Business Week*, Enterprise issue (June 9, 1997), pp. ENT32.

41. Dwight Hamilton, "Have Résumés: Fact or fiction?" *CAmagazine*, vol. 133 (April 2000), p. 16; on the Web, <www.camagazine.com>. (December 2006).

42. For a scholarly review, see John Van Maanen and Edgar H. Schein, "Toward a Theory of Socialization," in Barry M. Staw, ed., *Research in Organizational Behavior*, vol. 1 (Greenwich, CT: JAI Press, 1979), pp. 209–64. For a practitioner's view, see Richard Pascale, "Fitting New Employees into the Company Culture," *Fortune* (May 28, 1984), pp. 28–42.

43. Quote from Ronald Henkoff, "Finding, Training, and Keeping the Best Service Workers," *Fortune* (October 3, 1994), pp. 110–22.

44. This involves the social information processing concept as discussed in Gerald R. Salancik and Jeffrey Pfeffer, "A Social Information Processing Approach to Job Attitudes and Task Design," *Administrative Science Quarterly*, vol. 23 (June 1978), pp. 224–53.

45. Andy Holloway, "Mirror, Mirror," *Canadian Business*, vol. 79 (Summer 2006), p. 175ff.

46. Quote from Peter Petre, "Games That Teach You to Manage," *Fortune* (October 29, 1984), pp. 65–72; see also, the "Looking Glass" description on the Center for Creative Leadership website, <www.ccl.org>.

47. See Larry L. Cummings and Donald P. Schwab, *Performance in Organizations: Determinants and Appraisal* (Glenview, IL: Scott, Foresman, 1973).

48. Dick Grote, "Performance Appraisal Reappraised," *Harvard Business Review Best Practice* (1999), Reprint F00105.

49. See Mark R. Edwards and Ann J. Ewen, *360-Degree Feedback: The Powerful New Tool for Employee Feedback and Performance Improvement* (New York: AMACOM, 1996).

50. Information from "What Are the Most Effective Retention Tools?" *Fortune* (October 9, 2000), p. S7.

51. Charles Handy, *The Age of Unreason* (Cambridge, MA: Harvard Business School Press, 1990), p. 55.

52. Claudine Kapel and Catherine Shepherd, "Career Ladders Create Common Language for Defining Jobs," *Canadian HR Reporter*, vol. 17 (June 14, 2004), p. 15.

53. See Thomas P. Ference, James A. F. Stoner, and E. Kirby Warren, "Managing the Career Plateau," *Academy of Management Review*, vol. 2 (October 1977), pp. 602–12.

54. Information and quote from Carol Hymowitz, "Baby Boomers Seek New Ways to Escape Career Claustrophobia," *Wall Street Journal* (June 24, 2003), p. B1.

55. Timothy Butler and James Waldroop, "Job Sculpting: The Art of Retaining Your Best People," *Harvard Business Review* (September–October 1999), pp. 144–52.

56. See Betty Friedan, *Beyond Gender: The New Politics of Work and the Family* (Washington, DC: Woodrow Wilson Center Press, 1997); and James A. Levine, *Working Fathers: New Strategies for Balancing Work and Family* (Reading, MA: Addison-Wesley, 1997).

57. For reviews, see Richard B. Freeman and James L. Medoff, *What Do Unions Do?* (New York: Basic Books, 1984); Charles C. Heckscher, *The New Unionism* (New York: Basic Books, 1988); and Barry T. Hirsch, *Labor Unions and the Economic Performance of Firms* (Kalamazoo, MI: W.E. Upjohn Institute for Employment Research, 1991).

58. Yochi J. Dreazen, "Percentage of U.S. Workers in a Union Sank to Record Low of 13.5% Last Year," *Wall Street Journal* (January 19, 2001), p. A2.

59. D. Carter, G. England, B. Etherington, and G. Trudeau, *Labour Law in Canada* (The Hague, Netherlands: Kluwer Law International, Distributed by Butterworths Canada Ltd., 2002).

CHAPTER 13 NOTES

1. Source for the opening vignette:

   Information and quotes from Philip Preville, "For God's sake," *Canadian Business*, vol. 72 (June 25–July 9, 1999), p. 58–61.

TEXT NOTES

2. Information from the corporate website, <www.goldcorp.com>; and "The Fast 50 Leaders," *Fast Company* on the Web, <www.fastcompany.com>. (December 2006).

3. Tom Peters, "Rule #3: Leadership Is Confusing as Hell," *Fast Company* (March 2001), pp. 124–40.

4. Quotations from Marshall Loeb, "Where Leaders Come From," *Fortune* (September 19, 1994), pp. 241–42; Genevieve Capowski, "Anatomy of a Leader: Where Are the Leaders of Tomorrow?" *Management Review* (March 1994), pp. 10–17. For additional thoughts, see Warren Bennis, *Why*

Leaders Can't Lead (San Francisco: Jossey-Bass, 1996).

5. See Jean Lipman-Blumen, *Connective Leadership: Managing in a Changing World* (New York: Oxford University Press, 1996), pp. 3–11.

6. James M. Kouzes and Barry Z. Posner, "The Leadership Challenge," *Success* (April 1988), p. 68. See also their books *The Leadership Challenge: How to Get Extraordinary Things Done in Organizations* (San Francisco: Jossey-Bass, 1987); *Credibility: How Leaders Gain and Lose It; Why People Demand It* (San Francisco: Jossey-Bass, 1996); *Encouraging the Heart: A Leader's Guide to Rewarding and Recognizing Others* (San Francisco: Jossey-Bass, 1999).

7. Burt Nanus, *Visionary Leadership: Creating a Compelling Sense of Vision for Your Organization* (San Francisco: Jossey-Bass, 1992).

8. Quotation from the General Electric Company Annual Report (1997), p. 5. For more on Jack Welch's leadership approach at GE see *Jack Welch & the GE Way* (New York: McGraw-Hill, 1998).

9. See Kouzes and Posner, op. cit. and James C. Collins and Jerry I. Porras, "Building Your Company's Vision," *Harvard Business Review* (September–October 1996), pp. 65–77.

10. Bonnie Dupont, "Leadership—An Organization's Biggest Competitive Advantage," address given at the Faculty of Management Awards and Scholarship ceremony, University of Calgary, March 13, 2002, Calgary, Alberta.

11. Rosabeth Moss Kanter, "Power Failure in Management Circuits," *Harvard Business Review* (July–August 1979), pp. 65–75.

12. For a good managerial discussion of power, see David C. McClelland and David H. Burnham, "Power Is the Great Motivator," *Harvard Business Review* (March–April 1976), pp. 100–10.

13. The classic treatment of these power bases is John R. P. French, Jr. and Bertram Raven, "The Bases of Social Power," in Darwin Cartwright, ed., *Group Dynamics: Research and Theory* (Evanstion, IL: Row, Peterson, 1962), pp. 607–13. For managerial applications of this basic framework, see Gary Yukl and Tom Taber, "The Effective Use of Managerial Power," *Personnel*, vol. 60 (1983), pp. 37–49; and Robert C. Benfari, Harry E. Wilkinson, and Charles D. Orth, "The Effective Use of Power," *Business Horizons*, vol. 29 (1986), pp. 12–16; Gary A. Yukl, *Leadership in Organizations, 4th ed.* (Englewood Cliffs, NJ: Prentice-Hall, 1998), includes "information" as a separate, but related, power source.

14. Information from <www.wxnetwork.com>; and remarks by Rose Patten, Senior Executive Vice-President at BMO Financial Group to the Financial Women's Association of Chicago, February 24, 2005; available on the Web, <www2.bmo.com>. (December 2006).

15. Based on David A. Whetten and Kim S. Cameron, *Developing Management Skills, 2nd ed.* (New York: Harper-Collins, 1991), pp. 281–97.

16. Ibid., p. 282.

17. Ibid.

18. Chester A. Barnard, *Functions of the Executive* (Cambridge, MA: Harvard University Press, 1938).

19. Andy Holloway, "Live and Learn: Derek Oland," *Canadian Business* (October 24–November 6, 2005); available on the Web, <www.canadianbusiness.com>. (December 2006).

20. Jeff Sanford, "Clean and green: Suncor uses sustainability performance to track business," *Canadian Business* Online, February 22, 2006, <www.canadianbusiness.com>. (December 2006).

21. Jay A. Conger, "Leadership: The Art of Empowering Others," *Academy of Management Executive*, vol. 3 (1989), pp. 17–24.

22. The early work on leader traits is well represented in Ralph M. Stogdill, "Personal Factors Associated with Leadership: A Survey of the Literature," *Journal of Psychology*, vol. 25 (1948), pp. 35–71. See also Edwin E. Ghiselli, *Explorations in Management Talent* (Santa Monica, CA: Goodyear, 1971); and Shirley A. Kirkpatrick and Edwin A. Locke, "Leadership: Do Traits Really Matter?" *Academy of Management Executive* (1991), pp. 48–60.

23. See also John W. Gardner's article, "The Context and Attributes of Leadership," *New Management*, vol. 5 (1988), pp. 18–22; John P. Kotter, *The Leadership Factor* (New York: Free Press, 1988); and Bernard M. Bass, *Stogdill's Handbook of Leadership* (New York: Free Press, 1990).

24. Kirkpatrick and Locke, op. cit. (1991).

25. See, for example, Jan P. Muczyk and Bernie C. Reimann, "The Case for Directive Leadership," *Academy of Management Review*, vol. 12 (1987), pp. 637–47.

26. See Bass, op. cit.

27. Robert R. Blake and Jane Srygley Mouton, *The New Managerial Grid III* (Houston: Gulf Publishing, 1985).

28. This terminology comes from the classic studies by Kurt Lewin and his associates at the University of Iowa. See, for example, K. Lewin and R. Lippitt, "An Experimental Approach to the Study of Autocracy and Democracy: A Preliminary Note," *Sociometry*, vol. 1 (1938), pp. 292–300; K. Lewin, "Field Theory and Experiment in Social Psychology: Concepts and Methods," *American Journal of Sociology*, vol. 44 (1939), pp. 86–896; and K. Lewin, R. Lippitt, and R. K. White, "Patterns of Aggressive Behavior in Experimentally Created Social Climates," *Journal of Social Psychology*, vol. 10 (1939), pp. 271–301.

29. See Jason Kirby, "In the Vault," *Canadian Business*, vol. 77 (March 1–4, 2004), p. 68–72.

30. For a good discussion of this theory see Fred E. Fiedler, Martin M. Chemers, and Linda Mahar, *The Leadership Match Concept* (New York: Wiley, 1978); Fiedler's current contingency research with the cognitive resource theory is summarized in Fred E. Fiedler and Joseph E. Garcia, *New Approaches to Effective Leadership* (New York: Wiley, 1987).

31. Paul Hersey and Kenneth H. Blanchard, *Management and Organizational Behavior* (Englewood Cliffs, NJ: Prentice-Hall, 1988). For an interview with Paul Hersey on the origins of the model, see John R. Schermerhorn, Jr., "Situational Leadership: Conversations with Paul Heresy," *Mid-American Journal of Business* (fall 1997), pp. 5–12.

32. See Claude L. Graeff, "The Situational Leadership Theory: A Critical View," *Academy of Management Review*, vol. 8 (1983), pp. 285–91.

33. See, for example, Robert J. House, "A Path-Goal Theory of Leader Effectiveness," *Administrative Sciences Quarterly*, vol. 16 (1971), pp. 321–38; Robert J. House and Terrence R. Mitchell, "Path-Goal Theory of Leadership," *Journal of Contemporary Business* (autumn 1974), pp. 81–97. The path-goal theory is reviewed by Bass, op. cit.; and Yukl, op. cit. A supportive review of research is offered in Julie Indvik, "Path-Goal Theory of Leadership; A Meta-Analysis," in John A. Pearce II and Richard B. Robinson, Jr., eds., *Academy of Management Best Paper Proceedings* (1986), pp. 189–92.

34. See the discussions of path-goal theory in Yukl, op. cit.; and Bernard M. Bass, "Leadership: Good, Better, Best," *Organizational Dynamics* (winter 1985), pp. 26–40.

35. See Steven Kerr and John Jermier, "Substitutes for Leadership: Their Meaning and Measurement," *Organizational Behavior and Human Performance*, vol. 22 (1978), pp. 375–403; Jon P. Howell and Peter W. Dorfman, "Leadership and Substitutes for Leadership among Professional and Nonprofessional Workers," *Journal of Applied Behavioral Science*, vol. 22 (1986), pp. 29–46.

36. Victor H. Vroom and Arthur G. Jago, *The New Leadership: Managing Participation in Organizations* (Englewood Cliffs, NJ: Prentice-Hall, 1988). This is based on earlier work by Victor H. Vroom, "A New Look in Managerial Decision-Making," *Organizational Dynamics* (spring 1973), pp. 66–80; and Victor H. Vroom and Phillip Yetton, *Leadership and Decision-Making* (Pittsburgh: University of Pittsburgh Press, 1973).

37. For a related discussion see Edgar H. Schein, *Process Consultation Revisited: Building the Helping Relationship* (Reading, MA: Addison-Wesley, 1999).

38. Vroom and Jago, op. cit.

39. For a review see Yukl, op. cit.

40. See the discussion by Victor H. Vroom, "Leadership and the Decision-Making Process," *Organizational Dynamics*, vol. 28 (2000), pp. 82–94.

41. The distinction was originally made by James McGregor Burns, *Leadership* (New York: Harper & Row, 1978) and was further developed by Bernard Bass, *Leadership and Performance Beyond Expectations* (New York: Free Press, 1985) and Bernard M. Bass, "Leadership: Good, Better, Best," *Organizational Dynamics* (winter 1985), pp. 26–40.

42. This list is based on Kouzes and Posner, op. cit.; Gardner, op. cit.

43. Daniel Goleman, "Leadership That Gets Results," *Harvard Business Review* (March–April 2000), pp. 78–90. See also his books *Emotional Intelligence* (New York: Bantam Books, 1995) and *Working with Emotional Intelligence* (New York: Bantam Books, 1998).

44. Daniel Goleman, "What Makes a Leader?" *Harvard Business Review* (November–December 1998), pp. 93–102.

45. Goleman, op. cit., (1998).

46. Information from "Women and Men, Work and Power," *Fast Company*, Issue 13 (1998), p. 71.

47. A. H. Eagley, S. J. Daran, and M. G. Makhijani, "Gender and the Effectiveness of Leaders: A Meta-Analysis," *Psychological Bulletin*, vol. 117 (1995), pp. 125–45.

48. Research on gender issues in leadership is reported in Sally Helgesen, *The Female Advantage: Women's Ways of Leadership* (New York: Doubleday, 1990); Judith B. Rosener, "Ways Women Lead," *Harvard Business Review* (November–December 1990), pp. 119–25; and Alice H. Eagly, Steven J. Karau, and Blair T. Johnson, "Gender and Leadership Style Among School Principals: A Meta Analysis," *Administrative Science Quarterly*, vol. 27 (1992), pp. 76–102; Jean Lipman-Blumen, *Connective Leadership: Managing in a Changing World* (New York: Oxford University Press, 1996); and Alice H. Eagley, Mary C. Johannesen-Smith, and Marloes L. van Engen, "Transformational, Transactional and Laissez-Faire Leadership: A Meta-Analysis of Women and Men," *Psychological Bulletin*, vol. 124 (2003), pp. 569–591.

49. Vroom, op. cit., (2000).

50. Data reported by Rochelle Sharpe, "As Women Rule," *Business Week* (November 20, 2000), p. 75.

51. Rosener, op. cit., (1990).

52. For debate on whether some transformational leadership qualities tend to be associated more with female than male leaders, see "Debate: Ways Women and Men Lead," *Harvard Business Review* (January–February 1991), pp. 150–60.

53. Quote from "As Leaders, Women Rule," *Business Week* (November 20, 2000), pp. 75–84. Rosabeth Moss Kanter is the author of *Men and Women of the Corporation*, 2nd ed. (New York: Basic Books, 1993).

54. Peter F. Drucker, "Leadership: More Doing than Dash," *Wall Street Journal* (January 6, 1988), p. 16. For a compendium of writings on leadership sponsored by the Drucker Foundation, see Frances Hesselbein, Marshall Goldsmith, and Richard Beckhard, *Leader of the Future* (San Francisco: Jossey-Bass, 1997).

55. Based on the discussion by John W. Dienhart and Terry Thomas, "Ethical Leadership: A Primer on Ethical Responsibility," in John R. Schermerhorn, Jr., *Management, 7th ed*. (New York: Wiley, 2003).

56. Gardner, op. cit.

57. Fred Luthans and Bruce Avolio, "Authentic Leadership: A Positive Development Approach," in K. S. Cameron, J. E. Dutton, and R. E. Quinn, eds., *Positive Organizational Scholarship* (San Francisco, Berrett-Koehler, 2003), pp. 241–258.

58. Doug May, Adrian Chan, Timothy Hodges, and Bruce Avolio, "Developing the Moral Component of Authentic Leadership," *Organizational Dynamics*, vol. 32 (2003), pp. 247–60.

59. Conference Board of Canada, "Pat Daniel: An Authentic Voice," Leaders on Leadership series, July 2003, on the Web, <www.conferenceboard.ca>. (December 2006).

CHAPTER 14 NOTES

1. Sources for the opening vignette:

   B. Morris, "Genentec: The best place to work now," *Fortune* (January 20, 2006), p. 79; on the Web, <www.money.cnn.com>. (December 2006).

   Information from the corporate website, <www.gene.com>. (April, 2006).

TEXT NOTES

2. Quotes from Charles O'Reilly III and Jeffrey Pfeffer, *Hidden Value: How Great Companies Achieve Extraordinary Results Through Ordinary People* (Boston, MA: Harvard Business School Press, 2000), pp. 5–6.

3. A. Holloway, "Find out why your employee is disgruntled and fix it," *Canadian Business* (November 7–20, 2005).

4. For a comprehensive treatment of extrinsic rewards, see Bob Nelson, *1001 Ways to Reward Employees* (New York: Workman Publishing, 1994).

5. The Baytech case study is taken from "Employee Retention/Turnover and Knowledge Transfer Report," commissioned by the Canadian Plastics Sector Council, on the Web, <www.cpsc-ccsp.ca>. (November 2006).

6. For a research perspective, see Edward Deci, *Intrinsic Motivation* (New York: Plenum, 1975); Edward E. Lawler III, "The Design of Effective Reward Systems," in Jay W. Lorsch, ed., *Handbook of Organizational Behavior* (Englewood Cliffs, NJ: Prentice-Hall, 1987), pp. 255–71.

7. Michael Maccoby's book, *Why Work: Leading the New Generation* (New York: Simon & Schuster, 1988), deals extensively with this point of view.

8. Information from Ellen Graham, "Work May Be a Rat Race, But It's Not a Daily Grind," *Wall Street Journal* (September 19, 1997), pp. R1, R4. The story of Starbucks is told in Howard Schulz and Dori Jones Yang, *Pour Your Heart Into It: How Starbucks Built a Company One Cup at a Time* (New York: Hyperion, 1999).

9. See Abraham H. Maslow, *Eupsychian Management* (Homewood, IL: Richard D. Irwin, 1965); Abraham H. Maslow, *Motivation and Personality, 2d ed.* (New York: Harper & Row, 1970). For a research perspective, see Mahmoud A. Wahba and Lawrence G. Bridwell, "Maslow Reconsidered: A Review of Research on the Need Hierarchy," *Organizational Behavior and Human Performance*, vol. 16 (1976), pp. 212–40.

10. See Clayton P. Alderfer, *Existence, Relatedness, and Growth* (New York: Free Press, 1972).

11. The complete two-factor theory is in Frederick Herzberg, Bernard Mausner, and Barbara Block Synderman, *The Motivation to Work, 2d ed.* (New York: Wiley, 1967); Frederick Herzberg, "One More Time: How Do You Motivate Employees?" *Harvard Business Review* (January–February 1968), pp. 53–62; and reprinted as an HBR Classic (September–October 1987), pp. 109–20.

12. Critical reviews are provided by Robert J. House and Lawrence A. Wigdor, "Herzberg's Dual-Factor Theory of Job Satisfaction and Motivation: A Review of the Evidence and a Criticism," *Personnel Psychology*, vol. 20 (winter 1967), pp. 369–89; Steven Kerr, Anne Harlan, and Ralph Stogdill, "Preference for Motivator and Hygiene Factors in a Hypothetical Interview Situation," *Personnel Psychology*, vol. 27 (winter 1974), pp. 109–24.

13. Frederick Herzberg, "Workers' Needs: The Same around the World," *Industry Week* (September 21, 1987), pp. 29–32.

14. For a collection of McClelland's work, see David C. McClelland, *The Achieving Society* (New York: Van Nostrand, 1961); "Business Drive and National Achievement," *Harvard Business Review*, vol. 40 (July–August 1962), pp. 99–112; David C. McClelland and David H. Burnham, "Power is the Great Motivator," *Harvard Business Review* (March–April 1976), pp. 100–10; David C. McClelland, *Human Motivation* (Glenview, IL: Scott, Foresman, 1985); David C. McClelland and Richard E. Boyatsis, "The Leadership Motive Pattern and Long-Term Success in Management," *Journal of Applied Psychology*, vol. 67 (1982), pp. 737–43.

15. Developed originally from a discussion in Edward E. Lawler III, *Motivation in Work Organizations* (Monterey, CA: Brooks/Cole Publishing, 1973), pp. 30–36.

16. See, for example, J. Stacy Adams, "Toward an Understanding of Inequity," *Journal of Abnormal and Social Psychology*, vol. 67 (1963), pp. 422–36; J. Stacy Adams, "Inequity in Social Exchange," in L. Berkowitz, ed., *Advances in Experimental Social Psychology, vol. 2* (New York: Academic Press, 1965), pp. 267–300.

17. See, for example, J. W. Harder, "Play for Pay: Effects of Inequity in a Pay-for-Performance Context," *Administrative Science Quarterly*, vol. 37 (1992), pp. 321–35.

18. Victor H. Vroom, "Work and Motivation (New York: Wiley, 1964; republished by Jossey-Bass, 1994).

19. The work on goal-setting theory is well summarized in Edwin A. Locke and Gary P. Latham, *Goal Setting: A Motivational Technique That Works!* (Englewood Cliffs, NJ: Prentice Hall, 1984). See also Edwin A. Locke, Kenneth N. Shaw, Lisa A. Saari, and Gary P. Latham, "Goal Setting and Task Performance 1969–1980," *Psychological Bulletin*, vol. 90 (1981), pp. 125–52; Mark E. Tubbs, "Goal Setting: A Meta-Analytic Examination of the Empirical Evidence," *Journal of Applied Psychology*, vol. 71 (1986), pp. 474–83; and Terence R. Mitchell, Kenneth R. Thompson, and Jane George-Falvy, "Goal Setting: Theory and Practice," Chapter 9 in Cary L. Cooper and Edwin A. Locke, eds., *Industrial and Organizational Psychology: Linking Theory with Practice* (Malden, MA: Blackwell Business, 2000), pp. 211–249.

20. Gary P. Latham and Edwin A. Locke, "Self-Regulation Through Goal Setting," *Organizational Behavior and Human Decision Processes*, vol. 50 (1991), pp. 212–47.

21. E. L. Thorndike, *Animal Intelligence* (New York: Macmillan, 1911), p. 244.

22. See B. F. Skinner, *Walden Two* (New York: Macmillan, 1948); *Science and Human Behavior* (New York: Macmillan, 1953); *Contingencies of Reinforcement* (New York: Appleton-Century-Crofts, 1969).

23. OB mod is clearly explained in Fred Luthans and Robert Kreitner, *Organizational Behavior Modification* (Glenview, IL: Scott, Foresman, 1975); and Fred Luthans and Robert Kreitner, *Organizational Behavior Modification and Beyond* (Glenview, IL: Scott, Foresman, 1985); see also Fred Luthans and Alexander D. Stajkovic, "Reinforce for Performance: The Need to Go Beyond Pay and Even Rewards," *Academy of Management Executive*, vol. 13 (1999), pp. 49–57.

24. Andrea Nierenberg, "How to Motivate a Staff," on the Web, <www.selfmarketing.com>. (November 2006).

25. For a good review, see Lee W. Frederickson, ed., *Handbook of Organizational Behavior Management* (New York: Wiley-Innerscience, 1982); Luthans and Kreitner, op. cit. (1985); and Andrew D. Stajkovic and Fred Luthans, "A Meta-Analysis of the Effects of Organizational Behavior Modification on Task Performance 1975–95," *Academy of Management Journal*, vol. 40 (1997), pp. 122–49.

26. Edwin A. Locke, "The Myths of Behavior Mod in Organizations," *Academy of Management Review*, vol. 2 (October 1977), pp. 543–53.

27. For a discussion of compensation and performance, see Rosabeth Moss Kanter, "The Attack on Pay," *Harvard Business Review*, vol. 65 (March–April 1987), pp. 60–67; Edward E. Lawler III, *Strategic Pay* (San Francisco: Jossey-Bass, 1990).

28. Karthryn M. Bartol and Cathy C. Durham, "Incentives: Theory and Practice," Chapter 1 in Cooper and Locke, op. cit. (2000).

29. "As CEO Pay Rockets Higher, Shareholders Urge Companies to Share the Rewards More Widely," report by *Responsible Wealth* (April 5, 2000).

30. "Pay-For-Performance, Shareholder Scrutiny and Disclosure Requirements Impacting CEO Compensation," based on the annual Watson Wyatt study, "CEO Compensation Practices in the S&P/TSX Composite Index," on the Web, November 28, 2005, <www.watsonwyatt.com/news>. (November 2006).

31. Information from Jaclyn Fierman, "The Perilous New World of Fair Pay," *Fortune* (June 13, 1994), pp. 57–61.

32. Tove Helland Hammer, "New Developments in Profit Sharing, Gain Sharing, and Employee Ownership," chapter 12 in John P. Campbell and Richard J. Campbell, eds., *Productivity in Organizations: New Perspective from Industrial and Organizational Psychology* (San Francisco: Jossey-Bass, 1988).

33. Edward E. Lawler III, *From the Ground Up: Six Principles for Building the New Logic Corporation* (San Francisco: Jossey-Bass, 1996), pp. 217–18. See also Lawler's *Rewarding Excellence* (San Francisco: Jossey-Bass, 2000).

34. Information from the "Employee Retention/Turnover and Knowledge Transfer Report," commissioned by the Canadian Plastics Sector Council, on the Web, <www.cpsc-ccsp.ca>. (November 2006).

35. Jaclyn Fierman, "The Perilous New World of Fair Pay," *Fortune* (June 13, 1994), pp. 57–61.

36. "Freybe Gourmet Foods Ltd.," *National Post* Entrepreneur Profile, on the Web, <www.canada.com/nationalpost/entrepreneur/freybe.html>. (November 2006).

37. Employee stock option information on the Web, <www.intel.com>. (November 2006).

38. Anonymous, "Planes, pains & automobiles," *Canadian Business*, vol. 76 (September 15, 2003), p. 104.

39. Information from Susan Pulliam, "New Dot-Com Mantra: 'Just Pay Me in Cash, Please,'" *Wall Street Journal* (November 28, 2000), p. C1.

CHAPTER 15 NOTES

1. Sources for the opening vignette:

    Neil Gross, "Mining a Company's Mother Lode of Talent," *Business Week* (August 8, 2000), pp. 135–37.

    Information from the corporate website, <www. monitor.com>.

TEXT NOTES

2. Jeffrey Pfeffer and John F. Veiga, "Putting People First for Organizational Success," *Academy of Management Executive,* vol. 13 (1999), pp. 37–48; see also Jeffrey Pfeffer, *The Human Equation: Building Profits by Putting People First* (Boston: Harvard University Press, 1998).

3. Charles O'Reilly III and Jeffrey Pfeffer, *Hidden Value: How Great Companies Achieve Extraordinary Results Through Ordinary People* (Boston: MA: Harvard Business School Publishing, 2000), p. 2.

4. Mieke Koehoorn, Graham Lowe, Kent V. Rondeau, and Grant Schellenberg, *Creating High-Quality Health Care Workplaces*, prepared for the Canadian Policy Research Networks on the Web, January 23, 2002, <www.cprn.com>. (December 2006).

5. See John R. Schermerhorn, Jr., James G. Hunt, and Richard N. Osborn, *Organizational Behavior, 8th ed*. (New York: Wiley 2003).

6. Steve Crabtree, "Stryker's Investment in Talent Pays Off," Gallup Management Journal on the Web, June 12, 2003, <www.gmj.gallup.com>. (December 2006).

7. John P. Kotter, "The Psychological Contract: Managing the Joining Up Process," *California Management Review*, vol. 15 (spring 1973), pp. 91–99; Denise Rousseau, ed., *Psychological Contracts in Organizations* (San Francisco: Jossey-Bass, 1995); Denise Rousseau, "Changing the Deal While Keeping the People," *Academy of Management Executive*, vol. 10 (1996), pp. 50–59; and Denise Rousseau and Rene Schalk, eds., *Psychological Contracts in Employment: Cross-Cultural Perspectives* (San Francisco: Jossey-Bass, 2000).

8. Linda Grant, "Unhappy in Japan," *Fortune* (January 13, 1997), p. 142.

9. For a thought provoking discussion of this issue, see Ben Hamper, *Rivethead: Tales from the Assembly Line* (New York: Warner, 1991).

10. Studs Terkel, *Working* (New York: Avon Books, 1975).

11. Information from the corporate website, <www.roots.com>.

12. See M. R. Barrick and M. K. Mount, "The Big Five Personality Dimensions and Job Performance: A Meta-Analysis,"

Personnel Psychology, vol. 44 (1991), pp. 1–26.

13. This discussion based in part on Schermerhorn, et al., op. cit., pp. 54–60.

14. J. B. Rotter, "Generalized Expectancies for Internal Versus External Control of Reinforcement," *Psychological Monographs*, vol. 80 (1966), pp. 1–28.

15. T. W. Adorno, E. Frenkel-Brunswick, D. J. Levinson, and R. N. Sanford, *The Authoritarian Personality* (New York: Harper & Row, 1950).

16. Niccolo Machiavelli, *The Prince*, trans. George Bull (Middlesex, UK: Penguin, 1961).

17. Richard Christie and Florence L. Geis, *Studies in Machiavellianism* (New York: Academic Press, 1970).

18. I. Briggs-Myers, *Introduction to Type* (Palo Alto, CA: Consulting Psychologists Press, 1980). For management applications and research, see William L. Gardner and Mark J. Martinko, "Using the Myers-Briggs Type Indicator to Study Managers: A Literature Review and Research Agenda," *Journal of Management*, vol. 22 (1996), pp. 45–83.

19. Developed from Donald Bowen, "Learning and Problem-Solving: You're Never Too Jung," in Donald D. Bowen, Roy J. Lewicki, Donald T. Hall, and Francine S. Hall, *Experiences in Management and Organizational Behavior, 4th ed.* (New York: Wiley 1997), pp. 7–13.

20. See M. Snyder, *Public Appearances/Private Realities: The Psychology of Self-Monitoring* (New York: Freeman, 1987).

21. "Deborah Alexander Gets the Job Done," *Osler Link* (Spring-Summer 2003); on the Web, <www.osler.com>. (April 2006).

22. Martin Fishbein and Icek Ajzen, *Belief, Attitude, Intention and Behavior: An Introduction to Theory and Research* (Reading, MA: Addison-Wesley, 1973).

23. See Leon Festinger, *A Theory of Cognitive Dissonance* (Palo Alto, CA: Stanford University Press, 1957).

24. For an overview, see Charles N. Greene, "The Satisfaction-Performance Controversy," *Business Horizons*, vol. 15 (1982), p. 31; Michelle T. Iaffaldano and Paul M. Muchinsky, "Job Satisfaction and Job Performance: A Meta Analysis," *Psychological Bulletin*, vol. 97 (1985), pp. 251–273; Paul E. Spector, *Job Satisfaction* (Thousand Oaks, CA: Sage, 1997); and Timothy A. Judge and Allan H. Church, "Job Satisfaction: Research and Practice," Chapter 7 in Cary L. Cooper and Edwin A. Locke, eds., *Industrial and Organizational Psychology: Linking Theory with Practice* (Malden, MA: Blackwell Business, 2000).

25. Information from Wallace Immen, "It's Time to Leave a Loveless Career," *Globe and Mail* (September 7, 2005), p. C1.

26. Data reported in "When Loyalty Erodes, So Do Profits," *Business Week* (August 13, 2001), p. 8.

27. Information from Sue Shellenbarger, "Employers Are Finding It Doesn't Cost Much to Make a Staff Happy," *Wall Street Journal* (November 19, 1997), p. B1. See also, "Special Consumer Survey Report: Job Satisfaction on the Decline," The Conference Board (July 2002). A summary is available on the Web, <www.readyminds.com>. (December 2006).

28. The Individual Performance Equation and its management and research implications are discussed in William L. Gardner and John R. Schermerhorn, Jr., "Strategic Operational Leadership and the Management of Supportive Work Environments," in Robert L. Phillips and James G. Hunt, eds., *Leadership: A Multi-Organizational–Level Perspective* (Beverly Hills, CA: Sage, 1992); Thomas N. Martin, John R. Schermerhorn, Jr., and Lars L. Larson, "Motivational Consequences of a Supportive Work Environment," in M. L. Maehr and C. Ames, eds., *Advances in Motivation and Achievement: Motivation Enhancing Environments*, vol. 6 (Greenwich, CT: JAI Press, 1989); John R. Schermerhorn, Jr., "Team Development of High Performance Management," *Training & Development Journal*, vol. 40 (1986), pp. 38–41; and John R. Schermerhorn, Jr., William L. Gardner, and Thomas N. Martin, "Management Dialogues: Turning on the Marginal Performer, *Organizational Dynamics* (Summer 1990), pp. 47–59.

29. See Melvin Blumberg and Charles D. Pringle, "The Missing Opportunity in Organizational Research: Some Implications for a Theory of Work Motivation," *Academy of Management Review*, vol. 7 (1982), pp. 560–69.

30. Information from "Reasonable Work Demands Equals Happy Employees," *Canadian HR Reporter*, vol. 19 (May 22, 2006), p. 7.

31. Information from David Whitford, "A Human Place to Work," *Fortune* (January 8, 2001), pp. 108–20.

32. Job rotation information on the Web, <www.jobquality.ca>. (November 2006).

33. Information from David Kosub, "Putting Theory into Practice," *Canadian HR Reporter*, vol. 16 (January 13, 2003), p. 9.

34. See Frederick Herzberg, Bernard Mausner, and Barbara Block Synderman, *The Motivation to Work, 2nd ed.* (New York: Wiley, 1967). The quotation is from Frederick Herzberg, "One More Time: Employees?" *Harvard Business Review* (January–February 1968), pp. 53–62, and reprinted as an HBR Classic in (September–October 1987), pp. 109–20.

35. Information from David Brown, "TD gives employees tool to chart career paths," *Canadian HR Reporter*, vol. 18 (June 20, 2005), p. 11.

36. For a complete description of the core characteristics model, see J. Richard Hackman and Greg R. Oldham, *Work Redesign* (Reading, MA: Addison-Wesley, 1980).

37. See Richard E. Walton, *Up and Running: Integrating Information Technology and the Organization* (Boston, MA: Harvard Business School Press, 1989); Richard Walton, "From Control to Commitment in the Workplace," *Harvard Business Review* (March–April 1985), pp. 77–94; and William A. Pasmore, *Designing Effective Organizations: A Sociotechnical Systems Perspective* (New York: Wiley, 1988).

38. Paul J. Champagne and Curt Tausky, "When Job Enrichment Doesn't Pay," *Personnel*, vol. 3 (January–February 1978), pp. 30–40.

39. Quote from William W. Winipsinger, "Job Enrichment: A Union View," in Karl O. Magnusen, ed., *Organizational Design, Development, and Behavior: A Situational View* (Glenview, IL: Scott, Foresman, 1977), p. 22.

40. Barney Olmsted and Suzanne Smith, *Creating a Flexible Workplace: How to Select and Manage Alternative Work Options* (New York: American Management Association, 1989).

41. See Allen R. Cohen and Herman Gadon, *Alternative Work Schedules: Integrating Individual and Organizational Needs* (Reading, MA: Addison-Wesley, 1978), p. 125; Simcha Ronen and Sophia B. Primps, "The Compressed Work Week as Organizational Change: Behavioral and Attitudinal Outcomes," *Academy of Management Review*, vol. 6 (1981), pp. 61–74.

42. Information from Donna Nebenzahl, "Workers, Companies Find Flex-time Offers Benefits," *Vancouver Sun* (December 27, 2003), p. H9.

43. Anusha Shrivastava, "Flextime is now Key Benefit for Mom-Friendly Employers," *The Columbus Dispatch* (September 23, 2003), p. C2; Sue Shellenbarger, "Number of Women Managers Rises," *Wall Street Journal* (September 30, 2003), p. D2.

44. Information from <www.conferenceboard.ca>.

45. Information from <www.hrsdc.gc.ca>. (December 2006).

46. Information from Ian Harvey and Ian Johnson, "Will the Workplace Ever Be the Same?" *Globe and Mail* (April 25, 2006).

47. Ibid.

48. For a review see Wayne F. Cascio, "Managing a Virtual Workplace," *Academy of Management Executive*, vol. 14 (2000), pp. 81–90.

49. Quote from Phil Porter, "Telecommuting Mom Is Part of a National Trend," *Columbus Dispatch* (November 29, 2000), pp. H1, H2.

50. Information from Robert Coleman, "Telecommuting Transitions," *CMA Management* (August–September 2004); on the Web, <www.managementmag.com>. (November 2006).

51. These guidelines are collected from a variety of sources for telecommuters such as InnoVisions Canada, on the Web, <www.ivc.ca>.

52. Information from <www.statcan.ca>.

CHAPTER 16 NOTES

1. Sources for the opening vignette:

   Based on an interview of Ron Estey conducted by the author.

   Information from Jared Mitchell, "Pixar, eh?" *Financial Post Business* (April 2006), pp. 34–39.

TEXT NOTES

2. Grove quote from John A. Bryne, "Visionary vs. Visionary," *Business Week* (August 28, 2000), pp. 210–14; Chambers quote from Charles O'Reilly III and Jeffrey Pfeffer, *Hidden Value: How Great Companies Achieve Extraordinary Results Through Ordinary People* (Boston, MA: Harvard Business School Publishing, 2000), p. 4.

3. See Edward E. Lawler III, *From the Ground Up: Six Principles for Building the New Logic Corporation* (San Francisco: Jossey-Bass, 1996), pp. 131ff.

4. Cited in Lynda C. McDermott, Nolan Brawley, and William A. Waite, *World-Class Teams: Working Across Borders* (New York: Wiley, 1998), p. 5.

5. See, for example, Edward E. Lawler III, Susan Albers Mohrman, and Gerald E. Ledford, Jr., *Employee Involvement and Total Quality Management: Practices and Results in Fortune 1000 Companies* (San Francisco: Jossey-Bass, 1992); Susan A. Mohrman, Susan A. Cohen, and Monty A. Mohrman, *Designing Team-based Organizations: New Forms for Knowledge Work* (San Francisco: Jossey-Bass, 1995).

6. Information from the corporate website, <www.pomerleau.ca>. (November 2006).

7. Jon R. Katzenbach and Douglas K. Smith, *The Wisdom of Teams: Creating the High Performance Organization* (Boston: Harvard Business School Press, 1993).

8. A classic work is Bib Latane, Kipling Williams, and Stephen Harkins, "Many Hands Make Light the Work: The Causes and Consequences of Social Loafing," *Journal of Personality and Social Psychology*, vol. 37 (1978), pp. 822–32.

9. J. D. Rothwell, *In the Company of Others: An Introduction to Communication*, 2nd ed. (New York: McGraw-Hill, 2004).

10. See Marvin E. Shaw, *Group Dynamics: The Psychology of Small Group Behavior*, 2nd ed. (New York: McGraw-Hill, 1976); Harold J. Leavitt, "Suppose We Took Groups More Seriously," in Eugene L. Cass and Frederick G. Zimmer, eds., *Man and Work in Society* (New York: Van Nostrand Reinhold, 1975), pp. 67–77.

11. John M. George, "Extrinsic and Intrinsic Origins of Perceived Social Loafing in Organizations," *Academy of Management Journal* (March, 1992), pp. 191–202; and W. Jack Duncan, "Why Some People Loaf in Groups While Others Loaf Alone," *Academy of Management Executive*, vol. 8 (1994), pp. 79–80.

12. For insights on how to conduct effective meetings see Mary A. De Vries, *How to Run a Meeting* (New York: Penguin, 1994).

13. Survey reported in "Meetings Among Top Ten Time Wasters," *San Francisco Business Times* (April 7, 2003).

14. Quotes from Eric Matson, "The Seven Sins of Deadly Meetings," *Fast Company* (April/May, 1996), p. 122.

15. Developed from ibid.

16. See Leavitt, op. cit.

17. The "linking pin" concept is introduced in Rensis Likert, *New Patterns of Management* (New York: McGraw-Hill, 1962).

18. See discussion by Susan G. Cohen and Don Mankin, "The Changing Nature of Work," in Susan Albers Mohrman, Jay R. Galbraith, Edward E. Lawler III and Associates, *Tomorrow's Organization: Crafting Winning Capabilities in a Dynamic World* (San Francisco: Jossey-Bass, 1998), pp. 154–78.

19. Information from "Diversity: America's Strength," special advertising section, *Fortune* (June 23, 1997); American

Express corporate communication (1998).

20. Information from Matthew de Paula, "Diversity is About Equality, and That's Good for Bank Business," *USBanker* (June 2004.), p. 32.

21. See Susan D. Van Raalte, "Preparing the Task Force to Get Good Results," *S.A.M. Advanced Management Journal*, vol. 47 (winter, 1982), pp. 11–16; Walter Kiechel III, "The Art of the Corporate Task Force," *Fortune* (January 28, 1991), pp. 104–6.

22. Developed from ibid.

23. Mohrman et al., op. cit.

24. Information from Jenny C. McCune, "Making Lemonade," *Management Review* (June 1997), pp. 49–53.

25. Information from TECSYS customer case studies on the Web, <www.tecsys.com>. (December 2006).

26. For a good discussion of quality circles, see Edward E. Lawler III and Susan A. Mohrman, "Quality Circles After the Fad," *Harvard Business Review*, vol. 63 (January–February, 1985), pp. 65–71; Edward E. Lawler III and Susan Albers Mohrman, "Employee Involvement, Reengineering, and TQM: Focusing on Capability Development," in Mohrman, et al. (1998), pp. 179–208.

27. See Wayne F. Cascio, "Managing a Virtual Workplace," *Academy of Management Executive*, vol. 14 (2000), pp. 81–90.

28. See Sheila Simsarian Webber, "Virtual Teams: A Meta-Analysis," SHRMOnline, October 24, 2005, <www.shrm.org>. (December 2006).

29. "Nortel and BP succeed through virtual teamwork," *Training Strategies for Tomorrow*, vol. 16 (May/June 2002), pp. 3–5.

30. R. Brent Gallupe and William H. Cooper, "Brainstorming Electronically," *Sloan Management Review* (winter, 1997), pp. 11–21; Cascio, op. cit.

31. Cascio, op. cit.

32. See, for example, Paul S. Goodman, Rukmini Devadas, and Terri L. Griffith Hughson, "Groups and Productivity: Analyzing the Effectiveness of Self-Managing Teams," Chapter 11 in John R. Campbell and Richard J. Campbell, *Productivity in Organizations* (San Francisco: Jossey-Bass, 1988); Jack Orsbrun, Linda Moran, Ed Musslewhite, and John H. Zenger, with Craig Perrin, *Self-Directed Work Teams: The New American Challenge* (Homewood, IL: Business One Irwin, 1990); Dale E. Yeatts and Cloyd Hyten, *High Performing Self-Managed Work Teams* (Thousand Oaks, CA: Sage, 1997).

33. Information from Grande Prairie website, <www.cityofgp.com>. (December 2006).

34. Bradley L. Kirkman and Debra L. Shapiro, "The Impact of Cultural Values on Employee Resistance to Teams: Toward a Model of Globalized Self-Managing Work Team Effectiveness," *Academy of Management Review*, vol. 22 (1997), pp. 730–57.

35. For a discussion of effectiveness in the context of top management teams, see Edward E. Lawler III, David Finegold, and Jay A. Conger, "Corporate Boards: Developing Effectiveness at the Top," in Mohrman, op. cit. (1998), pp. 23–50.

36. For a review of research on group effectiveness, see J. Richard Hackman, "The Design of Work Teams," in Jay W. Lorsch, ed., *Handbook of Organizational Behavior* (Englewood Cliffs, NJ: Prentice-Hall, 1987), pp. 315–42; and J. Richard Hackman, Ruth Wageman, Thomas M. Ruddy, and Charles L. Ray, "Team Effectiveness in Theory and Practice," Chapter 5 in Cary L. Cooper and Edwin A. Locke, *Industrial and Organizational Psychology: Linking Theory with Practice* (Malden, MA: Blackwell, 2000).

37. Ibid; Lawler, et al., op. cit., 1998.

38. Example from "Designed for Interaction," *Fortune* (January 8, 2001), p. 150.

39. See Warren Watson, "Cultural Diversity's Impact on Interaction Process and Performance," *Academy of Management Journal,* vol. 16 (1993); and Christopher Earley and Elaine Mosakowski, "Creating Hybrid Team Structures: An Empirical Test of Transnational Team Functioning," *Academy of Management Journal*, vol. 5 (February 2000), pp. 26–49.

40. J. Steven Heinen and Eugene Jacobson, "A Model of Task Group Development in Complex Organizations and a Strategy of Implementation," *Academy of Management Review*, vol. 1 (1976), pp. 98–111; Bruce W. Tuckman, "Developmental Sequence in Small Groups," Psychological Bulletin, vol. 63 (1965), pp. 384–99; Bruce W. Tuckman and Mary Ann C. Jensen, "Stages of Small-Group Development Revisited," *Group & Organization Studies*, vol. 2 (1977), pp. 419–27.

41. See for example, Edgar Schein, *Process Consultation* (Reading, MA: Addison-Wesley, 1988); and Linda C. McDermott, Nolan Brawley, and William A. Waite, *World-Class Teams: Working Across Borders* (New York: Wiley, 1998).

42. For a good discussion, see Robert F. Allen and Saul Pilnick, "Confronting the Shadow Organization: How to Detect and Defeat Negative Norms," *Organizational Dynamics* (spring 1973), pp. 13–16.

43. See Schein, op. cit., pp. 76–79.

44. Marvin E. Shaw, *Group Dynamics: The Psychology of Small Group Behavior* (New York: McGraw-Hill, 1976).

45. Information from the coporate website, <www.telus.com>. (December 2006).

46. A classic work in this area is K. Benne and P. Sheets, *Journal of Social Issues*, *vol. 2* (1948), pp. 42–47; see also, Likert, op. cit., pp. 166–69; Schein, op. cit. pp. 49–56.

47. Based on John R. Schermerhorn, Jr., James G. Hunt, and Richard N. Osborn, *Organizational Behavior*, 7th ed. (New York: Wiley, 2000), pp. 345–46.

48. Research on communication networks is found in Alex Bavelas, "Communication Patterns in Task-Oriented Groups," *Journal of the Acoustical Society of America*, vol. 22 (1950), pp. 725–30; Shaw, op. cit.

49. Schein, op. cit., pp. 69–75.

50. See Kathleen M. Eisenhardt, Jean L. Kahwajy, and L. J. Bourgeois III, "How Management Teams Can Have a Good Fight," *Harvard Business Review* (July–August 1997), pp. 77–85.

51. The APIRIG consensus policy can be viewed on the Web, <www.apirg.org>. (December 2006.)

52. Victor H. Vroom and Arthur G. Jago, *The New Leadership: Managing Participation in Organizations* (Englewood Cliffs, NJ: Prentice Hall, 1988); Victor H. Vroom, "A New Look in Managerial Decision-Making," *Organizational Dynamics* (spring 1973), pp. 66–80; Victor H. Vroom and Phillip Yetton, *Leadership and Decision-Making* (Pittsburgh: University of Pittsburgh Press, 1973).

53. Norman F. Maier, "Assets and Liabilities in Group Problem Solving," *Psychological Review,* vol. 74 (1967), pp. 239–49.

54. Ibid.

55. See Irving L. Janis, "Groupthink," *Psychology Today* (November 1971), pp. 43–46; *Victims of Groupthink, 2nd ed.* (Boston: Houghton Mifflin, 1982).

56. Rosie Steeves, "Group Think Kills Healthy Corporate Decision-making and Weakens Companies," <http://www.exceptionalleadership.com/pdfs/groupthink_apr05.pdf> (January 2007).

57. These techniques are well described in Andre L. Delbecq, Andrew H. Van de Ven, and David H. Gustafson, *Group Techniques for Program Planning* (Glenview, IL: Scott, Foresman, 1975).

58. A very good overview is provided by William D. Dyer, *Team-Building* (Reading MA: Addison-Wesley, 1977).

59. Information on the Web, <www.outwardbound.ca>. (November 2006).

60. Katzenbach and Smith, op. cit; see also Jon R. Katzenbach, "The Myth of the Top Management Team," *Harvard Business Review*, vol. 75 (November–December 1997), pp. 83–91.

61. Carl E. Larson and Frank M. J. LaFasto, *Team Work: What Must Go Right/What Can Go Wrong* (Newbury Park, CA: Sage, 1990).

62. Quote from "Teach Your Leaders that Their Main Priority Is to Energize and Grow Their Team Around Themselves," *Fast Company* (March, 2001), p. 95.

CHAPTER 17 NOTES

1. Sources for the opening vignette:

    Quotes from *Business Week* (July 8, 1991), pp. 60–61.

    Additional information from the Center's website, <www.ccl.org>.

TEXT NOTES

2. Henry Mintzberg, *The Nature of Managerial Work* (New York: Harper & Row, 1973).

3. John P. Kotter, "What Effective General Managers Really Do," *Harvard Business Review*, vol. 60 (November–December 1982), pp. 156–57; and *The General Managers* (New York: Macmillan, 1986).

4. "Relationships Are the Most Powerful Form of Media," *Fast Company* (March 2001), p. 100.

5. See Mintzberg, op. cit., Kotter, op. cit.

6. Mary Pat Barry, "Canadian Telephone Company Enhances Corporate Dialogue With CEO Mailbox," *Communication World*, vol. 21 (July–August 2004), p. 50–51.

7. Jay A. Conger, *Winning 'Em Over: A New Model for Managing in the Age of Persuasion* (New York: Simon & Schuster, 1998), pp. 24–79.

8. This discussion developed from ibid.

9. *Business Week* (February 10, 1992), pp. 102–8.

10. See Robert H. Lengel and Richard L. Daft, "The Selection of Communication Media as an Executive Skill," *Academy of Management Executive,* vol. 2 (August 1988), pp. 225–32.

11. Survey information from "What Do Recruiters Want?" *BizEd* (November–December 2002), p. 9; "Much to Learn, Professors Say," *USA Today* (July 5, 2001), p. 8D; and AMA-Fast Response Survey, "The Passionate Organization" (September 26–29, 2000).

12. See Eric Matson, "Now That We Have Your Complete Attention," *Fast Company* (February–March 1997), pp. 124–32.

13. David McNeill, *Hand and Mind: What Gestures Reveal about Thought* (Chicago: University of Chicago Press, 1992).

14. Adapted from Richard V. Farace, Peter R. Monge, and Hamish M. Russell, *Communicating and Organizing* (Reading, MA: Addison-Wesley, 1977), pp. 97–98.

15. Tom Peters and Nancy Austin, *A Passion for Excellence* (New York: Random House, 1985).

16. This discussion is based on Carl R. Rogers and Richard E. Farson, "Active Listening" (Chicago: Industrial Relations Center of the University of Chicago, n.d.).

17. A useful source of guidelines is John J. Gabarro and Linda A. Hill, "Managing Performance," Note 9-96-022 (Boston, MA: Harvard Business School Publishing, n.d.).

18. Developed from John Anderson, "Giving and Receiving Feedback," in Paul R. Lawrence, Louis B. Barnes, and Jay W. Lorsch, eds., *Organizational Behavior and Administration, 3rd ed.* (Homewood, IL: Richard D. Irwin, 1976), p. 109.

19. See Lengel and Daft, op. cit. (1988).

20. Information from Terry Curtis, "Business Best Practices Applied to Sport," paper presented at Sport Leadership Sportif Quebec, 2005.

21. Information from Esther Wachs Book, "Leadership for the Millennium," *Working Woman* (March 1998), pp. 29–34.

22. Anonymous, "Going back to the floor to shape culture at Vancity," *Business Communicator*, vol. 6 (October 2005), pp. 8–9.

23. Adam Appelbaum, Lessard Javeri, et al., "A Case Study Analysis of the Impact of Satisfaction and Organizational Citizenship on Productivity Management," *Research News*, vol. 28 (May 2005), pp. 1–26.

24. See Richard Lepsinger and Anntoinette D. Lucia, *The Art and Science of 360° Feedback* (San Francisco: Jossey-Bass, 1997).

25. Brian O'Reilly, "360° Feedback Can Change Your Life," *Fortune* (October 17, 1994), pp. 93–100.

26. Sue Bowness, "Full-circle feedback: 360-degree performance reviews," *Profit* (May 2006); on the Web, <canadianbusiness.com>. (December 2006).

27. A classic work on proxemics is Edward T. Hall's book, *The Hidden Dimension* (Garden City, NY: Doubleday, 1986).

28. Mirand Wewll, "Alternative Spaces Spawning Desk-Free Zones," *Columbus Dispatch* (May 18, 1998), pp. 10–11.

29. Information from Susan Stellin, "Intranets Nurture Companies from the Inside," *New York Times* (January 21, 2001), p. C4.

30. Example from Heidi A. Schuessler, "Social Studies Class finds How Far EMail Travels," *New York Times* (February 22, 2001), p. D8.

31. Alison Overholt, "Intel's got (Too Much) Mail," *Fortune* (March, 2001), pp. 56–58.

32. Developed from *Working Woman* (November 1995), p. 14; and Elizabeth Weinstein, "Help! I'm Drowing in E-Mail!" *Wall Street Journal* (January 10, 2002), pp. B1, B4.

33. See Edward T. Hall, *The Silent Language* (New York: Doubleday, 1973).

34. Anonymous, "*Workforce Development*," *Canadian HR Reporter*, vol. 18 (December 5, 2005), p. 7.

35. See H. R. Schiffman, *Sensation and Perception: An Integrated Approach, 3rd ed.* (New York: Wiley, 1990).

36. A good review is E. L. Jones, ed., *Attribution: Perceiving the Causes of Behavior* (Morristown, NJ: General Learning Press, 1972). See also John H. Harvey and Gifford Weary, "Current Issues in Attribution Theory and Research," *Annual Review of Psychology*, vol. 35 (1984), pp. 427–59.

37. With information from "Few Cracks in Glass Ceiling," CBC News, on the Web, March 1, 2006, <www.cbc.ca>. Based on the "2005 Catalyst Census of Women Board Directors of the FP500," and Virginia Gault, "Lots of Qualified Women, but Few Sit on Boards," *Globe and Mail* (March 2, 2006), B1.

38. Information from "Misconceptions About Women in the Global Arena Keep Their Numbers Low," Catalyst study on the Web, <www.catalystwomen.org/home.html>. (December 2006).

39. These examples are from Natasha Josefowitz, *Paths to Power* (Reading, MA: Addison-Wesley, 1980), p. 60. For more on gender issues see Gary N. Powell, ed., *Handbook of Gender and Work* (Thousand Oaks, CA: Sage, 1999).

40. Survey reported in Kelly Greene, "Age Is Still More Than a Number," *Wall Street Journal* (April 10, 2003), p. D2.

41. The classic work is Dewitt C. Dearborn and Herbert A. Simon, "Selective Perception: A Note on the Departmental Identification of Executives," *Sociometry*, vol. 21 (1958), pp. 140–44. See also J. P. Walsh, "Selectivity and Selective Perception: Belief Structures and Information Processing," *Academy of Management Journal*, vol. 24 (1988), pp. 453–70.

42. Richard E. Walton, *Interpersonal Peacemaking: Confrontations and Third-Party Consultation* (Reading, MA: Addison-Wesley, 1969), p. 2.

43. Information from Michael A. Roberto, "Making difficult decisions in turbulent times," *Ivey Business Journal*, vol. 66 (January–February 2002), pp. 15–20.

44. See Kenneth W. Thomas, "Conflict and Conflict Management," in M. D. Dunnett, ed., *Handbook of Industrial and Organizational Behavior* (Chicago; Rand McNally, 1976), pp. 889–935.

45. See Robert R. Blake and Jane Strygley Mouton, "The Fifth Achievement," *Journal of Applied Behavioral Science*, vol. 6 (1970), pp. 413–27; Alan C. Filley, *Interpersonal Conflict Resolution* (Glenview, IL: Scott, Foresman, 1975).

46. This discussion is based on Filley, op. cit.

47. Information from "A Tale of Two Hotels: Hilton and Delta," *UNITE HERE Reporter* (December 2004), p. 1; on the Web, <www.unitehere.ca>. (December 2006).

48. Portions of this treatment of negotiation originally adapted with permission from John R. Schermerhorn, Jr., James G. Hunt, and Richard N. Osborn, *Managing Organizational Behavior, 4th ed.* (New York: Wiley, 1991), pp. 382–87.

49. See Roger Fisher and William Ury; *Getting to Yes: Negotiating Agreement Without Giving In* (New York: Penguin, 1983); James A. Wall, Jr., *Negotiation: Theory and Practice* (Glenview, IL: Scott, Foresman, 1985); and William L. Ury, Jeanne M. Brett, and Stephen B. Goldberg, *Getting Disputes Resolved* (San Francisco: Jossey-Bass, 1997).

50. Fisher and Ury, op. cit.

51. Information from Julie Stauffer, "Making It Work" *National*, vol. 14 (September 2005), p. 32; on the Web, <www.cba.org/CBA/National/Main/>. (December 2006).

52. Fisher and Ury, op. cit.

53. Developed from Max H. Bazerman, *Judgment in Managerial Decision Making, 4th ed.* (New York: Wiley, 1998), Chapter 7.

54. Fisher and Ury, op. cit.

55. Roy J. Lewicki and Joseph A. Litterer, *Negotiation* (Homewood, IL: Irwin, 1985).

CHAPTER 18 NOTES

1. Sources for the opening vignette:

   With information from archived news releases dated February 16, 2005 and April 4, 2005. Retrieved from <www.meridiancu.ca> (January 2007).

   Susan Maclean, "In the Mail: Mailings Help Credit Union Members Smile on Mergers, Meridian Launch," *Direct Marketing News* (August 2005).

TEXT NOTES

2. Information from "On the Road to Innovation," in special advertising section. "Charting the Course: Global Business Sets Its Goals," *Fortune* (August 4, 1997).

3. Michael Beer and Nitin Nohria, "Cracking the Code of Change,"

Harvard Business Review (May–June 2000), pp. 133–41.

4. Quote from John A. Byrne, "Visionary vs. Visionary," *Business Week* (August 28, 2000), p. 210.

5. Tom Peters, *The Circle of Innovation* (New York: Knopf, 1997).

6. Quotes from David Kirkpatrick, "From Davos, Talk of Death," *Fortune* (March 5, 2001), pp. 180–82.

7. Peter Senge, *The Fifth Discipline* (New York: Harper, 1990).

8. Teresa Kirkwood and Ajay Pangarkar, "Workplace Learning: beyond the classroom," *CMA Management*, vol.77 (May 2003), p. 10.

9. Peter A.C. Smith, "The Learning Organization Ten Years On: A case study," *Learning Organization*, vol. 6 (1999), p. 217.

10. R. Duane Ireland and Michael A. Hitt, "Achieving and Maintaining Strategic Competitiveness in the 21st Century: The Role of Strategic Leadership," *Academy of Management Executive* (February 1999), pp. 43–57.

11. *Director's Breakfast Series: Testing the Limits of Innovation* (Toronto: Spencer Stuart, 2002).

12. Developed from Ireland & Hitt, op. cit.

13. See, for example, Roger von Oech, *A Whack on the Side of the Head* (New York: Warner Books, 1983) and *A Kick in the Seat of the Pants* (New York: Harper & Row, 1986).

14. See Peter F. Drucker, "The Discipline of Innovation," *Harvard Business Review* (November–December 1998), pp. 3–8.

15. Peter F. Drucker, *Management: Tasks, Responsibilities, and Practices* (New York: Harper & Row, 1973), p. 797.

16. Information from David Kirkpatrick, "Software's Humble Wizard Does It Again," *Fortune* (February 19, 2001), pp. 137–42.

17. Information from "Providing Rural Phone Service Profitably in Poor Countries," *Business Week* (December 18, 2000), special advertising section.

18. Based on Gary Hamel, *Leading the Revolution* (Boston, MA: Harvard Business School Press, 2000), pp. 293–95.

19. Based on Edward B. Roberts, "Managing Invention and Innovation," *Research Technology Management* (January–February 1988), pp. 1–19, and Hamel, op. cit.

20. This discussion is stimulated by James Brian Quinn, "Managing Innovation Controlled Chaos," *Harvard Business Review*, vol. 63 (May–June 1985). Selected quotations and examples from Kenneth Labich, "The Innovators," *Fortune* (June 6, 1988), pp. 49–64.

21. Peter F. Drucker, "Best R&D Is Business Driven," *Wall Street Journal*, (February 10, 1988), p. 11.

22. See Roberts, op. cit.

23. Drucker, op. cit., 1998.

24. Reported in Carol Hymowitz, "Task of Managing Changes in Workplace Takes a Careful Hand," *Wall Street Journal* (July 1, 1997), p. B1.

25. Reported in G. Christian Hill and Mike Tharp, "Stumbling Giant—Big Quarterly Deficit Stuns BankAmerica, Adds Pressure on Chief," *Wall Street Journal* (July 18, 1985), pp. 1–16.

26. Beer and Nohria, op. cit.; and "Change Management, An Inside Job," *Economist* (July 15, 2000), p. 61.

27. Reported in Robert Rose, "Kentucky Plant Workers Are Cranking Out Good Ideas," *Wall Street Journal* (August 13, 1996), p. B1.

28. Beer & Nohria, op. cit.

29. For a review of scholarly work on organizational change, see Arthur G. Bedian, "Organizational Change: A Review of Theory and Research," *Journal of Management*, vol. 25 (1999), pp. 293–315.

30. For a discussion of alternative types of change, see David A. Nadler and Michael L. Tushman, *Strategic Organizational Design* (Glenview, Il: Scott, Foresman, 1988); John P. Kotter, "Leading Change: Why Transformations Efforts Fail," *Harvard Business Review* (March–April 1995), pp. 59–67; and W. Warner Burke, *Organization Change* (Thousand Oaks, CA.: Sage, 2002).

31. Based on Kotter, op. cit.

32. See Edward E. Lawler III, "Strategic Choices for Changing Organizations," Chapter 12 in Allan M. Mohrman, Jr., Susan Albers Mohrman, Gerald E. Ledford, Jr., Thomas G. Cummings, Edward E. Lawler III and Associates, *Large Scale Organizational Change* (San Francisco: Jossey-Bass, 1989).

33. The classic description of organizations on these terms is by Harold J. Leavitt, "Applied Organizational Change in Industry: Structural, Technological and Humanistic Approaches," in James G. March, ed., *Handbook of Organizations* (Chicago: Rand McNally, 1965), pp. 1144–70.

34. Angela Lovell, "Winkler's Super Carpenter," *Manitoba Business*, vol. 28 (May 2006), p. 15.

35. Kurt Lewin, "Group Decision and Social Change," in G. E. Swanson, T. M. Newcomb and E. L. Hartley, eds., *Readings in Social Psychology* (New York: Holt, Rinehart, 1952), pp. 459–73.

36. Ron Knowles, "Continuous change," *CA Magazine*, vol.132 (May 1999), p. 43.

37. This discussion is based on Robert Chin and Kenneth D. Benne, "General Strategies for Effecting Changes in Human Systems," in Warren G. Bennis, Kenneth D. Benne, Robert Chin, and Kenneth E. Corey, eds., *The Planning of Change*, 3rd ed. (New York: Holt, Rinehart; 1969), pp. 22–45.

38. The change agent descriptions here and following are developed from an exercise reported in J. William Pfeiffer and John E. Jones, *A Handbook of Structured Experiences for Human Relations Training*, vol. 2 (La Jolla, CA: University Associates, 1973).

39. Ram N. Aditya, Robert J. House, and Steven Kerr, "Theory and Practice of Leadership: Into the New Millennium," Chapter 6 in Cary L. Cooper and Edwin A. Locke, *Industrial and*

Organizational Psychology: Linking Theory with Practice (Malden, MA: Blackwell, 2000).

40. Information from Mike Schneider, "Disney Teaching Excess Magic of Customer Service," *Columbus Dispatch* (December 17, 2000), p. G9.

41. Teresa M. Amabile, "How to Kill Creativity," *Harvard Business Review*, (September–October, 1998), pp. 77–87.

42. Sue Shellenbarger, "Some Employers Find Way to Ease Burden of Changing Shifts," *Wall Street Journal* (March 25, 1998), p. B1.

43. Ibid.

44. John P. Kotter and Leonard A. Schlesinger, "Choosing Strategies for Change," *Harvard Business Review*, vol. 57 (March–April 1979), pp. 109–12.

45. Wanda J. Orlikowski and J. Debra Hofman, "An Improvisational Model for Change Management: The Case of Groupware Technologies," *Sloan Management Review* (winter 1997), pp. 11–21.

46. Ibid.

47. Overviews of organization development are provided by W. Warner Burke, *Organization Development: A Normative View* (Reading, MA: Addison-Wesley, 1987); William Rothwell, Roland Sullivan, and Gary N. McLean, *Practicing Organization Development* (San Francisco: Jossey-Bass, 1995); and Wendell L. French and Cecil H. Bell, Jr., *Organization Development*, 6th ed. (Englewood Cliffs, NJ: Prentice-Hall, 1998).

48. See French and Bell, op. cit.

49. See Arthur P. Brief, Randall S. Schuler, and Mary Van Sell, *Managing Job Stress* (Boston: Little, Brown, 1981), pp. 7, 8.

50. Robert B. Reich, *The Future of Success* (New York: Knopf, 2000), p. 8.

51. Michael Weldholz, "Stress Increasingly Seen as Problem with Executives More Vulnerable," *Wall Street Journal* (September 28, 1982), p. 31.

52. "Sources of Workplace Stress," Statistics Canada on the Web, June 25, 2003, <www.statcan.ca>. (February 2006).

53. Sue Shellenbarger, "Do We Work More or Not? Either Way, We Feel Frazzled," *Wall Street Journal* (July 30, 1997), p. B1.

54. See, for example, "Desk Rage," *Business Week* (November 27, 2000), p. 12.

55. Carol Hymowitz, "Impossible Expectations and Unfulfilling Work Stress Managers, Too," *Wall Street Journal* (January 16, 2001), p. B1.

56. The classic work is Meyer Friedman and Ray Roseman, *Type A Behavior and Your Heart* (New York: Knopf, 1974).

57. See Hans Selye, *Stress in Health and Disease* (Boston: Butterworth, 1976).

58. Carol Hymowitz, "Can Workplace Stress Get Worse?" *Wall Street Journal* (January 16, 2001), pp. B1, B3.

59. See Steve M. Jex, *Stress and Job Performance* (San Francisco: Jossey-Bass, 1998).

60. The extreme case of "workplace violence" is discussed by Richard V. Denenberg and Mark Braverman, *The Violence-Prone Workplace* (Ithaca, NY: Cornell University Press, 1999).

61. See Daniel C. Ganster and Larry Murphy, "Workplace Interventions to Prevent Stress-Related Illness: Lessons from Research and Practice," Chapter 2 in Cooper and Locke, eds., op. cit. (2000).

62. Reported in Sue Shellenbarger, "Finding Ways to Keep a Partner's Job Stress from Hitting Home," *Wall Street Journal* (November 29, 2000), p. B1.

63. Quote from Shellenbarger, op. cit.

64. Raizel Robin, "Healthy, Wealthy and Wise," *Canadian Business* (December 2003), p. 129; on the Web, <www.candianbusiness.com>. (December 2006).

65. Ibid.

Photo Credits

Chapter 1
Opener: Courtesy Workopolis.com. **Page 6:** Courtesy IKEA. **Page 14:** Courtesy Apple. **Page 20:** Corbis Digital Stock

Chapter 2
Opener: AP/Ben Margot. **Page 39:** Courtesy Mercedes. **Page 45:** Courtesy Rafael Simon. **Page 51:** Courtesy The Coca-Cola Company.

Chapter 3
Opener: Courtesy Aldo. **Page 62:** Jim Daniels. **Page 80:** Courtesy Marc Kielburger. **Page 82:** Courtesy Social Accountability International.

Chapter 4
Opener: Courtesy Bank of Montreal. **Page 98:** Courtesy UPS. **Page 103:** Flat Earth. **Page 107:** Courtesy Home Depot Canada.

Chapter 5
Opener: Courtesy Gildan. **Page 118:** Harley-Davidson Photography & Imaging. **Page 121:** International Labour Organization/M. Crozet. **Page 132:** Courtesy Pfizer Inc.

Chapter 6
Opener: Courtesy ACE. **Page 147:** Courtesy Frank Stronach. **Page 148:** Courtesy Virgin. Courtesy Chapters-Indigo. Courtesy Sobeys Atlantic Region. Courtesy Teresa Cascioli. **Page 149:** CP/Aaron Harris. **Page 152:** Courtesy Honest Ed's. **Page 155:** Corbis Digital Stock. **Page 160:** Courtesy Domino's Pizza.

Chapter 7
Opener: Courtesy Chapters-Indigo. **Page 180:** Courtesy Russel Metals Inc. **Page 188:** Everett Collection/ CJ Contino. **Page 189:** AFP/Getty Images.

Chapter 8
Opener: Courtesy Cognos Inc. **Page 205:** ActionPress/Ingo Rohrbein. **Page 218:** Courtesy Alimentation Couche-Tard Inc.

Chapter 9
Opener: Courtesy Taxi. **Page 228:** Courtesy Skype. **Page 235:** Courtesy Canadian Tire Corporation, Limited. **Page 245:** Purestock.

Chapter 10
Opener: Courtesy Edward Jones. **Page 264:** Intel Press Relations. **Page 268:** Courtesy Toromont Industries Ltd. **Page 270:** Courtesy Nike.

Chapter 11
Opener: Courtesy KPMG. **Page 283:** Getty Images. **Page 285:** AP/Kathy Willens. **Page 292:** Purestock.

Chapter 12
Opener: Courtesy Dofasco. **Page 306:** Courtesy TD Bank Financial Group. **Page 319:** Courtesy Autodesk. **Page 322:** PhotoDisc, Inc./Getty Images.

Chapter 13
Opener: Courtesy Cordon Bleu International Ltée. **Page 347:** Courtesy Southwest Airline Co. **Page 350:** Courtesy Goodlife Fitness Clubs. **Page 351:** Grove/Atlantic, Inc.

Chapter 14
Opener: AP/Paul Sakuma. **Page 360:** Courtesy Nucor. **Page 374:** Lorella Zanetti Photography. **Page 377:** PhotoDisc, Inc.

Chapter 15
Opener: Courtesy Monitor Company. **Page 392:** Courtesy Steinway & Sons. **Page 398:** Toronto Star/Keith Beaty. **Page 400:** Flat Earth.

Chapter 16
Opener: Courtesy C.O.R.E. Digital Pictures Inc. **Page 422:** Courtesy Niagara Health Systems Foundation. **Page 429:** Courtesy Motorola Inc. **Page 433:** Courtesy Callaway Golf.

Chapter 17
Opener: Courtesy Center for Creative Leadership. **Page 447:** Courtesy Swiss Reinsurance Co. **Page 458:** International Labour Organization/J. Maillard. Page 464: Corbis Digital Stock.

Chapter 18
Opener: Courtesy Meridian Credit Union. **Page 477:** PhotoDisc/Getty Images. **Page 479:** Courtesy Royal Bank of Canada. **Page 485:** Julie Jeffries.

Name Index

A
Adams, Barry, 71
Adams, J. Stacy, 366
Adlerfer, Clayton, 362
Alexander, Pam, 443
Allen, Michael, 103
Amabile, Teresa M., 487
Argyris, Chris, 45–46
Ariss, Don, 471
Armacost, Samuel, 478
Athos, Anthony G., 52
Austin, James A., 121
Avolio, Bruce, 352

B
Babiec, Joseph, 383
Bachand, Stephen, 235
Balsillie, Jim, 5
Bamesberger, Ann, 452
Banks, Jordan, 102
Barnard, Chester, 47–48, 337
Barnevik, Percy, 124
Baron, James, 305
Barrett, Colleen, 347
Barron, James, 392
Barry, Megan, 69
Bass, Bernard, 347
Beer, Michael, 472
Bélanger, Brigitte, 285
Bensadoun, Aldo, 59
Bérard, Jocelyn, 359
Bezos, Jeff, 378
Black, D. Grant, 161
Blake, Robert, 340
Boehlert, Bart, 188
Bogomolny, Laura, 218
Boyer, Herb, 357
Brabeck-Letmathe, Peter, 280
Bragg, John, 242
Branson, Richard, 148
Brin, Sergey, 33
Budman, Michael, 387
Burke, James, 477
Burns, James MacGregor, 347, 351
Burns, Tom, 284

C
Caldwell, Christopher, 351
Caldwell, Doug, 169
Callaway, Ely, 433
Campbell, Glenn, 150
Carroll, Archie, 77
Cascioli, Teresa, 148
Case, Stephen M., 117
Chamandy, Glenn, 115
Chambers, John, 122, 175, 410, 473
Chandler, Alfred, Jr., 287
Chappell, Tom, 62
Clemons, Mike "Pinball," 374
Clifford, Paul, 461
Cobb, Liz, 161
Cohen, Herman, 71
Conger, Jay, 444
Connolly, Agnes, 71
Cornell, Camilla, 260

Covey, Stephen R., 198
Cox, Ed, 387
Crandall, Robert, 69
Crosby, Philip, 98
Currie, Teri, 306
Curtis, Terry, 451
Cutler, Allan, 71

D
Daniel, Pat, 352
Davidson, Terry, 452
Davis, Keith, 76
De Vault, Rich, 385–386
Dell, Michael, 95, 248
Deming, W. Edward, 49, 98
DePree, Max, 6
Disney, Walt, 485
Djukastein, Eric, 452
Dodd, Graham, 359
Donaldson, Thomas, 64
Donovan, Denis, 308
Drucker, Peter, 53, 175, 190, 229, 230, 232, 253, 350–351, 475, 478
Duane, R., 474
Dunbar, Robin, 225
DuPont, Bonnie, 334

E
Einstein, Albert, 474
El Akkad, Omar, 122
England, Dean, 175
Entwistle, Daren, 444
Estey, Ron, 409
Etzioni, Amitai, 201
Evans, Peter, 306

F
Falconer, Bill, 393
Fayol, Henri, 37–38
Feder, Barnaby J., 377
Fehr, Ralph, 482
Fiedler, Fred, 341
Filvaroff, Ellen, 357
Fisher, Roger, 462
Follett, Mary Parker, 39
Ford, Henry, 35, 227
Forzani, John, 390
Friedman, Milton, 75
Friis, Janus, 228
Fritz, Justine, 16
Fry, Art, 476
Fung, Joseph, 145

G
Gallup, Patricia, 451
Gardner, John, 53, 352
George, Bill, 16
Gerstner, Louis V., Jr., 91
Gianturco, Paola, 400
Gilbreth, Frank and Lillian, 37
Godbehere, Ann, 447
Godsoe, Peter, 340
Goizueta, Roberto, 179, 313
Goleman, Daniel, 24, 349
Goodnight, Jim, 322

Graham, Lawrence Otis, 306
Gray, John, 180, 218
Green, Don, 387
Greiner, Larry, 290
Grove, Andy, 410
Guenette, Rob, 225

H
Hackman, J. Richard, 397
Haeckel, Stephen, 227
Hall, Edward T., 130
Hallett, Bill, 422
Hamel, Gary, 196, 476
Hammer, Michael, 231, 295
Handley, Nancy, 212
Handy, Charles, 9, 322
Hays, Matthew, 285
Hendry, Bob, 131
Herzberg, Frederick, 363, 395
Hitt, Michael, 474
Hock, Dee, 285
Hofstede, Geert, 131, 136–137
Holmes, Deborah K., 20, 21
Hopper, Grace, 333
Horton, Tim, 149
House, Robert, 344
Howard, Philip, 195
Huizenga, H. Wayne, 147
Hunchak, Gord, 471
Hunt, James G., 426

J
Jackson, Sean, 471
Janis, Irving, 429
Jaques, Elliott, 202
Jobs, Steven, 14
Johnson, Robert, 283
Johnson, William R., 260
Johnston, Larry, 130
Jones, Dave, 71
Joyce, Ron, 149
Jung, Carl, 389
Juran, Joseph, 50, 91

K
Kanter, Rosabeth Moss, 117, 285, 350
Kantrow, Alan, 383
Katz, Robert L., 23
Kelleher, Herb, 347
Kellner, Peter, 103
Kelly, Maureen, 180
Kelly, Patrick, 359
Khosa, Veronica, 79
Kielburger, Marc, 80
Kirkpatrick, Shelley, 338
Knight, Charles, 458
Knowles, Ron, 484
Kochan, Thomas, 104
Konefal, Alicia, 145
Kotter, John, 23, 245, 442–443
Kouzes, Jim, 338
Krasner, James D., 160
Kreps, David, 305
Kunkel, Sonya, 456

NAME INDEX

L
LaFasto, Frank, 434
Laliberté, Guy, 285
Larson, Carl, 434
Laskawy, Philip A., 20
Lauper, Simone, 447
Lavoie, Paul, 225
Lawler, Edward, 376
Lawrence, Paul, 292
Lee, Leonard, 311
Lee, Mark, 374
Levinson, Art, 357
Levinson, Sara, 349
Lewin, Kurt, 483–484
Lewis, Richard, 137
Likert, Rensis, 414
Locke, Edwin, 338
Locke, John, 63
Lorsch, Jay, 292
Losey, Michael R., 109
Luthans, Fred, 352

M
Machiavelli, Niccolo, 389
Magnis, Ellen, 441
Mandela, Nelson, 121
Marion, Dean, 441
Marsden, Lorna, 456
Martin, Justin, 39
Martin, Paula, 451
Martinez, Angel, 478
Maslow, Abraham, 43, 361
Matthews, Jana, 61
Mayberry, John, 303
Mayo, Elton, 42
McClearn, Matther, 480
McClelland, David, 364
McEwen, Rob, 332
McGregor, Douglas, 44, 212
McGuire, Elizabeth, 462
McKinnell, Henry "Hank," 134
Meisenger, Susan, 308
Michael, Natalie, 434
Mill, John Stuart, 62
Milton, Robert, 198
Mintzberg, Henry, 15, 21, 22, 245, 254, 442
Mirvish, Ed, 152
Molander, Scott, 150
Molinaro, Kerri, 6
Moncer, Jason, 480
Mouton, Jane, 340

N
Nardelli, Robert, 308
Newsham, Margaret, 71
Nitsch, Judith, 204
Nixon, Gord, 479
Nohria, Nitin, 472
Norris, Gary, 122

O
Ogilvie, Robert, 268
Ohmae, Kenichi, 7, 137

Oland, Derek, 338
Oldham, Greg R., 397
Olijnk, Zena, 134, 235
O'Reilly, Charles, 384
Osborn, Richard N., 426
Ouchi, William, 52
Ouimet, J. Robert, 331
Ozley, Lee, 118
Ozzie, Ray, 475

P
Page, Larry, 33
Park, Darcie, 338
Pascale, Richard Tanner, 52
Patchell-Evans, David, 350
Patten, Rose M., 336
Peters, Susan, 323
Peters, Tom, 10, 50, 448, 473
Pfeffer, Jeffrey, 14, 305, 384
Pitts, Gordon, 447
Plante, Janet, 454
Platt, Lewis, 200
Plourde, Réal, 218
Pooley, Erin, 350
Porter, Michael, 228, 234, 240, 241
Posner, Barry, 338
Pratt, Dale, 416
Putnam, Howard, 69

Q
Quinn, James Brian, 244

R
Reich, Robert, 11, 90, 304, 492
Reisman, Heather, 148, 169
Richardson, H. Smith, Jr., 441
Ritchie, Cedric, 340
Roddick, Anita, 68
Rodgers, T. J., 196
Rokeach, Milton, 62
Rosenberg, David, 117
Rosenblum, Mort, 121
Rosener, Judith, 9
Ross, Richard, 480
Rothwell, J. D., 411
Rottenberg, Linda, 103

S
Sabia, Michael, 73
Saint-Onge, Hubert, 474
Sales, Wayne, 235
Samuelson, Paul, 76
Sanford, Jeff, 479
Sanford, Linda, 210
Schein, Edgar, 100, 427
Schermerhorn, John R., Jr., 426
Schneider, Mike, 485
Schultz, Howard, 360
Senge, Peter, 52, 190, 474
Shaughnessy, Susan, 399–400
Sheppard, Susan, 69
Shulgan, Chris, 398
Simon, Rafael, 45
Skinner, B. F., 371

Skoll, Jeff, 398
Smith, Adam, 35
Sobey, Frank, 148
Soignet, Michel, 160
Sood, Stephanie Curtis, 322
Sorenson, Ralph, 54
Spade, Andy, 188
Spade, Kate, 188
Stalker, George, 284
Stam, Jim, 488
Steinway, Henry Engelhard, 392
Strauss, Marina, 6
Stronach, Frank, 146, 147
Stymiest, Barbara, 479
Swanson, Bob, 357

T
Taylor, Andy, 292
Taylor, Frederick W., 35–37
Taylor, Jack, 292
Teerlink, Rich, 118
Terkel, Studs, 387
Thomas, Dave, 149
Thomas, R. Roosevelt, Jr., 104, 108, 109, 306
Thomson, Sarah, 107
Thorndike, E. L., 370
Toffler, Alvin, 170
Trompenaars, Fons, 133–134
Turner, Susan, 402
Tutu, Desmond, 61

U
Ury, William, 462

V
Vang, Cindy, 394
Veiga, John F., 14, 305
Verschuren, Annette, 107
Vroom, Victor, 349, 367

W
Wada, Yoshihiro, 445
Wahl, Andrew, 45, 172, 180, 218
Watanabe, Katsuaki, 124
Waterman, Robert, 50
Waugh, Richard, 341
Weber, Max, 40, 283
Welch, Jack, 189, 481, 485
Wesley-Clough, Marita, 477
Whitman, Meg, 244
Whitney, John, 376
Willet, Robert, 135
Williams, Scott, 155
Wilson, Craig, 477
Winters, Carole Clay, 185
Woodward, Joan, 288
Wren, Daniel, 35

Z
Zapanta, Albert C., 155
Zennstrom, Niklas, 228
Zimmer, George, 358

Subject Index

A
Ability stereotypes, 456
Above-average returns, 228
Absenteeism, 391
Acceptance theory of authority, 337
Accommodation, 460
Accommodative strategy, 78
Accountability, 17
ACE, 145
Achievement-oriented leadership, 344
Achievement *vs.* prescription, 133
Acquired needs theory, 364
Action research, 490
Active listening, 449–450
Adaptive organizations, 285–286
Adaptive strategies, 244
Adjourning stage, 422
Administration Industrielle et Générale (Fayol), 37
Administrative principles, 37–39
Administrator, 17
Advancing action, 108
Advancing Canadian Entrepreneurship (ACE), 145
Advisory authority, 274
Aetna Life & Casualty Company, 296
Africa, 120–121
After-action review, 208
Age of Unreason, The (Handy), 322
Age stereotypes, 456
Agile manufacturing, 99
Agreeableness, 387
AI, 176
Air Canada, 198
Alberta Public Interest Research Group (APIRG), 428
ALDO shoes, 59
Alimentation Couche-Tard, 218
All-channel communication network, 426
Alternative dispute resolution, 464
Alternative work arrangements, 399–403
Americas, 119
Analyzer strategy, 244
Anchoring and adjustment heuristic, 187
Andean Pact, 119
Angel investor, 161
Apple Computer, 14, 126, 162, 477
Application form, 314
Arbitration, 464
Area structure, 260
Argyris's theory of adult personality, 45–46
Art of Japanese Management, The (Pascale/Athos), 52
Arthur Andersen, 9, 60, 69
Artificial intelligence (AI), 176
Asea Brown Boveri (ABB), 126
Asia/Pacific Rim, 120–121
Assertiveness, 459
Assessing, 476
Assessment centre, 315
Athena Sustainable Materials Institute, 269
Attitude, 390
Attractive industry, 234
Attribution error, 455
Attribution theory, 455
Authentic leadership, 352
Authoritarianism, 388
Authority-and-responsibility principle, 272
Authority decision, 345
Autocratic style, 340
Autodesk, 319
Automation, 394
Autonomous work groups, 417
Autonomy, 397
Availability heuristics, 186
Avoidance, 460
A&W Food Services, 203

B
Background checks, 316
Backward vertical integration, 237
Bafflegab, 446
Ballard Power Systems, 7
Bank of Nova Scotia, 10
Bargaining zone, 463
Barrick Gold, 126
BARS, 320
Base compensation, 323
BATNA, 463
Baytech Plastics, 360
B2B e-commerce, 171
B.C. Hydro, 496
B2C business strategy, 241
B2C e-commerce, 171
BCG matrix, 243–244
Behavioural decision model, 184, 185
Behavioural management approaches, 41–46
Behaviourally anchored rating scale (BARS), 320
Bell Canada, 172
Bell Canada Enterprises (BCE), 73
Benchmarking, 206
Best alternative to a negotiated agreement (BATNA), 463
Best practices, 206
BET Holdings II, Inc., 283
Beyond Race and Gender (Thomas), 104
Beyond Reengineering (Hammer), 295
Biculturalism, 107
Big Five personality traits, 387–388
Birth stage, 157, 290
Blast Radius, 434
BMO Financial Group, 89, 209
Board of directors, 246
Body Shop, 68–69
Bombardier, 265
Bona fide occupational requirements, 309
Bonus pay, 376
Borderless World, The (Ohmae), 137
Bottom-up change, 480
Boundaryless organization, 267–269
Brainstorming, 431
Bre-X, 9, 60
Break-even analysis, 216–217
Break-even point, 216, 217
Breakfast cereals market, 229
Breakthrough stage, 157
British Airways (BA), 129
Budgets, 204
Bureaucracy, 40
Bureaucratic organization, 40–41
Business incubation, 162–163
Business incubator, 162
Business plan, 158–159
Business strategy, 235, 236
Business-to-business e-commerce, 171
Business-to-consumer e-commerce, 171

C
Cafeteria benefits, 324
Callaway Golf, 433
Caltex, 135
Campbell Soup, 204, 318
Canadarm, 476
Canadian Airlines, 378
Canadian Council of Human Resources Associations (CCHRA), 307
Canadian Human Rights Act, 8, 308
Canadian Red Cross Society, 159, 231
Canadian Securities Administrators (CSA), 69
Canadian Tire, 235, 465
Career, 322
Career development, 322–323
Career path, 322
Career planning, 322, 490
Career plateau, 323
Careers, 9–10
CARICOM, 119
Cash cows, 243, 244
CCI Thermal Technologies, 236
Celebrity entrepreneurs, 147–149
Center for Creative Leadership, 318, 441
Centralization, 273
Centralized communication network, 426
Certain environment, 180, 286
Chain communication network, 426
Chain of command, 269
Challenger shuttle disaster, 430
Change. *See* organizational change
Change agent, 478
Change leaders, 478–479
Change strategies, 484–487
Changing, 484
Changing nature of managerial work, 18–19
Channel richness, 450, 451
Chapters-Indigo, 169
Charismatic leader, 347
Chat rooms, 451
Chemical Bank, 71

Chevron-Texaco, 136
Chief knowledge officer (CKO), 190
Child labour, 128
China, 119–120
CIBC, 79, 474
Circle of Innovation, The (Peters), 473
Cirque du Soleil, 285
City of Grande Prairie, 418
Classical decision model, 184, 185
Classical management approaches, 35–41
Classical view of social responsibility, 75
Co-operative strategies, 239
Co-operativeness, 459
Coaching, 318
Coca-Cola, 33, 51, 179, 227, 237
Code of ethics, 72–73
Coercion, 488
Coercive power, 335
Cognitive dissonance, 391
Cognos, 195
Collaboration, 460, 461
Collective bargaining, 325–326
Communication, 443–454, 453–454
    barriers, 445–449
    channel, 445
    consultants, 451
    credibility, 444–445
    cultural challenges, 453
    defined, 443
    diversity, 453–454
    effective/efficient, 444
    feedback, 450
    interactive management, 450–452
    listening, 449–450
    networks, 426–427
    persuasion, 444
    process, 443
    proxemics, 452
    space design, 452
    technology utilization, 452–453
"Company of the Future, The" (Reich), 11
Comparable worth, 311, 367
Compensation and benefits, 323–324
Competing objectives, 459
Competition, 460, 461
Competitive advantage, 91
Compressed workweek, 399–400
Compromise, 460, 461
Computer-mediated group, 416
Computer-mediated meetings, 451
Concentration, 237
Conceptual skill, 24
Concurrent controls, 211
Conflict, 457–461
Conflict management styles, 459–461
Conflict of interest, 66
Confrontation meeting, 492
Confucian values, 137
Conscientiousness, 388

Constructive conflict, 457
Constructive stress, 494
Consultative decision, 345
Consumer protection, 82
Content theories of motivation, 361–365
Contingency approaches to leadership, 341–346
Contingency planning, 206
Contingency thinking, 48–49
Contingency workers, 403
Continuous improvement, 98–99
Continuous-process production, 289
Continuous reinforcement schedule, 372
Control equation, 210
Control process, 209–210
Controlling, 21, 208–219
    break-even analysis, 216–217
    defined, 208
    employee discipline, 214–215
    importance, 208
    information and financial controls, 215–216
    internal *vs.* external control, 212–213
    MBO, 213–214
    operations management and control, 217–219
    organizational control, 213–219
    planning, and, 200
    steps in process, 209–210
    types of controls, 211–212
C.O.R.E. Digital Pictures, 409
Core characteristics model, 396–398
Core competency, 232, 233
Core culture, 102
Core values, 102, 232
Corning, 376
Corporate culture, 100–103
Corporate governance, 9, 83, 246–247
Corporate portals, 176
Corporate social responsibility, 73
    classical view, 75
    corporate governance, 83
    defined, 73
    evaluating performance, 77–78
    social entrepreneurship, 79–81
    social responsibility strategies, 78
    socio-economic view, 76
    stakeholder issues and analysis, 73–75
Corporate strategy, 235, 236
Corporation, 159
Corruption, 127
Corruption of Foreign Public Officials Act, 127
Cost-benefit analysis, 183
Cost leadership strategy, 242
Cott Corporation, 148
C.R. England, 175
Crafts Council, 400
"Creating High Quality Health Care

Workplace," 385
Creativity, 474–475
Credibility, 444–445
Crisis, 178
Crisis management, 179
Crisis management plans, 179
Crisis management teams, 179
Critical-incident techniques, 320
Critical thinking, 248
Cross-functional teams, 415–416
Cultural awareness, 137
Cultural diversity, 133–134
Cultural relativism, 64
Culture shock, 128
Culture's Consequences: International Differences in Work-Related Values (Hofstede), 131
Currency risk, 135
Current ration, 216
Customer confidence, 66
Customer-driven organizations, 95–97
Customer relations management (CRM), 96–97, 172
Customer structure, 260
Customer wants, 96
Customers, 95
Cycle time, 99

D

DaimlerChrysler, 126
Data, 174
Davco Machine Ltd., 454
DBG Canada Limited, 281
Debate, 458
Debt financing, 160
Debt ratio, 216
Decentralization, 273
Decentralization with centralization, 273
Decentralized communication network, 426
Decima Research, 199
Decision, 178
Decision by authority rule, 427
Decision by consensus, 428
Decision by lack of response, 427
Decision by majority rule, 427
Decision by minority rule, 427
Decision by unanimity, 428
Decision environments, 179–181
Decision making, 178
    decision environments, 179–181
    errors/traps, 186–187
    ethics, 189
    heuristics, 186–187
    individual *vs.* group, 188, 427–431
    knowledge management, 190
    organizational learning, 190
    problem-solving styles, 181
    steps in process, 182–186
    teams, 427–431

types of decisions, 178–179
Decision-making process, 182–186
Decision support system (DSS), 176
Decisional roles, 21, 22
Defender strategy, 244
Defensive strategy, 78
Deficit principle, 43, 361
Delegating style, 343
Delegation, 271–272
Dell Computer, 95, 227, 239
Delta Hotel, 461
Deming Prize, 98
Deming's "14 points of equality," 98
Democratic style, 340
Design. *See* Organizational design
Design for disassembly, 99
Design for manufacturing, 99
Designing, 476
Destructive conflict, 457
Destructive stress, 494
Differentiation strategy, 242
Direct investment strategies, 123–124
Directive leadership, 344
Discipline, 215
Discrimination, 8, 66, 308–309
Disney, 102
Disney World Resort, 317
Dispute resolution, 464
Distress, 494
Distribution alliances, 239
Distributive justice, 63
Distributive negotiation, 462
Diversification, 237
Diversity, 104. *See also* Workplace diversity
Diversity maturity, 109
Diversity rationale, 306
Diversity trends in socio-cultural environment, 92
Divestiture, 238
Divisional structure, 259–262
Dofasco, 303
Dogs, 243, 244
Domino's Pizza, 160
Downsizing, 237–238, 290
Drucker's "old-fashioned" leadership, 350–351
DSS, 176
Dunbar's Number, 225
DuPont Canada, 75
Dynamic Administration: The Collected Papers of Mary Parker Follett, 39
Dysfunctional conflict, 457

E
E-business strategies, 239–240
E-commerce, 171
EAP, 324
eBay, 245
eBay Canada, 102

Economic order quantity (EOQ), 218
EDI, 176
Edward Jones, 253
Effective communication, 444
Efficient communication, 444
EI, 349
80/20 rule, 50
Electronic commerce, 171
Electronic data interchange (EDI), 176
Electronic grapevine, 453
Electronic group network, 416
EllisDon Corp., 202
Email workload, 453
Emergent strategy, 245
Emotional intelligence, 24
Emotional intelligence (EI), 349
Emotional stability, 388
Employee. *See* Human resource management (HRM)
Employee advisory council, 451
Employee assistance program (EAP), 324
Employee benefits, 322–323
Employee discipline, 214–215
Employee group, 451
Employee involvement teams, 416
Employee orientation, 317
Employee stock ownership, 377–378
Employment discrimination, 308–309
Employment equity, 309
Employment Equity Act, 81, 309
Employment interview, 310, 315
Employment tests, 315
Empowerment, 272, 273, 337–338
En Cana, 126
Enbridge International, 126
Endeavor Global, 103
Engineering comparison, 210
Enron, 9, 60, 69
Enterprise portals, 176
Enterprise Rent-a-Car, 292
Entrepreneur, 147
Entrepreneurship, 151–152
Entrepreneurship and small business, 144–167
 business incubation, 162–163
 business plan, 158–159
 celebrity entrepreneurs, 147–149
 characteristics of entrepreneurs, 149–150
 diversity and entrepreneurship, 151–152
 failure—small business, 155–156
 family business, 154–155
 financing new ventures, 160–161
 form of ownership, 159
 international business entrepreneurship, 153–154
 Internet and entrepreneurship, 153
 large enterprises and entrepreneurship, 162

 myths, 151
 new venture creation, 156–161
 SBDCs, 163
Environment and competitive advantage, 90–95
Environment of hypercompetition, 229
Environmental concern, 94
Environmental protection, 82, 128
Environmental Protection Act, 82
EOQ, 218
Equity financing, 160
Equity theory, 366–367
ERG theory, 362
Ernst & Young, 20, 21
Escalating commitment, 187
Escalation trap, 187
ESOP, 377–378
Essential managerial skills, 23–25
Esteem needs, 44
Ethical dilemma, 65
Ethical imperialism, 64
Ethical leadership, 352
Ethics, 9, 58–73. *See also* Corporate social responsibility
 alternative views of, 62–63
 checklist (ethical dilemmas), 70
 cultural issues, 64
 decision making, 189
 defined, 9, 61
 ethical behaviour, 61–62
 ethical codes, 72–73
 ethical role models, 72
 factors to consider, 67–70
 leadership, 351–352
 multinational corporations, 127–128
 negotiation, 465
 power, 337
 rationalization for unethical behaviour, 66–67
 reinforcement, 373
 training, 71
 whistle-blower protection, 71
 workplace ethical dilemmas, 65–66
Ethics advocate, 72
Ethics training, 71
Ethnic cultures, 105
Ethnocentric attitudes, 138
Ethnocentric view, 238
Ethnocentrism, 129
EU, 118
Euro, 118
Europe, 119
European Union (EU), 118
Eustress, 494
Evolution of Management Thought, The (Wren), 35
Executive briefing, 446
Existence needs, 362

Expatriate, 136
Expectancy, 368
Expectancy theory, 367–369
Experimenting, 476
Expert power, 335–336
Expert systems, 176
Exporting, 123
External control, 212
External customers, 95
External recruitment, 313
Extinction, 371
Extranet, 176
Extrinsic reward, 359
Extroversion, 387
Exxon, 125

F
Facilities plans, 203
Failures of process, 246
Failures of substance, 246
Fair labour practices, 81
Family business, 154–155
Family business feud, 154
Family-friendly benefits, 324
Fast-food industry, 229
Fayol's 14 principles of management, 37
Feedback, 450
Feedback controls, 212
Feedback from the job itself, 397
Feedforward controls, 211
Fifth Discipline, The (Senge), 52
Filtering, 448
Financial plans, 203
Financial ratios, 216
Financing new venture, 160–161
First-line managers, 16
First-move advantage, 157
Fixed budget, 204
Flat structure, 271
Flexible benefits, 324
Flexible budget, 204
Flexible manufacturing, 99
Flexible working hours, 400
Flexiplace, 401
Flexitime, 400
*flex*Space, 172
Flextime, 400
Flight Centre, 373
Focused cost leadership strategy, 243
Focused differentiation strategy, 242
Force-coercion strategy, 484–486
Forced distribution, 321
Forcing strategy, 484
Ford Motor Company, 7, 259
Forecasting, 205
Foreign subsidiary, 124
Formal group, 414
Formal presentation, 446
Formal structure, 256

Forming stage, 421
Forward vertical integration, 237
Forzani Group, 390
Founding story, 103
4–40 schedule, 399–400
Four Seasons Hotel, 42
Framing error, 187
Franchise, 153
Franchising, 123
Free Trade Area of the Americas (FTAA), 119
Freybe Gourmet Foods, 377
Friendship groups, 414
Fiedler's contingency model, 341–343
Fringe benefits, 322–323
Frustration-regression principle, 362
FTAA, 119
Functional authority, 274
Functional chimneys problem, 258
Functional conflict, 457
Functional managers, 17
Functional strategy, 235, 236
Functional structure, 257–259
Functional subcultures, 105
Functions of management, 19–21
Functions of the Executive (Barnard), 47
Future of Success, The (Reich), 90, 304, 492

G
Gain sharing, 377
Gap Inc., 73
GDSS, 176
GE Medical Systems, 312
Gender equity, 367
Gender subcultures, 106
General Electric, 16, 125, 219, 236, 267, 334, 481
General environment, 91–92
General managers, 17
General Motors, 125
General partnership, 159
Generational gaps, 106
Generational subcultures, 106
Genentech, 357
Geocentric attitudes, 138
Geocentric view, 238
Geographical structure, 260
Getting to Yes (Fisher/Ury), 462
Ghana, 121
Gildan Activewear Inc., 115
Glass ceiling, 9, 106, 455
Global area structure, 136
Global awareness, 51–52
Global dimensions, 125–133
Global dimensions of management, 114–142
    Africa, 120–121
    Americas, 120
    Asia/Pacific Rim, 120–121
    complications, 124–125

    contracts and agreements, 131
    controlling, 135
    cultural diversity, 133–134
    direct investment strategies, 123–124
    entrepreneurship, 153–154
    ethical issues, 127–128
    Europe, 119
    global organizational learning, 137–138
    home-country issues, 127
    host-country issues, 126–127
    international management, 117–118
    interpersonal space, 130
    language, 129–130
    management theories, 136–137
    market entry strategies, 123
    multinational corporation (MNC), 125–126
    organizing, 135–136
    planning, 135
    religion, 130–131
    staffing, 136
    time orientation, 130
    universal values, 67
    values and national cultures, 131–133
    why companies go international, 122
Global economy, 117
Global manager, 118, 135
Global organizational learning, 137–138
Global product structure, 136
Global sourcing, 123
Global strategies, 238
Globalive Communications, 216
Globalization, 7, 117
Globalization strategy, 238
Goal displacement, 246
Goal-setting theory, 369–370
Goldcorp Inc., 332
Golder Associates, 273
GoodLife Fitness Clubs, 350
Google, 33
Government influence, 81–83
Grameen Bank, 475
Graphic rating scale, 320
Great person theory, 338
Greenfield ventures, 124
Groove Networks, 475
Group decision, 345
Group decision making, 188
Group decision support systems (GDSS), 176
Group process, 420
Groupe Germain, 282
Groupthink, 429–430
Groupware, 176
Growth and diversification strategies, 236–237
Growth needs, 362
Growth strategy, 236

Gulf Canada, 433

H
Hallmark Cards, 477
Halo effect, 456
Harley-Davidson, 118
Hat World, 150
Hawthorne effect, 43
Hawthorne studies, 41–43
Hayes Forest Services, 286–287
Hazardous Products Act, 82
Heart and Stroke Foundation of Ontario, 206
Heroes, 101
Hersey-Blanchard situational leadership model, 343
Herzberg's two-factor theory, 363
Heuristics, 186–187
Hierarchy of needs theory, 361–362
Hierarchy of objectives, 200
High-context cultures, 130
Higher-order needs, 361
Hilton Hotel, 461
Hino Motors Ltd., 122
Historical comparison, 210
Home-country issues, 127
Home Depot, 75, 80, 308
Home Depot Canada, 107
Honda, 92, 101, 120
Horizontal loading, 395
Horizontal structure, 263
Host-country issues, 126–127
Hotelling, 402
House's path-goal leadership theory, 344–345
HRM. *See* Human resource management (HRM)
HRPAO, 307, 308
Hubbell Canada, 416
Human capital, 305
Human Equation: Building Profits by Putting People First, The (Pfeffer), 305
Human relations movement, 43
Human resource management (HRM), 302–329
    career development, 322–323
    compensation and benefits, 323–324
    discrimination, 308–309
    diversity advantage, 305–306
    labour-management relations, 325–326
    legal issues, 308–311
    organizational design, 291
    orientation, 317
    performance appraisal, 319–321
    planning, 312
    recruiting process, 313–314
    retention and turnover, 324–325
    selection process, 314–317
    strategic, 307–308
    training and development, 318
    work-life balance, 323
Human resource management process, 307
Human resource plans, 203
Human resources management, 305–306
Human Resources Professionals Association of Ontario (HRPAO), 307, 308
Human Side of Enterprise, The (McGregor), 44
Human skill, 24
Husky Injection Molding, 75
Hygiene factor, 363
Hyundai, 120

I
IBM, 7, 210, 291, 452
IBM Canada, 402
Idea generators, 478
IKEA, 6
ILO, 458
Imagining, 476
Imperial Oil, 289
Importing, 123
Improvement objectives, 214
In Search of Excellence: Lessons from America's Best-Run Companies (Peters/Waterman), 50
Inco, 339
Incremental change, 482
Incremental planning, 201–202
Incrementalism, 201, 245
Independent contractors, 311
India, 119
Indigo Books & Music, 148
Individual behaviour and performance, 382–407
    alternative work arrangements, 399–403
    core characteristics model, 396–398
    individual performance, 392–393
    job design, 393–395
    job enlargement, 395
    job enrichment, 395–399
    job rotation, 395
    job satisfaction, 391
    OB, 385–386
    personality traits, 387–389
    psychological contract, 386
    quality of work life (QWL), 387
    scientific management, 394
    work attitude, 390–393
Individual performance, 392–393
Individual performance equation, 392
Individual *vs.* group decision making, 188
Individual with flexibility, 199
Individual with focus, 199
Individualism-collectivism, 131, 132
Individualism view, 63

Individualism *vs.* collectivism, 133
Industry/environment analysis, 233–234
Influence, 336–337
Info-Tech Research Group, 402
Infocheck Ltd., 316
Infomediary model, 239
Informal group, 414
Informal network integration, 105
Informal structure, 256–257
Information, 174
Information and financial controls, 215–216
Information filtering, 448
Information gatekeepers, 478
Information systems, 175
Information technology (IT), 170–173
Informational roles, 21, 22
Initial public offering (IPO), 160
Initiative, 367
Inmet Mining, 480
Inner-directed culture, 134
Innovation, 475–478
Innovation leaders, 478
Input standard, 210
Instant messaging, 173
Instrumental values, 62
Instrumentality, 368
Integrated change leadership, 480–481
Integrated model of motivation, 374–375
Integrity, 352
Intel, 264, 378
Intellectual capital, 6, 171
Intelligence information, 174
Intensive technology, 289
Interactional justice, 63
Interactive management, 450–452
Interbrew SA, 133
Interest groups, 414
Intergroup team building, 492
Intermediate-range plans, 202
Intermittent reinforcement schedule, 372
Internal control, 212
Internal customers, 95
Internal recruitment, 313
International business. *See* Global dimensions of management
International business entrepreneurship, 153–154
International joint ventures, 123–124, 239
International Labour Organization (ILO), 458
International management, 117–118
Internet and entrepreneurship, 153
Internet time, 203
Interpersonal roles, 21, 22
Interpersonal skills, 440–469
    communication, 443–454. *See also* Communication
    conflict, 457–461
    negotiation, 461–465

perception process, 454–455
personal management, 443
Interpersonal space, 130
Interview, 315
Intranet, 176
Intrapreneurship, 162, 290
Intrinsic reward, 360
Intuitive-feeler, 389
Intuitive-thinker, 389
Intuitive thinking, 181
Inventory, 218
Inventory control, 218
Inventory turnover, 216
IPO, 160
IT, 170–173

J
Jaguar, 259
Japan, 120
JIT systems, 218
Job, 393
Job analysis, 312
Job description, 312
Job design, 393–395
Job discrimination, 107
Job enlargement, 395
Job enrichment, 395–399
Job enrichment checklist, 396
Job interview, 310, 315
Job involvement, 391
Job performance, 392
Job redesign, 490
Job rotation, 395
Job satisfaction, 391
Job sharing, 401
Job simplification, 394
Job specification, 312
Johari Window, 22
Johnson & Johnson, 9, 33, 477
Johnson Controls, 480
Joint venture, 123–124
Just-in-time scheduling (JIT), 218
Justice view, 63

K
Kickbacks, 66
Kimberly-Clark, 378
Knowledge management, 190
Knowledge sharing, 268
Knowledge worker, 6, 171
KPMG, 279

L
Labour contract, 325
Labour-management relations, 325–326
Labour union, 325
Lack of participation error, 185, 246
Laissez-faire style, 340
Language, 129–130

Language metaphors, 103
Law of contingent reinforcement, 372
Law of effect, 370
Law of immediate reinforcement, 372
Leadership, 333, 338–350
    behaviours, 339–340
    Grid, 340
    style, 339, 340–341
    traits, 338–339
Leading, 21, 330–355
    contingency approaches to leadership, 341–346
    Drucker's "old-fashioned" leadership, 350–351
    EI, 349
    empowerment, 337–338
    ethics, 337, 351–352
    Fiedler's contingency model, 341–343
    gender, 349–350
    Hersey-Blanchard situational leadership model, 343
    House's path-goal leadership theory, 344–345
    influence, 336–337
    leadership behaviours, 339–340
    leadership style, 340–341
    leadership traits, 338–339
    moral leadership, 351–352
    power, 334–336
    strategic leadership, 473–474, 475
    substitutes for leadership, 345
    teams, 434–435
    transactional leadership, 347
    transformational leadership, 347–348
    vision, 333–334
    Vroom-Jago leader-participation model, 345–346
Leading the Revolution (Hamel), 196
Lean production, 99
Learning organization, 52, 190, 286, 474
Learning style, 53
Least-preferred co-worker scale (LPC scale), 341
Lee Valley Tools, 311
Legitimate power, 335
Licensing agreement, 123
Lifelong learning, 23
Limited liability corporation (LLC), 159
Limited liability partnership, 159
Limited partnership, 159
Lincoln Electric, 377
Line managers, 17
Linear programming, 46
Liquidation, 237
Listening, 449–450
LLC, 159
Lobbying, 83
Locus of control, 388
Long-linked technology, 289

Long-range plans, 202
Lose-lose conflict, 460
Lotus, 291
Low-context cultures, 130
Lower-order needs, 361
LPC scale, 341

M
Machiavellianism, 389
Mackinnon Transport, 207
Magma Communications, 179
Magna International, 147
Maintenance activity, 425
Maintenance objectives, 214
Malaysia, 120
Management, 19–21
Management approaches. *See* Management theory
Management by objectives (MBO), 213–214, 369, 492
Management by wandering around (MBWA), 450–451
Management development, 318
Management learning framework, 25–26
Management Learning Workbook, 26
Management practices and systems, 246
Management process, 19–23
Management science, 46–47
Management theory, 32–57
    administrative principles, 37–39
    Argyris's theory of adult personality, 45–46
    behavioural management approaches, 41–46
    bureaucratic organization, 40–41
    classical management approaches, 35–41
    contingency thinking, 48–49
    continuing management themes, 49
    Fayol, 37–38
    Follett, 39
    global awareness, 51–52
    Hawthorne studies, 41–43
    human relations movement, 43
    learning organization, 52
    management science, 46–47
    Maslow's hierarchy of needs, 43–44
    modern management approaches, 47–49
    organizations as systems, 47–48
    quality and performance excellence, 49–51
    quantitative management approaches, 46–47
    scientific management, 35–37
    Theory X/Theory Y, 44–45
    21st-century leadership, 52–54
Management training, 490
Manager

competencies, 25
decision making. *See* Decision making
defined, 15
essential skills, 23–25
global, 118
information processors, as, 177
levels of, 16
required attributes, 53
roles, 21–22
teams, 411, 412
types of, 17
Managerial activities and roles, 21–22
Managerial agendas and networking, 22–23
Managerial competency, 25
Managerial performance, 17–18
Managing diversity, 108–109
Manipulation and co-optation, 488
Maple Leaf Foods, 433
Maquiladoras, 119
Market entry strategies, 123
Market structure, 260, 261
Marketing plans, 203
Mary Kay Cosmetics, 103
Mary Parker Follett–Prophet of Management: A Celebration of Writings from the 1920s, 34
Masculinity-femininity, 131, 132
Maslow's hierarchy of needs, 43–44
Mass customization, 99
Mass production, 288
Mathematical forecasting, 46
Matrix organization, 261
Matrix structure, 260–261
Maturity stage, 157, 290
MBO, 213–214, 369, 492
MBWA, 450–451
McDonald's, 117, 123, 126, 131, 211, 229
MDA, 477
Means-ends chain, 200
Mechanistic design, 284–285
Mediating technology, 289
Mediation, 464
Medical/physical examination, 316
Medium-sized enterprises, 152
Medtronics, 11, 394
Meetings, 412–413
Mentoring, 318
Mercedes Benz, 39
Merchant model, 239
Merck, 102, 378
MERCOSUR, 119
Meridian Credit Union, 471
Merit pay, 375–376
Merrill Lynch Misery Index, 117
Mexico, 119
Microenterprises, 152
Microsoft, 107, 126, 159, 229
Mid-life stage, 290
Middle managers, 16

Miles and Snow adaptive model of strategy formulation, 244
Minorities, 107–108
Mission, 231
Mission statement, 231
Mitsubishi, 125
MNOs, 126
Modelling, 318
Modern management approaches, 47–49
Monitor Company, 383
Monochronic cultures, 130
Monopoly environment, 228
Moose Deer Point First Nations Sustainable Community Project, 75
Moral leadership, 351–352
Moral quality circles, 72
Moral-rights view, 63
Most favoured nation status, 125
Motion studies, 37
Motivation, 356–381
acquired needs theory, 364
content theories, 361–365
defined, 359
equity theory, 366–367
ERG theory, 362
expectancy theory, 367–369
goal-setting theory, 369–370
hierarchy of needs theory, 361–362
incentive compensation systems, 376–378
integrated model of, 374–375
pay for performance, 375–376
process theories, 366–370
reinforcement theory, 370–373
rewards, 359–361
two-factor theory, 363
Motorola, 429
Mountain Equipment Co-op (MEC), 76
Multi-tasking, 417
Multicultural organization, 104–105
Multiculturalism, 104
Multidimensional thinking, 181
Multidomestic strategy, 238
Multinational corporation (MNC), 125–126
Multinational organizations (MNOs), 126
Multiperson comparisons, 321
Myers-Briggs Type Indicator, 389

N
NAFTA, 119
National cultures, 105
Nature of Managerial Work, The (Mintzberg), 21
Need, 43, 361
Need for achievement, 364
Need for affiliation, 364
Need for personal power, 364
Need for power, 364
Need for social power, 364

Negative reinforcement, 371
Negotiation, 461–465
Neptec, 476
Nestlé, 126, 280–281
Net margin, 216
Network models, 46
Network structure, 265–267
Networking, 335
Neutral *vs.* affective, 133
New venture creation, 156–161
Niagara Health Systems Foundation, 422
Nike, 128, 270
Nk'Mip Cellars, 161
No Easy Victories (Gardner), 53
Noise, 445
Nokia, 313
Nonprogrammed decisions, 178
Nordstrom, 102
Normative re-educative strategy, 486
Norming stage, 421–422
NORPAC Controls, 231
Nortel Networks, 69, 173, 257, 416
North American Free Trade Agreement (NAFTA), 119
NTT DoCoMo, 125–126
Nucor, 360

O
OB, 385–386
Objectives, 197, 232
Observable culture, 101–102
Obstructionist strategy, 78
Occupational health and safety, 81
Occupational Health and Safety Act, 81
Occupational subcultures, 105
OD, 489–492
OD intervention, 490
Off-the-job training, 318
Oligopoly environment, 229
Ombudsperson, 464
On-the-job training, 318
Online discussion forums, 451
Open office hours, 451
Open system, 12, 48
Openness, 388
Operant conditioning, 371
Operating objectives, 232
Operational plan, 203
Operations management and control, 217–219
Operations research, 46
Opportunity situation, 210
Optimizing decision, 184
Oral presentation, 446
Organic design, 285–286
Organization, *See also* Organizing
bureaucratic, 40
changing nature of, 13–14
defined, 11

government, and, 81–83
open system, as, 12, 47–48
performance measures, 12
upside-down pyramid, as, 18
Organization chart, 256
Organization development (OD), 489–492
Organization structure, 255. *See also* Organizing
Organization with flexibility, 199
Organization with focus, 199
Organizational behaviour, 43
Organizational change, 478–492
    bottom-up change, 480
    change leaders, 478–479
    change strategies, 484–487
    forces/targets for change, 482
    incremental change, 482
    integrated change leadership, 480–481
    OD, 489–492
    phases of planned change, 483–484
    resistance to change, 487–488
    technological change, 488–489
    top-down change, 479–480
    transformational change, 481–482
Organizational commitment, 391
Organizational control, 213–219
Organizational culture, 100–103, 232
Organizational design, 278–300
    checklist, 287
    defined, 281
    environment, 286–287
    framework, 282
    human resources, 291
    life cycle, 289–291
    mechanistic design, 284–285
    organic design, 285–286
    organizational effectiveness, 282–283
    size, 289
    strategy, 287–288
    subsystem differentiation, 293
    subsystem integration, 293–294
    technology, 288–289
    work process design, 294–297
Organizational design checklist, 287
Organizational design paradox, 293
Organizational ecology, 452
Organizational effectiveness, 282–283
Organizational flexibility, 281
Organizational learning, 190
Organizational life cycle, 289–291
Organizational performance, 12–13
Organizational resources/capabilities, 232–233
Organizational ritual, 102
Organizational size, 289
Organizational stakeholders, 73
organizational subcultures, 105–106
Organizing, 20, 252–277
    boundaryless organization, 267–269
    chain of command, 269

customer structure, 260
decentralization with centralization, 273
delegation, 271–272
divisional structure, 259–262
formal structure, 256
functional structure, 257–259
geographical structure, 260
horizontal structure, 263
informal structure, 256–257
matrix structure, 260–261
network structure, 265–267
process structure, 260
product structure, 260
span of control, 270–271
staffing, 273–274
team structure, 263–265
unity of command, 270
virtual organization, 268
Oriental Brewery, 133
Orientation, 317
Ouimet-Cordon Bleu Foods, 331
Outer-directed culture, 134
Outplacement services, 325
Output standard, 210
Outsourcing, 265, 266
Outsourcing alliances, 239
Outward Bound, 433
Oxford Frozen Foods, 242

P
PAC, 83
Paired comparisons, 321
PAR, 108
Pareto Principle, 50
Part-time work, 403
Participant Productions, 398
Participating style, 343
Participative leadership, 344
Participatory planning, 207
Partnership, 159
Pay discrimination, 106
Pay for knowledge, 376
Peer appraisal, 321
Peer-to-peer file sharing, 173
Pelmorex Incorporated, 306
People, 6
PeopleSoft, 295
PepsiCo, 237
Perception, 454
Perception process, 454–455
Performance appraisal, 319–321
Performance-contingent rewards, 361
Performance deficiency, 178
Performance effectiveness, 12
Performance efficiency, 13
Performance excellence, 51
Performance management systems, 319–321
Performance measures, 12
Performance norm, 423

Performance opportunity, 178
Performing stage, 422
Permatemps, 311, 403
Person-job fit, 385
Personal character, 72
Personal development objectives, 214
Personal power, 335–336
Personal staff, 274
Personal wellness, 496
Personality, 387
Personality and Organization (Argyris), 45
Personality traits, 387–389
Persuasion, 444
Pfizer Canada, 313, 372
Philippines, 120
Physical examination, 316
Physiological needs, 44
Plan, 197
Planning, 20, 197–207
    benchmarking, 206
    benefits of, 199–200
    budgets, 204
    contingency planning, 206
    defined, 197
    forecasting, 205
    importance, 197
    participation and involvement, 207
    policies and procedures, 203–204
    projects, 204
    scenario planning, 206
    short-range *vs.* long-range plans, 202–203
    staff planners, 206–207
    steps in process, 198
    strategic and operational plans, 203
    theories, 201–202
Planning process, 197–198
Planning theories, 201–202
Pluralism, 105
Polaroid Corporation, 264
Policy, 203
Political action committees (PAC), 83
Political maneuvering, 484
Political risk, 135
Political-risk analysis, 135
Polycentric attitudes, 138
Polycentric view, 238
Polychronic cultures, 130
Pomerleau, 411
Porter's five forces model, 234
Porter's generic strategies, 241–243
Portfolio planning, 243–244
Position power, 334–335
Positive reinforcement, 371, 372
Post-action controls, 212
Power, 334–336
Power distance, 131, 132
P2P file sharing, 173
Pratt & Whitney Canada, 324
Prejudice, 8

Preliminary controls, 211
PricewaterhouseCoopers, 268
Principles of Scientific Management, The (Taylor), 35
Proactive strategy, 78
Probability, 180
Problem avoiders, 181
Problem seekers, 181
Problem situation, 210
Problem solvers, 181
Problem solving, 178
Problem-solving styles, 181, 389
Procedural justice, 63
Procedure, 204
Process consultation, 490
Process failure, 246
Process innovation, 475
Process re-engineering, 294–297
Process structure, 260
Process theories of motivation, 366–370
Process value analysis, 295–296
Procter & Gamble, 117, 238
Product champions, 478
Product design, 99
Product innovation, 475
Product structure, 260, 261
Production plans, 203
Productivity, 12
Professionalism, 308
Profit sharing, 377
Programmed decision, 178
Progression principle, 43, 361
Progressive Aboriginal Relations (PAR), 108
Progressive discipline, 215
Project management, 204
Project managers, 16, 478
Project schedules, 204
Project team, 415
Projection, 457
Projects, 204
Promotion, 324
Prospector strategy, 244
Protectionism, 125
Proversity: Getting Past Face Value and Finding the Soul of People—A Manager's Journey (Graham), 306
Proxemics, 452
Prudential Grand Valley Realty, 314
Psychological contract, 386
Public information, 175
Public relations campaigns, 83
Punishment, 371, 373
Purchasing control, 217–218
"Putting People First for Organizational Success" (Pfeffer/Veiga), 14, 305

Q

Qualitative forecasting, 205
Quality and performance excellence, 49–51
Quality circle, 416

Quality control, 218
Quality cycle, 99
Quality-driven organizations, 97–99
Quality management, 99
Quality of work life (QWL), 18, 387
Quantitative forecasting, 205
Quantitative management approaches, 46–47
Question marks, 243, 244
Queuing theory, 46
QWL, 18, 387

R

Race and ethnicity. *See* Workplace diversity
Racial and ethnic stereotypes, 455
Racial subcultures, 105–106
Rank ordering, 321
Rational comprehensive planning (RCP), 201
Rational persuasion strategy, 486
Reactor strategy, 244
Realistic job previews, 314
Recruiting process, 313–314
Recruitment, 313
Reference checks, 316
Referent power, 336
Refreezing, 484
Reinforcement theory of motivation, 370–373
Related diversification, 237
Relatedness needs, 362
Relative comparison, 210
Reliability, 315
Religion, 130–131
Representativeness heuristics, 186
Research in Motion (RIM), 53
Resistance to change, 487–488
Resource scarcities, 458
Restricted communication network, 426
Restructuring, 237
Restructuring and divestiture strategies, 237–238
Retention and turnover, 324–325
Retirement, 324
Retrenchment strategy, 237
Reward power, 335
Rewards, 359–361
Rightsizing, 238
Risk environment, 180
Risk taking, 150
Rites and rituals, 102
Role ambiguity, 495
Role clarification, 495
Role negotiation, 490
Royal Dutch/Shell Group, 126
Rugmark Foundation, 128
Rule, 204
"Run for the Cure" event, 79
Russel Metals, 180

S

Safety needs, 44
Saint Francis Xavier Enterprise Development Centre (XEDC), 163
Sarbanes-Oxley Act, 69
SAS Institute, 322
Satisfier factor, 363
Satisficing decision, 184
SBDC, 163
SBU, 236
Scalar chain principle, 38
Scalar principle, 269
Scaling, 476
Scenario planning, 206
Scientific management, 35–37, 394
Scotiabank, 340
SEI Investments, 419
Selection, 314
Selection process, 314–317
Selective perception, 456
Self-actualization needs, 44
Self-awareness, 22
Self-confidence, 185
Self-fulfilling prophecies, 44
Self-managing work teams, 417–418
Self-monitoring, 389
Self-organization, 286
Self-serving bias, 455
Selling style, 343
Sensation-feeler, 389
Sensation-thinker, 389
Sensitivity training, 490
Sequential view of time, 134
Service technologies, 289
7-Eleven, 207
Sexual harassment, 66, 106, 204
Shamrock organization, 10
Shaping, 372
Shared power strategy, 486–487
Short-range plans, 202
SIFE, 145
Simulations, 46
Simultaneous systems, 290
Singapore, 120
Six pillars of character, 72
Six Sigma, 219
Skill
    conceptual, 24
    defined, 23
    human, 24
    survival, 11
    technical, 24
Skill and outcome assessment, 25
Skill variety, 396
Skills-based pay, 376
Skunkworks, 162
Skype, 228
SkyWave Mobile Communication, 288
Small-batch production, 288
Small business. *See* Entrepreneurship and

small business
Small business development centre (SBDC), 163
SMART goal, 214
Sobeys, 322
Social Accountability International, 82
Social entrepreneurship, 79–81
Social loafing, 411
Social needs, 44
Social responsibility. *See* Corporate social responsibility
Social responsibility audit, 77
Social responsibility strategies, 78
Socio-economic view of social responsibility, 76
Sociotechnical system, 398
Sole proprietorship, 159
Sony, 7, 102, 120
SOPs, 204
South Africa, 121
South Korea, 120
Southern African Development Community (SADC), 121
Southwest Airlines, 243, 347
Space design, 452
Span of control, 270–271
Specialized staff, 274
Specific environment, 93
Specific *vs.* diffuse, 133
Spillover effects, 495
Spotlight questions, 189
St. Luke's, 280
Staff managers, 17
Staff planners, 206–207
Staffing, 273–274
Stakeholder analysis, 183
Stakeholder issues and analysis, 73–75
Stakeholders, 93, 231
Standard operating procedures (SOPs), 204
Star communication network, 426
Starbucks, 231, 360
Stars, 243, 244
Statistical quality control, 218–219
Status effects, 448
Steering controls, 211
Steinway & Sons, 392
Stereotype(s), 454–456
Stock options, 378
Stories, 101
Storming stage, 421
Strategic alliance, 123, 239
Strategic business unit (SBU), 236
Strategic competitiveness, 227–229
Strategic constituencies analysis, 231
Strategic human resource management, 307–308
Strategic Human Resources: Frameworks for General Managers (Baron/Kreps), 305

Strategic intent, 227
Strategic leadership, 247–248, 473–474, 475
Strategic management, 224–251
    adaptive strategies, 244
    BCG matrix, 243–244
    co-operative strategies, 239
    core values, 232
    corporate governance, 246–247
    defined, 228
    e-business strategies, 239–240
    emergent strategy, 245
    global strategies, 238
    goals, 228–229
    growth and diversification strategies, 236–237
    incrementalism, 245
    industry/environment analysis, 233–234
    levels of strategy, 236
    management practices and systems, 246
    mission, 231
    objectives, 232
    organizational resources/capabilities, 232–233
    Porter's generic strategies, 241–243
    portfolio planning, 243–244
    restructuring and divestiture strategies, 237–238
    strategic leadership, 247–248
    strategy formulation, 240–245
    strategy implementation, 245–248
Strategic management goals, 228–229
Strategic management process, 229–234
Strategic opportunism, 181
Strategic plan, 203
Strategy, 227
Strategy formulation, 229, 240–245
Strategy implementation, 230, 245–248
Stress/stress management, 492–496
Stressor, 493
Strong cultures, 100–101
Structural differentiation, 459
Structural integration, 105
Structural redesign, 492
Structured problems, 178
Stryker Instruments, 385–386
Students in Free Enterprise (SIFE), 145
Sub-Saharan Africa, 121
Subscription model, 239
Substance goals, 462
Substantive conflict, 457
Substitutes for leadership, 345
Subsystem, 47, 292
Subsystem differentiation, 293
Subsystem integration, 293–294
Subway, 123
Succession plan, 155
Succession problem, 154

Sun Microsystems, 452
Supervisor, 16
Supplier alliances, 239
Supply chain management, 172
Support groups, 414
Supportive leadership, 344
Survey feedback, 492
Survival skills, 11
Sustainable competitive advantage, 227
Sustainable development, 128
Sweatshops, 128
SWOT analysis, 232
Symbolic leader, 103
Symbols, 102
Synchronic view of time, 134
Synergy, 413
System, 47
Systematic thinking, 181

T
Taiwan, 120
Takashimaya, 477
Tall structures, 271
Task activity, 425
Task environment, 93
Task force, 415
Task identity, 396
Task interdependencies, 458
Task significance, 396
Tateni Home Care Nursing Services, 79
Taxi, 225
TD Bank Financial Group, 306, 395
Team, 411
Team-building process, 431–433
Team decision making, 427–431
Team diversity, 420
Team leader, 16–17
Team management, 340
Team structure, 263–265
Teams/teamwork, 408–438
    cohesiveness, 424–425
    committee, 415
    communication networks, 426–427
    cross-functional teams, 415–416
    decision making, 427–431
    definitions, 411
    diversity, 420
    effectiveness, 419–420
    employee involvement teams, 416
    formal/informal groups, 414
    leadership challenges, 434–435
    meetings, 412–413
    norms, 423–424
    project team, 415
    pros/cons, 411–412
    self-managing work teams, 417–418
    size, 420
    stages of team development, 420–422
    success factors, 433–434

SUBJECT INDEX

synergy, 413
task and maintenance needs, 425
task force, 415
team-building process, 431–433
usefulness of teams, 413–414
virtual teams, 416–417
Teamwork, 411
Teamwork: What Can Go Right/What Can Go Wrong (Larson/LaFasto), 434
Technical skill, 24
Technological change, 488–489
Technological imperative, 289
Technology, 7–8, 288–289, 398
Technology utilization, 452–453
Telecommuting, 401–402
Telephone interview, 316
Telling style, 343
Telus, 50, 424, 444
Terminal values, 62
Termination, 325
Thailand, 120
Theory. *See* Management theory
Theory X, 44–45
Theory Y, 44–45
Theory Z, 52
Theory Z (Ouchi), 52
3M, 261, 476, 477
3M Canada, 50
360° feedback, 321, 452
Thrifty Foods, 395
Tim Hortons, 149, 227, 237
Time for Equality at Work, 458
Time management, 200, 202
Time orientation, 130, 132
Tolerance for ambiguity, 288
Tom's of Maine, 62
Top-down change, 479–480
Toromont Industries, 268
Total quality management (TQM), 14, 50, 97–98
Toxic workplaces, 15
Toyota, 92, 120, 122, 125
Toyotetsu Canada, 122
TQM, 14, 50, 97–98
Traditional recruitment, 314
Training, 318
Training and development, 318
Transactional leadership, 347
Transfer, 324
Transformational change, 481–482
Transformational leadership, 347–348
Transforming Leadership: A New Pursuit of Happiness (Burns), 351
Transnational corporation, 126
Transnational strategy, 238
Trilogy, 162

Tropicana, 237
Turnover, 391
21st-century leadership, 52–54
Two-factor theory, 363
Type A personality, 493

U

Unattractive industry, 234
Uncertain environment, 181, 286
Uncertainty avoidance, 131, 132
Unfreezing, 483–484
Unilever, 238
Union, 325
United Nations, 464
United Parcel Service (UPS), 37, 98, 260
Unity of command, 270
Unity of command principle, 38
Unity of direction principle, 38
Universalism, 64
Universalism *vs.* particularism, 133
Unrelated diversification, 237
Unresolved prior conflicts, 459
Unstructured problems, 178
Upside-down pyramid, 18
Upward appraisal, 321
Utilitarian view, 62

V

Valassis Communications, 377
Valence, 368
Validity, 315
Value chain, 50
Value creation, 12, 93–94
Values, 62
Valuing diversity, 108
Vancity, 451
Venture capitalists, 160
Verizon Communications, 296
Vertical integration, 237
Video conferences, 451
Vietnam, 120
Virgin Group, 148
Virtual offices, 402
Virtual organization, 268
Virtual teams, 416–417
Vision, 333–334
Visionary leadership, 333–334
Voice over internet protocol (VoIP), 173
VoIP, 173
Volunteer Now!, 80
Vroom-Jago leader-participation model, 345–346

W

Wal-Mart, 94, 125, 176, 212, 226, 227, 242
Walt Disney Company, 485

Walt Disney World, 486
Weather Network, 306
Web-based business models, 239
Web portals, 176
Wendy's, 123, 237
Westbridge PET Containers, 376
Western Electric Company, 41
Western Wear and Tack, 236
WestJet, 101, 243
Wheel communication structure, 426
Wheel of innovation, 476
Whistle-blower, 71
Willet International, 135
Win-lose conflict, 460
Win-win conflict, 461
Wipro Technologies, 189
"Wiring the Border," 155
Women, 106–107. *See also* Workplace diversity
Women Business Owners of Color: Challenges and Accomplishments, 151
Wood Gundy, 433
Work attitude, 390–393
Work-life balance, 323
Work process, 295
Work process design, 294–297
Work sampling, 315
Work sharing, 401
Workbrain, 260
Workflow, 295
Workforce 2000: Work and Workers for the 21st Century, 8
Workforce 2020, 8
Workopolis, 3
Workplace diversity, 8
communication, 453–454
diversity maturity, 109
diversity trends in socio-cultural environment, 92
Workplace privacy, 311
World Trade Organization (WTO), 125
WorldCom, 9, 60
WTO, 125

X

XEDC, 163
Xerox Canada, 108
Xerox North American TeleWeb, 50

Y

Youth stage, 290

Z

Zenon Environment, 45
Zero-based budget, 204